To Ruth, Nancy, and Ruth our best listeners

The Rhetoric of Western Thought

Seventh Edition

James L. Golden   Goodwin F. Berquist   William E. Coleman

KENDALL/HUNT PUBLISHING COMPANY
4050 Westmark Drive   Dubuque, Iowa 52002

CONTENTS

PREFACE

As we observed in the 6th edition of this work, The Rhetoric of Western Thought is a subject both broad and narrow. Broad in the sense that any survey of a popular field of study for 2,500 years is bound to introduce the reader to a host of new thinkers and ideas. Narrow in the sense that the topic deals mainly with the insights of Americans and Europeans.

To a large degree, a new edition of a college text provides its authors with a unique opportunity. Fresh new material can be introduced in place of that which has become dated. And the arcane writings of specialists can be replaced by paraphrasing summaries—all in the interest of making the new work more "user friendly." In this edition, as in the previous one, we have pursued each of these avenues of change.

CHANGES IN THE SEVENTH EDITION

First we have modified several chapters through the process of amplifications, deletions, or substitutions. A brief section on the role of imitation in discourse has been added to our discussion of Renaissance Rhetorical Theory in chapter 5. In addition, we have substituted an essay on "Moral Exclusion and the American Indian" for our earlier study on "Judging Presidential Candidates in Person and on Television" which was based on a 1992 Presidential Primary Contest in New Hampshire in 1992. This change, which occurs in chapter 17, accomplishes two goals. It removes, first of all, an analysis of a political contest which is dated; and, secondly, it introduces a theme which has long been neglected in modern rhetorical analysis—a focus on an important aspect of American Indian discourse.

The most significant changes in the present volume are the inclusion of two new chapters. One is designed to fill in gaps that marked our earlier editions; and the other is created for the purpose of anticipating what form rhetoric will need to take for the future if it is to remain vibrant and relevant. The first of these additions, labeled chapter 10, is called "Enlightenment Rhetoric in America." These essays on

John Witherspoon and John Quincy Adams show how two major political and intellectual leaders, during the Colonial and early National periods of American history, reinforced the essence of classical and British/Continental theories of discourse by their own rich experiences for the goal of elevating the citizens of an emerging democratic society. This chapter, we feel, constitutes a vitally significant transition leading us to the formation of contemporary rhetorical thought.

The second new chapter, designated number 19, is called "A Rhetorical and Communication Theory for the 21st Century." It consists of two separate but related parts. The first, written by Professor J. Michael Sproule of San Jose University, is appropriately titled "Toward a Rhetoric for the New Millennium." The second, authored by Professor Thomas McCain of Ohio State University, deals with the challenging topic of "Information and Knowledge On-line: Teaching and Learning in the Communication Age." These two studies, produced at the onset of the new century and millennium, make use of factual data in order to glimpse how a rhetoric of the future could maintain its relevance and influence.

In order to make room for the new chapters 10 and 19, we have eliminated chapter 16 on "Rhetoric and the Production of Knowledge," and deleted portions of other chapters. The 16th chapter of the Sixth Edition was not needed, we concluded, because it overlapped the theories advanced by Toulmin and Perelman. In making the other deletions, we made certain that the importance of the content of the affected chapters would not be lessened.

It is our hope that these various changes will result in a more readable, coherent book. If, after examining this new edition students decide that rhetorical theory is a fascinating, constantly evolving field of study of primary relevance in a democratic world, we will feel our efforts have not been in vain.

James L. Golden
Goodwin F. Berquist
William E. Coleman

ACKNOWLEDGEMENTS

We wish to express our appreciation to those colleagues whose writings have influenced our thinking in the composition of this work: Lloyd Bitzer, Wayne Brockriede, Donald Bryant, Melbourne Cummings, Jack Daniel, Douglas Ehninger, Marie Nichols, Lyndrey Niles, and Roichi Okabe.

A special thanks is extended to Thomas McCain for his essay on "Information and Knowledge Online: Teaching and Learning in the Communication Age"; and to J. Michael Sproule for his study on "Toward a Rhetoric for the New Millennium." These two works provide helpful insights on a rhetorical and communication theory for the future.

We have at times quoted generously from the works of several leading contemporary rhetoricians: Richard Weaver, Kenneth Burke, Michel Meyer, Stephen Toulmin, and Chaim Perelman. Fortunately, we have had the privilege of dialoguing freely with Meyer, Toulmin, and Perelman, and have heard Burke lecture on several occasions. To these thinkers we owe a special debt.

Finally, we are indebted to some of the most significant thinkers in the western world: Plato, Aristotle, Cicero, St. Augustine, Francis Bacon, John Locke, and David Hume. Without their imagination and creativity, there would be no meaningful rhetoric of western thought.

ABOUT THE AUTHORS

James L. Golden is Professor Emeritus of Communication and former head of the Department of Communication at Ohio State University. He received his B.A. from George Washington University in 1947, his M.A. from Ohio State University in 1948, and his Ph.D. from the University of Florida in 1953. His research efforts have focused on rhetorical theory and political communication. He was recipient of the Ohio State Speech Association Distinguished College Teaching Award in 1973, and the Ohio State University Distinguished Alumni Teaching Award in 1982.

He recently served as a member of the President's Commission in honor of the 250th anniversary of Thomas Jefferson. He also served as a member of the jury for the selection of the Outstanding Belgian Scholar sponsored by the Franqui Foundation. Jim coauthored a book with Alan L. Golden, *Thomas Jefferson and the Rhetoric of Virtue,* Madison House Publishers. To be published in the Spring, 2001.

Goodwin Berquist's vocation and avocation is teaching undergraduates. After receiving his doctorate from Penn State, he went on to teach at Ohio State University, the University of Wisconsin-Milwaukee, Dartmouth College, and at the Indiana University Branch Campus in Malaysia.

Interested in the development of speech theory, he led an international study tour to Greece and Italy in 1970 to explore the sites of classical rhetoric. Upon his return, he taught "The Rhetoric of Western Thought" at Ohio State University for fifteen years. Professor Berquist retired from college teaching in 1995. He currently resides in Prescott, Arizona.

William E. Coleman, Jr. has held the position of Professor of Communication, Mount Union College, since 1979. He has served as chair of the department since 1987. In 1985, he was awarded the Great Teacher Award, and in 1993 he was awarded the Teaching Excellence Award from the United Methodist Church. Previous to teaching at Mount Union College, he taught at Ohio State University-Newark, and at Central Ohio Technical College, where he was awarded the Teaching Excellence Award in 1978. He received his Ph.D. from Ohio State University. In 1989, while on sabbatical, he won a grant to visit Germany and study the German Greens. In the spring of 1996, he studied the rhetoric of the American Indian.

PERSPECTIVES ON THE NATURE AND RELEVANCE OF RHETORIC

One of the most commonly used words in contemporary society is the term "rhetoric." It is employed almost daily by politicians, educators, and lawyers, as well as by members of countless other groups. Regrettably, however, when one alludes to the notion of rhetoric the intended meaning often has no resemblance to the art first developed by Corax in the fifth century, B.C., and later amplified by Socrates, Plato, and Aristotle.

As we begin our survey of Western thought, it will be our purpose in this introductory chapter to provide an overview of what we believe to be the general nature and relevance of rhetoric. First, we will examine three representative perspectives that have appeared in communication journals during the past four decades. Secondly, we will show how these perspectives have helped shape the approach used in this volume.

THREE REPRESENTATIVE PERSPECTIVES ON RHETORIC

The Single Definition Perspective

In 1953, Professor Donald C. Bryant, responding to a request made by the editor of the *Quarterly Journal of Speech,* published a landmark essay, entitled "Rhetoric: Its Function and Scope."[1] Bryant's pur-

pose was to provide an overview of what the field of study called rhetoric was all about. His approach, as we will now undertake to show, may be classified as a single definition perspective.

In his beginning remarks, Bryant sought to establish the parameters of rhetoric with the following statement: "I take rhetoric to be the *rationale of informative and suasory discourse.*" He developed this point with the argument that rhetoric, unlike many other instrumental disciplines, is concerned primarily with "informed opinion" based on probability, rather than with certain truths resulting from scientific demonstration. Since rhetoric belongs in the contingent category, he therefore suggested that its ultimate goal "is the attainment of maximum probability as a basis for public decision."

As he next turned to the "subjects of rhetorical discourse," he spoke of the continuing relevance of Aristotle's classification system—deliberative, forensic, and epideictic topics. These are the subject areas out of which speeches are formed for the marketplace, legislative and judicial bodies, and ceremonial occasions. But, Bryant added, we must also include topics associated with the modern fields of propaganda, public relations, advertising, and salesmanship.

> **Three Representative Rhetorical Perspectives**
>
> ■ Single Definition Perspective
> ■ Systems Perspective
> ■ Evolutionary Perspective

> "I take rhetoric to be the *rationale of informative and suasory discourse.*"

In the remaining portion of the essay, Bryant described rhetoric's dynamic quality, its essential functions, its method of inquiry, its place in the educational system, and its relationship to poetics (i.e., poetry). Rhetoric's dynamism, he notes, stems from the fact that "it *does* rather than *is*." Among its principal functions are the tasks of adjusting "ideas to people" and "people to ideas"; and of promoting values. To these functions must be added rhetoric's goal of discovering and popularizing ideas. Because of the tasks assigned to rhetoric, Bryant asserts, this field of study deserves "a place of uncommon importance" in our academic curricula.

Not to be overlooked, moreover, is Bryant's claim that rhetoric and poetics are close allies that share many common characteristics that link them together. When we speak of rhetoric, therefore, we recognize the existence of boundaries broad enough to include written and oral discourse and oratorical, interpersonal, and poetic forms that are "informative" and "suasory" in nature.

Bryant concludes his analysis with the following paragraph summarizing the inferences that may be drawn from his arguments:

> *In brief we may assign to rhetoric a fourfold status. So far as it is concerned with the management of discourse in specific situations for practical purposes, it is an instrumental discipline. It is a literary study, involving linguistics, critical theory, and semantics as it touches the art of informing ideas, and the functioning of language. It is a philosophical study, so far as it is concerned with the method of investigation or inquiry. And finally, as it is akin to politics, drawing upon psychology and sociology, rhetoric is a social study, the study of a major force in the behavior of men in society.*

Within this perspective, it seems clear, rhetoric emerges as an instrumental discipline, and a literary, philosophical, and social study that seeks to inform and persuade citizens in a democratic society.

Bryant's effort remains today as the most comprehensive attempt undertaken by an American scholar to delineate the nature, the functions, and the scope of rhetoric. But this single definition perspective did not satisfy his University of Iowa colleague Douglas Ehninger who, as we will now see, moved in a different direction.

The Systems Perspective

Fifteen years after Bryant completed his influential essay, Ehninger published a study "On the Systems of Rhetoric."[2] Convinced that it was an unproductive undertaking to seek to discover a single definition of rhetoric that would encompass all periods, he chose instead to use the plural term "rhetorics," which would more accurately reflect the dominant thinking in a particular era of Western thought. The concept he decided to emphasize was the term "system," which he defined as "an organized, consistent, coherent way of thinking about something. . . . "The three systems, or rhetorics, singled out by Ehninger were the theories of discourse as taught in the classical, British, and contemporary periods. Each, he felt, was sufficiently distinctive to warrant special attention.

The classical system of rhetoric, Ehninger observes, arose from two forces that were operative in ancient Greece and Rome. One was the "development of democratic institutions." The other involved the need for a man to have the type of knowledge and training in discourse that would enable him to serve as his own lawyer or act as a legislator. The system the classical scholars devised to meet these rhetorical needs had three major characteristics that reflected the demands of the society. First, as a response to the oral world in which the Greeks and Romans lived, the theorists focused on oral discourse. Thus students were taught principles that had a special relevance for the art of public speaking.

A second characteristic was the emphasis on persuasion. This encompassed the three forms of proof—ethical or personal, logical or reasonable, and pathetic or emotional. Thirdly, and perhaps more central to the system, was its grammatical nature. In describing this distinguishing characteristic, Ehninger referred to the essential role that vocabulary played. The defining term "grammatical" went far beyond the meaning of words alone. It referred more to the concepts that were used to describe the essential elements that were a fundamental part of rhetoric. They included such notions as ethos, logos, and pathos; deliberative, forensic, and epideictic; and the five canons-*inventio* (message); *dispositio* (organization and adaptation); *elocutio* (language control and style); *memoria* (memory); and *pronunciatio* (voice usage and bodily activity). The classical system, in sum, organized its ideas around the nature of the speech, the speaker, the audience, and the occasion.

British and continental theories of rhetoric, which came into prominence in the sixteenth century and extended through the first half of the nineteenth century, represented to Ehninger the second major system. If the concept "grammatical" was the principal defining term for the classicists, the word "psychological" best describes this new system. The choice of this term was propitious because of the system's preoccupation with the nature of the audience. Investigations led British and continental rhetoricians to conclude that the mind is comprised of such faculties as the understanding, imagination, passions (emotions), and will. These, in turn, helped a rhetor decide whether to deliver a speech to inform, to stimulate, or persuade. In addition to their concern for the "message-mind" relationship, these authors had two other strong interests. They stressed the written as well as the oral mode of discourse; and they elevated evidence (inartistic proof as Aristotle called it) to a position of importance comparable to that of artistic proof or creative reasoning. The British and continental system, especially as it unfolded in the eighteenth and nineteenth centuries, was a natural outgrowth of the political, social, and cultural milieu of the times.

The emphasis again shifts as we move to the contemporary era, which, according to Ehninger, began around the year 1930. Since the two dominant rhetoricians, at the time of the writing of the essay on "Systems," were Kenneth Burke and I.A. Richards, Ehninger described the contemporary approach with the word "sociological." Using their writings as his launching point, he noted that the issue of human relations and of language or symbols as a means of transmitting messages have become central concerns. Only in this way could discourse fulfill the need of enhancing understanding, promoting message-receiver identification, and reducing community, national, and international tensions.

In the concluding section of his essay, Ehninger discussed several implications and advantages emanating from a systems approach. First, each system of rhetoric reveals clearly that the theory of discourse of a given era is "time-and-culture bound." Because of this fact, it is profitless to try to seek a definition of rhetoric that would apply equally to each major historical period. Secondly, the systems perspective demonstrates commonalities as well as differences between each system. Finally, it teaches us that theories of rhetoric, while containing elements that appear to be revolutionary, are perhaps more properly understood as evolutionary in their nature and scope. Each system, for example, builds upon, modifies, and refines dominant ideas that formed an earlier system.

Evolutionary Perspective

The final rhetorical perspective we wish to examine is that enunciated by James L. Golden at the Central States Speech Communication Association Convention in 1987.[3] The title of this essay was "Contemporary Trends and Historical Roots: A Personal View," and its theme was the significant part that *evolution* performs in the formulation of a rhetorical or communication theory. The paper contains three major claims, the first of which is stated as follows: *"The flow of knowledge as it relates to any discipline or field of study moves along an evolutionary path—a fact which motivates each generation of scholars to build upon the past for the purpose of gaining new intellectual insights for the present and future."*

Four witnesses were cited in support of the first claim. They included Teilhard de Chardin, the French paleontologist and Catholic priest; Michael Polanyi, a scientist and humanitarian; Kenneth Boulding, an economist and expert in image theory and ecodynamics; and Stephen Toulmin, a philosopher, historian of science, and rhetorician. These authors argue that man has risen in successive stages, each drawing upon preceding ones. As this evolutionary pattern takes place, the cumulative thought of mankind, which may be described as the *noosphere,* continues to expand at a rapid rate. This suggests that a rhetorician in the contemporary period should be able to see a concept more clearly because in effect he or she stands on the shoulders of earlier writers. In accepting this premise, we are forced to conclude that knowledge does not move in a revolutionary manner.

> *"The flow of knowledge as it relates to any discipline or field of study moves along an evolutionary path—a fact which motivates each generation of scholars to build upon the past for the purpose of gaining new intellectual insights for the present and future."*

There are, according to Golden, three implications resulting from an evolutionary interpretation. "It gives us, first of all, a reasonable view of the nature and importance of history." Such a view suggests that history is an ongoing, dynamic process, not a sterile and stagnant field of study. Secondly, it implies that anyone who wishes to cut our historical roots is unwise. Thirdly, it suggests a need to adopt a world view based on pluralism rather than embrace a monism approach that is content to teach the virtues of a single perspective.

The second main claim of the study is: *"When we trace the present health of the field of communication (or rhetoric) against the background of evolution and the related principle of noosphere, we will find that we have kept the faith in key representative areas."* This may be seen in the areas of argumentation or practical reasoning, knowledge of language, interpersonal communication, the canons of rhetoric (except for *memoria*), and ethics and values. All of these elements of rhetoric, in addition to others not mentioned, have been modified and refined through the years, thus making them more meaningful and viable concepts for the present age.

Despite the educational advantages accrued from the evolutionary progression of ideas, the author sounds a warning that is expressed in the third claim: *"The present and future directions of technology threaten to cut off the roots out of which theories of argument, language, interpersonal communication, and ethics and values have grown."* In this "Age of Compunicology," in which "The Chip" is changing our lives, it is probable, many futurists argue, "that the basic contents of the mind some day may be transferred to a machine that would ensure immortality." This prediction, along with other potential probabilities associated with the rapidly developing technology, requires students of rhetoric to consider these possible results:

1. "Argument as we have come to know it may undergo a radical discontinuity, separating us from the cumulative knowledge we have known."
2. "Language structure and usage may lose its aesthetic dimension."
3. "Interpersonal communication may become disassociated from the self which depends so much upon the relationship between 'I' and 'Thou.'"

Golden's essay concludes that the field of communication has "developed in an evolutionary manner," making it possible for the rhetorical scholars to contribute significantly to the *noosphere*. But, the author adds, the study also "has tried to demonstrate that technology, notwithstanding the essential role it plays in our daily lives, may if we lack vigilance, separate us from our roots."

How Three Rhetorical Perspectives Have Influenced the Approach of This Book

The three perspectives on rhetoric discussed in the foregoing pages have had a significant influence on the content and organization of this volume. We have felt the impact, for example, of Bryant's comprehensive effort to define the parameters of rhetoric; of his belief that rhetoric is both an "informative" and "persuasive" enterprise; and that it is a highly substantive field of endeavor that seeks to produce action, and is comprised of philosophical, literary, and social qualities. Most of all, we share with him that it is a subject that deserves a prominent place in education and society.

Ehninger's work on "Systems," more than any comparable study, has influenced the organizational structure of The *Rhetoric of Western Thought*. By singling out the three dominant periods, and calling each one a separate system reflecting the culture of the day, he provided an important rationale for organizing the materials around the writings of the classicists, the British and continental theorists, and contemporary authors. In order to make our chronological pattern more complete, we have incorporated a brief transitional section on medieval and renaissance rhetoric. In doing so, however, we agree with Ehninger's argument that this transitional period does not constitute a separate system.

One shortcoming of Ehninger's analysis needs to be mentioned. In labeling the contemporary period as being largely "sociological," he tended to overlook a major emphasis now referred to as "rhetoric as a way of knowing" or "rhetoric as epistemic." This oversight he corrected in his later writings-especially in his essay on the future directions of rhetoric.

The ideas presented in our third study, "Contemporary Trends and Historical Roots in Communication," have both influenced and been influenced by the courses we have taught in Western rhetorical theory during the past twenty-five years. By adopting an evolutionary emphasis in this volume, we have given credence, it is hoped, to the notion that knowledge proceeds on a progressive plane. It follows, therefore, that in studying the theories of any period, we need to know how these theories not only set forth a new emphasis but how they also may have been derived in part from earlier works. This approach makes it clear, on the one hand, that Aristotle, perhaps the single most influential rhetorician in Western history, did not say all that needs to be said on rhetoric. But, on the other hand, it suggests that what he wrote about rhetoric should be known when we analyze later theorists. Because of our strong commitment to the belief that cumulative thought of the ages is constantly expanding, the number of pages we have devoted to the contemporary era is somewhat larger than that of the two preceding systems.

Our goal in this volume, in brief, is to advance the notion that rhetorical theories as described in the three major periods have no real connection to the corrupted use of the term that so often appears in our print and electronic media, and falls from the lips of politicians. We concur with Chaim Perelman, one of the most important theorists we will be analyzing in the modern era, when he says that the goal of rhetoric "is to intensify an adherence to values, to create a disposition to act." Seen from such a perspective, Perelman adds, "rhetoric becomes a subject of great philosophic interest."[4] Instead of being divorced from reality, rhetoric is joined with it. Instead of being separated from action, it embraces it. Out of these dynamic relationships the relevance of rhetoric is derived.

The nature and relevance of rhetoric described here and to be depicted throughout this volume was brilliantly personified by the late Martin Luther King, Jr. who sought mightily throughout his career "to intensify an adherence to values" and "create a disposition to act."

We saw Dr. King and 200,000 of his followers as they came to the nation's capital on August 28, 1963. One of the authors watched them pass on Constitution Avenue waving their banners in the warm summer breeze. They stopped on the Washington Monument Grounds and chanted the word "freedom," then marched in unison toward the Lincoln Memorial. It

was, in short, a revolution of non-violent resistance that dramatized the African Americans' serious intent to assimilate as equals into the American society. What King said on this occasion in his "I Have a Dream Speech" already has gained a permanent place in literature. This address and his "Letter from the Birmingham Jail" demonstrated King's ability to speak to men's and women's noble nature. Through such messages and the thrust of his forceful personality and graphic style, he identified with the masses of his race and won the respect of the enlightened members of the white community. Later, as he was attacked by more militant leaders in the civil rights movement, he modified his attitudes on "black Power" but refused to alter his basic strategy of non-violence. Shortly after his tragic death the *New York Times,* in capsulizing his career, spoke the sentiments of the majority of Americans with these words.

Martin Luther King was a preacher, a man from Georgia and a Negro who became a golden-tongued orator, a spokesman for the Deep South and the Ghetto North, a symbol above color of undying yearnings and imperishable rights. He was an American in the truest sense: for he had a dream. . . . He was a Negro who made Americans aware that the better angels of our nature could dominate the struggle of the United States and its people. The dream of true equality of rights and opportunities without regard to race is nearer because in our lifetime there lived an American named Martin Luther King.

One of the writers went to Washington, D.C. during the days following King's death for the purpose of presenting a Delta Sigma Rho-Tau Kappa Alpha Award to Eric Sevareid for his outstanding achievements as a commentator and critic. During the course of our dinner conversation, Mr. Sevareid was asked to name the greatest speaker he had known. Without hesitation he ranked Martin Luther King first. His choice was a good one, for until the end, King's faith in the power of rhetoric to alter attitudes and exalt humankind never diminished.

Notes

1. *Quarterly Journal of Speech,* 39 (December 1953), pp. 401–424.

2. *Philosophy and Rhetoric,* 1 (Summer 1968), pp. 131–144.

3. *Central States Speech Journal,* 38 (Fall/Winter 1987), pp. 262–270.

4. "The New Rhetoric: A Theory of Practical Reasoning," reprinted in *Great Ideas Today* (Chicago: Encyclopedia Britannica, Inc., 1970), p. 279.

PART 1

Classical Rhetorical Theory

If any one group of people could be said to have invented rhetoric, it would be the ancient Greeks. For they were the first Westerners to systematically write down recommendations for making speech persuasive to others. Over three thousand years ago, men and women in this small land in the eastern Mediterranean spoke directly to one another, broadcast ideas, listened, and like us, often misunderstood their peers. Their world was oriented to the spoken word, as is our own. To be sure, there was an alphabet and some Greeks knew how to read and write, but the majority were not so educated. Written communication in early Athens tended to be expensive and laborious, and was usually reserved for such memorable events as the recording of laws and constitutions. Day-to-day communication was carried on by word of mouth in face-to-face settings.

We know a good deal about Greek culture because the Romans who succeeded them preserved so much of it. To the practical Roman mind, it made no sense to reinvent the wheel, to create new cultural institutions, if earlier people had already produced effective ones. So they simply absorbed what they considered to be the best of Greek culture into their own civilization. They assigned Latin names in place of earlier Greek terms, organized random Greek ideas, refined concepts from time to time, and preserved largely intact what had been created before their own time.

Since the systematic study of rhetoric began in ancient times, we start our narrative with the world of Greece and Rome.

Major Figures

The Greeks Before Christianity

Homer
9th–8th century, B.C.E.

Blind poet whose epic tales of the Trojan War introduce us to the use of the spoken word in early Greece. *Iliad, Odyssey*

Corax
5th century, B.C.E.

Sicilian Greek who developed the first written *early* rhetoric in the West, based on probability and designed to help courtroom pleaders.

Pericles
(495–429), B.C.E.

Athenian statesman and general whose sustained persuasive efforts resulted in the construction of the Parthenon, a magnificent temple considered one of the seven wonders of the ancient world. *Funeral Oration*

Gorgias
(483?–376? B.C.E.)

Sicilian ambassador and teacher of rhetoric whose flowery prose style fascinated Greek audiences for over fifty years.

Socrates
(470?–399 B.C.E.)

Plato's friend and teacher whose questioning search for truth provided the model for his philosophic dialogues.

Isocrates
(436–338 B.C.E.)

Foremost speech teacher of the ancient world whose school at Athens was dedicated to the training of responsible civic leaders. *Against the Sophists, Antidosis*

Plato
(427–347 B.C.E.)

Disciple of Socrates and founder of the Academy, he outlined the dimensions of a true and false rhetoric. *Gorgias, Phaedrus*

Aristotle
(384–322 B.C.E.)

Plato's most famous student whose notes on rhetoric are considered by many to be the most significant work on persuasion ever written. *The Rhetoric*

Demosthenes
(385?–322 B.C.E.)

The most famous orator of the ancient world whose speaking skills were primarily due to the diligent nurturing of limited talents. *On the Crown*

Aeschines
(389–314 B.C.E.)

Demosthenes' rival, a naturally talented orator who tended to favor Macedonian policies over the welfare of his native city. *Against Ctesiphon*

The Romans Before and After the Birth of Christ

Cicero
(106–43 B.C.E.)

Rome's leading orator-philosopher who wrote extensively about the theory and practice of public discourse. *De Oratore, Brutus, Orator*

Quintilian
(35–100 A.D.)

First imperial professor of rhetoric at Rome, he developed a comprehensive system of rhetorical education which later influenced European educators. *The Institutes of Oratory*

Longinus
(1st century A.D.)

His stimulating essay on great writing had a major impact on later British rhetoricians. *On the Sublime*

St. Augustine
(354–430)

Christian convert who introduced his co-religionists to Ciceronian rhetoric; wrote the first manual on preaching. *De Doctrina Christiana*

European Thinkers After Augustine

Desiderius Erasmus
(1466?–1536)

Dutch scholar who influenced many of his peers through his works on style and composition. *De Copia, De Ratione Studii*

Thomas Wilson
(1525?–1581)

British neoclassicist who published the first rhetoric written in English, based largely on the works of Cicero. *The Arte of Rhetorique*

Peter Ramus
(1515–1572)

French monk who re-defined rhetoric as the study of style and delivery only; he assigned invention and disposition to logic. *Dialectique*

Key Concepts

- Rhetoric

- Poetics

- Dialectic

- Rhetorical systems

- Evolution

- Noosphere

- Plato's moral-philosophical view of rhetoric

- Aristotle's scientific approach

- The educational-philosophical view of Isocrates, Cicero, and Quintilian

- The forms of oratory

- Forensic—speaking designed for courts of law

- Deliberative—speaking designed for the public assembly

- Epideictic—speaking designed for ceremonial occasions

- Fundamental processes of rhetoric
  A. Invention—the art of discovery
     1. Artistic forms of proof (created by the speaker)
        Logical proof (probability, signs, the enthymeme, the example, topoi, lines of argument, deduction, induction, stasis)
        Ethical proof (listener impressions of a speaker's character, intelligence, and goodwill; cardinal virtues)
        Emotional proof (appeals to listener feelings, types of character)
     2. Nonartistic forms of proof (not created by the speaker); documents, the depositions of witnesses
  B. Disposition—the art of organizing one's material
     1. Selection of ideas and evidence
     2. Order or sequence (proem, narration, argument, epilogue, exordium, proof, refutation, peroration)
     3. Apportionment (judgment and prudence in adapting to one's listeners)
  C. Style or language—the art of clothing ideas with words
     1. Clearness, propriety
     2. Metaphor, other forms of ornamentation
     3. Types of oral style (plain, middle, grand)
  D. Delivery—the art of oral presentation
     1. Voice control
     2. Gesture and bodily movement
  E. Memory—the art of recalling ideas and images

- Freedom of speech, freedom of choice

- The nature versus nurture controversy

- The sophists

- Second Sophistic (the encomium)

- The Christianization of rhetoric (apologists, polemics, sermons)

- Letter writing

- Ramus' truncated rhetoric

- The Renaissance

The World of Greece and Rome

Douglas Ehninger reminds us that the collective rhetorics of a particular time are culture bound. Consequently, if we wish to understand the major theories emanating from the two great classical civilizations of Greece and Rome, we must first examine the world in which they were conceived.

GREEK CULTURE

Let us begin with a consideration of geography and climate, two important cultural determinants. The land of the Greeks is a rugged, mountainous peninsula in eastern Europe, jutting southward into the Mediterranean Sea. Although countless islands in the Aegean and the Adriatic have from time to time been under Greek control, what interests us most is the Greek mainland, a land mass of some 40,000 square miles, about the size of the state of Ohio.

In Greece, you are never far from the mountains or the sea. The crisp, clear air and the bright, blue skies of the eastern Mediterranean are a delight to tourists and cameramen alike. Even amateurs return home with marvelous colored slides for both the scenery and atmosphere are spectacular.

What is not spectacular is the limited productivity of Greek soil. Tillable soil is at a premium here. Olive trees are carefully tended on hillside slopes because there is no other place for them to grow. Farmers struggle to eke out a living today as in ancient times. The modern visitor to Greece still sees coarse-garbed peasant women weeding their crops by hand, bent over as their forebears were centuries before. Donkeys haul precious twigs and prunings for fuel, along with hay to feed the cattle. The importation of food from abroad is a fact of life familiar to every Greek.

It was trade from abroad in fact which provided Athens with its opportunity to lead the ancient world. While Sparta, her primary rival, is ringed by

The Greek shoreline.

snow-capped peaks even in May, Athens is an easy dozen miles from a large natural harbor, the Piraeus. It was the Athenian navy which destroyed the Persians at sea in 480 B.C.E., after their city had been sacked. And it was the Athenians who replaced the Phoenicians as the leading traders of the Mediterranean world.

Scattered islands and isolated mountain communities had one thing in common in ancient times; both preferred strong local government. The Greeks

5

formed between two and three hundred city states, with Athens and its population of 200,000 being by far the largest. These mini-states shared much in common: all spoke the same language; all shared a common history and literature; all worshiped the same gods; each participated whenever it could in athletic games and in music, drama, and oratory contests.

Yet, strangely enough, these miniature city states rarely joined together in common defense. Local rivalries often seemed more threatening to them than distant barbarians in the north and east. The pleas of countless orators for pan-Hellenism, for a single Greek state, were of no avail. Only military dictators like Philip of Macedon and his son, Alexander the Great, would eventually force unification. What the city states seemed to want most was simply to be left alone.[1]

Culture is more than the sum of its parts. Oftentimes there is a spirit, an esprit de corps, a unique way of life which transcends geography, climate, agriculture, and government. In *The Greek Way,* Edith Hamilton tried to capture this thread, by contrasting the civilizations of East and West, of Egypt and Greece.[2] The Kingdom of the Nile was a vast, rich land area controlled by the pharoah, his priests, and his soldiers. An army of slaves made specialized vocations possible. There was ample sustenance for all and extended periods of peace. Yet Hamilton tells us that Egyptian society was preoccupied with death. The pharoahs erected giant monuments to themselves to impress future generations. As a result, Egypt became the land of tombs and pyramids. Priests counselled the downtrodden that they could look forward to an afterlife; regardless of their present state, a brighter future lay ahead. Given such advice, acceptance of servitude was widespread.

Athens was a world apart from such thinking. Individual perfection of mind and body dominated Greek thought; hence, the Greeks excelled at philosophy and sports. Life in all its exuberant potential was the keynote to Greek civilization. The free citizen of Athens was trained to be a generalist, able to do many things well. He might be asked at any time to judge a murder trial or oversee the strengthening of city fortifications, embark on an embassy abroad or participate as a member of the Executive Council in city government. Citizens were expected to join in Assembly debates on topics ranging from war and peace, to finance, legislation, national defense, and commerce.[3] Probably the historian Thucydides summed up Athen-

Greek statues emphasized perfection of form.

ian civic responsibility best when he wrote: "We do not say that a man who takes no interest in politics is a man who minds his own business; we say that he has no business here at all."[4]

The early Greeks worshiped perfection. It was, they thought, the domain of the gods. If man were to approach godliness, he must strive always to do his best, to be as perfect as he was able. The Greeks thought every object had a character of its own, an essence which they called *ethos.* Modern sociologists often speak of a society's ethos when they mean its distinctive flavor. Everything the Greek saw about him appeared to have just such a character. A perfect speaker, for example, was conceived of as a man of honesty, intelligence and good will.[5] The speaker did not himself necessarily possess such qualities; rather, others perceived such qualities in him. It was the appearance of perfection which mattered.

In Greek society, form often seemed to be more important than reality. The perfect statue revealed a superb, muscular body and a faultless face, devoid of human emotion. It is only later in the days of the Romans that a smile appears upon faces cut in stone. The perfect story conformed to a literary ideal rather than to factual accuracy. The way a soldier died in battle seemed to be more important in the eyes of his relatives than whether the battle was won or lost. Ritual and procession typified Greek religion rather than sermons and the worship of a personal God.

Greek society, like our own, was oriented to the spoken word. Take Homer's great epic poems, the *Illiad* and the *Odyssey,* for example. These works constitute the poetic cornerstone of Greek culture—part history, part mythology, part oratory, part patriotism.[6] It was as if a single great genius wrote the *Bible,* Chaucer's *Canterbury Tales,* and Shakespeare's plays all in one. Homer's epics involved events which took place about 1300 B.C.E. An Asian prince violated the Greek code of hospitality and had to be punished; ten years of bitter warfare followed. About six centuries later, a blind wanderer began to collect and narrate the many tales of the conflict. Homer's tales passed from generation to generation by word of mouth until at last they became so much a part of Greek heritage that Homerology was taught to every schoolboy. Years later, at Olympia, Delphi, and Epidaurus, when a Greek citizen heard Homer's tales repeated, he would at any moment pick up the narrative himself if the storyteller paused unduly. Known throughout history as the first great work of European literature, Homer's epic poems were not finally written down until the third century, B.C.E. Oral tradition was as much a part of Greek culture as it is today in modern Africa or India.

> Since the city state of Athens was a democracy governed by some 40,000 free citizens, the power of every citizen to speak effectively was highly valued.

The Greeks depended upon trade for survival. Because of their geographic isolation, they were committed to strong local government. These independent city states shared much in common however —language, religion, history, literature, the persistent drive to seek perfection in mind and body. Theirs was an oral society dedicated to self-actualization. Thus the theory and practice of speechmaking came to flourish among them.

The first written rhetoric in the Western world was composed about 465 B.C. at the Greek colony of Syracuse in Sicily. A change of government resulted when a tyranny was displaced by a democracy. In the aftermath, property holders presented conflicting claims to various parcels of land. Who were the true owners? An enterprising bystander by the name of Corax realized that if a claimant could establish a more plausible case than his opponent, he would win title to the disputed property. With this insight, the rhetoric of probability was born. Corax devised a system of rules for arranging and arguing a legal case and promptly made this knowledge available to others, for a fee.[7] His system was later introduced to Athens and other city states on the mainland.

Legal suits were an everyday occurrence in ancient Greece. In cases involving major crimes, the jury usually included five hundred members. Thus, oratory often was more critical to legal success than factual evidence. Greek law did not provide for an advocate system like the one we know in America.[8] Every free citizen spoke for himself. But it was possible to secure the services of a good speechwriter if one had the necessary means. Many of the leading orators of ancient Greece, such as the great Demosthenes, amassed considerable fortunes by serving as forensic logographers, legal ghost-writers for the well-to-do.

Since the city state of Athens was a democracy governed by some 40,000 free citizens, the power of every citizen to speak effectively was highly valued. Rule by precinct, or *deme* as the Greeks called it, meant that on almost any day one might be called upon to speak on a matter of public policy.[9] Except for generals, all city officials were chosen annually by lot. This ruling Executive Council of Fifty was chosen anew each month. Jury panels of 6,000 were regularly on call. In any given day, one out of every five Athenian citizens was engaged in some form of public service. The ability to speak, to listen critically to the arguments of others, and to utter appropriate response—these were deemed valuable skills by all.

At the foot of the Acropolis, the three hundred foot limestone hill which dominates the central city of Athens, stands the *agora* or marketplace. Here traders came to buy and sell. Here were located the minor courts, side by side with merchant stalls, and here was the *stoa* or porch where the philosophers liked to stroll. The agora was an international marketplace for goods and ideas—colorful, noisy, varied, unique in the world of the ancient Greeks. While most other city states had their acropolis and agora, none attracted the clientele, foreign and domestic, that Athens did.

Greek mythology tells us that a maiden named Cassandra possessed the power to prophesy the future, but the god Apollo decreed that her prophesies should never be believed. A prophet the Greeks (and later the Romans) *did* believe was the oracle at Delphi. For a thousand years men came to an isolated mountainside in central Greece to seek her advice. Petitioners presented their questions to the priests of the Temple of Apollo. The priests would then disappear into the bowels of the Temple to consult with the oracle herself, a peasant woman from a nearby village. In a semi-trance, the oracle mumbled a reply which was later relayed to the questioner. In gratitude, he would leave valuable gifts of goods and money. One such petitioner, a wealthy prince from Thrace, asked if his contemplated invasion of Persia would prove successful. The response was that as a result of the action he was about to undertake, a great empire would fall. The prince confidently led his army into battle and was badly defeated. Ruined and disillusioned he returned to Delphi and demanded to know what went wrong. As a result of your action, a mighty empire fell, the priest replied; we did not say that it would be the *Persian* Empire.

From 776 B.C.E. until the Christians took over the Roman Empire some thousand years later, competitive athletic contests were held every four years at the village of Olympia in southern Greece. Besides sports, Greeks from all over the Mediterranean world vied with one another for trophies in drama, music, and oratory. Distinguished visitors from foreign lands, such as the Sicilian, Gorgias of Leontini, were invited to address the assembled multitude.[10] Each city state had its own treasure house for the series of events often took weeks at a time. So much a part of the Greek world were these Olympic games that warring cities would declare a truce so they could compete peacefully with one another and resume battle once competitive activities ceased.

Of the many uses of the spoken word in ancient Athens, none was more important than education. Athenian boys were trained orally by private tutors. They learned music, reading, writing, and gymnastics in this way.[11] The dialogue method of question and answer was reserved for advanced work. At the start of the fifth century, B.C., an information explosion took place in Ionia and on the islands near Asia Minor. In Athens, there was keen interest in higher education and in the new discoveries. The need to disseminate this knowledge and to offer advanced work was met by a band of wandering teachers who travelled by foot from one city state to another offering short courses for a fee.[12] These itinerant professors were called *sophists,* after the Greek word *sophos* meaning knowledge. Their function was to supplement the elementary instruction of the day. Fluent lecturers with excellent memories, the Greek sophists offered courses in rhetoric, grammar, art, drama, architecture, mathematics, poetry, literature, and various other branches of knowledge.

Just who were these itinerant teachers? The principal sophists of this time were Protagoras from Abdera (born circa 490 B.C.E.), Prodicus from Ceos (born circa 460 B.C.E.), Hippias from Elis (born circa 485–445 B.C.E.), Gorgias from Leontini in Sicily (born circa 480 B.C.E.), and Thrasymachus from Chalcedon. Other sophists include Callicles, Anaxagoras and Antiphon. Although undoubtedly some of the above were acquainted, they were not organized nor did they necessarily teach similar philosophies. It can be said with some assurance, however, that they shared a common goal in that they aimed for practical knowledge. Their courses were "designed to teach the Greek ideal of *arete:* the knowledge and attitude for effective participation in domestic, social, and political life . . . . the sophists were progressive and innovative leaders in an educational reform characterized by highly functional instruction."[13]

The sophists were popular and successful teachers in their day. But, they had their critics led by Plato. In brief, the sophists were reproached by the traditionalists because they threatened the very core of the established educational system of the times on two fronts. First, as noted above, the sophists featured practical knowledge (subjects associated with governing and decision-making). This emphasis ran contrary to the traditional philosophers who were engaged in seeking truth. Second, the sophists were willing to teach anyone who could pay for their services. Although to us today this fact seems rather insignificant, it had profound repercussions in the ancient Greek world. Heretofore, education was available only to the aristocracy—those born into the elite/ruling class families. Now, however, the sophists made education available to anyone with the financial resources. Access to education, then, was no longer restricted by birthright and was now available to those with monetary means as well. Although this shift did not make possible the education of the masses, it did open the door for a more democratic approach to education. As Jarratt tells us, underlying Plato's criticism of the sophists is his "aristocratic resistance to making available the skills of governance to anyone, regardless of birth, who could pay for them . . . . The shift from birth to wealth as a criterion of rule was a major step to democracy."[14] Thus, the sophists posed a threat to the traditional educational system of the early Greeks. It is important to keep the above points in mind when we consider Plato's powerful critique of the sophists in Chapter 2 of this text.

Besides the broad criticisms mentioned above, Plato had a narrower concern that dealt with the early sophists' teachings on rhetoric. John Poulakes notes that "sophistical rhetoric emerged in a culture of competition and spectacles. When the Sophists started appearing on the Hellenic horizon, the highest form of competition was the Olympic Games, and the highest form of spectacle was the dramatic performance of the theatre" (*The Possibility of Rhetoric's Early Beginnings,* The Van Zelst Lecture in Communication, Northwestern University, Evanston, Illinois, May 11, 1991). Little wonder then that Plato, concerned with philosopher kings searching for truth, should condemn the "brilliant styles, colorful appearances, and flamboyant personalities" of his sophistic rivals.

The later fall of the sophists was partly due, Plato tells us in one of his dialogues, to the use of rhetoric as mere flattery and as a vehicle for misleading others.[15] If happiness meant a life founded on truth, sophists who disregarded the truth and made the worse appear the better cause were evildoers, clever but specious reasoners. Some sophists were suspect as agnostics who preferred man rather than god as the measure of all things. Others offered instruction on any subject at all for a fee and many promised more than they could deliver. For all these reasons sophistic education declined in importance early in the fourth century, B.C.E.

Athenian society was oriented to the spoken word; hence the study of rational discourse, of oral persuasion, and of drama was a natural outgrowth of Greek curiosity and inventiveness. Dialectic, rhetoric, and poetics were the terms the Greeks used for such studies. As we would expect in such a society, Greek rhetoric encompassed a variety of speech settings. Legal speaking in the law courts was referred to as forensic discourse; political speaking such as that which occurred in the Athenian Assembly was called deliberative; occasional ceremonial speeches were labelled epideictic. Greek interest in the language with which to clothe ideas produced a plain, middle, and grand style of address.[16] The perfect speaker was conceived of as bright, honest, and socially responsible, a man of truth and reason who could, when occasion demanded, move the mind and passions of his listeners.

The orator-general, Pericles, was just such a leader. Remarkably adept at political persuasion, Pericles succeeded in having the war treasury of the Delian defense league transferred from its island home to Athens for safekeeping. He then convinced his fellow Athenians to use these war funds for peaceful purposes by re-building the Acropolis, earlier destroyed by a Persian army. Pericles' dream was of structures made to last centuries, marble temples to dazzle and fascinate mankind for thousands of

The Parthenon, Athens, Greece.

Aechines and Demosthenes

Of the many Greek orators of note, two particularly merit our attention. The first was a man of great natural talent, a soldier-athlete, who began life as a teacher's aide in his father's school. Aeschines by name, this eloquent Greek was a professional actor of considerable ability. He was chosen as court clerk, a position of responsibility, and represented Athens in an important diplomatic mission to Philip of Macedon. Aeschines was graceful of movement, an easy, fluent speaker to whom success seemed to come without effort. He was, in short, naturally talented. As one who chose the course of political expediency, Aeschines was often in the public eye, a popular, if not always credible, leader.

In contrast stood Demosthenes, acclaimed by many as the world's greatest orator.[17] Demosthenes began life so inauspiciously we would today think of him as a "born loser." He was a sickly child who could not participate in athletic games like other youths. His patrimony was squandered by unscrupulous guardians and though he ultimately defeated them after five separate trials, he was penniless at the time of the final verdict. Demosthenes yearned to play a major role in the affairs of his city state but he labored under an awesome series of handicaps: a weak voice, awkward movement, sloppy diction, a lateral lisp, shortness of breath, and a tendency to compose long sentences, ill-suited for oral presentation. It is said that when he first spoke in the Athenian Assembly, men laughed at his fumbling ways and he retired in shame. Failure might deter a lesser man but not Demosthenes. He dreamed of fame and fortune and he meant to have both.

Legend tells us that an actor instructed him in voice and physical action.[18] To overcome his lisp, Demosthenes spoke with pebbles in his mouth. To project his voice, he delivered speeches by the seashore, shouting above the crashing waves. To strengthen his breath, he declaimed orations while running uphill. To strengthen his will to succeed, he shaved half his head so that he could no longer appear in public and could thus undertake his studies

unmolested in a hidden cave. Demosthenes, to a large degree, represented the triumph of nurture over nature.

Demosthenes and Aeschines were political and oratorical rivals whose final confrontation came in 330 B.C.E. in a famous trial known as the case "On the Crown." A well-meaning friend proposed that the Athenian Assembly award Demosthenes a golden crown for public service to the state.[19] The friend recommended that the crown be bestowed at the Theater of Dionysius where a large assembly of citizens and foreigners could observe the ceremony. Aeschines, who barely won a bribery suit brought against him by Demosthenes several years before, now saw his chance for revenge. He contested the crown on three bases: first, that Demosthenes could not receive such an award because the books he kept as a financial official had not yet been audited; second, that Athenian law required citizen honors to be given before the Assembly rather than at the Theater specified; and third, that Demosthenes did not deserve such an award for he had not always had Athens' best interests in mind.

Technically, Aeschines was in the right on the first two charges. Athenian law stipulated that unaudited officials were not eligible to receive public honors and that when public awards were given, they were to be awarded before the Assembly itself. But the critical issue was the third and it was here that Demosthenes was to score his greatest victory. His problem was one of self-vindication: how does a public man defend himself when his advice proves costly in men and property? For many years Demosthenes urged his fellow citizens to oppose Philip of Macedon—the father of Alexander the Great. Finally, they did so and were soundly defeated. How then could this advocate of defeat win an audience to his cause when many of his listeners counted relatives among the fallen?

The case Demosthenes devised has won the admiration of political advocates ever since. Knowing that his listeners would be annoyed by self-praise,

Demosthenes coupled his political career with the course taken by their ancestors. What he advised, their parents endorsed. To reject Demosthenes meant to reject what most recognized as the best of the Athenian past. The vindictive oratory of Aeschines was simply no match for Demosthenes' brilliant strategy. Heavily fined because he failed to get even one fifth of the jury's vote, Aeschines retired in defeat to the island of Rhodes. Exile from the mother city, Athenians believed, was a fate worse than death.

---

years. He secured the services of the best artisans known to man. And he presided over the entire grand operation for the better part of thirty years. If we would know what the Golden Age of Pericles was like, we need only look at the Parthenon in downtown Athens. A temple dedicated to the patron goddess Athena (whose forty-foot ivory and gold statue it housed), the Parthenon is one of the man-made wonders of the world—a living testimonial to the power of the spoken word.

The military defeat of the Greek city states by Philip of Macedon in 338 B.C.E. brought with it a dramatic change in Greek thinking. Forced at last into a pan-Hellenic mold, the Greeks now found themselves part of a much larger world. In the new Macedonian society, the individual citizen was no longer king. Greek philosophers sought to ease this dissonant situation in two ways.[20] The first involved reducing the importance of the world around the Greeks. This approach was championed by a thinker named Epicurus. By non-involvement in public affairs, the individual Greek could achieve a state of tranquility, of apathy or nonconcern. He could avoid pain simply by entering a non-feeling state. *Epicureans* defined pleasure not as physical indulgence and sexual license but as the absence of pain in the body or trouble in the mind. Satisfying momentary needs was essential; community involvement was not.

A second popular philosophy of the day was called stoicism, after the porch where Zeno and his followers roamed. Wisdom and self-control lay at the heart of this school of thought. The *stoics* declared there was a basic order to the universe, knowable to man. An individual achieved happiness by discovering this order or pattern and conforming to it. At various times, the pattern was referred to as nature, providence, the cosmos, god, reason, and law. The stoic was unaffected by such externals as wealth, beauty, and power. Conformity to the plan of the universe, even if this involved suffering, guided his behavior.

> The Romans found much to admire in Greek culture and they borrowed generously.

Greek stoics interpreted the Roman conquest of the Mediterranean world as the divine plan of life. Later when Christianity became the state religion in Rome, its ready acceptance throughout the Roman Empire was assured. Thus, a pagan Greek philosophy paved the away for the expansion of the Christian religion.

ROMAN CULTURE

If the culture of Greece contributed to the development of a viable and enduring rhetoric, so, too, did the setting which surrounded the Romans. Central Italy is blessed with a warm climate and fertile plains. Life is easy there as it had been earlier in ancient Egypt. Captive slaves did a thousand manual tasks, freeing the wealthy for entertainment and capricious whim. One of the Caesars, for example, liked horse races so much he set legions of workers to the task of creating a hippodrome in his back yard—a five story excavation and race course viewable to the tourist today on Palatine Hill. The Romans founded a vast empire that lasted a thousand years. Their mother city became the dominant center of Western civilization, a far more powerful metropolis than Athens had ever been.

Practicality dominated Roman thought. In order to control a vast empire from the steppes of Russia to the shores of the Atlantic the Romans created a powerful army, an efficient bureaucracy, and a set of universal laws. They also constructed a connecting network of all-weather roads and a system of aqueducts to carry water to inland towns far from river or sea. The Caesars sought to provide the citizens of Rome itself with spectacular diversions, so they built eight coliseums in addition to the one which still stands at one end of the Forum.[21] Here the people witnessed such spectacles as chariot races, naval battles, fights to the death among powerful animals and, of course, the confrontation of lions and early Christians. Inside plumbing and outside sewers were Roman in-

The Roman Coliseum.

ventions, too.[22] Remnant Greek temples were refurbished to become modern Roman temples and later, Christian churches. No structure went to waste when the Romans controlled the Mediterranean world.

The Romans found much to admire in Greek culture and they borrowed generously. Rhetoric struck them as a more practical art than philosophy, for their Republic was modeled after the Athenian city state. The twelve Greek gods became twelve Roman gods. Roman youth were taught by Greek tutors, thus insuring the preservation of much of earlier Greek civilization. Homer's epic poems inspired Virgil's *Aeneid*. Roman dramatists copied Greek dramatists. Roman history, architecture, philosophy—all contained much that was Greek in origin.

But the Romans were more than just borrowers. They were classifiers and refiners. They preserved and transmitted the heart of Hellenic civilization to the wide world they conquered, and later this same Roman network served the cause of Christianity, for it was the Romans who brought the new religion to Britain and Africa, Babylon and Scandinavia.

In the realm of education, Isocrates' Greek system of liberal arts wedded to the spoken word became the pattern everywhere. In Rome as in Athens earlier, the philosopher-orator became the ideal citizen. Cicero was the Latin embodiment of the ideal. A brilliant speaker, a lifelong student of philosophy and liberal studies, a clever politician, ambitious, expedient, marvelously literate and articulate, Cicero epitomized the Roman Republic a half century before Christ. When he desired to study rhetoric and philosophy, he sailed east to Athens and Rhodes.

Demosthenes, he perceived as the greatest of the Greek orators; men would later debate whether Cicero himself surpassed Athens' favorite son. Greek teachers, Greek ideals, Greek philosophy, Greek gods adopted with little or no change—that was the Roman way.[23]

The treatment presented here of Roman culture is admittedly brief. A helpful overview of that culture can be found in Edith Hamilton's *The Roman Way to Western Civilization* (1932; available in recent paperback reprint), a companion volume to her *Greek Way* mentioned earlier. M.L. Clarke's *Rhetoric at Rome* (1953) provides the interested reader with a coherent specialized treatment.

In 292 B.C.E. Egyptian and Greek scholars at the great library at Alexandria began the mammoth job of preservation, classification, and refinement of Greek culture. Here for the first time ever an authoritative text of Homer's *Iliad* was written down. Here were deposited and catalogued Aristotle's encyclopedic studies, including the *Rhetoric* salvaged by a Roman general from a cellar in Asia Minor. The concept of stock issues applicable in trial settings was identified here for the first time. Such central turning points in a criminal case included the following: that an alleged crime was committed, that the alleged act caused harm, that the harm was less than the prosecution charged, and that the alleged act was justified.

The *Rhetorica ad Herenium,* written in the first century, B.C.E., is the earliest Latin rhetoric of which we have knowledge. Characteristically, it is Greek to the core and tersely practical.[24] Here in this schoolboy manual we encounter for the first time the five great canons of classical rhetoric: *inventio, dispositio elocutio, memoria,* and *pronuntiatio.* In order to compose an effective speech, the speaker must first choose an appropriate topic. Then he must identify the whole range of relevant ideas and supporting evidence available. This initial process of discovery the Romans labelled *inventio;* modern rhetoricians call it invention. Next the speaker must select from the whole spectrum of ideas available to him those which best meet the needs of purpose, audience, and occasion. Further, he must arrange them in a sequence both clear and memorable. Then the speaker must determine the amount of detail needed for the proofs he intends to employ. Selection, sequence, and apportionment were what the Romans call *dispositio;* modern speech communication scholars prefer the term speech organization. *Elocutio* refers to style, to the words and rhetorical devices the speaker uses to clothe his ideas. *Memoria* or memory embraces the mental process of recall. In a day when manuscript speeches were drafted *after* a speech was delivered, when the question demanded discourse hours in length, memorization was a necessary skill for the orator. The Greeks and Romans like today's college students recognized the value of code words, mnemonic devices designed to aid instant recall. Finally, the Romans stressed *pronuntiatio* or delivery. Here they meant the speaker's voice and physical action. To Roman theorists rhetoric was one great *art,* composed of five lesser arts.

The Romans made other contributions to rhetorical theory as well. In contrast to Aristotle and the Greeks, they stressed the impact of the speaker's prior reputation upon his listeners.[25] The speaker, they noted, should adjust his material to the audience *while speaking* rather than serving as a slave to a set speech memorized earlier. In a court of law, the speaker should focus his attention upon the key issue in the case rather than provide equal stress to each argument he advanced. Like the Greeks, the Romans recognized the importance of emotion in persuasion, but what was new was their emphasis upon a moving peroration, an end to the speech deliberately calculated to influence the feelings of listeners throughout the audience.

The Roman lawyer-rhetorician, Quintilian, compiled a four-volume work on rhetoric which embodied a system of education from the cradle to the grave. So systematic was Quintilian's *Institutes of Oratory* that it served as the model for much of medieval education throughout Europe.[26] Clarity of language was stressed to the point where misunderstanding was virtually impossible. The apprenticeship of student speakers to master orators was encouraged in much the same way as masons and carpenters learned their trade. As a rule, Roman rhetoricians were better at amplification than innovation. Greek ideas became Roman ideas, often with little or no credit being given to the original source.

SUMMARY

Broadly speaking, speech theorists in Greece and Rome viewed the subject of rhetoric in one of three ways: as a moral instrument for conveying truth to the masses, as a culturally important subject which merited scientific classification and analysis, and as practical training essential for the active citizen. Plato typified the first view; Aristotle, the second; and Isocrates, Cicero, and Quintilian, the third.[27] Let us turn now to a sampling of the views of each.

—————————————————— **Notes** ——————————————————

1. This description is based on the following sources: Professor Berquist's travels in Greece and Italy in the spring of 1971; Walter Agard, *What Democracy Meant to the Greeks* (Madison, Wisconsin: University of Wisconsin Press, 1960 reprint of 1942 edition); C.M. Bowra et al, *Classical Greece* (New York: Time, Inc. Great Ages of Man series, 1965); *Greece and Rome: Builders of Our World* (National Geographic Book Service, 1968).

2. Cf. especially chaps. I and XVI in E. Hamilton, *The Greek Way to Western Civilization* (New York: Mentor reprint of 1930 edition; 1960).

3. R.C. Jebb, *The Rhetoric of Aristotle: A Translation* (Cambridge: University Press, 1909), pp. 16–18. Unless otherwise noted, further quotations from Aristotle's *Rhetoric* come from this source.

4. C.C. Arnold, D. Ehninger and J.C. Gerber, *The Speaker's Resource Book* (Chicago: Scott, Foresman, 1961), p. 218.

5. Cf. William M. Sattler, "Conceptions of Ethos in Ancient Rhetoric," *Speech Monographs,* 14 (1947), pp. 55–65.

6. Some observers assumed Homer's poems were fiction. For a quite different view, see M.B. Grosvenor "Homeward with Ulysses," *Nat. Geog. M,* 144, 1 (July, 1973), pp. 1–39.

7. For a fuller account of Corax's activities, see Bromley Smith, "Corax and Probability," *Quarterly Journal of Speech,* 7, 1 (Feb., 1921), pp. 13–42.

8. Cf. James G. Greenwood, "The Legal Setting of Attic Oratory," *Central States Speech Journal,* 23, 3 (Fall, 1972), p. 182, *et passim.*

9. Agard, *What Democracy Meant to the Greeks,* p. 70, *et passim.*

10. Cf. Bromley Smith, "Gorgias: A Study of Oratorical Style," *Quarterly Journal of Speech,* 7, 4 (Nov., 1921), pp. 335–59.

11. D.L. Clark, *Rhetoric in Greco-Roman Education* (New York: Columbia University Press, 1957), p. 21.

12. Bromley Smith's studies of the sophists, published in the *Quarterly Journal of Speech,* included the following: Protagoras (Mar., 1918), Prodicus (Apr., 1920), Corax (Feb., 1921), Gorgias (Nov., 1921), Hippias (June, 1926), Thrasymachus (June, 1927), and Theodorus (Feb., 1928).

13. Harold Barrett, *The Sophists* (Novato, California: Chandler and Sharp Publishers, Inc., 1987), p. 5.

14. Susan C. Jarratt, *Rereading the Sophists: Classical Rhetoric Refigured* (Carbondale, Illinois: Southern Illinois University Press, 1991), p. 84.

15. Plato, *Gorgias,* trans. by W.R.M. Lamb (Cambridge, Massachusetts: Harvard University Press, 1967), *passim.*

16. George Kennedy, *The Art of Persuasion in Greece* (Princeton, N.J.: Princeton University Press, 1963), p. 12, *et passim.* Cf. also the comprehensive work of R.C. Jebb, *The Attic Orators from Antiphon to Isaeus* (London: Macmillan, 2nd ed., 1893, 2 vols.).

17. For an enlightening account of the rivalry between Aeschines and Demosthenes, see *Demosthenes' On the Crown: A Critical Case Study of a Masterpiece of Ancient Oratory,* ed. by James J. Murphy (New York: Random House, 1967).

18. *Plutarch's Lives,* trans. Bernadotte Perrin (Cambridge, Mass.: Harvard University Press, 1967), p. 17ff

19. Demosthenes' friend, Ctesiphon, proposed the crown in 336 B.C.E. but the trial was repeatedly postponed.

20. The authors are indebted at this point to the research of Mr. James Dennison.

21. The other eight were destroyed because Christians were sacrificed to lions in their arenas.

22. The best view of a restored Roman city we have is ancient Pompeii, south of Naples. This thriving Roman community was buried under volcanic ash in 79 A.D., and later discovered at the time of the American Revolution. Even today there remains considerable work for the archaeologist at Pompeii.

23. Cf. Edith Hamilton, *The Roman Way to Western Civilization* (New York, N.Y.: Mentor, 1961 reprint of 1932 ed.).

24. *Rhetorica ad Herennium,* trans. Harry Caplan (Cambridge, Mass.: Hazard University Press, 1968).

25. Jebb, *Aristotle's Rhetoric,* p. 6.

26. Cf. Harold F. Harding, "Quintilian's Witnesses," *Speech Monographs,* 1 (1934), pp. 1–20.

27. The authors are indebted to Donald Lemen Clark for this three-fold designation of classical rhetorical theory. See his *Rhetoric in Greco-Roman Education,* pp. 24–25.

Plato's Moral-Philosophical View of Rhetoric

It is fitting that we begin our study of classical rhetorical theory by analyzing Plato who has had enormous impact on Western thought for the past twenty-five hundred years. Rhetoricians in each of the three periods we will cover in this volume have used superlatives in describing his character, his teaching ability, and his works. Cicero referred to him as "the divine Plato," as "an eminent master and teacher both of style and thought," and as "the first of all writers or speakers."[1] Eighteen centuries later, Giambattista Vico called him "the prince of Greek wisdom."[2] In the modern era, Kenneth Burke ranked him as "the greatest of dialecticians."[3] More importantly, he has been labeled by two contemporary scholars as the most influential philosopher in history.[4]

- Who was Plato?
- What did he say about rhetoric that deserves our attention?

We seek to answer these questions in this chapter. Plato, we may say at the outset, was a wealthy Athenian who rejected the customary practices of his own society. He perfectly symbolized the Greek spirit of inquiry and the Academy which he founded in 387 B.C.E. was to continue functioning for a thousand years. When Plato started his school, the prevailing mode of higher education in Athens was sophistic. The new professor was anxious, therefore, to establish his uniqueness, to distinguish his brand of learning from that already offered. A talented literary artist, Plato chose the medium of the dialogue. What he did was to compose a series of fictional conversations based on philosophical problems he deemed important. These dialogues, which invariably featured his friend Socrates as the questioning hero, were advertisements for the Academy, persuasive previews of the instruction that awaited the interested student. Apparently they accomplished this end, for the Academy soon had a goodly number of students.[5]

PLATO'S TWO MAJOR RHETORICAL DIALOGUES—THE *GORGIAS* AND THE *PHAEDRUS*

Our approach in describing Plato's principal views on rhetorical theory is to discuss, first of all, his two primary works on this subject—the *Gorgias* and the *Phaedrus;* and, secondly, to look at his dialogues as a whole in order to see what general conclusions may be drawn.

As you read the following sections, keep in mind the points made in the last chapter regarding Plato's general attitude toward the sophists who emphasized practical knowledge rather than philosophical inquiry, who made education available to anyone willing to pay for their services, and who emphasized style in their teaching of rhetoric.

The *Gorgias:* A Study of False Rhetoric

One of Plato's earliest dialogues was that known as the *Gorgias*. The principal character, Gorgias of Leontini, was a famous Sicilian sophist who introduced argument from probability and a florid style of rhetoric to Athens. Legend has it that Gorgias was sent to Athens as an ambassador and so charmed the Athenians that they persuaded him to remain in the city and instruct their sons in rhetoric. Using literary license, Plato makes Gorgias and his friends the butt of Socrates' ridicule. The Sicilian sophist was pictured as a speaker more concerned with form than content, one who recommended a rhetoric of appearance rather than reality.

In the *Gorgias,* Plato "undertakes to refute the claims made for rhetoric by Gorgias, Polus, and Callicles."[6] He then proceeds to define the rhetorical practice of the day as "the art of persuading an ignorant multitude about the justice or injustice of a matter, without imparting any real instruction."[7] As the dialogue unfolds, Socrates presents four arguments attacking the utility of rhetoric:

1. "Rhetoric is not an art."
2. "Rhetoric does not confer power."
3. "Rhetoric as a protection against suffering wrong is of little importance."
4. "Rhetoric as a means of escaping a deserved punishment is not to be commended."[8]

Quite clearly what Plato sought to accomplish in this dialogue was to set forth the parameters of false rhetoric that typified much of Greek public discourse in the 4th century, B.C.E.

In order to see how the arguments establishing the nature of false rhetoric unfold in the *Gorgias,* we present the following passages featuring a discussion between the youthful Polus and Socrates.

Polus: I will ask; and do you answer me, Socrates, the same question which Gorgias, as you suppose, is unable to answer: What is rhetoric?

Socrates: Do you mean what sort of an art?

Polus: Yes.

Socrates: Not an art at all, in my opinion, if I am to tell you the truth, Polus.

Polus Then what, in your opinion, is rhetoric?

Socrates: A thing which, in the treatise that I was lately reading of yours, you affirm to have created art.

Polus: What thing?

Socrates: I should say a sort of routine or experience.

Polus: Then does rhetoric seem to you to be a sort of experience?

Socrates: That is my view, if that is yours.

Polus: An experience of what?

Socrates: An experience of making a sort of delight and gratification.

Polus: And if able to gratify others, must not rhetoric be a fine thing?

Socrates: What are you saying, Polus? Why do you ask me whether rhetoric is a fine thing or not, when I have not as yet told you what rhetoric is?

Polus: Why, did you not tell me that rhetoric was a sort of experience?

Socrates: As you are so fond of gratifying others, will you gratify me in a small particular?

Polus: I will.

Socrates: Will you ask me, what sort of an art is cookery?

Polus: What sort of an art is cookery?

Socrates: Not an art at all, Polus.

Polus: What then?

Socrates: I should say a sort of experience.

Polus: Of what? I wish that you would tell me.

Socrates: An experience of making a sort of delight and gratification, Polus.

Polus: Then are cookery and rhetoric the same?

Socrates: No, they are only different parts of the same profession.

Polus: And what is that?

Socrates: I am afraid that the truth may seem discourteous; I should not like Gorgias to imagine that I am ridiculing his profession, and therefore I hesitate to answer. For whether or no this is that art of rhetoric which Gorgias practices I really do not know: from what he was just now saying, nothing appeared of what he thought of his art, but the rhetoric which I mean is a part of a not very creditable whole.

Gorgias: A part of what, Socrates? Say what you mean, and never mind me.

Socrates: To me then, Gorgias, the whole of which rhetoric is a part appears to be a process, not of art, but the habit of a bold and ready wit, which knows how to behave to the world: this I sum up under the word 'flattery'; and this habit or process appears to me to have many other parts, one of which is cookery, which may seem to be an art, and, as I maintain, is not an art, but only experience and routine: another part is rhetoric, and the art of tiring [i.e. attiring, dress] and sophistic are two others: thus there are four branches, and four different things answering to them. And Polus may ask, if he likes, for he has not as yet been informed, what part of flattery is rhetoric: he did not see that I had not yet answered him when he proceeded to ask a further question,—Whether I do not think rhetoric a fine thing? But I shall not tell him whether rhetoric is a fine thing or not, until I have first answered,

'What is rhetoric?' For that would not be right, Polus; but I shall be happy to answer, if you will ask me, What part of flattery is rhetoric?

Polus: I will ask, and do you answer: What part of flattery is rhetoric?

Socrates: Will you understand my answer? Rhetoric, according to my view, is the shadow of a part of politics.

Polus: And noble or ignoble?

Socrates: Ignoble, as I should say, if I am compelled to answer, for I call what is bad ignoble . . . .[9]

Initially, then, Plato rejected rhetoric as a knack comparable to cookery, and as a form of flattery designed to gratify the mob. Rhetoric, in short, was a pseudo-art of appearances rather than a vehicle for conveying truth.[10] In a way his criticism is still relevant. All of us can think of instances in which speech is used to deceive and disguise. The demagogue who pursues his own goals instead of the best interests of his followers is a case in point. So, too, is the salesman who is more interested in making a commission than in satisfying the needs of his customers.

Figure 1 should help the reader visualize the essential elements of this dialogue.

> To Plato, truth was the only reality in life. Truth existed, he thought, as an idea in the minds of gods; thus truth partook of the divine.

The *Phaedrus:* A Study of True Rhetoric

Plato's second dialogue on rhetoric, the *Phaedrus,* is of greater importance to us for it is here that the most eminent of the Greek philosophers articulates what he terms a "true rhetoric" in contrast to the "false rhetoric" he ridiculed earlier. Before proceeding to an analysis of this dialogue, let us review briefly Plato's theory of truth. To Plato, truth was the only reality in life. Truth existed, he thought, as an idea in the minds of gods; thus truth partook of the divine. He illustrated this notion in his most famous philosophical work, *The Republic.* There are, Socrates observes in this dialogue, three types or levels of beds or tables. First in priority ranking is the concept of bed or table which exists in pure form in the minds of gods. Second is that created by the carpenter. Third is the picture of a bed or table portrayed by the artist. Since the painter, therefore, is two steps removed from the perfect idea upheld by deity, he tends to rely on imperfect images of reality. What applies to painters and other artists also applies to poets and rhetoricians, for they, too, are two steps from certain knowledge. Thus they are ruled out of the ideal republic.[11] There truth articulated by "philosopher kings" would guide every decision.

The format of the *Phaedrus* is based on a series of three speeches about love. The technique Plato used here was the literary device known as the allegory, a story with a double meaning. Plato's phrase "love" is identified with rhetoric; thus the main theme of this dialogue is "the art of speaking."[12]

The scene involves two characters, Socrates and Phaedrus, who chance to meet one day on the outskirts of Athens. Phaedrus has just heard what he considers to be an exceptional speech on love and is anxious to share its contents with his older friend, Socrates. The two agree to sit beneath a shade tree by a stream where they may pursue their discussion in leisurely comfort.

The speech which caught Phaedrus' attention, Plato tells us, was presented by Lysias, a well-known Athenian orator of the day. Lysias took the position that "people should grant favors to non-lovers rather than lovers," that is that we ought to prefer a neuter brand of speech or rhetoric to that which arouses our thoughts or feeling.[13] So, the best language is that which generates no response or interest at all, according to this view. The value judgments of good and bad we daily pronounce should be eliminated from our language so that our discourse becomes semantically pure. Scientific report writing and the prose style used in business letters become the ideal; connotative language and the language of abstraction are to be avoided at all cost. Lysias' non-lover becomes the modern day objective reporter whose task is to describe and record, not to interpret or evaluate.

In his essay entitled, "The *Phaedrus* and the Nature of Rhetoric," Richard Weaver notes "there are but three ways for language to affect us. It can move us toward what is good; it can move us toward what is evil; or it can in hypothetical third place, fail to move us at all."[14] Plato's non-lover is the speaker who fails "to move us at all."

A second speech on love which appears in the dialogue is delivered by Socrates who feels Lysias'

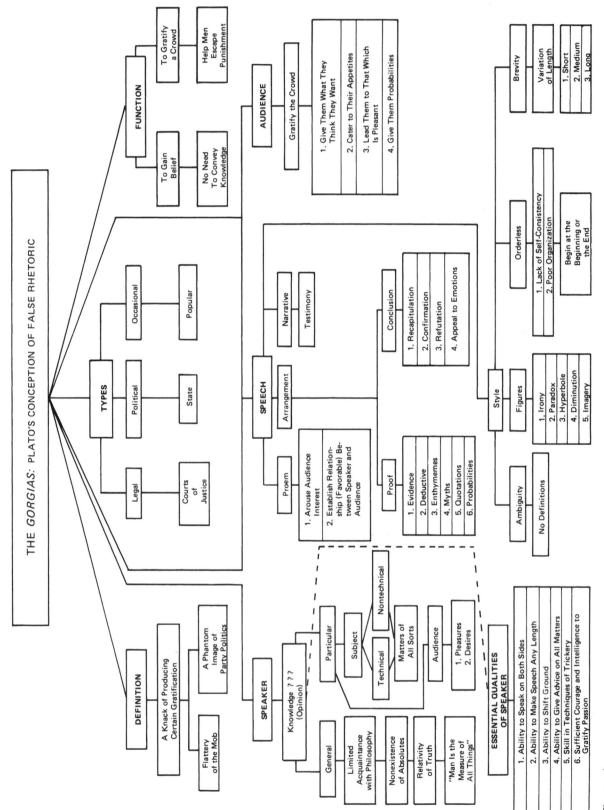

Figure 1

speech is so specialized as to be misleading. Accordingly the theme of this second speech is that love is a form of exploitation. The evil lover seeks to make the object of his attentions depend upon him and is jealous of any possible outside influence. Rhetorically speaking, the evil lover is one who uses language to enslave and deceive another. The mortician who sells a widow a casket for her husband more expensive than she can afford and the real estate agent who sells customers houses some thousands of dollars above their capacity to pay are cases in point. The evil lover, the base rhetorician, is out to serve himself. Colorful language laden with emotional appeal and spurious arguments are the tools he uses to sell his product. Distortion and delusion typify his approach. Anything goes as long as he gets *his* way. It is this type of lover, this abusive user of rhetoric, who gives persuasion its devilish, manipulative image. Those who make the worse appear the better cause, bad men skilled in speech, receive our condemnation today as they did in Plato's time. To cite only one recent example, governmental officials who make firm declarations and later label them "inoperative" insure our distrust and contempt.

In the first two speeches, Plato's view of love is incomplete, for most Greeks believed love to be a quality possessed by the gods. There must, therefore, be a third speech and indeed there is. Socrates proceeds to describe the noble lover, the skillful user of language, as one who seeks that which is best for his listeners rather than for himself. The attitude of the noble lover is the antithesis of that of the evil lover. His is a kind of "inspired madness," Plato tells us, for he ignores self-interest. Instead he uses language to teach and inspire, to reveal rather than conceal truth and value. Here, for example, is the wartime rhetoric of Winston Churchill or the presidential wisdom of an Abraham Lincoln. Here is virtue conjoined with eloquence, sublime oratory, superlative prose. The noble lover is Plato's ideal speaker, a rhetorician at once welcome in his ideal state. He is the conveyor and preserver of truth and morality. Moral users of language may never exist in great number but they are the pillars of a healthy society. Indeed in Plato's view, the noble lover approached divinity.

> The noble lover is Plato's ideal speaker, a rhetorician at once welcome in his ideal state. He is the conveyor and preserver of truth and morality.

At the close of the lengthy dialogue on the three lovers and their corresponding relationship to three types of speakers, Socrates and Phaedrus attempt to put true rhetoric into perspective. The flow of thought may be seen in the ensuing excerpt:

Phaedrus: Let us talk.

Socrates: Shall we discuss the rules of writing and speech as we were proposing?

Phaedrus: Very good.

Socrates: Is not the first rule of good speaking that the mind of the speaker should know the truth of what he is going to say?

Phaedrus: And yet, Socrates, I have heard that he who would be an orator has nothing to do with true justice, but only with that which is likely to be approved by the many who sit in judgment; nor with the truly good or honorable, but only with public opinion about them, and that from this source and not from the truth come the elements of persuasion.

Socrates: Any words of the wise ought to be regarded and not trampled under foot, for there is probably something in them, and perhaps there may be something in this which is worthy of attention.

Phaedrus: Very true.

Socrates: Let us put the matter thus: Suppose that I persuaded you to buy a horse and go to the wars. Neither of us knew what a horse was like, but I knew that you believed a horse to be the longest-eared of domestic animals.

Phaedrus: That would be ridiculous.

Socrates: There is something more ridiculous coming. Suppose, now, that I was in earnest and went and composed a speech in honor of an ass, whom I entitled a horse, beginning: "A noble animal and a most useful possession, especially in war, and you may get on his back and fight, and he will carry baggage or anything."

Phaedrus: That would be most ridiculous.

Socrates: Ridiculous! Yes; but is not even a ridiculous friend better than a dangerous enemy?

Phaedrus: Certainly.

Socrates: And when the orator instead of putting an ass in the place of a horse, puts good for evil, being himself as ignorant of their true nature as the city on which he imposes is ignorant; and having studied the notions of the multitude, persuades them to do evil instead of good, —what will be the harvest which rhetoric will be like to gather after the sowing of that fruit?

Phaedrus: Anything but good.

Socrates: Perhaps, however, rhetoric has been getting too roughly handled by us, and she might answer: What amazing nonsense is this! As if I forced any man to learn to speak in ignorance of the truth! Whatever my advice may be worth, I should have told him to arrive at the truth first, and then come to me. At the same time I boldly assert that mere knowledge of the truth will not give you the art of persuasion.

Phaedrus: There is reason in the lady's defense of herself.

Socrates: Yes, I admit that, if the arguments which she has yet in store bear witness that she is an art at all. But I seem to hear them arraying themselves on the opposite side, declaring that she speaks not true, and that rhetoric is not an art but only a dilettante amusement. Lo! a Spartan appears, and says that there never is nor ever will be a real art of speaking which is unconnected with the truth.

Phaedrus: And what are these arguments, Socrates? Bring them out that we may examine them.

Socrates: Come out, children of my soul, and convince Phaedrus, who is the father of similar beauties, that he will never be able to speak about anything unless he be trained in philosophy. And let Phaedrus answer you.[15]

Following the above exchange, Socrates offers a summary of his principal arguments delineating a true rhetoric.

Until a man knows the truth of the several particulars of which he is writing or speaking, and is able to define them as they are, and having defined them again to divide them until they can be no longer divided, and until in like manner he is able to discern the nature of the soul and discover the different modes of discourse which are adapted to different natures, and to arrange and dispose them in such a way that the simple form of speech may be addressed to the simpler nature, and the complex and composite to the complex nature—until he has accomplished all this, he will be unable to handle arguments according to rules of art, as far as their nature allows them to be subjected to art, either for the purpose of teaching or persuading; that is the view which is implied in the whole preceding argument.[16]

Two twentieth-century scholars have summed up the *Phaedrus* in a clear and precise manner. "The central idea [of the *Phaedrus*]," Richard Weaver observed, "is that all speech, which is the means the gods have given man to express his soul, is a form of eros, in the proper interpretation of the word. With that truth the rhetorician will always be brought face to face as soon as he ventures beyond the consideration of mere artifice and device."[17] Twenty-eight years before Weaver's analysis, Everett Lee Hunt, then Dean of Swarthmore College, presented the following seven points as a summary statement of Plato's suggestions in the *Phaedrus* "for the organization of rhetoric into a scientific body of knowledge".

A diagram of Plato's conception of true rhetoric as depicted in the *Phaedrus* may take the form as shown in Figure 2.

In sum, Plato in these well-known works conceived of two different types of rhetoric. The first or "false rhetoric," he perceived as all too common in the Athenian society around him. This rhetoric he rejected as showy in appearance, self-serving, and artificial. The second or "true rhetoric" he himself exemplified. The rhetoric he embraced was truthful, self-effacing, and real. Plato's noble lover was part philosopher, part logician, part psychologist. He must know the truth. He must be a master of dialectic, the Platonic instrument for the discovery and dissemination of the truth. And he must understand the human soul in order that he may appeal to the better side of mankind. The moral rhetoric of Plato as conceived in the *Phaedrus* continues to represent an ideal for all of us, even though history demonstrates the ideal is seldom achieved.

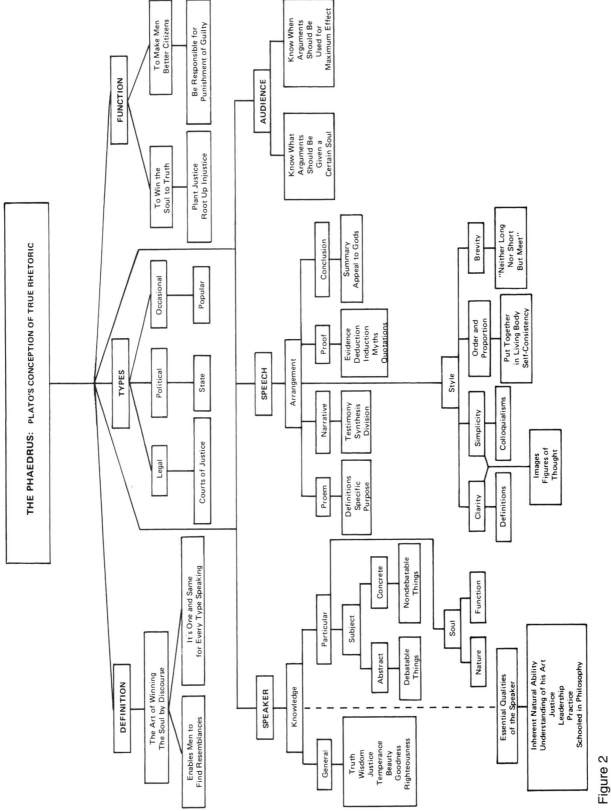

Figure 2

SEVEN POINTS

1. "The first rule of good speaking is that the mind of the speaker should know the truth of what he is going to say." This cannot be interpreted as an injunction to speak the truth at all times. It is rather to *know* the truth in order (a) to be persuasive by presenting to the audience something which at least resembles truth, and (b) to avoid being oneself deceived by probabilities. In order to know the truth, the rhetorician must be a philosopher.

2. The rhetorician must define his terms, and see clearly what subjects are debatable and what are not. He must be able to classify particulars under a general head, or to break up universals into particulars. The rhetorician, then, must be a logician.

3. Principles of order and arrangement must be introduced. "Every discourse ought to be a living creature, having its own body and head and feet; there ought to be a middle, beginning and end, which are in a manner agreeable to one another and to the whole."

4. The nature of the soul must be shown, and after having "arranged men and speeches, and their modes and affections in different classes, and fitted them into one another, he will point out the connection between them—he will show why one is naturally persuaded by a particular of argument, and another not." In other words, the rhetorician must be a psychologist.

5. The rhetorician must "speak of the instruments by which the soul acts or is affected in any way." Here we have the division under which comes practically all of rhetoric when viewed more narrowly and technically. The "instruments" by which rhetoric affects the soul are style and delivery. Plato believed style to be acquired, however, as Pericles acquired it, by "much discussion and lofty contemplation of nature."

6. The art of writing will not be highly regarded; nor will continuous and uninterrupted discourse be regarded as equal to cross-examination as a means of instruction. This is Plato's way of saying that any method of attempting to persuade multitudes must suffer from the very fact that it is a multitude which is addressed, and that the best of rhetoric is unequal to philosophic discussion.

7. The rhetorician will have such a high moral purpose in all his work that he will ever be chiefly concerned about saying that which is "acceptable to God." Rhetoric, then, is not an instrument for the determination of scientific truth, nor for mere persuasion regardless of the cause; it is an instrument for making the will of God prevail. The perfect rhetorician, as a philosopher, knows the will of God.[18]

PLATO'S OTHER DIALOGUES

As the foregoing discussion suggests, Plato turned his full attention to rhetoric, pointing out both its shortcomings and its potential in the *Gorgias* and the *Phaedrus.* But it would be a mistake to consider these dialogues as constituting all that Plato had to say about rhetoric as a field of study. We have found that the general subject of rhetoric is featured with varying degrees of emphasis in every dialogue that Plato wrote.[19]

In these writings he touched on all aspects of human discourse. Insights on the nature of eloquence, the need for ethics in communication, and the use of pathos are discussed in the *Apology;* rhetoric as a means of generating meaning and knowledge in *Cratylus;* criticism and taste, speech introductions, ethos, humor, and persuasion in *Laws;* learning as recollection in *Meno;* first principles and dimensions of intrapersonal communication in *Phaedo;* types of speech forms and recommendations concerning the length of speeches in *Protagoras;* the cardinal virtues, ideal forms, audience analysis and adaptation, and the notion of conversion in *The Republic;* genuine and sophistical discourse, and refutation in the *Sophist;* model speeches on love by Agathon and Socrates in the *Symposium;* the use of examples and analogies, and appeals to the motives in *Statesman;* and the noble lover, probability, and knowledge versus opinion in *Theaetetus.*

Of the numerous ideas on rhetoric advanced in these dialogues, we would like to single out three for special emphasis as a means of extending our knowledge of what Plato taught us in the *Gorgias* and the *Phaedrus.* These three elements include his discussion of delivery, of audience analysis and adaptation, and of his theory of dialectic.

The Canon of Delivery

It cannot be denied that delivery was far less important to Plato than was the content of the message. Nevertheless, he felt that it could not be totally ignored because of its power to give clarity and force to the meaning the rhetor wishes to generate. With this thought in mind, he gave suggestions in his dialogue *Cratylus* for adapting one's bodily activity to the basic characteristics of the object or thing being described. He used these words to develop this point:

We should imitate the nature of the thing; the elevation of our hands to heaven would mean lightness and upwardness; heaviness and downwardness would be expressed by letting them drop to the ground; if we were describing the running of a horse, or any other animal, we should make our bodies and their gestures as like as we could to them . . . . For by bodily imitation only can the body ever express any thing.[20]

In the highly significant dialogue *Laws,* Plato again emphasized the role that gestures, movement, and countenance may play in communication. Here he related bodily activity to a speaker's or actor's emotions, a pattern which was to become a central feature in the teachings of the British elocutionists. One who is experiencing a feeling of intense pleasure, Plato says, will use vigorous gestures. If the dominant emotion is fear on the part of the speaker, the gestures and movements will be "vehement," and, at times, "violent." By contrast, a person of fortitude and sobriety of thought is inclined to tone down his movements.[21]

Plato's analysis of voice control had a similar emphasis. The voice, like that of gestures and movement, he noted, must be integrally related to the description being articulated. "And when we want to express ourselves, either with the voice, or tongue, or mouth, the expression is simply their imitation of that which we want to express."[22] An additional point on this facet of delivery deserves mention. The vocal organs, if used properly, will make the body move, and when this movement occurs, it must be in tune with the "utterance."[23]

The ideas developed by Plato on bodily activity and voice control led him to reach a conclusion that was to foreshadow what later authors would write in the classical, British, and contemporary periods. This conclusion was put forth in the following exchange between Socrates and Hermogenes in the dialogue *Cratylus:*

Socrates: Who speaks as he pleases? Will not the successful speaker rather be he who speaks in the natural way of speaking, and as things ought to be spoken, and with the natural instrument? Any other mode of speaking will result in error and failure.

Hermogenes: I quite agree with you.[24]

What makes this exchange noteworthy is that it constitutes one of the earliest statements presented on the value of using a natural, conversational pattern of delivery.

Audience Analysis and Adaptation

A second, and far more vital, theme that commanded the attention of Plato in his dialogues as a whole was the subject of audience analysis and adaptation. Although we touched on this topic in a general way in our treatment of the *Gorgias* and the *Phaedrus,* more specific details may now be provided by turning to such works as the *Republic,* the *Sophist, Parmenides,* and the *Apology.* What we learn from this survey is that Plato not only dealt with a particular individual or group but with the highly elevated and moral audience called philosophical.

It was Plato's general practice, as we saw in the *Phaedrus,* to dissect souls, breaking them down into several distinct categories. He followed the same procedure in the *Republic.* Those souls who are "lovers of wisdom" and "lovers of honour," he said in this dialogue, are motivated almost entirely by ideal forms and cardinal virtues. "Lovers of gain," however, give a preeminent value to worldly goods.[25]

Plato's reflections on the nature and types of souls enabled him to note that since the soul has the power to initiate an action and to respond to a plea for action, it is incumbent upon the speaker to place each listener on an imaginary action scale, both as a potential initiator and respondent. This thought process will then determine, in part, the type of arguments that should be used.[26]

Other conditioning factors that influence a particular soul, according to Plato, are age, sex, and locale. In his discussion of each of these characteristics, he was innovative and provocative. He gave a special warning to those who address young people. Their immaturity, he said, prevents them from distinguishing between the literal and the allegorical, and between reality and appearances.[27] Moreover, they are excessively preoccupied with "what the world will think."[28] Thus they are too easily duped. Since the weaknesses in the young generally do not characterize the old, youth should yield to the leadership role their elders have earned through their superior wisdom and experience.[29]

Plato went beyond most of his contemporaries in his delineation of sex differences and the influence they might exert in rhetorical situations. Arguing that men and women are similar in kind, though not necessarily in degree, he concluded: "There is no special faculty of administration in a state which a woman has because she is a woman, or which a man has by virtue of his sex, but the gifts of nature are alike diffused in both; all the pursuits of men are the pursuits of women."[30] We may infer, therefore, that comparable appeals could be made to each group.

Not only did Plato show how a particular group is affected by age and gender, but he was one of the first classical authors to recognize the relationship between the geographical locale of an audience member and the way he or she responds to an argument. He firmly held that where one lives is an important determinant of that person's world vision. He illustrated this concept by drawing a comparison between the people of Athens and those of neighboring countries. With an attitude bordering on condescension, he proclaimed that a quest for knowledge "is the special characteristic of our part of the world." But, he added, the natives of Egypt and Phoenicia are primarily motivated by a "love of money."[31] He continued by asserting that if men are conditioned in different ways by the place in which they reside, they experience a universal pride in their country and home town. In elaborating on this point, Plato commented: "Had the orator to praise Athenians among Peloponnesians, or Peloponnesians among Athenians, he must be a good rhetorician who could succeed and gain credit. But there is no difficulty in a man's winning applause when he is contending for fame among the persons he is praising."[32]

The foregoing discussion of Plato's attitudes on adapting to a particular audience provides an insight into his general views on persuasion. But more central to his overall philosophy were his ideas on a second type of audience—the philosophical. The essence of what he said on this subject may be found in the *Apology*. This dialogue focuses on the eloquent defense delivered by Socrates to the Athenian leaders who charged him with corrupting the youth

he consistently had sought to challenge with his dialectical method of discourse. Whether or not the words that Plato placed in Socrates' mouth represent a true historical account or a dramatic recreation by a masterful stylist is difficult to determine.[33] What is beyond dispute, however, is that Socrates' trial was the "single most important courtroom scene" in ancient Greece.[34] Moreover, the trial gave Plato, who apparently was present at the proceedings, a chance to demonstrate how his theory of the philosophical audience came together with the world view of Socrates to create an ethical form of rhetoric that has profoundly influenced Western thought.

A close reading of the speech suggests that Socrates developed standards to be followed by the group that had assembled to hear and evaluate his defense and by himself. He challenged the jury members, for example, to perceive themselves as being more than a particular body of people with specific values and needs that must be satisfied. This required of them a need to push aside their prejudices and desires. It also demanded, as Socrates reminded them, that they concentrate more on the criterion of truth in his message than on his speaking manner and reluctance to use ornamental language.

But it was not enough for the listeners to meet the standards Socrates had set for them in this rhetorical situation. He as speaker must also fulfill certain goals in order to achieve the level of argument needed for the philosophical audience he wished to address. For such an audience, he believed, would be motivated entirely by value-centered, reasonable arguments that transcend time and place. He thus adopted the strategy of seeking to generate the same meaning in himself as in the members of the jury. To do this, he had to subject himself to the same standard of excellence in reasoning that would be applied to the judges.[35] It is not surprising, therefore, that Socrates, as Cicero later noted, refused to accept Lysias' offer to ghostwrite a speech for him on this occasion that presumably would gain a favorable verdict.[36]

Once he had urged his auditors to rise to the level of the philosophical audience, and had similarly prepared himself to carry out his own responsibilities, Socrates was ready to develop two major claims. His first contention was a refutation of the general charges made against him by the state, and the specific charges used by his enemy Meletus. In response to the state's charges, he denied that he was a boaster who flaunted his knowledge, and a meddler who justified his positions with needless philosophical speculations. Similarly, he rejected the notion that he was a sophist who relied on clever arguments to defeat his enemies and an unfair persuader who encouraged unthinking youth to follow his lead.

At this juncture, Socrates turned to the specific charges of Meletus, and proceeded as if Meletus were on the stand. This rhetorical strategy permitted him to follow his dialectical method of raising probing questions, listening closely to answers, refuting claims of the respondent, and offering a justification for the position that was taken at the end of the dialogue. Against the background of this approach, Meletus failed to uphold his persistent claim that Socrates had polluted the minds of the youth.

The stage was now set for treatment of Socrates' second major argument. As a prelude to this point, he advised the audience to adopt a system of ethics and values based on an appropriate hierarchical order that should function as a guide for our lives. This gave him the opening to assert the premise that death is preferable to dishonor. In support of this claim, Socrates boldly argued that no circumstances could exist that would prompt him to modify his mode of conduct for the purpose of escaping death or other types of painful punishment. Next he urged the jury to act at all times in accordance with what is right and good. Our principal end in life, he added, is to practice philosophy and advance the cause of truth. With persuasive force he then described the limited power of money or worldly possessions: "Wealth does not bring goodness, but goodness brings wealth."

Socrates completed the discussion of his second contention by noting that a speaker has a moral obligation to rely on reason buttressed by telling facts. This means that even if our goal is to protect ourselves or our children, we are not justified to use improper emotional appeals. It further implies that our arguments should be grounded in the universal values of wisdom, justice, honor, and truth. In his most moving passage, Socrates eloquently described his full commitment to the idea that the requirements and demands of the philosophical audience transcend those of a particular audience. With compelling force he observed:

> an important step that the rhetor needs to follow in assisting the audience to understand and appreciate the eternal verities is to persuade themselves that they should not react as a particular group with personal interests and biases but as a philosophical audience committed to reasonable arguments.

No doubt you think, gentlemen, that I have been condemned for lack of the arguments which I could have used if I had thought it right to leave nothing unsaid or undone to secure my acquittal. But that is far from the truth. It is not a lack of arguments that has caused my condemnation, but a lack of effrontery and impudence, and the fact that I have refused to address you in the way which would give you most pleasure. You would have liked to hear me weep and wail, doing and saying all sorts of things which I regard as unworthy of myself, but which you are used to hearing from other people. But I did not think then that I ought to stoop to servility because I was in danger, and I do not regret now the way in which I pleaded my case. I would much rather die as the result of this defense than live as the result of the other sort. In a court of law, just as in warfare, neither I nor any other ought to use his wits to escape death by any means.[37]

The concluding part of the speech reaffirmed Socrates' conviction that death may be a blessing. Indeed, he prophesied, it might provide a rhetorical situation for one to participate in dialectical exchanges with virtuous people who have preceded us. As he departed from the witness stand, Socrates put his attitude toward death in terms that jury members and posterity could not forget: "Now it is time that we are going, I to die, and you to live, but which of us has the happier prospect is unknown to anyone but God."[38]

What conclusions may be drawn from this discussion of Plato's memorable dialogue *Apology*? First, the speech of Socrates emphasizes the principle that a rhetor should seek to help an audience glimpse eternal truths, and then let these truths serve as guides for ordering their lives. To fulfill this task it is necessary for the speaker to function as a noble lover who subordinates his or her own welfare to the principles that are being espoused.

Secondly, an important step that the rhetor needs to follow in assisting the audience to understand and appreciate the eternal verities is to persuade themselves that they should not react as a particular group with personal interests and biases but as a philosophical audience committed to reasonable arguments. If such a vision is adopted, the controlling factors responsible for action will be what any reasonable and ethical person believes is right and good, not only for the present but for the future as well.[39]

Theory of Dialectic

Thirdly, these other writings now under review, particularly when combined with the *Gorgias* and the *Phaedrus,* tell us that "the single most useful and effective communicative method is the dialogue form which Plato invented and called dialectic."[40] This was the pattern he used in constructing most of his dialogues; and it is the one he repeatedly recommended in his works for philosophical conversation. Described as the essence of science and the guide for all discourse, dialectic chooses as its subject matter such abstract and enduring notions as knowledge and being. It is through dialectic that one resists the temptation to speak about people, and seeks instead to glimpse the noble verities and the eternal truths of ideal forms.

The sequence and rhetorical strategies that are used give dialectic its uniqueness and scientific thrust. Adhering to a chronological pattern, it begins with a definition of terms and proceeds through analysis and synthesis to an ultimate conclusion based on enlightened understanding. The particular communication strategy also unfolds in a sequential manner that, as we saw in Socrates' approach in the *Apology,* utilizes four steps. One of the participants initiates the discussion by phrasing one or more questions. Among the points considered here will be the defining of appropriate terms. This is followed by the presentation of a response that sets forth hypotheses that are developed through demonstration. As soon as these answers are introduced, the third step, comprised of refutation and cross-examination, takes place. The final phase hopefully will consist of a modification of the original position held by each participant.[41] The desired end result is shared meaning and enlarged understanding. What has been described here may be summarized in the following outline.

SUMMARY

Plato's theory of dialectic bears a resemblance to John Dewey's reflective thinking process, and, as will be seen in our analysis of the contemporary period, contains striking similarities to some of the principal ideas advanced in the current popular trend: "rhetoric as a way of knowing." In all, the innovative ideas Plato set in motion were to have an evolutionary power rarely matched by subsequent authors.

PLATO'S THEORY OF DIALECTIC

I. Definitions
   A. "The coping stone of the sciences"
   B. "The guide on the voyage of discourse"
II. Subject Matter
   A. Things
   B. Knowledge
   C. Being
III. Purposes
   A. To generate understanding concerning ideal forms
   B. To stimulate recollection
IV. Structure
   A. Definition of terms
   B. Analysis
      1. Dividing forms into particulars
      2. Dividing particulars until no further separation is possible

   C. Synthesis
      1. Moving upward from the concrete to the abstract
      2. Combining particulars so as to form universals
V. Rhetorical Strategies
   A. Questioning
   B. Answering and Justifying
   C. Cross-Examining and Refuting
   D. Modifying original views until agreement is reached on the problem.[42]

Notes

1. Cicero, *De Optimo,* vi, 17; *Orator,* iii, 10; and xix, p. 62.
2. Max Harold Fisch and Thomas G. Bergin, tr., *The Autobiography of Giambattista Vico* (Ithaca: Cornell University Press, 1944), p. 139. In summarizing Plato's enormous impact, Vico further said: "A Plato. . . among the ancients was the equivalent of an entire university of studies of our day, all harmonized in one system." Ibid., p. 199.
3. Kenneth Burke, *Grammar of Motives and Rhetoric of Motives* (Cleveland: World Publishing Co., 1962), p. 253.
4. Pierre Léveque has observed: "His (Plato's) influence was so profound, so enduring and so varied that. . . all the philosophers of the western world have only been able to add footnotes to his work." *The Greek Adventure* (Cleveland: World Publishing Co., 1968), p. 357; and Bertrand Russell observed: "Plato and Aristotle were the most influential of all philosophers, ancient, medieval, or modern; and of the two, it was Plato who had the greatest effect upon subsequent ages." *A History of Western Philosophy* (New York: Simon and Schuster, 1945), p. 104.
5. Plato, *Gorgias,* tr. by W.R.M. Lamb (Cambridge, Mass.: Harvard University Press, 1967), p. 250.
6. Everett Lee Hunt, "Plato and Aristotle on Rhetoric and Rhetoricians," *Studies in Honor of James Albert Winans* (New York: The Century Co., 1925), p. 25. Hereafter cited as "Plato and Aristotle."
7. Ibid., p. 26.
8. Ibid., p. 27.
9. B. Jowett, tr. *The Dialogues of Plato,* 4 vols. (New York: Scribner, Armstrong, and Co., 1874), III, pp. 47–49.
10. "Plato and Aristotle," p. 32.
11. Cf. *The Republic,* tr. by Paul Shorey (Cambridge, Mass.: Harvard University Press, 1963).
12. "Plato and Aristotle," p. 32.
13. Richard M. Weaver, "The *Phaedrus* and the Nature of Rhetoric," reprinted in *Language is Sermonic,* ed. by R.L. Johannesen, R. Strickland, and R.T. Eubanks (Baton Rouge: Louisiana State University Press, 1970), p. 60.
14. Ibid. The reason for the use of the term "hypothetical" in the above passage is that Weaver
took the position that language virtually always affects the reader or listener. See his "Language is Sermonic," in Part III of this work.
15. Jowett, *The Dialogues of Plato,* I, pp. 564–65.
16. Ibid., pp. 582–83.
17. *Language is Sermonic,* p. 83.
18. "Plato and Aristotle," pp. 37–38.
19. This claim is covered at length in the following essay: James L. Golden, "Plato Revisited: A Theory of Discourse for All Seasons," in Robert J. Connors, Lisa Ede, and Andrea Lunsford, eds, *Essays on Classical Rhetoric and Modern Discourse* (Carbondale: Southern Illinois University Press, 1984), pp. 16–36. Hereafter cited as "Plato Revisited."
20. Edith Hamilton and Huntington Cairns, eds, *The Collected Dialogues of Plato* (New York: Bollingen Series, 1961), pp. 457–58.
21. *Laws,* in Hamilton and Cairns, p. 1386.
22. *Cratylus,* in Hamilton and Cairns, p. 458.
23. *Laws,* in Hamilton and Cairns, p. 1386.
24. *Cratylus,* in Hamilton and Cairns, p. 424.
25. Jowett, *Plato's Republic* (New York: The Modern Library, n.d.), p. 344.
26. *Sophist,* in Hamilton and Cairns, pp. 924–25.
27. Ibid., p. 977.
28. *Parmenides,* in Hamilton and Cairns, pp. 924–25.
29. *Sophist,* in Hamilton and Cairns, p. 977.
30. Jowett, *Plato's Republic,* p. 176.
31. Ibid., p. 151.
32. *Menexenus,* in Hamilton and Cairns, p. 188.
33. George Kennedy, *The Art of Persuasion in Greece* (Princeton: Princeton University Press, 1963), p. 149. A similar description of Socrates' speech as discussed here may be found in the following essay: Golden, "The Universal Audience Revisited," in James L. Golden and Joseph J. Pilotta, eds., *Practical Reasoning in Human Affairs* (Dordrecht: D. Reidel Publishing Co., 1986), pp. 298–300.
34. Ibid., p. 149.
35. Ibid.
36. J.S. Watson, tr, *Cicero on Oratory and Orators* (New York: Arthur Hinds and Company, n.d.), Bk. I, p. liv.
37. *Apology,* in Hamilton and Cairns, p. 23.
38. Ibid., p. 26.
39. When we analyze the works of Chaim Perelman

in the contemporary period, we will see how remarkably similar his ideas on the "Universal Audience" are to Plato's notion of the "Philosophical Audience."

40. "Plato Revisited," p. 30.

41. For a helpful insight on this argument, see Michel Meyer, "Dialectic and Questioning: Socrates and Plato," in the *American Philosophical Quarterly.* 17 (October 1980), p. 283.

42. For a more detailed account of Plato's theory of dialectic, see "Plato Revisited," pp. 30–34.

The Scientific Approach of Aristotle

Of all the students educated at Plato's Academy, none was so distinguished as Aristotle. The son of the court physician at the kingdom of Macedonia to the north of Greece, Aristotle was trained as a field biologist. He was an expert at observing and describing all living and nonliving things and in classifying such data for the use of others.[1] Unlike today's scientists, Aristotle's investigations were not limited to specialties like botany and zoology. Instead he took the whole Greek world as his laboratory. Thus we find works by Aristotle on law and political science, ethics and drama as well as what we currently think of as "the sciences." Of over 170 works he authored, thirty survive today, embracing over 2,000 printed pages.[2]

Every subject to which an Athenian turned his attention received the diligent attention of Aristotle, and among these was rhetoric, the art of effective speaking. So comprehensive and fundamental were Aristotle's views on rhetoric that it is no exaggeration to say that his treatise on the subject is the most important single work on persuasion ever written.

GENERAL NATURE OF RHETORIC

Rhetoric, like dialectic, is common to all men. Yet the art of persuasion like the art of reasoned discourse belongs to no one field of study. "All men in a manner use both; for all men to some extent make the effort of examining and of submitting to inquiry, of defending or accusing."[3] Earlier works on rhetoric, Aristotle maintained, dealt with only part of the field. They concerned themselves, he declared, with irrelevant appeals to the emotions of a jury, while they neglected reason in public discourse. They prescribed how a speech should be organized but ignored the speaker's role in creating proof. Further, they stressed legal speaking while neglecting the deliberative rhetoric of the political assembly, a branch of the art "nobler and worthier of a citizen," Aristotle noted, "than that which deals with private contracts."[4]

Aristotle perceived this subject to be both significant and challenging and when he established his own school, he made it part of the regular curriculum. Rhetoric is useful, Aristotle wrote,

first, because truth and justice are naturally stronger than their opposites; so that, when awards are not given duly, truth and justice must have been worsted by their own fault. This is worth correcting. Again, supposing we had the most exact knowledge, there are some people whom it would not be easy to persuade with its help; for scientific exposition is in the nature of teaching, and teaching is out of the question; we must give our proofs and tell our story in popular terms—as we said in the Topics with reference to controversy with the many. Further—one should be able to persuade, just as to reason strictly, on both sides of a question; not with a view to using the twofold power—one must not be the advocate of evil—but in order, first, that we may know the whole state of the case; secondly, that, if anyone else argues dishonestly, we on our part may be able to refute him. Dialectic and Rhetoric, alone among all arts, draw indifferently an affirmative or a negative conclusion: both these arts alike are impartial. The conditions of the subject-matter, however, are not the same; that which is true and better being naturally, as a rule, more easy to demonstrate and more convincing. Besides it would be absurd that, while incapacity for physical self-defense is a reproach, incapacity for mental defense should be none; mental effort being more distinctive of man than bodily effort. If it is objected that an abuser of the rhetorical faculty can do great mischief, this, at any rate, applies to all good things except virtue, and especially to the most useful things, as strength, health, wealth, generalship. By the right use of these things a man may do the greatest good, and by the unjust use, the greatest mischief.[5]

The foregoing passage clearly shows that rhetoric, in Aristotle's opinion, has an important four-fold function:

1. to uphold truth and justice and play down their opposites;
2. to teach in a way suitable to a popular audience;
3. to analyze both sides of a question; and
4. to enable one to defend himself.

Viewed from this perspective, rhetoric is a moral, but practical art grounded in probability or the contingent nature of things.

Aristotle's analytical approach to rhetoric is most apparent in his definition of the term: "the faculty of discovering in every case the available means of persuasion."[6] It was not enough that a speaker conceive of a single approach to persuasion. He must examine *all* the means available. Only then would he be likely to choose the best course of action rather than that which first came to mind. A *comprehensive* view of one's subject and audience is much to be preferred over a narrow one, Aristotle told his students.

> Aristotle regarded the enthymeme as a method of persuasion which has the same relationship to rhetoric that the syllogism has to logic. Both of these forms of reasoning begin with a general premise and proceed to a particular case.

FORMS OF PROOF

Proof is either invented for the occasion or already existent, "artistic" or "nonartistic," Aristotle tells us.[7] A speaker may create support for his ideas or he may use documents or depositions already at hand. Of the first type, proofs artistically created by the speaker, there are three kinds: those which demonstrate that a thing is so *(logos),* those which depend for their effectiveness on the believability of the speaker *(ethos),* and those designed to sway a listener's feelings *(pathos).* Logical proof, Aristotle declared, "is wrought through the speech itself when we have demonstrated a truth or an apparent truth by the

means of persuasion available in a given case." Ethical proof, he wrote, "is wrought when the speech is so spoken as to make the speaker credible; for we trust good men more and sooner, as a rule, about everything; while, about things which do not admit of precision, but only guesswork, we trust them absolutely." Lastly, "the hearers themselves become the instruments of proof when emotion is stirred in them by the speech; for we give our judgments in different ways under the influence of pain and joy, of liking and of hatred."[8] Aristotle's threefold analysis of proof is every bit as appropriate to persuasion today as it was when written twenty-three centuries ago.

THE ENTHYMEME

The heart of Aristotle's theory of logical proof was the rhetorical syllogism or enthymeme. Because Aristotle believed that "enthymemes are the very body and substance of persuasion,"[9] we will treat this concept in detail, first by summarizing its nature, and then by applying it to a portion of one of Shakespeare's plays. Although many approaches to the study of the enthymeme have appeared in our literature in recent years, the one we will use is in keeping with the traditional interpretation presented by James McBurney of Northwestern University.[10]

Aristotle regarded the enthymeme as a method of persuasion which has the same relationship to rhetoric that the syllogism has to logic. Both of these forms of reasoning begin with a general premise and proceed to a particular case. The ideas may be presented in three steps: a major premise, a minor premise, and a conclusion. The initial or major premise was usually a categorical statement such as *All Athenians love to argue.* A second or minor connecting premise might be *Socrates is an Athenian.* The conclusion which then follows is *Socrates loves to argue.* It is significant to note that while the enthymeme and syllogism are structurally the same, they differ in one major respect: that is, the degree of certainty of the sources from which they draw their premises. The enthymeme deals with probable knowledge, whereas the syllogism is concerned with scientific truths. Consider, for instance, the following argument:

The degree of certainty in this major premise is stronger than that in the previously cited statement: "All Athenians love to argue." The degree of probability, therefore, constitutes an essential difference between enthymematic and syllogistic reasoning. Some writers have overlooked this fact, and, consequently, have defined the enthymeme as a truncated syllogism. There is, of course, some justification for this point of view. For nowadays rarely does one give formal speeches using all three steps of an enthymeme. Nor did the Greek orators. Usually the persuasive speaker would omit one or even two of the parts of the rhetorical syllogism, for they already existed in the minds of the listeners. As Aristotle put it, "if one of these elements is something notorious, it need not even be stated, as the hearer himself supplies it."[11] But while a characteristic of the enthymeme is its capacity to suppress one of its parts, the point which we are here stressing is that the enthymeme is a rhetorical syllogism "drawn, not from universal principles belonging to a particular science, but from probabilities in the sphere of human affairs."[12]

The three sorts of premises from which enthymemes are drawn are probabilities, signs [fallible and infallible], and examples.

Probability

By *probability* Aristotle meant arguments that are generally true and contain an element of cause. For example, since "sons tend to love their mothers, Orestes will love his mother." In this connection McBurney has observed that "when one concludes that Orestes loves his mother, because 'love [usually] attends the objects of affection,' the argument does not attempt to prove [to give a sign] that Orestes actually does love his mother; but rather [assuming it probable that he loves his mother] attempts to account for or explain this phenomenon."[13]

Signs

The *sign,* which is the second premise of the enthymeme, is a proposition setting forth a reason for the existence of a particular fact. No attempt is made to explain what has caused the fact.[14] According to Aristotle there are two types of signs: the fallible and the infallible. When a speaker, in seeking to demonstrate the truth of the statement that "wise men are just," asserts that "Socrates was wise and also just," he is employing a fallible sign because the conclusion does not establish with certainty. Further, to observe that one has "a fever for he is breathing rapidly" does not necessarily indicate illness. If, on the other hand, a speaker states that a woman "has had a child because she is in milk," he is relying on an infallible sign; for, in every instance, assumption of this kind can be scientifically verified.

Example

Aristotle is not so specific in his discussion of the *example,* the third premise of the enthymeme. He made it evident, however, that the enthymeme can be formed either from historical or invented examples. In *Book II* he tells us that enthymemes taken from examples are those which proceed by induction from one or more parallel cases until the speaker abstracts a general rule, from which he argues to the case in point.[15] Let us assume, for instance, that a speaker wishes to establish the relationship between military ingenuity and political acumen. He first examines the life of General Grant and immediately discovers that the Civil War hero is regarded as one of America's worst presidents. Next he finds that General DeGaulle failed to organize a strong political party in France. He then sees that Colonel Peron, as a political leader, alienated Argentina from the free world. Finally he notes that Dwight Eisenhower is ranked by contemporary historians in the lower one-fifth of American presidents. From these parallel examples he may conclude that military leaders make poor politicians. The speaker is now ready to argue the case in point. Thus he claims that General Colin Powell should not be elected president in 1996.

Not only was Aristotle interested in analyzing the premises of the enthymeme but also in a consideration of its proper subject matter. Here he was concerned with the problem of the sources or places which furnish arguments. The rhetorician may draw his material from either universal or particular *topoi.* Universal topics are broad, general sources which are equally applicable to physics or politics. The four common topics are the possible and impossible, past fact, future fact, and size. Special topics, on the other hand, are associated with a "particular species or class of things." They provide the speaker with a thorough insight into a specific problem. Aristotle advises his readers that most enthymemes are formed from special subjects such as ethics and politics.

After the speaker has chosen his premises from the available special and universal *topoi,* he must next turn to what Aristotle calls "lines of argument." These topics are to be interpreted as "methods of reasoning rather than material propositions."[16] Twenty-eight types of valid arguments and nine which are referred to as "sham" are discussed in Book II. They are shown in the table below. Whenever one of these lines of argument is combined with a premise derived from a general or special topic an enthymeme is formed.[17]

The *Rhetoric* also distinguishes between the two primary species of the enthymeme, the demonstrative and the refutative. The demonstrative begins with consistent propositions and reaches affirmative conclusions. The converse is true of the refutative enthymeme. Since its purpose is to controvert the demonstrative the conclusions are obtained from "inconsistent propositions," and its purpose is not to affirm but to destroy a premise. One should remember, however, that both the enthymeme and the counter syllogism are constructed from the same *topoi.*

In discussing the question of refutation Aristotle carefully emphasizes the fact that the enthymeme is not properly refuted by simply pointing out the existence of probability in one of the premises. For by its very nature the enthymeme embraces the probable and, as a result, cannot be expected to set forth conclusions of scientific certainty. The same is true with respect to refutation of any argument from sign. It is not a question, therefore, of the presence of probability in either the premise or the conclusion, but rather one of how closely the probability or the sign resembles truth.

It would appear from the discussion thus far that Aristotle was thinking of the enthymeme only as a mode of logical proof. If this were true, however, the organizational pattern of the *Rhetoric* cannot be adequately understood.[18] If Aristotle were sincere in assuming that the enthymeme is "the body and substance of persuasion," he would not have given such spatial emphasis to ethical and pathetic appeals, unless he felt these proofs were directly related to the rhetorical syllogism.

In his explanation of the maxim, which is a shortened enthymeme, Aristotle suggests two advantages produced by this type of general truth. First, the audience will be delighted in hearing an expression of an oft repeated generalization which corresponds to their own beliefs. Thus, an audience comprised exclusively of men, would react favorably to the assertion that women drivers are poor drivers. While the form of the argument is enthymematic the degree of pathos is strong.

Secondly, by employing maxims the speaker often enhances his own character in the eyes of his auditors. Aristotle, commenting on this point, observed that "maxims always produce the moral ef-

VALID LINES OF ARGUMENT		SHAM ENTHYMEMES
1. Opposites 2. Inflections 3. Correlative terms 4. More and less 5. Time 6. Definition 7. Induction 8. Existing decisions 9. Turning the tables 10. Part to whole 11. Simple consequences 12. Criss-cross consequences 13. Inward thoughts, outward show 14. Proportional results	15. Identical results and antecedents 16. Altered choices 17. Attributed motives 18. Incentives and deterrents 19. Incredible occurrences 20. Conflicting facts 21. Meeting slander 22. Cause to effect 23. Meaning of names 24. Actions compared 25. Course of action 26. Previous mistakes 27. Division 28. Ambiguous terms	1. Diction (Structure of and homonyms) 2. Fallacious combination and separation 3. Indignation 4. A "sign" 5. The accidental 6. Consequence 7. Post hoc propter hoc 8. Time and manner 9. Substituting the absolute for the particular

fect, because the speaker in uttering them makes a general declaration of ethical principles (preferences); so that, if the maxims are sound, they give us the impression of a sound moral character in him who speaks."[19] Only by recognizing the relationship of the enthymeme to ethos and pathos can we fully comprehend the integral part which that mode of persuasion played in Aristotle's rhetorical system.

In summary, the enthymeme may be defined as a rhetorical syllogism which draws its premises from probabilities, signs, and examples. It has two species, the demonstrative and refutative, both of which derive their materials from particular or universal *topoi*, and then combine that material with the various lines of argument. Further, while the enthymeme is technically a form of logical proof, it frequently produces an emotional and ethical effect.

Mark Antony's Speech on the Death of Julius Caesar

Most of the principles which we have discussed are clearly illustrated in Shakespeare's historical play, "Julius Caesar." An analysis of Mark Antony's speech on the death of Caesar should suffice to show that Shakespeare was evidently acquainted with the theory of the enthymeme. Moreover, it will tend to demonstrate how the enthymeme is a vital component of practical argument.

Antony's address was delivered primarily for the purpose of counteracting the influence of a previous oration by Brutus. Antony knew that he must refute the charge that Caesar was ambitious. To do this he used enthymematic reasoning based on Aristotelian principles both to disarm his hearers and motivate them to action.

The introduction contains two maxims which adequately express the sentiment of the audience. "The evil that men do lives after them; the good is oft interred with their bones." This statement is, in effect, a truncated enthymeme constructed from probable knowledge. Antony next states that "the noble Brutus hath told you Caesar was ambitious; if it were so, it was a grievous fault, and grievously hath Caesar answered it." Such an assertion may be restated in enthymematic form as follows:

Ambition is a grievous fault. ⟶ *Major Premise*
Caesar had ambition. ⟶ *Minor Premise*
Caesar had a grievous fault. ⟶ *Conclusion*

Of course Antony did not accept the minor premise or the conclusion of this argument, but since the audience concurred with Brutus it was necessary to give them sufficient proof to show the fallibility inherent in the reasoning. He chose to do this by developing a counter syllogism utilizing signs. Caesar could not have been ambitious, he argued, because

1. "He hath wrought many captives home to Rome, whose ransoms did the general coffers fill."
2. "When the poor have cried Caesar hath wept."
3. "You all did see that on the Lupercal I thrice presented him with a kingly crown which he did thrice refuse."

The orator naturally concluded that these signs are the substance of non-ambition.

Antony next turned to the line of argument based on "time." "You all did love him once not without cause; what cause withholds you then to mourn for him?" The following enthymeme is implied in this plea:

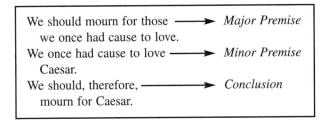

We should mourn for those ⟶ *Major Premise*
we once had cause to love.
We once had cause to love ⟶ *Minor Premise*
Caesar.
We should, therefore, ⟶ *Conclusion*
mourn for Caesar.

Antony's persuasion was complete as he demonstrated the enormity of Brutus' crime. "For Brutus as you know was Caesar's angel. Judge O you Gods how dearly Caesar loved him! This was the most unkindest cut of all." Actually he was telling his listeners that

Those who kill their friends are the unkindest of men.
Brutus killed his friend.
Brutus is the unkindest of men.

This is an enthymeme expressing the argument of "more or less."

The rhetorical syllogisms which Antony used are consonant with the teachings of Aristotle. All of the premises of the enthymemes are drawn from the particular topoi of ethics and politics, those branches of knowledge dealing with the conduct of man in human affairs. In addition, many of the twenty-eight lines of argument suggested by Aristotle can be seen. They may be summarized as follows:

1. Antony succeeds in "turning the utterances" of Brutus against him.
2. The question of "time" is noted in the reference that "you all did love him once."
3. Throughout the oration there seems to be an ambiguity with respect to the meaning of the term "ambition." To Brutus it had one connotation; to Antony it had another.
4. The enthymeme constructed from signs is an argument "from part to whole."
5. The "consequence" of envy and hate as seen in Casca is murder.
6. Although Brutus professed to love Caesar his testimony is not sincere. It is nothing more than "inward thoughts and outward show."
7. The problem of "incentives and deterrents" permeates the discussion.
8. It seems "incredible" that Brutus would commit such a crime.
9. The doctrine of "more or less" is implicit in the charge that there is no greater crime than that of killing your friend.

By combining the special *topoi* of ethics and politics with these lines of arguments, Antony strengthened his own character and obviously aroused the emotions of his hearers. In short, his persuasion, which is expressed through the media of ethos, logos, and pathos, originates with the enthymeme.

What we have said about the enthymeme is based upon Aristotle's discussion of this concept in the *Rhetoric*. But he also dealt with various aspects of this element of logos in his *Topica*. In Book III of this work, for example, he analyzed twenty or more commonplace arguments involving decision-making choices between two alternatives that may confront a speaker on a particular issue. In each case, he pointed out what he perceived to be the stronger argumentative position that should be chosen as the major premise of an enthymeme. Here are some of the representative claims he believed to be on superior ground:

1. "That which is more permanent and constant is more worthy of choice than that which is less so . . . ."

2. "That which commends itself to the wise and good is preferable . . . ."
3. "What is desirable for its own sake is preferable."
4. "What is *per se* the cause of good is preferable to what is accidentally so."
5. The "end is usually . . . more worthy of choice than the means to the end . . . ."
6. The "practicable is more worthy of choice than the impracticable . . . ."
7. "That which is in itself more noble and more valued and more praiseworthy is more worthy of choice . . . ."
8. "That of which the consequence is a greater good is more worthy of choice . . . ."
9. "A greater number of good things is preferable to a lesser number . . . ."
10. "Everything is preferable at the time when it has greater importance . . . ."[20]

What Aristotle is suggesting in these commonplaces has relevance for contemporary discourse. Let us reflect, for instance, on his statement (point "10") that "everything is preferable at a time when it has greater importance," and then relate the claim to the presidential contest of 1996. In the early autumn of 1995, two potential political leaders—General Colin Powell and Ross Perot—were confronted with a need to make a choice concerning what action they should take with respect to the upcoming campaign, and at what point in time it would be taken. Both ended up making choices on the question of appropriate timing. General Powell announced in late September, 1995 that if he were to enter the nominating process as a Republican, it would be desirable to do so by November. If, on the other hand, he were to run as an Independent candidate, he concluded that the best time to take this action would be in the spring of 1996. By contrast, Perot was faced with a more daunting challenge because he was contemplating the formation of a new political party.

He came to believe that the superior moment for him to make public his intentions was in the last week of September. If the timing were delayed, he correctly concluded, it would be highly improbable that his new "Independence Party" would be able to fulfill all of the requirements for getting his presidential candidate on the ballot in each of the fifty states.

This reasoning process utilizing a commonplace statement as the major premise of an enthymematic claim was, in Aristotle's opinion, an effective method for enabling a communicator to produce sound and relevant choices in a rhetorical situation.

ETHICAL AND PATHETIC APPEALS

In Book II of his three-book treatise, Aristotle focuses his attention on the listener. It is here that he describes ethos as the hearer's perception of a speaker based on the speech itself. The Greeks conceived of the perfect speaker as one who possessed character, intelligence, and good will. A speaker's integrity was judged on the basis of the apparent truthfulness of the statements he made (character). Listeners judged the soundness of his ideas in terms of their own experience and the evidence presented in support of a proposal (intelligence). The speaker's attitude toward his listeners was judged in terms of the listeners' best interests (good will).

Aristotle amplifies his ideas on ethical proof with these words:

The speakers themselves are made trustworthy by three things; for there are three things, besides demonstrations, which make us believe. These are, intelligence, virtue and good will. Men are false in their statements, and their counsels, from all or one of the following causes. Either through folly, they have not right opinions; or having right opinions, they say through knavery what they do not think; or they are sensible and honest, but not well-disposed; which they may happen not to advise the best course, although they see it. Besides these cases there is no other. It follows that the man who is thought to have all the three qualities must win the belief of the hearers. Now the means of appearing intelligent and good are to be got from the analysis of the virtues.[21]

Just prior to providing this description of the constituent elements of ethical proof, Aristotle developed the important notion that the persuasive power of ethos is to be demonstrated within the speech not only by the choice of arguments but by the speaker's frame of mind and relationship to the audience. He explained this principle as follows.

> The Greeks conceived of the perfect speaker as one who possessed character, intelligence, and good will.

And since Rhetoric has a view to judgment, for, both in debates and in law suits, there is judging, the speaker must not only see that the speech shall prove its point, or persuade, but must also develop a certain character in himself and in the judge, as it matters much for persuasiveness—most of all in debate, but secondarily in lawsuits too—that the speaker should appear a certain sort of person, and that the judges should conceive him to be disposed towards them in a certain way, further, that the judges themselves should be in a certain mood. The apparent character of the speaker tells more in debate, the mood of the hearer in lawsuits. . . .[22]

Despite the fact that Aristotle stressed the rationality of people in his emphasis upon logical proof, he came to believe that ethical appeals are "the most potent of all the means to persuasion."[23]

Since Aristotle equated rhetoric with the whole man, he also analyzed human emotions. The method he used was that of contrast as he discussed the following pairs: anger and mildness, friendship and enmity, fear and boldness, shame and shamelessness, gratitude and ingratitude, pity and indignation, envy and emulation.[24] As he probed into the nature of these emotions and related them to the challenge facing a rhetor, Aristotle revealed his orderly mind and scientific technique. He asked such questions as these: What type of person feels a given emotion? What is the state of mind of one experiencing a particular emotion? Under what circumstances is the emotion aroused or allayed? Out of the response to these inquiries, Aristotle was able to define the emotion. Typical explanations used in describing the emotions are the following statements:

1. "Anger (is) an appetite, attended with pain, for revenge, on account of an apparent slighting of things which concern one, or of oneself, or of one's friends, when such slighting is improper."
2. "Friendship (is) wishing for a person those things which one thinks good—wishing them for his sake, not for one's own—and tending, in so far as one can, to effect these things."
3. "Fear (is) a pain or trouble arising from an image of coming evil, destructive or painful; for

36 ■ Part 1 Classical Rhetorical Theory

men do not fear all evils—as, for instance, the prospect of being unjust or slow; but only such evils as mean great pain or losses, and these, when they seem not distant, but close and imminent."

4. "Shame (is) a pain or trouble about those ills, present, past or future, which seem to tend to ignominy; shamelessness is a kind of negligence or indifference about these things."

5. "Pity (is) a pain for apparent evil, destructive or painful, befalling a person who does not deserve it, when we might expect such evil to befall ourselves or some of our friends, and when, moreover, it seems near."[25]

Taken as a whole this early analysis of human nature merits the attention of those interested in psychology.

Forms of Discourse or Speaking Occasions

Aristotle classified speaking in ancient Athens in three ways

- *forensic* discourse—that which deals with happenings in the past as in the case of alleged criminality;
- *epideictic*—that which deals with praise and blame as in the case of ceremonial address; and
- *deliberative*—that which deals with future policy as in the case of legislative debate.

> Aristotle classified speaking in ancient Athens in three ways:
> - *forensic* discourse—that which deals with happenings in the past as in the case of alleged criminality;
> - *epideictic*—that which deals with praise and blame as in the case of ceremonial address; and
> - *deliberative*—that which deals with future policy as in the case of legislative debate.

Forensic

Crucial to an understanding of Aristotle's theory of forensic speaking is his treatment of wrongdoing. Criminal acts, he said, are either voluntary or involuntary and are caused by such forces as chance, nature, reason, and passion.[26] Since the major concern of both the prosecution and the defense focuses on whether or not an act was committed and the causes that were operative, forensic discourse emphasizes fact past. The forensic addresses Lysias wrote for wealthy patrons parallel the later rhetoric of Clarence Darrow and Edward Bennett Williams. Notwithstanding its usefulness as a practical art in the Western world, however, forensic discourse did not have a strong appeal for Aristotle because of its susceptibility "to unscrupulous practices."[27]

Epideictic

Epideictic or ceremonial speaking occurs when a speaker praises or blames an individual, an idea, or organization, a locale, or a nation. In view of the fact that the substance of epideictic discourse is drawn largely from the field of ethics, "we have in the *Rhetoric. . .* a summary view of the needed ethical material—happiness, goods, virtue and vice, wrongdoing and injustice, pleasure, equity, laws, and friendship."[28] Of particular importance to this type of rhetorical occasion is the subject of cardinal virtues. Plato doubtless influenced Aristotle with his summary of the four virtues which he believed to be essential for the formation of an ideal republic—courage, temperance, wisdom, and justice. The trait Plato held to be the great integrating virtue which could only exist if the other three were present is justice.[29] When Aristotle turned to an analysis of epideictic discourse, he discussed these four cardinal virtues of Greek culture and added five others including magnanimity, liberality, gentleness, prudence, and magnificence.[30] The epideictic speaker's task is to relate the virtues to the theme being discussed. Evidence would be cited, for example, to show that a praiseworthy individual exemplified specific virtues, while a blameworthy person practiced vices. Pericles' Funeral Oration is the ancestor of Lincoln's Gettysburg Address and Douglas MacArthur's Farewell Speech to Congress. Demosthenes' attacks on Philip of Macedon established the pattern for Cicero's philippics against Mark Antony and Winston Churchill's addresses against Adolph Hitler. Epideictic discourse eulogizing our founding fathers typified much of the speaking during the bicentennial of the Declaration of Independence (1976), the Constitution (1989), and the Bill of Rights (1991).

Deliberative

Of the three types of discourse, Aristotle was most interested in the deliberative. Partly because other writers had ignored this speaking form, and partly because it embraced all of those subjects dealing with fact future, Aristotle felt justified in giving to deliberative speaking his major attention. If ethics permeated all aspects of the epideictic genre, politics performed the same function for the deliberative. Thus a rhetor using this speaking form must be a student of each type of government—an aristocracy, an oligarchy, a monarchy, and a democracy. Only in this way can he adapt to the political views of his hearers. From our contemporary American perspective it is instructive to note what Aristotle perceived to be the main topics about which people debate in a democracy: ways and means (i.e. public revenue), war and peace, national defense, commerce (i.e., imports and exports), and legislation.[31] No modern political scientist would disagree.

Aristotle's discussion of the nature of public discourse is significant for several reasons. First, he implies that the speaker's starting point is the occasion. Secondly, he notes that epideictic discourse is primarily concerned with fact present, forensic discourse with fact past, and deliberative discourse with fact future. Thirdly, he reinforces the notion that the principal subject matter fields utilized by rhetoric are ethics and politics.

To summarize Aristotle's notions on types of speeches and occasions, we have provided the chart developed by Forbes Hill in his essay on "The Rhetoric of Aristotle."[32]

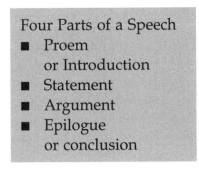

Four Parts of a Speech
■ Proem or Introduction
■ Statement
■ Argument
■ Epilogue or conclusion

Organization of Ideas and Audience Analysis and Adaptation

In his discussion of forms of proof and the types of speaking occasions, Aristotle developed his views on content or the speaker's intended message—a canon of rhetoric described by the Romans as *inventio*. The arrangement and adaptation of the speaker's ideas became a second canon, which later was labeled *dispositio*. Any speech, Aristotle observed, has four parts which unfold in a chronological order:

1. proem or introduction,
2. statement,
3. argument,
4. epilogue or conclusion.[33]

Most essential to Aristotle were the statement and argument; for it is in these parts of the discourse that logical appeals are used. A speech introduction is designed to capture the attention of the audience and to create good will with one's listeners. The conclusion is meant to arouse emotion, to stir up enthusiasm for the speaker's proposal.

Another facet of *dispositio* was audience analysis and adaptation. On this point Plato and Aristotle held widely divergent views. "Aristotle did not share Plato's notion that a true art of rhetoric would enable a speaker to adapt himself to each of the persons of an audience as the dialectician adjusts himself to one deuteragonist."[34] What should concern the rhetor, argued Aristotle, was not "a given individual like Socrates or Hippias, but with what seems probable to men of a given type."[35]

Forms of Discourse

Kind of Speech	Kind of Auditor	Time	Ends	Means
Forensic	Decision-maker	Past	The unjust and just	Accusation and defense
Deliberative	Decision-maker	Future	The advantageous and disadvantageous	Persuasion and dissuasion
Epideictic	Spectator	Present	The noble and the shameful	Praise and blame

Groups

Because of his preoccupation with the characteristics of groups as a whole rather than with the special traits of a particular person, Aristotle approached audience analysis in a comprehensive way. To begin with, he pointed out, all men seek happiness. Speakers must, if they mean to be persuasive, propose those things which either create or enhance the happiness of their listeners. Aristotle listed the following traits as those most treasured by his fellow Greeks: good birth (as measured by the eminence of one's family), numerous children, wealth, good repute, honor, health, physical beauty, strength, size, long life, many friends, good fortune, and virtue.[36] The wise speaker related his proposals to those goods which bring happiness to his listeners. Thereby, he adapted to his audience.

Age

A second dimension of audience analysis involved the traits one associates with audiences of different ages. Compare, for example, Aristotle's description of the young with America's male college students:

> *Young men are lustful in character, and apt to do what they lust after. Of the bodily desires, they are most apt to indulge, and to exceed in, the sexual. They are changeable and fickle in their desires, which are violent but soon appeased; for their impulses are rather keen than great, like the hunger and thirst of the sick. They are passionate, quick to anger and apt to obey their impulse; and they are under the dominion of their passion, for, by reason of ambition, they cannot bear to be slighted, and they are indignant, if they think they are wronged. They are ambitious, or rather contentious; for youth covets preeminence, and victory is a form of preeminence. They are both ambitious and contentious rather than avaricious; this they are not at all, because they have not yet experienced want— as goes the saying of Pittakos about Amphiaraos. They think no evil, but believe in goodness, because as yet they have not seen many cases of vice. They are credulous, because, as yet, they have not been deceived. They are sanguine, because they are heated, as with wine, and also because they have not had many disappointments. They live for most part*

all men seek happiness.

> *by hope; for hope is of the future, as memory of the past, and for young men the future is long and the past short; since, on the first day of a life, there is nothing to remember and everything to hope. They are easily deceived, for the same reason,—since they hope easily. They are comparatively courageous; for they are passionate and hopeful, and passion keeps men from being fearful, while hope makes them bold: no one fears while he is angry, and to hope for a good thing is emboldening. They are shy; for, as yet, they have no independent standard of propriety, but have been educated by convention alone. They are high-minded; for they have not yet been abased by life, but are untried in its necessities; and to think oneself worthy of great things is high-mindedness; and this is characteristic of the hopeful man. They choose honourable before expedient actions; for they live by habit rather than by calculation; and calculation has the expedient for its object, as virtue has the honourable. They are fond of their friends, their relations, their companions, more than persons of the other ages, because they delight in society, and because, as yet, they judge nothing by the standard of expediency, and so do not apply it to their friends. All their mistakes are on the side of excess or vehemence— against the maxim of Chilon; they do everything too much; they love too much, hate too much, and so in all else. They think they know everything and are positive; this, indeed, is the cause of their overdoing all things. Their wrong deeds are done insolently, not viciously. They are ready to pity, because they think all men good, or* rather *good; for they measure their neighbours by their own innocence, and so conceive that these are suffering wrongfully. And they are lovers of laughter,—hence also lovers of wit; for wit is educated insolence.[37]*

How does the following analysis of senior citizens accord with your view of, say, your grandparents?

> *As they have lived many years, and have been deceived or have erred more often, and as most things are disappointing, they are positive about nothing, and do all things much too fee-*

bly. They think, *but are never* sure; *in their uncertainty, they always add 'maybe,'—'perhaps'; they speak thus on all subjects, and positively about nothing. They think evil; for evil-thinking is to put the worst construction upon everything. Further, they are suspicious through their incredulity, being incredulous through their experience. For these reasons they neither like nor hate strongly, but according to the advice of Bias, like, as if they would afterwards hate, and hate, as if they would afterwards like. They are meansouled, through having been abased by life; for they desire nothing great or extraordinary, but only the appliances of life. They are illiberal; for property is one of the necessaries; and, at the same time, they know from their experience, that it is hard to acquire, but easy to lose. They are cowardly, and afraid of everything; for they are of the opposite temperament to youth; they are chilled, while youth is hot; and so old age has prepared the way to cowardice, since fear is a chill. They cling to life, and the more on their latest day, since the object of desire is the absent, and since, too, men most desire that in which they are deficient. They are unduly selfish; for this, too, is a meanness of soul. And, because they are selfish, they live too much for the expedient, too little for the honourable; the expedient being a relative good, the honourable an absolute good. They are not shy, but rather shameless; for, as they do not care, in the same degree, for what is honourable, as for what is expedient, they disregard appearances. They are slow to hope, owing to their experience,—since most things which happen are unsatisfactory and turn out for the worse,—and also from their cowardice. They live in memory more than in hope; for the remainder of their life is small, and the past part large—and hope is of the future, as memory of the past. This is the reason of their talkativeness;—they are for ever speaking of the past, since the retrospect gives them pleasure. Their fits of passion are sharp, but feeble; hence they are not lustful, nor apt to act after lust, but rather for gain. Hence men of this age appear temperate, their desires have become slack, and they are slaves to lucre. And their life is regulated by calculation rather than by moral instinct; calculation having expedi-*

ency for its object, while moral instinct has virtue. Their wrong deeds are done viciously, not insolently. Old men, like young; are compassionate, but not for the same reason as young men; the latter are so from benevolence, the former from weakness; for they think that every possibility of suffering is near themselves, and this, we saw, was a condition of pitying. Hence they are given to lamentation, and are not witty or lovers of mirth; for the love of lamentation is opposite to the love of mirth.[38]

Unlike our own culture in which youth is worshipped, the Athenians admired a later period they termed the "prime of life." Aristotle described that ideal state this way:

Men in their prime will evidently be of a character intermediate between these, abating the excess of each;—neither excessively bold, for this is rashness, nor over-timid, but rightly disposed in both respects, neither trusting nor distrusting all things, but rather judging by the true standard, and living neither for the honourable alone, nor for the expedient alone, but for both; inclining neither to frugality nor to extravagance, but to the just mean. And so, too, in regard to passion and desire, they will be courageously temperate and temperately courageous. Young men and old men share these qualities between them; young men are courageous and intemperate, old men are temperate and cowardly. To speak generally— those useful qualities, which youth and age divide between them, are joined in the prime of life; between their excesses and defects, it has the fitting mean. The body is in its full vigour from thirty to five and thirty; the mind at about forty-nine.[39]

Aristotle's partiality for the "golden mean" prompted him to suggest that whenever a speaker addresses an audience comprised of all three groups, he should gear his remarks to the prime of life. In this way he would not deviate too far from the interests of the young and the old.

STYLE AND DELIVERY

In the preceding analysis we have seen how Aristotle was a message-centered rhetorician whose principal concern was to help his student discover, organize, and adapt the available means of persuasion to a particular rhetorical situation or occasion. But he also recognized that a speaker must reinforce his invention and disposition with a compelling style and delivery. Even though these canons held a subordinate position, they, like the spectacle in a dramatic production, are essential tools in persuasion. Thus style (the use of language to express ideas) and delivery (the management of the voice) form part of the focus of Book III. The inclusion of physical action as a part of delivery was a later Roman innovation.

Style

In his treatment of style, Aristotle deals with the traditional elements of language such as accuracy of word choice, clarity, appropriateness, and vividness. He was especially interested in delineating the characteristics of the metaphor or implied comparison.

Metaphor

"Metaphor," said Aristotle, "is the application of a strange term either transferred from the genus and applied to the species or from the species and applied to the genus, or from one species to another or else by analogy."[40] Aristotle then clarifies this definition by giving an example of each type of metaphor. A transferral of a term from genus to species can be seen in the statement, "Here *stands* my ship." When we say that a ship stands we actually mean that it is "riding at anchor," for the latter is a species of standing. The sentence, "Indeed *ten thousand* noble things Odysseus did," is an example of transference from one species to another. The term "ten thousand" is akin to "many," since they are both members of the same species, one can be substituted for the other.

The fourth and most commonly used method of deriving metaphors is that of analogy. Here we have four terms which have a proportional relationship to each other, such as B is to A as D is to C. By analogy the D may be substituted for the B and the B for the D. Replacing these letters with names, we let A be Plato, B a goblet, C Ares, and D a shield. By def-

inition the goblet is to Plato as the shield is to Ares. A metaphor is obtained by referring to the goblet as a shield of Plato or the shield as a goblet of Ares. Since the shield and the goblet are both characteristic of deity, they come under the same genus and can therefore be interchanged.[41]

In developing his theory of style, Aristotle further observed that one of the most important functions of a metaphor in public address is to teach. If words are strange, foreign, or archaic, they are not known to all and, consequently, do not give any new information. Proper and ordinary words, on the other hand, are already known by the audience. It is the metaphor, more than any other figure of speech, therefore, that increases our knowledge. When Homer calls old age a stubble, he conveys learning and knowledge through the medium of the genus, because they are both withered.[42]

The metaphor, Aristotle states, teaches by bringing into view resemblances between things which appear on the surface as dissimilar. It is most effective when it is drawn from objects that are related, but not too obvious to everyone at first sight. Whenever the significance of the metaphor is comprehended at first glance, the mind is not stirred into action. If people are to engage in reflective thinking, the figure must arouse curiosity.

Similarly Aristotle suggests that metaphors should also "be derived from something beautiful . . . ."[43] When a speaker plans a speech of praise he must take his metaphors from the superior things that fall under the same genus. Thus it makes a difference whether we say "rosy-fingered dawn" or "red-fingered dawn" because the rose reminds us of something that is agreeable to sight and smell. It is essential, therefore, that the forms of the word express an agreeable sound.

Aristotle, finally emphasizes the point that metaphors cannot be derived from anyone else.[44] This does not imply that one writer or speaker cannot borrow a metaphor from another; but that the invention of metaphor is an innate talent, and therefore cannot be taught. Although metaphors are not confined to men of genius, they do show originality and

> "Metaphor," said Aristotle, "is the application of a strange term either transferred from the genus and applied to the species or from the species and applied to the genus, or from one species to another or else by analogy."

are definite marks of natural ability. It is obvious, then, that a proportional relationship exists between one's intellect and his success in using metaphors.

Delivery

Aristotle was far less enthusiastic about analyzing delivery. It was to him an external quality, a low priority canon that does not lend itself to philosophical speculation or scientific inquiry. As a result he subordinates it to style—a fact which disturbed the Roman rhetoricians.

SUMMARY

The *Rhetoric* of Aristotle is not a well-organized textbook by modern standards. Rather it appears to be Aristotle's own lecture notes collected over a twelve-year period. Topics are treated briefly, dropped, and reconsidered elsewhere. Illustrative material is limited, perhaps because Aristotle resorted to impromptu examples at the time of utterance, examples which undoubtedly changed over the years. Clearly Aristotle himself made no effort to edit this material for later publication. What we have instead are rough lecture notes used intermittently when needed. But despite these reservations the *Rhetoric* remains the most significant rhetorical work in Western thought. Indeed, as Lane Cooper correctly points out, "Aristotle's treatise on Rhetoric is one of the world's best and wisest books."[45]

the *Rhetoric* remains the most significant rhetorical work in Western thought.

In 1951, Herbert James, then a graduate student at Ohio State University, constructed the following model of *The Rhetoric*. We include it here as an excellent summary of the major components of Aristotle's theory of persuasive discourse.

The RHETORIC OF ARISTOTLE

Rhetoric is the counterpart of dialectic (1-1). Rhetoric is the faculty of discovering in the particular case all the available means of persuasion (1-2). The functions of rhetoric are to make truth prevail, to instruct, to debate, and to defend, (1-1).

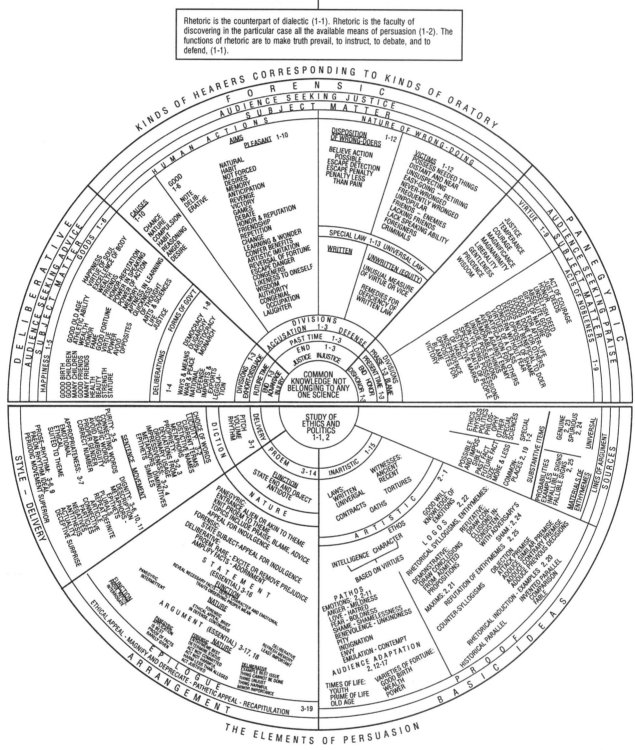

Notes

1. For a more extended analysis of Aristotle's methodology, see Donal J. Stanton and Goodwin Berquist, "Aristotle's *Rhetoric:* Empiricism or Conjecture?", *Southern Speech Communication Journal,* 41, 1 (Fall, 1975), pp. 69–81.
2. *Britannica, Macropaedia, XIV,* 62.
3. *The Rhetoric of Aristotle: A Translation* (Cambridge: University Press, 1909), p. 1.
4. *Ibid,* p. 3.
5. *Ibid,* pp. 4–5.
6. *Ibid,* p. 5.
7. The use of the terms "artistic" and "nonartistic" comes from the Lane Cooper translation of *"The Rhetoric* (New York: Appleton-Century-Crofts, 1932), p. 8. These terms seemed to the authors more meaningful than Jebb's "artificial" and "nonartificial."
8. *The Rhetoric,* trans. by Jebb, p. 6.
9. Rhetorical scholars now generally seem to agree that what distinguishes the enthymeme from the syllogism is its *probable* nature and that some enthymemes may include a statement of all three terms, rather than one or two.
10. James H. McBurney, "The Place of the Enthymeme in Rhetorical Theory," *Speech Monographs,* 3 (1936), pp. 49–74.
11. *The Rhetoric,* trans. by Jebb, p. 9.
12. Everett Lee Hunt, "Plato and Aristotle on Rhetoric and Rhetoricians," *Studies in Rhetoric and Public Speaking in Honor of James Albert Winans* (New York: The Century Co., 1925), p. 50.
13. McBurney, "The Enthymeme," p. 57.
14. *Ibid.,* p. 56.
15. *The Rhetoric,* trans. by Cooper, p. 147
16. McBurney, "The Enthymeme," p. 61.
17. *Ibid.,* p. 62.
18. *Ibid.,* p. 63.
19. *The Rhetoric,* trans. by Cooper, p. 154.
20. E.S. Forster, trans., *Topica* (Cambridge, Mass.: Harvard University Press, 1966), Book III, chs. 1–5.
21. *The Rhetoric,* trans. by Jebb, p. 69.
22. *Ibid.,* p. 68.
23. *The Rhetoric,* trans. by Cooper, p. 9.
24. *Ibid.,* pp. 90–131.
25. *The Rhetoric,* trans. by Jebb, pp. 71–89.
26. *The Rhetoric,* trans. by Cooper, pp. 56–57.
27. Hunt, "Plato and Aristotle," p. 52.
28. *Ibid.*
29. See *The Republic.*
30. *The Rhetoric,* trans. by Cooper, p. 47.
31. *Ibid.,* pp. 21–23.
32. James J. Murphy, ed., *A Synoptic History of Classical Rhetoric* (New York: Random House, 1972), p. 24.
33. *The Rhetoric,* trans. by Cooper, pp. 221–241.
34. Hunt, "Plato and Aristotle," p. 58.
35. *Ibid.*
36. *The Rhetoric,* trans. by Cooper, pp. 24–29.
37. *The Rhetoric,* trans. by Jebb, pp. 99–100.
38. *Ibid.,* pp. 100–102.
39. *Ibid.,* p. 102.
40. Aristotle, *Poetics,* trans. by W. Hamilton Fyfe (Cambridge, Mass.: Harvard University Press, 1955), p. 81.
41. *Ibid.*
42. *The Rhetoric,* trans. by Cooper, pp. 206–207.
43. *Ibid.,* p. 189.
44. *Poetics,* p. 91.
45. *The Rhetoric,* trans. by Cooper, p. vii.

The Education
of the Citizen-Orator

In Chapters Two and Three we saw how Plato's dialogues and Aristotle's treatise constitute major contributions to the rhetoric of Western thought. The first provided moral guidelines for the persuasive speaker so timeless in appeal no one has improved upon them since. The second circumscribed the field of rhetoric so broadly modern writers on persuasion inevitably become constant borrowers. But Plato and Aristotle were not the only early thinkers to write on this subject. The insights of dozens of other theorists, practitioners, and critics have survived as well.[1] Our purpose here is not to provide a compendium of the thoughts of every Greek and Roman who ever wrote about rhetoric but to survey important representative contributions to the field. In particular, we will focus in this chapter on what might be called the educational-philosophical school of thought as seen in the writings of Isocrates, Cicero, and Quintilian.

ISOCRATES OF ATHENS

Well educated but early deprived of his patrimony, Isocrates began his career as a logographer or speech writer for wealthy Athenians. He wanted desperately to play a leading role in the affairs of his city state but was unable to do so for two reasons. First, he had a weak voice; he was unable to be heard by large groups out-of-doors, and this after all was how the Athenian Assembly conducted its business. Further, he was naturally timid; he had what we would today call an advanced case of stage fright. In a society oriented to the practice of oratory, Isocrates was a man of ambition without promising prospects.

Isocrates' School of Speech

At age forty-three, he finally found a solution to his dilemma. If he could not himself become an outstanding citizen-orator, then he would do the next best thing: he would train Athens' future leaders. In 392 B.C.E., some five years before Plato established his Academy, Isocrates founded a school of speech, the first permanent institution of higher learning in his native city. For over fifty years, he conducted his school single-handedly. Here he tutored as many as one hundred students at a time, setting forth his ideas for the future leaders of Athens and much of the Greek world. And here he became "the foremost speech teacher of the ancient world."[2]

In a society dominated by the spoken word, rhetoric was of critical importance. No one before or since, we submit, has put the matter as well as Isocrates did in the passage that follows:

We ought. . . to think of the art of discourse just as we think of the other arts, and not to form opposite judgments about similar things, nor show ourselves intolerant toward that power which, of all the faculties which belong to the nature of man, is the source of most of our blessings. For in the other powers which we possess. . . we are in no respect superior to other living creatures; nay, we are inferior to many in swiftness and in strength and in other resources; but, because there has been implanted in us the power to persuade each other and to make clear to each other whatever we desire, not only have we escaped the life of wild beasts, but we have come together and founded cities and made laws and invented arts; and,

generally speaking, there is no institution de-
vised by man which the power of speech has
not helped us to establish. For this it is which
has laid down laws concerning things just and
unjust, and things honourable and base; and if
it were not for these ordinances we should not
be able to live with one another. It is by this
also that we confute the bad and extol the
good. Through this we educate the ignorant
and appraise the wise; for the power to speak
well is taken as the surest index of a sound un-
derstanding, and discourse which is true and
lawful and just is the outward image of a good
and faithful soul. With this faculty we both con-
tend against others on matters which are open
to dispute and seek light for ourselves on things
which are unknown; for the same arguments
which we use in persuading others when we
speak in public, we employ also when we delib-
erate in our own thoughts; and, while we call
eloquent those who are able to speak before a
crowd, we regard as sage those
who most skillfully debate their
problems in their own minds.
And, if there is need to speak in
brief summary of this power, we
shall find that none of the things
which are done with intelli-
gence take place without the
help of speech, but that in all
our actions as well as in all our
thoughts speech is our guide, and is most em-
ployed by those who have the most wisdom.[3]

Speech separates men from all other animals; speech underlies all of the important institutions of our society—law, education, morality. We use speech to debate public policy; we also use speech to resolve problems in our own minds. Nothing of substance in society is accomplished without the aid of speech. Those who use speech best are the men of greatest wisdom among us. These were Isocrates' views on the subject he taught for over half a century. Is it any wonder that a subject so conceived should form the nucleus of a whole system of education in both Greece and Rome?

Students were admitted to Isocrates' school of speech at age fifteen. To be accepted, they had to demonstrate competence in science and mathematics and promise in voice control, intellect, and nerve. Their master felt that geometry and astronomy

served as a sort of mental gymnastics which prepared the mind for philosophy and civics.[4] Further, he knew by his own experience that lung power and self-confidence were crucial ingredients to oratorical success. To be a leader in a democratic state meant to be a capable if not outstanding speaker. The tuition for a three to four-year course of study was roughly $200, a large sum for those days when the normal curriculum might extend six weeks and cost far less.

Isocrates maintained that there were three essentials for learning: natural ability, training, and practice. Those who were unwilling to work hard at developing their talents soon dropped out.

The Curriculum

Instruction began with introductory lectures on writing, speaking, and Greek culture. The sole texts available were a set of "speeches" written by the master himself. These set pieces, together with student essays were studied, criticized, revised, rewritten, and reexamined again and again. Students were sent to the Assembly and the law courts to study the compositions of experienced orators as well.

The core of Isocrates' curriculum was public speaking, for he believed speech was the best available instrument for sharpening human judgment. To find the right expression demanded a sensitivity to both thought and language no other method then in use required. The right word, Isocrates declared, was a sure sign of good thinking. Taken in its broadest sense, learning to speak properly was tantamount to learning to think properly. Isocrates advised his students that the liberally educated man was conspicuous for his eloquence rather than for his wealth or valor. Note that effective speech-making was the sign of sound training, *not* its principal goal.

The curriculum also included writing, debate, classical prose and poetry, philosophy, mathematics, and history. The brand of education Isocrates offered was literary in its stress upon the development of a graceful style, psychological in its emphasis upon influencing human behavior, political in its use of contemporary issues in government, and pragmatic in its preparation of students to serve as citizen leaders in Greek society. Isocrates had no interest in idle speculation, in a search for knowledge unrelated to

---

Isocrates' Three Learning Essentials
■ Natural Ability
■ Training
■ Practice

human conduct. Nor did he believe in the existence of absolute truth. Rather, he recommended that his students pursue that conduct which all Greeks acknowledged to be good. To him, the moral man was one who chose wisely in a given situation. Education in "the wisdom of choice" was as essential an exercise for the soul, he believed, as gymnastics was for the body. Thus a sharp contrast existed between the truthseeking of students at Plato's Academy and the practical training in civic leadership offered by Isocrates.

Isocrates' set speeches, the texts his students studied with care, were propagandistic in nature for they mirrored the master's lifelong belief in pan-Hellenism. Like many thinkers in his day, Isocrates was justly proud of the many cultural accomplishments of the Greek people. But he was dismayed by the endless squabbling of the various city states. He yearned for a united Greece, a goal achieved only at his life's end with the military conquests of the Macedonians.

Unlike other teachers of his time, Isocrates did not pretend to have a monopoly on wisdom. He often sent his students to learn from others, from whomever was best qualified to teach them. Even though his own curriculum was richly diverse, he recognized special talent in others.

> The Greeks invented rhetoric but the Romans perfected it.

Approach to Education

Isocrates' approach to education was innovative in that he made widespread use of imitation and models. He insisted on providing each of his students with individual attention. Pupils came from every corner of the Mediterranean world. At the end of their extended stay in Athens, many wept. Some initiated a life-long correspondence with the master and some erected a statue to his memory at the Temple of Apollo at Delphi.

The aim of Isocrates' system of education was the development of citizen-orators, not of orators *per se*. Graduates of his school became prominent generals, philosophers, historians, and statesmen. Isocrates attracted more students than all the other sophists and philosophers combined.

Plato perceived "something of philosophy" in Isocrates' work and predicted he would excel all those who studied rhetoric and "leave them far-

ther behind than children."[5] *Against the Sophists,* Isocrates' attack on the itinerant professors of his day, served as the prototype of Plato's *Gorgias,* the dialogue he wrote several years later.

Isocrates' name is cited more often than that of any other rhetorician in Aristotle's *Rhetoric.* And his broad influence may well exceed even this enviable record. Consider, for example, his treatment of the character of a speaker, written when Aristotle was still a student at Plato's Academy:

> *Mark you, the man who wishes to persuade people will not be negligent as to the matter of character; no, on the contrary, he will apply himself above all to establish a most honourable name among his fellow citizens; for who does not know that words carry greater conviction when spoken by men of good repute than when spoken by men who live under a cloud, and that the argument which is made by a man's life is of more weight than that which is furnished by words?*[6]

Cicero, with his notable gift for imagery, summed up the impact of the great Athenian teacher best: "Then behold Isocrates arose, from whose school as from the Trojan horse, none but real heroes proceeded."[7]

THE ROMAN RHETORICIANS: CICERO AND QUINTILIAN

Practical, thorough, intellectually diverse—Isocrates' version of rhetorical education stimulated the thinking of Roman philosophers and educators two centuries later. Rhetoric at Rome began with the mastery of Greek rhetoric.

Training Exercises for Students

Young Romans were "expected to memorize the system and might be subjected to a thorough catechism on it."[8] The Greek language was taught in Roman schools and oftentimes the teachers themselves were Greek so there was no way around the "system"— the student had no choice but to learn.

The Greeks invented rhetoric but the Romans perfected it. Consonant with their stress on thoroughness and practicality, the Romans believed in an early start. Before all things let the talk of the child's nurses be grammatical, Quintilian counseled.

To their morals, doubtless, attention is first to be paid; but let them also speak with propriety. It is they that the child will hear first; it is their words that he will try to form by imitation. We are by nature more tenacious of what we have imbibed in our infant years; as the flavour, with which you scent vessels when new, remains in them . . . those very habits, which are of a more objectionable nature, adhere with the greater tenacity; for good ones are easily changed for the worse, but when will you change bad ones into good? Let the child not be accustomed, therefore, even while he is yet an infant, to phraseology which must be un-learned.[9]

Elementary education was placed in the hands of a teacher called a *grammaticus:* his duties involved correcting spelling, grammar and punctuation together with reading and interpreting poetry and history. He provided students with a solid introduction to language and culture; others were responsible for instruction in arithmetic, geometry, music, and astronomy.

Advanced rhetorical education involved a rich variety of skills, perhaps the most distinctive of which was declamation. The instructor would present a case similar to those debated in the Roman Forum and the students would argue its merits as closely as possible to reality.[10] If we were to walk into a Roman classroom where rhetoric was being taught we might hear a debate on the following typical themes:

1. A certain commander, being surrounded by the enemy and unable to escape, came to an agreement with them, by which he was to withdraw his men, leaving behind their arms and equipment. This was done, and so his men were saved from a hopeless situation with the loss of arms and equipment. The commander was accused of high treason . . . .
2. The law forbids the sacrifice of a bull calf to Diana. Some sailors caught by a storm on the high seas vowed that if they reached a harbour which was in sight they would sacrifice a bull calf to the deity of the place. It so happened that at the harbour there was a temple of Diana, the very goddess to whom a bull calf might not be sacrificed. Ignorant of the law, they made their sacrifice on reaching shore and were brought to trial.[11]

The mastery and skillful use of argument and language were nurtured through such exercises, along with those in writing, paraphrase, translation, imitation, and memorization. Students were also assigned readings in poetry, history, and oratory and they undertook as well the study of law and politics.

The ultimate goal of such training was the production of the philosopher-orator-statesman. Cicero, the greatest of the Roman orators, articulated the ideal program in his most famous rhetorical work, *de Oratore.*

In my opinion . . . no man can be an orator possessed of every praiseworthy accomplishment, unless he has attained the knowledge of every thing important, and of all liberal arts, for his language must be ornate and copious from knowledge, since, unless there be beneath the surface matter understood and felt by the speaker, oratory becomes an empty and almost puerile flow of words.[12]

Cicero himself was a life-long student and would travel anywhere in the Mediterranean world at his own expense to enhance his education.

To be thus widely read and broadly educated insured the speaker ample subject matter for his speeches. But the Romans went further by amplifying Greek concepts in filling in gaps on various aspects of discourse. Consider, for example, their treatment of the five canons of rhetoric. They created a fresh vocabulary to designate these elements. The first of the canons they called *inventio* (the message); the second, *dispositio* (organization and adaptation of the message); the third, *elocutio* (style and language control); the fourth, *memoria* (memory), and the fifth, *pronunciatio* (voice control, bodily activity, and appearance). Our purpose here is to summarize the salient issues they emphasized in discussing these canons. As we do so, our principal concern will be to give special attention to those points of view which both amplified what the Greeks had discussed, and filled in areas they had tended to ignore or neglect.

THE CANONS OF RHETORIC

Inventio: Logical Proof

Both Cicero and Quintilian accepted the Aristotelian notion that a rhetorical message consists of effective use of logical, ethical, and pathetic proof. The rhetor who has command of these three persuasive strategies, they held, is in a good position to motivate an audience. We begin our analysis of this first canon with a discussion of Roman views on logos. Since the Romans concurred with Aristotle's interpretation of commonplaces, lines of argument, and enthymematic reasoning, we will stress primarily what they said on the crucial logical element of stasis. This aspect of logos came to mean the central turning point in a case—the issue upon which a debate may hinge. Cicero and Quintilian argued that the state of any case could be determined by asking certain questions: Whether a thing is, what it is, and of what kind it is. Did a case turn on a question of fact, definition, or quality? Quintilian analyzed Cicero's defense of Milo, as an example: "First, Did Milo kill Claudius? (Fact). Yes, fact admitted. Second, Did Milo murder Claudius? (Definition). Claudius lay in wait and attacked Milo. Therefore, the killing was not premeditated. It must be defined as self-defense, not as murder. Third, Was the act good or bad? (Quality). Good, because, Claudius was a bad citizen, and the Republic was better off with him dead."[13] Let the student examine the nature of the cause with these three questions in mind, Cicero wrote, and the point at issue becomes immediately apparent.[14]

When we apply the Roman theory of stasis to representative controversial issues in the past three decades, it is easy to see its relevance. We will cite as examples two contentious cases—one political and the other legal—which produced typical central turning points that led to a division of thought among Americans. The first was the heated debate generated during the Vietnam War. Here are the questions that speakers on both sides had to answer.

1. Was the Vietnam War essentially a Civil War? (Stasis of Definition)
2. Were the My Lai killings justified? (Stasis of Quality)

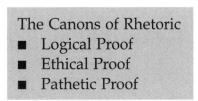

The Canons of Rhetoric
■ Logical Proof
■ Ethical Proof
■ Pathetic Proof

Since the Romans concurred with Aristotle's interpretation of commonplaces, lines of argument, and enthymematic reasoning, we will stress primarily what they said on the crucial logical element of stasis. This aspect of logos came to mean the central turning point in a case—the issue upon which a debate may hinge.

3. Did the South Vietnamese Army or the Viet Cong first violate the cease-fire agreements? (Stasis of Fact)

How these questions were answered frequently determined whether members of the Administration and Congress would be identified as "Hawks" or "Doves."

The second case we would like to use as a graphic illustration of how the concept of stasis works was the recent O.J. Simpson Murder Trial which captivated millions of Americans and other world citizens as they viewed the hearings on television. The stasis of fact, observers soon learned, played a prominent role whenever members of the prosecution and the defense cross-examined witnesses and delivered their closing speeches. These five factual questions were at all times before the jury:

1. Did O.J. Simpson murder Nicole Simpson and Ronald Goldman?
2. Did the murder take place between 10:15 P.M. and 10:50 P.M. on the night of June 12, 1994?
3. Did prosecution investigators, through careless handling and testing of blood samples, contaminate their findings?
4. Did the Los Angeles police plant evidence with respect to blood drops and the glove found at Simpson's estate?
5. Was the act of murder committed by more than one person?

If the jury concluded that the factual data did not establish guilt on the part of the defendant, an acquittal must take place. But if they decided that Simpson did commit the act, they would then be faced with a stasis of definition phrased as follows:

1. Was the act of murder first degree? (Premeditated in nature, thereby proving intent)
2. Was the act of murder second degree? (An unplanned act of rage)

Not present among the issues was a stasis of quality, for neither side argued that the killings were justified.

Arguments and information were to be found in certain "places," as the Romans metaphorically phrased it. Quintilian described the process this way. "I now come to *things,* among which *actions* are most closely connected with persons, and must therefore be first considered. In regard, then, to everything that is done, the question is, either *why,* or *where,* or *when,* or *in what manner,* or *by what means,* it was done. Arguments are consequently derived from *the motives for actions done* or *to be done.*"[15] The ancient student of rhetoric, like the modern student of journalism, used these questions to guide him in the discovery of a case. "The places pointed to by Quintilian's questions were cause, place, time, manner, means."[16]

Inventio: Ethical Proof

In the area of ethical proof the Romans also expanded the concept of *inventio.* Aristotle, you may recall, spoke of the constituent elements of ethos as being intelligence, character, and good will. But his interest in these notions was largely limited to the period of speech presentation itself. He did not feel that the listener should concern himself unduly with the orator's actions outside of the immediate rhetorical situation. The Romans, however (perhaps influenced by Isocrates' earlier view), broadened ethical proof to include the thrust and image of the speaker's life as a whole. Thus they constructed a theory consistent with their notion of the "perfect orator." Because this aspect of Roman thinking was to have importance for centuries to come, let us turn to the personification of this idea of antecedent ethical proof—Quintilian's "good man theory."

In Book XII of his *Institutes of Oratory,* Quintilian develops his concept of the perfect orator. First, he is a good man and after that he is skilled in speaking, Quintilian declared.[17] Although technical skill is important, it is subordinate to the moral strength of the speaker. So strong were Quintilian's convictions on this subject that he believed "no man can be an orator unless he is a good man." It is not difficult to understand this strong emphasis on the character of the speaker if we analyze Quintilian's views on the function of a speech. "Oratory," he tells us, "is in the main concerned with the treatment of what is just and honorable." A speech which does not exemplify these traits is suitable only to a "hireling pleader" or a "hack advocate." The orator "is sent by heaven to be a blessing to all mankind." Consequently, he is not only a leader but a servant of the people. When he speaks in the forum he pleads with the judge to acquit the innocent defendant. As he speaks in the senate in time of war he encourages the citizens to abandon their fear. As he orates on special occasions he inspires his hearers to emulate the great heroes of the past. In short, whether the speech is forensic, deliberative, or epideictic in nature, it is designed for the sole purpose of guiding the hearers along a righteous path.

Quintilian, therefore, concludes that only the individual "who is a good man skilled in speaking" can hope to perform these essential duties of the orator. Who is this good man? What traits does he possess? Quintilian answers that he is a man who is free from all vice, a lover of wisdom, a sincere believer in the cause which he advocates, and a servant of the state and the people.

Quintilian believed that "vileness and virtue cannot jointly inhabit in the selfsame heart." A man is either good or evil. It is impossible for him to yield to the lusts of the flesh and, at the same time, carry out the great responsibility which belongs to the orator. "Surely the advocate who is called upon to defend the accused," asserts Quintilian, "requires to be a man of honor, honor which greed cannot corrupt, influence seduce, or fear dismay."

Quintilian, like Aristotle, Plato, and Cicero, stressed the importance of knowledge as an essential requisite of the orator. To acquire understanding of the subject matter of a particular case, the speaker must assiduously study all pertinent material. Since study, however, requires considerable effort the heart and mind must be free from those distractions which turn the attention of the orator away from the "object of preparation." Arguing from less to greater, Quintilian points out that if many of the necessary daily activities interfere with our speech preparation, how much more will such violent passions as "envy,"

> In Book XII of his *Institutes of Oratory,* Quintilian develops his concept of the perfect orator. First, he is a good man and after that he is skilled in speaking, . . .

"avarice," and "greed" hamper serious contemplation.

Further, the orator cannot hope to achieve his end unless he sincerely believes in the cause which he advocates. First, be inspired yourself, advises Quintilian, then you are ready to "inspire such good feelings in others." Quintilian disagrees with those who state that a speaker may have the ability to simulate an attitude of sincerity. "For however we try to conceal it," he noted, "insincerity will always betray itself, and there was never in any man so great eloquence as would not begin to stumble and hesitate as soon as his words ran counter to his inmost thoughts."

The ideal orator, likewise, places the interests of the people before his own welfare. His actions will not be motivated by ambition, but rather his duty to his countrymen. It is clear, Quintilian argues, that the evil man is a slave to his own fleshly desires. In time of emergency he may sacrifice the people at the altar of cowardice or greed. The good man, on the other hand, even in the moments of greatest adversity, remains just and honorable.

Not content with a philosophical explanation alone of the nature of the good man, Quintilian turns to more practical considerations. He answers his critics who charge that his theory is impractical and inconsistent. The ideal orator must know how to speak on both sides of a question, and, in addition, may frequently be forced to tell a falsehood in defense of a good cause. We cannot understand the nature of virtue until we have seen vice. Since it is incumbent on the orator to teach honor and justice, he must analyze the opposite traits of dishonor and injustice. In this connection, Quintilian observes that "the schemes of his adversaries should be no less known to the orator than those of an enemy to a commander in the field."

How can the orator express untruths and still be a virtuous man? Quintilian points out that the end, rather than the means, is the leading principle of life. Any methods which the orator might use are acceptable if the cause which he defends is just. In each of the following situations, for example, a lie would, in Quintilian's opinion, serve a more useful purpose than the truth:

1. To divert an assassin from his victim.
2. To deceive an enemy to save our country.
3. To convince an unjust judge that certain righteous acts were never done.
4. To forgive enemies who may serve the state to advantage.
5. To comfort a child who is sick.

Quintilian next considers the problem of teaching the prospective orator how to become a good man. He is careful to note that virtue is not an innate gift from God. Instead it is something that comes from study, contemplation, and training. The student would be wise, therefore, to concentrate on the subject of ethics and logic; "for no one will achieve sufficient skill in speaking, unless he makes a thorough study of all the workings of nature and forms his character on the precepts of philosophy and the dictates of reason." Although the powers of a particular student are "inadequate to such an achievement," his efforts will not be in vain. For he will be rewarded according to the distance which he travels toward that goal.

What is distinctive in this theory is the stress upon "goodness" as the Romans understood that word. "Goodness," to them, meant dutiful service to family and state. Thus Quintilian, as the chief propagator of the "good man theory," felt content in upholding an ends-means philosophy. Situational ethics which typified Roman morality was later ignored by the Christian Church when it sought an educational system for its believers. Quintilian's comprehensive system of education with its central focus on the "good man" appealed at once to ethical Christians: no matter that Roman and Christian ideas of morality failed to coincide. From the fifth century, A.D. to the Renaissance, the educational concepts of Quintilian dominated Western thought.

Inventio: **Pathetic Proof**

As we turn from ethical to pathetic proof, we again see that the Romans both reinforced and extended Aristotle's theories. Accepting the view that man is basically rational, they agreed with Aristotle that emotional proof should be used as a reinforcement of logos. But they went far beyond Aristotle and Isocrates in highlighting the value of pathos. In the *Orator,* Cicero suggested that impressive pathetic appeals must be used to strengthen the logos.[18] The speaker, he said, who inflames the court accomplishes far more than the one who merely instructs it. Non-emotional speech produces yawning, gossiping, and poor eye contact. Only when a speaker stirs the audience to pity or hate and has them hang on every word is a genuine orator present.

Cicero further observed that he owed his reputation as an outstanding orator to his ability to appeal to sympathy and pity. It is for this reason, he noted, that he frequently was selected as the speaker to deliver a closing plea to a jury. Moreover, he freely participated in rhetorical acts designed to arouse emotions. On one occasion Cicero and other members of a defense team told a defendant to stand up and raise his small son so that all could see. The result was "a wailing and lamentation" throughout the forum.[19]

Cicero set the stage for Quintilian's theory of pathetic proof. Fully convinced of the need for compelling pathos, Quintilian observed: "There is room for addresses to the feelings. The nature of the feelings is varied, and not to be treated cursorily; nor does the whole art of oratory present any subject that requires greater study."[20]

With Cicero, Quintilian viewed humor and laughter as important emotions which have the power to dispel hatred or anger. The following statements taken from Quintilian's theory of humor, we feel, are timely and useful suggestions for twentieth-century speakers:

1. "There are three things out of which we may seek to raise a laugh, to wit, others, ourselves, or things intermediate."
2. "There is such a thing as a humorous look, manner or gesture . . . ."
3. Humor should "never be designed to wound, and we should never make it our ideal to lose a friend sooner than lose a jest."

Dispositio

The Roman rhetoricians sought to amplify the other four divisions of classical rhetoric as well. The four parts of a speech outlined by Aristotle—proem, statement, argument, and epilogue—were enlarged to five—exordium, narration, proof, refutation, and peroration. In developing these points, Cicero gave practical suggestions that still have a contemporary relevance. The purposes of an exordium or introduction, he said, are to arouse attention, to orient the listeners regarding the theme, and to conciliate. If the proof or body portion of the discourse contains three main ideas, he added, the strongest argument should come first and the weakest should be placed in the middle. Finally, the peroration or concluding action step is the appropriate section to use forceful emotional appeals.[21]

Cicero's inclusion of refutation as a separate element of *dispositio* foreshadows later theories of argumentation and debate. Both he and subsequent writers held that the weight of an argument is often sustained unless it is countered by strong reasoning and evidence. Cicero himself offers us a splendid model of persuasive refutation in his historically significant essay "On Old Age." First, he lists the following arguments which are frequently used to relegate older people to a position of inferiority and unhappiness:

1. elderly citizens are inactive;
2. they lack physical vitality and stamina;
3. they are unable to experience "sensual pleasures";
4. they are rapidly approaching death.

Cicero next turns to each of the four indictments against old age and presents a point-by-point refutation. The inactivity of older people, he argued, does not prevent them from engaging in intellectual pursuits. Nor does it keep them from remembering what is important in maintaining the good life. Secondly, the loss of physical vigor due to age is more than offset by an improvement in vocal melody and a mastery of a subdued style. Thirdly, an older person, by being deprived of sensual pleasures becomes more temperate, refrains from engaging in unrewarding activities, and strengthens his appetite for conversation. Fourthly, the issue of death not only confronts the elderly but also the young. More importantly one's success in life is not determined by the number of years spent on earth but by the quality of his existence. Nor can we overlook the fact that since death is followed by immortality, grief is unwarranted.[22]

By the time that Cicero finishes his refutation, he has successfully established the claim that old age has positive merits as well as shortcomings. For this reason his argument not only gives us a valuable insight concerning the use of refutation, but provides

> The four parts of a speech outlined by Aristotle—proem, statement, argument, and epilogue—were enlarged to five—exordium, narration, proof, refutation, and peroration.

comfort and encouragement to senior citizens in the 21th century.

Cicero also amplified the classical notion that *dispositio* embraces audience analysis and adaptation as well as arrangement.[23] Prudence and judgment, he stated, must be used by the orator in choosing and organizing arguments and speech details so that they will be suitable to the listeners and occasion. This implies the need, in some instances, to make major adjustments on an impromptu basis.

Quintilian approached speech organization from the viewpoint of a defendant in a legal case. He considered the methods for responding to single and multiple accusations, the importance of ordering arguments to best advantage, the order of speakers, and the nature of one's defense. Himself a courtroom pleader of note, Quintilian relied partly on personal experience and partly on the wisdom of those who preceded him. The Romans devoted more attention to forensic speaking than to any other type. This explains in part why refutation became one of the five parts of a speech.

Elocutio

The Roman tendency to amplify and fill in gaps was also evident in their handling of the canon of style or language control. In his discussion of style, Cicero declared the speaker's purpose would determine his use of language: *to prove* he will resort to the "plain" style typified by Greek orators in the province of Attica; *to please* he will employ a "middle" style championed by Isocrates; *to persuade* he will choose the "grand" style of discourse first used by Gorgias. In his dialogue, *Orator,* Cicero described the ideal orator as one who mastered all three styles. "He in fact is eloquent who can discuss commonplace matters simply, lofty subjects impressively, and topics ranging between in a tempered style."[24]

The "plain" speaker had as his main concern, propriety. He talked in a subdued voice and used the most common of words. His attention was directed to thought rather than language, so he disregarded rhythm and smoothness and avoided ornamentation. His goal was to speak adroitly and neatly, clearly and properly. He might employ mild metaphors and maxims, but only when they enhanced understanding, never for effect. His discourse, then, was plain and direct, expeditious and ordinary.

The speaker who sought to entertain his listeners would choose a "middle" style. Vigor was sacrificed

for charm. Any and every form of ornamentation was appropriate, including the use of wit and humor. Such a speaker possessed the skill to develop arguments with breadth and erudition; he was master at amplification. His words were chosen for the effect they would produce on others. Harsh sounds were avoided. Euphony and imagery were cultivated. The overall effect was one of moderation and temperance, of polish and urbanity. This style of discourse, more than any other, typified Cicero himself and would later influence us in English through the marvelous prose style of Edmund Burke.

The "grand" style of oratory Cicero described was magnificent, stately, opulent, and ornate. The grand orator was fiery, impetuous; his eloquence "rushes along with the roar of a mighty stream."[25] Such a speaker might sway thousands if conditions were right. But if he resorted to dramatic delivery and majestic speech without first preparing his listeners, he would be "like a drunken reveller in the midst of sober men." Timing and a clear understanding of the speaking situation were critical. The grand orator must be familiar with the other two forms of style or his manner would strike the listener as "scarcely sane." The "eloquent speaker" was Cicero's ideal. No one ever achieved the eminence he had in mind but like Plato's philosopher king, the ideal sometimes motivated man's best efforts.

Memoria

The canon of memory which goes unmentioned in Aristotle's *Rhetoric* was also viewed by the Romans as an area the orator must master. A Greek by the name of Simonides was the first to teach this mental discipline, according to Quintilian. The story goes that Simonides was attending an athletic banquet when he was informed that two messengers on horseback wished to speak with him. While he was absent from the banquet hall, the building collapsed, crushing the guests so horribly "that those who went to look for the bodies of the dead, in order to bury them, were unable to recognize by any mark, not only their faces, but even their limbs." Then Simonides, by the aid of his memory, "pointed out the bodies to the friends in the exact order in which they had sat."[26]

The essential rule recommended as a first requisite by Simonides, Cicero, and Quintilian was the association of words with visual images which could be remembered against some familiar background. The common system was to identify words or topics with physical objects and place. Convinced that it is chiefly order that gives distinctness to memory, Cicero suggested that certain places must be firmly fixed in the mind; then symbols to be used in a discourse should be mentally arranged in those places. Thus "the order of places would preserve the order of things, and the symbols of the things would denote the things themselves; so that we should use the places as waxen tablets, and the symbols as letters."[27]

Quintilian was more specific in developing the method of association. He asked potential speakers to familiarize themselves with a series of visual images such as the rooms of a house and furniture in each room. They should associate part of what they have written or planned with each chair, statue, or the like in a room. Then when they speak they can imagine they are going into the vestibule of the house so as to be reminded of words or thoughts associated with it.

Let us consider the following hypothetical speech using Quintilian's method. The specific purpose of the address is to discuss the principal causes of cheating in academic institutions. With such a theme, the speaker might come into the classroom and concentrate upon five places and things: (1) chairs; (2) blackboard; (3) lectern; (4) hallway; and (5) windows. He would then be ready to associate these objects with the ensuing potential main ideas:

1. The *chairs* = an overemphasis on grades.
2. The *blackboard* = unfair testing procedures.
3. The outside *hallway* = peers who cheat in order to survive academically.
4. The *lectern* = poor teaching and lectures.
5. The *windows* = the general public that cheats on such matters as income taxes.

Other suggestions for improving the memory were also given. Although Cicero argued that nature actually endows us with a good, average, or poor memory, he nevertheless gives several hints. Chief among these are the need to use a proper sequence that has a logical structure, and to imprint ideas firmly in our mind through the senses.

Quintilian spelled out some rules for memorizing a manuscript speech or a part in a dramatic production. These he summarized as follows:

RULES FOR MEMORIZING

- ✔ Learn the manuscript "piecemeal."
- ✔ Mark those sections that prove difficult to learn.
- ✔ Practice the passages aloud. ("The mind should be kept alert by the sound of the voice, so that the memory may derive assistance from the double effort of speaking and listening.")
- ✔ Test frequently, repeating passages which tend to slip from memory.
- ✔ Use an artistic sequence so that if interruption occurs in the middle of a speech the train of thought will not be lost.[28]

The best overall method of improving the memory, argued Quintilian, is through practice and industry.

Pronunciatio

The Greeks were aware that a speaker's manner of presentation was important to his success. Indeed, Cicero tells us that when Demosthenes was asked to name the three most important qualities an orator must have, his reply was "Delivery, Delivery, Delivery."[29] But Aristotle, as we have observed, was message-oriented. He considered the management of the speaker's voice largely extraneous to his main business. It remained for the Romans, therefore, to explore this canon in depth.

Complaining that no previous rhetorician had ever undertaken a systematic treatment of delivery, the Roman author of *Rhetorica ad Herennium* observed: "I believe (that it) deserves serious consideration."[30] Included in this author's system is a discussion of three speaking tones—the conversational, the debating, and the pathetic. The debating tone is "sustained or broken," and characterized by "an occasional quick gesture of the arm, a mobile countenance, and a knowing glance." Moreover, it often features pacing, stamping of the foot, and a "look of intense concentration." The pathetic tone frequently is accompanied by slapping "one's thigh" and beating "one's head." The author concludes his analysis of delivery by ensuring that what the orator is saying should appear to come from the heart.

Cicero stood high among those rhetoricians who gave a significant position to delivery. In his *Brutus,* one speaker is rebuked for his lackadaisical manner. "Did you smite your brow, slap your thigh, or at least stamp your foot? No! In fact, so far from touching my feelings, I could scarcely refrain from going to sleep then and there."[31] Despite this extreme, Cicero elevated delivery to a respectable place in rhetorical practice. He defined it as the control of the voice and body in a manner suited to the dignity of the subject and style of the speech. Holding that nature and training go hand in hand in producing a specific voice for each emotion, he declared: The whole "frame of a man, and his whole countenance, and the variations of his voice, sound like strings in a musical instrument, just as they are moved by the affections of the mind."[32] He then added that while we look to nature for a musical voice, clarity can be improved by practice.

Quintilian agreed with Cicero and other predecessors that a good delivery comes largely from nature but that it can be enhanced by nurture. Similarly, he, too, placed emphasis on the association of the emotions with delivery, and gave suggestions concerning the voice. It should be easy, powerful, fine, flexible, firm, sweet, well sustained, clear, pure, and one that cuts the air and penetrates the ear. One should not hiss, pant, cough, wheeze, or sing. Most of all, vocal tones should be suited to the occasion and to the speech.

Quintilian was the first rhetorician to provide an extensive treatment of gesture and facial expression. Here are some of his suggestions:

GESTURE AND FACIAL EXPRESSION

- Gesture of the head can indicate humility, haughtiness, languor, or rudeness.
- The face can be suppliant, menacing, soothing, sad, cheerful, proud, humble.
- With your arms and hands, ask, promise, threaten, supplicate; show fear, joy, grief, doubt, acknowledgment, penitence; indicate measure, quantity, number, time.
- Strike the thigh to indicate indignation, but do not stamp the foot too often.
- As for the speech as a whole, open calmly and gain fire and momentum as you go.
- The fingers may be used to designate specific ideas.

In utilizing an educational-philosophical approach to rhetoric, the Romans, following in the tradition of Isocrates, were influential and relevant. They are to be commended for seeing the relationship between nature and nurture, for identifying and stressing all five classical canons of rhetoric, for alerting students regarding the significance of antecedent ethical proof, and for filling in vital gaps concerning memory and delivery. They also recognized that since rhetorical situations may have permanence, a speech too should have permanence.

In the foregoing treatment of the educational-philosophical approach to rhetoric which formed one of the major trends in the classical period, we have sought to develop general concepts and guidelines as articulated in representative treatises and in the classrooms. To see more graphically how Roman scholars provided specific and detailed suggestions for achieving the goal of constructing enduring speeches, we will now examine some of the ideas advanced by Cicero and Quintilian on how an orator may be formed.

Cicero, who was consistently influenced by Isocrates' theory of culture approach to learning, had a special interest in producing rhetorical works that have artistic form. He warned prospective authors, therefore, to avoid faulty use of content, organization, and language so that they would not be charged with "an unpardonable abuse of letters and retirement."[33] Cicero expressed a similar view shortly after the murder of Caesar. Concerned that his friend Brutus might risk his reputation as a scholar and, indeed, endanger his life, he sent the following note to Atticus: "Brutus has sent me his speech that he delivered before the Assembly on the Capitol. He wants me to correct it frankly before he publishes it. . . . I should like you to read the speech . . . and to let me know what you think of it."[34] This letter typifies Cicero's career-long devotion to the idea of challenging a speaker or writer to take care in using strong scholarship that would give a degree of permanence to a rhetorical work.

In addition to stressing the value of an artistic form that would gain the approval of people of culture, Cicero and Quintilian set forth three other requirements for the formation of an accomplished speaker. Such an ideal orator, they noted, should have

- an inherent natural ability,
- an extensive reading knowledge of the arts and sciences,
- a program of practice in writing.

So related are these three requirements, according to Quintilian, that if one were diminished in power the others would lose much of their effectiveness. He phrased this belief in the following excerpt drawn from *Institutio Oratoria*:

> *For eloquence will never attain to its full development of robust health, unless it acquires strength by frequent practice in writing, while such practice without the models supplied by reading will be like a ship drifting aimlessly without a steersman. Again, he who knows what he ought to say and how he should say it, will be like a miser brooding over his hoarded treasure, unless he has the weapons of his eloquence ready for battle and prepared to deal with every emergency.*[35]

The importance of nature in the development of an orator stems from the fact that it influences a speaker's inventive and organizational ability, the use of language control, and the pattern of delivery. But this natural talent must be reinforced by a daily schedule of reading and study. "No man can be an orator complete in all points of merit," observed Cicero, "who has not attained a knowledge of all important subjects and arts. For it is from knowledge that oratory must derive its beauty and fullness, and unless there is such knowledge, well-grasped and comprehended by the speaker, there must be something empty and almost childish in the utterance."[36]

These views on the role of nature and reading as they relate to the development of an ideal orator were shared by other ancient scholars—especially Isocrates. On the next requirement, that of writing practice, Cicero and Quintilian went beyond earlier authors in citing its importance. Even in the area of extemporaneous speaking, they argued, one who has perfected a pleasing writing style will have the advantage over those who have not done so. Thus they urged such orators to write out specific portions of a speech such as the introduction and transitional statements. The style used in these sections would then influence, in a positive way, the other parts of the discourse. Cicero makes this claim in an impressive manner in the *De Oratore*.

In addition to stressing the value of an artistic form that would gain the approval of people of culture, Cicero and Quintilian set forth three other requirements for the formation of an accomplished speaker. Such an ideal orator, they noted, should have

- an inherent natural ability,
- an extensive reading knowledge of the arts and sciences,
- a program of practice in writing.

Frequent practice in writing, he says, will give the speaker an oral style that resembles the language usage that characterizes the polished written word. When written paragraphs are introduced in a speech and then articulated, the word choice and sentence structure that ensue in an extemporaneous mode will flow in a similarly easy fashion. To illustrate this point, Cicero draws an analogy to oarsmen who row their boat at full speed; and when the rowing ceases, the boat will continue for awhile in the same direction and with a comparable force. From this analogy Cicero concludes that "in an unbroken discourse, when written notes are exhausted, the rest of the speech still maintains a like progress, under the impulse given by the similarity and energy of the written word."[37] In endorsing Cicero's perspectives on the significance of writing, Quintilian called this discipline the "roots and foundations" of eloquence.[38]

As a means of emphasizing the importance of writing, Cicero and Quintilian separated orators of the Greek and Roman eras into three categories:

1. those who, as was the case of Pericles, could speak but not write;
2. those who, like Isocrates, could write but not speak; and
3. those who, in the tradition of Demosthenes, were outstanding speakers and writers.

The palm, of course, was given to the latter group.

With writing assuming such a vital function, the Romans offered guidelines for improving this skill so that the most challenging thoughts could be expressed in the most appealing style. Quintilian presented, for instance, such practical suggestions as the need to limit the time spent on the first draft, and to avoid the habit of dictating a speech to a secretary. He also informed students to know when and where to write, to adopt an appropriate speed, and to revise freely by using the methods of "addition, excision, and alteration."[39]

Cicero and Quintilian, it would appear, developed their interest in the relationship between speaking and writing out of their concern for producing an orator who could not only address an immediate audience but who could speak to posterity as well.

Although the major emphasis in this section has been on "the education of the orator," it is vitally important to note that Cicero, in particular, recognized the need to relate rhetoric to conversation or interpersonal communication. Indeed, in his famous essay "On Moral Duties," he not only called for an in-depth analysis of the "science of conversation" but presented preliminary guidelines which have relevance for contemporary discourse. After observing that "speech is a great power in the world," he said:

It is of two kinds, formal discourse and conversation. Formal discourse is appropriate to judicial argument and to political and deliberative orations; conversation finds its natural place in social gatherings, learned discussions, and in friendly reunions and banquets. There is a science of rhetoric, and I am inclined to think a science of conversation possible though none exist. The demand for masters creates the supply, and though the world is full of students of rhetoric, there are neither students nor masters of conversation. Still the rules of rhetoric are equally applicable to conversation. Since the voice is the organ of speech, we should try to make it clear and pleasant. These qualities, it is true, are natural gifts, but the first may be improved by practice, the second by the imitation of calm and articulate speakers. There was nothing about the two Catuli to make you think they possessed a fine literary sense; for the culture they had was nothing extraordinary, and yet it was thought they spoke Latin with the greatest purity. Their pronunciation was agreeable, the sounds were neither mouthed nor minced, obscure nor affected; and they spoke without effort, yet without monotony or excessive modulation. The diction of L. Crassus was more copious and not less brilliant, but the eloquence of the Catuli ranked as high as his. In wit and humour Caesar, the brother of the elder Catulus, was the first speaker of his time; even at the bar his easy conversational style surpassed the laboured speeches of his rivals. If, then, we aim at decorum in everything we do, we should strive to perfect ourselves in all these qualities. Forming our conversation on the admirable model of the disciples of Socrates, let us put forward our opinions in an easy tentative way and not without a spice of humour. Above all, we should never monopolize the conversation but allow every one in turn to have his fair share. First of all it is necessary to consider the subject, and, whether it be grave or gay, let our language correspond. Again it is important not to betray any defect of character, such as the malice of the slanderer who delights in attacking the absent either in jest or with the serious purpose of covering them with abuse and contumely. Conversation generally turns upon family affairs, politics or learning and culture. These are the subjects to which we must endeavor to bring it back if it has drifted into another channel, but we must always study the company; for tastes differ, and nothing pleases all men at all times or to the same degree. It is well to mark the moment when the subject palls and to end as we began with tact. The sound principle, that in all our conduct we should be free from passion or wild irrational feeling, ought naturally to govern our conversation. Let us betray no symptom of anger, or intense feeling, or of apathy, listlessness, or similar defects, and endeavor to exhibit respect and consideration for those with whom we converse. If at times reproof is required, it may be necessary to speak in a louder tone and in stronger language and to assume the appearance of anger. But like the cautery and the lance, that is an extreme measure which we should seldom and reluctantly employ and only as a last resource. Anger itself we must put far away, for with it we can do nothing right or well-advised. Often it will suffice to administer a gentle, but calm, reproof and to exhibit sternness without insolence. Nay more, let us show that even the severity of our censure is only intended for the good of the offender. Again, in the quarrels we have with our bitterest enemies, it is proper to stifle our feelings and maintain our composure whenever insults may be offered to us. If we are under the dominion of excitement we lose our balance and forfeit the respect of the company. Another offence against decorum is to boast of oneself, especially without ground, and to expose oneself to derision by playing the 'Braggart Captain.'
(Basic Works, *pp. 50–52*)

Cicero, in sum, is telling us that in order to be an effective conversationalist, we should focus on a worthy and timely subject such as family affairs, politics, or the arts and sciences; know when and how long to speak; adapt to the interests of our guests and colleagues; exemplify decorum, tact, self-control, and rationality; utilize humor to liven the discussion; and channel our ideas through a clear, pleasant, and articulate vocal pattern. Above all, we should avoid playing the role of the braggadocio. Such procedures, we feel, constitute useful rules that may be applicable for present-day situations involving interpersonal communication.

What makes Cicero such a compelling rhetorical figure, both to us and to his disciple Quintilian, was his ability to put into practice each of the five canons of rhetoric. Throughout his writings Cicero, who perhaps more than anyone else, personified the Roman Republic, preached action. His rhetorical treatises are reinforced with practical personal illustrations showing rhetors on the Rostrum or in the Curia. His great essay "On Moral Duties," written in the year of his death, placed action above philosophical speculation.[40] How difficult it was for the medieval scholars to recognize this need for action. They idolized Cicero for his thoughtful essays and treatises, and for his eminent position as a Stoic sage. Moreover they perhaps would have agreed with the modern classical historian Chester Starr who said that Cicero was the most important man of letters in a thousand years.[41] Yet they denigrated his orations because they were part of action. Why, they asked, did he challenge the monarchy that Caesar was to initiate? Petrarch, writing in 1345, bemoaned the fact that his fallen idol Cicero refused to accept the clemency offered by Caesar.

Why did you choose to involve yourself in so many vain contentions and unprofitable quarrels? Why did you abandon the retirement proper to your age, profession and fortune? What false dazzle of glory led you, an old man, to implicate yourself in the wars of the young? What tempted you to dealings that brought you to a death unworthy of a philosopher? . . . How much better it would have been for you, the philosopher, to have grown old in country peace, meditating, as you yourself write somewhere, on eternal life, not on this transitory existence: How much better if you had never held

the faces of power, never longed for triumphs, never corrupted your spirit with Catilines?[42]

Several years ago we stood in the Roman Forum and relived the public life of Cicero. We stood near the Rostrum and the Curia where he had made so many of his famous speeches on behalf of the Roman Republic. Then we remembered how he left public life and enjoyed a few years in contemplation as an essayist and historian of Roman culture—a scholar who placed the original stamp of his genius on the Latin language. With Petrarch we found ourselves asking why Cicero left the life of an author to come back into the Forum following the assassination of Caesar. But had Petrarch and we paused to reflect on the unmistakable connecting links that bind rhetoric and action, we would perhaps not have raised the question. It simply was unthinkable that Cicero would place contemplation on a higher plane than action. For the action-centered quality inherent in its nature gave to rhetoric, according to Cicero, the power of relevance.

SUMMARY

The foregoing analysis of classical rhetorical theory may be summarized under three broad headings. First, we saw how the culture of ancient Greece and Rome provided the ambience for the flowering of rhetoric. All facets of Greek and Roman life suggested a strong need for knowledge of and skill in rhetorical theory and practice. The democratic political system in 4th Century-Greece and 1st Century-Rome (until the death of Cicero in 43 B.C.E.) encouraged the discussion of controversial issues affecting the state; the legal system called to the attention of the populace the role that rhetoric could play in self-defense; the literary, dramatic, and historical productions featured rhetorical strategies and techniques in communicating their subject matter; and the society, in general, promoted dialogue. Against this background of prevailing interest in communication, the sophists, schools, and academies found a rationale for giving instruction in rhetoric.

Secondly, we have observed that in the classical period three major approaches, all of which were related, dominated rhetorical theory and training.

■ The *moral-philosophical* view represented by *Plato* established as its ideal the noble lover—a speaker who seeks to lead the audience to an understanding of truth centered in the will of the gods.

■ The *scientific-philosophical* view epitomized by *Aristotle* described in specific detail a communication model comprised of speaker, speech, and audience; and recognized the vital notion that rhetoric deals almost exclusively with probability and contingent propositions.

■ The *educational-philosophical* view typified by *Isocrates, Cicero,* and *Quintilian* admitted the superiority of nature over nurture in the formation of an orator, yet created an effective model for teaching rhetoric in the classroom.

Thirdly, our survey has demonstrated that there were several distinguishing characteristics of classical rhetorical theory which affected later thought. With varying degrees of emphasis the Greek and Roman scholars made these claims:

■ Rhetoric is a field of study worthy of scientific speculation and inquiry.

> while public speaking was the dominant rhetorical form preoccupying the attention of the ancients, there were telltale signs pointing to a developing theory of interpersonal communication.

■ Rhetoric has a unique vocabulary and category system consisting of such elements as forms of discourse and the canons of *inventio, dispositio, elocutio, memoria,* and *pronunciatio.*

■ Rhetoric, for the most part, is concerned with persuasion.

■ Rhetoric is essentially an oral activity.

■ Artistic proof, with its stress on enthymematic reasoning, is more important than inartistic proof comprised largely of evidence.

■ The ethical dimension is a central aspect of rhetoric.

Perhaps we should also add that while public speaking was the dominant rhetorical form preoccupying the attention of the ancients, there were telltale signs pointing to a developing theory of interpersonal communication. Illustrative of this emerging trend were Plato's reliance on dialectic and the Socratic method and Cicero's guidelines for constructing an "art of conversation."

Notes

1. For an overview of the varied contributions of Greek and Roman rhetoricians, see L. Thonssen, A.C. Baird, and W. Braden, *Speech Criticism,* 2nd. ed. (New York: The Ronald Press Co., 1970. Excerpts of representative classical works in rhetoric appear in T. Benson and M. Prosser, *Readings in Classical Rhetoric* (Boston: Allyn and Bacon, Inc., 1969).

2. For the principal objectives which guided Isocrates' school, see G. Berquist, "Isocrates of Athens: Foremost Speech Teacher of the Ancient World," *The Speech Teacher,* 8 (September 1959), pp. 251–255.

3. "Antidosis," *Isocrates,* trans. by George Norlin (Cambridge: Harvard University Press, 1929; reprinted 1956), II, pp. 327–329.

4. "Antidosis," II, p. 333.

5. *Phaedrus,* trans. by Lane Cooper (London: Oxford University Press, 1938), pp. 70–71.

6. "Antidosis," II, p. 339.

7. *Cicero on Oratory and Orators,* trans. by J.S. Watson (New York: Harper and Brothers, 1860), p. 108.

8. M.L. Clarke, *Rhetoric at Rome* (London: Cohen and West Ltd., 1953), p. 15.

9. Quintilian's *Institutes of Oratory,* trans. by J.S. Watson (London: George Bell and Sons, 1875). I, pp. 9–10.

10. So long as the Roman Republic existed, this form of training continued, but once the Caesars came to power, the themes declaimed became fictitious or hypothetical.

11. Cited in Clarke, *Rhetoric at Rome,* p. 18.

12. *Cicero on Oratory and Orators,* p. 11.

13. Cited in D.L. Clark, *Rhetoric in Greco-Roman Education* (New York: Columbia University Press, 1957), pp. 72–73.

14. *Cicero on Oratory and Orators,* p. 119.

15. *Institutes of Oratory,* 1. p. 340.

16. Clark, *Rhetoric in Greco-Roman Education,* p. 76.

17. The references used in this discussion of ethos are taken from *The Institutio Oratoria of Quintilian,* trans. by H.E. Butler (London: William Heinemann, 1961), IV, Book XII.

18. Cicero, *Orator,* trans. by H.M. Hubbell (London: William Heinemann, 1962), pp. 403–409.

19. *Ibid.,* p. 405.

20. *Institutio Oratoria,* I, p. 421.

21. Cicero, *De Oratore,* trans. by E.W. Sutton (Cambridge, Mass.: Harvard University Press, 1959), II, 78. p. 314.

22. Moses Hadas, ed. *The Basic Works of Cicero* (New York: The Modern Library, 1951), pp. 127–158.

23. Russell Wagner, "The Meaning of *Dispositio."* *Studies in Speech and Drama in Honor of Alexander Drummond* (Ithaca, New York: Cornell University Press, 1944), pp. 285–294.

24. *Orator,* XXIX, p. 100.

25. *Ibid.,* XXVIII, p. 97.

26. *Institutio Oratoria,* XI, 2, pp. 11–14.

27. *Cicero on Oratory and Orators,* p. 187.

28. *Institutio Oratoria,* XI, 2, pp. 27–50.

29. *Orator,* XVII, p. 56.

30. *Ad Herennium,* trans. by Harry Caplan (Cambridge, Mass.: Harvard University Press, 1964), III, XI, p. 19. It is generally believed that Cicero was the author of this work.

31. *Brutus,* trans. by G.L. Hendrickson (Cambridge, Mass.: Harvard University Press, 1942), LXXX, p. 278.

32. *Cicero on Oratory and Orators,* p. 256.

33. *Tusculan Disputations,* C.D. Yonge, ed., I, p. 3.

34. Cicero to Atticus, Sinuessa, May 18, 44 B.C., in Hadas, *The Basic Works of Cicero,* pp. 418–419.

35. Butler, tr., *The Institutio Oratoria of Quintilian,* Book, X, 1, 2.

36. Sutton, tr. *Cicero, De Oratore,* Book I, vi, p. 20.

37. Sutton, *Cicero, De Oratore,* Book I, 33, pp. 152–153.

38. *Institutio Oratoria,* Book X, 3, pp. 2–3.

39. *Institutio Oratoria,* Book X, 3 and 4.

40. Hadas, *The Basic Works of Cicero,* p. 57.

41. *A History of the Ancient World* (New York: Oxford University Press, 1965), p. 526.

42. To Marcus Tullius Cicero: from Verona, 16 June 1345. Cited in Morris Bishop, ed., *Letters from Petrarch* (Bloomington: Indiana University Press, 1966), pp. 206–207.

The Christianization
of Rhetorical Thought

To this juncture, we have traced the evolution of rhetorical thought through the writings of the early Greek and Roman theorists using Plato, Aristotle, Isocrates, Cicero, and Quintilian as our main guides. Plainly, the evolution of rhetorical thinking throughout the classical period was not as tidy nor as simple as the previous chapters might have suggested. Indeed, numerous rhetorical notions and ideas were commonplace during these formative years. However, by concentrating on a few of the foremost and respected theorists we hope to have introduced the reader to the mainstream of rhetorical thought that flowed during the classical period.

Unfortunately for the novice student, the evolution of rhetorical thinking now becomes fragmented, taking several very different twists and turns. The time lapse between the classical and the British and continental periods of over a dozen centuries is characterized by a richness and diversity created literally by hundreds of writers who pulled rhetoric in directions that would have been quite disturbing to Plato, Aristotle, and Cicero.

Of all the factors affecting the formation of rhetorical thought during these centuries, two were most prominent. One primarily was political and the other religious in nature. First, as the Roman Empire declined, so did the democratic spirit that was embodied in the once mighty Roman Senate. Deliberative and forensic oratory were no longer welcome in this unstable political atmosphere as emperors became dictators clinging fiercely onto power while dominating the decision-making process. Rhetoric entered a period known today as the "Second Sophistic."

The second factor which affected the growth of rhetorical studies was the birth of Christ and the subsequent unfolding of the Christian faith. The Chris-

tianization of rhetoric was a process which not only left its mark on the British theorists, but continues to influence the contemporary scene as well. As the church matured, the classical rhetorical tradition was severely challenged, sometimes endorsed, oftentimes rejected, and thoroughly refined by countless Christian teachers, preachers, and philosophers. We feel that the title for this chapter is most appropriate because it highlights the chief development in theory as well as practice during this time period. Before discussing the religious impact on rhetoric, a consideration of the Second Sophistic needs to ensue.

THE SECOND SOPHISTIC

The transition from the classical to the British period of rhetorical history is marked by an interlude called the Second Sophistic—a span of time lasting from about 50 A.D. through 400 A.D. As the reader might surmise, the label for this era was derived from the Greek word "sophist"—a term introduced in two earlier chapters. Flavius Philostratus (b. 170 A.D.) in his work titled *Lives of the Sophists,* claims the origins of the term "Second Sophistic" could be traced back to the orator Aeschines:

As an extempore speaker he was easy and fluent and employed the inspired manner, in fact he was the first to win applause by this means. For hitherto the inspired manner in oratory had not become a regular device of the sophists, but it dates from Aeschines who extemporized as though he were carried away by a divine impulse, like one who exhales oracles. . . . For in his orations shines the light of perfect lucidity, he is at once sublime and seductive, energetic and delightful, and in a word his sort of eloquence defies the efforts of those who would imitate it.[1]

In brief, the Second Sophistic "was a period of oratorical excess in which the subject matter became less important than the interest in safer matters like the externals of speech, especially style and delivery."[2] These were times, then, when rhetoric was no longer concerned with "giving effectiveness to truth; it [was] conceived alike by the earlier and later sophists and by their successors as the art of giving effectiveness to the speaker."[3]

It is no coincidence that the second sophistic flourished during the final decades of the Roman Empire—years marked by extraordinary political unrest. Until the empire fell in 410 A.D., free and open debate and public discussion, which at an earlier time were encouraged, were often rewarded with death or prison. These were times when emperors came and went, when the dictatorship mentality prevailed and the authority of the once forceful Roman Senate waned and was eventually extinguished. In the unending struggle for power within the paranoid atmosphere characteristic of this era, democratic ideals were smothered as deliberative oratory in the hitherto lively public forums was suppressed. It was simply unwise to argue with the Emperor and to debate the courses of action and decisions he made. Oratory and rhetorical theory, forced to adapt to political and social exigencies, turned toward "safe" considerations such as style and delivery.

The development of inventio was also halted since the topics that were discussed in public had to be harmless. Philostratus lists popular themes that were frequently addressed in declamations of the day. One category considered historical or semi-historical contained such topics as: "Demosthenes swears that he did not take the bribe," "Should the trophies erected by the Greeks be taken down?" "The Cretans maintained that they have the tomb of Zeus," and "Isocrates tries to wean the Athenians from their empire of the sea." Another grouping of themes called fictitious included: "The instigator of a revolt suppresses it," "A tyrant abdicates on condition of immunity," and "The man who fell in love

> the Second Sophistic "was a period of oratorical excess in which the subject matter became less important than the interest in safer matters like the externals of speech, especially style and delivery."

with a statue."[4] A quick glance at these topics reveals that they are apolitical and because declamations on such themes generally lacked substance, they became forms of entertainment for the populace. Besides the theme approach, orators of the period also focused on the "*panegyric,* which is technically a speech at a festival, *gamelion,* or speech at a marriage, *genethliac,* or speech on a birthday, *prosphonetic,* or address to a ruler, and *epitaphios,* or funeral oration."[5] Thus, rhetoric was emptied of its concern for substantive matters and was focused on clever and creative expression. In the main, the practice of rhetoric as a relevant, vibrant art preventing the triumph of fraud and injustice ceased for some 400 years.

Even though the politics of the day tended to thwart the progress of rhetorical thought, a few writers made positive contributions to rhetorical studies.

Two such authors were Hermogenes and Longinus. Hermogenes wrote On *Types of Style* in which he elaborated on seven qualities of style that the effective speaker should emulate:

1. clarity
2. grandeur
3. beauty
4. rapidity
5. character
6. sincerity
7. force

In addition, Hermogenes composed a set of exercises for the practicing orator. One such exercise thoroughly discussed the form of oratory known as encomium. Baldwin summarizes:

> *Encomium is the setting forth of the good qualities that belong to some one in general or in particular: in general, an encomium of man, in particular, an encomium of Socrates. We make encomia also of things, such as justice; and of animals without reason, such as the horse; and even of plants, mountains, and rivers. It has been called encomium, they say, from poets singing the hymns of the gods in villages long ago. . . .*
>
> *Encomium differs from praise (in general) in that the latter may be brief, as "Socrates was wise," whereas encomium is developed at some length. . . .*

Subjects for encomia are: a race, as the Greeks; a city, as Athens; a family, as the Alcmaeonidae. You will say what marvelous things befell at the birth, as dreams or signs or the like. Next, the nurture, as, in the case of Achilles, that he was reared on lions' marrow and by Chiron. Then the training, how he was trained and educated. Not only so, but the nature of soul and body will be set forth, and of each under heads: for the body, beauty, stature, agility, might; for the soul, justice, self control, wisdom, manliness. Next his pursuits, what sort of life he pursued, that of philosopher, orator, or soldier, and most properly his deeds, for deeds come under the head of pursuits . . . . Then external resources, such as kin, friends, possessions, household, fortune, etc. Then from the (topic) time, how long he lived, much or little; for each gives rise to an encomia. A long-lived man you will praise on this score; a short-lived, on the score of his not sharing those diseases which come from age. Then, too, from the manner of his end, as that he died fighting for his fatherland, and, if there were anything extraordinary under that head . . . .[6]

Longinus

A work titled *On the Sublime* composed by a source known as Pseudo-Longinus about 200 A.D. is recognized today as perhaps the major work authored during the Second Sophistic. As revealed in the title of the treatise, the author's attention is focused on sublimity (hypsos) or that "eminence and excellence in language" achieved by only the greatest poets and prose writers.

To provide insight into Longinus's ideas on style and language use, consider the following passage from his work which is in the form of a letter addressed to his friend Terentianus.[7]

Writing to you, my good friend, with your perfect knowledge of all liberal study, I am almost relieved at the outset from necessity of showing at any length that Sublimity is always an eminence and excellence in language; and that from this, and this alone, the greatest poets and writers of prose have attained the first place and have clothed their fame with immortality. For it is not to persuasion but to ecstasy that passages of extraordinary genius carry the hearer; now the marvelous, with its power to amaze, is always and necessarily stronger than that which seeks to persuade and to please: to be persuaded rests usually with ourselves, genius brings force sovereign and irresistible to bear upon every hearer and takes its stand high above him. Again, skill in invention and power or orderly arrangement are not seen from one passage nor from two, but emerge with effort out of the whole context; Sublimity, we know, brought out of the happy moment, parts all the matter this way and that, and like a lightning flash, reveals, at a stroke and in its entirety, the power of the orator. These and suchlike considerations I think, my dear Terentianus, that your own experience might supply . . . .

After this introduction, Longinus states that "the nature of the soul is raised by true sublimity" and then moves to a discussion of the sources of sublimity.

Now there are five different sources, so to call them, of lofty style, which are the most productive; power of expression being presupposed as a foundation common to all five types, and inseparable from any. First and most potent is the faculty of grasping great conceptions, as I have defined it in my work on Xenophon. Second comes passion, strong and impetuous. These two constituents of sublimity are in most cases native-born, those which now follow come through art: the proper handling of figures, which again seem to fall under two heads, figures of thought, and figures of diction; then noble phraseology, with its subdivisions, choice of words, and use of tropes and of elaboration; and fifthly, that cause of greatness which includes in itself all that preceded it, dignified and spirited composition. . . .

The centuries during which the Second Sophistic reigned were marked by an emphasis on style rather than substance. The remaining canons of rhetoric dropped out of serious consideration. Ceremonial speaking overshadowed political and legal. In essence, the progress rhetorical studies made during the classical period was abruptly halted. It was simply wiser to adapt to the political milieu of the times. With the rise of the Christian faith, rhetorical theory and practice were influenced yet in other ways.

THE CHRISTIANIZATION OF RHETORIC

Whereas the Second Sophistic stressed ceremonial speaking, the early Christians generated forms of oratory primarily concerned with propagating the Word of God and defending the faith from political and religious adversaries. But, as they examined the classical theorists, the first Christians had serious doubts about their ideas and approach to communication. One such concern centered on the fundamental assumption upon which much of classical rhetoric rested: the concept of "probability" as developed by Aristotle and refined by the Romans. Harper explains,

Christian leaders saw the rhetorical tradition as a threat to their most fundamental beliefs. Classical human communication theory was predicated upon "probability," the premise that in human affairs "the truth" is unknowable, that human realities are socially constructed. Christianity, however, was predicated upon "fact," the premise that absolute truth is knowable through divine revelation. The problem for the Christian communicator is not to "persuade" himself and others of likelihoods, but to discover for himself and instruct others in the "will of God." Thus Christian leaders condemned the study of the "pagan" art of rhetoric.[8]

the early Christians generated forms of oratory primarily concerned with propagating the Word of God and defending the faith from political and religious adversaries.

Even though many of the first Christians were critical of classical rhetoric, they nonetheless borrowed many of its concepts. The fact that several leaders of the early church were thoroughly trained in the classical tradition is evident in their work.

Four types of Christian oratory flourished during the three centuries between the death of Paul and the writings of Augustine: *apologies, polemics, sermons,* and the *panegyrical sermon.*[9] Beginning with Jesus Christ, the Apostles, Paul, and other missionaries, this period was distinguished by a flurry of oratorical activity as the new faith sought to establish itself in an inhospitable world.

Apologies

As a young, rapidly expanding faith, early Christianity was confronted by the established Roman religious and secular authorities. The results were predictable: persecution for their beliefs and mar-

tyrdom. When these Christian zealots refused to affirm the Roman gods, they were labeled as "atheists" and when they resisted the authority of the Emperor, they were called "anarchists." After all, only Jesus the Christ was worthy of worship and obedience. As the new faith encountered criticism and resistance from society at large, Christian orators mounted a defense. These so-called *"apologists"* geared their oratory toward the nonbelievers—attempting to persuade them of the legitimacy of the faith. Often the strategy of the apologists was a simple refutation of the criticisms directed toward the church by an unsympathetic pagan society. Walker elaborates,

Charges against Christians, and the hostile attitude of the Roman government, aroused a number of literary defenders, who are known as the Apologists. Their appearance shows that Christianity was making some conquest of the more intellectual elements of society. Their appeal is distinctly to intelligence. Of these Apologists the first was Quadratus, probably of Athens, who about 125 A.D. presented a defense of Christianity, now preserved only in fragments, to the Emperor Hadrian. Aristides, an Athenian Christian philosopher, made a similar appeal, about 140 A.D., to Antoninus Pius.[10]

Justin was a noted apologist whose most famous work is appropriately titled "The Apology." Composed around 153 A.D., this work also was addressed to the Emperor Antoninus Pius. Herein, Justin argued that,

Christians, if condemned at all, should be punished for definite crimes, not for the mere name without investigation of their real character. They are atheists only in that they count the popular gods demons unworthy of worship, not in respect to the true God. They are anarchists only to those who do not understand the nature of the kingdom they seek.[11]

Justin, then, is a representative of the first type of oratory that naturally evolved from the expansion of the faith. This rhetoric of defense was a useful weapon as the believers struggled for legitimacy in an antagonistic world.

Polemics

The second type of oratory that sprang from the Christian movement involved the *"polemicists."* These persuaders directed their energies toward the splinter groups that were abandoning the "true" faith. These heretics—the Monatists and agnostics, for example—had to be coaxed into rejoining the fold. Irenaeus, Bishop of Lyons, was an early polemicist who wrote *Against Heresies,* which attacked Gnosticism—a particularly popular sect active during the middle of the second century. Influenced heavily by a mixture of oriental and Hellenic thinking, the Gnostics advocated among other ideas "the wholly evil character of the phenomenal world."[12] Irenaeus, and others, rhetorically took on the gnostics, arguing in favor of the faith as defined by the Apostles.

It is not surprising that during the early developmental stages of any new faith, factions break off from the main body of believers. When these breaks occurred in early Christianity, polemics were directed toward the heretical groups. Besides Irenaeus, other well-known polemics were authored by Hippolytus and Augustine.

Sermons

Preaching (*sermons*), the third type of fellow Christians in an attempt to reinforce the believers' faith. The most popular form of preaching was the homily—a form of address based on scripture which was generally delivered within the order of the worship service. One of the eminent early preachers specializing in homilies was John, the Patriarch of Constantinople, who was known as Chrysostom and who lived around 337–407 A.D. Brilioth comments on Chrysostom's lively oratorical style:

> *Chrysostom's attempts to restrain profane applause are well known, but they did not always succeed: we notice in an extant address how the art he employs in such an exhortation itself calls forth the applause which he sought to avoid. The addresses are, however, full of instances which show a lively contact between the speaker and his hearers. His whole career as a speaker contains many evidences that his preaching was a power both in the church and in the community and that his speeches were regarded as significant events.*[13]

Panegyrical Sermons

The final type of oratory that evolved with the early church was the Christian *epideictic* or the *panegyrical sermon*—a form of oratory that bordered on rhetorical excess. More than the three types of oratory previously discussed, the panegyrical sermon was inspired by the emphasis on stylistic matters characteristic of the Second Sophistic. Gregory of Nazianzus was a renowned expert here. Again, Brilioth explains: "In his uncontrolled use of rhetorical flourish, antithesis, parallelism, rhyming articulation, and in the rushing flow of his short sentences, Gregory breaks the restraints of the classic art of oratory. In his most lofty outpourings he transcends the boundary between prose and poetry."[14]

As the Christian faith expanded throughout the civilized world, Eastern and Western church structures emerged. Likewise, eloquent spokespersons surfaced. The Eastern church was represented by Chrysostom (previously mentioned), Origen, and Basil to name a few. Among the compelling figures of the Western church were Jerome, Ambrose, and Augustine. Of the above, Augustine was the most influential writer and thinker on rhetorical matters. He had a profound impact on both rhetorical and religious studies.

Saint Augustine

The Second Sophistic with its emphasis on style over content flourished until it was challenged by a few of the early Christians around 400 A.D. Its most formidable opponent was Augustine (b. 354) whose *De Doctrina Christiana* in four books has become a monumental work in rhetorical circles. A native of northern Africa, Augustine was educated at Carthage where he taught sophistic rhetoric. He later traveled to Rome and Milan as a professor. While in Milan, he heard Ambrose preach and was so impressed with the Christian message that he consequently converted in 386. His fervent involvement in the early church led to his appointment to the bishopric at Hippo in 395.

The magnitude of Augustine's contribution to rhetorical theory is well documented. Baldwin, for instance, declares that the fourth book of *De Doctrina Christiana* "Begins rhetoric anew. It not only ignores sophistic; it goes back over centuries of the lore of personal triumph to the ancient idea of moving men to truth; and it gives to the vital counsels of

Cicero a new emphasis for the urgent tasks of preaching the word of God."[15]

As a convert, Augustine faced the problem of how to adapt the pagan rhetorical thinking of the Second Sophistic to the Christian message. This was no easy assignment as sophistry "was often criticized by Christians because of its celebration of the beauties of pagan mythology or because of the emphasis it gave to style, ornament, and the cleverness of the orator."[16] In approaching this difficult task, Augustine returned to the ancient writings of Cicero.

Book four of *De Doctrina Christiana* was composed around 427 while the earlier three books were completed around 397. The first three books are concerned with inventio as it relates to the study of scriptures. Herein Augustine writes about discovering the meaning of the scripture through a study of signs. This was a critical task for the preacher as the Christian sermon had to be based on the scriptures. So, Augustine's first thoughts in his four volume work were on assisting the preacher to critically interpret the text. In writing about such matters, Augustine was contributing to the field known today as exegesis. The fourth book extends beyond inventio into the realm of expression: preaching and teaching. After a brief introduction, book four explores Christian eloquence, the duties of the orator as espoused by Cicero, the three kinds of style, and ethos.

Augustine began the fourth book with an argument supporting the value of rhetorical studies. The rationale Augustine constructed here is significant for it provided the Christians with the much needed justification for their study of rhetoric. In a very real sense, Augustine's remarks signal the end of the second sophistic and the birth of a new Christian rhetoric. Augustine notes:

For since by means of the art of rhetoric both truth and falsehood are urged, who would dare to say that truth should stand in the person of its defenders unarmed against lying, so that they who wish to urge falsehoods may know how to make their listeners benevolent, or attentive, or docile in their presentation, while the defenders of truth are ignorant of that art? Should they speak briefly, clearly, and plausibly while the defenders of truth speak so that they tire their listeners, make themselves difficult to understand and what they have to say dubious? Should they oppose the truth with fallacious arguments and assert falsehoods, while the defenders of truth have no ability either to defend

the truth or to oppose the false? . . . While the faculty of eloquence, which is of great value in urging either evil or justice, is in itself indifferent, why should it not be obtained for the uses of the good in the service of truth if the evil usurp it for the winning of perverse and vain causes in defense of iniquity and error?[17]

The above proclamation on the value of rhetoric to the Christian was courageous. It is important to note that when Augustine referred to rhetoric he was thinking in terms of the classical writers—especially Cicero. Thus, he did not accept nor grant legitimacy to the rhetorical preoccupation with style and the epideictic. In the fifth chapter of book four, Augustine warns, "We must beware of the man who abounds in eloquent nonsense, and so much the more if the hearer is pleased with what is not worth listening to, and thinks that because the speaker is eloquent what he says must be true."[18]

Outside a very few references such as the above, Augustine ignored sophistry and refused to criticize it directly. "No denunciation could be more scathing than this silence. In Augustine's view of Christian preaching sophistic simply has no place. A good debater, instead of parrying he counters. He spends his time on his own case. A good teacher, he tells his neophytes not what to avoid, but what to do."[19]

Now that Augustine's feelings on the excesses of the second sophistic have been addressed, let us highlight a few of the ideas Augustine discussed in this fourth book.

To begin, Augustine clearly details the duties of the Christian teacher.

It is the duty, then, of the interpreter and teacher of Holy Scripture, the defender of the true faith and the opponent of error, both to teach what is right and to refute what is wrong, and in the performance of this task to conciliate the hostile, to rouse the careless, and to tell the ignorant both what is occurring at present and what is probable in the future.[20]

Augustine next discusses the importance of uniting eloquence with wisdom providing examples of eloquence from the writings of Paul and Amos. Moving from a consideration of the significance of perspicuity for an effective style, Augustine considers the aims of the orator. Here he quotes Cicero: "Accordingly a great orator has truly said that 'an eloquent man must speak so as to teach, to delight, and to persuade.' Then he adds: 'To teach is a necessity, to delight is a beauty, to persuade is a triumph.' Now of these three, the one first mentioned, the teaching, which is a matter of necessity, depends on what we say; the other two on the way we say it."[21]

In Augustine's thinking, it is vital that the audience members are not only instructed, but that they are also moved. "The eloquent divine, then, when he is urging a practical truth, must not only teach so as to give instruction, and please so as to keep up the attention, but he must also sway the mind so as to subdue the will. For if a man be not moved by the force of truth, though it is demonstrated to his own confession, and clothed in beauty of style, nothing remains but to subdue him by the power of eloquence."[22]

A final major area covered by Augustine was style. Here he discusses the subdued, temperate, and majestic styles and provides appropriate examples of each drawn from the Bible, Ambrose, and Cyprian. Throughout, he stresses the importance of variety in style, their effects, and uses. His remarks in this area are concluded when he mentions the three qualities of an effective style: perspicuity, beauty, and persuasiveness.

It is essential to note the gravity of *de Doctrina Christiana*. In the midst of a world where democratic ideals were stifled by a series of autocratic Roman emperors, where public communication became a form of entertainment favoring ornamentation and ceremonial speaking, and where a new religious faith (fighting for legitimacy) was suspicious of rhetoric, Augustine came forth and reconnected rhetoric to its classical roots. Once this was accomplished, theories of rhetoric were free to grow, develop, and branch out within the spirit of the Greek rhetoricians. Augustine put rhetoric back on track.

> In the midst of a world where democratic ideals were stifled by a series of autocratic Roman emperors, where public communication became a form of entertainment favoring ornamentation and ceremonial speaking, and where a new religious faith (fighting for legitimacy) was suspicious of rhetoric, Augustine came forth and reconnected rhetoric to its classical roots.

RHETORIC AND THE MIDDLE AGES

To provide a meaningful description of the evolution of rhetorical thought for the 1,200 years between the writings of Augustine and the British period is an imposing assignment. In the following paragraphs, we will attempt to highlight a few of the more sig-

nificant authors and ideas that affected the flow of Western rhetorical thought. For the most part, the course that rhetoric took during these twelve centuries was uneven. However, roughly five directions can be identified:

1. the classical tradition,
2. grammar and poetry,
3. letter writing,
4. preaching, and
5. logic.

First, rhetorical theory influenced by the Greek and Roman writers continued to develop during the Middle Ages. Aristotle and Cicero were especially important. Parts of Aristotle's work on logic, *Organon,* and his *Topics* were known, but his *Poetics* was not. The *Rhetoric,* though, seems to have had more of an influence toward the end of the Middle Ages when it "reached the Latin West in the form of thirteenth-century translations from Arabic commentators."[23]

The writings of Cicero, on the other hand, played more of a prominent role in keeping the classical tradition alive—both in the universities and pulpit. According to Murphy, "the most frequently used Ciceronian books before the fifteenth century were his youthful *De inventione* (known as *rhetorica vetus* or 'old rhetoric') and the Pseudo-Ciceronian *Rhetorica ad Herennium* (called *rhetorica nova* or 'new rhetoric' to distinguish it from *De inventione*)."[24] Furthermore, when rhetoric was taught as a subject in the medieval universities it was in all likelihood the rhetoric of Cicero.[25] Most probably, then, the medieval university student's rhetorical education was based on the three types of discourse: deliberative, forensic, and epideictic and rhetorical theory attending each. Certainly the preachers of this period were familiar with Augustine who, as we noted earlier, was heavily influenced by Cicero. Finally, it should be noted that Cicero's rhetoric was the only rhetoric translated into the vernacular during this time.[26]

A few authors who kept the classical tradition viable during the Middle Ages include: Cassiodorus (c. 490–585), Isidore of Seville (560–636), Alcuin (c. 735–804), and Boethius (c. 475–524).

Boethius, short for Anicius Manlius Severinus Boethius, was well grounded in the classics and languages. One of his major ambitions, which he failed to complete, was to translate the works of Plato and Aristotle from Greek into Latin. He did succeed, however, in translating Aristotle's *Organon*. As Baldwin notes, "The logic of Aristotle was mediated to the whole middle age by the translations and commentaries of Boethius."[27] The classical influence on Boethius's thinking is evident as the following passages from his "Overview of the Structure of Rhetoric" illustrate.

> *By genus, rhetoric is a faculty; by species, it can be one of three: judicial, demonstrative, deliberative. . . . There is one special kind of rhetoric for judicial matters, based upon their specific goals; there are other kinds for deliberative and demonstrative purposes. These species of rhetoric depend upon the circumstances in which they are used; all cases deal either with general principles or with the specific application of those principles, in either case using one of three species we have already identified. For example, judicial rhetoric can treat either of general topics like rendering just honor or demanding satisfaction, or of individual cases, like paying honor to Cornelius or demanding satisfaction of Verres . . . Rhetoric has five parts: invention, disposition, style, memory, and delivery. These are referred to as parts because if an orator lacks any of them, then his use of the faculty is imperfect . . . .*[28]

The classical influence is clearly evident here. The first direction that rhetoric took during the Middle Ages, then, was a restatement and building upon the classical authors.

A further path taken by rhetoric was in the direction of grammar and verse writing: ars poetriae of "the study of rhetoric as a matter of style, particularly poetic style."[29] Authors in this tradition were concerned not only with correctness in writing and speaking, but also with the analysis and interpretation of literature.[30] Before 1200, theorists led by Donatus and Priscian examined the parts of speech, syntax, and the figures. After 1200, works by Alexander of Villedieu and Evard of Bethune domi-

nated this school of thought. These later writers extended the thinking of this school laying "claim to the jurisdiction over all uses of language: the grammarians produced preceptive doctrine for poets, for prose-writers, and for preachers."[31]

Letter writing, ars dictaminis, also became an important rhetorical emphasis during the Middle Ages. As the church expanded, the population grew and commerce crossed national boundaries, the simple organization of people and resources became increasingly complex. In other words, the management of the legal, political, economic, social, and religious affairs required coordination. Effective communication was vital so an interest in letter writing developed.[32] Several letter-writing manuals were composed. C. Julius Victor (1097–1141) and Alberic of Monte Cassino (c. 1087) are two notable authors of this rhetorical emphasis.

Usually texts on the ars dictaminis were heavily classical in their approach. For instance, "the parts of the oration . . . were adapted into a standard five-part epistolary structure: the *salutation,* or greeting; the *capratio benevolentiae* or exordium, which secured the goodwill of the recipient; the *narratio;* the *peririo,* or specific request, demand, or announcement; and a relatively simple *conclusio*."[33]

Following is an excerpt from a popular letter-writing manual:

> *An epistle or letter, then, is a suitable arrangement of words set forth to express the intended meaning of its sender. Or in other words, a letter is a discourse composed of coherent yet distinct parts signifying fully the sentiments of its sender.*
>
> *There are, in fact, five parts of a letter: the Salutation, the Securing of Goodwill, the Narration, the Petition, and the Conclusion.*
>
> *The Salutation is an expression of greeting conveying a friendly sentiment not inconsistent with the social rank of the persons involved.*
>
> *Now, every salutation is said to be either "prescribed," "subscribed," or "circumscribed." It is said to be "prescribed" if the name of the recipient is written first, followed by those things which are joined with that person's name . . . .*[34]

Although information given in these manuals seems rather simple by today's standards, remember that the standardization of letter forms was being worked out during the Middle Ages. The influence of these early manuals is evident in much of the style of contemporary letter writing.

The ars praedicandi, the art of preaching, was also an area of rhetorical development during the Middle Ages. The Christianization of rhetoric that had begun 300 years before Augustine made further inroads during these centuries—so much so that Baldwin considers preaching as "the characteristic form of oratory"[35] during the Middle Ages. Leo the Great (395–461), Gregory the Great (540–604), Bede the Venerable (673–735), Charlemagne (742–814), Bernard of Clairvaux (d. 1153), and Thomas Aquinas (1225–1274) are only a handful of the exceptional Christian orators of this period. Authors composing theoretical works on the art of preaching include Guibett de Nogent (c. 1084), *A Book About the Way a Sermon Ought to Be Given*, Alain de Lille (c. 1100–1200) *A Compendium on the Art of Preaching*, Alexander of Ashby (c. 1200–1250) On *the Mode of Preaching*, and Jacques de Vitry (d. 1240) *Manual for Sermons*.

Finally, the tradition of logic that followed from Aristotle and Cicero was refined and transformed during the Middle Ages. Some authors assimilated rhetoric into dialectic and located the study of rhetoric in the field of logic. When this occurred, a philosophical struggle between rhetoric and logic ensued. It continued throughout the Renaissance. In the work of Peter Ramus, for example, rhetoric was truncated into style and delivery. Invention and disposition were assigned to logic. We will have more to say about the relation of rhetoric to logic later. For now, note that a significant battle between rhetoric and logic was initiated in the Middle Ages—a battle that lasted for centuries.

Richard McKeon, who has written the definitive essay on rhetoric in the Middle Ages, summarizes for us:

In application, the art of rhetoric contributed during the period from the fourth to the fourteenth century not only to the methods of speaking and writing, of composing letters and petitions, sermons and prayers, legal documents and briefs, poetry and prose, but to the canons of interpreting laws and scripture, to the dialectical devices of discovery and proof, to the establishment of the scholastic method which was to come into universal use in philosophy, theology, and finally to the formulation of scientific inquiry which was to separate philosophy from theology.[36]

RENAISSANCE RHETORICAL THEORY

The years roughly between 1400 A.D. and 1600 A.D. are referred to as the Renaissance. "The Italians called this coming of age la Rinascita, Rebirth, because to them it seemed a triumphant resurrection of the classic spirit after a barbarous interruption of a thousand years."[37] This was an age when commerce flourished while sculpture, literature, philosophy, poetry, architecture, and the arts were infused with energy and creativity from the likes of such giants as Leonardo da Vinci, Raphael, Michelangelo, Titian, and Machiavelli. This was a time when civilization stepped out of the Dark Ages and into a new dawn—an era that was aesthetically and intellectually stimulating.

Likewise, the Renaissance proved to be an exciting time for the development of rhetorical thought. A major reason for the renewed interest in rhetoric was the Greek and Latin texts. During the Middle Ages, few Greek texts were known, but during the two hundred years of the Renaissance, "the entire body of Greek rhetorical literature became accessible to the West, both through the original texts and through Latin and vernacular translations . . . . To the theoretical treatises on rhetoric we must add the actual products of ancient Greek oratory. The Attic orators, especially Lysias, Isocrates, and Demosthenes, were all translated, read and imitated."[38] In the fifteenth century Cicero's *Orator* and *De oratore* were recovered as well as the complete texts of Quintilian. These materials had been "lost" for the thousand or so years known as the Middle Ages. With their recovery, a new excitement and interest in the rhetorical was ignited.

As the Latin and Greek rhetorical texts were uncovered during the Renaissance, excitement ran high throughout the scholarly community. Of the innumerable issues that arose as the classics were uncovered, none was more debated than that surrounding the rhetorical concept of imitatio or imitation. At first, the debate revolved around how faithfully one should follow the style as well as the teachings of the early classical writers. Eventually, however, the Italian Renaissance scholars focused the debate on Cicero. Before examining the positions regarding the imitation of Ciceronian thought and style, we need to discuss the concept of imitation as Renaissance scholars generally approached it.

The idea of a renaissance or a "new beginning" fostered an examination of the contemporary use of Latin within the scholarly community. Italian scholars were especially active in this discussion and an examination of the leading Italian voices will highlight the debate. First, there were those who idealized classical Latin and strongly advocated it as the model of eloquence. "Latin style must conform to the habits of its great period; and this restoration was a prime object of Renaissance classicism."[39] This call for a return to classical Latin was essentially a repudiation of medieval Latin as well as the use of vernacular languages (Italian, French and English) — languages that were rapidly evolving and changing. Conformity to the stability inherent in the classical Latin "of Vergil, Caesar, Sallust, above all Cicero, the Latin of the great period,"[40] to the point of imitation was the goal of these scholars. In this regard, the "exclusive imitation of Cicero as the ideal prose style"[41] was urged by some. The term "Ciceronianism" became a pivotal term for this school of thought, which is sometimes referred to as "Renaissance humanism" for which the restoration of Augustan Latin was of prime importance. In general this school of thought maintained that,

1. Latin, or any other language, attains in a certain historical period its ideal achievement and capacity,
2. that within such a great period style is constant,
3. that a language can be recalled from later usage to earlier in scholastic exercises,
4. that such exercises can suffice for personal expression,
5. that a single author can suffice as a model, even for exercises.[42]

The views on imitation held by the Italian Renaissance scholars can best be gleaned by examining important letters that were exchanged during this period. Writing in the 16th century to his friend Giovanni Battista Giraldi Cinzio, Celio Calcagnini articulated this preoccupation with Cicero.

But when we come to M. Cicero, good gods, is there any description of body or soul that is lacking? How boldly he drives his points? What uproar, what commotion he elicits? How often is he indignant! What grief, what mourning he inspires in people's souls when he stretches the sails of pity! His statement, 'How wretched, how unhappy I am: you, Milo, have been able to recall me to the fatherland through these men; will I not be able to retain you through the

same?' and what follows convey so much fire that the listener's entire soul begins to see. What is in those books that he wrote on philosophy? How concisely he proceeds! How brilliantly he narrates the matter! How boldly he refutes! How soundly he confirms! But in his books on rhetorical method, he has produced something really remarkable. Although there is the least room for eloquence there, he has nevertheless ornamented these books so much that you would not need any other account of eloquence. And what of the countless praises that this most eminent and clearly incomparable orator has earned? Aren't they greater than any envy? No one but Cicero has easily tallied so many.[43]

Continuing,

But if everyone agrees that one should choose each best writer to imitate, he will also agree that Cicero is indisputably preferable to anyone else. For we can seek one virtue or another from other writers; but Cicero satisfies all our needs at once and alone had advanced the boundaries of Roman eloquence more than any of the emperors extended the empire by military strength. So it was not without reason that Apollonius Molo, after he had heard Cicero speaking at Rhodes, lamented for the Greeks, from whom, after Roman virtue had seized their power, Cicero took the only thing that remained—their eloquence—and brought it back to the Roman capitol like the spoils of conquered genius.[44]

Writing to Renaissance scholar Giovanni Franscesco Pico della Mirandola (a specialist in Hebrew grammar and scripture) in 1513, Peter Bembo (1470–1547) who held positions at the courts of Ferrana, Urbino, and Rome, expresses a similar sentiment,

Wherefore Pico, our general rule can be as follows; first, that we propose to imitate whoever is the best of all; then we should imitate him in the effort to reach his level; and once we are equal we should finally aim at surpassing him. . . . Yet imitating Cicero will certainly be able to satisfy anyone that wants to write in rhetorical prose about whatever matter and material they must address.[45]

This call for imitation of Cicero did not go unchallenged. Indeed, a significant criticism of this position was articulated by scholars such as Pico della Mirandola who responded to Peter Bembo as follows.

Still I shall not agree that, although exceptional, only Cicero is a risk-free model for rhetorical prose, that he is so accomplished in all rhythms that we should despise everyone else and give him our exclusive thought and interest. We should rather select the features that he excels in and consult other writers who, though inferior in some way, are still judged to outshine him in other areas.[46]

Other critics included Erasmus and Angelo Poliziano (b. 1454) who was university professor in Florence. First Poliziano:

To me whoever composes only by imitation seems like either a parrot or a magpie, merely voicing what he does not understand. For what sort writes lacks force and life; it lacks drive, emotion, talent; it falls flat, dozes, snores. Nothing there is truthful, nothing solid, nothing effective. You do not express Cicero, someone says. So what? Indeed, I am not Cicero. Still, I think I do express myself. . . . I ask that you not so shackle yourself with this superstition that you be pleased with nothing of your own and never shift your eyes from Cicero. But after you have read Cicero and other good writers widely and at length, after you have consumed, thoroughly learned and digested them, and have filled your heart with the knowledge of many matters, and you prepare to compose something yourself, then at last I would wish you to swim without a preserver, as they say, take your own counsel sometimes, put away that excessively morose and anxious preoccupation that you have with imitating Cicero alone and finally put your own general powers to the test. . . . if you strain to put your feet only in others' tracks, neither can you write well unless you dare depart from what has been prescribed, as it were. Finally, I hope you know that only a barren talent produces nothing of its own but always imitates.[47]

Erasmus, whose rhetoric is considered below, also expressed concern over this preoccupation with imitating Cicero. He penned a dialogue titled "Dialogus Ciceronianus" or "The Ciceronian: A Dialogue on the Ideal Latin Style," where he offered his cri-

tique. The following lengthy quote is included here so the reader can grasp the full force of Erasmus' thought.

What effrontery then on the part of anyone to demand that we speak in a totally Ciceronian manner! He must first give us back the Rome of long ago, the senate, and the curia, the conscript fathers, the equestrian order, the people distributed into tribes and centuries. . . . The religious rites, the gods and goddesses, the Capitol and the sacred fire; he must restore the provinces, colonies, municipalities and allies of the city that was mistress of the world. Since the entire scene of human activity has been transformed, the only speaker who can respond to it appropriately is one who is very different from Cicero. . . . You say that no one can speak well unless he reproduces Cicero; but the very facts of the matter cry out that no one can speak well unless he deliberately and with full awareness abandons the example of Cicero. Wherever I turn I see everything changed, I stand on a different stage, I see a different theatre, a different world. What am I to do? I am a Christian and I must talk of the Christian religion before Christians. If I am going to do so in a manner befitting my subject, surely I am not to imagine that I am living in the age of Cicero. . . .[48]

Continuing,

We should shun with equal determination those persons who are always loudly proclaiming that anything that fails to conform to Cicero's pattern in vocabulary, phraseology, and rhythm should be rejected as quite unfit to be read; for it is possible, with different stylistic virtues, to be, if not like Cicero, at least comparable to him. Let us have nothing to do with this fault-picking censoriousness.[49]

I welcome imitation with open arms—but imitation which assists nature and does not violate it, which turns its gifts in the right direction and does not destroy them. I approve of imitation—but imitation of a model that is in accord with, or at least not contrary to, your own native genius, so that you do not embark on a hopeless enterprise, like the giants fighting against the gods. Again, I approve of imitation—but imitation not enslaved to one set of rules, from the guidelines of which it dare not depart, but imitation which gathers from all authors, or at least from the most outstanding, the thing which is the chief virtue of each and which suits your own cast of mind; imitation which does not immediately incorporate into its own speech any nice little feature it comes across, but transmits it to the mind for inward digestion, so that becoming part of your own system, it gives the impression not of something begged from someone else, but of something that springs from your own mental processes, something that exudes the characteristics and force of your own mind and personality. Your reader will see it not as a piece of decoration filched from Cicero, but a child sprung from your own brain . . . .[50]

And so the debate over imitatio and the imitation of Cicero in particular played itself out during the Renaissance. As the history of rhetoric goes, the school of thought represented by Erasmus won out. Although some theorists have urged the imitation of great writers over the centuries, the strict adherence to the style and language of a single author such as Cicero is no longer advocated.

The Renaissance was also a period that produced original writers and works on rhetoric. Rudolf Agricola, Leonard Cox, Desiderius Erasmus, Philip Melanchthon, Henry Peacham, George Puttenham, Peter Ramus, Joannes Susenbrotus, George Trapezuntius, Juan Luis Vives, and Thomas Wilson are just a few of the significant authors active during the Renaissance.[51]

Desiderius Erasmus

Desiderius Erasmus (1466?–1536) was born in Rotterdam and spent time in France, England, Italy, Switzerland, and Germany. Corbett claims that Erasmus was the most influential rhetorician on the European continent after the Middle Ages. "Although this illustrious scholar spent only five years in England (1509–14), he set the pattern for the English grammar-school curriculum and for rhetorical training in the schools."[52] Two significant textbooks authored by Erasmus were *De Ratione Studii* and *De Duplici Copia Verborum ac Rerum.* "Originally published in 1512 both of these texts went into an astounding number of editions in subsequent years. (The *De Copia,* for instance, had at least 150 editions—only a few of those, it should be pointed out,

issuing from presses in England.)"[53] *De Copia* begins:

The speech of man is a magnificent and impressive thing when it surges along like a golden river, with thoughts and words pouring out in rich abundance. Yet the pursuit of speech like this involves considerable risk. As the proverb says, 'Not every man has the means to visit the city of Corinth.' We find that a good many mortal men who make great efforts to achieve this godlike power of speech fall instead into mere glibness, which is both silly and offensive. . . . Such considerations have induced me to put forward some ideas on copia, the abundant style, myself, treating its two aspects of content and expressions, and giving some examples and patterns.[54]

The central rhetorical concerns that unify *De Copia* are what Erasmus calls "richness in content" and "richness of expression." Richness in content or subject matter "involves assembling, explaining, and amplifying of arguments by the use of examples, comparisons, similarities, dissimilarities, opposite and other like procedures."[43] Richness of expression "involves synonyms, heterosis or enallage, metaphor, variation in word form, equivalence, and other similar methods of diversifying diction."[56] It is clear, then, that Erasmus is quite traditional in his treatment of rhetoric. Both content and expression are important considerations in his thinking. Erasmus and others writing in the Renaissance continue the Ciceronian legacy articulated by Augustine where subject matter as well as its expression are critical topics for the rhetorician. Besides his dependence on Cicero ("the great father of eloquence"), Erasmus notes that Quintilian, Homer, Ovid, Seneca, Pindar, and Plato were also important contributors to rhetorical thought.

The *De Ratione Studii* stipulates that the way to improve writing is through practice. In this regard, Erasmus "recommends the exercise of keeping a commonplace book; of paraphrasing poetry into prose and vice versa; of rendering the same subject in two or more styles; of proving a proposition along several different lines of argument; and of construing from Latin into Greek."[57] In addition to the above texts, Erasmus composed a work on letter writing titled *Modus Conscribendi Epistotlas* in 1522, thus continuing the interest in letter writing begun in the Middle Ages. Also, following the lead of the Middle

Ages, Erasmus authored a book on preaching called *Ecclesiastes sire de Rationa Concionandi.*

Thomas Wilson

A second major thinker representing this phase of rhetorical development is Thomas Wilson who was the author of a very popular vernacular rhetoric titled *The Arte of Rhetorique* (1553). The significance of Wilson's *Rhetorique* is that he "was the first to re-assemble, in English, the lost, strayed, or stolen doctrines of rhetoric."[58] Wilson's work was largely modeled after Cicero. He begins his text by defining rhetoric:

> *Rhetorique is an Arte to let foorth by vtter-aunce of words, matter at large, or (as Cicero doth say) it is a learned, or rather artificiall declaration of the mynd, in the handling of any cause, called in contention, that may through reason largely be discussed.*[59]

He next examines the ends of rhetoric or the "three things" required of an orator: to teach, to delight, and to persuade.[60] Following the classical authors, Wilson explores the canons of rhetoric. Invention is defined as a searching out of things true, or things likely which may reasonably set forth a matter and make it appear probable. He suggests that logic will help in the invention process claiming that the orator who will prove any cause and seek only to teach the truth must search out the places of logic. Disposition is defined as an orderly placing of things declaring where every argument should be set and in what manner every reason should be applied for confirmation of the purpose. Elocution is the process of applying "apt" words and "picked" sentences to the matter, found out to confirm the cause. Memory is a "fast holding" both of the matter and the words and pronunciation is utterance of or "a framing of the voice, countenance and gesture after a comely manner."[61]

Wilson continues examining the seven parts of an oration: the entrance or beginning, narration, proposition, division, confirmation, confutation, and conclusion. Attention is given also to the three types of orations (demonstrative, deliberative, and exhortation), figures of speech, amplification, style, memory, and delivery. Throughout, examples and illustrations from Greek literature as well as the Bible abound. Wilson, like Erasmus, remains faithful to the classical tradition as it was interpreted by Cicero.

Peter Ramus

A third major figure representative of Renaissance rhetorical theory is Pierre de la Ramee, better known today as Peter Ramus (1515–1572). Of Ramus' writings, perhaps his most noted is the *Dialectique* published in 1555. Largely influenced by the writer Agricola and the new logic of the Middle Ages, Ramus redefined rhetoric as the study of style and delivery only. The content and subject matter normally considered as parts of invention and disposition by the classical authors were placed into the domain of dialectic by Ramus. Thus, a clear break from the classics was made. Through the efforts of Ramus and likeminded writers, the movement to separate rhetoric from logic begun in the Middle Ages succeeded during the Renaissance. This separation of the classical canons of rhetoric exists today as logic is taught in philosophy departments, and rhetoric is studied in speech, communication, and English departments in most of our colleges and universities.

Ong and others consider Ramus from the perspective of the educational reformer.[62] As a professor at the University of Paris, Ramus closely examined the curriculum focusing on the organization of the disciplines and teaching practices. His criticisms of the educational system were grounded in three laws that could be traced to Aristotle's *Posterior Analytics*.[63] The first was called the Law of Truth, which "required any principle in any liberal discipline to be universally true."[64] Second was the Law of Wisdom, which "required the principle of any liberal discipline to be ordered in relation to their generality of particularity."[65] Finally, and most importantly for our discussion on the relation of rhetoric to dialectic or logic, the Law of Justice stated that "each liberal discipline must keep to its own subject matter, must share no doctrine with a sister discipline."[66] By applying these laws to the curriculum, Ramus was carefully categorizing and compartmentalizing subject matter. A result of this approach was the rhetoric-dialectic split mentioned above. Ramus' *Dialectique* was translated into English in 1574 and his well-articulated position concerning the relationship between logic and rhetoric was introduced to the English-speaking world.

In conclusion, consider this statement made in Ramus' *Arguments in Rhetoric Against Quintilian*:

> *I propose . . . that we should argue and deliberate quite differently the questions concerning the proper nature and the true divisions of the*

arts. I consider the subject matters of the arts to be distinct and separate. The whole of dialectic concerns the mind and reason, whereas rhetoric and grammar concern language and speech. Therefore dialectic comprises, as proper to it, the arts of invention, arrangement, and memory; this is evident because, as we find among numerous dumb persons and many people who live without any outward speech, they belong completely to the mind and can be practiced inwardly without any help from language or oration. To grammar for the purposes of speaking and writing well belong etymology in interpretation, syntax in connection, prosody in the pronunciation of short and long syllables, and orthography in the correct rules for writing. From the development of language and speech only two proper parts will be left for rhetoric, style and delivery; rhetoric will possess nothing proper and of its own beyond these.[67]

SUMMARY

The intellectual and artistic energy of the Renaissance provided fertile soil for free-thinking in every area of life. New ideas were tried and tested during this two-hundred year span; some caught on while others quickly faded. One individual whose ideas were accepted and who forever changed the thrust of Christianity was Martin Luther (1483–1546). Troubled over what he perceived as the suffocating authority of the Roman Church—especially as revealed in the handling of indulgences and papal taxation—Luther set out to challenge the religious establishment. Justification by faith became his central creed. When Luther posted his ninety-five theses on the door of the castle church in Wittenberg on October 31, 1517, a reformation of the Christian church was set in motion. As Martin Luther orchestrated his break with the Pope and the Roman hierarchy, he relied heavily on preaching to convey his message. He wrote in several places that preaching was the most important part of public worship, that the preacher should base his oratory on the Scriptures, that a sermon should instruct and exhort, and that a clear, simple, direct style should be used. Luther also took a stand on the logic-rhetoric debate saying,

> *Logic gives us a clear, correct, and methodical arrangement, showing us the grounds of our conclusions, and how we may know, to a certainty, from the nature of the subject itself, what is right or wrong, and what we should judge and decide. Logic teaches, rhetoric moves and persuades; the latter controls the will, the former the understanding.*[68]

> Martin Luther wrote in several places that preaching was the most important part of public worship, that the preacher should base his oratory on the Scriptures, that a sermon should instruct and exhort, and that a clear, simple, direct style should be used.

From Martin Luther and the Christian Reformation of the sixteenth century, it is a short leap in both time and geography to the British and continental rhetoricians. As we have seen, rhetorical theory and practice took several twists and turns during the centuries between Plato and Luther. Many of the issues raised—especially the relationship of rhetoric to logic—continue to be contested by the British and continental writers. However, the enormous impact of the Christian experience on rhetorical development cannot be underscored enough. Both in theory and practice the Christians forever influenced the development of rhetorical thought. It is not coincidence, then, that the three outstanding theorists of the next period—Hugh Blair, Richard Whately, and George Campbell—were Christian ministers who further imprinted the faith on rhetorical theory. Nor should it come as a surprise that some of the greatest orators—George Whitefield and John Wesley to name two—were to come out of this tradition, which began sometime in the first century in and around the quiet village of Nazareth.

Notes

1. Flavious Philostratus, *Lives of the Sophists,* in Wilmer C. Wright, trans., *Philostratus and Eunapius: The Lives of the Sophists* (Cambridge, Mass.: Harvard University Press, 1952), p. 61.

2. James J. Murphy, *A Synoptic History of Classical Rhetoric* (New York: Random House, 1972), p. 177.

3. Charles Sears Baldwin, *Medieval Rhetoric and Poetic* (Glouster, Mass.: Peter Smith, reprint 1959), p. 3.

4. *Ibid.,* pp. 10–11.

5. George Kennedy, *Classical Rhetoric and Its Christian and Secular Tradition from Ancient to Modern Times* (Chapel Hill: University of North Carolina Press, 1980), p. 39.

6. Baldwin, op. cit., pp. 30–33.

7. The following paragraphs are from A.O. Pickard, trans., *Longinus: On the Sublime* (Oxford, Clarendon Press, 1906).

8. Nancy L. Harper, *Human Communication Theory: The History of a Paradigm* (Rochelle Park, N.J.: Hayden Book Company, 1979), p. 70.

9. George Kennedy, op. cit, pp. 132–146.

10. Williston Walker, *A History of the Christian Church* (New York: Charles Scribner's Sons, 1958), p. 45.

11. *Ibid,* pp. 46–47.

12. *Ibid.,* p. 52.

13. Yngve Brilioth, *A Brief History of Preaching* (Philadelphia: Fortress Press, 1965), p. 35.

14. *Ibid.,* p. 30.

15. *Ibid.,* p. 51.

16. Kennedy, op. cit., p. 39.

17. D.W. Robertson, trans., *On Christian Doctrine: Saint Augustine* (Indianapolis: Bobbs-Merrill, 1958), pp. 118–119.

18. Phillip Schaff, ed., *A Select Library of the Nicene* and *Post-Nicene Fathers of the Christian Church: St. Augustin's City of God and Christian Doctrine* (Grand Rapids, Michigan: Wm. B. Eerdmans Publishing Company, 1956), p. 576.

19. Baldwin, op. cit., p. 53.

20. Schaff, op. cit. p. 576.

21. *Ibid.,* p. 583.

22. *Ibid.,* p. 584.

23. James J. Murphy, *Rhetoric in the Middle Ages: A History of Rhetorical Theory from Saint Augustine to the Renaissance* (Berkeley: University of California Press, 1974), p. 90.

24. *Ibid.,* p. 90.

25. *Ibid.,* p. 90.

26. *Ibid.,* p. 337.

27. Baldwin, op. cit., p. 88.

28. Joseph M. Miller, trans., "An Overview of the Structure of Rhetoric," in Patricia Bizzell and Bruce Herzberg, eds. *The Rhetorical Tradition: Readings from Classical Times to the Present* (Boston: Bedford Books of St. Martin's Press, 1990), pp. 425–426.

29. John Bliese, "The Study of Rhetoric in the Twelfth Century," *Quarterly Journal of Speech,* 63 (December 1977): p. 364.

30. Murphy, op. cit., p. 136.

31. *Ibid.,* p. 193.

32. Bliese, op. cit., p. 344.

33. George Kennedy, op. cit., p. 186.

34. James J. Murphy, trans., "Principles of Letter Writing," in Bizzell and Herzberg, op. cit, p. 432.

35. Baldwin, op. cit, p. 230.

36. Richard McKeon, "Rhetoric in the Middle Ages," *Speculum: A Journal of Medieval Studies,* 17 (January 1942): pp. 1–32.

37. Will Durant, *The Renaissance: A History of Civilization in Italy from 1304–1576.* (New York: Simon and Schuster, 1953), p. 67.

38. Paul O. Kristeller, "Rhetoric in Medieval and Renaissance Culture," in James J. Murphy, ed., *Renaissance Eloquence: Studies in the Theory and Practice of Renaissance Rhetoric.* (Berkeley: University of California Press, 1983), pp. 4–5.

39. Charles S. Baldwin, *Renaissance Literary Theory and Practice (Gloucester, MA: Peter Smith, 1959), p. 7.*

40. *Ibid.,* p. 18.

41. *Ibid.,* p. 44

42. *Ibid.,* p. 45.

43. Brian Duvick, (unpublished manuscript) trans,. "Letter of P. Bembo to Giovanni Franscesco Pico della Mirandola, p. 79.

44. Ibid.

45. Duvick, trans., "Letter Pietro Bembo to Giovanni Franscesco Pico della Mirandola," pgs. 38–39.

46. Duvick, trans., "Letter from Giovanni Franscesco della Mirandola to Pietro Bembo," p. 58.

47. Duvick, trans., "Letter of Angelo Poliziano to Paulo Cortesi," p. 58.

48. Betty I. Knott, "The Ciceronian: A Dialogue on the Ideal Latin Style" in the *Collected Works of*

Erasums (Toronto: University of Toronto Press, 1986), vol. 27, p. 383.

49. *Ibid.,* p. 446.

50. *Ibid.,* p. 441.

51. Cf. James J. Murphy, *Renaissance Eloquence,* pp. 20–36.

52. Edward P.J. Corbett. *Classical Rhetoric for the Modern Student,* 2nd ed., (New York: Oxford University Press, 1971), p. 605.

53. *Ibid.,* p. 605.

54. Craig R. Thompson, ed., *Collected Works of Erasmus.* (Toronto: University of Toronto Press, 1978), vol. 24, *Literary and Educational Writings 2: De Copia/De Ratione Studii,* p. 295.

55. *Ibid.,* p. 301.

56. *Ibid.*

57. *Classical Rhetoric for the Modern Student,* p. 605.

58. Russell H. Wagner, "Thomas Wilson's Contributions to Rhetoric," in Raymond F. Howes, ed., *Historical Studies of Rhetoric and Rhetoricians.*

(New York: Cornell University Press, 1961), p. 108.

59. G.H. Mair, ed., *Wilson's Arte of Rhetorique.* (Oxford Clarendon Press, 1909), p. 1.

60. *Ibid.,* p. 2.

61. *Ibid.,* p. 6.

62. Walter J. Ong, *Rhetoric, Romance, and Technology.* (Ithaca: Cornell University Press, 1971), chapters 6 and 7.

63. Nancy Harper, op. cit., p. 95.

64. Wilbur S. Howell, "Ramus and English Rhetoric: 1574–1681," *Quarterly Journal of Speech,* 37 (October 1951), p. 301.

65. *Ibid.,* p. 301.

66. *Ibid.,* p. 301.

67. Carole Newlands, trans., *Arguments in Rhetoric Against Quintilian,* in Bizzell and Herzberg, op. cit., p. 570.

68. Frederick Eby, *Early Protestant Educators* (New York: McGraw-Hill, 1931), p. 171.

PART 2

British/Continental Theory and Enlightenment Rhetoric

In the preceding chapters we have seen how classical rhetorical theory flourished in Greece and Rome. So successful was the system of training used by the ancients that it constituted a model for rhetorical scholars in the Middle Ages, the Renaissance, and, to some extent, the seventeenth century. "At different periods, of course, the system was subjected to retrenchments, amplifications, shifts of emphasis, revitalizations, innovations, and changes in terminology, sometimes to suit the whim of a particular teacher or group, at other times to make the system more relevant to the needs and moods of the time."[1] Following the development of the printing press, for example, "and during periods when a great deal of political and mercantile business was carried on through the medium of letters, the emphasis both in the classroom and in the rhetoric texts shifted more and more from oral to written discourse."[2] The influence of Christianity and humanism also contributed to some modifications of classical theory. But these changes were primarily in degree rather than substance.

It seems evident that despite innovations which occasionally altered its scope or emphasis, rhetoric at the close of the sixteenth century was still primarily an integral part of an old and cherished system dating back to the early Greeks and Romans. The classical strain which dominated the period found expression in Thomas Wilson's *Arte of Rhetorique* published in 1553. This historically significant study, as we saw in the last chapter, was the first modern English rhetoric text that gave full treatment to the basic tenets set forth by the ancients. In all, it was essentially an English version of the rhetorical theories of Cicero, Quintilian, and the author of *Ad Herennium*.

But if classical doctrine was a vital element in sixteenth-century British thought, it encountered a serious challenge in the early decades of the seventeenth century. With dramatic suddenness, revolutionary scientific, philosophical, and psychological developments modified traditional theories of knowledge, thereby creating the demand for a "new rhetoric" rooted not only in the past but in modern epistemology. These happenings gave rise to four rhetorical trends which interacted with each other during the next two hundred years:

1. neoclassicism;
2. the eclectic method of the belletristic scholars;
3. the psychological-epistemological school of rhetoric; and
4. the truncating approach of the elocutionists.

In chapters 6 through 9, we will examine each of these trends. In approaching the study of British rhetoric from the point of view of trends, we are fully aware of the fact that we must move back and forth in chronology. We feel, however, that this is necessary in order to see the flow of thought within a particular school. We begin with neoclassicism and belles lettres because they most clearly reflect the major teachings of the classical writers. We then move to the epistemologists whose interest in the social and behavioral sciences led them to go far beyond the ancients in exploring the human mind. Following these two steps, we turn to the elocutionists whose tendency to focus primarily on a single canon of delivery set them apart from the other major trends. It is hoped that by the time we have completed our survey, we will be able to appreciate both the diversity and the similarities in British rhetoric.

Moreover, we feel that these British/Continental rhetorical trends, when viewed in their entirety, helped create what has become an important part of the Enlightenment movement in America in the last half of the 18th and early part of the 19th centuries. How this movement unfolded will be made in chapter 10 which centers its attention on the rhetorical teachings of John Witherspoon and John Quincy Adams.

Major Figures

Francis Bacon
(1561–1626)

English philosopher, lawyer, scientist whose ideas on faculty psychology, style and invention strongly influenced later theorists. *Advancement of Learning*

René Descartes
(1596–1650)

French philosopher-mathematician who favored certainty over probability, experimentation over disputation. *Discourse on Method*

John Locke
(1632–1704)

English philosopher and political theorist who helped to lay the groundwork for modern science. Novel ideas on pathos, doctrine of association, and faculties of the mind. Essay *Concerning Human Understanding*

Giambattista Vico
(1668–1744)

Italian philosopher and cultural historian who rejected Descartes' ideas and reemphasized probability; father of modern social science. *On the Study Methods of our Time*

David Hume
(1711–1776)

Scottish philosopher-historian who probed deeply into the nature of man, Hume taught that empiricism was the basis of modern science. Rejected Christian miracles on the basis of inadequate evidence. Major influence on Campbell and Whately. *A Treatise of Human Nature*

Edmund Burke
(1729–1797)

English-Irish philosopher-orator deeply interested in taste, emotion, and the motivational power of words. *A Philosophical Enquiry into the Origin of our Ideas of the Sublime and the Beautiful*

John Ward
(1679?–1758)

Author of the most extensive treatment of classical rhetorical theory in English. *A System of Oratory*

Thomas Sheridan
(1719–1788)

Lecturer-theater manager, father of the naturalist school, and perhaps the most famous of the British elocutionists. *Lectures on Elocution*

Adam Smith
(1723–1790)

Scottish philosopher and political economist concerned with criticism, style, and the forms of discourse. *Lectures on Rhetoric and Belles Letters*

Hugh Blair
(1718–1800)

Popular Scottish preacher whose lectures at the University of Edinburgh introduced students to taste, criticism, style, and sublimity. *Lectures on Rhetoric and Belles Lettres*

George Campbell
(1719–1796)

Scottish minister and educator. The most original thinker among the British and continental rhetoricians. Campbell was concerned with moral reasoning, pathos, audience analysis, and the doctrine of usage. *The Philosophy of Rhetoric*

John Walker
(1732–1807)

Lexicographer-grammarian who believed that every internal emotion has an external expression; father of the mechanical school of elocution. *Elements of Elocution*

Joseph Priestley
(1733–1804)

Scientist, theologian, educator interested in the association of ideas, style, and taste. *A Course of Lectures on Oratory and Criticism*

Gilbert Austin
(1753–1837)

English elocutionist interested in body language. Austin sought to elevate delivery to the level of a science. *Chironomia or a Treatise on Rhetorical Delivery*

Richard Whately
(1787–1863)

Anglican bishop interested in argumentation as a tool for combatting heresy and reforming society. *Elements of Rhetoric*

John Witherspoon
(1723–1794)

Presbyterian minister and President of the College of New Jersey, later known as Princeton University. *Lectures on Moral Philosophy* and *Eloquence*

John Quincy Adams
(1767–1848)

Professor of Rhetoric and Belles Lettres at Harvard University, and 6th President of the U.S. *Lectures on Rhetoric and Oratory*

Key Concepts

- Four schools of rhetorical thought

- Neoclassicists

- Belletristic school

- Epistemologists

- Elocutionists

- Rhetoric of style

- Bacon's barriers to perception (idols of the tribe, cave, marketplace, theater)

- Belles lettres
  - A. Taste
  - B. Criticism
  - C. Genius
  - D. The sublime
  - E. Perspicuity
  - F. Precision
  - G. Beauty

- Psychological and philosophical concepts
  - A. Faculty psychology
  - B. Doctrine of association
  - C. Common sense
  - D. Ends of discourse (understanding, imagination, passions, the will)

- E. Wit, humor, ridicule
- F. Moral reasoning (experience, analogy, testimony, calculation of chances)
- G. People in general
- H. People in particular
- I. Doctrine of usage (reputable, national, present)
- J. Doctrine of sympathy
- K. Conviction/persuasion duality
- L. Verisimilitude
- M. Miracles

- Argumentative discourse
  - A. Presumption
  - B. Burden of proof
  - C. A priori arguments
  - D. Deference
  - E. Refutation
  - F. Rebuttal

- Enlightenment Rhetoric
  - A. Virtue
  - B. Types of Oratory (demonstrative, deliberative, judicial, and pulpit)
  - C. Faculties of the mind
  - D. Moral philosophy
  - E. Eloquence
  - F. Jurisprudence

6

Neoclassicism, the Belletristic Movement, and the Rhetoric of Hugh Blair

NEOCLASSICISM

The period roughly covering the years 1700 to 1740 represents a flowering of the classical tradition in English letters. Frequently described as a new "Augustan Age" after its first century Roman predecessor, this era was under the dominating influence of Jonathan Swift, Alexander Pope, and John Dryden. These classicists, motivated to some degree by eminent French critics, happily joined the ranks of the ancients. Aristotle's *Poetics,* Horace's *Ars Poetica,* and Longinus' *On the Sublime* were to them the desiderata of effective literary composition. They came to believe that if the English language hoped to live as a virile instrument of expression, it must be patterned after the eternal precepts set forth in these works. Consequently, they had little sympathy for those who sought to establish an experimental methodology as a basis for criticism. Such an approach, they were convinced, minimized the importance of classical learning.

Taking their cue from Horace, the Augustans set up a standard for effective writing. The first crucial step that must be observed by all prospective authors is imitation; that is, after diligently studying the ancients, one should strive to imitate the classical precepts. This means that to be a good writer, there is no need for originality, except in the mode of expression. It is the duty of every writer, therefore, to de-velop a style which describes old truths in a new and interesting manner. The criteria upon which the success of this style depends are correctness and lucidity. It follows that ornate images, ambiguous words and phrases, and verbose expressions, have no place in good style.[3]

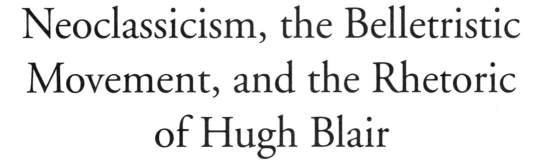

One of the leading characteristics of the Augustans was their inflexible attitude toward those who questioned the value of classicism.

Jonathan Swift

One of the leading characteristics of the Augustans was their inflexible attitude toward those who questioned the value of classicism. Jonathan Swift was the first to voice his disapproval. He had witnessed the advance of experimental science and had envisioned it as a definite threat to all forms of art. Out of this feeling of fear and bitterness came the "Battle of the Books," a masterpiece of satirical criticism. In this account, Swift tells of a battle that occurred in the Public Library between the Ancients and Moderns. He vividly portrays scenes depicting the utter futility of the modern forces. Bacon, Descartes, Locke, and Boyle all received telling blows at the hands of Aristotle, Plato, and Horace. One of the highlights of the narration is an animated conversation carried on by the spider, a modernist, and the bee, an ancient—the latter revealing Swift's position in the conflict. This delightful episode does more than serve as a dramatic relief. It clearly states the issues that are involved.[4]

In the "Tale of a Tub," Swift throws more light on the long literary controversy. He ridicules the modern methods of research by pointing out the tendency of contemporary scholars to read introductions, and prefaces rather than books. "I do utterly disapprove and declare against the pernicious custom, of making the Preface a bill-of-fare to the book," said Swift.[5] In an ironical vein, Swift next condemns the egotistical moderns who set themselves up as aesthetic authorities. "We of this age have discovered a shorter and more prudent method, to become scholars and wits, without the fatigue of reading or thinking."[6] Thus we have the paradoxical statement implied by the rebels that they, not the Greeks or Romans, are the true ancients. Swift concluded his indictment with these words: "Our illustrious moderns have eclipsed the weak glimmering lights of the ancients, and turned them out of the road of all fashionable commerce, to a degree, that our choice town wits, of most refined accomplishments, are in grave dispute, whether there have been ever any ancients or not. . . ."[7]

Alexander Pope

Probably the most popular Augustan was Alexander Pope who ruled for over fifty years as the dominant figure in English literature. His "Essay on Criticism," written at the age of twenty, was considered by his contemporaries as a model of critical theory. Samuel Johnson, in commenting on this work, said that if Pope had never written another line, the "Essay" would be sufficient to establish him as the foremost critic and poet of his day.[8] The "Essay on Criticism" played a significant part in the ancient-modern struggle. In this poem, Pope sets down certain rules which must be observed if a high standard of criticism is to be achieved. These tenets are built around the underlying principle of nature. Follow nature, says Pope, and then frame your judgments by her standards.[9] A writer cannot hope to succeed unless he absorbs this spirit and willingly accedes his will to the will of nature. True art, therefore, is an imitative art—nature being the original, art the copy.

But how is the poet to determine what is "natural" in poetry? Pope answers by saying that it is to be found in the best works of the ancients.

> Follow nature, says Pope, and then frame your judgments by her standards.

You then whose judgment the right course would steer,
Know well each ancient's proper character.
His fable, subject, scope in every page.
Religion, country, genius of his age
Without all these at once before your eyes,
Cavil you may, but never criticize.[10]

Herein lies Pope's strong classical leanings. It is a clear, terse statement of the respective genius of the two schools. If the modernist is to understand the universal truths of nature, he must call upon the ancients to intercede on his behalf. It is like Plotinus' "One," the first member of the Trinity, which fills up and overflows, then emanates into the second member of the Trinity and this, in turn, into the third member. Nature is the One, the classical writers are the second part of the Trinity, and the true modern genius, the third. The effulgence of nature descends upon the ancients, and they in turn radiate the way for us. Thus there is a hierarchical arrangement in which the moderns, as third members of the Poetical Trinity, are dependent upon their ancient masters. This can be further illustrated by showing the relationship of Homer and Virgil. The former looked directly to nature for his source of inspiration; the latter looked to Homer. In Pope's opinion, both poets imitated nature. Homer chose the direct method, Virgil the indirect. The fact that Virgil was not original in his approach did not mean that he possessed inferior genius. It simply meant that he saw nature through his master's eyes.[11]

The combined efforts of the Augustans in supporting the classical tradition were instrumental in temporarily preventing an encroachment of scientific methodology in the field of art. Once again men's minds were turned back to the cherished teachings of the past. But while generating a renewed feeling of reverence for the classics, Pope and his school failed to appreciate the challenge of the scientific philosophical thinkers who prevailed in the seventeenth century.

John Lawson

Notwithstanding the fact that neoclassicism began to wane in the middle of the century, some rhetoricians were not yet ready to alter either the content or the structure used by the ancients in their analyses of oral discourse. Chief among these authors were John Lawson and John Ward whose books were published at the time when Hugh Blair was beginning his lectures at the University of Edinburgh. Lawson's *Lectures Concerning Oratory,* which appeared in Dublin in 1758, was little more than an Anglicized version of the theories of Aristotle, Cicero, and Quintilian. Although he often drew upon English literature for illustrative material, attempted to incorporate a few of the concepts of Baconian faculty psychology in his discussion of emotions, and sought to make adaptations for students seeking a career in preaching, Lawson seemed content to summarize and apply classical rhetorical doctrines. He turned primarily to Aristotle for guidelines on invention, and to Cicero and Quintilian for ideas on disposition, style, and delivery.[12] The end product was an unimaginative and sterile work which not only was ignored by Blair and Campbell but by subsequent scholars.

John Ward

If Lawson's *Lectures* were an unoriginal and tedious summary of classical views, so too was John Ward's *Systems of Oratory,* published one year later. This two volume study, which covers more than eight hundred pages, is the most extensive treatment of classical rhetorical theory in the English language.[13] Without criticism, Ward accepts the format and treatment employed by the ancients. Like them, he equates rhetoric with persuasion; recognizes the three forms of oratory—deliberative, forensic, and epideictic; and highlights the numerous elements of invention, disposition, style, and delivery. Early in Volume I he objects to the inclusion of memory as one of the five canons because it was not a unique aspect of rhetoric. Yet at the close of Volume II he apparently changes his mind and decides to devote a chapter to it. So firm is Ward's commitment to the ancients that he, unlike Lawson, derives most of his illustrations from classical documents. At heart he is a Roman. He thus turns principally to Cicero and Quintilian, rather than to Aristotle, for guidance and inspiration. His work, in short, is a comprehensive summary of the best of Roman rhetorical thought and practice. De-

> Among the unique features of the belletristic movement was the tendency to broaden rhetoric to include writing and criticism, along with speaking, as forms that should be studied in a single course or text.

spite its obvious lack of originality, it had considerable appeal for students and professors in American colleges and universities during the nineteenth century.[14]

What set the neoclassicists apart from their contemporaries such as Hume, Campbell, and, as we will later note, the belletristic scholars was not their admiration for classical notions but their slavish devotion to them and their tendency to reject newly developing trends. This failure to incorporate relevant social and behavioral science data into their theories of discourse prevented the neoclassicists from advancing our knowledge of rhetoric.

THE BELLETRISTIC MOVEMENT: BELLES LETTRES

A second major trend in British rhetorical thought was the work of the belletristic scholars. Consistent with the practice of the epistemologists, these students of communication theory borrowed heavily from the ancients and the modernists in producing a "new" type of rhetoric. From Aristotle they derived a communication model comprised of source, message, and receiver; an understanding of ethical, logical, and pathetic proof; a recognition of the effect of the occasion on a speaker's choice of material and development of themes; and an appreciation for perspicuity in style. From Cicero and Quintilian they accepted the definition of rhetoric as one great art consisting of five lesser arts (invention, disposition, style, memory, and delivery); the tripartite separation of the ends of discourse into instructing, pleasing, and moving, and of style into plain, medium, and grand; and the role of nature, imitation, and the use of models in the formation of an orator or writer. Finally, from Longinus they learned the value of combining rhetoric and poetics into a single, coherent system; and the meaning and significance of taste and sublimity. The professors of rhetoric and belles lettres were unwilling to rely on classical ideas and models alone. From modern works they derived principles of faculty psychology, a knowledge of the function of reason in criticism, insights into genius, and examples of eloquence depicting the potentialities inherent in the native idiom.

Among the unique features of the belletristic movement was the tendency to broaden rhetoric to include writing and criticism, along with speaking, as forms that should be studied in a single course or text. The student, therefore, received training not only in oral discourse but in poetry, drama, historical and philosophical writing, and, occasionally, in miscellaneous matters pertaining to education. This technique of joining rhetoric and polite literature, and in employing classical and contemporary models, proved to be, as we shall see in the case of Hugh Blair, a pedagogically attractive approach to the study of communication.

The principal works employing the belletristic approach can be understood only against the background of an important movement that began in the latter part of the seventeenth century. Longinus' celebrated treatise *On the Sublime,* virtually unknown to modern rhetoricians, suddenly appeared in 1674 with a translation and commentary by Boileau. Almost at once the essay caught the imagination of French and English scholars, stimulating in them a strong interest in taste, sublimity, and genius as potentially useful criteria to be employed in criticism. In his brief but penetrating analysis, Longinus made several points with telling effect—points which we feel are worth repeating because of their impact on the belletristic trend. He set the tone of his study by asserting that the goal of genius "is not to persuade the audience but rather to transport them out of themselves."[15] Observing that this aim could not be attained by using language that was inflated or frigid, he listed the five genuine sources of the sublime: (1) "the command of full blooded ideas"; (2) "the inspiration of vehement emotion"; (3) figures of thought; (4) figures of speech; and (5) "dignity and elevation."[16] Here Longinus was suggesting that when a communicator unites profound ideas with strong emotion and nobility of phrase, he transports or lifts the audience. So essential is this ability, he added, that one may redeem "all his mistakes by a single touch of sublimity and true excellence."[17]

Joseph Addison

The subject of sublimity, along with its related theme of taste, commanded the attention of Joseph Addi-

son, an English essayist and poet. What is it, he asked, that gives pleasure to the imagination when we survey outward objects? The pleasure results from viewing what has the characteristics of greatness, novelty, and beauty. Greatness, by which Addison meant the sublime, was the perceiving of an object in its fullest view. It is present during those moments when the eye or the imagination focuses on open country, vast uncultivated deserts, lofty mountain ranges, high rocks and precipices, wide expanses of water, and a spacious horizon. "Our imagination loves to be filled," said Addison, "with an object, or to grasp anything that is too big for its capacity."[18] To the grandeur stemming from greatness may be added beauty and novelty. Together they make their way to the soul of man through his imagination.

Addison defined taste as "that faculty of the soul, which discerns the beauties of an author with pleasure and the imperfections with dislike."[19] Convinced that taste was to a certain degree innate, he nevertheless argued that it could be improved and cultivated by those who gained a knowledge of the writings of the best authors and critics, and who conversed with men of genius. Addison was not reluctant to apply his theory of taste to contemporary British works which he found to be overly partial to epigrams, turns of wit, and forced conceits.

> The subject of sublimity, along with its related theme of taste, commanded the attention of Joseph Addison,

John Baillie

Students of taste in the middle of the century moved steadily in the direction of psychology as they sought to draw their precepts from human nature. Locke's treatment of the senses and Hume's discussion of associationism became driving forces for Dr. John Baillie who wrote *An Essay on the Sublime* that was published posthumously in 1747. Starting with the premise that nature conveys the sublime to our senses, Baillie then used an analogy to the works of art, saying that they likewise may produce a similar experience. An appealing object of nature or of *art* in and of itself may activate immediately the senses causing sublimity. This does not preclude, however, a second possibility. For those objects which lack this power when standing in isolation may when united with other concepts through association become a stimulus for the sublime.[20]

Edmund Burke

Two other essays in the late 1750's similarly relied extensively upon psychology. The first was Edmund Burke's *A Philosophical Enquiry into the Origin of our Ideas of the Sublime and Beautiful,* to which was attached an introductory discourse on taste. Burke accepted the hypothesis that the mind is comprised of faculties, and that taste results from the senses, the imagination, and judgment. Since all men have these traits, they have taste. Differences that arise among observers are due to natural sensibility, knowledge, and training—those elements that strengthen the judgment.[21]

The discussion of taste formed the rationale for Burke's comprehensive analysis of the sublime and beautiful. After speaking of general emotions, he described the effect upon the senses of such passions as astonishment, terror, obscurity, vastness, infinity, uniformity, magnitude, difficulty, darkness, color, and loudness. These passions have in common the power to create strong impressions upon the imagination of the beholder. Some of Burke's favorite terms to pinpoint the meaning of sublime were "vast," "rugged," "dark," "gloomy," "solid," "massive," and "terror." If these qualities caused pain, that is part of the cost that one must pay in order to experience the sublime.[22]

More gentle and pleasant than sublimity is the beautiful which has as its object love. Contrary to popular opinion, Burke suggested, proportion, fitness, and perfection are not causes of beauty. The following traits are the real causes: smallness, smoothness, variation, delicacy, color, physiognomy, and clarity. The sublime and beautiful, therefore, are built on different principles: the one has terror for its basis and leads to astonishment; the other depends on pleasure to stimulate the affection of love.

Burke's theory of the sublime is noteworthy not only because of his stress on emotion, but because of his unusual faith in the power of words to arouse the senses needed to promote the sublime and beautiful. Words, he said, are generally more motivating than pictures or scenes. With such a belief he found it easy to claim: "Eloquence and poetry are . . . more capable of making deep and lively impressions than any other arts, and even than nature itself in very many cases."[23] In evaluating the worth of Burke's discussion, Samuel Monk has observed that the *Enquiry,* despite its shortcomings, was "one of the most im-portant aesthetic documents that eighteenth-century England produced."[24]

Alexander Gerard

In 1759, two years after the appearance of Burke's *Enquiry,* Alexander Gerard published a similarly significant volume, entitled *An Essay on Taste.* Like his predecessors, Gerard equated taste with ideas relating to the powers of the imagination. His major sources were Locke, Hume, and Baillie. From them he gained an enthusiasm for the doctrines of reductionism and associationism which became the key for his aesthetic theory. Gerard broke down taste into the simple principles of novelty, grandeur and sublimity, beauty, imitation, harmony, ridicule, and virtue. Throughout his analysis the impact of association is evident. Objects which are not by nature sublime, he argued, may possess this quality when united with other concepts in a proper manner. Examples of this may be seen in the fine arts, in color combinations, and in all aspects of imitation.

Gerard endorsed the views of earlier writers who spoke of the development and improvement of a standard of taste. "Goodness of taste," he said, "lies in its maturity and perfection. It consists in certain excellencies of our original powers of judgment and imagination combined." These may be reduced to the elements of sensibility, refinement, correctness, and "proportion or comparative adjustment of its separate principles."[25] To eliminate a defect in taste, Gerard recommended a strengthening of the internal senses and of judgment, and the need for establishing general precepts that conform to "the common feelings of men."[26]

Another important facet of Gerard's theory was his discussion of the relationship between taste and genius and the influence of taste on criticism. A man of genius, Gerard pointed out, has a comprehensive and perceptive imagination which enables him to see associations or connections between ideas regardless of their remoteness. This talent to unite concepts quickly is a product not of practice but of imagination. Genius, the leading quality of invention, "is the grand architect which not only chooses the materials, but disposes them into a regular structure."[27] The function of taste, on the other hand, is to guide, moderate, and give the finishing touches to the efforts of genius. Without genius one cannot perform, but he may be able to judge. For taste provides the critic with a discernment that assists him in interpreting his own feelings with accuracy, and in explaining these sentiments to others. These descriptions of taste, genius, and criticism—strongly rooted in eighteenth-century psychology—anticipated the philosophy of Hugh Blair.

Charles Rollin

It was within the context of a renewal of interest in the classics, of revolutionary advances in epistemological thought, and of an evolving theory of taste that the trend toward belletristic rhetoric developed. Of the many works that were belletristic in function and scope, three stand out: Charles Rollin's *The Method of Teaching and Studying the Belles Lettres* (1726–28); Adam Smith's *Lectures on Rhetoric and Belles Lettres* (1762–63); and Hugh Blair's *Lectures on Rhetoric and Belles Lettres* (1783). Rollin's four volume study, which was translated into English in 1734,[28] doubtless was influenced by early French rhetorics. Consciously avoiding any real pretense of originality, Rollin confesses at the outset that the ideas espoused in his volumes represent the combined thinking of classical rhetoricians and seventeenth and eighteenth-century scholars at the University of Paris.[29] Despite this disclaimer, Rollin departed markedly from his predecessors in his selection and development of materials.

The Method of Teaching and Studying the Belles Lettres was designed to improve the understanding, manners, and religious affections of students, and possibly their parents and friends. The work is separated into six parts: grammar, poetry, rhetoric, history, philosophy, and educational administration and procedures. In the amplification of these units, all of the elements of the belletristic tradition to be covered later by Smith and Blair are present. Rollin establishes guidelines for future studies by analyzing taste, sublimity, the rhetorical canons, ends of discourse, forms of proof, and the eloquence of the bar, pulpit, and sacred writings.[30] It is, in fine, a comprehensive bringing together of the major tenets of communication under the rubric of a single discipline. For his efforts Rollin won the praise of Bishop Atterbury and Voltaire who regarded the book as "one of the completest Treatises ever published on the Subject of polite literature."[31]

Adam Smith

The English counterpart to Rollin was Adam Smith whose *Inquiry into the Nature and Causes of the Wealth of Nations* (1776) carried for him the reputation as "father of political economy." In 1748, Smith began under the sponsorship of Lord Kames a series of public lectures in Edinburgh on rhetoric and belles lettres which were repeated during the following two years. Largely as a reward for the popularity of these lectures, Smith received a coveted appointment in 1751 as Professor of Logic at the University of Glasgow. One year later he moved to the discipline of Moral Philosophy, an academic specialty which he taught for thirteen years. Steeped in the classics and well versed in French and Italian as well as in English history, literature, and psychology, Smith sought both in his lectures and in his writings to present a systematic analysis of style, oratory, and criticism.

Crucial to an understanding of Smith's rhetorical lectures was his emphasis on the various forms of discourse. Whenever he developed one of the traditional canons, he related his discussion to oratorical, poetical, dramatic, and historical writing. He compared the function, ends, structure, and substance of each, demonstrating wherein each conformed to and deviated from the other. Since the common element present in all methods of communication is style, Smith gave to this canon a central position. Throughout the lectures he summarized the origin and progress of language, trumpeted the virtues of perspicuity in style, and cited the danger of an excessive reliance on tropes and other figures of speech and thought.

In his discussions of the purposes and ends of discourse and of the three forms of eloquence—demonstrative, judicial, and deliberative—Smith hewed closely to classical teachings. Persuasion, epitomized by well reasoned arguments and moving emotional appeals, he regarded as the primary aim of rhetoric. But Smith, who was also a student of the faculty psychologists, made room in his system for a secondary purpose—to inform. This method, which he called didactic, adheres to the narrative form and is designed to instruct.[32]

Interspersed throughout the lectures are numerous comments on literary criticism. Smith's aesthetic theory was an outgrowth of his philosophy of taste which had deep roots in the classical and modern psychological traditions. A proper taste, he remarked, is one that conforms to the fashions and customs of a particular age and locale, and to a majority sentiment. Since a thorough understanding of the nature of man is an essential requisite for one who seeks to make delicate and discriminating judgments, the critic must begin his task by searching his own mind in order to assess his genuine feelings. But if he stops here, he is in danger of measuring perfection against the yardstick of his own interests and sensibilities. So he needs, secondly, to come to an appreciation of the feelings of others. "We must look at ourselves," he argued, "with the same eyes with which we look at others; we must imagine ourselves not the actors, but the spectators of our own character and conduct. . . ."[33]

The most fitting summary of Smith's views on taste is found in his *Lectures on Justice, Police, Revenue and Arms.* Here he suggested that the three essential ingredients of beauty, which he held to be the principal substance of taste, are "proper variety," "easy connexion," and "simple order."[34] These traits, which combine to form the general neoclassic concept of "decorum" or "propriety," pervade Smith's approach to all phases of rhetorical criticism. With Dryden, the first great English poet to discuss this doctrine at length, he embodied extensively in his criticism the principles of "refinement," "correctness," "strict unity," and "simple clarity."[35] Smith's impatience with the Greek dramatists grew out of his belief that they had violated these rules by placing an undue emphasis on bodily pain. Shakespeare annoyed him by constantly violating the unity of place: his practice of making one scene in France, the following one in London, and the next in York, warned Smith, creates distances of such magnitude that we wonder what has happened in the intervals. No such fault, he added, could be found in the plays of Racine and Sophocles who were content to concentrate on one place.[36] But if Smith showed impatience with a work that lacked decorum or propriety, he applauded those productions that exemplified these traits. He thus placed John Dryden, Alexander Pope, and Thomas Gray upon pedestals because of the conciseness, beauty, harmony, and movement of their poetry. Pope, he held, was the "most correct, as well as the most elegant and harmonious of all the English poets." In Gray he recognized but one fault, namely that he wrote too little. Although he viewed Swift as basically more talented than these three poets because of his superior style and sentiment, he regretted that the articulate and clever doctor frequently descended to the level of "a gossiper writing for the entertainment of a private circle."[37]

Smith's lectures as reported in his students' notes are not, on the whole, well organized or profound. All too often he relied on the Roman rhetoricians and the neoclassicists to buttress his evaluations. Such a procedure led Wordsworth to say with biting sarcasm that Smith was "the worst critic, David Hume not excepted, that Scotland, a soil to which this sort of weed seems natural, has produced."[38] Yet Smith's importance as a major rhetorician is incontrovertible. His treatment of the ends of discourse, his rejection of commonplaces, his recognition of arguments from the essential nature of things, his stress on passions and sympathy, and, most of all, his belletristic methodology triggered the imagination of Hugh Blair who achieved permanent fame for his remarkably successful attempt to blend the best elements of rhetoric and poetics.

THE RHETORIC OF HUGH BLAIR

In 1759, eleven years after Smith delivered his first public lectures, Lord Kames assisted Hugh Blair in setting up a similar series of discourses. Though the initial lectures were presented at the University of Edinburgh, no college credit was given. In the following year, the Town Council appointed Blair Professor of Rhetoric, making his course a recognized part of the college curriculum.[39] It was not until 1762, however, that he officially received the title of Regius Professor of Rhetoric and Belles Lettres. After serving in this capacity for more than twenty years, Blair retired in 1783, and immediately thereafter published his *Lectures on Rhetoric and Belles Lettres.* This work was, for the most part, a reproduction of the discussions he had delivered at the University since 1759. Blair explains in the preface that many students, relying on superficial notes, were circulating imperfect copies of his lectures. The purpose of the volume, therefore, was to give to the public an accurate account of his teachings.[40]

When Blair's lectures appeared, they received a warm reception. Schools in England and America introduced them into their curricula, and within a short time "half of the educated English-speaking world studied" the rhetorical theories of Blair with approbation.[41] The immediate reaction proved more than a passing fancy. From the beginning the public demand was so great that the first edition was followed by many other editions in England, in America, and on the continent. From 1783 to 1873, sixty-two complete editions and fifty-one abridgments were published. In addition, there were ten translations in French, Italian, Russian, and Spanish. Ten textbooks containing representative lectures were also used in English and American schools.

It is difficult to appreciate Blair's position as a rhetorician unless the extrinsic and intrinsic sources of his enormous popularity are understood.[42] The general resurgence of interest in culture and human nature, the restoration of rhetoric to its earlier status, and Blair's reputation as an eloquent divine, perceptive critic, and stylist were factors that contributed to the success of his *Lectures on Rhetoric and Belles Lettres*. But there were at least three other causes with still greater import. First, the organizational structure and educational philosophy were appealing to students who, with little prior background study, wanted a comprehensive, coherent, and rational overview of rhetoric, literature, and criticism. Taken in their entirety, Blair's lectures—forty-seven in all—were systematic discussions of five major subject areas. Five of the discourses dealt with criticism, taste, and genius; four with language; fifteen with style; ten with eloquence; and thirteen with literary themes such as poetry and historical and philosophical writing. The lectures begin with the construction of a base consisting of the ingredients of taste, and, then moving in an upward spiral, they survey the history of language and analyze the nature and constituent parts of style. In a total of twenty-four lectures, or slightly more than one half of the course, the foundation was laid for a consideration of eloquence and polite literature.

If Blair's hierarchical structure had popular appeal, so, too, did his pedagogical technique and pleasing style. He was pragmatic enough to realize that abstract statements lacking concrete evidence were, at best, dry and uninteresting. Consequently, whenever he made an important observation, he substantiated it with a specific example. The lectures, therefore, contain exemplary models from the works of leading authors past and present. Additionally, Blair expressed his ideas in language that exemplified the precision, propriety, and perspicuity he held to be essential to good style.

A second cause responsible for Blair's effectiveness was the fact that his brand of eclecticism epitomized the dynamic, developing nature of rhetoric. Determined to avoid the extremes of classicism on the one hand and excessive novelty on the other, he wanted to demonstrate the continuity as well as the changing aspects of rhetoric. He had come to believe that a rhetorical system grounded only in the classics was static and sterile, while one based exclusively on modernism was without historical roots. He met this challenge by bringing together "the best ancient and contemporary thought on rhetoric and belles lettres."[43] The influence of the Roman rhetoricians and Longinus is at all times evident. The lectures on the conduct of the discourse in all its parts, for example, are modern versions of the ideas of Cicero and Quintilian on organization; the sections on style incorporate many of the precepts of Quintilian; and the discussions on taste and sublimity reveal a keen awareness of Longinus' *On the Sublime*.[44] Similarly, Blair made frequent use of modern teachings. His analysis of the ends of discourse and his belief in the *conviction/persuasion* duality, the notion that a reader or listener could be convinced that a thing was true without feeling compelled to act on this belief, grew out of his reading of the faculty psychologists; his attack on the commonplaces (standardized arguments) and his acceptance of the managerial function of invention stemmed from contemporary theories of logic; his appreciation of the tenets of neoclassicism, romanticism, rationalism, and common sense philosophy shaped the direction of his critical theories; his partiality for Thomas Sheridan's emphasis on the natural method and the conversational pattern affected his recommendations on delivery; and his favorable response to the course structure outlined by Rollin and Smith gave him a philosophy and format that he could strive to perfect. The versatility and range which Blair displayed in making his lectures derivative constituted proof of the existence of an ongoing quality in rhetorical thought.

To suggest that Blair was primarily a masterful synthesizer of the ideas of others is to imply that he lacked originality.[45] A careful scrutiny of the lectures, however, yields compelling evidence to refute this claim. As a result, a third major factor contributing to Blair's popularity was his innovative treatment of key principles of rhetoric and criticism. He modified, for instance, the traditional practice of placing all forms of oratory in the categories of epideictic, deliberative, and judicial. He endorsed the classical concept of judicial eloquence, but combined demonstrative and deliberative speaking under one head which he called the eloquence of the public assembly, and added to these, the eloquence of the pulpit. He then discussed the purpose of each communication form and its rank in the trilogy. The first division of demonstrative speaking, which Blair designated special occasional oratory, has as its function to please. Judicial rhetoric has a higher aim, the convincing of the intellect. The supreme goal in communication, that of persuasion, characterizes the purpose of deliberative speaking and of pulpit oratory. In making a distinction between convincing and persuading, Blair affirmed his faith in the faculty psychology notion of a conviction-persuasion duality. In writing his essay on "pulpit oratory," moreover, he made one of his most original contributions to rhetorical theory. As a prominent minister in the Scottish Presbyterian Church, he knew first hand the problems confronting a preacher in preparing a sermon. Because the lecture he delivered on this theme was the result of an empirical study covering many years, it has permanent relevance.

Blair's handling of invention, though sketchy in detail, was, like his analysis of the nature and function of discourse, fresh and imaginative. He was innovative in the way he phrased his indictment against commonplaces, in his tendency to relate genius to inventive ability, and his attitude toward rules. The ancient doctrine of "Loci Communes" or topics, he felt, was of little aid to the speaker in preparing either the introduction or the line of reasoning. He supported the view by pointing out that "knowledge and science must furnish the materials that form the body and substance of any valuable composition."[46] To those who believed that knowledge of the commonplaces would increase their inventive talent, Blair recommended the reading of Aristotle, Cicero, and Quintilian. But when one is faced with the task of preparing a persuasive speech, he continued, he should disregard the ancient topics and concentrate on his subject. Blair clinched his argument with the following allusion: "Demosthenes, I dare say, consulted none of the loci, when he was inciting the Athenians to take arms against Philip; and where Cicero has had recourse to them, his orations are so much the worse on that account."[47]

Blair's discussion of invention was similar to his treatment of genius. Although these terms were not synonymous, they shared a similar meaning. To say that a man possesses genius, Blair asserted, is to imply that he has unusual inventive and creative

> George Saintsbury asserted that Blair "is to be very particularly commended for accepting to the full the important truth that 'Rhetoric' in modern times really means 'Criticism.'"

powers.[48] Invention, on the other hand, requires a thorough knowledge of the subject, and the ability to reason adequately concerning the theme. It is clear, then, that the man of genius has a greater capacity to analyze the particular problem.

A defect in genius or invention, Blair further held, cannot be supplied by art. The only source from which these powers can be derived is nature. All that rhetoric or art can do is to guide genius in the proper direction or to assist the speaker in arranging arguments that invention discovers. Because rhetorical rules, therefore, have little, if any, effect on the improvement of invention, Blair apparently felt justified in giving this subject a minimum amount of space in his lectures.

Many of the conclusions Blair reached, such as his recognition of the managerial nature of invention and the limited value of topics, were a part of the teachings of the epistemologists. But it was Blair's innovative approach in applying and phrasing these ideas that gave them a prominent place in the "new rhetoric" of the eighteenth century.

Blair must be credited, finally, with being one of the first modern writers to think of rhetoric as a form of criticism. Indeed, the lectures, to a large degree, are composed of a series of critical precepts pertaining to the arts of writing and speech. This preoccupation with criticism has motivated some recent authors to study Blair as a critic rather than a rhetorician. In sanctioning this method of approaching the study of communication, George Saintsbury asserted that Blair "is to be very particularly commended for accepting to the full the important truth that 'Rhetoric' in modern times really means 'Criticism.'"[49] If Saintsbury's assessment is correct, Blair is to be praised for his use of a critical method that was soundly conceived and executed. The principles he established and their application to nature and works of art constituted the base, as we have seen, upon which all of his judgments on taste derived. Refusing to limit himself to a single school of critical thought, he was part neoclassicist, part rationalist, part epistemologist, and part romanticist. His genius in drawing these varied philosophies together in an innovative and coherent manner gave to his lectures and to the belletristic movement an enduring fame seldom equaled in rhetorical history.[50]

Since Blair personifies the high degree of effectiveness associated with the belles lettres approach to rhetoric, we would like to single out several important concepts and recommendations he discussed which influenced the direction rhetoric was to take both in Europe and America for many years. First was his clear and concise treatment of taste—the rhetorical element forming the base upon which much of Blair's theory was constructed. Taste, which he described as "the power of receiving pleasure from the beauties of nature and of art,"[51] is a faculty of the mind common to all men and women and can be influenced by exercise and reason. Taste, like the body, responds to exercise. The role of exercise is particularly useful in sharpening one's taste. Before relating this principle to discourse, Blair, as the following excerpt shows, believed "that exercise is the chief source of improvement in all our faculties":

We see how acute the senses become in persons whose trade or business leads to nice exertions of them: Touch, for instance, becomes infinitely more exquisite in men whose employment requires them to examine the polish of bodies, than it is in others. They who deal in microscopical observations, or are accustomed to engrave on precious stones, acquire surprising accuracy of sight in discerning the minutest objects; and practice in attending to different flavours and tastes of liquors, wonderfully improves the power of distinguishing them, and of tracing their composition.

What is true of the influence of exercise on our physical senses is similarly applicable in the areas of rhetoric and criticism. In delineating this perspective, Blair notes that our taste may be refined by studying "the most approved models," by frequently examining the works "of the best authors," and by comparing "lower and higher degrees of the same beauties. . . ."

Taste is also influenced by reason. Although these qualities are separate faculties of the mind, they are closely related. Taste produces pleasure; reason explains the nature of that pleasure. It is the duty of reason to determine the accuracy of a production of nature. Whenever a pleasure derived from

nature or art is consonant with sound judgment, the taste is perfected.

Blair graphically shows in the ensuing paragraph how reason contributes importantly to our understanding of why we experience pleasure from a work of art, and why this, in turn, enhances our taste:

In reading . . . such a poem as the Aeneid a great part of our pleasure arises from the plan or story being well conducted, and all the parts joined together with probability and due connexion, from the characters being taken from nature, the sentiments being suited to the characters, and the style to the sentiments. The pleasure which arises from a poem so conducted, is felt or enjoyed by taste as an internal sense; but the discovery of this conduct in the poem is owing to reason; and the more that reason enables us to discover such propriety in the conduct, the greater will be our pleasure. We are pleased, through our natural sense of beauty. Reason shows us why, and upon what grounds we are pleased. . . .

That person who has elevated his or her taste to the highest potential level through exercise and reason, Blair goes on to say, produces two important characters of taste-delicacy and correctness. To have a delicate taste means to feel "strongly" and "accurately." Further, it makes it possible for one to see differences and distinctions, however slight, and to see a latent beauty or a small blemish that would escape the attention of others. Correctness of taste, which also implies delicacy, enables the critic to see logical connections, to perceive the comparative merit between two beauties, and to recognize counterfeit efforts. Blair puts it this way in summarizing the major characteristics of these two traits:

The power of delicacy is chiefly seen in discerning the true merit of a work; the power of correctness, in rejecting false pretensions to merit. Delicacy leans more to feeling; correctness, more to reason and judgment. The former is more the gift of nature; the latter, more the product of culture and art. Among the ancient critics, Longinus possessed most delicacy; Aristotle, most correctness. Among the moderns, Mr. Addison is a high example of delicate taste; Dean Swift . . . would perhaps have afforded the example of a correct one. . . .

> Taste produces pleasure; reason explains the nature of that pleasure.

Thus far we have probed the nature of taste and the characteristics that give refinement to this quality. Yet to be analyzed is Blair's answer to the following question which he raised at the end of Lecture II: "Is there anything that can be called a standard of taste by appealing to which we may distinguish between a good and bad taste?" Prior to giving a direct answer to this query, Blair provides a rationale for the discussion that will ensue. It is based upon the fact that to argue there is no standard of taste is tantamount to saying "that all tastes are equally good." Moreover, it further suggests that one would be justified in saying the taste of an uncultured person is as strong as that of a Longinus or an Addison; and that a journeyman newspaper reporter compares favorably to Tacitus as a historian. Since this position is untenable, Blair argues, we must conclude that one person's taste may be superior to another's; and that there is such a thing as a good and bad, and a right and wrong taste.

From this perspective, the discussion proceeds to a description of the role that diversity plays in the treatment of standards. The existence of divergent views with respect to multiple objects does not in and of itself mean that there is present a corruption of taste. It may imply instead that different preferences are characterized by similarly good taste. Blair illustrates this notion by drawing these comparisons: some may prefer poetry, others history; some comedy, others tragedy; and some a simple style, others an ornate one. The next two comparisons stress the impact that age and nationality may have on taste. The young, for example, may like "gay and sprightly compositions," while the old may prefer graver specimens of discourse. Finally, the people of one nation may respond warmly to passionate appeals, while those from another country are inclined towards "more correct and regular elegance both in description and sentiment."

Blair's description of diversity, as we have seen, has been concerned up to this point with different perspectives that may be held regarding a variety of objects. The situation changes significantly, however, when attitudes toward a single object are considered. If two observers look at a particular work of art, for instance, and one describes it as beautiful and the other calls it ugly, we have a "direct opposition of taste," not diversity. In discussing this condition, Blair repeated his earlier claim that one point of view "must be in the right," and the opposing perspective "in the wrong, unless that absurd paradox were allowed to hold, that all tastes are equally good and true."

In sum, Blair realized that taste is a fluctuating quality which varies with the nature and cultural background of an individual. It is quite conceivable that two people may react differently to the virtues of a given writer. One might be impressed by Virgil's style; another by his thought. Such differences are not inconsonant with reason. If, however, one denies the existence of any virtues in Virgil, then the views of the critics are diametrically opposed. Who is going to decide, in these cases, which judgment is the better? The response to this question, as will now be noted, is covered in the last section of Lecture II.

As Blair laid the groundwork for developing a meaningful standard for the judgment of taste, he advised us of the dangers of seeking to discover arbitrary principles that have scientific validity. We should turn instead, he suggested, to an analysis of human nature. To do so would lead us to conclude that a "just and true" taste is one "which coincides with the general sentiments of men."

If we use "reason and sound judgment" in the study of human nature, we will learn that taste at its highest incorporates appeals to the understanding and to our feelings as well. Here are some of the inferences, Blair tells us, that may be drawn from an analysis of our own intellect and emotions, and those of others:

- "Mankind universally" has a preference for a "simple and natural" style over an "artificial and affected" one.
- It believes that "a regular and well connected story" is superior "to loose and scattered narratives."
- It responds more favorably to a passionate description of a catastrophe than to an unmoving account.

At first glance, this standard for measuring the quality of taste appears to be overly general and simplistic. But it has the saving merit of being consistent with the overriding concern that British rhetoricians as a whole had in devising a rhetoric that has as its starting point the audience.

Blair's theory of taste is integrally connected to two additional qualities that commanded the attention of the belletristic scholars—sublimity and beauty. Indeed, these two qualities, he tells us, constitute the two main sources of the pleasure of taste.

Sublimity may be found in inanimate objects and in human nature. It implies vastness, force, and power. Nature, with its oceans, its heavens, and its infinite space, pleases the imagination. That which is most effective, however, is mighty power and strength. Ideas that express solemnity, obscurity, disorder, and, above all, the Supreme Being, exemplify force.

The sublime is often seen in human nature. A magnanimous or heroic spirit instills in the mind a feeling of admiration. When a story is told of a courageous warrior, the grandeur of character displayed usually produces the noblest form of pleasure. Sublimity in writing or speaking is characterized by simplicity, conciseness, and strength. The truly sublime passage is an expression of bold, pathetic thoughts in language that is not profuse nor superfluous, not bombastic nor frigid, but, at the same time, is sufficiently strong to give a clear and full impression of the object described.

Beauty is a calmer, but more lasting quality than the sublime. It is portrayed in nature in the form of color, figure, and motion. Color simply suggests these sensory stimuli that come to us through one source only, the structure of the eye. Figure is composed of two categories: regularity and variety. The truly beautiful object is one that combines regularity, variety, and motion. The human countenance is an excellent illustration of this pleasing combination.

In the next lecture Blair dealt with the related theme of criticism. The application of reason and good sense to the pleasures of nature and art (he said) is the criterion by which the merit of a production can be determined. True criticism, he further held, is not based on abstract reasoning; rather it is the result of a careful analysis of facts. To substantiate this belief, Blair pointed out that Aristotle's opinions concerning the three unities were formed after a thorough examination of the works of the great writers of antiquity. Criticism is an empirical art, therefore, which is never independent of facts and observations. In all, the purpose of critical rules is to help the writer or speaker avoid faults in his compositions; beyond this, criticism cannot go.

What Blair said on taste and criticism not only cuts to the heart of his rhetorical doctrine, but it lays the foundation for subsequent modern ideas on rhetoric grounded in judgment and evaluation. As a final consideration in our attempt to show the contemporaneity of several of Blair's major theories, we will now summarize what we perceive to be the advice he would give to twentieth-century students of rhetoric enrolled in American colleges and universities. The suggestions presented here are derived primarily from that portion of Lecture XIX dealing with "Directions for forming a Proper Style," and from Lecture XXXIV focusing on "Means of Improving in Eloquence."

The Modern Age

Before summarizing Blair's recommendations, however, let us review briefly the challenging situation he would find in the last decade of twentieth-century America. Unlike his own era in which the fortunate few were sent to the university and the vast majority of the citizenry were illiterate, he would be shocked with the magnitude of college enrollments. But he would feel quite at home with the visible desire for educated persons to be able to read, write, and speak effectively. At the same time he would not be surprised to learn that the goal of achieving widespread student proficiency in basic communication skills had fallen far short of the mark.

Here is what Blair would soon come to know. A 1977 nationwide poll of 4,400 college faculty members employed at 161 colleges and universities indicated that a sizable majority find their students "seriously underprepared" in oral and written communication.[52] Additionally a midwestern university student newspaper reported that four out of ten incoming freshmen were unable to write a coherent paragraph and must consequently enroll in remedial English. In the twenty-three years that have passed since these surveys were completed, numerous studies, such as those sponsored by the Princeton University Testing Services, indicate that these disturbing conditions have steadily worsened.

As an eighteenth-century visitor to modern America, Blair would have difficulty in understanding the role that the electronic media would play in

> Sublimity in writing or speaking is characterized by simplicity, conciseness, and strength.

> The application of reason and good sense to the pleasures of nature and art (he said) is the criterion by which the merit of a production can be determined.

causing a sharp decline in the quality of communication practice. Among the data that would come to his attention are the following:

- American preschool children "watch television 6,000 hours before they spend a single hour in the classroom."[53]
- By the time students "graduate from high school, they will have spent 16,000 hours in front of television sets and only 11,000 hours in the classroom."[54]
- An increasing number of United States citizens rely on television as their principal information source.
- The television viewer is a passive observer who typically turns on the tube to amuse himself rather than to engage his mind.
- Thirty and sixty second television advertisements endlessly repeated have more staying power than an in-class discussion of an eloquent speech or a thoughtful essay by renowned political and literary leaders.
- It is faster and easier to call by telephone than to take the time to compose a letter.

These facts doubtless would cause Blair to reflect that time spent in this way is time taken away from standard communication-oriented activities such as reading, writing, speaking, or critical listening.

More disturbing to Blair than the deleterious effect of the electronic media on communication skills would be the knowledge that the current tendency to endorse the "social pass" in the public school system ultimately means that a high school diploma is more a certificate of attendance than a measure of achievement. But he would take comfort in learning from the *Chronicle of Higher Education* that the thirty-four high schools nationwide whose test averages have not dramatically declined in the past ten years have continued to require basic instruction in communication.

Against this background that would prove both familiar and strange to Blair, he would deliver his universal and timely lecture on forming a good style and in improving eloquence. The presentation would proceed in the following vein.

The effective writer should begin with clear ideas. Not to know what one means to say is to guarantee reader confusion. If it takes several drafts of an essay before the author has satisfied himself on this point, so be it. Further, the student writer needs practice, the more the better. Admittedly, English composition classes are costly to the university because they must necessarily be small in size; yet how else can sustained individual attention be ensured? Also of importance is the need to read the best literary works available. In doing so, however, the prospective communicator should avoid slavish imitation, for a good written style is a personal asset nontransferable to others.

It is necessary, Blair continues, to adapt ideas to a specific target audience; thus a speaker or writer should consider the purpose and the occasion. In adhering to these suggestions, one should remember that thought precedes style; substance comes before form or ornamentation. The goal at all times should be correctness, precision, propriety, and lastly, polish.

In turning to a consideration of methods for achieving eloquence, Blair prescribes a similar pattern. First of all, a beginning speaker, he says, should put forth his best effort by reading and studying widely, and striving never to be at a loss for selecting an appealing subject. Once this is done the following rules should prove helpful:

1. Speak regularly and often for speakers require practice every bit as much as do athletes.
2. Study the best models, not necessarily those you hear most frequently.
3. Learn from the mistakes of others.
4. Let your aim be verbal fluency; do not be governed by a set of mechanical rules as a grammarian is.
5. Remember that repetition is both necessary and appropriate in oral discourse for a listener cannot re-read.

Notwithstanding the fact that the above advice was first given at the University of Edinburgh during the time of the American Revolution, there can be little doubt concerning its continuing relevance for modern students. The college senior who misspells words in his letter of application or reveals himself to be inarticulate in a job interview will learn the hard way that few skills in our society are more valuable and useful than those which involve communication.

Notes

1. James L. Golden and Edward P.J. Corbett, Jr., eds. *The Rhetoric of Blair, Campbell, and Whately* (New York: Holt, Rinehart and Winston, Inc., 1968), p. 5.
2. *Ibid.*
3. A. Bosker, *Literary Criticism in the Age of Johnson,* 2nd ed. (New York: Hafner Publishing Co., 1952), pp. 1–7.
4. Jonathan Swift, "The Battle of the Books," in Sir Walter Scott, ed., *The Works of Jonathan Swift,* 19 vols. (Boston: Houghton Mifflin and Co., 1883), X, pp. 21–25.
5. "A Tale of the Tub," in *ibid.,* p. 124.
6. *Ibid.,* p. 136.
7. *Ibid.,* p. 120.
8. Arthur Murphy, ed., *The Works of Samuel Johnson,* 12 vols. (London: Thomas Tegg, et. al. 1824), XI, p. 176.
9. Alexander Pope, "Essay on Criticism," in *Works,* 10 vols. (London: C. and J. Rivington, 1824), V, pp. 68–69.
10. *Ibid.,* pp. 118–24.
11. *Ibid.,* pp. 130–38.
12. John Lawson, *Lectures Concerning Oratory* (Dublin: George Faulkner, 1758). For a detailed analysis of Lawson's rhetorical theories, see Ray E. Keesey, "The Rhetorical Theory of John Lawson," Ph.D. Dissertation, The Ohio State University, 1950.
13. W.P. Sandford, *English Theories of Public Address, 1530–1828* (Columbus, Ohio, 1931), p. 110. For Ward's full work, see A *System of Oratory,* 2 vols. (London: John Ward, 1759).
14. Warren Guthrie, "Rhetorical Theory in Colonial America," in Karl Wallace, ed., *History of Speech Education in America* (New York: Appleton-Century-Crofts, Inc., 1954), p. 54.
15. *On the Sublime,* 1.4.
16. *Ibid.,* VIII.I.
17. *Ibid.,* XXXVI.1.–2.
18. Richard Hurd, ed., *The Works of the Right Honorable Joseph Addison,* 6 vols. (London: T. Cadell and W. Davies, Strand, 1811), IV, p. 340.
19. *Ibid.,* p. 330.
20. For a brief but penetrating overview of Baillie's philosophy, see Samuel H. Monk, *The Sublime* (Ann Arbor: The University of Michigan Press, 1960), pp. 73–77.
21. Edmund Burke, *The Works and Correspondence of the Right Honourable Edmund Burke,* 8 vols. (London: Francis and John Rivington, 1852), II, pp. 566–77.
22. *Ibid.,* pp. 598–620.
23. *Ibid.,* p. 679.
24. Monk, p. 87.
25. Alexander Gerard, *An Essay on Taste,* Walter J. Hipple, ed. (Gainesville, Fla.: Scholars-Facsimilies & Reprints, 1963), p. 95.
26. *Ibid.,* p. 249.
27. *Ibid.,* p. 166.
28. Charles Rollin, *The Method of Teaching and Studying the Belles Lettres,* 4 vols. (London: A. Bettesworth and C. Hitch, 1734).
29. *Ibid.,* I, p. 63.
30. Most of these discussions appear in volume II.
31. *Ibid.,* I, A 2.
32. Adam Smith, *Lectures on Rhetoric and Belles Lettres,* John M. Lothian, ed. (London: Thomas Nelson, 1963), p. 140.
33. Adam Smith, *The Theory of Moral Sentiments* (London: A Millar, 1759), p. 257.
34. *Lectures on Justice, Police, Revenue and Arms,* Edward Cannan, ed. (New York: Kelly & Millman, 1956), p. 171.
35. See Walter Jackson Bate, ed., *Criticism: The Major Texts* (New York, 1952).
36. Smith, *Lectures on Rhetoric and Belles Lettres,* p. 119.
37. James Anderson, *The Bee or Literary Weekly Intelligencer, consisting of original Pieces and Selections from Performances of Merit, Foreign and Domestic,* 18 vols. (London, 1791), III, p. 4.
38. William Wordsworth, "Essay Supplementary to Preface," in Charles W. Eliot, ed., *Prefaces and Prologues to Famous Books* (New York, 1909), p. 338 n. For more favorable views of Smith's contributions as a rhetorician, see the following essays: Vincent Bevilacqua, "Philosophical Influences in the Development of English Rhetorical Theory, 1748 to 1783," *Proceedings of the Leeds Philosophical and Literary Society Literary and Historical* Section, XII (April, 1968), pp. 191–215; Bevilacqua, "Adam Smith and Some Philosophical Origins of Eighteenth-Century Rhetorical Theory," *The Modern Language Review,* 63 (July, 1968), pp. 559–68; and Wilbur S. Howell, "Adam Smith's Lectures on

Rhetoric: An Historical Assessment," *Speech Monographs, XXXVI* (November, 1969), pp. 393–418.

39. Sir Alexander Grant, *The Story of the University of Edinburgh,* 2 vols. (London: Longman, Green and Company, 1884), I, p. 276. For an informative essay on the history of this chair, see Henry W. Meikle. "The Chair of Rhetoric and Belles Lettres in the University of Edinburgh." *University of Edinburgh Journal,* XIII (1945), pp. 89–103.

40. Hugh Blair, *Lectures on Rhetoric and Belles Lettres* (Philadelphia: T. Ellwood Zell, 1862), p. 3.

41. William Charvat, *The Origins of American Critical Thought,* 1810–1835, (Philadelphia: University of Pennsylvania Press, 1936), p. 44.

42. For an analysis of these influences, see Douglas Ehninger and James L. Golden, "The Intrinsic Sources of Blair's Popularity," *The Southern Speech Journal,* XXI (Fall, 1955), pp. 12–30; and "The Extrinsic Sources of Blair's Popularity," *The Southern Speech Journal,* XXII (Fall, 1956), pp. 16–32.

43. Robert Schmitz, *Hugh Blair* (New York: King's Crown Press, 1948), p. 66.

44. Blair's view on sublimity and taste also reflect the teachings of Burke and Gerard.

45. As late as 1948, one of the authors expressed the prevailing view concerning Blair's status as a rhetorician in the following manner: ". . . it is clear that the *Lectures on Rhetoric and Belles Lettres,* for the most part, is not an original work. Many writers have condemned Blair for his lack of originality." James L. Golden, "The Rhetorical Theory and Practice of Hugh Blair," M.A. thesis, The Ohio State University, 1948, p. 167.

46. Blair, *Lectures on Rhetoric and Belles Lettres,* p. 11.

47. *Ibid.,* p. 354.

48. *Ibid.,* p. 29.

49. George Saintsbury, *A History of Criticism and Literary Taste in Europe,* 3 vols. (New York: Dodd, Mead, and Company, 1902), II, p. 462.

50. Blair's long range influence may be seen in D. Josef Gomez Hermosilla, *Arte De Hablar, En Prosa Y Verso* (Paris: Liberia De Gamier Hermanos, 1866). This volume, first published in 1842 and revised in 1866, relies so heavily on Blair that the author confesses he often actually uses the words that appear in the *Lectures on Rhetoric and Belles Lettres;* and he does so without the use of quotation marks in many instances.

51. All quotations on Blair's theory of taste are drawn from Lecture II. See *Lectures on Rhetoric and Belles Lettres,* pp. 16–26.

52. E.C. Ladd, Jr., and S.M. Lipset, "The Faculty Mood: Pessimism is Predominant," *The Chronicle of Higher Education,* October 3, 1977, p. 14.

53. Ernest L. Boyer and Arthur Levine, *A Quest for Common Learning: The Aims of General Education* (Washington, D.C.: Carnegie Foundation, 1981), p. 37.

54. *Ibid.*

The Epistemologists

We place those authors in the psychological-philosophical or epistemological school of thought whose principal concern was to relate communication theory to the basic nature of man. With determination and skill, reinforced by painstaking research in the natural and social sciences, they set for themselves the task of unraveling the mystery of man's mind and soul. Notwithstanding the fact that their fame was derived primarily from writings generally associated with psychology and philosophy, these epistemologists left an indelible imprint upon the direction rhetoric was to take for generations to come.

Our discussion of this trend will be divided into two parts. First we will deal with four great innovators of Western thought who made their contributions during the period from 1600 to 1725: Francis Bacon, René Descartes, John Locke, and Giambattista Vico. What these great thinkers had to say about the knowledge in general and communication theory in particular remains provocative and challenging to contemporary students.

We then move on to the 18th Century Epistomologists

> **The Four Innovators**
> **1600–1725**
> ■ Francis Bacon
> ■ René Descartes
> ■ John Locke
> ■ Giambattista Vico

THE FOUR INNOVATORS, 1600–1725

Francis Bacon

Shortly after Copernicus made the startling discovery that the earth with clockwise precision rotates around the sun; his European followers—including Kepler, Gilbert, Galileo, Bacon, Descartes, and Boyle—initiated a scientific movement that challenged the classical preoccupation with deduction, and stressed the value of an experimental method based on the inductive process. Of this group of modern thinkers, Bacon and Descartes had the most impact on rhetoric. Described as "the greatest poet of science" and the "herald of the scientific movement," Bacon, who had come to realize the importance of the recent discoveries—"printing, gunpowder, and the compass"—recommended to his contemporaries "a total reform of human knowledge, a true advancement of learning, and a revolution in the conditions of life."[1] Convinced that progress was an inherent principle of life, he sketched in 1605 a philosophy of optimism in his first monumental work, the "Advancement of Learning." In this treatise may be found Bacon's innovative discussion of the faculties of the mind.[2] "The parts of human learning," he argued, "have reference to the three parts of Man's Understanding which is the seat of learning: History to his Memory, Poesy to his Imagination, and Philosophy to his Reason."[3] To the faculties of understanding, reason, imagination, and memory, he then added will and appetite. These categories explaining the mind of man led to Bacon's celebrated statement that "the duty and office of Rhetoric is to *apply Reason* to *Imagination* for the better moving of the will."[4]

An integral part of Bacon's rhetorical theory was his concept of invention. Unlike the ancients, he played down the role of discovery in the formulation of arguments and the gathering of source data, emphasizing instead the element of "remembrance." A speaker, in effect, reaches back into his memory to summon forth knowledge that he already knows; then he applies it to the rhetorical situation at hand.[5]

How, it might be asked, does the communicator get the knowledge that is to be stored in the memory for appropriate use in a given situation? Bacon's response to this question is both traditional and original. He is strikingly similar to the classical scholars in suggesting that knowledge may be obtained from general and special or particular topics. But he is innovative in his discussion of four commonplaces as aids to invention. The first, he calls *Colours of Good and Evil.* "The persuader's labour," Bacon argues, "is to make things appear good or evil, and that in higher or lower degree. . . ."[6] To assist potential speakers in the use of this commonplace, Bacon provided a "Table of Colours or appearances of Good and Evil" which contains shades of meaning and a list of possible accompanying fallacies associated with a particular argument.[7] Since the commonplace of "Colours of Good and Evil" often deals with premises that appear on the surface to be true, Bacon warns us to examine such claims critically. Consider, for instance, the following statement: "What men praise and honour is good; what they dispraise and condemn is evil." At first glance the thought expressed in this argument seems to be a high level "good" grounded in the idea that public sentiment is infallible. But to Bacon this argument is a sophism which deceives people by appealing to their ignorance, factional spirit, prejudices, and "natural disposition" to "praise and blame."[8]

The second commonplace, which is labeled "antitheta," consists of theses which may be argued pro and con. In his *De augmentis,* Bacon lists forty-seven theses expressed both in affirmative and negative terms. Similar to a modern day debate brief, this technique helps the advocate answer possible objections to his claims; it is also useful in making decisions. Assume, for example, that we are confronted with the difficult and challenging task of rendering a decision on a controversial issue. If we use Bacon's method of "antitheta," we might take a sheet of paper, draw a vertical line down the middle of the page, and then place the affirmative contentions on the left side and the negative counter claims on the right. By weighing all of the arguments for and against, Bacon implies, we should be able to reach a thoughtful conclusion.

"Formulae" constitute a third type of commonplace or aid to invention. They are "small parts of a

speech, fully composed and ready for use. . . ."[9] They may take the form of a stock phrase, sentence, or paragraph designed to serve as a transition or summary; or a humorous thrust devised for the purpose of blunting the attack or image of an adversary. Here Bacon, perhaps drawing upon his own rich experience in law courts and in Parliament, illustrates how "formulae" may be employed to diminish the impact of an opponent's argument. "When one's adversary declares, 'you go from the matter,' you reply: 'But it was to follow you.' When he demands that 'you come to the point,' you answer: 'Why, I shall not find you there.' If he says, 'You take more than is for granted,' you retort: 'You grant less than is proved.'"[10] Admittedly, such examples appear contrived and artificial. But this kind of rhetorical strategy is still prevalent in contemporary political, forensic, and religious discourse.

The fourth and final commonplace discussed by Bacon is that of *"apothegms."* These are "pointed speeches" or pithy statements which may be "interlaced in continued speech" or "recited upon occasion of themselves." Like salt, they can be "sprinkled where you will."[11] In compiling a list of "apothegms," Bacon alluded to the classics, British and continental history, and to his own works. The ensuing examples are representative:

> These categories explaining the mind of man led to Bacon's celebrated statement that "the duty and office of Rhetoric is to *apply Reason* to *Imagination* for the better moving of the will."

- When the oracle of Delphi pronounced Socrates to be the wisest man in Greece, Socrates is reputed to have said: "I am not wise, and know it; others are not wise, and know it not."
- "Queen Isabella of Spain used to say, 'Whosoever hath a good presence and a good fashion, carries continual letters of recommendation.'"[12]

Nor was Bacon content to describe the nature and utility of the commonplaces; he also gave three useful hints for collecting them. First, he asserted, we should *observe* the world around us, taking special note of particular instances, similarities and contrasts in events, and the "utterances of others."[13] Secondly, we should *converse* freely in order to generate fresh insights. The well-known political leaders—Charles James Fox of the eighteenth century and Robert Kennedy of our own—relied on this method, more than any other, for gaining the knowledge needed to cope with knotty domestic and international problems. Thirdly, Bacon adds, we should *study* widely, especially in the area of history.

Bacon next turns to a consideration of how to record the data gathered from the process of observing, conversing, and studying. His advice was the use of commonplace "note books or phrase books." To make certain that the source material in these books be etched in the memory, Bacon suggested: "One man's notes will little profit another. . . ."[14] The act of writing one's own notes, he felt, contributed importantly to the practice of recall. Among those contemporary figures we have known who used a commonplace book for preparation of speeches was John F. Kennedy.

Perhaps more vital in appreciating Bacon's contribution to knowledge is to examine his analysis of sense perception. Motivated by a desire to establish progressive stages of certainty, he rejected the widely practiced inductive method that moved from particular instances to general premises, and then proceeded to "judgment and the discovery of middle axioms." Instead, he observed, we should derive "axioms from the senses and particulars, rising by a gradual and unbroken ascent, so that it arrives at the most general axioms last of all."[15] Bacon's interest in psychology led him to conclude that faulty sense perception could hinder man's quest for establishing reliable and valid conclusions through the method of induction. He was particularly concerned with the need to clear the human mind of four potential fallacies which he called the "Idols of the Tribe," "Idols of the Cave," "Idols of the Market Place," and "Idols of the Theatre."[16] These terms used to designate the fallacies were both novel and meaningful. The "Idols of the Tribe" represented the inherent limitations in the general nature of man. As a whole, suggested Bacon, mankind shared a homogeneous spirit that often exemplifies obsessions, narrowness, restlessness, and excessive emotionality. Moreover it is a spirit formed in part by an inadequate response to sense messages that may be blurred or inaccurate. Thus it is wrong, asserted Bacon, to argue "that the sense of man is the measure of things."[17]

If the "Idols of the Tribe" stem from human nature itself as seen in the generality of man, the "Idols of the Cave" are derived from those unique qualities and experiences of the individual man. One's basic personality, intellectual capacity, educational training, occupation, or value system may serve as "a cave or den of his own, which refracts, and discolours the light of nature."[18] The life style that results from these elements significantly affects an individual's attempt to interpret his sense impressions.

Not only is a man influenced by his general and particular nature, but by his close associations with others in the "Market Place." Here Bacon, anticipating the twentieth-century semanticist, warned of the pitfalls confronting those who failed to use words with precision and care while communicating with others. Such writers and speakers, he said, confuse words with things, and hastily conceived definitions with reality. This idol, consequently, is the most troublesome fallacy because "the ill and unfit choice of words wonderfully obstructs the understanding."[19]

The final idol, that of the Theatre, describes how untested information that has "immigrated into men's minds from the various dogmas of philosophy, and also from wrong laws of demonstration," are "but so many stage plays, representing worlds of their own creation after an unreal and scenic fashion."[20] Bacon used this idol to attack those philosophical systems that have been handed down from generation to generation with no effort on the part of the recipients to apply scientific criteria for the purpose of judging their validity.

To conclude his perceptive analysis of the idols, Bacon stressed its meaning for his theory of knowledge. Since his purpose was to construct an epistemological system that would lead men to an earthly kingdom "founded on the sciences," he saw the idols

> Bacon's interest in psychology led him to conclude that faulty sense perception could hinder man's quest for establishing reliable and valid conclusions through the method of induction. He was particularly concerned with the need to clear the human mind of four potential fallacies which he called the "Idols of the Tribe," "Idols of the Cave," "Idols of the Market Place," and "Idols of the Theatre."

as barriers that would block the entrance. Thus these fallacies "must be renounced and put away with a fixed and solemn determination, and the understanding thoroughly freed and cleansed." In fine, man in search of scientific certainty must assume the purity and simplicity of a little child which Christianity holds to be essential for "entrance into the kingdom of heaven."[21]

To gain further insight into Bacon's notions on the Idols, consider the following passage drawn from his *Novum organum:*

There are four classes of Idols which beset men's minds. To these for distinction's sake I have assigned names—calling the first class Idols of the Tribe; *the second,* Idols of the Cave; *the third,* Idols of the Marketplace; *the fourth,* Idols of the Theatre.

The formulation of ideas and axioms by true induction is no doubt the proper remedy to be applied for the keeping off and clearing away of idols. To point them out, however, is of great use; for the doctrine of Idols is to the interpretation of Nature what the doctrine of the refutation of Sophisms is to common logic.

The Idols of the Tribe have their foundation in human nature itself, and in the tribe or race of men. For it is a false assertion that the sense of man is the measure of things. On the contrary, all perceptions as well of the sense as of the mind are according to the measure of the universe. And the human understanding is like a false mirror, which, receiving rays irregularly, distorts and discolours the nature of things by mingling its own nature with it.

The Idols of the Cave are the idols of the individual man. For everyone (besides the errors common to human nature in general) have a cave or den of his own, which refracts and discolours the light of nature; owing either to his own proper and peculiar nature; or to his education and conversation with others; or to the reading of books, and the authority of those whom he esteems and admires; or to the differences of impressions, accordingly as they take place in a mind preoccupied and predisposed or in a mind indifferent and settled; or the like. So that the spirit of man (according as it is meted out to different individuals) is in fact a thing variable and full of perturbation, and governed as it were by chance. Whence it was

well observed by Heraclitus that men look for sciences in their own lesser worlds, and not in the greater or common world.

There are also idols formed by the intercourse and association of men with each other, which I call Idols of the Marketplace, on account of the commerce and consort of men there. For it is by discourse that men associate; and words are imposed according to the apprehension of the vulgar. And therefore the ill and unfit choice of words wonderfully obstructs the understanding. Nor do the definitions or explanations wherewith in some things learned men are wont to guard and defend themselves, by any means set the matter right. But words plainly force and overrule the understanding, and throw all into confusion, and lead men away into numberless empty controversies and idle fancies.

Lastly, there are idols which have immigrated into men's minds from the various dogmas of philosophies, and also from wrong laws of demonstration. These I call Idols of the Theatre; because in my judgment all the received systems are but so many stage-plays, representing worlds of their own creation after an unreal and scenic fashion. Nor is it only of the systems now in vogue, or only of the ancient sects and philosophies, that I speak; for many more plays of the same kind may yet be composed and in like artificial manner set forth; seeing that errors the most widely different have nevertheless causes for the most part alike. Neither again do I mean this only of entire systems, but also of many principles and axioms in science, which by tradition, credulity, and negligence have come to be received.

Two other aspects of Bacon's philosophy are not without significance for the role they played in helping to mold eighteenth-century rhetorical theory. First was his rejection of the syllogism as a productive means for establishing principles. That the syllogism with its emphasis on opinion and probability and its usefulness in checking reasoning was important to popular arts such as rhetoric, Bacon was willing to admit. Indeed, he, like Aristotle, recognized the function of topics and commonplaces in constructing arguments. But he excluded the syllogism as a part of his scientific method on the grounds that it had little correspondence to the essential nature of things. He put it this way in his essay on "The Great Instauration," written in 1620—fifteen years after "The Advancement of Learning."

The syllogism consists of propositions; propositions of words; and words are the tokens and signs of notions. Now if the very notions of the mind. . . be improperly and overhastily abstracted from facts, vague, not sufficiently definite, faulty in short in many ways, the whole edifice tumbles. I therefore reject the syllogism; and that not only as regards principles. . . but also as regards middle propositions; which, although obtainable no doubt by the syllogism, are, when so obtained, barren of works, remote from practice, and altogether unavailable for the active department of the sciences. Although therefore I leave to the syllogism and these famous and boasted modes of demonstration their jurisdiction over popular arts and such as are matter of opinion (in which department I leave all as it is), yet in dealing with the nature of things I use induction throughout, and that in the minor propositions as well as the major. For I consider induction to be that form of demonstration which upholds the sense, and closes with nature, and comes to the very brink of operation, if it does not actually deal with it.[22]

In later discussions we will observe how Bacon's reservations concerning the syllogism prepared the way for similar attacks by Descartes, Locke, Hume, and Campbell.

Secondly, it is instructive to note that Bacon was among the early English prose authors who sought to replace the copious style, then in vogue, with a language control featuring Attic simplicity. He was content to break with the Elizabethan tradition even though it led to a "schizm of eloquence" because of his conviction that scientific ideas may best be expressed in a clear, unadorned style.[23] Bacon thus contributed importantly to the doctrine of perspicuity that was to become a benchmark of eighteenth-century rhetorical thought.

Bacon's pioneering theories set into motion a movement toward a new empiricism that achieved focus and symbolic effect in the experimental studies of the Royal Society. In his history of the Society published in the 1660s, Thomas Sprat eulogized Bacon for providing the inspiration and direction of his "Enterprize, as it is now set on foot. . . ."[24] Ad-

ditionally he praised him for his cogent defense of "Experimental Philosophy" and his model of excellence in style. Sprat's assessment of Bacon's accomplishments has been widely shared by subsequent writers.

René Descartes

While the theories of Bacon and the Royal Society were being disseminated throughout England, similar probings into the nature of man and methods of study were taking place in France. These inquiries began in earnest in 1637 with the publication of Descartes' celebrated *Discourse on Method*. Partly autobiographical, this study contains the heart of Descartes' philosophy. He relates that when he had completed his studies, he resolved to devote his remaining years to an analysis of himself rather than to the reading of books. By then, however, Descartes already had formed strong convictions concerning branches of learning that were a part of the humane tradition. He regarded "eloquence highly, and was in raptures with poesy (i.e. poetry)," but thought that "both were gifts of nature rather than fruits of study."[25] He complained that the syllogism was incapable of investigating the unknown and separating truth from error. It was, instead, useful only in communicating "what we already know."[26] Most of all, he was "delighted with the mathematics, on account of the certitude and evidence of their reasonings."[27] The remarkable similarity between these views and those expressed by George Campbell in his *Philosophy of Rhetoric* will be observed later.

This preference for mathematical certainty as opposed to syllogistic probability may be seen in Descartes' four-fold study method. With unwavering resolution he was determined to accept only those claims which could be verified with proof containing no ground for doubt; to divide all difficult aspects of a subject into as many segments as possible; to follow a pattern of inquiry utilizing a climactic order and a cause to effect sequence; and to use an all-inclusive system of enumeration that prevents omissions.[28]

Central to Descartes' study design was his faith in the power of reason to determine truth and to discipline the imagination. The mind of man, he suggested, was capable of reaching unchallenged conclusions such as: "I think, therefore I am"; and "God exists." Similarly the mind had the ability to regulate the senses in such a way that the fallacy of the idols could be brought under control. Like Bacon, he further believed in an advancement of learning made possible for an enlightened society through the means of experiments.[29] But he went beyond his predecessor's grasp of understanding abstract scientific principles and in appreciating the full implications of rationalism for the experimental process.[30]

Despite his apparent indebtedness to Bacon, Descartes was, in many respects, unique and prophetic. In arguing that experiment takes precedence over disputation, inquiry over communication, and action over speculation, he broke with the logicians of the past.[31] His mathematical contribution to science and his stress on reasoning enabled him to make bold predictions "which became the assumptions of nineteenth-century science."[32] This overall impact prompted Leon Roth to observe that the *Discourse on Method* "marks an epoch. It is a dividing line in the history of thought. Everything that came before it is old; everything that came after it is new."[33] What is more relevant for this study is the fact that Descartes' work influenced the direction and thrust of the French Academy and, indeed, became a textbook for the Port-Royal logicians and rhetoricians who, in turn, influenced British thought.

Descartes' impact on later scholars can best be seen by turning to the publication of the second edition of Arnauld and Nicole's *Logique of Port-Royal.* This provocative edition contained from the beginning to end the cardinal tenets of Cartesian philosophy and shook the foundations of traditional rhetorical theory. With Descartes and Boileau, Arnauld and Nicole held that truth is the transcendent goal in life. Thus the only acceptable communication model is one which adheres to the principles of geometry requiring demonstration based on clear definitions, axioms, and cause to effect relations. In such a system there could be no place for the scholastic art of syllogizing, commonplaces which substitute verisimili-

> Central to Descartes' study design was his faith in the power of reason to determine truth and to discipline the imagination. The mind of man, he suggested, was capable of reaching unchallenged conclusions such as: "I think, therefore I am"; and "God exists."

> Locke concluded that since the mind has the power to *perceive* and *prefer,* it must be comprised of two major faculties, the understanding and the will.

tude for reality, or highly emotional appeals. Nor was there a need for a method of expression or invention because of man's natural facility in these areas. In short, since rhetoric cannot produce truth it is, at best, relegated to the simple task of communicating principles that logic and experimentation can discover.[34] These views, as we shall later note, produced a strong counter response from the brilliant Italian scholar, Giambattista Vico.

John Locke

Many of the ideas of Bacon and Descartes, as well as those of the members of the French Academy and Royal Society, found eloquent expression in John Locke's monumental *Essay Concerning Human Understanding* written in 1690. To a large extent Locke succeeded in summarizing the central features of seventeenth-century scientific thought. Additionally, however, he presented novel and penetrating insights into the nature of man. Although Locke is well known for his claim that rhetoric was a "powerful Instrument of Error and Deceit,"[35] he had a positive influence on the psychological-philosophical theories of discourse that evolved in the eighteenth century, culminating in Campbell's *Philosophy of Rhetoric.* Of the many concepts included in Locke's *Essay,* four have special meaning for students of rhetorical theory. They are his treatment of the faculties of the mind, association of ideas, pathetic proof, and the syllogism.

Locke concluded that since the mind has the power to *perceive* and *prefer,* it must be comprised of two major faculties, the understanding and the will.[36] In explaining the nature of the faculty of understanding, Locke developed his famous theory of ideas. Reflection upon sensory experience, he observed, produces ideas which are, in turn, held together in a meaningful pattern through the talent of the mind to trace relationships that show natural correspondence and connection. Reason likewise enables us to unite ideas that are apparently unrelated by relying on the laws of association. Here we may observe from past experiences that whenever a particular idea reaches the understanding an "associate appears with it." Under such conditions, the doctrine of association permits us to connect these concepts so that they will form an inseparable unit in our minds.[37]

Locke's thesis caused him to reject the syllogism on the grounds that it neither demonstrates nor strengthens the connection that two ideas may have with each other. Nor does it advance an argument or lead to moral truth. The power of inference, a gift presented to man by God, makes it possible for us to perceive associations and to determine whether or not ideas are coherent or incoherent. Thus the understanding, concludes Locke, "is not taught to reason" by the "methods of syllogizing."[38] Quite clearly Locke gave a new dimension to the reservations pertaining to the syllogism articulated by Bacon, Descartes, and the Port-Royal logicians.

As one of the early proponents of faculty psychology, Locke came to believe that an idea which reaches the understanding does not necessarily have the power to motivate the will. The rational process, he argued, must be reinforced by a pathetic appeal that ultimately becomes the major determinant of action. All of the emotions have one common element which Locke called "uneasiness," and described as the absence of some good. Whenever the mind experiences "uneasiness," it feels pain and generates the compelling desire to remove it. The will, in short, may be influenced when the passions are stirred, for the arousal of an emotion inevitably causes pain. There is little opportunity for persuasion, however, if the mind is at ease since the desire for happiness has already been achieved.[39] To some extent Locke's views anticipated the twentieth-century theory of cognitive dissonance.[40]

Giambattista Vico

By the time Locke's probings into the human mind had attracted attention in England and on the continent, another European epistemologist, the Italian rhetorician and social scientist Giambattista Vico was elaborating his theory of ideas at the University

> Locke's thesis caused him to reject the syllogism on the grounds that it neither demonstrates nor strengthens the connection that two ideas may have with each other.

of Naples.[41] Launching his career in 1699, he immediately began a series of annual lectures which formed the germinal seed of his innovative philosophy.[42] Steeped in the classics—especially in the works of Homer, Plato, Cicero, and the Roman historian, Tacitus—Vico turned to the origin of language and to ancient rhetoric and poetics as a starting point in his quest to unlock the mysteries of man's nature, culture, and history. When he wished to improve his own style, "on successive days he would study Cicero side by side with Boccaccio, Virgil with Dante, and Horace with Petrarch, being curious to see and judge for himself the differences between them."[43] But the two classicists he admired above all others were Plato and Tacitus. He explains this preference in the following manner: "For with an incomparable metaphysical mind Tacitus contemplates man as he is, Plato as he should be,"[44] In the writings of these two ancient authors, Vico saw the model he hoped to imitate—that which presented both the virtues of pragmatism and idealism.

But if he derived much of his early basic philosophy and method from Plato and Tacitus, he received his greatest help in the area of communication from Homer and Cicero. From the readings of Homer who represented much of the early knowledge of the Greeks, Vico first saw a close relationship between rhetoric and human nature. Man alone, he came to believe, knows with a high degree of accuracy his own feelings and attitudes and expresses these sentiments to others with a wide range of universal communication procedures such as verbal and nonverbal symbols, art, and music. Since people of all ages adhere to this practice of communicating a language that can be interpreted, each person through sympathy can know, at least approximately, the feelings of his contemporaries. Equally important, by studying the communicative patterns of earlier societies, one may similarly come to appreciate what they have believed and experienced.[45]

The prime source of Vico's rhetorical theory was Cicero who held that rhetoric is a useful art designed to help men adjust to the exigencies of life, thereby rendering them more productive and influential. It was Cicero who taught him that rhetoric, a form of practical knowledge based on probability, is as significant in the sphere of human relations and conduct as a mathematical truth stemming from geometry is to the physical world. Cicero's orations, moreover, persuaded him that the generality of mankind cannot be motivated unless the passions are stirred.[46] Most of all, it was Cicero who convinced him that verisimilitudes constructed from topics or lines of arguments, rather than a recitation of physical facts, constituted the pivotal element needed to alter one's behavior through speech.[47]

Vico, it would appear, equated invention with the topics, and regarded the Ciceronian theory of the verisimilar with its emphasis on probability as the key to knowledge.[48] He did so with the conviction that "absolute truth, as preached by the Cartesians, does not appeal to all the faculties of the mind."[49] By supplanting certainty with verisimilitude, Vico pointed the way to the social scientist's use of the concept of "hypothesis," and "illustrated the practical end toward which knowledge should tend."[50]

Up to this point the analysis tends to suggest that Vico was an uncompromising classicist who was preoccupied with the obsession to use ancient doctrines to diminish the appeal of Descartes and other seventeenth-century modernists. Such an assessment is not responsive to the evidence. For Vico's early devotion to Homer, Plato, Tacitus, and Cicero was matched by his later zeal for Bacon. Indeed, he found the "esoteric wisdom" of Plato and the "common wisdom" of Tacitus both present in the comprehensive and ingenious mind of Bacon.[51] After making this discovery, he developed an abiding belief in the premise that the "constant of human nature" could be "reduced to scientific principles."[52] He admired the successes of Galileo and Newton in systematizing and explaining the scientific characteristics inherent in the world of nature, and became convinced that he could, by using the tools of social and behavioral science, discover similar valid axioms pertaining to the world of nations.[53] What he found was to have far-reaching significance for historiography and anthropology. His researches led him to conclude that there was "an ideal eternal history traversed in time by the history of every nation in its rise, development, maturity, decline, and fall."[54] In observing that every na-

> By supplanting certainty with verisimilitude, Vico pointed the way to the social scientist's use of the concept of "hypothesis," and "illustrated the practical end toward which knowledge should tend."

tion goes through a series of stages beginning with inception and concluding with disintegration, Vico became the first major proponent of the cyclical view of history.[55] Moreover, in suggesting that a society begins with a primitive belief in magic and progresses to an advanced commitment to philosophy, he gave support to the sociological tenet that nature is not static, but an ongoing process of growth. Whatever occurs in the historical evolution of a nation, therefore, takes place at the appropriate point in the cyclical pattern.[56]

After Vico had established the essential principles of his new science, he enthusiastically compared it with the natural sciences. In fact, he was willing to argue that the geometrical propositions which Descartes and his followers held to be the key to our understanding of the physical world were merely creations of man. It is easy, concluded Vico, to demonstrate mathematical principles because they are man-made concepts designed to conform to our perception of the universe. As such, these propositions are no more reliable than the knowledge derived from scientific historical methods depicting the story of man.[57] In thus avoiding the polarities of rationalism on the one hand and empiricism on the other, Vico developed for himself the task of providing a synthesis of the two approaches to knowledge.

At this juncture it is useful to summarize the arguments which Vico used in his attempt to refute some of the major tenets advanced in Descartes' *Discourse on Method*. To make these ideas salient, we present the brief on the preceding page containing the central arguments both of Descartes and of Vico. Three points should be remembered as you examine Descartes' contentions and Vico's rejoinder. First, the sequence of the arguments has been determined by us in order to ensure clarity and to see appropriate relationships. Secondly, Vico, in constructing his response approximately seven decades after Descartes had written his treatise, had the advantage of hindsight. Thirdly, it is of interest to note that the opposing views articulated here are often reproduced in the 1990s with a group of philosophers on one side and the rhetoricians on the other.

Descartes vs. Vico: Debate on the Theory of Knowledge

Descartes

I. The Cartesian Method is grounded in Mathematical Certainty.
   A. It insures a systematic and orderly process guided by rules.
      1. Through intuition we have a vision of clarity and truth.
      2. Through deduction we make inferences from truth.
   B. Observe how the method is modeled after Mathematics.
      1. It is based on axioms which are known directly and clearly. (Intuition)
      2. It uses mathematical reasoning from axioms to the unknown. (Deduction)
   C. We must discover the one absolute truth with certainty and then move step by step without losing clarity and certainty along the way.
      1. We should accept only those claims which can be verified with proof containing no grounds for doubt.
      2. We should divide all difficult aspects of a subject into as many parts as possible.
      3. We should follow a pattern of inquiry utilizing a climactic order and cause-to-effect structure.
      4. We should use an all-inclusive system of enumeration that prevents omissions.

Note: The following statement, which is the cornerstone of my philosophy, meets the above criteria: "I think, therefore I am."

II. My theories have led me to conclude that rhetoric is not a worthy field of study.
   A. It makes use of the scholastic art of syllogizing.
   B. Rhetoric fails to rely exclusively on reason.
      1. Reason determines truth and disciplines the imagination.
      2. Experimentation is the key to knowing.

Vico

I. There are inherent limitations in Descartes' attempt to equate truth with mathematical propositions.
   A. Consider his claim that we should only accept that which can be proved beyond any reasonable doubt.
   B. Mathematical Certainty has nothing to do with the following subject areas that influence our daily lives.
      1. Politics
      2. Military Science
      3. Medical Science
      4. Jurisprudence
      5. History and Religion
   C. The mathematical-formal logic approach also runs counter to man's nature.
      1. It deemphasizes the faculty of memory.
      2. It ignores imagination, thereby thwarting our genius for invention.

II. Despite his commitment to mathematics, Descartes' use of reasoning and evidence is unduly subjective. Thus he is inconsistent.
   A. The mind, he argues, is the criterion of truth.
      1. The mind, not the senses, he says, gives us knowledge of the external world.
      2. His argument, "I think, therefore I am," is a subjective claim.
      3. So, too, is his argument that "God exists."
   B. Furthermore, in his preoccupation with mathematics, he overlooks the subjective nature of that discipline.
      1. Mathematics was created by man.
      2. In effect, mathematics is not on as high a level as Descartes claims.

III. Descartes is an enemy of rhetoric.
   A. He errs in faulting rhetoric on these grounds.
      1. It is beneath the level of philosophical speculation.

Descartes—continued

    C. Rhetoric is non-philosophical.
       1. It uses verisimilitude; that is, appearances of being real.
       2. By relying on commonplaces and topics, it deals only with probabilities.
       3. It is incapable of producing truth.
    D. Rhetoric is limited to communicating what is already known.

Vico—continued

       2. It places undue stress on pathos.
       3. It can only communicate what is already known.
    B. Rhetoric, contrary to what Descartes believes, is rooted in a probability-based reality.
       1. By using topical philosophy, it has the power to create knowledge.
       2. Rhetorical invention precedes demonstration; and rhetorical discovery precedes truth.
       3. Rhetoric creates data and hypotheses.
       4. Only through rhetoric can we communicate our ideas and impressions to others.

The immediate failure of Vico to attract widespread support for his creative attempt to synthesize classical and modern precepts is surprising. René Wellek has argued that Vico's supposed impact on England and Scotland in the eighteenth century is, at best, marginal.[58] Yet so pervasive was his influence on the social sciences during the nineteenth and twentieth centuries that Sir Isaiah Berlin—President of Oriel College at Oxford—calls him "one of the boldest innovators in the history of human thought." Berlin further adds that Vico virtually invented the idea of culture; his theory of mathematics has to wait until our own century to be recognized as revolutionary; he anticipated the esthetics of both romantics and historicists, and almost transformed the subject; he virtually invented comparative anthropology and philology and inaugurated the new approach to history and the social sciences that this entailed; his notions of language, myth, law, symbolism, and the relationship of social to cultural evolution, embodied insights of genius; he first drew that celebrated distinction between the natural sciences and human studies that has remained a crucial issue ever since.[59] When it is remembered that Vico's social science philosophy was developed during his long tenure as a Professor of Rhetoric at the University of Naples, his status as a pioneering communication theorist is remarkable. To him we are indebted for his reaffirmation of the role of probability in rhetoric and for his brilliant attempt to place rhetoric squarely in the tradition of the emerging field of social and behavioral science.

SUMMARY

It is difficult to overestimate the impact that Bacon, Descartes, Locke, and Vico had on the development of rhetorical thought. Approaching their study of the nature of man from similar starting points, they did not always reach the same conclusions. This was particularly true of Descartes who alone among the four innovators tended to embrace a form of absolutism patterned on the model of mathematics. Yet Descartes was an influential figure in the history of British and continental rhetorical theory because he created a rhetorical situation which demanded Vico's response upholding the value of probability and the integrity of the social sciences. Taken as a whole the imaginative writings of these epistemologists served as a model and inspiration for later authors representing the psychological-philosophical school of rhetoric.

EIGHTEENTH-CENTURY EPISTEMOLOGISTS

At the time of Vico's death in 1744, the philosophy of rationalism, which had received its major impetus from the writings of Descartes and Locke, began to take hold among many of the leading literati in Britain and on the continent. In varying degrees the works of David Hume, David Hartley, Lord Kames, Adam Smith, Joseph Priestley, Samuel Johnson, Edward Gibbon, François Voltaire, Jean Jacques Rousseau, and Thomas Paine reflect this emphasis. As rationalism unfolded in the eighteenth century there were three clearly delineated features. First, there was a heightened consciousness for the need of logic in the study of man and his institutions. Secondly, there was an absolute belief in the attainability of reliable knowledge. Thirdly, there was a faith in the capacity of man to make society better. Reason, in sum, was no longer the property of philosophers but a weapon for social improvement.[60]

The telltale signs of rationalistic thought were highly visible. Despite the enormous appeal of traditional Christianity promulgated by John Wesley, religion, for instance, contracted sharply in the eighteenth century. Prior to 1660, the world was viewed as a place of sin, peopled with men who were wicked. God and the devil haunted man. But from 1660 onward religion was less influential. The messages of Bishop Tillotson reflected changing attitudes induced by rationalism. To him, religion was a matter of right behavior; and since there was nothing evil in riches, places, or profits, the world was a happy spot in which to live.[61] As the ideas of rationalism began to secularize society, many prominent thinkers embraced a highly generalized deism. Some felt that they no longer had a need to look to God; others made a polite nod to the unknown. It was against this background of declining interest in orthodox religion in the latter part of the century that Hugh Blair delivered his popular sermons at St. Giles Church in Edinburgh.[62] The fact that Blair gained such prominence as a Protestant divine was not due to his eloquence or to his grasp of theology, but to his talent to construct relevant and inoffensive moral discourses that kept alive the latent religious sentiment of his audience.[63]

Another sign of the steadily increasing impact of rationalism was its influence in governmental and social affairs. In the 1690s Locke and Newton advised the government on currency affairs. Of still greater significance was the fact that a realistic attitude toward experimentalism developed. Statistics were used in decision-making, and a rational approach to social and economic matters began to be introduced.

A third sign could be observed in the continued advance of the scientific revolution which had been initiated in the seventeenth century. Even though there was an active decline in the number of scientists by 1730, science nevertheless continued to move forward. By the 1740s and 1750s scientific societies and lectures prepared for large popular audiences became the order of the day. These public discourses were designed for adults who wished to explore the physical world through scientific meth-

ods. The undiminished thirst for knowledge produced an age of circulating libraries, encyclopedias, and dictionaries.[64] In addition, it brought on an era in which young people alarmed their elders by wanting to read radical writers like Thomas Paine.[65] It was the age of Josiah Wedgwood's scientific approach to pottery-making—an enterprise whose products stand for quality to this very day.

To what extent did the rhetoricians make use of the basic tenets of rationalism? How did they view the classical tradition? What were the immediate and long range influences of this modern epistemology on the rhetoric of Western thought? The answers to these questions should provide an insight into what might be called the eighteenth-century British version of the psychological-philosophical theory of discourse.

One of the distinguishing characteristics of the rationalists, as noted earlier, was a compelling desire to study human nature. Their probings convinced them of man's *unique* power to engage in abstract thought and to communicate on the level of symbolism. To understand the mind of man, they came to believe, was to recognize the nature and function of discourse. Consequently, writers of diverse orientation developed a considerable interest in rhetoric. The works of David Hume and David Hartley, in particular, demonstrate how a philosopher and a physician could be rhetoricians.

Before proceeding to an analysis of the theories of the British epistemologists, we should observe briefly their method and sources. With a goal to construct a rhetoric consistent with the principles of man's nature, they brought to their task a knowledge of and appreciation for the elements of classicism that had a permanent relevance, and precepts of modernism that possess contemporary scientific and social value. They were, in essence, synthesizers who applied scholarly criteria in evaluating the worth of all information handed down to them. In doing so, they strove hard to free themselves from the four fallacies of sensory experience and educational training outlined by Bacon.

The principal British epistemologists concerned with rhetoric were David Hume, David Hartley, Lord Kames, Joseph Priestley, George Campbell, and Richard Whately. Although we will discuss each of these representative authors, far greater attention will be given to Campbell and Whately because of the substantial influence they exercised. Thus, a later chapter will be devoted to their theories and contributions.

David Hume

If John Locke was the pillar of rational thought, David Hume, a close disciple, was the leading world philosopher and interpreter of humanism to write in English.[66] In any analysis of the writings of Hume it is important to remember that he, like his associates Blair and Campbell, was a native of Scotland—a small country which experienced "unrivaled literary brilliance" during the period from 1739 to 1783.[67] Among those who initiated the "second golden age" of Scottish letters were Hume and Thomas Reid in philosophy, William Robertson in history, Adam Smith in political economy, Robert Burns in poetry, and Sir Joshua Reynolds in art. The hub of Scottish literary activity was the capital city of Edinburgh. Described by contemporary observers as "a hotbed of genius" and the "Athens of the North."[68] Edinburgh was a cultural center which could take just pride in its celebrated educational institution, the University of Edinburgh. To city and college came students from England, America, and the continent. Thus Blair was able to write to Hume on July 1, 1764: "Our education here is at present in high reputation. The English are crowding down upon us every season."[69]

To Hume must go the major credit for setting the literary revolution in motion. In 1739 he wrote his greatest work, *A Treatise on Human Nature*. Within a few years he published *An Enquiry Concerning Human Understanding* and *An Enquiry Concerning the Principles of Morals*. In these psychological-philosophical works, Hume showed a remarkable capacity to synthesize classical and modern thought, and to generate fresh ideas. Just as Vico had combined a devotion to Plato and Tacitus with an enthusiasm for Bacon, Hume traced his intellectual heritage to Cicero and Locke. Early in his career Hume turned to the writings of Cicero for both instruction and entertainment.[70] Nursing this interest throughout his life, he freely included quotations from and footnotes to Cicero's moral essays, rhetorical works, and orations. By 1742 he had become so familiar with Cicero's speeches that he wrote a critique of them in a letter to Henry Home (Lord Kames).[71] In his *Enquiry Concerning the Principles of Morals* published a few years later, he used a lengthy excerpt from *De Oratore* to illustrate his theory of virtue; and he patterned his *Dialogues* so closely after the model of *De Natura Deorum* that he all but lost his originality.[72] It is not surprising, therefore, that he could at the middle of the century take comfort in affirming that "the fame of Cicero flourishes at present; but that of Aristotle is utterly decayed."[73]

What makes Hume a central figure in the history of British rhetorical thought, however, was not his admiration for Cicero, but his strong pull toward Locke's philosophy of ideas. He was intrigued by Locke's tendency to compartmentalize the faculties, his theory of association, and his belief in the primacy of the emotions. The teachings of Locke and the example of Isaac Newton, who achieved far-reaching success in applying the experimental method to natural science, spurred Hume to become "the first to put the whole science of man upon an empirical footing, and to appeal to experience exclusively and systematically in teaching his results."[74] The researches that ensued led him to probe the innermost workings of the mind and to devise a theory of reasoning adapted to human nature. What we will find in this analysis is that Hume laid the groundwork for the epistemological approach in Britain in the eighteenth century. So successful was he in achieving his goal that he set the standard for later writers, particularly George Campbell, to follow.

The Nature of the Mind

As he undertook the task of dissecting the nature of the mind, Hume centered his attention on the major areas that are of importance to students of rhetoric.

- two perceptions of the mind
- four faculties
- doctrine of association

Perceptions of the Mind

Hume held that the mind is characterized by two classes or species, which he called ideas or thoughts, and impressions. Ranking these perceptions according to degree of force, he noted that ideas often are abstract, faint, and obscure; and have little vivacity and motivating power. By contrast, impressions are lively concepts that enable us to "hear, or see, or feel, or love, or hate, or desire, or will."[75]

One of the more insightful points emphasized by Hume was his contention that since "ideas are nothing but copies of impressions,"[76] it "is impossible for us to *think* of anything which we have not antecedently *felt*, either by our external or internal senses."[77] Similarly whenever we are confused about the meaning of a term, we are obligated to search for the impression that gave birth to the idea. In sum, an idea, which by its nature lacks force and liveliness, must at all times be clearly associated with a particular impression, the characteristics of which are dynamic and moving sensations. The distinction that we have drawn here between these two concepts will again be evident as we turn to a consideration of the four faculties of the mind highlighted by Hume.

Faculties of the Mind

In his *Enquiry,* Hume repeatedly refers to what he believes to be the four faculties of the mind—understanding, imagination, passions, and the will. The first and fourth of these faculties, as we earlier noted, were stressed by Locke. By treating imagination and the passions as the second and third elements respectively, Hume was convinced that men and women are affective as well as cognitive beings. This suggests that a speaker who wishes to be persuasive must stimulate all of the faculties.

> In his *Enquiry,* Hume repeatedly refers to what he believes to be the four faculties of the mind—understanding, imagination, passions, and the will.

The faculty of understanding is concerned with ideas that are well developed, "clear and determinate," and epitomized by carefully-drawn distinctions between terms. One who instructs in the area of the mathematical sciences limits his rhetorical goal primarily to an informative appeal to the understanding. But a rhetor who seeks to address the whole person uses the faculty of understanding as a starting point or logical base upon which the other faculties rest.

The next two faculties, the imagination and the passions, are tied in closely with impressions. Through the power of imagination, for example, one conjures up vivid images which, in turn, produce strong feelings that go beyond correct judgments associated with the understanding. "The imagination of man," Hume asserts, "is naturally sublime, delighted with whatever is remote and extraordinary"; and with beauty and taste. It is the faculty, in sum, that has a compelling attraction for poets, priests, and politicians.[78]

In his description of the faculty of the passions, Hume was original and influential. Since he held that human motivation stems from man's emotional nature, he, as Locke had done earlier, argued that appeals to the passions of pleasure and pain are necessary to persuade the will to act. But he departed from Locke and the classical scholars in boldly claiming that "reason is and ought only to be the slave of the passions, and can never pretend to any other office than to serve and obey them."[79] At first glance, it appears difficult to reconcile this statement with Hume's career-long commitment to the use of soundly-conceived and well-executed arguments. Upon a closer examination, however, we may glimpse the true meaning of this startling observation. What he is trying to say, we believe after studying all of his major writings, is that the understanding and the passions must be in tune with each other. If a person is not emotionally committed to a course of action recommended by reason, the result will be ineffective in the long run. It is the purpose, therefore, of reason to serve the passions by guiding them toward a thoughtful conclusion.

> "reason is and ought only to be the slave of the passions, and can never pretend to any other office than to serve and obey them."

Further evidence of Hume's concern in having the understanding and the passions to reinforce each other may be noted in the following excerpt taken from his *Enquiry:*

> *Eloquence, when at its highest pitch, leaves little room for reason or reflection; but addressing itself entirely to the fancy or the affections, captivates the willing hearers, and subdues their understanding. Happily, this pitch it seldom attains. But what a Tully or a Demosthenes could scarcely effect over a Roman or Athenian audience, every Capuchian, every itinerant or stationary teacher can perform over the generality of mankind, and in a higher degree, by touching such gross and vulgar passions."*[80]

The ultimate faculty of the mind is the will. It is this fourth element that must be stimulated if appropriate action is to take place. For this to occur, as Hume conceives it, a sequential, hierarchical pattern is helpful. First of all, the understanding receives logically-constructed arguments that meet the test of consistency with facts and with themselves.[81] Next these claims, which often begin as ideas, are transformed into impressions by the imagination; and as these strong impressions stir the passions, belief is generated.[82] It is at this juncture that persuasion of the will results.

The Principles of Association

Another major aspect of Hume's description of the nature of the mind that has important implications for rhetorical theory is his discussion of the principles of "connexion or association." This doctrine explains how thoughts are united together by three different, but related processes—resemblance, contiguity, and cause to effect. When we observe a particular object, event, or person, for instance, our mind is inclined to turn to its counterpart, which projects the image of being very similar. Hume illustrates this point with the following argument:

> We may . . . observe, as the first experiment of our present purpose, that upon the appearance of the picture of an absent friend, our idea of him is evidently enlivened by the resemblance, and that every passion which that idea occasions, whether of joy or sorrow, acquires new force and vigour. In producing this effect, there concur both a relation and a present impression. . . .[83]

As might be expected, the associative principle of resemblance, which gains its thrust from experience, helps the rhetor create arguments from analogy. Resemblance, in short, teaches us to recognize ideas and impressions that are "conjoined with each other."[84]

Hume uses the term "contiguity" to depict the second element of association. This concept refers to such ideas as geographical position in a sequential pattern or to the issue of time as it pertains to the moment an event occurred. If two points converge in a spatial sequence, thus rendering them adjacent, they are contiguous; as a result, a strong associative bond exists between them. Similarly if two related objects are present concurrently, there is a tendency for the mind to connect them.

The questions of time and space have a special significance when analyzing contiguity because, as Hume puts it, "distance diminishes the force of every idea." Consequently, the closer an object or an idea appears to us, the stronger the relationship will be. For this reason, the presence of an object is able to transport the mind to what is a connecting link or uniting bond with far greater vivacity and force than what is possible merely by thinking about it.[85]

Hume's discussion of the third element of association—cause and effect—was perhaps his most significant contribution to philosophical and rhetorical thought. Throughout the pages of the *Enquiry* he constantly affirms and reaffirms his views on causal relationships. He does so by defining what is meant by the terms, shows how they are a central part of the doctrine of association, and demonstrates the unique role that experience plays in establishing the reciprocal connection between cause and effect.

Cause is defined as "an object, followed by another, and where all the objects similar to the first are followed by objects similar to the second. . . ."[86] In other words, whenever we observe that B consistently follows the appearance of A, we may infer that A is the cause and B is the effect. This inference is made possible by the doctrine of association. For what it suggests is that our mind has made a connection between A and B in such a way that "they become proofs of each other's existence. . . ."[87] A typical example of how this causal relationship operates, Hume notes, may be seen when our mind focuses on a wound (Object A) that we have received. This reflection immediately stimulates our senses thereby reminding us of the pain (Object B) that accompanied the wound.

Hume makes it clear that we cannot determine causal relationships by relying on a *priori* reasoning. Such knowledge can only be learned through experience based on repeated observations. This method of analysis, which is the centerpiece of his experimental theory, is the principal means of enabling us to evaluate all matters of fact.[88] How, for instance, do we come to know that a dry piece of wood thrown into a fire will strengthen rather than extinguish a flame? We know this, Hume points out, by recalling similar incidents throughout our lifetime.

Hume's experimental probes into the nature of the mind, as the preceding discussion demonstrates, prompted him to deal with such topics as ideas and impressions; the four faculties—understanding, imagination, passions, and the will; and the concept of cause and effect. It is also of importance to note, as we conclude this section, that he viewed the mind as a bundle of sensory perceptions held together by association, and that a belief may be defined as "a lively idea related to or associated with a present impression."[89] It remains now for us to see how these explanations of the nature of the mind form the basis for creating a theory of reasoning.

The Two Types of Reasoning

Hume used the terms "demonstrative" and "moral" to identify the two kinds of reasoning that result from the nature of the mind. The major difference between these argumentative approaches, as we shall now see, is the degree of certainty inherent in the claims.

Demonstrative Reasoning

This form of reasoning emphasizes the "relations of ideas," and premises that are "either intuitively or demonstratively certain. . . ."[90] It typifies the reasoning process associated with the mathematical sciences, including arithmetic, algebra, and geometry. Of this type of high level reasoning, Hume says "that the ideas . . . being sensible, are always clear and determinate, the smallest distinction between them is immediately perceptible, and the same terms are still expressive of the same ideas, without ambiguity or variation. . . ."[91] Since demonstrative reasoning leads us to claims that are certain, they cannot be disputed; thus they are outside of the field of rhetoric, which is incapable of rising above the level of probability. This, then, is the rationale for Hume's introduction of his theory of moral reasoning.

Moral Reasoning

This is the designation that Hume uses to explain the kind of reasoning that takes place in human affairs. To him, moral reasoning is the principal source of our knowledge and the moving force responsible for our behavior and actions.[92] Its subject matter consists of factual data—particularly cause to effect relationships—related to existence. If a speech or written treatise does not utilize abstract reasoning concerning "quantity or number," he argues, it fails to fulfill its duty to enlighten us on matters of fact or existence. When this is the case, the work contains "nothing but sophistry and illusion" and should, therefore, be cast into the "flames."[93]

The four elements of moral reasoning are experience, testimony, analogy, and calculation of probabilities. The most important of these, according to

Hume, is experience because of its powerful influence on the other three. As we observed in our treatment of the doctrine of association, it is experience that informs us of the relation between cause and effect and "enables us to infer the existence of one object from that of another."[94] Moreover, it is experience that guides our reasoning on all issues involving particular facts. With these firmly-held beliefs etched in his mind, Hume felt justified in asserting that "a uniform experience amounts to a proof. . . ."[95] By the same token, however, experience may be used to show how an adversary's claim, which runs counter to custom, must be rejected because of its deviation from known facts.

A by-product of experience is testimony, which constitutes a second significant element of moral reasoning. This pervasive form of evidence, based on the accounts of expert or lay witnesses, is always grounded in experience. Hume lists five criteria for evaluating the worth of testimony. These tests may be phrased in the following interrogatory form:

> ### Hume's Four Elements of Moral Reasoning
> - Experience
> - Testimony
> - Analogy
> - Calculation of Probability

1. Are there a sufficient number of witnesses?
2. Is the testimony offset by contrary testimony?
3. Do the witnesses have a strong character?
4. Do the witnesses "have an interest in what they affirm?"
5. Is the testimony presented in a manner free from hesitation and from "too violent asservations?"[96]

If the testimony does not meet all of the above criteria, it falls short of the probability needed to convince a thoughtful listener or reader.

Arguments from analogy, like those from testimony, are drawn from experience. Consequently, personal observations made throughout one's career have instilled in that individual knowledge of the associative quality of resemblance, making it possible to see connections between two objects or events. If the relationships we perceive between two ideas or things conform to known reality, the analogical argument we construct in this instance should be persuasive. But Hume recommends that we take special care not to overstate a perceived similarity. "Nothing so like eggs," he asserts; "yet no one, on account of this appearing similarity, expects the same taste and relish in all of them."[97]

The last element of moral reasoning is called "calculation of probabilities." Hume divides this discussion of this point into two categories: (1) "probability of chances" and (2) "probability of causes." We measure the effectiveness of a probability of chance by contrasting the possibilities on one side with those on another. By weighing the numerical strength of each position, we may determine which side contains the higher degree of probability.

The same procedure is followed when assessing the probability of causes. Again we weigh the experimental findings in support of each case, and act in accordance with the superior evidence. The following excerpt should prove helpful in seeing how the notion of calculation of probabilities is an important rhetorical strategy in moral reasoning:

> *A wise man . . . proportions his belief to the evidence. In such conclusions as are founded on infallible experience, he expects the event with the last degree of assurance, and regards his past experience as full proof of the existence of that event. In other cases, he proceeds with more caution: he weighs the opposite experiments; he considers which side is supported by the greater number of experiments; to that side he inclines, with doubt and hesitation; and when at last he fixes his judgement, the evidence exceeds not what we properly call* probability. *All probability, then, supposes an opposition of experiments and observations, where the one side is found to over balance the other, and to produce, a degree of evidence, proportioned to the superiority. . . .*[98]

By stressing the significance of the use of statistical-based probability as an essential part of the decision-making process, Hume, it would appear, laid the foundation for an important dimension of modern experimental methodology.

The last point to be considered in examining Hume's philosophy of moral reasoning is to see how it makes use of audience analysis and adaptation. What we will find later on is that his ideas on adapting discourse to its end, and to an audience were to have a profound influence both on his contemporary Campbell and on the twentieth-century scholar Chaim Perelman.

Audience Analysis and Adaptation

Since the audience, in Hume's opinion, is the primary focal point in the initiation of discourse, it is necessary for the rhetor to anticipate from the outset how his or her appeal will be received. To succeed in this endeavor, appropriate responses must be given to these two questions:

1. Is the discourse, as it relates to the discipline or field of study under consideration, adapted to its end?
2. Is it adapted to the nature of the audience?

Hume's theory of moral reasoning will provide answers to these queries.

Adapting Discourse to Its End

Each discipline or field of study, Hume tells us, has a specific purpose that should be achieved. Adhering to the teachings of Cicero, he noted that history, for example, has as its goal "to instruct"; poetry seeks to please; and eloquence, or oratory, is designed to persuade. To implement their ends, history is concerned with the faculty of understanding; poetry with the imagination and the passions; and eloquence with all four faculties, beginning with the understanding and proceeding in order to the imagination, the passions, and the will. Hume gives this advice to a critic who wishes to ascertain whether or not a rhetor has succeeded in reaching his or her goal: "These ends we must carry constantly in our view when we peruse any performance, and we must be able to judge how far the means employed are adapted to their respective purposes. . . ."[99]

Adapting to the Nature of the Audience

The two types of hearers or readers who captured the interest of Hume were the particular and the philosophical audience. A particular audience consists of men and women who not only share the general traits of human nature but those characteristics peculiar to the specific group of people who have assembled to receive a message. The author of an address, for instance, knows in advance that the hearers consist of human beings who have four faculties of the mind; the knowledge to distinguish the feelings produced by ideas and by impressions; and the ability to make associations with respect to objects and events through the power of resemblance, contiguity, and cause-to-effect connections. The author is also aware that all people have a sense of taste, even though "few are qualified to give judgment on any work of art or establish their own sentiment as the standard of beauty. . . ."[100] Further, the rhetor can know that people as a whole are dogmatic beings who are inclined to affirm their own positions and to reject outright all counter arguments regardless of their merit.[101]

From these considerations of a person in general, the rhetor or the critic must next focus on the composition of the particular auditors. This would include an analysis of such points as their educational and cultural background, their geographical locale, their religious affiliation, their occupational status, the question of time when they assembled, and their strongly-held beliefs. An orator whose duty it is to persuade, Hume points out, is constrained to adapt the message to the listeners' "genius, interests, opinions, passions, and prejudices. . . ."[102]

In emphasizing the above points, Hume offers two suggestions for helping the rhetor or the critic to adapt to a particular audience. First, he notes that if the auditors are biased toward the speaker, it will be necessary to break down the hostility by using conciliatory appeals in the introduction.[103] Secondly, he advises the critic whose purpose is to evaluate an address delivered in an earlier historical period not to rely wholly on the standards of taste that are operative at the time the critique is written. Rather the critic should seek to place himself or herself in the audience that heard the presentation firsthand. In this way the perceptions would have a greater degree of accuracy and relevance.[104]

Hume's discussion of a particular audience had its roots in the works of numerous previous authors. Notwithstanding this fact, the phrasing of his ideas, as observed here, was fresh and influential because of the way it was integrated into his principles of moral reasoning.

As he turned to an analysis of the second kind of audience—the philosophical, Hume showed a greater degree of originality. For us to be a member of this ideal audience, he felt, is to strive for "a proper impartiality in our judgments," to free ourselves from all prejudices, and to show a capacity for comprehending the speaker's arguments. These high

standards, he asserts in one of his written dialogues, could not be met by an Athenian mob. They could, however, be fulfilled by those who have a strong philosophical nature and training. When addressing this thoughtful audience, Hume suggests that we follow these guidelines:

To begin with clear and self-evident principles, to advance by timorous and sure steps, to review frequently our conclusions and examine accurately all their consequences. . . are the only methods, by which we can ever hope to reach the truth, and attain a proper stability in our determinations. . . .[105]

Although the philosophical audience, with its seemingly excessive reliance on idealism, may be outside the scope of typical discourse presentations, it is, as we shall see in the final section of this volume, strikingly consistent with Perelman's notion of the universal audience and with Jurgen Habermas' views on the "ideal speaking situation."

Hume, we may conclude, contributed vitally to the evolution of rhetorical thought. More than any other British epistemologist, he taught us the value of experience as a source of knowledge; and of using moral reasoning rather than syllogistic arguments to buttress our claims. In short, he has revealed to us forcefully that rhetoric is not only a humane field of study, but is a major part of the social science tradition as well.

David Hartley

The conclusions reached by the physician David Hartley in his *Observations on Man, His Frame, His Duty, and His Expectations,* published in 1749—ten years after *The Treatise on Human Nature*—are strikingly similar to those set forth by Hume. Although he makes no reference to Hume's works, Hartley doubtless is indebted to them. Throughout his volume he draws upon general classical rhetorical principles and upon Locke, seeking "to do for human nature what Newton did for the solar system."[106] Thus the doctrine of association, which was the basic element in Hartley's theory of knowledge, is as fundamental to man's intellectual nature as gravitation is to the planets. All ideas, he argued, are

> Hume has revealed to us forcefully that rhetoric is not only a humane field of study, but is a major part of the social science tradition as well.

derived from sensations caused by vibrations in the nerves of the muscles. As ideas in their elementary form enter the mind they are gradually transformed through the power of association into complex beliefs and attitudes that stimulate human action.

An essential aspect of Hartley's system is the view that all developments in life, including persuasive communication events, "are links in an eternal chain of cause and effects."[107] The subject of pleasure and pain illustrates how causal relationships are a part of one's daily life. From the basic starting point of sensation six other pleasures and pains are generated, each dependent upon those that precede it. The seven classes and the order in which they occur are sensation, imagination, ambition, self-interest, sympathy, theopathy, (i.e. religious emotion), and moral sense.

In formulating his psychological and moral theories, Hartley, unlike Vico and Hume, rarely alluded to specific rhetoricians or their works. Yet his debt to classical rhetorical precepts is unmistakable. When analyzing propositions and the nature of assent, he urged that a plain didactic style should be used to appeal to the understanding, and figurative language to stimulate the passions.[108] More importantly he recognized the role of rhetoric in producing the pleasures and pains of imagination. Convinced that rhetoric like history conforms to reality, he defined invention as "the art of producing new Beauties in Works of Imagination, and new Truths in Matters of Science."[109] To describe how the communicator stirs the imagination, Hartley turned to traditional rhetorical doctrines. He advocated an inventive process characterized by forceful logical, emotional, and ethical appeals. Further he recommended that these available means of persuasion should be properly arranged and expressed in moving language designed to excite the passions. Out of such an approach human conduct is altered.[110]

In still another important respect Hartley found a helpful ally in rhetoric. More than most of his contemporaries, he used classical persuasive strategies to outline his book and to argue his thesis. Employing many of the Aristotelian and Ciceronian elements of logos, he attempted to show, for example, the relevancy and reliability of Christianity. Repeatedly he relied upon cause to effect reasoning, the argument from sign, and indirect testimony. Additionally he incorporated refutation in his discussion in an effort to demonstrate the good consequences of Christian piety. It would appear, then, that Hartley's

elaborate system of associational psychology, which was to have a noticeable impact on Campbell and Priestley as well as on nineteenth-century writers, used traditional rhetorical theory and modern epistemological thought as important sources.

Lord Kames

The attempts of Hume and Hartley to produce a philosophy of human nature based upon classical theories and modern science gave a new dimension to psychological and sociological thought, and created a challenge for literary critics to employ a similar method. One of the leading proponents of this approach was Henry Home [Lord Kames] whose efforts contributed to the "Age of Reason" in Scottish literature. That Kames was influenced by experimental methodology is observable in his rigid adherence to the Newtonian theory and to Locke's doctrine of the association of ideas. In his work *Elements of Criticism*, published in 1762, Kames combines the analytical and synthetic methods. He begins with effects and by tracing a series of particular causes, reaches a general concept. From here he descends slowly, explaining consequences by the universal law which he has established.

Kames was especially intrigued with Locke's principle of connections; that is, "perceptions and ideas in a train." There is, he believed, a definite connection of ideas in one's mind. "It is required [in every work of art]," said Kames, "that, like an organic system, its parts be orderly arranged and mutually connected, bearing each of them a relation to the whole."[111] Working from this premise, Kames found fault with many of the ancients. Homer, Pindar, Horace, and Virgil are criticized for not observing the rules of connection, order, and arrangement."[112] He likewise was one of the first writers to fault Aristotle's *Poetics*. He agreed with Aristotle on the unity of action, but thought he put too much emphasis on the unities of time and place. On this point, he said, "we are under no necessity to copy the ancients; and our critics are guilty of mistake, in admitting no greater latitude of place and time than was admitted in Greece and Rome."[113]

Kames was willing to endorse any of the ancient teachings which were based on reason. He found it easy, therefore, to praise Aristotle's doctrine of tragedy because it "depends upon natural operations of the human mind."[114] But Kames was quick to condemn an unwarranted imitation of the classics. In all,

Kames' wide-ranging scholarship, his openness to new ideas, and his leadership capacity, made him a favorite in Edinburgh society and a literary model to be emulated by such men as Adam Smith, Hugh Blair, and James Boswell.

Joseph Priestley

Like many earlier epistemologists who turned their attention to rhetoric, Joseph Priestley was a man of many interests and accomplishments. He was a Unitarian preacher and theologian, as well as an educator. Most of all he was a renowned scientist who discovered oxygen and invented soda water. His major contribution to the rhetoric of Western thought was his *Course of Lectures on Oratory and Criticism.*[115] Published in 1777, this volume contains many of the benchmarks of belletristic rhetoric. In its basic thrust, however, it more correctly belongs to the epistemological school of thought. At least this was Priestley's intention, agreeing to put his lectures in print only after he had convinced himself that he would be the first author to apply Hartley's principles of association to the field of oratory and criticism. That he fulfilled his promise of relating Hartley's teachings to rhetoric cannot be denied. Even when Priestley is giving the appearance of subscribing to Aristotle's treatment of topics, he is actually superimposing upon them Hartley's doctrine of association. Topics and ideas, he argues, are tied in with experience and recollection which, in turn, are "associated by means of their connection with, and relation to one another."[116]

Hartley is again the source for Priestley's discussion of style and taste. After acknowledging that pleasure derived from a discourse results from a stimulation of the imagination and passions, he rejects the popular interpretation that those "delicate sensations" and "sensible feelings" experienced by the listener or reader are "reflex, or internal senses."[117] Priestley explains his own position as follows:

> *According to Dr. Hartley's theory, those sensations consist of nothing more than a congeries or combination of ideas and sensations, separately indistinguishable, but which were formerly associated either with the idea itself that excites them, or with some other idea, or circumstance, attending the introduction of them. It is this latter hypothesis that I adopt, and, by the help of it, I hope to be able to throw some new light on this curious subject.*[118]

In a subsequent lecture on imagination and taste, Priestley likewise alludes to Hartley to explain how the pleasures that are received from a "country landscape," a "rural scene," or a "romance" come from the mental principles of association.[119]

The *Lectures on Oratory and Criticism,* it should be pointed out, are more than a practical application of Hartley's psychology. Indeed, the study is so dependent upon other seventeenth and eighteenth-century works such as Locke's *Essay Concerning Human Understanding,* Hume's *Enquiry into the Principles of Morals,* Kames' *Elements of Criticism,* and John Ward's *Systems of Oratory* that Priestley has been called "more an 'index scholar' in rhetoric than an original thinker."[120] It is of interest to note, however, that the two critics who made this assessment also observed that Priestley's "psychological reinterpretation of traditional rhetorical principles in terms of associational psychology" gives him a permanent place in the history of Western rhetorical thought.[121]

SUMMARY

What we have seen in the foregoing discussion are major contributions to rhetorical thought made by a group of epistemologists who achieved fame in a wide variety of scholarly areas. Well versed in psychology, philosophy, and science, they drew ideas from their field of special knowledge, and applied them to theories of human communication. In doing so, they profoundly influenced George Campbell and Richard Whately, the writings of whom will constitute our principal focus in the next chapter.

Notes

1. Hugh C. Dick, ed., *Selected Writings of Francis Bacon* (New York: The Modern Library, 1955), p. X.
2. Karl Wallace has observed that the "central pillars" of the *Advancement of Learning* "are the psychological faculties." *Francis Bacon on the Nature of Man* (Urbana, Ill: University of Illinois Press, 1967), p. 2.
3. *Selected Writings of Francis Bacon,* p. 230.
4. *Ibid.,* p. 309.
5. Francis Bacon, "Advancement of Learning," in *The Works of Lord Bacon,* 2 vols. (London, Bohn, 1871), I, p. 48.
6. *Ibid.,* p. 254.
7. *Ibid.,* p. 255.
8. Karl R. Wallace, *Francis Bacon on Communication & Rhetoric* (Chapel Hill, N.C., 1943), p. 66.
9. *Ibid.,* p. 71.
10. *Ibid.,* p. 73.
11. *The Works of Lord Bacon,* 1, p. 310.
12. *Ibid.,* pp. 315, 319.
13. *Francis Bacon on Communication & Rhetoric,* p. 78.
14. *Ibid.,* p. 81. Also see pp. 82–83.
15. "Novum organum," in *ibid.,* p. 465.
16. See *ibid.,* pp. 469–487.
17. *Ibid.,* p. 470.
18. *Ibid.*
19. *Ibid.*
20. *Ibid.,* p. 471.
21. *Ibid.,* p. 487.
22. "The Great Instauration," in *ibid.,* pp. 441–42.
23. Dick makes this claim in the introduction of *ibid.,* XVII.
24. Thomas Sprat, *History of the Royal Society,* Jackson I. Cope and Harold W. Jones, eds. (St. Louis: Washington University Press, 1959), p. 35.
25. René Descartes, *A Discourse on Method* (London: J.M. Dent and Sons, 1941), p. 7.
26. *Ibid.,* p. 15.
27. *Ibid.,* p. 7.
28. *Ibid.,* pp. 15–17.
29. *Ibid.,* p. 50.
30. This conclusion appears in the editor's commentary in the introduction of *Discourse on Method,* XI.
31. Wilbur S. Howell, *Logic and Rhetoric in England, 1500–1700* (New York: Russell & Russell, Inc., 1961), pp. 346–49.
32. *Discourse on Method,* XI.
33. Cited in Howell, *Logic and Rhetoric in England,* p. 343.
34. Hugh Davidson, *Audience, Words, and Art: Studies in Seventeenth-Century French Rhetoric* (Columbus, Ohio: The Ohio State University Press, 1965), p. 82.
35. John Locke, *An Essay Concerning Human Understanding,* 2 vols. (London: D. Browne, et al, 1760), II, p. 106.
36. *Ibid.,* I, p. 192.
37. *Ibid.,* p. 367.
38. *Ibid.,* II, pp. 290–99.
39. *Ibid.,* I, pp. 203–210.
40. Leon Festinger, *A Theory of Cognitive Dissonance* (New York: Row, Peterson, 1957).
41. Vico was born in 1670 and died in 1744. In honor of the tercentenary year of his birth, the following comprehensive volume was published: Giorgi Tagliacozzo and Hayden White, eds., *Gambattista Vico: An International Symposium* (Baltimore: The Johns Hopkins Press, 1969).
42. The most famous of these lectures was presented in 1708 under the title *De nostri temporis studiorum ratione.* It was first published in English with the title: "On the Study Methods of our Time." See Elio Granturco, ed., Giambattista Vico, *On the Study Methods of our Time* (Indianapolis: Bobbs Merrill, 1965).
43. Max H. Fisch and Thomas G. Bergen, eds., *The Autobiography of Giambattista Vico* (Urica, N.Y.: Great Seal Books, 1963), p. 120.
44. *Ibid.,* p. 138.
45. Thomas G. Bergin and Max H. Fisch, eds, *The New Science of Giambattista Vico* (Ithaca, N.Y.: Cornell University Press, 1958), pp. 65, 755–76.
46. Grassi has observed: "The thinker who tried, at the end of the humanistic tradition, to overcome the dualism of *pathos and logos* . . . was Vico; and the basis of his effort was a discussion of the preeminence of topical versus critical philosophy." Ernesto Grassi, "Critical Philosophy or Topical Philosophy?" in *Giambattista Vico: An International Symposium,* pp. 41–42.

47. This is a major premise in *On the Study Methods of our Time.* For an instructive criticism, see Grassi's essay.

48. Alfonsina A. Grimaldi, *The Universal Humanity of Giambattista Vico* (New York: S.F. Vanni, 1958), p. 52.

49. *Ibid.*

50. *Ibid.*, p. 53.

51. *Autobiography,* p. 139. In addition to Plato, Tacitus, and Bacon, Vico selected Grotius as one of his four favorite authors. See Enrico De Mas, "Vico's Four Authors," in *Vico:* An *International Symposium,* pp. 3–14.

52. Grimaldi, p. 3.

53. *The New Science,* XXXIII.

54. *Ibid.*, p. 104.

55. Isaiah Berlin, "One of the Boldest Innovators of the History of Human Thought," *The New York Times Magazine,* November 23, 1969.

56. *The New Science,* pp. 104–105.

57. *Ibid.*, p. 104.

58. René Wellek, "The Supposed Influence of Vico on England and Scotland in the Eighteenth Century," in *Vico: An International Symposium.* pp. 215–23.

59. *The New York Times Magazine,* November 23, 1969.

60. J.H. Plumb, "Reason and Unreason in the Eighteenth Century," Unpublished address delivered at Ohio State University, April 9, 1969.

61. *Ibid.*

62. For an analysis of Blair's preaching techniques, see James L. Golden, "Hugh Blair: Minister of St. Giles," *Quarterly Journal of Speech,* XXXVIII (April, 1952), pp. 155–60.

63. *Ibid.*

64. Samuel Miller, A *Brief Retrospect of the Eighteenth Century,* 2 vols. (New York: T. and J. Swords, 1803), II, p. 425; and Hugo Arnot, *History of Edinburgh (Edinburgh:* T. Tumbull, 1818), pp. 516, 567.

65. "Reason and Unreason in the Eighteenth Century in England."

66. V.C. Chappell, ed., *The Philosophy of David Hume* (New York: The Modern Library, 1963), VII.

67. James Golden and Douglas Ehninger, "The Extrinsic Sources of Blair's Popularity," *Southern Speech Journal,* XXII (Fall, 1956), p. 28.

68. Michael Joyce, *Edinburgh: The Golden Age* (London: Longmans, Green, 1951), pp. 1, 6.

69. John Hill Burton, *Life and Correspondence of David Hume* (Edinburgh: W. Tait, 1846), II, p. 229.

70. J.Y.T. Greig, *David Hume* (New York: Oxford University Press, 1931), p. 59.

71. David Hume to Henry Home, June 13, 1742, in John Burton, pp. 144–45.

72. The quotation was drawn from *De Oratore,* II, LXXXIV, pp. 343–44. Greig criticized Hume for relying too heavily upon Cicero's *De Natura Deorum* when writing his *Dialogues.* Greig, *David Hume,* p. 231.

73. L.A. Selby-Bigge, ed., *Enquiries Concerning the Human Understanding* and *Concerning the Principles of Morals by David Hume* (Oxford: The Clarendon Press, 1936), p. 7.

74. It is important to note that the term "philosophy" in the eighteenth century was used to cover a broad range of disciplines including psychology.

75. *An Enquiry Concerning Human Understanding* (Buffalo, N.Y.: Prometheus Books, 1988), p. 21.

76. *Ibid.*, p. 24.

77. *Ibid.*, p. 59.

78. *Ibid.*, pp. 57 and 146.

79. *A Treatise of Human Nature,* ed. By T.H. Green and T.H. Grose, 2 vols. (New York: Longmans, Green, and Co., 1898), II, p. 195.

80. *An Enquiry Concerning Human Understanding,* pp. 107–108.

81. *Ibid.*, p. 88.

82. Although this may be the usual pattern, Hume states in his *Treatise of Human Nature* that a belief may come first and then proceed to influence the imagination and the passions. See Mossner edition, Penguin Books, New York, 1984, pp. 169–170.

83. *An Enquiry Concerning Human Understanding,* p. 50.

84. *Ibid.*, p. 134.

85. *Ibid.*, p. 51.

86. *Ibid.*, p. 72.

87. *Ibid.*, p. 71.

88. On this point, Hume asserts: "All reasonings concerning matter of fact seem to be founded on the relation of cause and effect." *Ibid.*, p. 29.

89. *A Treatise of Human Nature,* I, p. 396.

90. *An Enquiry Concerning Human Understanding,* pp. 28 and 36.

91. *Ibid.*, p. 58.

92. *Ibid.,* p. 148.

93. *Ibid.,* p. 149.

94. *Ibid.,* p. 148.

95. *Ibid.,* p. 106.

96. *Ibid.,* p. 103.

97. *Ibid.,* p. 101.

98. *Ibid.*

99. "Of the Standard of Taste," in V.C. Chappell, ed.; *The Philosophy of David Hume* (New York: The Modern Library, 1963), p. 494.

100. *Ibid.*

101. *An Enquiry Concerning Human Understanding,* p. 145.

102. "Of the Standard of Taste," p. 492.

103. *Ibid.*

104. *Ibid.*

105. *An Enquiry Concerning Human Understanding,* p. 136.

106. Leslie Stephen, *History of English Thought in the Eighteenth* Century, 2 vols. (London: G.P. Putnam's Sons, 1876), II, p. 66.

107. *Ibid.,* p. 64.

108. David Hartley, *Observations on Man, His Frame, His Duty, and His Expectations* (1749) (Gainesville, Fla., 1966), p. 357.

109. *Ibid.,* p. 434.

110. *Ibid.,* p. 432.

111. Henry Lord Kames Home, *Elements of Criticism,* ed. by Abraham Mills (New York: Huntington & Savage, 1849), p. 23.

112. *Ibid.,* pp. 23–24.

113. See the discussion on "The Three Unities," in *ibid.,* pp. 429–440. In particular, observe p. 432.

114. See chapter on "Three Unities."

115. Vincent Bevilacqua and Richard Murphy. eds. *A Course of Lectures* on *Oratory and Criticism by Joseph Priestley* (Carbondale, Ill.: Southern Illinois University Press, 1965).

116. *Ibid.,* p. 22.

117. *Ibid.,* p. 72.

118. *Ibid.,* pp. 72–73.

119. *Ibid.,* p. 130.

120. *Ibid.,* p. 111.

121. *Ibid.*

The Rhetorics of Campbell and Whately

GEORGE CAMPBELL

The rhetorical trend we have chosen to call the epistemological school of thought reached its zenith in the writings of George Campbell, a Scottish Presbyterian minister and educator, and in the works of Richard Whately, Archbishop of the Anglican Church. In the epochal year of 1776, Campbell published his *Philosophy of Rhetoric*. Among the greatest books on communication theory written in the modern era, Campbell's work, more than any preceding volume devoted exclusively to rhetoric, brought together the best knowledge available to eighteenth-century scholars.[1] Few men could roam so freely over classical and contemporary thought, and sift from these ideas the most relevant concepts that would contribute significantly to the development of a theory of discourse rooted in human nature and interdisciplinary in its thrust.

As an admirer of the classics, Campbell reminded his theological students to immerse themselves in such specific works as Quintilian's *Institutio Oratoria,* Cicero's *De Inventione* and *De Oratore,* the *Ad Herennium,* Longinus' *On the Sublime,* and the critical essays of Dionysius. What he liked most of all was the classical emphasis on rules as an art form. In his *Lectures on Pulpit Eloquence,* Campbell taunted his contemporaries for their inability to extend the highly artistic approach to rhetoric developed by the ancients. "As to the rhetorical art itself," he said, "in the particular the moderns appear to me to have made hardly any advance or improvement upon the ancients. I can say, at least, of most of the performances in the way of institute, which I have had an opportunity of reading on the subject, either in French or English, every thing valuable is servilely copied from Aristotle, Cicero, and Quintilian."[2]

Underlying Campbell's philosophy was the idea that rhetoric is a dynamic, developing process. He most earnestly wished, therefore, to incorporate into his inventional theory not only relevant classical precepts but the principal findings of the social and behavioral sciences and select experimental evidence from the natural sciences. In this way, he thought, could be avoided the sterility that results from an undue reliance upon the Greek and Roman rhetoricians.

Faculties of the Mind

Book I of the *Philosophy of Rhetoric* contains Campbell's most original contributions to rhetorical theory. Included in this section are basic elements of faculty psychology, the laws of association, sympathy, moral reasoning, and what the Scots called "common sense." Campbell began his inquiry by examining the nature of people. The writings of Bacon, Locke, and Hume, reinforced by his own observations and experience, taught him that the mind is separated into faculties. To Locke's categories of understanding and will, he, like Hume, added imagination and the passions. These were to be viewed not so much as discrete elements but as a hierarchy, ranging from the elementary faculty of the understanding to the more complex faculty of the will. Persuasion, therefore, is the final result of a four-step process that starts with instruction, and proceeds through the imagination and passions until it motivates the will. Campbell explains these relationships in the following way:

In order to evince the truth considered by itself, conclusive arguments alone are requisite; but in order to convince me by these arguments, it is moreover requisite that they be understood, that they be attended to, that they be remembered by me; and in order to persuade me by them to any particular action or conduct, it is further requisite, that by interesting me in the subject, they may, as it were, be felt. It is not therefore the understanding alone that is here concerned. If the orator would prove successful, it is necessary that he engage in his service all these different powers of the mind, the imagination, the memory, and the passions. These are not the supplanters of reason, or even rivals in her sway; they are her handmaids, by whose ministry she is enabled to usher truth into the heart, and procure it there a favourable reception.[3]

From these general considerations, Campbell moved to a more detailed discussion of the mental faculties and their relationship to rhetorical practice. As he did so, he drew heavily from the ideas of Hume. In many instances (as we shall see) he developed the same points, often using identical terminology and reaching similar conclusions. But since Campbell's central focus was on rhetoric rather than on philosophy, he was able to take Hume's ideas on human nature and give them a strong communication emphasis; and herein lies the principal legacy of Campbell's major contribution to rhetorical thought.

> Campbell drew heavily from the ideas of Hume. In many instances (as we shall see) he developed the same points, often using identical terminology and reaching similar conclusions.

Faculty of the Understanding

Appeals to the understanding, Campbell suggested, consist of explanation and proof. The communicator may have as his purpose to clarify an unknown doctrine or a complex idea. The predominant quality of this end of discourse is perspicuity in language. When the listener, however, approaches a rhetorical situation with an attitude of disbelief or doubt concerning a thesis, the speaker is constrained to use argument in such a way that conviction is achieved.

Faculty of the Imagination

Campbell felt obliged to begin his discussion of imagination with a brief refutation of those who tended to regard this faculty as beneath the level of serious scholarly inquiry. He then defined imagina-

tion as "that faculty of mind, whereby it is capable of conceiving and combining things together, which in that combination have neither been perceived by the senses, nor are remembered."[4] It follows, therefore, that such communication forms as fables, parables, allegories, and poetry are addressed to the imagination; and that part of the discourse most suitable to this appeal is narration. For here the speaker or writer may employ vivid and impelling language, imitation, and resemblances to portray lively and beautiful representations of his subject.

Faculty of the Passions

The stimulation of the passions grows naturally out of the descriptions directed to the imagination. Through an association of images, Campbell observed, the emotions are stirred. These lively associations hurry the audience along into feelings of "love, pity, grief, terror, aversion or desire."[5]

Campbell added that the emotions experienced by the auditor are especially strong when they are seen operating in the speaker.

Faculty of the Will

The best means of influencing the will, which Campbell called the most difficult task facing a communicator, is to combine in an artful manner strong arguments designed to convince the judgment and graphic emotional appeals related to the passions.[6] In holding that conviction operates on the understanding and persuasion on the will and resolution, Campbell supported the notion that a conviction-persuasion duality exists. Such a dichotomy not only was endorsed by Blair but by rhetoricians for generations to come.

The significance of Campbell's belief in the faculties may be seen in his definition of eloquence as "that art or talent by which the discourse is adapted to its end."[7] In this system, the listener, rather than the occasion or speaker, becomes the starting point in the construction of a message.

Forms of Proof

Campbell's discussion of the forms of proof, long considered the substance of invention, is a comprehensive, yet uneven, analysis revealing his grasp of classical rhetoric, the Bible, and the principal writings of Bacon, Descartes, Locke, and Hume. The fact that Campbell was an orthodox Presbyterian divine, opposing the extremist views of the enthusiasts on the one hand and the scepticism of Hume on the other, is also visible in the development of his inventional theory. This influence is reflected in his treatment of the requirements of a speaker, his positioning of emotional proof, and his partiality for moral reasoning. How Campbell blended these ancient and modern secular and religious forces into a tightly-knit, eclectic system of invention is our present concern.

Ethical Proof

There are no well-defined sections in any of his works in which Campbell handles the subject of ethical proof. Yet it is possible to go to his *Philosophy of Rhetoric, Lectures on Systematic Theology,* and occasional sermons to pull out relevant passages that deal with this theme. On April 7, 1752, he delivered a sermon "The Character of a Minister of the Gospel as a Teacher and Pattern." In this address, Campbell asserted that a preacher trebles his effectiveness whenever his teachings correspond to his practice. Using an argument from less to greater, he pointed out that the minister, whose chief end is persuasion, must adhere to Quintilian's good man theory.[8] Twenty-four years later, in his *Philosophy of Rhetoric,* Campbell acknowledged the importance of intelligence, yet placed it on a lower plane than character. "Men generally will think themselves in less danger of being seduced by a man of weak understanding, but of distinguished probity," he said, "than by a man of the best understanding who is of a profligate life."[9] In making this claim, Campbell in no way meant to denigrate the worth of knowledge on the part of the speaker. He admonished all prospective ministers, for example, to steep themselves in the writings of the classical rhetoricians and orators, and to be conversant with modern authors including Rollin, Fenelon, and Hugh Blair.[10]

No summary of Campbell's attitudes toward ethical proof is complete without a reference to the doctrine of sympathy. Cicero, Hume, and Smith taught him to believe that genuine sympathy between the communicator and the listener can only exist when

> "Nothing is more tasteless, and sometimes disgusting," he asserted, "than a joke that has become stale by frequent repetition."

trust is present. It is for this reason that the speaker who demonstrates sincerity and good will has the best chance to create a bond with his audience, and thereby establish the necessary interaction that leads to the influencing of the will.

Pathetic Proof

Campbell was more systematic and original in his treatment of pathetic proof. His conviction that Aristotle was right in assuming the basic rationality of man and in dissecting emotions for the purpose of showing how they may react upon logos was tempered by what he had learned from Locke and Hume about human nature. He accepted Locke's dichotomy of passions—the "pleasant" and the "painful," and his contention that passions are held together by an attraction or association. Pity, for instance, is a group of emotions "comprised of commiseration, benevolence, and love." Campbell further suggested "that pain of every kind generally makes a deeper impression on the imagination than pleasure does, and is retained longer in the memory."[11] Hume's notions are also present. Although his belief in the dominance of impressions over ideas did not cause Campbell to modify his hierarchy of ends progressing from the understanding to the will, it did persuade him to see the causal relationship between lively ideas and the imagination and passions.

A peripheral aspect of Campbell's views on pathetic proof was his penetrating discussion of wit and humor. The mind, he said, is agreeably surprised when a speaker presents novel ideas that debase pompous or seemingly grave things, aggrandizes small and frivolous concepts, or places in juxtaposition dissimilar objects or incongruous events. The process of debasing or aggrandizing a notion derives its strength from appeals to the imagination which may incorporate the method of burlesque. Incongruity, on the other hand, gets its thrust from unlikely associations that generate a surprise meaning. We do not, says Campbell, expect a well-dressed man to fall into a kennel. Thus when a rhetor describes such a happening, we are amused by the incongruity inherent in the situation.

Since wit essentially is a result of novelty and surprise, Campbell came down hard on the use of old jokes as a rhetorical technique. "Nothing is more tasteless, and sometimes disgusting," he asserted, "than a joke that has become stale by frequent repetition."[12] His belief that the surprise element is a central aspect of wit led him to conclude that "a witty repartee is infinitely more pleasing than a witty attack." Wit, in short, has as its primary aim to paint and divert. Consequently, it must be clothed in clever language employing figures of speech and thought that titillate the fancy.

Humor, Campbell goes on to observe, is more pathetic than wit, but since it addresses itself to contempt rather than to imagery and resemblances, it is inferior in nature and function. Notwithstanding this reservation, Campbell proceeds to give several practical hints for employing humor in discourse. Here are a few of his suggestions, all of which pertain to the foibles of human character:

- Describe a person's "caprices, little extravagances, weak anxieties, jealousies, childish fondness, pertness, vanity, and self-conceit."
- Relate familiar stories in a whimsical manner, sometimes assuming a particular character and relying on mimicry and "peculiarities in voice, gesture, and pronunciation."
- Describe your own shortcomings and blunders.
- A serious countenance may prove to be beneficial in order to conceal your art.

In his discussion of wit and humor, Campbell observed that these rhetorical strategies designed to produce laughter may have as their goal either to divert, "or to influence the opinions and purposes of the hearers. . . ." The related art of ridicule seeks more to dissuade than to persuade. "It is," he said, "fitter for refuting error than for supporting truth, for restraining from wrong conduct, than for inciting to the practice of what is right." Moreover, "it is not properly leveled at the false, but at the absurd in tenets."

What Campbell said about wit, humor, and ridicule grew out of his theory of human nature. To see how practical these insights have proved to be, we need only look at the writings and speeches of such well-known British figures as Samuel Pepys, James Boswell, George Bernard Shaw, and Winston Churchill.

Throughout his famous *Diary,* written in the seventeenth century, Pepys engaged in self-disclosure, revealing himself as a humorous man who took great pleasure in describing his "caprices," "jealousies," "childish fondness," and "self-conceit." With a frankness matched only by Boswell a century later, Pepys lets the reader in on his combative dialogues and other encounters with his wife, his unpredictable and irreverent behavior in church during the preaching of a sermon, and the spying techniques he used to check up on his subordinates. On one occasion following a highly successful speech in the House of Lords, he fancied himself a reborn Cicero. But in order to protect his sudden fame as an eloquent orator, he contemplated an abrupt retirement from the podium so that he could savor his newly-discovered eminence.

If Campbell perhaps had Pepys in mind when he constructed his theories on wit, humor, and ridicule, he also had ample opportunity to learn of the antics of his fellow Scotsman, James Boswell, who had a unique talent for telling stories about himself and others. When he did so, he often employed mimicry and a whimsical manner as suggested by Campbell. Never was this more evident than in his vivid account of the evening when he and Hugh Blair sat "together in the pit of Drury Lane playhouse. . . ." "In a wild freak of youthful extravagance," said Boswell, "I entertained the audience prodigiously by imitating the lowing of a cow." He then added with some degree of enjoyment: "I was so successful in this boyish frolic that the universal cry of the galleries was, 'Encore the cow! Encore the cow!' In the pride of my heart I attempted imitations of some other animals, but with inferior effect. My reverend friend, anxious for my *fame,* with an air of utmost gravity and earnestness, addressed me thus: 'My dear sir, I would confine myself to the cow.'"

The humor in Boswell's story was enhanced by the presence of incongruity caused by Blair's participation in the event. The "Minister of St. Giles" was by nature both pompous and discreet. Moreover, since his conservative parishioners in Edinburgh did not permit him to attend a theatrical production, he had to escape to London in order to indulge his aesthetic tastes regarding drama.

Shaw and Churchill, like Pepys and Boswell, were also scintillating story tellers who could arouse

What Campbell said about wit, humor, and ridicule grew out of his theory of human nature.

the fancy of their audiences. But they also had a remarkable capacity for witty repartee designed to throw an opponent off balance. Their brilliant exchanges presented to each other have formed the basis for numerous dinner-table conversations centering on the theme of humor.

Logical Proof

The uniqueness of Campbell's theory of rhetorical proof may be measured not so much in terms of what he had to say on ethos and pathos as in his remarks on logos. His comments on this phase of invention exemplify the brilliant analytical powers he had sharpened through his reading, writing, and platform presentations. Never was he more prone to depart from the classical teachings and embrace modern psychological and philosophical theory. Notwithstanding the fact that Campbell's fresh approach led Whately to indict him for apparently failing to understand even the most rudimentary elements of logic,[13] he went beyond his contemporaries in synthesizing seventeenth and eighteenth-century scientific thought and applying it to rhetoric.

The heart of Campbell's theory of logical proof is found in his description of evidence. The first type, which he designates intuitive in nature, bears a close resemblance to the method of knowledge delineated by Bacon and Descartes. It consists of *mathematical axioms,* derived from intellection, *consciousness* kept alive by sensory messages, and *common sense* shared in varying degrees by all mankind. Almost instantly the mind can gain an insight into the meaning and worth of a principle or a reputed fact. But despite the high degree of reliability of this intuitive evidence, Campbell, like Descartes and other rationalists, grew impatient with those who accepted it without a probing analysis. Rarely was this more evident than in a fast day sermon on the duty of allegiance, delivered on December 12, 1776. Observe how he taunted the American colonists for their uncritical acceptance of certain axioms:

Indeed the most consistent patrons of the American cause deny that the legislative power of the British senate can justly extend to the colonies in any thing. . . . This appears to them an axiom *in politics as clear as any in mathematics. And though for a first principle, it has been wonderfully late of being discovered, they are so confident of its self-evidence, that*

they never attempt to prove it; they rather treat with contempt every person who is so weak as to question it. These gentlemen, however, will excuse me, as I am not certain that I understand them, and am a little nice about first principles, when I ask, what is the precise meaning they affix to the term consent? *For I am much afraid, that if they had begun with borrowing from the mathematicians, the laudable practice of giving accurate* definitions *of their terms, and always adhering to those definitions, we had never heard of many of their newfangled axioms. . . .*[14]

In his *Philosophy of Rhetoric,* Campbell, following Hume closely, subdivided deductive evidence into scientific proof and moral reasoning. The former is, in effect, a restatement of Cartesian philosophy and, for the most part, resides outside the sphere of rhetoric. It deals with abstract independent truths, relies on a single coherent series, and excludes from its domain any demonstration which contains multiple degrees of certainty or contradictions.[15]

What, then, is the kind of evidence available to the speaker who seeks to convince or persuade? Moral reasoning is Campbell's answer. It stands above possibility and probability but below absolute certainty. In the highly important discussion that follows, Campbell draws heavily upon Bacon, Descartes, Locke, and especially Hume; but because of his religious orientation, he moves in other directions as well. With Hume, he held that there are four species of moral evidence: experience, analogy, testimony, and calculation of chances. Experience, Campbell points out, is based upon our own observation and provides a useful method of proceeding inductively from a particular example to a universal premise. Further it enables us to isolate the constituent elements of a fact. When an experience is replicated by experimental research, its persuasive appeal is substantially strengthened.

Analogy, in Campbell's view, is an "indirect experience, founded on some remote similitude."[16] The more distant or ambiguous the relationship between two objects or events, the less rewarding is the comparison. Because of this shortcoming the analogy generally is a weak form of support. To offset this inherent problem, Campbell recommends that numerous analogies be used, but primarily for defensive reasons. Thus while it cannot advance truth, it diminishes the power of an opponent's refutation.

Campbell's discussion of the third species of moral reasoning, testimony, constitutes a landmark in argumentation theory. In asserting that it was "an original principle of our nature,"[17] Campbell lifted testimony from the inartistic plane described by Aristotle to the level of artistic proof. In a sermon delivered before the Synod of Aberdeen on April 9, 1771, he drew a parallel between history and the Bible to show that both rely upon testimony for their primary source material.

The history of past ages we derive solely from testimony. Our knowledge of countries which we never saw, and the much greater part of natural history, must proceed to us entirely from the same source. It will be admitted, that on these topics, without such extraneous information, a man of the most enlightened reason, and the most acute discernment, could never investigate aught beyond the sphere of his corporeal senses. If then we receive from a book, pretending to contain a divine revelation, the account of what happened in a period preceding the date of civil history, can it be justly sustained an objection to the veracity of the writer, that he unravels a series of facts, which, by no use or improvement of reason, it would have been in our power to discover? This identical objection would operate equally against all the histories, natural or civil, foreign or domestic, and travels and voyages, that ever were, or ever will be in the world. Nor is this reasoning applicable only to such events as the creation, the fall, and the deluge. Its application to the discoveries revelation brings concerning the designs of Heaven for our recovery, and final happiness, stands precisely on the same footing.[18]

Campbell thus found in testimony the type of proof he needed to affirm his belief in the authenticity of the Bible. But he was quick to point out that every Biblical account must be subjected to a critical analysis before the evidence could be accepted. "The credibility of the facts related," he said, "is no proof of their truth, though it be a foundation for inquiry. The next province of reason is, to examine the evidence by which the veracity of the writer is supported. . . ."[19] Such a conclusion is similar to Descartes' *Discourse on Method.*

These well-honed ideas on testimony which Campbell had formulated as part of his theology form the nucleus of his remarks on this subject in the *Phi-losophy of Rhetoric.* Again he argued that testimony is experiential in nature because it is based upon the observations of others. Similarly, he maintained that it provided the source material for many disciplines including philosophy, history, grammar, languages, jurisprudence, criticism, and revealed religion. But Campbell added a new dimension when he asserted that testimony is stronger for single facts than is experience. The latter has a higher position only when it leads to a generalized conclusion resulting from experimental studies. Even this advantage can be offset in part, Campbell added, with concurrent testimonies that support a particular observation.[20]

Although Campbell does not provide a detailed discussion of the guidelines to be used in evaluating the reliability of a rhetor's testimony, he does list the following criteria that may be used in corroborating or invalidating the claims of a witness:

1. The "reputation" of the author and the manner of his or her "address."
2. The nature "of the fact attested."
3. The "occasion" and the "disposition of the hearers to whom it was given."
4. The "design" or motives of the witness.
5. The use of "concurrent" testimony.

When these criteria are met, and are consistent with experience, a high level of persuasion may be achieved.[21]

The inclusion of calculation of chances as the fourth species of moral reasoning gave Campbell pause because of its mixed nature. Sharing some of the characteristics of both demonstrative and moral evidence, it is difficult to categorize with precision. What Campbell hoped to do was to devise some type of method that would assist the communicator in establishing a strong probability when the elements of experience, analogy, and testimony were contradictory and incapable of further experimental validation. With the aid of mathematics, one might predict on the basis of past experiences stored in his memory what the likely statistical probability of an occurrence may be. In this sense it is demonstrative. But one might also use reason for the purpose of balancing all of the possibilities inherent in both sides of a question. The calculation of chances is then made on the grounds of degree of moral certainty. This kind of proof which relates mathematics and logic to experience and chance can be illustrated, concluded Campbell, "in the computations that have been made of the value of annuities, insurances, and several other commercial articles."[22]

A final elaboration of Campbell's theory of moral evidence appears in his discussion of the syllogism. Following in the tradition of Descartes, Locke, and Hume, he rebelled against what he called the scholastic art of syllogizing. In his attack he presented four indictments. First, the syllogism, in proceeding by synthesis and from universals to particulars, runs counter to moral reasoning which proceeds by analysis and from particulars to universals. Secondly, it has not been used by mathematicians as an appropriate means of demonstrating theorems. Thirdly, it is of little utility in applying knowledge stemming from experience. Lastly, since it is confined primarily to the adjustment of language to express previously-known concepts, it contributes nothing to our understanding.[23]

> A final elaboration of Campbell's theory of moral evidence appears in his discussion of the syllogism. Following in the tradition of Descartes, Locke, and Hume, he rebelled against what he called the scholastic art of syllogizing.

Campbell's inventional theory, in sum, partook more of the modern scientific thought than of classical precepts. The investigatory nature of the Greek and Roman inventional system, with its stress on topics and commonplaces as a means of generating new arguments and evidence, was largely discounted. Since every man is endowed with a memory, he may begin construction of a discourse, not by following the road of inquiry in search of new materials, but by recalling the information that had come to him earlier by way of intellection and experience, and by familiarizing himself with the findings already engendered by logic. "As logic therefore forges the arms which eloquence teacheth us to wield," Campbell observed, "we must first have recourse to the former, that being made acquainted with the materials of which her weapons and armour are severally made, we may know their respective strength and temper, and when and how each is to be used."[24] This decision to accept the Baconian distinction between inquiry and transmission gave to invention a managerial rather than an investigatory function.

> With considerable foresight Campbell told prospective speakers what they need to know about audiences in general and audiences in particular.

AUDIENCE ANALYSIS AND ADAPTATION

If Campbell's provocative notions on inventional theory stand as his greatest single contribution to rhetorical thought, his notions on audience analysis and adaptation and on language control and style perhaps have had the longest range influence on rhetorical practice and pedagogy. With considerable foresight he told prospective speakers what they need to know about audiences in general and audiences in particular. We can assume as a starting point in speech preparation, he argued, that all men and women are endowed with an understanding, an imagination, a memory, and passions. It behooves persuasive speakers, therefore, to use arguments that can be understood, to employ language that is vivacious and lively, to provide an organizational pattern and form of repetition that stimulate the memory, and to utilize appeals that arouse the emotions. Concluding that "passion is the mover to action" and "reasoning the guide," Campbell listed the following seven "circumstances that are chiefly instrumental in operating on the passions":

1. Probability
2. Plausibility
3. Importance
4. Proximity of Time
5. Connexion of Place
6. Relation to the Persons addressed
7. Interest in the Consequences

From these general considerations, he moved to an analysis of the things which a speaker should know about his particular audience. These include such matters as educational level, moral culture, habits, occupation, political leanings, religious affiliation, and locale. The excerpt which follows, while revealing some of Campbell's biases, nevertheless is a useful reminder regarding the speaker's need to know the characteristics of a particular audience.

Now, the difference between one audience and another is very great, not only in intellectual but in moral attainments. That may be clearly intelligible to a House of Commons, which would appear as if spoken in an unknown tongue to a conventicle of enthusiasts. That may kindle fury in the latter, which would create no emotion in the former but laughter and contempt. . . . Liberty and independence will ever be prevalent motives with republicans, pomp and splendour with those attached to monarchy. In mercantile states, such as Carthage among the ancients, or Holland among the moderns, interest will always prove the most cogent argument; in states solely or chiefly composed of soldiers, such as Sparta and ancient Rome, no inducement will be found a counterpoise to glory. Similar differences are also to be made in addressing different classes of men. With men of genius the most successful topic will be fame; with men of industry, riches; with men of fortune, pleasure.[25]

Doctrine of Usage in Style

Campbell's discussion of language and style was similar to that expressed by Blair and other belletristic scholars. He supported the element of perspicuity because of its importance in developing appeals to the faculty of understanding. Similarly, figurative language performs an essential role in stimulating the imagination and the passions. The use of language, therefore, has a strong correlation with invention. While it is not our purpose here to present a thorough review of Campbell's theory of style, we feel it is appropriate to highlight his doctrine of usage. We do so because of the tremendous impact which this theory has exerted on subsequent rhetorical literature.

Campbell introduces his discussion of proper usage with the rationale that a speaker or writer, as well as the members of the audience, must have an acceptable standard by which to measure the appropriateness of a word, phrase, or idiom. The first criterion he offers is that of "reputable use." He makes it clear from the outset that this term does not mean general use, for common practice frequently employs "vulgarisms" and other undesirable words and sentence constructions. To be a reputable spokesman in the use of language, therefore, one must not only be perceived as being knowledgeable in the liberal arts and sciences, but must also be recognized as having "the talent of communicating knowledge." In brief, those rhetors who meet these two tests of reputability should function as our models with respect to this criterion of language.

In describing the second element of the doctrine of usage, Campbell used the word "national." To achieve a national standard, he said, one must strive mightily to avoid excessive reliance upon provincial and foreign terms that have meaning only to special groups. Quite clearly, he argues, provincial pronunciations and word choices that cannot be understood or appreciated by other provinces and the nation at large constitute an inappropriate standard in language. This point is illustrated by referring to the term "good," which on the national level is fully understood. As a result, the word "good" is superior to its provincial counterparts in Wales ("goot") and in southern Scotland ("gude").

Closely related to "impure," local terms associated with a particular province are "professional dialects." We must be aware, Campbell informs us, of the tendency of business people, medical doctors, and military spokespersons, for example, to use the vocabulary of their professions when communicating to the public. This dependence upon professional "cant" or jargon is an enemy of appropriate usage.

If we are to uphold national usage as a desirable standard, Campbell further argues, we should resist the tendency to substitute foreign terms and phrases for our native idiom. Those who yield to this troubling practice not only may be misunderstood but also render themselves vulnerable to the charge that they are motivated by "affectation" and undue pride.

To conclude his analysis of language usage, Campbell emphasized the importance of a third standard, which he labeled "present use." In claiming that our style should be "regulated" not by ancient practice but by present use, he was careful to point out that the boundary of time related to this criterion varies according to the type of discourse that is being employed. In the fields of poetry, science, and the

> a speaker or writer, as well as the members of the audience, must have an acceptable standard by which to measure the appropriateness of a word, phrase, or idiom.

Bible, for instance, there is a wider latitude in what constitutes present use. Consequently, the language of Milton, of Newton, and of the King James version of the Old and New Testaments may still be applicable in 1776—the date of the publication of *The Philosophy of Rhetoric.*

But what is true of the above specialized forms of discourse does not apply to such subject areas as "history," "romance," "travels," "moral essays," "familiar letters," public address or polite conversation. These communication types, which represent the largest share of human discourse, should be guided by the principle of present use as evidenced in "the writings of a plurality of celebrated authors." It should be remembered, Campbell reminds us, that novel words and phrases, as introduced by popular orators and writers, may be in vogue for a short period of time; but in the long run, they may be little more than a passing fancy in the eyes of a fickle public.[26]

Campbell's doctrine of usage, it would appear, is rooted firmly in the belief that a stylistic standard is required in order to produce a degree of stability, accuracy, and propriety in our language. Notwithstanding the fact that this doctrine is still highly influential in academia and in other professional fields in the latter part of the twentieth century, it came under heavy fire, as we will note later, from contemporary theorist I.A. Richards.

Whately limited the scope of rhetoric to a study of argumentation.

Campbell, it is clear, stood at the transitional period in the evolution of rhetorical thought. The full force of the classical tradition and modern science made a deep imprint upon his mind. In the general area of rules and in his lengthy treatment of language control and style, he followed closely the ancients. But it was the modernists like Hume who directed his attention to the study of the nature of man. Out of this interest came his historic discussion of the ends of discourse, the nature of proof, and the meaning of rhetorical invention.

RICHARD WHATELY

Although George Campbell's *Philosophy of Rhetoric* is often viewed as the benchmark of the psychological-philosophical trend in British rhetorical thought, it was Richard Whately who carried this approach "to its logical completion."[27] First published in 1828—fifty-two years after the appearance of Camp-

bell's work, Whately's *Elements of Rhetoric* is significant both as an historical document and as a moulder of contemporary argumentation theory.

Argument Whately's Central Focus

As in the case of the twentieth-century authors Stephen Toulmin and Chaim Perelman, Whately limited the scope of rhetoric to a study of argumentation. "I propose in the present work," he said in the introduction to *Elements,* "to treat of 'Argumentative Composition,' *generally* and *exclusively.* . . ."[28] Later in his discussion of the parameters of rhetoric, he observed that "the only province that Rhetoric can claim entirely and exclusively is 'the art of inventing and arranging arguments. . . .'"[29] In his analysis of invention, however, Whately subscribed to Campbell's notion that rhetoric is less concerned with investigation and discovery than with "management."[30]

It is the function of logic and inquiry to provide the substance of truth out of which reasoning is formed and conveyed to others by means of the rhetorical process.[31] "The orator," in short, "approaches the process of rhetorical invention not as an investigator but as a communicator" who is "already armed with a general proposition he will advance and with a knowledge of the substantive resources, factual and inferred, by which that proposition may be established."[32]

Key Elements in Whately's Theory

A Priori Arguments and Reasoning Based on Sign

If argumentation is the central focus of Whately's rhetorical system, what, we might ask, did he say on this subject that was distinctive? To answer this question let us turn first to his categorization of two classes of argument—*a priori* and sign. An *a priori* argument, according to Whately, is reasoning from cause to effect which he describes as "an accounting for." To be effective this type of argument should contain a sufficiently strong cause to establish plausibility.[33] In modern parlance, to establish an *a priori* case is to present a case which will stand unless challenged. More important from an historical point of view is Whately's second classification—the argument from sign. Whereas an *a priori* argument proceeds from a cause to an effect, an argument from sign moves in the direction of an "effect to a condition." Of significance here is Whately's inclusion of testimony as "a kind of sign." In his discussion of testimony, he distinguishes between "matters of fact and opinion," and emphasizes the impact that character has upon the persuasibility of witnesses.[34]

Testimony as a Special Kind of Argument From Sign

Three specific types of testimony highlighted by Whately deserve special mention. First is that called "undesigned." This incidental and unplanned testimony gains its strength and uniqueness from the fact that it has the appearance of genuineness and disarming simplicity. Second is that labeled "negative testimony." If an advocate is challenged to deal with a particular question or charge that is widely known by the general public, his failure to contradict the claim constitutes negative testimony. For it is assumed that the uncontradicted statement has validity. The third testimonial form to be singled out here is termed "concurrent." When several witnesses who have had no contact with each other affirm a similar conclusion, the independent nature of their claims has greater force.

Whately advises his readers that a given kind of testimony when presented is less effective than the use of a combination of several types. Thus the advocate who can offer varied testimony including undesigned, negative, and concurrent, and who can demonstrate that the witnesses he cites have a strong character and are large and representative in number, significantly enhances the strength of his claims. It follows, therefore, that a "progressive approach" is the ultimate aim of every advocate. On this point, Whately observes: "The combined force of the series of Arguments results from the *order* in which they are considered, and from their *progressive* tendency to establish a certain conclusion." He then proceeds to show how progressive arguments may be used to establish the law of inertia, the "being and attributes of God," and tolerance.[35] Observe how Whately utilizes the progressive argumentative pattern to set forth the nature of God.

> **Key Elements in Whately's Theory**
> ■ A Priori Arguments and Reasoning Based on Sign
> ■ Testimony as a Special Kind of Argument From Sign
> ■ Presumption and the Burden of Proof

Again, in arguing for the existence and moral attributes of the Deity from the authority of men's opinions, great use may be made of a like progressive course of Argument, though it has been often overlooked. Some have argued for the being of God from the universal, or at least, general, consent of mankind; and some have appealed to the opinions of the wisest and most cultivated portion, respecting both the existence and the moral excellence of the Deity. It cannot be denied that there is a presumptive force in each of these Arguments; but it may be answered, that it is conceivable, an opinion common to almost all the species, may possibly be an error resulting from a constitutional infirmity of the human intellect; that if we are to acquiesce in the belief of the majority, we shall be led to Polytheism; such being the creed of the greater part:—and that more weight may reasonably be attached to the opinions of the wisest and best-instructed, still, as we know that such men are not exempt from error, we cannot be perfectly safe in adopting the belief they hold, unless we are convinced that they hold it in consequence *of their being the wisest and best-instructed. . . . Now this is precisely the point which may be established by the above-mentioned progressive Argument. Nations of Atheists, if there are any such, are confessedly among the rudest and most ignorant savages: those who present their God or Gods as malevolent, capricious, or subject to human passions and vices, are invariably to be found (in the present day at least) among those who are brutal and uncivilized; and among the most civilized nations of the ancients, who professed a similar creed, the more enlightened members of society seem either to have rejected altogether, or to have explained away, the popular belief. The Mahometan nations, again, of the present day, who are certainly more advanced in civilization than their Pagan neighbors, maintain the unity and the moral excellence of the Deity; but the nations of Christendom, whose notions of the Divine goodness are more exalted, are undeniably the most civilized part of the world, and possess, generally speaking, the most cultivated and improved intellectual powers. Now if we would ascertain and appeal to, the sentiments of Man as a rational Being, we must surely look to those which not only prevail most among the most rational and cultivated, but towards which also a progressive tendency is found in men in proportion to their degrees of rationality and cultivation. It would be most extravagant to suppose that man's advance towards a more improved and exalted state of existence should tend to obliterate true and instill false notions. On the contrary, we are authorized to conclude, that those notions, would be the most correct, which men would entertain, whose knowledge, intelligence, and intellectual cultivation should have reached comparatively the highest pitch of perfection; and that those consequently will approach the nearest to the truth, which are entertained, more or less, by various nations, in proportion as they have advanced towards this civilized state.*[36]

What comes through in the above passage is not only Whately's faith in the power of the progressive approach as an argumentative strategy, but his extreme devotion to Christianity. He could not forget his role as a Christian minister who would achieve the position of Archbishop of the Anglican Church. Such a commitment went far to formulate what might be designated an ecclesiastic rhetoric.[37] The whole fabric of Whately's system of argumentation reflects this influence. In no instance is this more evident than in his famous discussion of presumption and burden of proof. Motivated by his Christian beliefs and stimulated by his study of law, he constructed a theory of presumption that is largely upheld by modern textbooks on argumentation and debate. The heart of this influential theory, we feel, is contained in the following discussion based upon the *Elements of Rhetoric.*[38]

> Whately begins his analysis of presumption and burden of proof by defining terms. Concerned with the misunderstanding often associated with the meaning of presumption, he argues that this concept may not be defined as "a preponderance of probability" in favor of a proposition, but rather as a "preoccupation of the ground," which the claim implies.

Presumption and the Burden of Proof

Whately begins his analysis of presumption and burden of proof by defining terms. Concerned with the misunderstanding often associated with the meaning of presumption, he argues that this concept may not be defined as "a preponderance of probability" in favor of a proposition, but rather as a "preoccupation of the ground," which the claim implies. In other words, a proposition "must stand good till some sufficient reason is adduced against it." The burden of proof, on the other hand, belongs to that rhetor who seeks to dispute the presumption.

But, in Whately's opinion, it is not enough to recognize the distinction between these related concepts. Of equal importance is the need to know on which side the presumption lies, and how to construct arguments accordingly. If one has the presumption on his or her side but tends to overlook this fact in the course of the debate, then the initial advantage that may have been present would be lost. Whately uses the following military analogy to illustrate his point:

A body of troops may be perfectly adequate to the defence of a fortress against any attack that may be made on it; and yet, if, ignorant of the advantage they possess, they sally forth into the open field to encounter the enemy, they may suffer a repulse. At any rate, even if strong enough to act on the offensive, they ought still to keep possession of their fortress.

This military example, suggests Whately, has a special relevance for students of rhetoric. Not to recognize that the presumption is on your side may cause a speaker to leave out one of the strongest potential arguments, thereby causing him or her to make "a feeble attack, instead of a triumphant defence."

Whately next considers a series of sample cases in which he demonstrates where the presumption lies in a debate. Alluding first of all to the field of law, he notes that in all instances of alleged wrongdoing, the accused person is presumed to be innocent at the start of a trial. This does not mean that "the accused is innocent." Nor can we conclude that it is highly probable that he or she is innocent. Finally, we are not justified in assuming "that the majority of those brought to trial" are innocent. What we can say, however, is that the accused is not expected to prove his or her innocence. Moreover, we can argue that since the accusers must prove guilt, they have the burden of proof.

As a second illustrative point, Whately maintains that there is a presumption "in favour of existing institutions." In the British Isles, he would say, the Christian Church, the two houses of parliament, the system of royalty, and the two celebrated universities—Oxford and Cambridge—are representative examples of existing institutions that are presumed to merit an enduring status. Even though such institutions may from time to time be in need of repair, a rhetor who demands a major "alteration" in any of them "should show cause for it" in view of the fact that "change is not a good in itself." In completing this discussion, Whately informs us that a speaker who has the presumption in this case is not required to defend the existing institution unless an opponent, who has the burden of proof, has leveled arguments against it.

Thirdly, Whately asserts that there is a "presumption against anything paradoxical," which is defined as a claim that is "contrary to prevailing opinion." In responding to an adversary's use of a paradoxical argument, we may use three different types of strategies:

1. if we have knowledge that the claim is false, we may reject it outright;
2. if the claim is presented with inadequate evidence, we may state that it lacks needed substantiation; and
3. if the claim appears to be true, we are morally obligated to deal with it as a serious challenge.

This discussion of a paradoxical argument is especially important for two reasons. First, it shows that a rhetor who has the presumption on his or her side does not necessarily have an advantage. In the second place it enables Whately to uphold his fundamental religious belief that Christianity, at the time of its onset, was a paradox containing a novel truth that could not be easily ignored.

Whately is similarly instructive when he turns, fourthly, to a consideration of where he believes presumption lies with respect to the Christian religion as a whole. Departing from his usual tendency to identify specifically where the presumption resides, he observes in this instance that it is dependent upon the historical period that is being used as a starting point. In the first century, A.D., for example, the presumption was against Christianity. But its widespread acceptance and influence in the world during the subsequent eighteen centuries elevated it to the level of the status quo. This in turn, according to Whately, creates a current presumption in favor of Christianity. As a result, a rhetor who seeks to refute it has the burden of proof.

The pro and con approach used by Whately in describing the presumption related to Christianity is also applied to the group he calls the "learned." To demonstrate this fifth example, he notes that often there is a presumption favoring these well-educated people because of their superior knowledge. When they speak in the area of their expertise, therefore, we are inclined to accept their statements as being authoritative. It is instructive to note, however, that the presumption may change when a learned person's views are challenged by a comparable authority whose refutation functions as a counter-presumption.

A sixth illustration will serve to show how Whately assigned presumption to the area of tradition. Those who develop arguments based on tradition usually have presumption on their side. This would apply both to religious and to secular beliefs. For a rhetor to appeal to tradition, Whately asserts, he or she must

> *prove, not merely generally, that there is such a thing as Tradition, and that it is entitled to respect, but that there is a tradition relative to each of the points which he thus maintains; and that such tradition is, in each point, sufficient to establish that point.*

During the past two hundred years, American political leaders, either consciously or unconsciously, have sought to implement Whately's ideas on the influence of tradition by rooting their arguments in the teachings of the Constitution in particular and of the founding fathers in general.

Two additional aspects of Whately's theory of presumption and burden of proof are worthy of our attention. First is his notion that the burden of proof may be transferred and the presumption overthrown in a debate. "It is to be observed," he says, "that a Presumption may be *rebutted* by an opposite presumption, so as to shift the Burden of Proof to the other side." The following hypothetical instance is used to highlight this claim:

Suppose you had advised the removal of some existing restriction: you might be, in the first instance, called on to take the Burden of Proof, and allege your reasons for the change, on the ground that there is a Presumption against every Change. But you might fairly reply, "True, but there is another Presumption which rebuts the former; every Restriction is in itself an evil; and therefore there is a Presumption in favour of its removal, unless it can be shown necessary for prevention of some greater evil. . . ."

A second vitally significant aspect of Whately's views on this subject is the connection he makes between deference and presumption. Here he articulates the notion that there is a strong tendency to defer to a person who has, in the eyes of the judges of a debate, a high level ethos. If such a person who is being cited is universally recognized as one who commands deference, a presumption concerning his or her "decisions or opinions" exists. It is for this reason that an American spokesperson may with good cause invoke the names of Thomas Jefferson, Abraham Lincoln, or Martin Luther King, Jr., to buttress an argument.

It is difficult to overestimate the importance of Whately's pioneering analysis of presumption and burden of proof. What makes his discussion a significant landmark in the rhetoric of Western thought is the reminder that presumption rests not on the side where a "preponderance of probability" exists, but on that side which consists of a "preoccupation of the ground." (i.e. that side which the majority of a given audience favors at the outset of a speech.) And he also was on target in reminding his students that no meaningful debate on a controversial question can proceed intelligently unless it is first determined where the presumption lies. Finally, Whately contributed vitally to argumentation theory when he pointed out that, in most circumstances, there is a presumption in favor of existing institutions," "innocence," "tradition," and people who command "deference." Such insights paved the way for modern high school and college debate practices. Since a negative team often begins with an initial presumption in favor of the status quo, the affirmative team has the burden of proof to overthrow the prevailing presumption. To counter this starting point, the affirmative debaters are given the right to begin and end the contest. This type of format supports Whately's contention that there is "no necessary advantage to the side on which the presumption lies."[39]

In concluding our discussion of the past two chapters centering on the rhetorical theory of leading British epistemologists, we would like to analyze briefly a historically-significant case study that puts their ideas on argument in perspective. This case study, or representative anecdote as Kenneth Burke labels it, has as its subject matter the issue of whether or not a belief in miracles may be supported by compelling reasoning and evidence. After considerable self-reflection and dialogue with his friends, Hume decided to include his now famous "Essay on Miracles" as Section X in his *Enquiry Concerning Human Understanding.*

THE DEBATE ON MIRACLES

Hume's Essay on Miracles

This work, published in 1748, produced an enormous negative response, including at least seven volumes of refutation in a four-year period. What gives it a special significance for students of rhetoric is the influence it had upon Campbell and Whately. Our purpose, then, in this closing section on the psychological-philosophical trend is to discuss the substance of Hume's arguments and the vigorous responses of Campbell and Whately. It is our hope that the debate will give us a strong insight into the question of what constitutes proof.

Drawing upon his ideas on the nature of the mind and on his theory of moral reasoning, Hume took the position that no one is capable of providing proof that miracles have ever existed. To substantiate this central idea, he developed four major claims, each utilizing one of the elements of moral reasoning. *First, he said, a belief in miracles does not conform to experience.* Since a miracle, he contended, is "a violation of the laws of nature," it contradicts uniform "experience and observation." The following excerpt, which makes use of clear and vivid language, explains his stance on this point:

Why is it more probable, that all men must die; that lead cannot, of itself, remain suspended in the air; unless it be that these events are found agreeable to the laws of nature, and there is required a violation of these laws, or in other words, a miracle to prevent them.[40]

None of the arguments in support of miracles, Hume stated in his second claim, have been demonstrated by persuasive testimony leading to a proof.

He buttressed this contention by drawing data from history and psychology. In the first place, he asserted, the historical testimony in defense of miracles does not meet the standards of evidence required for establishing a proof. The testimony, for example, was given by an insufficient number of competent witnesses; by people whose integrity and motives were questionable; by people who had nothing to lose in case their statements proved to be false; and by those who came from a geographical locale where detection of inappropriate testimony would be unlikely.

History further shows, Hume proceeded to say, that those who have tended to testify that miracles have existed are usually residents of a "barbarous nation." Such untrained, uncultivated, and overly-credulous persons are inclined to perpetuate a doctrine handed down to them as being true. Finally, noted Hume, we are taught by history that those who cite testimony in support of miracles are refuted by an equal or greater number of witnesses who take an opposing view.

The field of psychology, as well as that of history, informs us that the testimony given to generate a belief in miracles does not produce a proof. Those who endorse the concept of miracles, for instance, all too often have an inclination to favor what they perceive to be an extraordinary or supernatural event that directly challenges experience and common sense. A belief in such occurrences, it would appear, provides a feeling of psychological pleasure that is associated with the emotions of "wonder" and "surprise." Additionally, Hume notes, when the passions of "wonder" and "surprise" are joined with religious affection, it will cause one to see "what has no reality." Not to be discounted, moreover, is the fact that even if a witness comes to realize that his or her narrative in defense of a miracle is false, that person might "persevere in it, with the best of intentions in the world, for the sake of promoting so holy a cause. . . ."[41]

Hume summarized his treatment of testimony with a premise that has often been stated by both his supporters and his adversaries: "Upon the whole, then it appears, that no testimony for any kind of miracle, has ever amounted to a probability, much less to a proof. . . ."[42]

For his third claim, Hume argued that *analogies based on unmistakable resemblances show that those who believe in miracles do so without depending on convincing reasoning and evidence.* Of the numerous analogies that appear in the "Essay" for the purpose of clarifying Hume's position on miracles, two stand out. Both were phrased in the form of hypothetical illustrations. In the first analogy, he asks his readers to imagine that all authors who have written on the subject agree that on January 1, 1600, the earth was covered by darkness that persisted for eight days. The second analogy again uses as a starting point the first of January, 1600. This time he suggested that we imagine all the authorities in English history have agreed that on this date Queen Elizabeth died. This death, moreover, presumably was followed by these remarkable happenings:

1. The Queen's physicians reportedly saw her;
2. parliament appointed her successor;
3. she was interred for a month; and then
4. she "reappeared, resumed the throne and governed for three years."

In assessing the degree of probability inherent in these two analogies, Hume suggested that the first involving the blackout of the earth could be classified as believable, but the second must be discounted. He defended his opposing conclusions by noting, first, that the "decay, corruption, and dissolution of nature" have frequently occurred in the past; thus "any phenomenon which seems to have a tendency towards . . . catastrophe" comes within the sphere of believability. He then, secondly, offered three reasons for rejecting the miraculous account of Queen Elizabeth's reputed experience. First, the Queen and members of the court may have pretended the alleged death; secondly, it is highly improbable that the deception could go undetected; and, thirdly, it is much more probable that a person's testimony could be wrong than that the laws of nature could be violated.[43]

When we employ the fourth element of moral reasoning, calculation of probabilities, we are, states Hume, also forced to conclude that arguments supporting a belief in miracles cannot adequately be substantiated. What Hume does when discussing this last category of moral reasoning is to consider the combined persuasive power of the arguments rooted in experience, testimony, and analogy. To do this, he said, we must rely on such mathematical terms as weighing, counting, balancing, and subtracting in order to determine where the strongest probability rests. When we apply this procedure to the question of miracles, we must ascertain which side has "the greatest number of supporting experiments"; the superior quantity of "past observations"; and the most weight when pro and con data are balanced. To accomplish this goal, we subtract the evidence on one side from that of the other. The remainder then constitutes the ultimate conclusion we embrace. Such an arithmetical process, Hume boldly asserts, inevitably requires us to reject a belief in miracles.[44]

Satisfied that he had demonstrated with his four claims that reason is incapable of proving that miracles have existed, Hume presented several reminders to his audience in his closing statements. He told them to remember that the Biblical teachings on miracles were written by men; that this doctrine was first received and promulgated to others by uneducated men; and that even in the present day the Christian religion "cannot be believed by any reasonable person" without a miracle. If in light of what has been said a person still insists on believing in miracles, he or she should know that such a belief is the result of faith, not reason.[45]

Campbell's "Dissertation on Miracles"

Shortly after the "Essay on Miracles" appeared in print, Campbell, who for years had been a close student of Hume's philosophical theories, contemplated the thought of offering a rebuttal. To prepare himself for the task, he became an active participant in the debates and discussions held at the Aberdeen Philosophical Society where Hume and his writings were a favorite subject for analysis. Although Campbell felt indebted to Hume for enlarging his understanding of abstract reasoning and of human nature, he was alarmed at the content of the "Essay on Miracles." As a result, he published his response in 1762, entitling his work *A Dissertation on Miracles*. Before doing so, however, he forwarded a copy of the manuscript to Hugh Blair and then asked him to pass it on to Hume for his reaction. Hume, who had a career-long policy of never answering his critics, made an exception in this case by submitting a response both to Blair and Campbell.[46]

In his introductory statements in the *Dissertation*, Campbell thanked Hume for the influence he had exerted on him and pointed out changes that were made in language usage and in several interpretations of Hume's arguments. But Campbell insisted that despite the criticism Hume had made on specific points, the substance of his own positions had remained the same.

Campbell's arguments in defense of miracles may be summarized under three headings. The first contention he presented was a point by point refutation of Hume's four major contentions. The second and third claims consist of positive premises revealing why reason is fully capable of proving that the Biblical stories of miracles are true. His first contention, which we will now discuss, is covered in Part I of the two-part *Dissertation*.

Hume's arguments against miracles, Campbell states at the outset, are grounded in false hypotheses. The first shortcoming in the "Essay," in Campbell's opinion, is its misuse of the term experience. By suggesting that experience, for example, is essentially concerned with natural, ordinary events involving circumstances that "are entirely similar," Hume overlooks the fact that this phenomenon also deals with particular occurrences. What makes this distinction significant is that experience loses much of its relevance and power when it is lowered to the level of particulars.

Campbell also points out that Hume from time to time shifts the sense of meaning with respect to the term experience. Observe for instance, he notes, Hume's reference to the probability of a dead man's coming back to life. If such a bizarre and unusual occurrence were to take place, Hume argued, it would doubtless be a miracle. But in then proclaiming that no such extraordinary happening could ever take place, he first cites as his evidence that it has "never been observed by us." Not content to let this interpretation stand, Hume then incorporates the modified assertion that it has "never been observed in any age or country." At this point, Campbell faults his adversary for suggesting that it is probable to know "what has been observed, and what has not been observed, in all ages or countries." Such comprehensive knowledge, Campbell argued, is beyond the reach of any person.[47]

The argument on experience is concluded with an attack on Hume's favorite thesis that "a miracle is a violation of the laws of nature." In this part of his refutation, Campbell charges Hume with using the fallacy of begging the question. He puts his charge this way:

I leave it . . . to the author to explain with what consistency he can assert, that the laws of nature are established by an uniform experience . . . and at the same time allow that almost all human histories are full of the relations of miracles and prodigies which are violations of these laws.[48]

Campbell presents similar specific arguments in his attempt to refute Hume's stand on testimony. Citing children as an example, he argues that Hume is mistaken in his belief that testimony relies entirely on experience. This is followed by the assertion that since testimony may occasionally precede experience, such an occurrence should be regarded as acceptable evidence until it is "properly refuted by experience."

At this stage in the formulation of his argument against Hume's claims on testimony, Campbell made what he perceived to be one of his most telling points. Testimony, he declared, derives its persuasive thrust from particular facts that in many instances are more convincing than "the general conclusions from experience can afford us."[49]

Campbell knew that his refutation of Hume's contentions could not be complete until he had answered the psychological notions advanced regarding the anti-intellectual effects that supposedly are produced by a "passion of the marvellous" and "religious affection." Here he defended the virtues of the "marvellous," arguing that it has a close connection with the principle of curiosity. The innate quality of curiosity, he asserted, gives us an attachment to the quality of wonder associated with miracles, and it also helps us appreciate "the philosophical wonders in electricity, chemistry," and "magnetism."[50]

As he continued to use the same four principles of moral reasoning employed by Hume, Campbell introduced an important analogy to strengthen his case. It was directed at the claim that a miracle is "a violation of the laws of nature." Hume's entire argument on this central issue, he asserted, rests upon the notion that only the visible material world is governed by established laws. We know by virtue of analogy, however, that there are similarly impressive invisible laws that are "moral and intellectual" in nature. Consequently, when we view this issue in a broader sense, we may conclude that a miracle does not necessarily imply a suspension of the laws of nature has occurred.[51]

Nor did Campbell neglect to respond to Hume's arguments on the calculation of probabilities. In attacking this point, he highlighted what he came to believe was the fallacy of Hume's approach. This was the proclivity to focus on the total number of specific items of evidence on each side of the issue

of miracles. We cannot, Campbell argued, make the assumption that each piece of evidence is comparable in substance and, therefore, should be treated as having the same degree of persuasive power. To adhere to this policy is to ignore the fact that a particular datum has a particular strength or quality. All that is required to illustrate this point is to see what happens when specific testimony is given. For it is quite clear that the arithmetical procedure designed by Hume does not take into account the problem of a witness's veracity.

Convinced now that he had answered Hume's four claims in opposition to miracles, Campbell presented two arguments in Part II of his *Dissertation* that he felt would corroborate the thesis that the descriptions of miracles in the Bible and related literature are true. The first contention he stated as follows: *Biblical and other historical testimony provide the type of probability that is needed to establish a proof.* The reliability of the Biblical accounts, for example, may be seen by examining the testimony of the early evangelists. If you scrutinize the statements of these witnesses, he stated, you will learn that they conformed to the standards outlined by Hume. Their testimony and character have not been successfully challenged; they had nothing to gain in making their assertions; they had large numbers; and they presented their claims with confidence and with controlled emotions.[52]

Historical testimony, Campbell went on to argue, provides additional evidence. Contrary to what Hume has said, he pointed out, no other religious group, including Mahomet and his followers, has listed miracles as being a central aspect of their teachings. Christianity alone upholds this position.

Campbell's final argument upheld the proposition that *a belief in miracles may be proved by causal reasoning.* In developing this claim, he asked his audience to reflect on the remarkable effect of Christianity in the 1,700 years since its inception. He then traced that effect to its principal cause—the generative power emanating from miracles.[53] Campbell now felt ready to conclude that he had proved by reason, and not faith, that miracles as detailed in the Holy Scriptures, are indeed true.

Whately's Historic Doubts Relative to Napoleon Bonaparte

Seven decades after Hume had initiated the discussion on miracles, and fifty-seven years following Campbell's response, Whately entered the debate.

His interest in the theme not only stemmed from his religious convictions but from an article he read in the *Edinburgh Review* praising Hume's "Essay" for being the first work that recognized the close connection between experience and testimony as forms of evidence. The author also noted that the "Essay" was filled with "maxims of great use in the conduct of life."[54] This article angered Whately, thereby giving him a strong determination to respond to Hume's arguments.

Unlike Campbell, who he had long admired, Whately decided not to use a standard refutation based on direct attack. He chose instead to speak about Napoleon Bonaparte, who at the time of Whately's publication in 1819, was living in exile on the isle of Elba. Titling his work *Historic Doubts Relative to Napoleon Bonaparte,* he sought to demonstrate that by using Hume's arguments against miracles it is possible to show that the man called Napoleon may never have existed. This ironical approach using satire as its rhetorical weapon went through fourteen separate editions during Whately's lifetime alone. In addition, it launched his career as a thoughtful and productive scholar.

Historic Doubts develops two major contentions, each containing reservations about the incredible events associated with Napoleon's presumed life and character. In his first argument, Whately asserted that *we do not have the type of persuasive proof, as required by Hume, to have confidence in the belief that Napoleon has ever lived.* Since most of what we think we know about Napoleon comes from newspapers, according to Whately, our information is inaccurate because such a source has proved to be unreliable.

Several practices contribute to the print medium's lack of dependability. First, the owners are excessively preoccupied with increasing circulation. Secondly, by copying verbatim from other newspapers, editors rely on inadequate means to obtain "correct information." Thirdly, they too easily contradict each other on such important matters as Napoleon's achievements and character. The numerous inconsistencies in newspaper accounts, for example, prevent us from gaining an accurate picture of Napoleon's performance at the bridge of Lodi and in the battle of Waterloo. Nor do we know whether or not he destroyed a garrison of his soldiers in Europe because they had surrendered.[55]

Comparable discrepancies are evident in the depiction of Napoleon's character. Some newspaper reports describe him as a magnanimous and insightful military leader; others portray him as an insane man whose meanspirited and cruel nature is intolerable to bear. These strikingly contradictory assessments of what Napoleon has done and who he is force us to conclude that either there are multiple Napoleons or we must "doubt the existence of any."[56]

But newspapers, states Whately, are not the only faulty and confusing source. Equally misleading are the contradictory and inconsistent reports emanating from political and governmental leaders. A representative instance of this tendency is what happened following the battle of Trafalgar. Both an English officer and the French people were given the false information that France had won a victory in this important contest.[57]

Further evidence of contradictory and exaggerated accounts given by authorities, Whately observed, may be seen in their frequent efforts to substitute fiction for reality, and to use hyperbolic terms. The adjective "great," for example, is used repeatedly to describe "armies," "victories," "frosts," and "reverses." These grandiose terms, Whately pointed out, suggest that the commentators are hypnotized by, what Hume calls, a love of events that are "marvellous," "wonderful," and "miraculous."[58]

Whately next considered the question of the relationship between testimony and our senses or experience. Reminding his readers of Hume's demand that this connection must be explored closely, he presented a hypothetical illustration. Let us imagine, he said, that a person goes to Plymouth to catch a personal glimpse of Napoleon. Even though this eyewitness is present on the scene and has good vision, he cannot know with certainty that the officer he observes in a tilted hat and French uniform is indeed Napoleon. Similarly, by studying his physical appearance and demeanor, he would be unable to discover his real name or learn of his public or personal history. By the same token, we cannot be sure that a soldier who produces scars that he claims resulted from his fighting Napoleon is being truthful.[59]

The contradictions and inconsistencies seen thus far clearly revealed to Whately's satisfaction that most of the claims made about Napoleon were highly improbable. None, however, could match the fact that notwithstanding Napoleon's alleged decisive and pivotal defeat at Waterloo, large numbers of French citizens urged him to create a new army for the sixth time. This incredible occurrence, when measured by Hume's standards of evidence, must, asserted Whately, be regarded as improbable.[60]

To make his stance on the first claim more graphic and compelling, Whately paraphrased Biblical language in listing other "marvellous" and "wonderful" accomplishments of Napoleon. But he then warned that all reasonable people must reject this recitation of remarkable events because it exceeded the limits of probability articulated by Hume. With this affirmation, he was now prepared to consider his climactic second claim, which says in essence that *Hume and his followers are obligated to apply the same standards of evidence in investigating Napoleon as they have utilized in their treatment of miracles.*

Although Whately devoted far less space to this concluding argument, it was similarly critical to his case. He first told them what they had not done. They had not to date engaged in a thoughtful inquiry of Napoleon's character and achievements. Thus we have no clear idea if they "are conformable to experience." Instead, moreover, of making use of their own tests of reliability and validity concerning testimony, they have been content to abide by "the stream of public opinion."[61]

In his closing appeal, Whately challenged those who endorse Hume's views on miracles to do what is right according to their own doctrine. If in view of the evidence he had provided, they still persist in their belief that Napoleon exists, they must in the name of fairness admit that a different standard in this case has been used. As a result, honor dictates they must renounce the reasoning method employed on the issue of miracles.[62]

> the debate on miracles involving three of the most significant rhetoricians in Western thought was a landmark event in the history of argument.

Significance of the Debate on Miracles

In retrospect, the debate on miracles involving three of the most significant rhetoricians in Western thought was a landmark event in the history of argument. Its effect on each of the protagonists cannot easily by overestimated. Hume's "Essay" attracted such widespread attention that critics began to look more closely at all of his works; and this, in turn, has helped elevate him to the lofty position of Britain's greatest philosopher.[63] Campbell also profited tremendously from his experience in writing his *Dissertation.* Much of what he said in his use of the four principles of moral reasoning and in his discussion of human nature—ideas that he drew heavily from Hume—later became a central emphasis in his *Philosophy of Rhetoric.* This book subsequently has been described as the most important book on rhetorical theory published in the eighteenth century;[64] and it was this book Hume held in his hand a few days before his death.[65] Finally, Whately's *Historic Doubts,* described by one critic as a "brilliant satire" and by another observer as his greatest work, profoundly influenced his *Elements of Logic* (1826) and his *Elements of Rhetoric* (1828).[66]

But the greatest legacy of the debate is what it informs us about reasoning, evidence, and proof. More than any other single event, it put in clear perspective how the British epistemologists elevated evidence, or what Aristotle called inartistic proof, to the artistic level. Thus as reasoning and evidence united as equal partners, the stage was set for the onset of modern theories of argumentation.

--- **Notes** ---

1. One of the most important recent publications on Campbell is Lloyd F. Bitzer, ed., *The Philosophy of Rhetoric by George Campbell* (Carbondale, Ill.: Southern Illinois University Press, 1963).

2. George Campbell, *Lectures on Systematic Theology and Pulpit Eloquence* (Boston: Lincoln and Edwards, 1832), p. 99.

3. George Campbell, *The Philosophy of Rhetoric* (Boston: Charles Ewer, 1823), p. 101.

4. *Lectures on Systematic Theology and Pulpit Eloquence,* p. 131.

5. *Ibid.,* p. 132.

6. *Ibid.* Also see *The Philosophy of Rhetoric,* pp. 23–30.

7. *Ibid.,* p. 23.

8. George Campbell, "The Character of a Minister of the Gospel as a Teacher and Pattern," A Sermon preached before the Synod of Aberdeen at Aberdeen, April 7, 1752 (Aberdeen, Scotland, 1752).

9. *The Philosophy of Rhetoric,* p. 129.

10. *Lectures on Systematic Theology and Pulpit Eloquence,* pp. 99–100.

11. *The Philosophy of Rhetoric,* pp. 165–168.

12. All quotations on wit and humor are taken from *The Philosophy of Rhetoric,* pp. 30–33; 39–42; 43–48.

13. Douglas Ehninger, ed., *Elements of Rhetoric by Richard Whately* (Carbondale, Ill.: Southern Illinois University Press, 1963), p. 9.

14. George Campbell, "The Nature, Extent, and Importance of the Duty of Allegiance," A Sermon preached at Aberdeen, December 12, 1776, Being the Fast Day Appointed by the King, on account of the Rebellion in America," in George Campbell, *A Dissertation on Miracles* (London, 1824), p. 275.

15. *The Philosophy of Rhetoric,* p. 70.

16. *Ibid.,* p. 80.

17. *Ibid.,* p. 83.

18. "The Spirit of the Gospel, a Spirit Neither of Superstition Nor of Enthusiasm," *ibid.,* pp. 152–53.

19. *Ibid.,* p. 154.

20. *The Philosophy of Rhetoric,* pp. 82–84.

21. *Ibid.*

22. *Ibid.,* p. 86.

23. *Ibid.,* pp. 90–99. This discussion resembles closely earlier attacks on the syllogism cited above.

24. *Ibid.,* p. 59.

25. *Ibid.,* pp. 127–128.

26. *Ibid.,* pp. 178–188.

27. *Elements of Rhetoric* by Richard Whately, XXVIII. (Boston and Cambridge: James Munroe and Co., 1855).

28. *Ibid.,* p. 4.

29. *Ibid.,* p. 40.

30. *Ibid.,* p. xxviii.

31. *Ibid.,* pp. xxviii–xxix.

32. *Ibid.,* p. xxix.

33. *Ibid.,* p. 46.

34. *Ibid.,* pp. 60–62.

35. *Ibid.,* p. 82.

36. *Ibid.,* pp. 106–107.

37. *Ibid.,* p. ix.

38. *Ibid.,* pp. 139–146; 152–160.

39. In our analysis of Whately we have dealt almost entirely with his theories of argument. What he had to say on delivery will be briefly examined in our forthcoming discussion of the Elocutionary Movement.

40. *An Enquiry Concerning Human Understanding* (Buffalo, N.Y.: Prometheus Books, 1988), p. 106.

41. *Ibid.,* p. 107.

42. *Ibid.,* p. 115. A similarly significant statement on p. 105 says: ". . . no testimony is sufficient to establish a miracle, unless the testimony be of such a kind that its falsehood would be more miraculous, than the fact, which it endeavors to establish . . . ."

43. *Ibid.,* pp. 116–17.

44. *Ibid.,* p. 115.

45. *Ibid.,* p. 119.

46. See David Hume to Hugh Blair, London, Autumn, 1761, in J.Y.T. Greig, *The Letters of David Hume,* 2 vols. (Oxford: Clarendon Press, 1931), I, pp. 348–351; and David Hume to George Campbell, Edinburgh, June 7, 1762, in ibid., pp. 360–361.

47. *A Dissertation on Miracles* (London: Thomas Tegg, 1824), p. 30.

48. *Ibid.,* p. 31.

49. *Ibid.,* p. 28.

50. *Ibid.,* p. 47.

51. *Ibid.,* p. 38n.

52. *Ibid.,* p. 58.

53. *Ibid.,* pp. 59–60.

54. Cited in David Akenson, *A Protestant in Purgatory: Richard Whately, Archbishop of Dublin* (Hamden, Conn.: Archon Books, 1981), p. 30.

55. *Historic Doubts Relative to Napoleon Bonaparte* (New York: Robert Carter & Brothers, 1867), p. 30.

56. *Ibid.,* p. 34.

57. *Ibid.,* p. 37.

58. *Ibid.,* p. 42.

59. *Ibid.,* p. 39.

60. The use of the term "improbable" is central to Whately's argument because he is suggesting that this is what Hume had in mind when he denied the existence of miracles. Campbell held a similar view. See his *Dissertation,* p. 55.

61. *Historic Doubts Relative to Napoleon Bonaparte,* p. 70.

62. *Ibid.,* p. 72.

63. See Ernest Mossner, "Hume and the Legacy of the Dialogues," in G.P. Morice, ed., *David Hume: Bicentary Papers* (Edinburgh: Edinburgh University Press, 1977), p. 1.

64. Whately ranked *The Philosophy of Rhetoric* above Blair's extremely popular *Lectures on Rhetoric and Belles Lettres.* See *Elements of*

Rhetoric ed. by Douglas Ehninger (Carbondale: Southern Illinois University Press, 1963), p. 8.

65. Boswell, who visited Hume on this occasion noted: "Dr. Campbell's Philosophy of Rhetoric" was "before him." Geoffrey Scott and F.A. Pottle, eds., *The Private Papers of James Boswell of Malahide Castle. . . ,* 18 vols. Boswell's delightful description of the whole visit appears in Vol. XII, pp. 227–32.

66. Not only does Whately allude often to the debate on miracles, but he also discusses several aspects of moral reasoning that were used both by Hume and Campbell. The influence of the debate on the *Elements of Logic* is especially important because Hume's arguments are frequently listed under the heading of fallacies.

The Elocutionary Movement

A final group of British scholars responsible for initiating a major trend in rhetorical thought in the eighteenth century were the elocutionists who devoted their attention primarily to delivery. In their practice of singling out a particular canon for emphasis, they used a strategy similar to that of the sixteenth-century stylists. Functioning as truncators who separated a specific canon from the other four treated by the ancients, both the elocutionists and the stylists reflected the influence of Peter Ramus and his disciple Omer Talon. In the second half of the sixteenth century, as we noted in the chapter on "The Christianization of Rhetorical Thought," Ramus, a French philosopher, sought to realign logic and rhetoric. Under logic or dialectic, he argued, belonged the canons of invention and disposition. Since rhetoric, on the other hand, should not be permitted to share the same subject matter, it should consist merely of style and delivery.[1] Although Ramus "is not the originator of the idea" that rhetoric should be limited to style and delivery, he proved to be such a popular and influential persuader that he won the devotion of numerous followers who proclaimed him as a seminal thinker.[2] What makes him particularly significant in this historical survey is the fact that the Ramistic dichotomy not only provided the rationale for rhetorical works on style such as Henry Peacham's *Garden of Eloquence* (1577) but established a framework in which the elocutionary movement could build.

EIGHTEENTH-CENTURY ELOCUTIONISTS

Although the first book written in English limiting itself to the subject of delivery appeared as early as 1617,[3] the elocutionary movement did not progress in earnest until the following century. In the 1700s and in subsequent decades, students of speech and polite literature saw three pressing needs which, they believed, had to be met before effective oral communication in English could develop.

First, their research of ancient and modern works proved much to their dismay that no previous writer had come to grips adequately with delivery. The author of *The Art of Speaking* observed in 1768 that Greek, Roman, French, and Italian scholars had spoken copiously of invention, disposition, and style, but had neglected the last canon.[4] Four decades earlier John Henley noted that Aristotle, in considering delivery a gift of nature, gave no rules on the subject. Moreover, he added, many of the helpful hints appearing in Quintilian's *Institutio Oratoria* were more appropriate for eloquence of the bar than for other forms of public address, and more suitable for the classical period than the modern era.[5] These elocutionists found it hard to understand why a subject reputed to be Demosthenes' favorite rhetorical canon had been so poorly handled.

Thomas Sheridan, perhaps the most famous British elocutionist,[6] took special notice of the failure of contemporary authors to analyze delivery. Locke, he said regretfully, wrote in a brilliant and speculative manner about the theoretical nature of man, but completely ignored the challenge to apply his doctrines to a practical theme such as voice and gesture.[7]

The elocutionists saw a second major need that made the study of delivery a fertile field for future research. Everywhere they looked they could see an increased demand for expressing ideas in oral English. Speaking opportunities were developing rapidly in parliament, at the bar, in the pulpit, and in public recitations and polite conversation. The pulpit in particular fascinated the elocutionists. Thus they often wrote their treatises with the minister in mind.

The interest in private and public speech was matched by a corresponding concern for the study of language and pronunciation. The time had come, the elocutionists believed, not only for a comprehensive English dictionary such as that of Samuel Johnson, but for a rhetorical grammar setting forth a standard of punctuation. Both Sheridan and John Walker wrote books dealing exclusively with this theme.[8] What they hoped to accomplish in doing so was to lift oral English to the high status level enjoyed by written English.

As the elocutionists became aware of the omissions in rhetorical literature with respect to delivery, and as they witnessed expanding opportunities in public speaking and oral reading and a developing interest in language study, they surveyed contemporary practices in oral presentation. What they saw was disheartening. In the church, at the bar, and in parliament they could find no Demosthenes or Cicero who could move the passions with a dynamic voice control and properly-motivated bodily activity. Two neoclassicists, Addison and Swift, made commentaries on this weakness that were to be quoted often in the middle of the century. Additionally, they compared the ancients with the moderns, and they concluded that "had we never so good an ear, we have still a faultering tongue, and a kind of impediment in our speech."[9] After condemning preachers who "stand stock-still in the pulpit, and will not so much as move a finger to set off the best sermons in the world," Addison gave a ringing indictment against speaking practices at the bar.

How cold and dead a figure . . . does an orator often make at the British bar, holding up his head with the most insipid serenity, and stroking the sides of a long wig that reaches down to his middle? The truth of it is, there is often nothing more ridiculous than the gestures of an English speaker; you see some of them running their hands into their pockets as far as ever they can thrust them, and others looking with great attention on a piece of paper that has nothing written on it; you may see many a smart rhetorician turning his hat in his hands, moulding it into several different cocks, examining sometimes the lining of it, and sometimes

the button, during the whole course of his harangue. . . . I remember, when I was a young man, and used to frequent Westminister-hall, there was a counsellor who never pleaded without a piece of pack-thread in his hand, which he used to twist about a thumb, or a finger, all the while he was speaking: the wags of those days used to call it the thread of his discourse, for he was not able to utter a word without it.[10]

Nor had the situation improved by 1762, the publication date of Sheridan's *Lectures on Elocution.* It is common knowledge, said Sheridan, that British natives as a whole do not have the ability to speak or read with grace and propriety in public; nor have they had to date a methodology to overcome this difficulty. He later taunted his English contemporaries with the claim that a country with a limited vocabulary has an inadequate supply of ideas, and a nation with a limited system of tones and gestures has an inferior use of feelings.[11]

> As the elocutionists became aware of the omissions in rhetorical literature with respect to delivery, and as they witnessed expanding opportunities in public speaking and oral reading and a developing interest in language study, they surveyed contemporary practices in oral presentation.

Apart from the three major needs outlined above, the elocutionists noted several subsidiary reasons for concentrating on the area of delivery. While these factors were not as urgent, they, along with the others, helped create the rationale for focusing on one canon of rhetoric. First, the study of delivery, the elocutionists argued, would extend our knowledge of human nature. Whatever we learn about symbolic vocal expression and gesture assumes importance because these characteristics belong exclusively to man. In this regard they thought of themselves as empiricists who derived their conclusions from observation, experience, and social science methodology. They used the information resulting from their investigations to study the effects of delivery on the mental faculties. Some used an approach similar to that employed by twentieth-century students of speech and hearing science. In his *Introduction to the Art of Reading,* for instance, John Rice considered the relationship between sense and sound, and discussed vocal anatomy.[12] Sheridan, moreover, used scientific instruments as a part of his public demonstrations. James Boswell reports that in April, 1781, he, along with fifty men and twenty ladies, went to hear Sheridan discuss his favorite subject. There he was impressed with the apparatus which was used to "clear and smooth and mellow" the voice.[13]

Secondly, delivery was the only major canon, the elocutionists pointed out, that had not yet been under a concerted attack during the modern era. The inventional system of topics and the stylistic movement's stress on schemes and tropes, for example, had received a withering indictment from the Port-Royal logicians, the Royal Academy, and Locke. Similarly, Ramus and his English followers had separated invention and disposition from rhetoric. No one thus far, however, had succeeded in launching a campaign against the canon of delivery.[14] Finally, the elocutionists believed that English was peculiarly suited to public speaking and oral reading. James Burgh summarized the attitude of his colleagues on this point. "Whoever imagines the English tongue unfit for oratory, has not a just notion of it. . . . And in oratory, and poetry, there is no tongue, ancient, or modern, capable of expressing a greater variety of humours, or passions, by its sounds than the English. . . ."[15]

Once the elocutionists had demonstrated a need and articulated their rationale, they proceeded to discuss the theory of delivery and offer practical suggestions for improving voice control and bodily activity. They defined elocution in essentially the same manner. John Henley referred to his book *The Art of Speaking in Public* as "An Essay on the Action of the Orator as to his Pronunciation and Gesture." In their introductory remarks the editors explained that the work "treats of Pronunciation and Gesture in particular, which are the very life, soul and quintessence of Rhetoric. . . ."[16] Expressing a comparable opinion, Sheridan described elocution as "the just and graceful management of the voice, countenance, and gesture in speaking,"[17] Included within the sphere of elocution were both oratory and oral reading. The former was identified with persuasion; the latter with "that system of rules, which teaches us to renounce written composition with justness, energy, variety, and ease. . . ."[18]

That the elocutionary movement as it developed in the eighteenth century was firmly entrenched in the principles of faculty psychology there can be little doubt.

That the elocutionary movement as it developed in the eighteenth century was firmly entrenched in the principles of faculty psychology there can be little doubt. Sheridan noted that much of the world was still in the dark about the understanding and the imagination, and was unaware that "the passions and the fancy have a language of their own, utterly independent of words"; and this language can be instrumental in bringing forward the four faculties of the mind with such force that persuasion ensues.[19] Later, in his "Two Dissertations on the State of Languages," Sheridan reaffirmed his belief in the faculties and asserted that they should be strengthened. Rice also incorporated the tenets of faculty psychology into his elocutionary system. Adhering to the conviction-persuasion duality, he deplored the practice of political speakers and ministers who bypassed appeals to the understanding and moved directly to a stimulation of the passions. Eleven years before the publication of Campbell's *Philosophy of Rhetoric,* Rice called for a type of public speaking that progressed in a hierarchical order beginning with the understanding and ending with the influencing of the will. It was wrong, he added, for parliamentary leaders like Lord Chatham to stir the emotions without first instructing the intellect.[20]

Burgh and Walker similarly reinforced their theories with principles drawn from psychology and the related school of taste. The faculties, Burgh observed, are always responsive to elegant speakers who with the aid of a pleasing voice and gesture transport the mind to the lofty plane of the sublime and beautiful.[21] Walker turned to Burke's *Enquiry* for information pertaining to emotional proof. He praised Burke for recognizing the connection between the internal feeling of a passion, and the external expression of it. "Hence it is," concluded Walker, "that though we frequently begin to read or express, without feeling any of the passion we wish to express, we often end in full possession of it."[22]

This reliance on the psychological theories then in vogue prevented the elocutionists from playing down the significance of invention as a vital element in the communication process. They were upset, as noted earlier, with the practice of circumventing the understanding. But they were even more disturbed with orators who had inferior content and superior vocal skill and gesture, for such communicators had an impressive power to persuade without providing thoughtful and relevant information to an enlightened auditory. This was the basis for Sheridan's tendency to denigrate the Methodists. He confessed their effectiveness in delivery but castigated them for using what he perceived to be shallow ideas. Placing them in the category of "wild orators," he nevertheless cited them as an example of how a dynamic delivery pattern could influence the reception of a message.

> *Sure I am, that the advantages which the Methodist teachers have obtained over the regular clergy, in seducing so many of their flocks from them, have been wholly owing to this. For were they to read their nonsense from notes, in the same cold, artificial manner, that so many of the clergy deliver rational discourses, it is to be presumed, that there are few of mankind, such idiots, as to become their followers; or who would not prefer sense to nonsense, if they were cloathed in the same garb.*[23]

It would appear that Sheridan's caricature of the Methodists was motivated to some degree by prejudice, but also by a sincere desire to illustrate to the Anglican clergy the role that delivery can play in affecting the faculties.

The practical application of knowledge which Sheridan found missing in the writings of Locke was a central feature of the works on elocution. Within their method of instruction was the underlying belief that theory had no value unless it was accompanied by carefully arranged training periods in front of a critical observer. This theory-practice pedagogical system had three distinctive characteristics. It recommended the natural manner, along with prescriptive rules for achieving it, and taught the need to know the internal and external traits of a passion. Students who wished to use the natural method were told to study the normal dispositions and affections of themselves and others, and to observe people in action during conversational situations. Whatever is considered natural in informal face-to-face communication sessions was the model to be followed on the platform either for public speaking or oral reading. It was a technique, in sum, that urged prospective orators and interpreters to be true to their own genuine feelings and to avoid imitating the performance of others.[24]

The elocutionists were quick to advocate rules for the management of the voice and gesture. Sheridan's practice was typical. He consistently advised speakers to learn their shortcomings in vocal control and to work on these defects in the presence of an auditor. A few representative rules that show his prescriptive method are listed.

RULES FOR MANAGEMENT OF VOICE AND GESTURE

---

1. To get more force a communicator should "fix his eyes upon that part of his auditory which is farthest from him," and "mechanically endeavour to pitch his voice so as that it may reach them."
2. In striving for more force one should "never utter a greater quantity of voice, than he can afford without pain to himself, or any extraordinary effort."
3. To correct an excessive speed in utterance, "the most effectual method will be, to lay aside an hour every morning, to be employed in the practice of reading aloud, in a manner, much slower than is necessary."
4. To improve the pronunciation of vowels and consonants, these sounds should be repeated over and over again.
5. The rule to be remembered concerning the proper use of accent "is to lay the accent always on the same syllable, and the same letter of the syllable, which they usually do in common discourse, and to take care not to lay any accent or stress, upon any other syllable."[25]

More detailed and artificial were the rules for bodily activity presented by Walker. He gave suggestions, first of all, to oral readers.

> *When we read to a few persons only in private, it may not be useless to observe, that we should accustom ourselves to read standing; that the book should be held in the left hand; that we should take our eyes as often as possible from the book, and direct them to those that hear us. The three or four last words, at least, of every paragraph, or branch of a subject, should be pronounced with the eye pointed to one of the auditors. When any thing sublime, lofty, or heavenly, is expressed, the eye and the*

right hand may be very properly elevated; and when any thing low, inferiour, or grovelling is referred to, the eye and hand may be directed downwards; when any thing distant or extensive is mentioned, the hand may naturally describe the distance or extent; and when conscious virtue, or any heartfelt emotion, or tender sentiment occurs, we may as naturally clap the right hand on the breast, exactly over the heart.[26]

In turning to public speaking, Walker advised that this type of communication requires more action than oral interpretation. His detailed, mechanical suggestions contained in the following passage, at first glance, appear to be inconsistent with his conviction that gestures should comply with the taste of a society, and with his commitment to the natural manner of delivery.

In speaking extempore, we should be sparing of the use of the left hand, which may not ungracefully hang down by the side, and be suffered to receive that small degree of motion which will necessarily be communicated to it by the action of the right hand. The right hand, when in action, ought to rise extending from the side, that is, in a direction from left to right; and then be propelled forwards, with the fingers open, and easily and differently curved: the arm should move chiefly from the elbow, the hand seldom be raised higher than the shoulder, and when it has described its object, or enforced its emphasis, ought to drop lifeless down to the side, ready to commence action afresh. The utmost care must be taken to keep the elbow from inclining to the body, and to let the arms, when not hanging at rest by the side, approach to the action we call a-kimbo; we must be cautious, too, in all action but such as describes extent or circumference, to keep the hand, or lower part of the arm, from cutting the perpendicular line that divides the body into right and left; but above all, we must be careful to let the stroke of the hand, which marks force, or emphasis, keep exact time with the force of pronunciation; that is, the hand must go down upon the emphatical word, and no other.[27]

Walker's ideas undoubtedly were influenced by what he had observed in music and dancing, and, to some extent, by what he had seen in theatrical productions. If his rules were too artificial and prescriptive for a natural mode of delivery, they had the saving merit of attempting to make gesturing a science.

The habit of establishing rules for voice production and bodily activity was perhaps most noticeable in the field of pronunciation. Sheridan, who was the leader in an effort to have a fixed, universal standard of pronunciation for English, devised a system of visible marks to designate how a particular word should be articulated. Rice, in supporting Sheridan's goal of producing an acceptable standard, included an appendix in his *Art of Reading* which he subtitled: "The Sketch of a Plan for establishing a criterion, by which the Pronunciation of Languages may be ascertained; and, in particular that of the English Tongue, reduced to a certain fixt Standard."[28]

Not content to limit their investigations to an analysis of the natural method and to rules and standards, the elocutionists also sought to determine the connection between bodily movement and the passions. Burgh was one of the first to become persuaded that each internal emotion has an accurate external manifestation that could be detected by any discerning eye. As he put it in his *Art of Speaking*: "Nature has given every emotion of the Mind its proper outward expression, in such a manner, that what suits one, cannot, by any means, be accommodated to another. . . ."[29] He next undertook to list and discuss seventy-one emotions ranging from "tranquility" and "cheerfulness" to "fainting" and "death." Observe the description of the emotion he labels "persuasion." "Persuasion," he said, "puts on the looks of moderate love. Its accents are soft, flattering, emphatical and articulate."[30]

Burgh's method of describing and illustrating the passions impressed Walker, prompting him to use the same plan. Here is a typical sampling of the passions appearing in the *Elements of Elocution*:

Tranquility *appears by the composure of the countenance, and general repose of the whole body, without the exertion of any one muscle. The countenance open, the forehead smooth, the eyebrows arched, the mouth just not shut, and the eyes passing with an easy motion from object to object, but not dwelling long upon any one. To distinguish it, however, from insensibility, it seems necessary to give it that cast of happiness which borders on cheerfulness.*

A pleasing emotion of mind, on the actual or assured attainment of good, or deliverance from evil, is called Joy. *Joy, when moderate, opens the countenance with smiles, and throws, as it were, a sunshine of delectation over the whole frame: When it is sudden and violent, it expresses itself by clapping the hands, raising the eyes towards heaven, and giving such a spring to the body as to make it attempt to mount up as if it could fly: When Joy is extreme, and goes into transport, rapture, and ecstasy, it has a wildness of look and gesture that borders on folly, madness, and sorrow.*

Pity is benevolence to the afflicted. It is a mixture of love for an object that suffers, and a grief that we are not able to remove those sufferings. It shows itself in a compassionate tenderness of voice, a feeling of pain in the countenance, and a gentle raising and falling of the hands and eyes, as if mourning over the unhappy object. The mouth is open, the eyebrows are drawn down, and the features contracted or drawn together.

Fear is a mixture of aversion and sorrow, discomposing and debilitating the mind upon the approach or anticipation of evil. When this is attended with surprise and much discomposure, it grows into terror and consternation. Fear, violent and sudden, opens wide the eyes and mouth, shortens the nose, gives the countenance an air of wildness, covers it with deadly paleness, draws back the elbows parallel with the sides, lifts up the open hands, with the fingers spread, to the height of the breast, at some distance before it so as to shield it from the dreadful object. One foot is drawn back behind the other, so that the body seems shrinking from the danger, and putting itself in a posture for flight. The heart beats violently, the breath is quick and short, and the whole body is thrown into a general tremour. The voice is weak and trembling, the sentences are short, and the meaning confused and incoherent.[31]

Walker's procedure, notwithstanding its obvious superficiality, emanated from the belief that covert bodily activity should be consistent with overt behavior, and that well-planned and meaningful gestural motions can generate an accurate inner feeling and outward expression of the passion being displayed.

GILBERT AUSTIN'S CHIRONOMIA

In their scope, scientific grounding, and use of specific notational or marking systems, none of the eighteenth-century works on elocution could equal Gilbert Austin's *Chironomia,* published in 1806. This monumental study, which was to exert a strong influence "upon the history and teaching of rhetoric and oral interpretation in Europe and America,"[32] was impressive in its design and goals. The following complete title of the text suggests the wide range of Austin's interest in elevating the fifth canon of rhetoric to the level of a science: "Chironomia; or a *Treatise on Rhetorical Delivery:* Comprehending Many Precepts, Both Ancient and Modern, For the Proper Regulation of the *Voice, the Countenance, and Gesture.* Together With An *Investigation of the Elements of Gesture, and a New Method for the Notation Thereof: Illustrated by Many Figures.*"

As he begins his task Austin expressed the hope that he would complete the rules needed "for the better study and acquisition of rhetorical delivery. . . ." It soon becomes quite clear, however, that what the Irish author and clergyman wished to stress was not so much delivery as a whole but the science of gesturing. He devotes two chapters to the voice and one each to the countenance, reading, declamation, oratory, and acting. At the same time he sets aside fifteen chapters to a consideration of gesture. Here are but a few of the topics he considers:

- Of Notation and Gesture
- Of the Position of the Feet and Lower Limbs
- Of the Positions, Motions, and Elevation of the Arms
- Of the Positions and Motions of the Hands
- Of the Head, the Eyes, the Shoulders, and Body

An essential element in Austin's detailed system was the creation of a marking method to show proper facial expressions, eye contact, hand or bodily action, and stance. Had such notations been used in the classical period or in the time of Shakespeare or Milton, he said, prospective orators or actors in the present day would have models to emulate and rules to follow. Thus instead of relying on conjecture we would know how Demosthenes and Cicero performed and how Shakespeare and Milton wanted their writings to be read orally.

Austin's complicated method of teaching delivery, along with its impact on the elocutionary movement, cannot be fully appreciated unless we see the visual drawings and markings he used. At the conclusion of this chapter is a reproduction of four of the eleven plates he used to depict appropriate posture and stance, the systematic positions of the arms and hands, and complex significant gestures. The plates, in all, contain 122 separate items which constitute a reference chart alluded to in the last half of the volume. Robb and Thonssen have observed:

(The plates) explain that Austin's system of gesture and movement is based upon the speaker's position in an imaginary sphere, and that notations are made to indicate changes of position, especially of the arms as they move in the sphere. The notations for arms, hand, and head are placed above the line of literature to be read, and the movement about the stage indicated below; for example, AR2 means that the speaker advances two steps to the right.[33]

The elocutionary movement, on balance, has left an influence on Western rhetorical thought which is both detrimental and fruitful. While expressing a preference for the natural method, many of the elocutionists unwittingly gave prescriptive mechanical rules which frequently led to excesses—a practice soundly condemned by Whately.[34] Moreover, by centering their attention primarily on delivery, elocutionists were inclined to ignore the close relationship between the message and the channel. This tendency prompted Howell to observe

that voice and gesture seem much more trivial when studied by themselves than they are when studied within the context of the best possible conceptions of invention, arrangement, and style. It was the solidest virtue of Cicero's and Quintilian's rhetorical writings that they saw delivery as an activity allied with but never separable from, the speaker's need to know his subject, to arrange it properly, and to give it effective expression. Indeed, Cicero and Quintilian had learned this virtue from Aristotle, and the lesson should never be forgotten. . . .[35]

Howell concludes his indictment of the elocutionists by suggesting that they mistakenly "sought to save classical rhetoric by rediscovering its precepts of delivery and by emphasizing them by themselves, whereas in reality classical rhetoric could best have been saved by modernizing those precepts and by teaching them only within the context of philosophi-

cally-reconstituted theories of invention, arrangement, and style."[36]

Despite the shortcomings outlined by Howell, the elocutionists exerted a positive effect in several respects. Sheridan's "principles of elocution," for example, "lie somewhere at the roots of much of the present teaching of oral interpretation."[37] Perhaps even more important, Austin's comprehensive notational system "anticipated the electronic wizardry of tape and disc that today preserves the images and the voices of poets, actors, orators, and public officials who record memories for the archives of oral history projects."[38] The elocutionists, in sum, showed a strong preference for applying science and the scientific method to their study of human communication. On this crucial point, Frederick Haberman notes:

It is the elocutionists' primary claim to fame in rhetorical history that they applied the tenets of science to the physiological phenomena of spoken discourse, making great contributions to human knowledge in that process. The spirit of the elocutionary movement, like that of science, was one of independence, of originality, of a break with tradition. The methodology of the elocutionary movement, like that of science, was a combination of observing and recording. Just as the astronomer observed the movements of the planets and recorded them in special symbols, so the elocutionists observed certain phenomena of voice, body, and language, and recorded them in systems of notation. The elocutionists who contributed most to the movement are those whose work is characterized by exhaustive analysis based on observation, by systematic organization, and by the invention of systems of symbolic representation. The philosophy of the elocutionary movement, like that of the scientific-rationalistic creed, was a conception of man controlled by natural law. The elocutionists believed that the nature of man was governed by the same law and order which seventeenth-century science had discovered in the nature of the universe. They could claim that their rules and principles and systems represented the order that is found in nature; they were 'nature still, but nature methodized.' The phrase 'follow nature' meant in general that the rational order found in the universe should be reproduced in books;

and it meant in the field of delivery that the laws of elocution must approximate as closely as possible the laws of life.[39]

SUMMARY

Scholars who have debated the worth of the elocutionary movement, as we can see, have marshalled strong arguments on one side or the other of the issue. All agree, however, that the elocutionists hold an important place in Western rhetorical thought because of their attempt (though artificial at times) to derive a theory of delivery based on science and human nature, and because of the great influence which their efforts had on the teaching of speech in the American classroom for more than a century.

In our survey of British and continental rhetoric, which covered the period roughly from 1600 to 1828, we have observed how distinguished figures renowned in other fields turned their attention to the study of human communication, thereby leaving their mark on Western rhetorical thought. Francis Bacon, René Descartes, Giambattista Vico, David Hume, and Adam Smith were among the leading philosophers and/or social scientists of the modern era. Edmund Burke was a celebrated political leader. Hugh Blair, George Campbell, and Archbishop Richard Whately were influential Protestant ministers. Because of the eminence these scholars and practitioners achieved in their professional occupations, and the courage they possessed in applying their wide knowledge to an analysis of rhetoric, they were able to contribute new insights

> the elocutionists hold an important place in Western rhetorical thought because of their attempt (though artificial at times) to derive a theory of delivery based on science and human nature, and because of the great influence which their efforts had on the teaching of speech in the American classroom for more than a century.

which both reinforced and modified the classical heritage.

Most of the rhetorical notions emanating from the British period fall under the major categories of neoclassicism, belles lettres, the psychological-epistemological school of thought, and the elocutionary movement. Except for neoclassicism, which tended to use traditional classical symbols, the other trends featured six emphases which gave fresh impetus to the idea that rhetoric is a dynamic developing process. These may be summarized as follows:

1. Rhetoric should be broadened to include the written genre and criticism.
2. Communicators should use a variety of ends of discourse rather than limit themselves to persuasion.
3. The audience, including their general human traits and their particular conditioning forces, should become a starting point in preparation for a rhetorical transaction.
4. Invention should be treated as a managerial function instead of a discovery process.
5. Inartistic proof or evidence deserves a place of importance comparable to artistic proof or reasoning.
6. The canon of delivery, long relegated to a state of "benign neglect," is worthy of scientific analysis.

How many of these emphases worked their way into contemporary rhetorical theory will be evident as we consider the next chapters of this volume.

Notes

---

1. For an excellent discussion of Ramus' philosophy of rhetoric, see Wilbur Samuel Howell, "Ramus and English Rhetoric: 1574–1681," *Quarterly Journal of Speech,* 37 (October 1951), pp. 299–310.
2. *Ibid.,* pp. 11–12.

3. Warren Guthrie, "The Elocution Movement— England," in Joseph Schwartz and John A. Rycenga, eds, *The Province of Rhetoric* (New York: The Ronald Press Company, 1965), p. 257. This essay first appeared in *Speech Monographs* (March, 1951).

4. James Burgh, *The Art of Speaking* (London: T. Longman and J. Buckland, 1768), pp. 1–2.

5. John Henley, *The Art of Speaking in Public,* 2nd. ed., (London: N. Cox, 1727), p. 9.

6. The most impressive study of Sheridan's theories may be found in Wallace A. Bacon, "The Elocutionary Career of Thomas Sheridan," Speech *Monographs,* XXXI (March, 1964), pp. 1–53.

7. Thomas Sheridan, A *Course of Lectures on Elocution,* 1762 (Menston, England: The Scholar Press Limited, 1968), VI–VII.

8. See Thomas Sheridan, *A Rhetorical Grammar of the English Language,* 1781 (Menston, England: The Scholar Press Limited, 1969); and John Walker, *A Rhetorical Grammar* (Boston: Cummings and Hilliard, 1822). This volume first appeared in 1785.

9. Joseph Addison, *The Works of the Right Honorable Joseph Addison,* ed. by Richard Hurd, 6 Vols. (London: T. Cadell and W. Davies, Strand, 1811), VI, p. 452.

10. *Ibid.,* IV, p. 328.

11. Thomas Sheridan, "Two Dissertations on the State of Languages," in *A Course of Lectures on Elocution,* pp. 168–69.

12. John Rice, *An Introduction to the Art of Reading with Energy and Propriety* (London: J. and R. Tonson, 1765).

13. James Boswell, *Private Papers of James Boswell from Malahide Castle,* ed. Geoffrey Scott, 18 vols. (Mount Vernon, N.Y.: W.E. Rudge, privately printed, 1928–34), 1, p. 70.

14. Wilbur S. Howell, "Sources of the Elocutionary Movement in England," *Quarterly Journal of Speech* XLV (February 1959), pp. 1–18.

15. Burgh, p. 4.

16. Henley, p. xvii.

17. Sheridan, *A Course of Lectures on Elocution,* p. 19.

18. John Walker, *Elements of Elocution* (Boston: D. Mallory & Co., 1810), p. 18.

19. Sheridan, *A Course of Lectures on Elocution,* X.

20. Rice, pp. 288–89.

21. Burgh, p. 30.

22. Walker, *Elements of Elocution,* p. 311.

23. Sheridan, *A Course of Lectures on Elocution,* p. 128.

24. *Ibid.,* pp. 119–20.

25. *Ibid.* pp. 32–38, 55–56, and 85–88.

26. Walker, *Elements of Elocution,* pp. 304–305.

27. *Ibid.,* p. 305.

28. Rice, p. 307.

29. Burgh, p. 12.

30. *Ibid.,* p. 22.

31. Walker, *Elements of Elocution,* pp. 317–36. The most comprehensive analysis dealing with Walker's methods is M. Leon Dodez, "An Examination of the Theories and Methodologies of John Walker with Emphasis upon Gesturing," Ph.D. Dissertation, The Ohio State University, 1963.

32. Mary Margaret Robb and Lester Thonssen, eds, *Chironomia or A Treatise on Rhetorical Delivery by Gilbert Austin* (Carbondale, Ill.: Southern Illinois University Press, 1966), V.

33. *Ibid.,* IX–X.

34. In the last chapter of *Elements of Rhetoric,* Whately articulated the need for a natural mode of delivery, and criticized the elocutionists for devising a mechanical marking system that promoted artificiality.

35. Howell, "Sources of the Elocutionary Movement in England," pp. 17–18.

36. *Ibid.,* p. 18.

37. Bacon, "The Elocutionary Career of Thomas Sheridan," p. 46.

38. *Chironomia,* p. Ix.

39. Frederick W. Haberman, "English Sources of American Elocution," in Karl Wallace, ed., *History of Speech Education in America* (New York: Appleton-Century-Crofts, Inc., 1954), pp. 109–110.

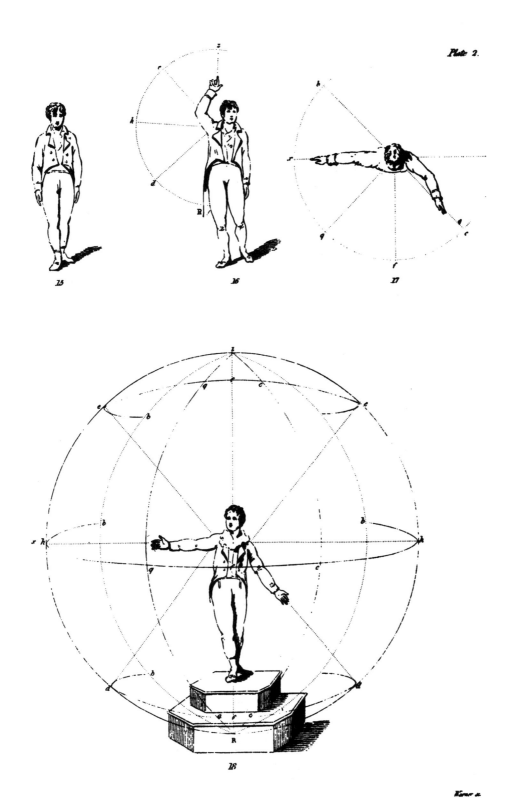

Plate 2.

Plate. 10.

Complex Significant Gestures.

99   100   101   102

103   104   105   106

107   108   109   110

Kelly del.   Warner sc.

Plate. 11.

Complex Significant Gestures.

Kelly del.

Warner sc.

Enlightenment Rhetoric in America

During the Colonial and early National Periods in American history, a dominating concern of the Founding Fathers and their disciples was to elevate the educational and cultural levels of professional leaders in particular and the public in general. They sought to achieve this goal by teaching the citizens the basic principles of Enlightenment thought as seen in the works of major classical scholars and the writings of a group of significant British and Continental theorists such as Francis Bacon, John Locke, Lord Shaftesbury, Francis Hutcheson, Lord Kames, and David Hume. Among the subject areas stressed by these Enlightenment scholars were moral philosophy and rhetoric.

In the development of this chapter, we have selected two men who, notwithstanding their enormous political commitments and influence, took time out from their pressing schedules to articulate a philosophy of discourse which may aptly be called "The Beginnings of an American Rhetoric." They are John Witherspoon and John Quincy Adams. Witherspoon's ideas are contained in his "Lectures on Moral Philosophy" and his "Lectures on Eloquence," both of which were delivered while he served as President of the College of New Jersey, currently known as Princeton University. Adams' reflections are treated in his *Lectures on Rhetoric and Oratory,* first presented at Harvard University from 1806 through 1809, and later published as a two-volume work in 1810.

A third member of the triumvirate of rhetorical scholars who were part of the Enlightenment movement in America was Thomas Jefferson. In naming Jefferson the preeminent person of the 18th century, the editors of *Time Magazine* [12/31/99] stated: "With the Declaration [of Independence]

Jefferson gave the Enlightenment its most eloquent and succinct political expression" which "lifted the human race into a higher orbit." Although Jefferson's philosophy of discourse will not be analyzed here, it is interesting to note that he knew and respected John Witherspoon and John Quincy Adams not only as men of virtue but as distinguished teachers of rhetoric.*

JOHN WITHERSPOON'S LECTURES ON MORAL PHILOSOPHY AND ELOQUENCE

The first person to offer a systematic course in rhetoric in America was a clergyman by the name of John Witherspoon. Witherspoon was born in 1723 and was educated at the University of Edinburgh. Like Hugh Blair, who was his college classmate, and George Campbell, he became a prominent Presbyterian minister. In 1768, at the age of forty-five, he agreed to travel across the Atlantic to become the president of the College of New Jersey, or as it is now called, Princeton University.

An active spokesman in civic and religious matters, Witherspoon was elected to the Continental Congress in 1776 where he became a friend of Franklin, Adams, and Washington, along with other leaders of the new republic. During the course of the debates on the Declaration of Independence, Witherspoon became an eloquent supporter of the document, often challenging those who expressed reservations about breaking ties with Great Britain. At one point a delegate suggested that America was "not yet ripe" to take such a revolutionary action. Witherspoon responded with these words: "In my judgment, Sir, we are not only ripe but rotting."[1] When the time

---

*For an extensive analysis of Thomas Jefferson's philosophy and practice of discourse, see James L. Golden and Alan L. Golden, "Thomas Jefferson and the Rhetoric of Virtue," to be published by Madison House Publishers in the Spring of 2001.

arrived for a final vote, he became the only clergy-man to sign the Declaration of Independence.

Nor did Witherspoon forget his responsibilities as a Christian minister and polemicist in the area of theology. With enthusiasm, he helped establish the Presbyterian Church in America, making it a strong force in promoting virtue. In sum, he was a religious conservative who often took issue with such moderates as Blair and Campbell by vigorously advancing the cause of Calvinism.

As an influential educator, Witherspoon not only recognized the importance of preparing young men for the ministry, but also believed that it was the duty of the college "to prepare its students to fill . . . secular positions of colonial leadership."[2] He himself taught classes in history, philosophy, divinity, and eloquence, and could take pride in knowing that "under his auspices were educated many ministers and early patriots and legislators of the United States, among them James Madison."[3] These students appreciated the fact that the President and Professor brought with him from Scotland a new instructional system based on lecturing. It was this method he used as he discussed the two related arts of moral philosophy and eloquence.

From the first year he arrived in the New World until a brief period before his death, Witherspoon delivered lectures on moral philosophy and eloquence, which together constituted the core of his thinking about rhetoric. Six years before these courses began, Witherspoon's alma mater, the University of Edinburgh, had elected Hugh Blair Regius Professor of Rhetoric and Belles Lettres so we should not be surprised to learn that the new college president included the subject of rhetoric among those required for his students. But despite the fact Witherspoon and Blair were influenced by the same professors, and were ministers in the same denomination, they developed different emphases in rhetorical theory. Blair, for example, instituted "rhetoric by its ties to polite literature," while Witherspoon, on the other hand, redefined "classical rhetoric and moral philosophy to suit the social needs" of his new American environment.[4]

Witherspoon's "Lectures on Eloquence" were published posthumously, first appearing in 1801 in his

> all humans are born with a "moral sense" or "conscience" which helps us to determine the difference between right and wrong, and creates in us a desire to stand on the side of both private and public good.

Works and then in a separate edition with his "Lectures on Moral Philosophy" in 1810.[5] His practice was to make a syllabus of his lectures, a series of bare statements each student was expected to copy and use as a text. "At recitation the President would amplify the bare statements."[6] It appears that his approach was similar to that used by Aristotle in his *Rhetoric*.

The procedure we will now follow is to begin with an analysis of Witherspoon's "Lectures on Moral Philosophy" because they establish a foundation for his "Lectures on Eloquence." Each of these sets of lectures contain sixteen separate presentations. The source for our discussion is Thomas Miller's *Selected Writings of John Witherspoon,* published by the Southern Illinois University Press in 1990.[7]

Lectures on Moral Philosophy

The first two lectures are comprised of preliminary observations on the parameters of moral philosophy which, according to Witherspoon, consists of three subject areas—Ethics, Politics, and Jurisprudence. The first subject pertains "to personal duties"; the second to the constitution of a government and to the rights of society; and the third to "the administration of justice." This brief overview of the constituent parts of moral philosophy is followed by references to three faculties of the mind—the Understanding, the Will, and the Affections. He then pointed out how a person gains knowledge through the "external senses" of "seeing, hearing, feeling, tasting, and smelling." These senses, he suggested, are reinforced by the "internal sensation" of perception.

The ensuing three lectures [III–V] focus their attention on the general nature of virtue—the subject which Shaftesbury, Hutcheson, and Jefferson believed to be the essence of moral philosophy. With these three contemporaries, Witherspoon argued that all humans are born with a "moral sense" or "conscience" which helps us to determine the difference between right and wrong, and creates in us a desire to stand on the side of both private and public good. When this is done, an integrative relationship between these forms of "good" will develop. To be moral, he further held, is to embrace the notion that virtue possesses "its own intrinsic excellence," and produces "happy consequences" in our present lives. It also generates in us a "sense of duty" toward God, and "a hope of future happiness" as a reward.

Particular aspects of virtue became the theme of lectures VI through IX. Chief among these are duties toward God, toward others, and toward ourselves. Since God represents "holiness, justice, truth, goodness and mercy," it is only natural for us to honor and love Him. But we also have a duty to man. In discussing this obligation, Witherspoon endorsed the concept of benevolence featured by Hutcheson. Like his fellow Scotsman, he believed that this branch of virtue is concerned with our duty regarding others. Commenting on the law of love to others, he said that "it ought to have for its object their greatest and best interest, and therefore implies wishing and doing them good in soul and body." If this love begins with our family and our friends, he added, it can then be extended to "promote the general happiness."

Duties to ourselves, Witherspoon maintained, requires, first of all, an appreciation of the relevance and power of the cardinal virtues highlighted by the ancients. We thus owe it to ourselves to show a commitment to "justice, temperance, prudence, and fortitude" in our thoughts and actions. In describing this point, Witherspoon reflected on the teachings of Hutcheson when he observed: "An action good in itself may be made criminal by an evil intention. But no action, in itself evil, can be made lawful or laudable by a good intention." Consequently, our motives in performing an act must be pure, not guided by excessive self-interest.

The foregoing analysis of the first nine lectures, as we have seen, emphasized the general and specific aspects of ethics, a subject of which Witherspoon was familiar because of his experience as a philosopher and Christian minister. But his active participation in governmental affairs during the formation of the United States made him feel equally at home in discussing politics, the second element of moral philosophy. Three lectures [X–XIII] were devoted to this theme. "Politics," he thought, contain the principles of social union and the rules of duty in state of society."

Witherspoon's particular concern was with the nature of a "Civil Society," which he defined as a "union of a number of families in one state for the mutual benefit" of all. Such a society, he asserted, consists of "rulers" and the "ruled." In his discussion of the three major forms of government—democracy, monarchy, and aristocracy—he made his preference clear. In a democracy, he said, "the multitude collectively always are true in intention to the interest of the public because it is their own." Moreover, since a democracy upholds "freedom of speech" and depends on "persuasion," it is "the nurse of eloquence." By contrast, a monarchy "is but another name for tyranny, where the arbitrary will of one capricious man disposes of the lives and properties of all ranks." Similarly unappealing, he noted, is an aristocracy which "always makes vassals of the inferior ranks, who have no hand in government . . . ." When we reflect on these pointed descriptions showing the superiority of a democracy over a monarchy and an aristocracy, we can understand why Witherspoon found it easy to sign the Declaration of Independence and had such an enduring influence on his students, not the least of whom was Madison.

The final three lectures [XIV–XVI] deal with "Jurisprudence," defined by Witherspoon as "the method of enacting and administering civil laws in any constitution." To some extent this element of moral philosophy overlaps what was said about the unit on politics. For in both instances, the object of civil laws is introduced and explained. What makes this section of special interest to students of rhetoric, however, is the question of what constitutes persuasive jurisprudential arguments. To answer this query, Witherspoon expresses his views on testimony, direct and circumstantial evidence, contracts and truth, and oaths and vows.

When seeking to determine the guilt or innocence of one charged with a crime, Witherspoon believed it to be necessary "to consider the number and character of the witnesses." Here he noted that at least two witnesses are required in order "to guard against the danger of hired evidence," and to provide an opportunity for the judge or jury to see if the testimony of each person is consistent with that of the other. If witnesses base their testimony on what they have seen or otherwise experienced firsthand, the evidence is classified as "direct." But if what is affirmed is the result of "certain facts which cannot be supposed to have existed unless the crime had been committed," it is considered to be "circumstantial." He illustrated this principle by noting that when a man is found dead at the site of a crime, and another is present holding a bloody weapon and wearing bloody clothes, it is reasonable to assume that he is probably responsible for the murder.

Such an argument from sign was repeated in Witherspoon's discussion of contracts. This type of legal transaction, he believed, must be "lawful," "formal," and "made with a capable person." Of utmost importance is the fact that a contract, in all its provisions, must meet the test of truthfulness. On this subject he took issue with Hutcheson, his favorite moral philosopher, for claiming that on some occasions it is acceptable to permit a "voluntary departure from truth" so long as a good end might be achieved. This, said Witherspoon, "is wrong" because deception in all its forms is "base and unworthy." As a result, "a good end cannot justify it." In rejecting the "end justifies the means" philosophy, Witherspoon stood squarely on the side of Jefferson.

The theme of oaths and vows, which represented the message of the last lecture on moral philosophy, gives a meaningful explanation of the serious consequences that would ensue for one who lied after promising to tell the truth before God. "An oath," declared Witherspoon, "is an appeal to God . . . for the truth of what we say and always expresses or supposes an imprecation of his judgment upon us if we prevaricate." To give increased force to this sentiment, he added these words: Oaths and vows have "been adopted by all nations in their administration of justice in order to discover the truth." Inherent in this claim is the belief that while lies and/or deceptions are in direct violation of both personal and public virtue, the most egregious testimony that can be given in a court of law is that which breaks a vow.

Witherspoon's lectures on moral philosophy were not designed to be completely original in their conception and execution. But they nevertheless represented to 18th-century American students the essence of Enlightenment thought in the areas of ethics, politics, and jurisprudence. Sprinkled throughout the lessons were instructive references to the writings of the English philosophers Locke and Hobbes; to the Scottish epistemologists Hume, Hutcheson, Kames, Thomas Reid, and Adam Smith; and to the French political philosopher Montesquieu. Witherspoon, in short, shared with Jefferson similar intellectual heroes whose commitment to virtue occupied a central place in their teachings.

Lectures on Eloquence

The first three lectures on eloquence were preliminary discourses designed to prepare the student for what should follow. After noting that eloquence is concerned with "composition, taste, and criticism," Witherspoon next raised this question: "Does art or nature contribute most to the production of a complete orator?" As might be anticipated, he argued that "very great natural powers" must be combined with "great cultivation." The ideal orator, in short, must be born and made. On the subject of improving a writer's and speaker's communication skills, Witherspoon offered suggestions similar to those advanced by Blair and Jefferson. A student, he said, should study specimens of eloquence of outstanding classical and modern authors, and imitate those rhetorical elements they deem relevant in their own compositions and delivery patterns. To prepare for their exercises, as well for their public performances, it would be useful, suggested Witherspoon, to become acquainted with principles of grammar, orthography, and pronunciation; and to avoid stylistic "blemishes" such as relying on "peculiar phrases," "improper epithets," "unnecessary words," and "vulgarisms."

Following this preliminary overview in his first three presentations, Witherspoon, in Lectures IV and V, itemized the seven principal subject areas that would be covered in the subsequent class sessions. This was in keeping with his love of systematic order. He next made some comments on the nature of eloquent speech and its history, observing that commentators on oratory have tended to concentrate on the teachers of this art rather than on "its progress and effects." Quite clearly the two classical scholars who impressed Witherspoon most were Aristotle and Cicero. In comparing these early communication pioneers, he drew this distinction between them. "Aristotle has laid open the principles of eloquence and persuasion as a logician and philosopher, and Cicero has done it in a still more masterly manner as a philosopher, scholar, orator, and statesman." By giving the palm to Cicero instead of to Aristotle, Witherspoon was reminding his pupils in the Colonial and Early Nationalism eras that a rhetorical theorist has much to gain by serving in a public capacity which would give him an opportunity to put his principles into practice.

Lectures VI–IX focus on three kinds of oratory—"the sublime," "the simple," and the "mixed." For each of the types, the distinctive characteristics are delineated. The first is called "sublime writing" which often typifies "epic poetry," "tragedy," and speeches on highly significant themes. Using Longinus' *On the Sublime* as his model, Witherspoon compressed the celebrated Greek scholar's five points into three. An initial source for producing the sublime, he suggested, along with Longinus, is "greatness or elevation of the mind." The second is "the power of moving the passions." This can be done in the following four ways:

1. Probe deeply into the "knowledge of human nature," learning as much as possible about the emotions.
2. Orators must feel the emotions in themselves they wish to arouse in others.
3. The subject under discussion should determine the emotional appeals to be used.
4. A rhetor "in attempting the pathetic" should examine his own character and personality as well as the top being discussed in order to ascertain whether or not the two dimensions are consonant with each other.

These four recommended guidelines reflect the teachings of the Scottish epistemologists, and, in turn, of the British Enlightenment Movement, by examining human nature as a starting point in a rhetorical situation.

A third source which gives "sublimity to discourse" is an appropriate use of figures of speech. These tropes should meet three tests: (1) They should be used in such a manner that they exemplify naturalness and spontaneity; (2) They should be propitious and consistent; and (3) They should be informative, thereby contributing to the knowledge of the hearer or reader.

Moving from the sublime to the simple style, Witherspoon indicated that the most frequent communication forms which feature simplicity as their hallmark "are narration, dialogue, epistolary writing, essay writing, and all the lighter species of poetry, as odes, songs, epigrams, elegies, and such like." For effective examples demonstrating how this style achieved distinction, Witherspoon singled out the ancients as exemplars of simplicity in their word choice and arrangement. He also warned that the ensuing enemies of simplicity should, for the most part, be avoided: an undue reliance on abstraction instead of specificity; frequent dependence on allegories; "an affectation of learning"; and a visible "ambition to excel."

The mixed style, as Witherspoon conceived it, is what it implies—a blending of the sublime and the simple. It is particularly appropriate in historical writing, essay writing, and on questions that are controversial. Usually present in this form of discourse are the characteristics of plainness, conciseness, and perspicuity because the principal ends in view are "to be understood" and pleased. Witherspoon alluded to Hume as a masterful essay writer who "happily joined conciseness and perspicuity." Although Jefferson severely criticized Hume for the tory sentiments expressed in his *History of England,* he nevertheless praised him as one of the best stylists in the English language.

When Witherspoon turned to the canons of rhetoric in Lectures XI and XII, he anglicized the categories employed by the ancients. He worded them as "invention," "disposition or distribution," "language," and "pronunciation, including gesture." The category of "memory" was omitted. Surprisingly, despite his strong interest in moral philosophy, his discussion of invention was disappointing. He was on target when he spoke of the need of rhetors to discover arguments that must be developed in support of a proposition. And he correctly pointed out, as did Blair and Campbell, that the ancient practice of recommending commonplaces was of "little use, unless to a person that has no fund of his own." Yet, unlike Hume and Jefferson, he did not discuss the elements of argument or tests for evaluating their soundness and relevance. Indeed, he went so far as to suggest that "in by far the greatest number of cases, there is no need of teaching [invention], and where it is necessary," he believed, "it exceeds the power of a man to teach it with effect." For this reason, he concluded that he would "not spend much time on invention."

It would appear that Witherspoon's unsatisfactory analysis of the first canon of rhetoric resulted from the mistaken belief that invention is almost exclusively controlled by a rhetor's natural talents, thus placing it outside the realm of instruction. Fortunately for his students, he was far more effective in his discussion of organization.

The arrangement or distribution of ideas, he asserted, is of "utmost importance" in developing a message because it gives "light" and "force" to the theme, produces the elegant traits of "beauty" and "brevity," and assists the "memory" of the audience. To achieve these results, a speech, for instance, must have a clearly delineated specific aim which reduces the subject "to one single proposition." This controlling purpose should then be directly supported by subordinate points which are distinct, yet at the same time maintain a connection with each other. Finally, the arguments and supporting details should "exhaust the subject."

To add more specificity to his views on the canon of disposition, Witherspoon explained how speakers in creating a persuasive speech have two choices, each of which provides an "equal advantage." One option, he described as an "ascending climax," proceeds from weaker to stronger arguments; the other, labeled a "descending climax," begins with stronger premises and ends with weaker ones. He illustrated how this could be done by an orator whose central purpose is to recommend "a pious and virtuous life." The first arrangement pattern would take this form:

Specific Purpose: "A pious and virtuous life is desirable," for
  I. "It is amiable, honorable, pleasant, profitable even in the present life."
  II. It "makes death itself a friend, and leads to a glorious immortality."

The second outline would rely on this structure:

Specific Purpose: "A pious and virtuous life is desirable, for
  I. "It is the one thing needful, that eternity is the great decisive argument that should determine our choice, though everything else were in favor of vice."
  II. "Even in the present life it is a great mistake to think that bad men are gainers."

From these examples, we can see that those speakers who prefer to end a speech on a high note would choose the first organizational model; those, on the other hand, who prefer an address to begin with the most compelling idea because of its strong initial interest value would select the second pattern. That Witherspoon chose the topic of virtue for his illustration is not surprising in view of his professional status as a minister, educator, and political leader who was an active participant in the American Enlightenment Movement which was inspired by every phase of private and public morality.

Witherspoon's treatment of the canon of language, or of composition, was brief in this section of his lectures because of his previous description of the three writing styles. He did, however, reinforce what he had earlier said by giving three new suggestions. First, rhetors should possess a thorough knowledge of their native language. Secondly, care should be taken when arranging the clauses within a sentence so that the "proportion and sound" could be featured. Lastly, an effort should be made to promote variety in word choice and structure.

Of the final rhetorical canon, pronunciation and gesture, Witherspoon acknowledged its universal importance. On the element of enthusiasm or animation, he argued, despite the fact he was a Scotsman, that "the French and Italians have much more warmth and fire in their manner than [do] the British." The major emphasis of his discussion centered on suggestions for avoiding improprieties. These included the need for conveying an attitude of sincerity and a "decency of manners"; and expressing syllables with a "distinct articulation." Similarly significant was his recommendation of this rule: ". . . keep to the tone and key of dialogue, or common conversation, as much as possible." These guidelines were consistent with some of the advice offered by the elocutionists. As a concluding point, he asserted the need to adapt the delivery to the subject, to the situation, and to the speaker's "own capacity."

The thirteenth lecture was devoted to the ends of discourse which he listed as information, demonstration, persuasion, and entertainment. Since a speech to inform relies on description, and is designed to appeal to the understanding, the stylistic elements of "plainness," "precision," and "order" are essential. These are the characteristics which should be found in historical narration, letter writing, fables, and business transactions. The closely related discourse end, demonstration, has a special relevance for scientific writings expressed in the form of "essays, systems, or controversy." To be effective, demonstration requires "perspicuity, order, and strength," and should never utilize wit.

When speaking of persuasion as a purpose in discourse, Witherspoon asserted that this end is

> When speaking of persuasion as a purpose in discourse, Witherspoon asserted that this end is achieved "when we would bring the reader or hearer to determinate choice, either immediately upon the spot for a particular decision, as in an assembly or court of justice, or in a more slow and lasting way, as in religious and moral writings.

achieved "when we would bring the reader or hearer to determinate choice, either immediately upon the spot for a particular decision, as in an assembly or court of justice, or in a more slow and lasting way, as in religious and moral writings." Most often, he added, it occurs "as the effect of a single discourse."

Entertainment, the last purpose of discourse, has no other goal than to amuse. Poetical compositions, Witherspoon believed, were an ideal medium for entertaining a reader or hearer. He further held, as did Jefferson, that Cervantes' Don Quixote is a splendid example of this rhetorical end because of its mastery of humor.

On the whole, Witherspoon's analysis of the ends of discourse was consistent with traditional thought. But the following observation was groundbreaking in its implications: "The intention of all speech or writing, which is but recorded speech, is to persuade. . . ." Such a statement anticipated our contemporary thinking.

The remaining lectures on eloquence dealt with the three forms of discourse—the pulpit, the bar, and deliberative assemblies—and with taste and criticism. To fulfill their obligations as Christian ministers, according to Witherspoon, preachers should possess a wide range of knowledge, make certain that their arguments and evidence are accurate, and reveal at all times an attitude of piety and reverence toward the gospel. In addition, they should deliver their sermons with "simplicity," "force and vehemence." For there are no speakers who have "a greater right to exert themselves to the utmost, or who may properly interest their hearers more, than" ministers "of the gospel." Witherspoon's former classmate Hugh Blair echoed similar sentiments about pulpit eloquence in his *Lectures on Rhetoric and Belles Lettres.*

In speaking of legal eloquence, Witherspoon emphasized the overridingly crucial element of virtue. If lawyers in their presentations, he noted, epitomize the moral elements of integrity, prudence, and firmness, they will have the rhetorical tools to be "an overmatch for all the villains upon earth." These virtuous traits, moreover, should be revealed in the causes that are undertaken and in those that are rejected. Every lawyer, he asserted, "should make it a point of honor not to undertake a cause" which is unjust. This same level of integrity is needed in the manner of conducting causes. It should further be remembered that lawyers are never justified in engaging in "sinister acts," "equivocation," and in the

"concealment of the truth." Victory, in sum, is far less important than maintaining one's honor.

Extensive knowledge and training on the part of the legal advocate are also essential qualities in forensic discourse. Thus the lawyer should be schooled in the arts and sciences in general and in history in particular. Even more important, he must have knowledge of human nature and the way life is lived. Finally, successful lawyers are those who demonstrate "quickness and vivacity" when presenting their arguments.

With his own experience as a member of the New Jersey delegation which was sent to the Continental Congress, Witherspoon knew what it was like to participate in legislative assemblies, including the debates on the Declaration of Independence. From these experiences and his research, he was able to conclude with confidence that fervor and passion on the part of an orator in a public assembly are as appropriate for this type of discourse as it is for pulpit eloquence. To support this claim, he cited the opinion of David Hume who he praised "for his accuracy of judgment in matters of criticism." Hume has asserted, noted Witherspoon, "that human nature is always the same and that eloquence which kindles and governs the passions will always have great influence on large assemblies, let them be of what station or rank so ever." To make these appeals to the passions culminate in persuasion, legislative orators will enhance their chances for success if they display "dignity in character" and an in-depth "knowledge of men and manners, of history, and of human nature."

Witherspoon appropriately chose for his last lecture on eloquence the subject of taste and criticism because of its application to all the fine arts, but particularly to oratorical and poetical discourse. His strategy in discussing this theme was to summarize and evaluate what leading contemporary scholars have said about taste, and then to draw his own conclusions. In seeking to explain "why one person, one thing, or one composition is more excellent than another," he thought the answer could be discovered by considering the foundations of taste. Some have suggested, he observed, that the source of taste "is an immediate and simple perception . . . ." Other have probed more deeply into human nature, he added, to find the real foundation of taste. Hutcheson, for example, described "the powers or perceptions in human nature" as "reflex senses" or "internal sensations" which are derived "from outward objects" which may be called "external sensations." With this description, Witherspoon concurred. But, unlike Hutcheson, he did not believe that taste was a part of virtue.

Although Witherspoon accepted the premise that the foundation of taste "is laid . . . in our natures," at the same time, he felt there is "great room for improvement and cultivation." This could be accomplished, he observed, "by investigating the grounds of approbation, by comparing one thing with another, by studying the best examples, and by reflection and judgment. . . ." Reasoning, it is clear, is an important part of the process. If critics follow these procedures, Witherspoon believed, they will develop "a well-formed taste" which, in turn, will enable them "to perceive the beauty of the whole" in an oratorical or poetical work, as well as the relation of one part to another.

> Witherspoon's lectures on moral philosophy and on eloquence were eclectic in nature, bringing together the core ideas of neoclassicism, British and Continental epistemology, and rhetoric and polite literature.

What emerges from the preceding discussion of the lectures on eloquence is, first of all, a broad-range philosophy of discourse which embraces oral and written communication, and combines rhetoric with belles lettres. Repeatedly, Witherspoon used the words "speaker" and "writer" as he described what was required to become an effective orator, debater, essayist, poet, and critic. All of these forms of discourse, he noted, must meet the tests of virtue and of a refined taste. Moreover, with their persistent emphasis on epistemological thought, the lectures drew heavily from the principles of human nature, thus using the audience as a starting point in preparing for a rhetorical transaction.

Not content to stress theory alone as he strove to acquaint his students with the nature and significance of eloquence, Witherspoon also provided opportunities for implementing the theoretical principles in a rhetorical situation. His attitude toward practicum may be seen in the following statement: "The College erected a stage for formal speaking, and at least three evenings a week Princeton students were pronouncing orations from this platform."[8] It soon became known throughout America that speech was important to Witherspoon and he was determined that rhetoric play a major role in undergraduate instruction. Aware of what his former colleague in the Continental Congress was accomplishing in his lectures, Jefferson, then serving as Secretary of State in Washington's first cabinet, wrote to Witherspoon with this request:

The bearer [of this letter], Mr. Bennet Taylor, a young gentleman from Virginia, goes on to your seminary for the prosecution of his studies. Being recommended to me by a good friend of mine, I feel an interest in his success, and therefore take the liberty of naming him particularly to you. His principal objects will be mathematics and Natural Philosophy. Rhetoric also, I presume is taught with you, and will be proper for him as destined for the bar. . . .[9]

Witherspoon's lectures on moral philosophy and on eloquence, in brief, were eclectic in nature, bringing together the core ideas of neoclassicism, British and Continental epistemology, and rhetoric and polite literature. This heritage was then strengthened by his rich personal experiences as a pulpit orator, legislative assembly speaker, and college administrator. He thus took his place, along the side of other influential leaders, who sought to make available to their students those basic rhetorical principles which proved to be a vital part of Enlightenment thought during the formative years of the American nation.

Notes

1. "John Witherspoon," in *Dictionary of National Biography.* p. 744. During another phase of the debates on the Declaration, in which a rough draft was being considered, Witherspoon objected to a clause which read: "Scotch and foreign mercenaries. . . ." He "sprang to his feet and said that he would not have the Scottish nation insulted." As a result of this objection, the words "Scotch and" were "deleted." Samuel Eliot Morison, *The Oxford History of*

the American People (New York, 1965), pp. 221–22.

2. Varnum Collins, ed., *John Witherspoon's Lectures on Moral Philosophy* (Princeton, 1912), p. xi.

3. "John Witherspoon," *Dictionary of National Biography,* p. 743.

4. Thomas Miller, ed., *Selected Writings of John Witherspoon* (Carbondale, Ill., 1990), p. 1.

5. Ibid., p. vii.

6. Collins, ed., *John Witherspoon's Lectures on Moral Philosophy,* p. xi.

7. Miller's work, which also begins with the *Lectures on Moral Philosophy,* contains an excellent introduction.

8. Jack Scott, ed., *An Annotated Edition of Lectures on Moral Philosophy by John Witherspoon* (Newark, Del., 1982), p. 15.

9. Thomas Jefferson to John Witherspoon, Philadelphia, January 12, 1792, in Julian Boyd, ed., *The Papers of Thomas Jefferson,* 27 vols. to date (Princeton, 1990), XXIII, p. 40. Apart from serving together as members of the Continental Congress in 1776, Jefferson and Witherspoon were both elected as Councillors in the American Philosophical Society in February, 1781.

JOHN QUINCY ADAMS' LECTURES ON RHETORIC AND ORATORY

John Quincy Adams was the gifted first son of John and Abigail Adams. His father helped draft the Declaration of Independence, served as a diplomat in France, England, and the Netherlands, and went on to become our first Vice President. The senior Adams succeeded to the presidency in 1796 and served one tumultuous term before being replaced by Thomas Jefferson in 1801.

A brilliant student, John Quincy served as his father's secretary during negotiations that ended the Revolutionary War. At fourteen, he became secretary to the American minister in Russia. Much of his education was received abroad in France and the Netherlands. He was fluent in French and could read Greek and Latin with ease. He entered Harvard at age eighteen and completed his undergraduate degree in two years. He next studied law and was admitted to the bar at age twenty-three.

A year later, young Adams published a reply to Thomas Paine's *Rights of Man* "so brilliantly written, it was attributed to his father." His writings in defense of President Washington's foreign policy attracted such favorable attention he was appointed Minister to the Netherlands at twenty-eight. In 1803, the Massachusetts Legislature chose Adams to be their representative in the United States Senate. Nominally a Federalist but in fact an Independent, Adams voted for President Jefferson's Embargo Act, a piece of legislation highly unpopular in his native New England. With his Senate career at an end, he accepted appointment as the first Boylston Professor of Rhetoric at Harvard University in 1806.[1]

In 1809, Adams resigned his professorship to accept a presidential appointment as United States Minister Plenipotentiary to Russia. Later he would serve as President Monroe's Secretary of State and pen the famous "Monroe Doctrine." In 1824, John Quincy Adams was elected sixth President of the United States. Two years after leaving office, much to the surprise of his friends, he agreed to accept election to the House of Representatives. His distinguished career there on behalf of the right of petition in protecting slavery earned him the title "Old Man Eloquent." He died in the Speaker's chambers in 1848.

In his role as professor of rhetoric, Adams drafted a set of thirty-six lectures designed to be delivered on successive Fridays. At the request of his students, these presentations representing three years of concentrated study and writing, were published in a two-volume set in 1810, one year after he resigned from Harvard.[2]

The subject matter of these two volumes may be categorized into four major parts. The first is the Inaugural Oration which is in addition to the thirty-six lectures. The second category consists of a general view of rhetoric and oratory including a summary of their origin in Greece and Rome, and specific lectures on Cicero and Quintilian. Category III, comprised of twenty-four lectures, deals with the canons of rhetoric. The final area, focusing its attention on the four forms of public address, contains five lessons. Our plan is to examine these parts as a whole rather than one lecture at a time.

Part One—The Inaugural Oration

What Adams told his students on opening day went far beyond a simple explanation of the nature of the course for which they had enrolled. This memorable initial address was marked not only by appeals to the understanding but also by vivid and compelling descriptions designed to stir the imagination and the passions concerning the enormous potential value that competence in rhetoric and oratory could produce in their future professional lives. After beginning with the claim that reason was the foundation of eloquence in the classical world, and that eloquence in the ancient culture meant virtue and power, Adams suggested that "the whole *duty* of man" consisted in revealing himself as a good person and "an accomplished speaker." The relevance and power of speech, he added, were equally applicable in the present day. He expressed this sentiment in the following language that opened the doors of the mind: "At the revival of letters in modern Europe, eloquence, together with her sister muses, awoke and shook the poppies from their brow."

With language direct and personal, Adams began his conclusion with these words of identification: "Sons of Harvard!" What followed next were remarks directed to the three primary groups of students enrolled in the course—those planning careers in religion, in law, and in governmental service. The art of rhetoric and oratory, he told the future ministers, would help them to preach the gospel "in the temples of Almighty God, to be the messenger of heaven upon the earth," and "to enlighten with the torch of eternal truth the path of your fellow-mortals to brighter worlds." This art of discourse, he next reminded prospective lawyers, would assist them in defending "the fame of your fellow-citizens from the open assaults of violence and the secret encroachments of fraud." Finally, to those who have opted to serve their country, he suggested that communication effectiveness was needed to prepare them to participate in their government's "councils" so that they could help direct "her affairs" through the power of "persuasion."

Adams concluded his Inaugural Oration with this challenge:

> *Gather fragrance from the whole paradise of science, and learn to distil from your lips all the honies of persuasion. Consecrate above all, the faculties of your life to the cause of truth, of freedom, and of humanity. So shall your country ever gladden at the sound of your voice, and every talent, added to your accomplishments, become another blessing to mankind.*

In this early National period, as this inaugural oration suggests, Adams came down hard on the side of private and public virtue; and he made it clear that rhetoric and oratory were the principal means of transmitting the power of virtue to the American citizens. Against the background of this initial overview of the course, he was now ready to begin his lectures.

Part Two—A General Overview of the Nature and History of Rhetorical Theory. With his strong devotion to the classics, Adams began his lectures by summarizing the definitions of rhetoric presented by Aristotle, Cicero, and Quintilian. To make these definitions resonate with his students, he drew illustrations from the Old Testament, Shakespeare, and Pope. Rhetoric, he concluded, was a science; and oratory an art.

Early in his preliminary lectures, Adams confronted the issue of the relevance of rhetoric. He did so by considering three common objections to this subject area. First, he noted, it has been called a "pedantic science" characterized by an excessive use of "scholastic subtleties," and "divisions and subdivisions" which run counter to one's "genius" and "memory." Secondly, it is described as a "frivolous science," more suitable "to the pageantry of a public festival" than to the real concerns of our daily existence. Thirdly, it is labeled a "pernicious science" which all too often substitutes appeals to the imagination for ideas addressed to the understanding.

Adams refuted the above charges by again alluding to the leading Greek and Roman rhetoricians, all of whom believed that eloquence is a "useful and honorable" enterprise which constitutes the engine of a democracy. His particular hero was Cicero who he regarded as "the friend of the soul" who always produces in his readers "a gleam of pleasure." This enthusiasm for Cicero, also shared by Hume and Jefferson, led Adams to recommend the reading not only of *de Oratore* but of *Brutus, Orator,* and *The Offices* as well. Since Cicero and his disciple Quintilian believed that the ideal orator should be a virtu-

> "Sons of Harvard!" Gather fragrance from the whole paradise of science, and learn to distil from your lips all the honies of persuasion.

ous person, Adams argued that what they taught has an enduring relevance because "virtue is the oxygen, the vital air of the [modern] world."

Part Three—The Canons of Rhetoric. A lover of the classics, Adams followed closely the teachings of Aristotle, Cicero, and Quintilian when discussing the canons of rhetoric. Like his ancient forbears, he described the characteristics of invention, disposition, language, memory, and delivery. But he made one slight variation by tending to combine, in some instances, invention and disposition. This was evident in his treatment of argument which is both a part of the inventive process and the organizational structure. We will include argument in our analysis of invention as we now turn to the three traditional forms of proof.

Ethical proof was for Adams, as it was for the Greeks and Romans, the moral and intellectual qualities of an orator as they were revealed in the course of a speech. For rhetors to have strong personal proof, he believed, they must project an image of integrity, honesty, and uprightness. But these virtues of the heart must be reinforced by a speaker's "universal knowledge" and "endowments of the understanding." Adams, in sum, upheld Aristotle's notion that ethical proof is derived largely from an orator's character, intelligence or knowledge, and good will.

A more detailed analysis occurs in Adams' discussion of logical proof, covering such themes as "state of the controversy," "commonplaces," and methods of reasoning. Here as elsewhere in his comments on invention, he was more derivative than innovative. As a lawyer, statesman, and educator, he expressed faith in what the ancients said about the "state of the cause" or stasis. With them he sanctioned the idea that there are three types of stasis, or turning points in a debate—the issues of definition, quality, and quantity. Every word which is uttered in a controversy must directly or indirectly support one or more of these ends. So committed was he to this conviction that he made the following assertion: If I were "required to point out any one thing, which most forcibly discovers the inventive powers of a speaker, the infallible test or oratorical ability, the stamp,

> If I were "required to point out any one thing, which most forcibly discovers the inventive powers of a speaker, the infallible test or oratorical ability, the stamp, which distinguishes the orator from the man of words; I should say, it is the adaptation of the speech to the state of the controversy."

which distinguishes the orator from the man of words; I should say, it is the adaptation of the speech to the state of the controversy."

On the question of "topics" or "commonplaces," Adams had much less to say. He did not, as was the case with Witherspoon, Blair, and Campbell, look upon these commonplaces as artificial and sterile sources for creating arguments. He chose instead to take a middle ground position. "A perfect master of the topics," he suggested, "may be a miserable orator; but an accomplished orator will not disdain a thorough knowledge of the topics."

In developing the argumentative step, Adams alluded to this phase of the discourse as "its living soul." It includes a blending of reasoning and evidence, utilizing either the deductive or inductive process. Deduction, which he equated with "ratiocination," is based on conclusions drawn from high probability statements or self-evident premises—a type of reasoning which often is expressed in the form of rhetorical syllogisms or enthymemes. Induction, on the other hand, begins with factual data produced by experience and testimony. Deduction at its highest, he thought, approaches the level of the mathematical sciences; induction, by contrast, is more appropriate for "polite literature and the works of taste."

To illustrate what he had said about argumentation, Adams cited the examples of Cicero and Edmund Burke who, he believed, resembled the Roman orator. He was particularly motivated by the high standards Burke set in his renowned speech "On Conciliating America" in 1775, and his Bristol election speech in 1780. In the first of these addresses, Burke presented arguments in support of the proposition that there was a need to adopt steps that would alleviate the tension between Great Britain and the American colonies. In the second discourse, Burke told his constituents in Bristol why he had to vote his conscience rather than tell the electors what they wanted to hear. In both of these instances, Burke, in Adams' opinion, conformed to the tests required for an argument to be sound, relevant, and convincing.

For Adams, the third form of proof, the use of pathos, was described as an "excitation, and management of the passions." Although he believed the arousal of the emotions was necessary to complete the process of persuasion, he did not feel the need to probe the issue in depth. The main reason for this attitude may be found in his conviction that Aristotle's treatment of the passions "is one of the profoundest and most ingenious treatises upon human nature, that ever issued from the pen of man." Adams, it would appear, might have been more insightful in this assessment if he had taken a similar position about the writings of Locke and Hume on the emotions.

Notwithstanding the foregoing reservation, Adams did advance several premises worthy of note. First, he praised the Christian system of morality because it commands us "to suppress the angry and turbulent passions in ourselves, and forbids us to stimulate them in others." Secondly, he argued that appeals to "malevolent passions" could never be associated with the noblest "efforts of eloquence." Thirdly, he asserted that if the goal is "to stir the passions" and "the tempests of the soul" in an acceptable way, an orator must display a "grandeur of expression," a "boldness and irregularity of thought," a "spirit of gravity" and "seriousness," and "an inflexibility of manner. . . ." To see how this could be done, he again urged his students to study the speeches of Burke.

We have seen how Adams tended in several cases to unite invention with disposition. This was especially noticeable in his treatment of the forms of proof. There were, however, some parts of the discourse which relate more directly with the canon of disposition or order. This was true in his lectures on the "Proposition and Partition," on "Digression and Transition," and on the "Conclusion." In keeping with the recommendations of Cicero and Quintilian, Adams favored the use of partitions because they promoted "clearness and perspicuity" in a discourse. With them he also agreed that a conclusion in an oration is strengthened when it makes use of amplification and of a structural climax. Altogether, eleven lectures were devoted to an analysis of invention and disposition.

Adams developed ten lectures on language control and style, two of which dealt with purity and perspicuity and five with figures of speech. The other three focused on comparison and order, juncture and number, and sentence structure. We see in these lectures an increased interest in the writings of modern authors, both as theorists and as exemplars of excellence in composition. Among the scholars and practitioners cited are Locke, Campbell, Shakespeare, Milton, Pope, Dryden, and Swift.

When discussing the stylistic elements of purity and perspicuity, Adams suggested that these rhetorical components of language represent "oratorical elegance." As he developed this point, he, for the first time in his lectures, became a critic of George Campbell's *Philosophy of Rhetoric,* calling it "a work of great learning and ingenuity." But he proceeded to argue that Campbell was mistaken in his view that the universal standard for evaluating purity was determined by its usage and custom. This standard alone, he concluded, runs the risk "of cramping too much the liberties of language and the powers of oratory." Moreover, this criterion, if carried too far, would significantly limit "improvement in language." What is needed instead is a purity unhampered by the rigors of reputable, national, and present usage advocated by Campbell. With this view, Jefferson, because of his faith in neology, would strongly concur.

Perspicuity which, according to Adams, is comparable in importance to purity, may be violated in two ways: (1) the use of inappropriate words; and (2) a reliance on a "defective arrangement." Of these two faults, he noted, the latter tends to be more frequent and serious.

As he moved to the area of figurative language, Adams again chose not to limit himself to the teachings of the classical scholars who had shaped his ideas on invention and disposition. Early in his analysis he quoted Locke as saying "that all human ideas are ultimately derived from one of two sources; either from objects perceptible to the senses, or from the reflections of our own minds upon such subjects." He also showed the influence of Locke when he said: "The great foundation of figurative language rests on the association of ideas."

Since Adams believed that the most widely used and beautiful trope is the metaphor, he listed the ensuing five rules for using this stylistic device:

1. The figure and the literal object to which it refers must have a strong resemblance with each other.
2. After the figure is introduced, care should be taken in not spending too much time on it.
3. A metaphor should not be produced from "mean or disgusting subjects."
4. The figures should not be crowded together.

5. A distinction should be made between metaphors that are suitable to "oratorical discourse" and those appropriate for poetry.

For his illustrations showing how figurative language may achieve distinction, Adams turns to the Old and New Testaments and to English poets, dramatists, and essayists, and to his favorite British orator Edmund Burke.

In his treatment of the following two canons—memory and delivery—Adams was influenced both by the British epistemologists and the elocutionists. When discussing memory, he alluded to Locke's searching analysis of the understanding and of the concept of sensation. Similarly, without identifying Bacon as his source, he was able to conclude that memory "is the faculty of the human mind, by which we are enabled to call up at pleasure ideas, which have before been lodged in it." He also recognized, as did the ancients, that exercises may be performed for the purpose of preserving the memory.

Delivery for Adams related to all aspects of voice control and articulation, and to the various forms of bodily activity. After discussing with approval what Cicero and Quintilian said about this canon, he strongly recommended that his students give particular attention to the works of two major British elocutionists—Sheridan and Walker. From them, he held, they could gain valuable insights on pronunciation, vocal inflections, and the rules of gesturing.

Part Four—The Forms of Public Address. The final question to be answered in this survey of Adams' perspectives on rhetoric and oratory is this: What were his basic ideas on demonstrative, deliberative, judicial, and pulpit oratory? All that is to be done in analyzing the first of these two forms, he asserted, is "to receive and register in our memory the instruction of our ancient guides." This premise led him to criticize Blair for his seemingly lack of "knowledge of the critical principles, upon which demonstrative orations ought to be composed. Apparently, Adams was referring to Blair's decision to omit demonstrative oratory as a separate category in his *Lectures on Rhetoric and Belles Lettres.* This omission, Adams suggested, degraded an important form of public address.

As he sought to "reinstate demonstrative oratory" to the high place given it by the ancients, Adams emphasized the point that since this oratorical form is concerned with praise and blame, its principal theme is virtue. It is virtue, he said, which contributes "to the happiness of its possessor and of other men." Moreover, he noted, "virtue alone unites the double praise of enjoyment and of beneficence." An orator, therefore, whose task is to praise a person whose life has epitomized private and public virtue should make use of the stylistic principle of amplification so that these noble traits may be highlighted. What the audience is being told in a panegyric is that those elements of virtue exemplified by the recipient should be applied to their own lives. A speech of blame has an opposite goal, that of indicting someone who has violated those ideas or practices deemed to be good.

On the subject of deliberative oratory, Adams admitted that he subscribed fully to the stance taken by the ancients. He shared with them the view that this public address form stresses utility and relates primarily to issues pertaining to the future. As a result, orators addressing a public democratic assembly concerning actions that should be taken to ensure their future happiness must make certain that the audience has a favorable opinion of them as persons of virtue.

Adams' discussion of judicial oratory, which covered two lectures, was influenced by his own training as a lawyer. He embraced a number of the legal precepts advanced by Aristotle, Cicero, and Quintilian, including the ideas that "the common standard of all judicial arguments . . . is justice or equity," and that this rhetorical form is concerned with what happened in the past. But his own experience taught him that modern law is so complex that "the bar is beyond all question the scene of the greatest difficulty to the speaker. . . ." The reason for this claim is that an advocate opens "to public view all the strength and weakness of the mind." One of these possible weaknesses is a tendency for a lawyer to be "susceptible to digression," thus breaking the continuity of thought. Steps should be taken to avoid this fault, Adams observed, since the duty of a judicial orator is to emphasize the importance of understanding and to produce conviction.

We have noted how Adams freely acknowledged his indebtedness to the ancients in his analysis of demonstrative and deliberative oratory. Similarly he suggested that his perspectives on judicial oratory were partly classical and partly modern because of the way this form had evolved through the centuries. But when turning to pulpit discourse, he confessed that the ancients were completely unable to serve as guides to 19th-century students. This condition, he said, has created a significant challenge since "the pulpit is essentially the throne of eloquence," and thus must be assigned a "distinguished place by itself." In reaching this conclusion, Adams mentioned little about the fact that Blair had likewise produced a thoughtful lecture on pulpit eloquence.

Despite his failure to comment on Blair's contribution to religious instruction, Adams developed several premises he wanted his students to remember about pulpit oratory. Although this type of public address arose at the time Christianity was introduced, Adams argued that "it remains among the most energetic instruments of power, exercised upon mankind." What makes it so meaningful and influential, he thought, is its emphasis on "knowledge and virtue." Consequently, "one of the essential obligations of a preacher" is to acquaint his parishioners with the "moral duties" that must be performed in order to strengthen their private lives and the good of the people as a whole. Adams further pointed out that a sermon should not necessarily be limited to the primary audience assembled in a particular church on a Sunday morning. It also has the power to address a future audience provided that a written manuscript is produced at the time of delivery. This is what great ministers of the past have done.

So pleased was Adams with his decision to present a separate lecture on this rhetorical form that he drew this comparison: "The eloquence of the pulpit is to the science of rhetoric what this Western Hemisphere is to that of geography."

Adams' *Lectures on Rhetoric and Oratory* abound with simile and metaphor as well as simple, direct language. Not since Cicero, as we saw in his inaugural oration, had a theorist written so well about the art of rhetoric. So strong was his devotion to the classics that it may safely be said the torch of ancient Greece and Rome was safely passed across the sea. Although his work is more of a precedent than an innovation, it was consistent with evolving thought in the early part of the nineteenth century as reflected in the pace set by Harvard University. Fol-

lowing in the footsteps of Hugh Blair and George Campbell, he paid particular attention to the ministry for, after all, the majority of his hearers expected to enter this profession. In all, Adams the legislator, lawyer, and educator stood squarely in the tradition of the Enlightenment movement in America so ably championed by Jefferson and Witherspoon.

We conclude this overview of John Quincy Adams' *Lectures on Rhetoric and Oratory* with a brief story showing how this work helped produce a reconciliation between John Adams and Thomas Jefferson early in 1812. Shortly after Jefferson defeated Adams in his campaign for a second term as president in 1800, a rift, resulting from a misunderstanding, developed between these two founding fathers who had worked so closely together during the debates on the Declaration of Independence. Jefferson also had served as Vice President under Adams. This alienation lasted approximately eleven years before mutual friends began to call for a reconciliation. What followed was a body of correspondence between these remarkable American leaders which lasted until a few months before they both died on July 4, 1826. The quality and importance of this correspondence have achieved lasting distinction in the annals of American history.[3]

On January 1, 1812, Adams wrote the first letter, stating: "I take the liberty of sending you by the Post a Packett containing two pieces of Homespun." This "Homespun" was John Quincy Adams' two volumes on *Lectures on Rhetoric and Oratory*. The letter then noted that this work was "lately produced in this quarter by one who was honoured in his youth with some of your Attention and much of your kindness."[4] Jefferson later responded, praising John Quincy's volumes for their "fine texture," "delicate character," and "display of imagination which constitutes excellence in Belles Lettres. . . ."[5] He then apologized for the Virginia "Homespun" he had sent to Adams in return, suggesting that when it is compared to the *Lectures* it will prove to be "a mere sober, dry and formal piece of logic" since "the subject itself refuses to be embellished."[6]

> "The eloquence of the pulpit is to the science of rhetoric what this Western Hemisphere is to that of geography."

Notes

1. John Adams explained to Jefferson how the Boylston Chair was established at Harvard University: "A Relation of mine, a first Cousin of my ever honoured, beloved and revered Mother, Nicholas Boylston, a rich Merchant of Boston, bequeathed by his Will a Donation for establishing a Professorship, and John Quincy Adams . . . was most earnestly solicited to become the first Professor." John Adams to Thomas Jefferson, Quincy, February 3, 1812, in Lester J. Cappon, ed., *The Adams-Jefferson Letters,* 2 vols. (Chapel Hill: The University of North Carolina Press, 1959), II, p. 294.

2. (Cambridge: Hilliard & Metcalf, 1810).

3. Cappon observed in the Preface: "No correspondence in American history is more quotable or more readily recognized for its historical significance than that of John Adams and Thomas Jefferson." Later in the Introduction, Cappon noted: "The reconciliation of Adams and Jefferson in 1812 . . . brought about a rich and voluminous correspondence that has no counterpart in any other period of American intellectual history." I, xlvi.

4. John Adams to Jefferson, Quincy, January 1, 1812, in ibid., II, p. 290.

5. Thomas Jefferson to John Adams, Monticello, April 20, 1812, in ibid., II, p. 298.

6. The "Homespun" Jefferson sent to Adams on April 20, 1812 was the most important and thorough legal brief he ever wrote. It was produced at the request of William Wirt who was Jefferson's defense lawyer in which he was being sued by Edward Livingston for action he had taken as President. The lengthy title of the brief reads: *The Proceedings of the United States, in maintaining the Public Right to the Beach of the Mississippi, Adjacent to New-Orleans, against the Intrusion of Edward Livingston.* Prepared by Thomas Jefferson for the use of Counsel (New York, 1812). In his response to Jefferson's "Homespun," Adams wrote: "You have brought up to the view of the Young Generation of Lawyers in our Country Tracts and Regions of Legal Information of which they had never dreamed: but which will become, every day more and more necessary for our Courts of Justice to investigate." Adams to Jefferson, Quincy, May 1, 1812, in Cappon, II, p. 298. Although the case was eventually thrown out of Court on jurisdictional grounds, it remains an important incident in Jefferson's legal career. The Massachusetts and Virginia "Homespuns," it would appear, played an interesting and crucial role in cementing a warm relationship between the two Adamses and Thomas Jefferson.

PART 3

Contemporary Rhetorical Theory

The last major rhetorician we discussed in the British period was Richard Whately whose seven editions of the *Elements of Rhetoric* appeared during the years from 1828 to 1846. It is also significant to observe that the works of Blair and Whately, along with those of the elocutionists, had some influence on rhetorical training in American colleges and universities. There were, for example, thirty-two separate printings of Blair's work published in America between 1784 and 1873. Nor did these include the numerous abridgments as well as the extensive cuttings which appeared in other texts.

We also saw how Witherspoon and Adams, drawing upon the classical and British/Continental philosophies of discourse and upon their own personal experiences, sought to acquaint their American students with Enlightenment thought. Despite these important advances, up until 1890 "the writings in rhetoric" in America, emanating primarily from scholars in grammar and literature, "were concerned with written forms of communication."[1] By 1893–1894, however, the trend began to change. With the opening of the academic year, fifty-two colleges could boast separate departments of speech.[2] Twenty-one years later in 1914, seventeen men met for the purpose of creating a national organization of speech teachers—a decision which was to go a long way toward providing respectability to speech programs.

In these formative years numerous prominent scholars taught courses and wrote textbooks on varying aspects of rhetoric. Of this group we would like to mention three who were both representative and influential: Thomas Trueblood, James Winans, and Charles Woolbert. Trueblood, who served as Chairman of the Department of Elocution and Oratory at the University of Michigan from 1902 to 1926, emphasized the classical canon of *pronunciatio.* His volume on *Practical Elements of Elocution (1893),* co-authored with Robert Fulton, helped revitalize the elocutionary movement in the United States.

While Trueblood devoted most of his energy to the study of a single canon, James Winans, who taught first at Cornell University and later at Dartmouth College, combined traditional and modern theories in his efforts to formulate a broad-based relevant rhetoric suitable for twentieth-century students. His pioneering work on *Public Speaking,* written in 1915, is exemplary in its use of classical precepts and the application of contemporary principles of psychology. Students found it profitable to turn to his volume for valuable insights on traditional doctrines, on the conversational pattern of delivery, and on methods for gaining attention and maintaining interest. Just as Campbell had borrowed heavily from Locke and Hume to develop his ideas on faculty psychology and moral reasoning, Winans borrowed freely from William James to devise his theory of persuasion. His scholarly, eclectic approach helped make Cornell University the undisputed center of rhetorical inquiry and research during the first quarter of the twentieth century.

Meanwhile Charles Woolbert, like Trueblood, was advancing the cause of rhetorical training in the Middle West. First at the University of Illinois and then at the University of Iowa, Woolbert, utilizing behavioral psychology, dealt at length with the subject of persuasion. In a series of widely-publicized articles in the *Quarterly Journal of Speech,* and in the revised edition of *The Fundamentals of Speech* (1927), he highlighted the role of logic in persuasion, challenged the value of adhering to belief in a conviction-persuasion duality, and described the important part that bodily activity played in oral communication.

Winans and Woolbert, far more than Trueblood, set the stage for a resurgence of interest in rhetoric as a field of study beginning in the 1930s. Theories which were to evolve in the next five decades form the core of what we call our third great system of rhetoric. As we examine the enormous amount of literature pertaining to rhetorical theory in the contemporary period, we see four general themes under which most material can be classified; (1) rhetoric as meaning; (2) rhetoric as value; (3) rhetoric as motive and drama; and (4) rhetoric as argument and a way of knowing.

I.A. Richards and Marshall McLuhan highlight "meaning" as an inherent communication problem in social relations. Richard Weaver cogently reminds us of the impact of values on our language systems. Kenneth Burke bases his rhetorical system largely on human motivation. In fact, he entitled two of his most important treatises *The Grammar of Motives* and *The Rhetoric of Motives.* Chaim Perelman and Stephen Toulmin approach rhetoric as an instrument for the creation and advancement of knowledge. Finally we turn our attention to the suggestive works of four important European thinkers: Ernesto Grassi, Jurgen Habermas, Michel Foucault, and Michel Meyer.

Major Figures

I.A. Richards
(1893–1979)

British semanticist keenly interested in language, meaning, and misunderstanding, devised the semantic triangle. *The Meaning of Meaning* (coauthor)

Kenneth Burke
(1897–1993)

American critic-theorist who greatly expanded the sphere of rhetoric. Burke has developed a new lexicon for explaining the influence of speakers and writers. *A Grammar of Motives, A Rhetoric of Motives*

Richard Weaver
(1910–1963)

American neo-Platonist and conservative humanist who argued that all language is value-laden; he believed in a hierarchy of arguments. *The Ethics of Rhetoric, Language is Sermonic*

Marshall McLuhan
(1911–1980)

Canadian professor of communication whose theories revolutionized our thinking about media and meaning. *The Gutenberg Galaxy, Understanding Media*

Stephen Toulmin
(1922–   )

British logician and historian of science whose model of argument broke with formal logic; a fresh perspective of the human reasoning process. *The Uses of Argument, Human Understanding*

Chaim Perelman
(1912–1984)

Belgian lawyer-philosopher who stressed the importance of rhetoric as the key to how we reason with one another. *The New Rhetoric: A Treatise on Argumentation* (coauthor)

Ernesto Grassi
(1902–   )

Italian humanist who believes a rhetorician can transcend sensory awareness. Grassi views the metaphor as a creative vehicle for helping listeners perceive relationships not readily apparent. *Rhetoric as Philosophy*

Jurgen Habermas
(1929–   )

German philosopher and social theorist interested in communicative competence, argument, and speech act theory. *Communication and the Evolution of Society, Reason and the Rationalization of Society*

Michel Foucault
(1926–1984)

French philosopher-historian concerned with power relationships, language structure, and usage. *The Archaeology of Knowledge, Power/Knowledge*

Michel Meyer
(1950–   )

Belgian professor of rhetoric and philosophy concerned with argumentation and the role questioning plays in the rhetorical process. *Meaning and Reading*

Key Concepts

- Rhetoric as meaning
  A. Context theorem of meaning
  B. Proper meaning superstition
  C. Semantic triangle (thought, symbol, referent)
  D. Medium
  E. Medium as message
  F. Interinanimation
  G. Metaphor
  H. "Hot" and "cool" media
  I. Speech act
  J. Significant symbols
  K. Gutenberg galaxy
  L. Cultural archetype
  M. Sorting

- Rhetoric as value
  A. Axiology
  B. Values
  C. Argument from definition
  D. Argument from circumstance
  E. The three lovers
  F. Language is sermonic
  G. Ultimate terms (devil and god terms)
  H. Ethos and image

- Rhetoric as motive
  A. Motive
  B. Identification (consubstantiality)
  C. Pentad (act, agent, agency, scene, purpose)
  D. Magic
  E. Dramatism
  F. Hierarchy of argument
  G. Terministic screens
  H. Pentadic ratios
  I. Administrative rhetoric

- Rhetoric as a way of knowing
  A. Toulmin model of argument
  B. Presence
  C. Association/dissociation

  D. Universal audience
  E. Quasi-logical arguments
  F. Rule of justice
  G. Rational/reasonable
  H. Ingenium-work-metaphor
  I. Poet as orator
  J. Universal Pragmatics
  K. Performative acts: imperatives
                        constatives
                        regulatives
                        expressives
                        communicatives
  L. Argumentation: procedures
                    products
                    process
  M. Valid claims
  N. Consensus theory of truth
  O. Ideal speech situation
  P. Epistemes
  Q. Archaeological/genealogical mode of inquiry
  R. Power
  S. Problematology
  T. Questioning
  U. Question-answer pair
  V. Apocritical answers
  W. Propositions

- Rhetoric for the 21st Century
  A. Premodernism, Modernism, and Postmodernism
  B. Media innovations
  C. Millennial communicator
  D. Popular culture
  E. Values
  F. Virtues
  G. Information Abundance
  H. Digital communication
  I. Digital differences
  J. On-line
  K. Transmissional and dialogical views of teaching and learning

I.A. Richards and Marshall McLuhan: Toward a Meaning-Centered Theory of Rhetoric

The exploration into contemporary rhetorical trends begins with the question of meaning. Although several modern theorists could easily be included in this discussion, we have chosen to focus in this chapter upon the ideas of I.A. Richards and Marshall McLuhan. At first glance, it seems as if these two individuals, separated by a half century in time, are quite dissimilar in their theoretical positions. They are. But, at several crucial points, the construct of "meaning" mysteriously serves to unite Richards and McLuhan. Thus, we have sorted out the "meaning" theme and have highlighted this issue as a significant bridge between the thoughts of McLuhan and Richards.

Marshall McLuhan opens his provocative text, *Understanding Media: The Extension of Man,* with the following insight.

In a culture like ours, long accustomed to splitting and dividing all things as a means of control, it is sometimes a bit of a shock to be reminded that, in operational and practical fact, the medium is the message. This is merely to say that the personal and social consequences of any medium—that is, of any extension of ourselves—result from the new scale that is introduced into our affairs by each extension of ourselves, or by any new technology.[3]

Thus, McLuhan begins his intellectual search for the nature of meaning in the various media which engulf men in a technological society.

In *The Meaning of Meaning*—a work jointly compiled by I.A. Richards and C.K. Ogden, a similar idea is echoed.

Language, though often spoken of as a medium of communication, is best regarded as an instrument; and all instruments are extensions, or refinements, of our sense organs. The telescope . . . the microscope . . . are . . . capable . . . of introducing new relevant members into the contexts of our signs. And as receptive instruments extend our organs. . . .[4]

Both Richards and McLuhan are concerned with the social consequences and inherent nature of meaning characteristic of media. Richards narrows his focus to the language medium, the meanings elicited by words, and the implications thereof to human thinking, and ultimately to social relationships. McLuhan, on the other hand, widens his emphasis to include the meanings which occur in all the diverse media abounding in our atomic age.

So, both McLuhan and Richards attack a portion of the psycho-philosophical problem of meaning. Each, however, launches his own personal strategy, tactics, and assumptions into the arena. The results of such inquiry are intriguing and thought-provoking. It must be remembered, however, that Richards and McLuhan have been selected as representatives of the "meaning school" for pedagogical purposes only. That is, Richards and McLuhan have each woven theories and hypotheses far "richer" than is evident in the following pages. Nevertheless, the meaning issue is functional in that it serves as an intellectual handle or key into the thinking of two unique writers of the twentieth century who are concerned with sociological aspects in human communication.

RICHARDS' RHETORIC OF MEANING

Ivor Armstrong Richards has extensively inquired into the impact which language and symbols have on human relationships. His chief concern is with *meaning:* how language and words come to mean. Richards' contribution to rhetorical thought is predicated on the ideas of Francis Bacon concerning perception—specifically Bacon's Idols of the Market Place. Although Bacon is classified as a British theorist, his metaphor of the Market is, as we now see, distinctly modern:

> *There are Idols formed by the intercourse and association of men with each other, which I call Idols of the Marketplace on account of the commerce and consort of men there. For it is by discourse that men associate, and words are imposed according to the apprehension of the vulgar. And therefore the ill and unfit choice of words wonderfully obstructs the understanding . . . words plainly force and overrule the understanding, and throw all into confusion, and lead men away into numberless empty controversies and idle fancies.*[5]

Bacon, then, considers man's use of language as a potential barrier to human understanding and relationships. As he puts it: ". . . the Idols of the Marketplace are the most troublesome of all, idols which have crept into the understanding through the alliances of words and names."[6]

I.A. Richards has considered the language issue raised by Bacon perhaps more seriously than any contemporary author. In the ensuing discussion of Richards' contribution to modern rhetorical theory, we shall focus on two of his major works. The first, *The Meaning of Meaning*, was published in 1923 in conjunction with C.K. Ogden. The second work considered herein is Richards' *Philosophy of Rhetoric* (1936).

These texts and their theoretical contribution have been chosen because they provide, we think, a brief but meaningful introduction into Richards' thinking. Richards' contribution to the field of rhetoric certainly goes far beyond the concepts discussed in the ensuing pages. For those who wish to further their study of Richards' ideas, we recommend the following works: *The Foundations of Aesthetics* (with C.K. Ogden and James Woods, 1922), *Principles of Literary Criticism* (1924), *Science and Poetry* (1926), *Practical Criticism* (1929), *Basic Rules of Reason* (1933), *How to Read a Page* (1942), and *Speculative Instruments* (1955).

Richards' theoretical bias is quickly discerned in his unique definition of rhetoric which appears in the *Philosophy of Rhetoric:*

> *Rhetoric, I shall argue, should be a study of misunderstanding and its remedies. We struggle all our days with misunderstandings and no apology is required for any study which can prevent or remove them.*[7]

With this premise, Richards launches into a discussion of the context theorem of meaning, the interinanimation of words, the Proper Meaning Superstition, and the metaphor. A brief consideration of each of these rhetorical concepts ensues.

Perhaps the integrating conceptual dimension of Richards' system is his "Context Theorem of Meaning." To understand this central theorem it is necessary to sketch Richards' theory of abstraction—or *how* words come to mean.

Richards postulates that as human beings we are all responsive to incoming data; hence, we continually respond to "things" in our perceived environment. Furthermore, our *reactions to* and *interpretations of* environmental stimuli or data are dependent on past confrontations and experiences with *similar* stimuli. Accordingly, effects from more or less similar happenings in the past give our responses their character or meaning.[8] In conclusion, the *meanings* we attach to the stimuli in our environments are thus rooted far in our past and grow out of one another.[9] Richards, then, underscores the importance of the *context* in relation to past experience with similar stimuli. In this connection, he observes:

> *Our interpretation of any sign is our psychological reaction to it, as determined by our past experience in similar situations, and by our present experience.*
>
> *If this is stated with due care in terms of causal contexts or correlated groups we get an account of judgment, belief and interpretation which places the psychology of thinking on the same level as the other inductive sciences . . . .*

A theory of thinking which discards mystical relations between the knower and the known and treats knowledge as a causal affair open to ordinary scientific investigation, is one which will appeal to common sense inquirers.[10]

Therefore, while we live in the present, our reactions to the here-and-now world are directly correlated to our individual and collective histories. We are engaged in perpetual *sorting* activity whereby we *perceive* incoming bits of information (Richards denies that we have "sensations" or data which "stand on their own"), *compare* them with our past, *analyze* them, *classify* and *process* them, and attach *meaning* accordingly—hence, we come to understand the data bits. So, our reactions and decisions in the here-and-now situation are tied to our past histories. All *perceived* events and things are automatically processed by the mind which continuously *compares* the here and now with the individual's past.

We have perceptions, responses whose character comes to them from the past as well as the present occasion. A perception is never just of an it; *perception takes whatever it perceives as a thing of a certain sort. All thinking from the lowest to the highest—whatever else it may be—is sorting.*[11]

In the *sorting* process, stimuli within the present field of awareness are analyzed and classified with similar past stimuli: categories of contexts are thus created and maintained by each individual. The issue of *how* meaning develops in individuals is therefore a complex phenomenon rooted in personal histories. Summarizing Richards to this point, we may say: humans are *perceiving* beings who respond to present stimuli in their environment by interpretations based on past contexts and experience.[12]

We need to mention at this point, however, an essential characteristic of the human sorting process which Richards considers. Given the nature of thinking and sorting, Richards states that when any *part* of a context appears (a context is "a set of entities—things or events—related in a certain way. . . .")[13] the possibility exists that the *entire* context will be remembered and the organism will act *as if* the total context were present. In other words, the *part* has the power to elicit the *whole*. Richards cites the case of a chicken who, when attempting to bite into a striped yellow and black caterpillar, found its taste offensive and immediately dropped the small creature. From

that time hence, the chicken refused to touch any yellow and black striped caterpillar for the mere sight of it conjured up the previous bitter taste context. Richards elaborates:

This simple case is typical of all interpretation, the peculiarity of interpretation being that when a context has affected us in the past the recurrence of merely a part of the context will cause us to react in the way in which we reacted before. A sign is always a stimulus similar to some part of an original stimulus and sufficient to call up the engram (i.e., 'to call up an excitation similar to that caused by the original stimulus') formed by that stimulus.[14]

A further illustration of this ability to "abridge" from the immediate external context to previous and similar contexts when only one segment or part of the whole is perceived may also prove helpful. Several years ago a young boy was playing on the front lawn of his home—a small, quiet, Midwestern town. He was lying on his back clutching his neighbor's small black kitten—holding it above his face. With his arms extended the boy was trying to shield the sun from his eyes by placing the kitten between him and the fiery ball. Alas, however, the game was cut short. It seems that the young boy became so engrossed in his hide and seek game with the sun and kitten that he clenched the poor creature a bit too firmly. And, as the kitten had just eaten a large breakfast, she reacted naturally to the young man's grip by expelling the contents of her stomach on the young man's once smiling, gleeful face. This strange episode took place almost forty years ago and to this day, the young man has avoided all kittens and, as expected, becomes very anxious in their presence. Thus the mere perception of a kitten at once evokes the former context.

We have detailed Richards' theory of abstraction precisely because it is the foundation of his rhetorical theory. In essence, humankind's sorting activity is basic to an understanding of his rhetorical behavior. Thus far, Richards has considered only man's response to things and events in his environment. However, *words* and *symbols* are also important stimuli; accordingly, Richards turns his attention to the character and uniqueness of symbols.

Words are symbols and unique, says Richards, in that they are "substitutes exerting the powers of what is not there."[15] That is, words and symbols transcend the here and now and *stand for* that which is missing. Richards terms the study of words and symbolism the science of Symbolism. However, he further narrows the traditional definition of "symbol" to include only words which refer to verifiable "things" in our environment. Symbols are "words that refer, through thoughts, to things. Everything inside the skin that relates to feelings, attitudes, hopes, dreams, etc., is excluded. This is the distinguishing characteristic of the science of symbolism."[16] Richards' focus, then, is *only* on words which have a definite referent in reality. Words which do not refer to "things," are termed "emotive language" and are *not* the locus of Richards' theory. It is important to keep this distinction in mind throughout the ensuing discussion. Marie Nichols provides an instructive illustration:

THREE SETS OF SYMBOLS

Let us take the following three sets of symbols to illustrate Richards' analysis of language and the classification of its uses:

1. Winston Churchill is eighty-three years old.
2. The grand old man who occupied 10 Downing Street during the Second World War is eighty-three years old.
3. Four-score and three he counts his years, proud England's mighty son.

The **first** sentence Richards would identify as a purely referential statement, and, therefore, a *scientific* use of language. The context out of which the symbol grew would include recurrent experiences with the process of explicit naming and counting. The referent is the person bearing the name and having those years.

The **second** sentence represents a change in symbolization. The references, or psychological context, out of which the symbols were composed might include an affectionate attitude on the part of the composer of the symbol, a remembering of the events of the war, a recollection of others who had occupied the house at 10 Downing Street, in addition to a strict reference to the number of years of life. The referent is still to a person. The symbol, however, has not been produced for merely referential uses. Attitudes, reminiscences, and perhaps other factors have exerted strong influence. This use of language Richards labels 'emotive' or 'mixed,' hence, 'rhetorical.'

The **third** set of symbols represents still further change in symbolization. The purely referential function of language has almost completely vanished. Who is being talked about is no longer definite. The psychological context out of which this symbolization grew might contain feelings about age and England and some queries about relations, sonship, fatherhood. It might even include feelings about Lincoln at Gettysburg. This use of language represents almost completely the "emotive" function of language and would be regarded as poetry, good or bad.

When Richards and his collaborator published *The Meaning of Meaning,* they claimed among their peculiar contributions the following: 'An account of interpretation in causal terms by which the treatment of language as a system of signs becomes capable of results,' and second, 'A division of the functions of language into two groups, the symbolic and the emotive.' The symbolic use of words is 'statement; the recording, the support, the organization and the communication of references.' The emotive use of words is the 'use of words to express or excite feelings and attitudes.' There are, in other words, 'two totally distinct uses of language.'[17]

The *Meaning of Meaning* was published in 1936. Thirteen years later, Richards published "Emotive Language Still" (*Yale Review,* xxxviii, Autumn 1949) wherein he refined his thinking regarding emotive language and what he called "descriptive language" arguing that almost all our word use is simultaneously both emotive and descriptive. But, in 1936 he made a clear distinction between the two uses of language.

How, then, do words which refer to "things" in our environments come to *mean?* Similar to our previous discussion on *how* stimuli come to mean, the meaning attached to words also depends on past encounters with the word and what it correspondingly *stands for.* The summation of past experience with a symbol together with the present instance of the word determine meaning. Thus, the immediate external context together with past psychological contexts determine meaning. Richards labels this *total* of past and present experience the *technical context.* So, in Richards' terms, words attain meaning through the technical context which surrounds them.

If we sum up thus far by saying that meaning is delegated efficacy, *that description applies above all to the meaning of words, whose virtue is to be substitutes exerting the powers of what is not there. They do this as other signs do it, though in more complex fashions, through their contexts.*[18]

Consider the word-symbol "kitten." Suppose you hear this word in a conversation with a colleague. To interpret the immediate event (i.e., the hearing of the word "kitten"), you abstract from the technical context (the psychological context plus the external context) and arrive at a meaning for the symbol "kitten." So, you *abridge* from the immediate instance of the symbol back through your past "kitten" contexts—i.e., you sort through your category of "kitten." In so doing, you attach a meaning to the word "kitten"—a meaning which is actually the missing part of the context.

Richards' theory of *how* words *mean,* then, is based on the concept of context and the sorting process. With these thoughts underlying Richards' thinking, it is logical that he would be critical of the doctrine of usage discussed by the British rhetorician, George Campbell. Whereas Campbell believed that every word has a "proper" and "correct" usage or meaning, such thinking is foreign to Richards who insists that meanings are in people, not words or symbols. So, Richards discusses the Proper Meaning Superstition.

A chief cause of misunderstanding, I shall argue later, is the Proper Meaning Superstition. That is, the common belief . . . that a word has a meaning of its own (ideally, only one) independent of and controlling its use and the purpose for which it should be uttered. This superstition is a recognition of a certain kind of stability in the meanings of certain words. It is only a superstition when it forgets (as it commonly does) that the stability of the meaning of a word comes from the constancy of the contexts that give it its meaning. Stability in a word's meaning is not something to be assumed, but always something to be explained. And as we try out explanations, we discover, of course, that—as there are many sorts of constant contexts—there are many sorts of stabilities.[19]

Thus, contexts determine and shape the meaning of words and symbols. It follows that since every human being is a unique entity who has had different past and immediate experiences (contexts), everyone will attach slightly different meanings to symbols. That is, we operate from personal contexts—therefore, meaning becomes individualized precisely because it is context dependent.

How, then, do we happen to understand one another? How do we agree on meanings? Richards partly answers these questions when he considers the literary context "as the other words before and after a given word which determines how it is to be interpreted. . . ."

The familiar sense of 'context' can be extended further to include the circumstances under which anything was written or said; wider still to include, for a word in Shakespeare, say, the other known uses of the word about that time, wider still finally to include anything whatever about the period, or anything else which is relevant to our interpretation of it.[20]

Thus, the literary context is certainly an essential component which enables us to determine "collective" meaning and understanding. In sum, words never appear in isolation but in literary contexts, which in turn provide clues as to possible responses.

The result of literary contexts is "interinanimation." Richards states that "no word can be judged as to whether it is good or bad, correct or incorrect, beautiful or ugly, or anything else that matters to a writer, in isolation."[21] So, it follows that words in a sentence, a phrase, or a paragraph are *dependent* upon one another and their *interaction* (interinanimation) provides the literary context. "But in most prose, and more than we ordinarily suppose, the opening words have to wait for those that follow to settle what they shall mean—if indeed that ever gets settled."[22] Interinanimation, then, refers to the mutual dependency and interaction which links words and symbols together in a literary relationship.

The best known rhetorical device developed in the *Meaning of Meaning* is perhaps the "semantic triangle." Ogden and Richards concluded that a major problem in human communication is man's tendency to treat words as if they were *things in reality.* So, in saying the word "dog" we tend to behave as if the three letter symbol **DOG** is an actual four-legged animal that barks, growls, runs, eats, and sleeps. That is, as the general semanticists argue, we confuse the symbol or word with the "thing" or object in reality. Richards and Ogden, in turn, say that we tend to make a one-to-one correspondence or a *necessary connection* between the word and reality object (referent). Ogden and Richards argue that there is only an *indirect* relationship between symbol and reference since the symbol is merely an *abstraction* of reality rather than reality itself. Recall that words and symbols *stand for* "things" in the real world, according to Richards.

Thus, humans communicate with symbols which in turn stand for or refer to verifiable "things." But, there is a third element involved in the semantic triangle. Besides the symbol and referent Ogden and Richards consider the *thought* or *reference*. Often when we use words we are tempted to conclude that our partner in communication is operating from *our* thought/reference perspective. That is, we assume that our *references* are identical or universal—something which in all probability seldom occurs because of the individual's abstraction process. Such an assumption can effectively obstruct communication between individuals. Now, recall the earlier discussed incident of the young man and the kitten. As stated, this event took place years ago, but the young man of our story will vividly remember that traumatic moment in his youth. In fact, to this day, he avoids all kittens. He rarely touches them and becomes quite uncomfortable in their presence. We might diagram this situation as follows.

> The best known rhetorical device developed in the *Meaning of Meaning* is perhaps the "semantic triangle."

In this situation, the meaning of the symbol "kitten" has been determined by the context and the sorting activity inherent in the abstraction process. So, meaning is delegated efficacy. Thus, there is *not* a necessary connection between symbol and referent. This is an impossibility in Richards' rhetorical system.

Now, what happens when the young man is engaged in a conversation with another individual who has a quite different Thought or Reference for "kitten"?

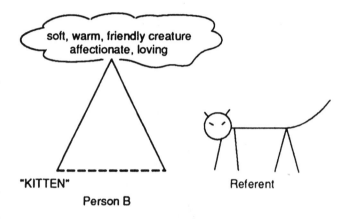

When the young man and person B are discussing kittens they are (a) using the identical symbol: "Kitten," and (b) they are reacting to a similar referent, *but* (c) their thought/references are quite different. Such an incongruence can easily lead to a misunderstanding between these two individuals discussing cats. The semantic triangle is thus a practical tool because it makes clear the relationship of thought, reference, and referent and demonstrates that meanings exist not in symbols or words but in people. Stated differently, the identical symbol or word does not often evoke *identical* meanings from two or more participants in human communication.

Richards' theory of abstraction leads him to consider meaning as the "missing parts of a context." This leads to a discussion of the nature of context (external and psychological) and the importance of the literary aspects of context and interinanimation. The semantic triangle makes clear the distinction between symbol, reference, and referent—describing the *lack* of necessary connection between symbol and referent. This indirect relationship is a logical conclusion of the delegated efficacy concept central

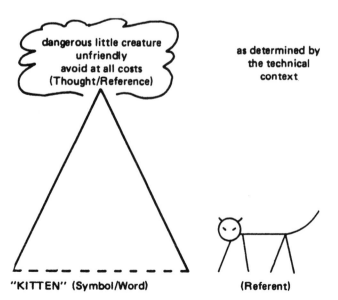

to Richards' thinking. Finally, we need to examine briefly the *metaphor* whereby Richards' ideas are brought to culmination.

As we have seen, Richards maintains that all human thinking is a matter of sorting—i.e. the individual's mind is continually engaged in establishing and refining categories of stimuli. Incoming data are quickly processed, analyzed, compared, and classified. Thus, Richards' theory of abstraction leads him to conclude that the metaphor is really the heart of our language systems.

We early begin to use language in order to learn language, but since it is no mere matter of the acquisition of synonyms or alternative locutions, the same stressing of similarities between references and elimination of their differences through conflict is required. By these means, we develop references of greater and greater abstractness, and metaphor, the primitive symbolization of abstraction, become possible. Metaphor, in the most general sense, is the use of one reference to a group of things between which a given relation holds, for the purpose of facilitating the discrimination of an analogous relation in another group.

In the understanding of metaphorical language one reference borrows part of the context of another in an abstract form.[23]

Richards continues this line of inquiry.

The view that metaphor is omnipresent in speech can be recommended theoretically. If you recall what I said in my second lecture about the context theorem of meaning; about meaning as the delegated efficacy of signs by which they bring together into new unities the abstracts, or aspects, which are missing parts of their various contexts, you will recollect some insistence that a word is normally a substitute for (or means), not one discrete past impression but a combination of general aspects. Now that is itself a summary account of the principle of metaphor. In the simplest formulation, when we use a metaphor we have two thoughts of different things active together and supported by a single word, or phrase, whose meaning is a resultant of their interaction.[24]

Therefore, within Richards' theory of abstraction, the metaphor "is a borrowing between and intercourse of *thoughts*, a transaction between contexts.

Thought is metaphoric, and proceeds by comparison, and the metaphors of language derive therefrom."[25]

Richards believes that we need to examine the metaphorical nature of language more closely. Thus, he proposes two concepts which enable us to speak intelligently about metaphor.

We need the word 'metaphor' for the whole double unit, and to use it sometimes for one of the two components in separation from the other is as injudicious as that other trick by which we use 'the meaning' here sometimes for the work that the whole double unit does and sometimes for the other component—the tenor, as I am calling it—the underlying idea or principal subject which the vehicle or figure means.[26]

So, the vehicle and tenor become conceptual tools helpful in analyzing our language. Perhaps an illustration would prove beneficial. In Monday morning coffee breaks in the fall, the normal conversation centers on the "big" football game. In the course of the discussion it is not uncommon to hear these words about your favorite linebacker. "He was a real animal last Saturday, wasn't he, Tom?" The tenor (underlying idea to which the vehicle refers) in this metaphor is "he" or the linebacker. The vehicle ("animal") attributes the characteristic of "savage or ferocious" behavior to the brutal play of the linebacker. Daniel Fogarty summarizes Richards' thinking on the metaphor and its importance or centrality to human language and social relationships.

Richards' most emphatic contention about metaphor, thus explained, is that language is naturally metaphor. Since metaphor is just abstraction for the purpose of clearer and more vivid communication, since it seems to be the nature of our thinking to be perpetually busy with sorting and classifying references and comparing contexts and their parts, and since our language symbolizes this thinking, it seems to Richards that our language must be highly, habitually, and even naturally metaphoric.[27]

Since language is metaphoric in nature, an understanding of the basic nature of metaphors (tenor and vehicle interaction) will help one to comprehend better the "workings" of language.

I.A. Richards provides us with a unique philosophy of rhetoric founded on his theory of abstraction, the semantic model, the context theorem of meaning, interinanimation, and metaphor. He is chiefly concerned with how words mean and how they work in discourse. With such an analysis of language, Richards believes that we can begin to understand *how* misunderstanding occurs. By appreciating the complexities of meaning, perhaps we can begin to break down the communication barriers which exist in human discourse: we can begin to understand one another. An understanding of contexts as the basis for human thinking is thus developed to the logical

conclusion concerning the metaphorical nature of language. Therefore, context, delegated efficacy, interinanimation, semantic triangle, and metaphor are all inextricably related.

In conclusion, Richards claims that we can study *how* man thinks by examining *how* he uses language. Conversely, one can study how man uses language by studying how he thinks. In either case, we can study both language use and thinking through an understanding and appreciation of the metaphor.

Notes

1. Giles W. Gray, "Some Teachers and the Transition to Twentieth-Century Speech Education," *A History of Speech Education* in *America,* Karl R. Wallace, ed. (New York: Appleton-Century-Crofts, Inc., 1954), p. 424.
2. *Ibid.,* p. 422.
3. Marshall McLuhan, *Understanding Media: The Extension of Man* (New York: Signet Books, 1964), p. 23.
4. C.K. Ogden and I.A. Richards, *The Meaning of Meaning: A Study of the Influence of Language Upon Thought and of the Science of Symbolism,* 4th ed. (New York: Harcourt, Brace and Company, 1936), p. 98.
5. Francis Bacon, *Idols of the Mind,* in Richard Hughes and P. Albert Duhamel, *Rhetoric: Principles and Usage,* 2nd ed. (Englewood Cliffs, New Jersey: Prentice-Hail, Inc., 1967), pp. 361–362.
6. *Ibid.,* p. 365.
7. I.A. Richards, *The Philosophy of Rhetoric* (New York: Oxford University Press, 1965), p. 3.
8. *Ibid.,* pp. 29–30.
9. *Ibid.,* p. 30.
10. *Meaning of Meaning,* pp. 244–245.
11. *Philosophy of Rhetoric,* p. 30.
12. Richards' ideas concerning perception and sortings differentiate him from the Nominalists and Realists of the Eighteenth-Century controversy concerning "about whether we have and how we come by abstract ideas and what they are. This theorem alleges that meanings from the very beginning, have a primordial generality and abstractness. . . . It is behaving of thinking with a concept—not, of course *of* one. . . . The theorem holds that we *begin* with the general abstract anything, split it, as the world makes us, into sorts and then arrive at concrete particulars by the overlapping or common membership of these sorts." *Philosophy of Rhetoric,* pp. 30–31.
13. *Meaning of Meaning,* p. 58.
14. *Ibid.,* p. 53.
15. *Philosophy of Rhetoric,* p. 32.
16. Bess Sondel, *The Humanity of Words: A Primer of Semantics* (New York: The World Publishing Company, 1958), p. 56.
17. Marie H. Nichols, "I. A. Richards and the New Rhetoric," *Quarterly Journal of Speech,* XLIV (February 1958), in Richard L. Johannesen, ed., *Contemporary Theories of Rhetoric: Selected Readings* (New York: Harper and Row, 1971), pp. 131—132.
18. *Philosophy of Rhetoric,* p. 32.
19. *Ibid.,* p. 11.
20. *Ibid.,* pp. 32–33.
21. *Ibid.,* p. 51.
22. *Ibid.,* p. 50.
23. *Meaning of Meaning,* p. 213.
24. *Philosophy of Rhetoric,* p. 93.
25. *Ibid.,* p. 94.
26. *Ibid.,* pp. 96–97.
27. Daniel Fogarty, *Roots for a New Rhetoric* (New York: Russell and Russell, 1959), p. 38.

THE SIGNIFICANT SYMBOL

The works of I.A. Richards, especially the volume on *The Meaning of Meaning,* stimulated considerable interest in the study of the nature of symbols

and how they may be used to generate meaning and produce action. Soon numerous authors, from a wide variety of disciplines and orientations, began to build upon the theories of Richards. Of particular relevance to us here are the ideas developed by George Herbert Mead and his student Charles Morris regarding "significant symbols."

What Mead has in mind in using the term "significant symbol" was a communicator's use of signs for the purpose of arousing meaning in himself at the same time it occurs in another. "The significant symbol," he said, "is the gesture, the sign, the word which is addressed to the self. . . ."[1] Mead put it more graphically when he observed: "A person who is saying something is saying to himself what he says to others; otherwise he does not know what he is talking about. . . ."[2] Any communication which occurs that does not lead to a shared meaning between the speaker and the listener falls short of significance.

In addition to enabling a speaker to convey an intended meaning to himself as well as to one or more other listeners in a specific situation, "significant symbols" are a means by which a universe of discourse is established. Drawing upon the logicians, Mead gives the following definition of this phenomenon:

A universe of discourse is always implied as the context in terms of which, or as the field within which, significant gestures or symbols do in fact have significance. The universe of discourse is constituted by a group of individuals carrying on and participating in a common process of experience and behavior, within which these gestures or symbols have the same or common meanings for all members of that group. . . . A universe of discourse is simply a system of common or social meanings.[3]

The effect of the creation of a universe of discourse on socialization and the democratic process as a whole is clear. For the very existence and preservation of a society are fully dependent upon the capacity of the members of that group to employ "significant symbols."[4]

Morris, whose behavioral approach owes much to Mead's philosophy of the act, ably summarizes his colleague's interpretation of "significant symbols."

For Mead, it is characteristic of the human being that he can react to his own (or some

of his) actions as other human beings will react. . . . Mead calls these symbols to which their producer is disposed to react like their receiver 'significant symbols.' He equates mind with the operation of such symbols. Mentality is thus for him a kind of behavior or disposition to behavior. . . . This capacity to respond by significant symbols is an intelligible basis for the analysis of the term 'freedom' and for the conception of man as a moral agent. Mead thus brings within his behavioral analysis what the traditional behaviorist ignores or denies or what the more complicated behaviorism of the present is still seeking after—a psychology equated to the full person.[5]

What is the procedure, we may next ask, that should be employed in order to produce "significant symbols?" This query may be answered in part by turning to the advice which Hugh Blair gave to prospective ministers two centuries ago. Observe how Blair anticipated Mead in his lecture on the "Eloquence of the Pulpit:"

In studying a sermon he (the preacher) ought to place himself in the situation of a serious hearer. Let him suppose the subject addressed to himself; let him consider what views of it would strike him most; what arguments would be most likely to persuade him; what parts of it would dwell most upon his mind. Let these be employed as his principal materials; and in these, it is most likely his genius will exert itself with the greatest vigour. . . .[6]

To approach from a different but related angle the question of formulating a method to develop "significant symbols," we may use a hypothetical illustration involving Blair's city of Edinburgh. Let us assume, for example, that you are a Scottish native standing on the corner of Princes Street and Waverly Bridge and an American tourist approaches you to ask: "Could you please tell me how to get to the Church of St. Giles?" Immediately you turn to the south and point to a large steeple several blocks away. You then tell the tourist to cross Waverly

> What Mead has in mind in using the term "significant symbol" was a communicator's use of signs for the purpose of arousing meaning in himself at the same time it occurs in another.

Bridge and continue south until he reaches a series of steep outdoor steps. You then instruct him to climb the steps, several hundred in number, and proceed through a close at the top which leads to the famous Royal Mile. The Church of St. Giles, you conclude, stands several hundred yards to the left on the right side of the block. What is required in this rhetorical transaction if a "significant symbol" is to be used is a need for the speaker to place himself in the perspective of the tourist and to respond to the signs he generates from the perspective. The communicator thus also functions as one of the communicatees as he hears the combination of signs that sets forth the directions. "In the process of communication," Mead observes, "the individual is an other before he is a self. It is in addressing himself in the role of the other that his self arises in experience."[7]

The most far-reaching implication of the notion of the "significant symbol," apart from its power to reduce misunderstandings, is the effect it has on the concept of audience. Many scholars have held that a person cannot persuade himself; nor can he be a part of the audience he is addressing. An attempt to persuade one's self, it is pointed out, is nothing more than an ideational process which does not qualify as communication. To embrace the idea of "significant symbols," however, is to argue that a communicator, by regarding himself as a candidate for action, experiences the meaning and alteration in behavior that his message, or sign usage, is intended to convey. This fact is convincing testimony of the shortcomings associated with the practice of ghostwriting techniques which permit a speaker to mouth, almost mechanically, the words of others. For whenever the encoder is not the source of the message being articulated, the signs he uses may not be achieving significance.

Speech Acts

The concept of "meaning" also has been studied by a unique group of scholars who focus not on individual words or significant symbols, but rather on the *acts* of speaking. Among those who have turned their attention to this theme are J.L. Austin, John Searle, Karl Wallace, and Douglas Ehninger.

Austin's provocative book *How to Do Things with Words*[8] is an excellent starting point to get at the notion of speech acts. He begins his analysis with a challenge to the traditional view that a statement is always an utterance which describes or reports, meets the requirements of a fact, and conforms to the criteria of truth and falsity. In many instances, he argues, words are used not for the purpose merely of "saying something" but for "the performing of an action." Consider the following examples:

1. "'I do' (sc. take this woman to be my lawful wedded wife)—as uttered in the course of the marriage ceremony."
2. "'I name this ship the Queen Elizabeth'—as uttered when smashing the bottle against the stern."
3. "'I give and bequeath my watch to my brother'—as occurring in a will."
4. "'I bet you a sixpence it will rain tomorrow.'"[9]

What is important in each of these utterances is not the question of fact or truth, but the performance of an act. The words, in short, become speech acts because they "do things." In developing this idea, Austin perceptively notes that if a marriage vow, the christening of an object, the bequeathing of a gift, or the making of a bet fails in any vital respect, the utterance should not be labeled false. Instead it should be characterized as "unhappy." On this point he observes: ". . . we call the doctrine of *the things that can be and go wrong* on the occasion of such utterances, the doctrine of the *Infelicities*."[10]

Frequently these "infelicities" are caused by a violation of the ensuing speech act rule developed by Austin: "There must exist an accepted conventional procedure having a certain conventional effect, the procedure to include the uttering of certain words by certain persons in certain circumstances."[11] In assessing the importance of the rhetorical situation in which symbols are used, Austin allies himself, at least partially, with the contextual theory of meaning emphasized by Richards.

There are numerous implications of Austin's theory for students of communication. Not the least of these are the following three inferences which

> The concept of "meaning" also has been studied by a unique group of scholars who focus not on individual words or significant symbols, but rather on the *acts* of speaking.

Rosenfield feels can be drawn from Austin's "performative conception of utterance as tactical behavior:"

- *For one, utterance, rather than linguistic units such as the word or sentence, comprises the minimal tactical unit of analysis.*
- *For another, an utterance differs from a simple statement in that it needn't describe or report; it is not pertinent to assess its truth value.*
- *Thirdly, the utterance may itself be the totality of the social act.*[12]

Expressing similar views to those of Austin, Searle begins his discussion of the speech act with remarks about language, claiming that "speaking a language is engaging in a rule-governed form of behavior."[13] In other words, "Talking is performing acts according to rules."[14] Searle elaborates:

Speaking a language is performing speech acts, acts such as making statements, giving commands, asking questions, making promises, and so on; and more abstractly, acts such as referring and predicting; and, secondly, that these acts are in general made possible by and are performed in accordance with certain rules for the use of linguistic elements.[15]

Thus, the appropriate study of meaning must focus not on words or symbols alone, but must consider the act of speech—which includes words, sentences, rules, and contexts. Regarding this idea, Searle observes: "The unit of linguistic communication is not, as has generally been supposed, the symbol, word or sentence . . . but rather the production or issuance of the symbol or word or sentence in the performance of the speech act."[16]

Wallace also considered the speech act as the appropriate unit of study for the communication scholar. Echoing the views of Searle, Wallace stressed that meaning is found/created by the *act*, not the word. He gives the following explanation:

The emphasis here is upon unit *or a* whole. *It is an event having terminals. Part of it is internal to the speaker and is accessible to sense; part of it is external and is available to ear and eye. This fact makes the event impossible to describe unless we regard it as an act. . . . What grammarian, logician, linguistician, and psycholinguist study are the last stages of a creative act. What the poet and rhetorician try to*

do, aided by students of language behavior, is to understand all stages of a creative act.[17]

Consequently, meaning is revealed in the act itself. "To see this is to see that the symbolic features of utterance do not lie in words alone."[18] Continuing, Wallace states: "What we call meaning thus seems to arise from, or be a function of, the entire field of experience that is brought into play by a communication context. . . . It is implicit in every stage of utterance and becomes explicit upon the completion of utterance."[19]

Those who, like Austin, Searle, and Wallace, hold that meaning resides in the act of utterance, further suggest that words or sentences—even paragraphs—are not the proper unit for investigation (unless, of course, they are in themselves acts of utterance). Rather, the speech act—with its underlying assumptions and rules–is the generator of meaning. In brief, this perspective provides the bridge from the rhetorical to the interpersonal.

Along with Wallace, the scholar who has made the most useful attempt to relate speech act theory to rhetoric, we feel, is Douglas Ehninger. In his former seminar course on this subject at the University of Iowa and in his unpublished paper entitled, "Toward a Taxonomy of Prescriptive Discourse," Ehninger examined several speech acts and the corresponding conditions which define each action. Such an examination is essential, said Ehninger, if the rhetorician intends to formulate meaningful theory. We will briefly summarize a few of the speech acts which are considered in the Ehninger study.

To begin, Ehninger claims that instructing is that form of discourse that tells someone *how* to do something. For example, the instructions telling you how to assemble your new charcoal grill are representative of instructive discourse—discourse aimed at a defined goal. It becomes a means, then, of accomplishing that goal or desired end. A major characteristic is that the receiver (who wishes to attain some goal) lacks certain expertise and so needs instruction of how to do so. Thus, instructing is a "means" rather than a goal-oriented act.[20] The assumptions accompanying the act include: (a) the listener *contracts* in advance to *perform as directed*, and (b) if he performs as directed, he will reach the defined and established goal.

A second speech act is advising or *telling* someone that he *ought* seriously to *consider* doing something. Such an act requires a unique rhetorical stance wherein the speaker must take a "superior" posture in relation to the listener. By definition, the proclamation of "ought" statements necessitates "special knowledge" in the form of advice. Subsequently, possession of "special knowledge" brings a moral obligation to the speech act of advising which is not found in instructing. The speaker, then, risks his name and reputation in the act of advising and must keep the best interests of the listener in mind at all times.

A further dimension of advising is the free choice assumption. In other words, the listener is free to decide whether to accept or reject the message. Obviously, the act of instructing does not possess such a latitude of freedom because the hearer *must* follow the instructions (and carefully) if he is to reach his goal.

During the speech act of arguing, the speaker aims at *providing reasons* which justify why the listener should *reconsider* the correctness of something he is doing, plans to do, or believes in.[21] Several assumptions define this speech act. First, arguing assumes that the listener is mistaken or wrong about something and needs to be corrected. Second, the speaker is obligated to provide reasons for the listener. This obligation is absent in instructing and advising. Thirdly, whereas advising is directed only to

something a listener is doing, arguing may be directed to beliefs as well as actions. Finally, the speech act of arguing is generally initiated by the speaker. In advising, the transaction is initiated by the listener.

The speech act of arguing propounds reasons for reconsidering a belief or behavior. The act of persuading, on the other hand, is to "cause a hearer to *decide* to behave or to do as the speaker desires."[22] Persuading, then, demands a commitment from the listener in the form of a change of mind or behavior. Such a commitment is lacking in the act of arguing. Thus, someone may argue with you without persuading you. So, the speech act of persuading does not necessarily require the use of reasons or rational discourse.

Rhetoricians, adhering to a speech act theory approach, need to study more than the words uttered during a communication transaction. Indeed, the assumptions, norms, roles, and stances taken by the speaker and listener need to be thoroughly described and categorized. Such an undertaking is a viable and necessary direction for the rhetorician wishing to have a firm understanding and appreciation of discourse. In a later chapter we will see how the European scholar Jurgen Habermas attempts to meet this challenge in his discussion of speech act theory.

--- **Notes** ---

1. "Significant Symbol," in *Selected Writings* (Indianapolis: The Bobbs-Merrill Co., 1964), p. 246.
2. *Mind, Self, and Society* (Chicago: University of Chicago Press, 1934), p. 147.
3. *Ibid.*, pp. 89–90.
4. Duncan has noted: "Symbols are the most easily, and most directly observable 'facts' in human relationships, for they are the forms in which relationships take place." Hugh Dalziel Duncan, *Symbols in Society* (New York: Oxford University Press, 1968), p. 152.
5. *Signification and Significance*, p. 30.
6. Hugh Blair, *Lectures on Rhetoric and Belles Lettres* (Philadelphia: S.C. Hayes, 1860), pp. 317–318.
7. *Selected Writings*, p. 312.
8. (Cambridge, Mass.: Harvard University Press, 1977).
9. *Ibid.*, p. 5.
10. *Ibid.*, p. 14.
11. *Ibid.*, p. 26.
12. Larry W. Rosenfield, "A Game Model of Human Communication," in *What Rhetoric (Communication Theory) is Appropriate for Contemporary Speech Communication?*, David Smith, ed., Minnesota Symposium, p. 34.
13. John S. Searle, *Speech Acts: An Essay in the Philosophy of Language* (London: Cambridge University Press, 1976), p. 16.
14. *Ibid.*, p. 22.
15. *Ibid.*, p. 16.
16. *Ibid.*
17. Karl Wallace, *Understanding Discourse: The Speech Act and Rhetorical Action* (Baton Rouge, Louisiana: Louisiana State University Press, 1970), p. 123.
18. *Ibid.*, p. 125.
19. *Ibid.*, pp. 127–128.
20. Douglas Ehninger, "Toward a Taxonomy of Prescriptive Discourse," unpublished paper, University of Iowa, p. 3. We also are indebted to Ehninger's former student Norman Elliott for his contributions to our thinking.
21. *Ibid.*, p. 6.
22. *Ibid.*, p. 9.

MARSHALL MCLUHAN ON THE MEDIUM AND THE MESSAGE

Few authors in the 1960s captured the fancy of the Western world more than did Marshall McLuhan. Trained as a Renaissance scholar and Professor of English, he nevertheless became aware of the declining influence of the print media in an age of electronics. This prompted him to make numerous probes into the field of mass media communication. These probes called to our attention the enormous impact of modern technology on our lives, and led to the introduction of a new vocabulary, including such descriptive terms as "hot" and "cool," "high definition" and "low definition," and "medium as message" and "massage."

In a wide-ranging interview appearing in *Playboy Magazine* in 1969, McLuhan described the image he had of himself and of his "explorations" and "probes." He was a "generalist, not a specialist," he argued; moreover, he rejected the notion of being a moralist whose principal task was to function as a critic of society and its communication forms. The purpose of his writings, he asserted, was "to employ facts as tentative probes, as means of insight, of pattern recognition. . . . "Even though the end result of such probes could not produce "revealed truth," it could, nevertheless, contribute "to an understanding of the problem." That this goal was achieved there can be little doubt.

McLuhan is an important figure in any survey of the rhetoric of Western thought because of his provocative insights on communication media. Early in the 1960s, he was among the first to tell us that man's image of the world is changed significantly by various media that have proved to be dominant during a given period of history.

There have been, in McLuhan's opinion, four important periods with special significance for students of rhetoric and culture.

1. First was the preliterate, tribal society that relied exclusively on rudimentary face-to-face communication patterns. It was an era typified by balanced senses and a strong emphasis on orality. By relying on the dominant discourse form—speech, people created an "acoustic space" that led to the formation of an "audile-tactile tribal man" who "partook of the collective unconscious." Because people during this tribal period relied on speech for their information, they tended to be "more spontaneous and passionately volatile."

2. With the development of the phonetic alphabet and the onset of manuscript technology, a second major communication period became prominent. It was one in which "tribal involvement" was replaced by "civilized detachment" as the eye gained supremacy over the ear. Not surprisingly, therefore, this newly-found literacy resulting from a stress on reading and writing led to the detribalization of men and women.

3. The third historically significant era, one which was ushered in by the printing press and labeled "The Gutenberg Galaxy," gave further impetus to "phonetic literacy." In describing the enormous impact of this mechanization process, McLuhan noted: "If the phonetic alphabet fell like a bombshell on tribal man, the printing press hit him like a 100-megaton H-bomb." What made this development so remarkable was its ability to produce books in mass quantities—a fact that enabled individuals to expand their personal libraries and, in turn, their overall knowledge.

4. The dominating influence of the print age, according to McLuhan, extended from about 1500 to the latter part of the nineteenth century. As the twentieth century neared, two forms of electronic media—the telegraph and the telephone—launched the beginning of a new period that culminated several decades later in the development of radios, films, televisions, and computers. That these types of electronic media have transcended in importance the influence of the three preceding areas will soon be made clear.

In a series of popular books, McLuhan described in graphic detail how the prevailing media operating at a particular time has stimulated man's senses.[1] His definition of media is so broad and encompassing that it includes such elements as "the spoken word," "the written word," "roads," "comics," "wheels," "bicycles," "airplanes," "photographs," "the press," "motor cars," "ads," "games," "the telegraph," "typewriters," "telephones," "phonographs," "movies," "radio," "television," "weapons," and "automation."[2] All of these media, or technologies, McLuhan argues, both extend and amputate our sensory perceptions. "The wheel," for example, "is an extension of the foot"; "the book is an extension of the eye"; "clothing is an extension of the skin"; and "electric circuitry is an extension of the central nervous system."[3] Moreover, whenever one of these senses is extended, others experience amputation. If we extend the eye, for instance, we may at the same time amputate the ear.

The application of the extension-amputation principle is easy to make when we examine the four periods mentioned earlier. In the preliterate, tribal society, the oral genre which predominated extended the ear and diminished the influence of the eye. The manuscript period launched by the phonetic alphabet gave an important extension to the eye, causing a break with the ear and "between semantic meaning and visual code. . . ." Phonetic writing, in short, "has the power to translate man from the tribal to the civilized sphere, to give him an eye for the ear."[4]

By far the greatest impact on man's senses, McLuhan proceeds to argue, came with the onset of the electronic age. The whole nervous system of man has undergone a radical change.

But it was not until Gutenberg's invention of movable type in the fifteenth century that the use of the eye was maximized to the point that other senses virtually were cut off. The effect on man was dramatic. In the preface of his most creative work, *The Gutenberg Galaxy*, McLuhan states:

Printing from movable types created a quite unexpected new environment—it created the Public. Manuscript technology did not have the intensity or power of extension necessary to create publics on a national scale. What we have called "nations" in recent centuries did not, and could not, precede the advent of Gutenberg technology. . . .
The unique character of the 'public' created by the printed word was an intense and visually oriented self-consciousness, both of the individual and the group. The consequences of this intense visual stress with its increasing isolation of the visual faculty from the other senses are presented in this book. Its theme is the extension of the visual modalities of continuity, uniformity, and connectiveness to the organization of time and space alike.[5]

It would appear then that the print-oriented society, responding to the technology of movable type, became so independent, isolated, and self-reliant that

there was progressively less need for social communion.

By far the greatest impact on man's senses, McLuhan proceeds to argue, came with the onset of the electronic age. The whole nervous system of man has undergone a radical change. In breaking the hold that the Gutenberg galaxy had on man for more than four centuries, "electric circuitry has overthrown the regime of 'time' and 'space' and pours upon us instantly and continuously the concerns of all other men. It has reconstituted dialogue on a global scale. . . ."[6] This enormous influence will be seen more clearly when we turn later to a discussion of radio and television.

Out of the foregoing general views, which constitute McLuhan's starting point, he reached his most celebrated conclusion: "The medium is the message." On November 12, 1967, an article dealing with "McLuhan and His Critics" appeared in the *Washington Star*. At the top of the page we see McLuhan seated on a swivel chair in front of twelve TV monitors, eight of which have superimposed upon the screen the words: "The Medium is the Message."[7] This recurring theme, grown stale by its repetition, wends its way through all of McLuhan's probes. The meaning that we experience in a communication transaction, he asserts, is more dependent upon the medium than upon content. To gain a better perspective of this revolutionary concept, let us observe the following distinction which he makes between "hot" and "cool" media:

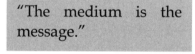
"The medium is the message."

There is a basic principle that distinguishes a hot medium like the movie from a cool one like TV. A hot medium is one that extends one single sense in 'high definition.' High definition is the state of being well filled with data. A photograph is, visually, 'high definition.' A cartoon is 'low definition,' simply because very little information is provided. Telephone is a cool medium, or one of low definition, because the ear is given a meager amount of information. And speech is a cool medium of low definition, because so little is given and so much has to be filled in by the lis-

tener. On the other hand, hot media do not leave so much to be filled in or completed by the audience. Hot media are, therefore, low in participation, and cool media are high in participation or completion by the audience. Naturally, therefore, a hot medium like radio has very different effects on the user from a cool medium like the telephone. . . .[8]

Of all of the above distinctions between "hot" and "cool" media, perhaps the most controversial is the designation of movies as "hot." Film, it has been argued, has the same characteristics which are present in television. McLuhan's position is that there are noticeable differences both in the scanning principle and size of the screen, and in the effect on the viewer. The latter claim is illustrated with a reference to members of the African culture who tend to respond less favorably to film than to television. "With film," McLuhan suggests, "you are the camera and the nonliterate man cannot use his eyes like a camera. But with TV you are the screen. And TV is two-dimensional and sculptural in its tactile contours."[9]

Because of the pervasive influence of radio and television on modern culture, it will be fruitful for us to examine more fully how "hot" and "cool" apply to these two media. To say that a radio is a "high definition" medium implies that it contains considerable specific data designed to stimulate the auditory sense, thus making it unnecessary for the audience to supply details or their own version of meaning. Since so much information is present, the listeners find it easy to respond even though the level of their participation is minimal. It is for this reason, McLuhan suggests, that radio is very effective as a tool for persuasion in an oral tribal society so characteristic of many African communities in the present century.

By contrast television is a "cool" medium, providing limited data and requiring an intense degree of audience participation. As in the case of a cartoon, a television picture permits the listener to produce much of the message. Consequently, in political situations calling for decision-making, such as in the War in Vietnam and Watergate, a person sitting in front of a TV set in his/her living room becomes part of a unified whole. The situation is experienced feelingly because not only the eye and the ear are sensitized but also the tactile sense as well. In explaining this phenomenon, Carey observes: "Television, as a result of the scanning system on which it operates, is capable of conveying or eliciting a sense of touch."[10]

According to McLuhan, color television creates even more listener involvement than does black and white.[11]

If radio and television illustrate the differences between "hot" and "cool" media, so, too, do glasses and sunglasses. On this point, McLuhan says:

The principle that distinguishes hot and cool media is perfectly involved in the folk wisdom: 'Men seldom make passes at girls who wear glasses.' Glasses intensify the outward-going vision, and fill in the feminine image exceedingly. . . . Dark glasses, on the other hand, create the inscrutable and inaccessible image that invites a great deal of participation and completion.[12]

The following diagram based upon the foregoing discussion and upon other writings will serve as a summary of how McLuhan classified a group of select media as being "hot" or "cool".

Hot	Cool
Photograph	Cartoon
Radio	Television
Print	Speech
Book	Telephone
Motion Picture	Conversation
Lecture	Seminar
Eyeglasses	Sunglasses

There can be little doubt that McLuhan's belief in the notion that "the medium is the message," or as he says in one of his books the "massage," is the central aspect of his theory of communication. This claim, more than any other conclusion we have analyzed in this survey of Western thought, is a radical thesis which runs counter to prior studies on meaning. Consistently we have demonstrated that the language symbols we use form the content of the message and generate meaning. But McLuhan has given us an antithetical interpretation of meaning by arguing that the medium, more than the content, is the essence of a message. Unfortunately, McLuhan's most widely publicized claim has made him an occasional victim of ridicule. Kenneth Burke's indictment typifies the problem. After criticizing McLuhan for placing an undue stress "upon the role of instruments (means, agencies) in shaping human dispositions, or attitudes and habits," Burke observed with telling sarcasm:

The medium is the message. Hence, down with content analysis. We should at least pause en route to note that the formula lends itself readily to caricature. Primus rushes up breathlessly to his friend Secundus, shouting, 'I have a drastic message for you. It's about your worst enemy. He is armed and raging and is—whereupon Secundus interrupts: 'Please! Let's get down to business. Who cares about the content of a message? My lad, hasn't McLuhan made it clear to you? The medium *is the message. So quick, tell me the really crucial point. I don't care what the news is. What I want to know is: Did it come by telegraph, telephone, wireless, radio, TV, semaphore signals, or word of mouth?'*[13]

McLuhan's probes into the nature and effects of media on our sensoria are, Burke argues, often overdrawn. Other critics claim that McLuhan was an armchair theorist and clever coiner of phrases whose ideas do not lend themselves to experimental verification.[14] Still others note that McLuhan rose to fame in the decade of the turbulent 1960s, only to see his influence and relevance wane in the succeeding decade.[15]

McLuhan is not without fault in creating doubts about the value of his probes. His background as a literary scholar did little to help him express his ideas in a clear and precise manner. Consequently he often is vulnerable to the charge that he used vague, conflicting, and exaggerated language that belied his true purpose. In response to these criticisms, McLuhan reputedly said: "I don't agree with everything I say," and "If there are going to be McLuhanites, I am certainly not going to be one of them."[16]

But if McLuhan had his detractors he also has an astonishingly large number of admirers. His two most important books, *The Gutenberg Galaxy and Understanding Media,* have become required reading in many college courses; and they won for McLuhan invitations to address executives in large corporations such as General Electric, I.B.M., and Bell Telephone. Moreover, he was a frequent guest on the network television shows. In the face of his wide acceptance as a seminal thinker, we raise the following question: What are the implications of McLuhan's theories for a contemporary rhetorical theory grounded in meaning? There are, we feel, four responses to this query.

> *we are indebted to McLuhan for alerting us to the great extent in which a medium affects the message and its reception.*

■ First, although we agree with Burke's claim that McLuhan went too far in equating the medium with the message, *we are indebted to him for alerting us to the great extent in which a medium affects the message and its reception.* One of the examples McLuhan uses to make this point was the Kennedy-Nixon debates in 1960. The verbal content of the message was the same for those who heard the presentations on radio and those who saw them on television. Yet in the crucial first debate the meaning was affected significantly by the medium. Kennedy was the acknowledged winner in the eyes of the television viewers, and Nixon the victor in the opinion of those who heard the debate on radio. These two groups found it difficult to witness the *same* rhetorical event. Nixon's point-by-point debate style, buttressed by numerous speech details, gave to the radio listener all the arguments he needed. The high definitional material extended the ear, and reduced the amount of audience involvement.

Kennedy, on the other hand, was less interested in offering a detailed rebuttal to Nixon's specific contentions and in directing his remarks to his opponent. Instead, he spoke self-confidently and engagingly to the American people, inviting them, as it were, to participate as an equal partner in the formulation of his arguments. His "cool" manner, strengthened by a youthful appearance, presented a dramatic contrast with the more stern, austere, and "hot" image projected by Nixon. Even Kennedy's full hair line and bronzed look, McLuhan would say, gave added force to the tactile image.[17] Thus the television audience tended to share Kennedy's view that he, not the Republican candidate, was the type of leader required in 1960.

■ A *second rhetorical implication stemming from McLuhan's probes is that since the nature of the medium affects the message reception, speakers should either choose that medium most suitable to their natural style or modify the style so as to make it appropriate to the medium.* If we again apply this principle to radio and television, we may conclude that a communicator whose manner is "hot" will perhaps be more effective on radio; and a speaker who exemplifies "coolness" will probably be more persuasive on television. McLuhan's examples illustrating this principle are instructive. Hitler, who was able to galvanize German sentiment by utilizing the "hot" medium of radio, would doubtless have failed as a persuader had he projected his high degree of intenseness on the "cool" medium of television. The same was true of former Senator Joseph McCarthy of Wisconsin. His aggressive anticommunist crusade, which aroused the radio audience in the early 1950s, ended abruptly and disastrously when it began to be transmitted on the emerging "cool" medium of television.[18]

Two other political leaders who had difficulty in adapting to the medium of television, McLuhan noted, were Lyndon Johnson and Hubert Humphrey during the troubling campaign year of 1968. Their "hot," forceful speaking manner proved to be inappropriate to a medium designed to "allow the viewer to fill in the gaps with his own personal identification. . . ."

But if Hitler, McCarthy, Johnson, and Humphrey—to name a representative few—were unable to adapt their styles to the cool medium of television, the same was not true of Kennedy and Fidel Castro. Kennedy, as suggested earlier, had a "compatible coolness and indifference to power" that made him an authentic child of television who was less persuasive on radio.[19] Despite his lengthy speeches, which often border on diatribes, Castro has the saving merit of being a masterful user of television for the purpose of developing a strong interactive relationship with his audience. McLuhan gives the following description of how the Cuban audiences respond to this type of appeal:

> *Castro is a good example of the new tribal chieftan who rules his country by a mass-participational TV dialog and feedback; he governs his country on camera, by giving the Cuban people the experience of being directly and intimately involved in the process of collective decision-making.*

Had McLuhan lived during the decade of the 1980s, we feel that he would have added the name of Ronald Reagan to those whose style and personality epitomized the coolness required by an effective television communicator.

McLuhan, we feel, does not mean to suggest that a speaker's use of radio or television is completely dependent upon his/her natural personality, style, or appearance. His probe into the area of "hot" and "cool" encourages a speaker, at least implicitly, to

alter the style and manner in order to make them suitable to a particular medium. A similar modification is also possible in the format that is to be used on radio and television. On the day following the first televised debate between Jimmy Carter and Gerald Ford in 1976, McLuhan said on the Today Show that the format should be modified. The stand-up debate technique featuring formal opening statements, planned questions by newsmen, and lengthy responses, he argued, was a "hot" approach presented in a "cool" medium which required an informal give-and-take between the participants, and involving the audience, a format first used in the second presidential debate of 1992.

■ *A third rhetorical implication related to McLuhanism is the resurgence of the oral mode of communication due to the influence of the electronic media.*[20] While we cannot concur with McLuhan's belief that the print medium with its eye-oriented emphasis is dead, our experience supports his claim that the oral genre during the age of television has gained so rapidly in popularity that it has contributed to the retribalization of man. Moreover, with this developing interest in orality accompanied by a decline in writing and reading skills has come an increased preference for the study of and practice in interpersonal communication.[21] Here McLuhan points out that the rhetoric of the classroom, if it is to keep pace with the change in the perception of our youth caused by the impact of the electronic media, should emphasize the seminar approach or other modes of informal dialogue rather than the sustained, uninterrupted lecture.[22]

■ *The fourth and final rhetorical implication pertaining to McLuhan's ideas "concerns the structure of public oral discourse," as Ehninger puts it, "and the modifications which may have to be made in our conceptions of that structure as we move into the electronic age."* Ehninger goes on to state the importance of McLuhan's contribution to the canon of *dispositio*:

> *Traditionally, of course, influenced by print culture or not, we have taught and used a linear pattern of speech development, whether the particular pattern in question be the classical parts of exordium through peroration, the Ramistic analysis and synthesis, the geometric or demonstrative development of the Port Royalists, or the reflective thinking process of John*

Dewey. All of these patterns, in one way or another, have assumed that if a discourse is to be organized properly some sort of ground work must be laid, a forward-moving thought line developed step by step in accordance with the logical demands of the subject or the psychological demands of the listeners, and, finally, a summarizing or applicative conclusion added. But if McLuhan is right, and the configurational all-at-once mode of presentation characteristic of television is changing our perceptual habits—or if, as he repeatedly suggests, it is the mosaic arrangement of the front page of our newspaper, with its stories developed according to the rule that makes the lead paragraph an all-at-once nutshell or capsule summary of what is to follow—if these and the similar configurational stimuli of contemporary art and literature are indeed affecting us as he suggests—then may not we as rhetoricians be called upon to follow suit by developing nonlinear patterns of speech organization, as well as to evaluate anew our predominantly linear systems of proof as couched in the enthymeme and example? At least, this seems to me to be worth thinking about, especially in the face of some of the evidence which the communication researchers now are gathering concerning the relative effectiveness of climactic and anticlimactic order.[23]

Ehninger's call for a need to consider alternative organizational patterns, as a result of McLuhan's probes, was perhaps more appropriate for the decade of the 1960s than it is for that of the 1990s. Even so, it still remains as an ongoing, provocative challenge to our traditional full commitment to the linear pattern that has been a benchmark of the canon of *dispositio* since the days of classical Greece and Rome.

SUMMARY

The four implications of McLuhanism singled out above, we believe, are worthy of the attention of students of rhetorical theory interested in the impact of technology on human communication practices. McLuhan, despite his frequent excesses and unsupported claims, has gone far beyond most of his predecessors and peers in describing the relationship between the medium and the message, and in challenging traditional views regarding the canons. More than any other rhetorician analyzed in this book, he helps us understand and appreciate the reciprocal relationships between rhetoric and the mass media and the influence of the latter on our sensory perceptions.[24]

--------- **Notes** ---------

1. The following are representative: *The Gutenberg Galaxy* (Toronto, 1962); *Understanding Media* (New York, 1964); *The Medium is the Message* (New York, 1967); *War and Peace in the Global Village* (New York, 1968); and *From Cliche to Archetype* (New York, 1970).
2. See chapter headings of *Understanding Media.*
3. *The Medium is the Message,* pp. 26–40.
4. *The Gutenberg Galaxy,* p. 38.
5. *Ibid.,* p. 7.
6. *The Medium is the Message,* p. 16.
7. "McLuhan and His Critics: Hot, Cool, and Baffling," F-3.
8. *Understanding Media,* p. 36.
9. *The Gutenberg Galaxy,* p. 52.
10. James W. Carey, "Harold Adams Innis and Marshall McLuhan," Douglas Ehninger, ed., *Contemporary Rhetoric* (Glenville, Ill.: Scott, Foresman and Co., 1972), p. 315.
11. *War and Peace in the Global Village,* p. 77.
12. *Understanding Media,* p. 44.
13. *Language as Symbolic Action* (Berkeley, Cal.: University of California Press, 1966), p. 414.
14. His writings, suggests one critic, are "impure nonsense, nonsense adulterated by sense." Another observes: "Marshall McLuhan. . . continually risks sounding like the body-fluids man in 'Doctor Strangelove.'" Richard Kostelanetz, "Understanding McLuhan," *New York Times Magazine,* January 29, 1967, p. 18.
15. One recent author has noted: "The fact that contemporary students of communication are only vaguely conversant with McLuhan's ideas is testimony of the failure of McLuhanism to exert a significant impact upon communication as a field of scholarly inquiry." B. Aubrey Fisher, *Perspectives on Human Communication* (New York: Macmillan Publishing Co., 1978), pp. 238–39. It should be noted, however, that as the decade of the 1970's came to a close,

McLuhan's ideas were being picked up by the French Structuralists who have a strong interest in forms and structures as suggested by McLuhan. Interview with Joseph Pilotta, Columbus, Ohio, January 30, 1978. Pilotta enrolled in McLuhan's University of Toronto year-long course, "Myth and Media."

16. Charles Cooke, "McLuhan and His Critics: Hot, Cool, and Baffling." *Washington Star,* November 12, 1967, F-3. Equally surprising is McLuhan's confession to his students at the University of Toronto that "he gets his insights from inspiration resulting from prayers to the Blessed Mary." Interview with Pilotta.

17. Interview with Pilotta.

18. It is necessary to observe, however, that McCarthy's tactical error of making a frontal attack on President Eisenhower and on the United States Army was also a factor in McCarthy's demise.

19. Even in death Kennedy's television appeal was enormous. Said McLuhan: "The Kennedy funeral. . . manifested the power of TV to involve an entire population in a ritual process." *Understanding Media,* p. 293.

20. See Douglas Ehninger, "Marshall McLuhan: Significance for the Field of Communication," (Connecticut) *Speech Journal,* Vol. VI (1969), pp. 17–24.

21. At the annual meeting of the ten Western Conference Chairmen of Departments of Communication in Detroit, Michigan, April, 1977, all of those present reported a steady increase in their undergraduate enrollments during recent years. This trend continued through the 1980's.

22. *Understanding Media,* p. 39.

23. "Marshall McLuhan: Significance for the Field of Speech Communication," VI, pp. 22–23.

24. For a comprehensive analysis of McLuhan's theories and influence, see the symposium on "The Living McLuhan," *Journal of Communication,* 31 (Summer 1981), pp. 116–198.

Richard Weaver and Rhetoric as Value

Rhetorical scholars from Plato to the present have studied the relationship between their "art" and ethics. Our purpose here is first to survey the views of various contemporary rhetoricians who have explored the ethical dimension of rhetoric, and then to direct your attention to the thoughtful work of a major value-oriented rhetorician, Richard Weaver.

Since rhetoric is concerned with probability and not scientific certainty, the communicator by definition possesses a certain measure of freedom to determine the structure of her message. During the exercise of this freedom, the concept of "choice" becomes apparent. Precisely because of the probable nature of rhetoric, the rhetor knowingly or unknowingly selects from her experiences and observations those elements of the persuasive process which best enable her to affect change in a given audience. It is this selection of specific ideas, evidence, language, structure, channels, and artistic proofs which underlies the study of rhetoric. Thus "choice" is basic to a study of rhetorical communication.

The communicator, according to most contemporary theorists, must exercise discretionary powers at several stages of the persuasion process; and it is precisely at these decision points that the ethics of rhetoric plays a role. To make the necessary choices inherent in the rhetorical process, the rhetor must possess a standard, a frame of reference, or a value system consonant with her personal philosophy at a given time. Everyone—acting as source or receiver—operates within an ethical perspective or value system which dictates her communicative behavior. In short, an individual's ethics affect her construction of messages as well as her perception of incoming communiques. Rhetoric, then, is a process grounded in "choice" which is dependent

on the values of those engaged in the communicative act. Inevitably, therefore, ethics and rhetoric are inseparable.

But how, we may ask at this point, may ethics be defined so that it will have meaning for students of communication? Ethics, according to Donald K. Smith, is the study of "value statements which identify the standards of conduct which an individual may acknowledge as constitutive of his person or personality, or which a group or society may acknowledge as constitutive of its character. We take it that men and societies universally acknowledge such system of values."[1] More specifically, Thomas Nilsen notes: "By ethics as a subject of study is meant systematic thinking and theorizing with respect to questions about good, right and wrong, and moral obligation."[2] For our purposes, ethics is concerned with the values of the communicator as revealed in her rhetorical behavior. In other words, are the rhetor's choices "good," "right," or "moral?" Karl Wallace and Richard Weaver begin to establish our perspective.

Wallace advocates that rhetoric must consider the basic "substance" or foundation of speech. In an oft-quoted passage, he observes:

What is this stuff? First, the underlying materials of speeches, and indeed of most human talk and discussion are assertions and statements that concern human behavior and conduct. They are prompted by situations and contexts that present us with choices and that require us to respond with appropriate decisions and actions. Second, such statements are usually called judgements and appraisals. They reflect human interests and values, and the nature of value judgements and the way of justifying them are the special, technical, and expert concern of ethics. Third, the appearance and use of value-judgements in practical discourse are the proper, although not the sole, concern of the theory and practice of rhetoric.[3]

Wallace next defines the substance of rhetoric as "good reasons" which he describes as "statements, consistent with each other, in support of an *ought* proposition or of a value judgement."[4] In a similar vein, Weaver equates ethics with "sermonic" language, saying: "As rhetoric confronts us with choices involving values, the rhetorician is a preacher to us, noble if he tries to direct our passion toward noble ends and base if he uses our passion to confuse and degrade us."[5] Both Wallace and Weaver emphasize the basis of rhetoric as "choice," pointing out that the rhetor's "choices" lie in the domain of ethics.

Convinced that ethical discourse consists of sermonic language dealing with ought propositions, numerous contemporary rhetoricians have suggested guidelines for helping a communicator to persuade in *a morally right way.* Richard Murphy, for example, states that an ethical rhetoric must not tolerate "offenses against common decency such as appeals to base motive, falsifying of evidence, the use of slanderous innuendo."[6] Any appeal, he adds, that falls short of responsible and informed communication fails to meet the test of honest expression, and should, therefore, be condemned.

Wayne Minnick is even more specific than Murphy in developing guidelines for the rhetor. An ethical communicator, he says, must:

reject all frauds, deceptions, concealments, specious arguments; cultivate the capacity for careful investigation and judicial and reflective deliberation of controversies and problems; endorse only those positions whose truth-claim merits his advocacy; must use intrinsically sound methods; use ethically neutral methods in ways that are consistent with and can be defended by reliable evidence and sound reasoning.[7]

Buttressing the views of Murphy and Minnick are the suggestions of Bryant and Wallace. The speaker, they point out, must have respect for the ends of speech; therefore, she should encourage goals which are in the best interest of the audience. The welfare of her listeners must be placed above the personal ambitions of the rhetor. Secondly, the speaker must respect the means of her communication. The means are more important than the ends for it is the quality of the production that counts. "What matters is how *well* the persuader spoke, how well he measured up to the standards of speechmaking."[8] Finally, the authors say that the speaker must honor the opinion of others as well as her own opinion. In this regard, the speaker must be convinced of her own viewpoint, she must be informed, and must not suppress or distort information.

Robert Scott agrees with the above guidelines, but then adds an important dimension. He elaborates the ethical demands or requirements for the communicator as "(1) taking responsibility for our choices, recognizing that we must assume the burden of harm done in our attempts to do good; (2) striving for honesty knowing the perils of arrogant self-deception; and (3) demanding toleration for those whose claims contradict our own."[9]

Crucial to an understanding of the nature of ethical discourse, many writers also agree, is the difficult and elusive concept of the intent of the agent. "A good intent," asserts Lawrence Flynn, "is so essential that without it an act cannot be morally good."[10] Predictably, Flynn further argues that the end does not justify the means for a good intent does not justify using an evil means."[11] Expressing a similar sentiment, James McCroskey gives the following perspective on the "intent" of the communicator:

Ethical judgments in rhetorical communication should be based exclusively on the intent of the communicator toward his audience. If the communicator seeks to improve the well-being of his audience through his act of communication, he is committing a moral act. If he seeks to produce harm for his audience, the communicator is guilty of an immoral act. If the intended effect upon the audience is neither to improve nor to harm their well-being, the communicator is committing an amoral act.[12]

As students of rhetorical theory we may agree or disagree with these ideas. Nevertheless we will find it useful to become aware of the philosophical problems inherent in the ethical system summarized here—problems which abound in any discussion of ethics. Perhaps more questions are raised here than are answered. What, for instance, is a "base emotion?" What is "intent?" Who measures "intent?" How is "intent" measured? What is meant by "deception?" Can deception in one circumstance be honest expression in another situation? "Is "honesty" a relative concept? Must the speaker really "tolerate" other viewpoints? As our discussion continues, we may find it profitable to examine carefully the considered viewpoints. In so doing, we will quickly realize that the issue of ethics in communication is an extremely complex problem area.

The next group of theorists to be analyzed are related in that they construct their ethical stance primarily around the democratic philosophy. These critics state that "in a democracy the standards of value by which a speaker and a speech are evaluated must be the standards established by the society."[13] Edward Rogge, Karl Wallace, Thomas Nilsen, and Franklyn Haiman are representatives of this school.

Wallace states that an ethics for communication must be built in relation to the political context of the society. An ethics of communication, therefore, for a free democratic society must encompass the following. First, the communicator must be thoroughly informed on her topic. Second, the speaker "must select and present fact and opinion fairly."[14] Third, the speaker should reveal her sources of fact and opinion. Finally, the speaker must tolerate other viewpoints and "acknowledge and . . . respect diversity of argument and opinion."[15] If a democratic society is premised on the free and open dialogue between individuals and groups and government, then Wallace's dictums are instructive.

Nilsen advocates an ethic based on the values of a democracy or "a belief in reason as an instrument of individual and social improvement; self-determination as the means to individual fulfillment of his potentialities as a positive good."[16] An ethical rhetoric, therefore, must enhance the values of the individual as guaranteed in the Bill of Rights.

Franklyn Haiman concurs with Nilsen's ideas concerning the intrinsic worth of the individual within a democracy. "Democracy is, in fact, primarily dedicated to the proposition that anything which helps in the development of the strength, productiveness, and happiness of the individual is good, and that anything which blocks or hinders his growth in these directions is immoral."[17] Thus, Wallace, Nilsen, and Haiman preface their ethic on the intrinsic worth of the individual—a worth inherently tied to the democratic political context.

A final group of writers needs to be mentioned. These are the theorists who are not content to limit their concern for traditional viewpoints already discussed. They go beyond previous authors by advocating a more active role for rhetoric as a device for proclaiming values. Typical of this approach is that expressed by Ralph Eubanks and Virgil Baker. These authors claim that rhetoric is a dynamic force which must nurture human values or "universal concepts basic to civil decisions and action." The function of rhetoric is to "crystallize and transmit human values." The end of rhetoric, therefore, is the realization of *justice* and order. "The concept of Justice synthesizes the classical trinity of democratic ideals, liberty, equality, and fraternity, whose central premise is the essential worthfulness and profound potentialities of the individual human being."[18] This suggests the wisdom of making "more direct the association between rhetorical method and axiology."[19]

Consistent with the emphasis of Eubanks and Baker is that used by Chaim Perelman and L. Olbrechts-Tyteca in their text, *The New Rhetoric: A Treatise on Argumentation.* In this volume, the authors discuss the centrality of values to all forms of discourse. "Values," they note, "enter, at some stage or other, into every argument."[20] An advocate, thus, "appeals to values in order to induce the hearer to make certain choices rather than others and, most of all, to justify those choices so that they may be accepted and approved by others."[21]

Up to this point we have summarized both prescriptive and descriptive means recommended by select contemporary authors as guidelines to be used by communicators in rhetorical transactions. Not to be overlooked is the challenge confronting the critic whose function it is to examine the discourse of others. In fact, of all the students of communication, the rhetorical critic perhaps most needs to be keenly aware of "choice" and its ethical imperative. As Nichols states: "The critic's function is to examine the speaker's premises, stated or implied, and to examine the truth of these premises."[22] She further shows, that the critic needs to become a vital force in society. "His place should be in the vanguard, not in the rear. . . . He should be ready to alert a people, to warn what devices of exploitation are being exercised, by what skillful manipulations of motives men are being directed to or dissuaded from courses of action."[23] If the critic ignores the ethical implications of his art, he engages in "pseudocriticism."[24]

In the foregoing discussion, we have attempted to survey the thoughts of a few writers who have dealt with ethics in relation to communication. Several different emphases and approaches have been stressed. Each perspective, as we have seen, is characterized by inherent philosophical problems, for such is the nature of ethics. From the earlier discussed prescriptive systems, to those ethical ideas tied into the intrinsic worth of the individual in his particular political context, to those which advocate an activist role in pursuit of justice and the integration of the human personality—we find limitations, drawbacks, and serious questions which need to be answered. However, it is not our purpose to offer a critique of ethics. Rather, we have sought only to present a brief overview of the ethical issue in communication as seen from the perspective of representative contemporary authors. To continue our discussion, we turn now to Richard Weaver and his axiological ideas on rhetoric.

RICHARD M. WEAVER

Weaver personifies (those) rhetoricians who have focused their attention almost exclusively on the relationship between rhetoric and ethics. In his widely circulated 1953 book, *The Ethics of Rhetoric,* he brought together a series of eight essays which probe various facets of the ethical dimension. The first essay on Plato's "Phaedrus and the Nature of Rhetoric" sets the tone for the volume. Equating Plato's "lovers" with evil, neuter, and noble speakers, Weaver revealed his close identification with the moral-philosophical emphasis in rhetoric. In the following excerpt he quotes Plato with approval.

> *What Plato has prepared us to see is that the virtuous rhetorician, who is a lover of truth, has a soul of such movement that its dialectical perceptions are consonant with those of a divine mind. Or, in the language of more technical philosophy, this soul is aware of axiological systems which have ontic status. The good soul, consequently, will not urge a perversion of justice as justice in order to impose upon the commonwealth. Insofar as the soul has its impulse in the right direction, its definitions will agree with the true nature of intelligible things.*[25]

Throughout the remaining portion of this essay, Weaver continually advocates the noble or virtuous rhetorician position wherein the rhetor is preoccupied with "truth," "justice," and the "good" in relation to the welfare of his listeners.

In the ensuing chapters of *Ethics of Rhetoric,* Weaver glimpses other themes that have strong moral implications. He opts for a rhetoric that has as its base dialectic. Knowledge and meaning derived from scientific inquiry, he argues, will constitute the foundation for appeals upholding values. He then articulates a distinction between two argumentative forms which he labels argument from circumstance and argument from definition or "the essential nature of things."[26] England's famous orator and literary scholar Edmund Burke becomes the focal point for illustrating an argument from circumstance. The historically significant "Conciliation with America" speech, delivered in 1775, is an example depicting an advocate's reliance on expedient principles. For Burke in this address, according to Weaver, never comes to grips with first principles grounded in human nature. Instead he upholds a policy of conciliation for such practical reasons as the great distance separating England and America, the high level of trade between the two areas, the large amount of legal works read by the colonists, and the independent spirit of the Southerners. At no time does he suggest that a policy of conciliation should be adopted because it is the inherent right of all men to be free, and to be exempt from taxation if they do not have representation. Weaver is to be commended for choosing a graphic model upon which to delineate the nature of an argument from circumstance. What he overlooks, however, is the fact that other speeches presented by Burke—particularly the Bristol Election address in 1780—are from beginning to end an argument from definition.

Weaver likewise selects a telling example for the purpose of describing an argument from definition. Alluding to the Lincoln-Douglas debates in 1858, he recreated the dramatic encounter between the two Illinois senatorial candidates regarding the doctrine of popular sovereignty. Douglas succeeded in convincing large segments of the voting public of the merits of permitting majority sentiment to determine whether or not a state should have slavery. Encouraged by the response to this political philosophy, Douglas taunted Lincoln by asking him where he stood on the question. Eventually Lincoln replied that he was opposed to it, saying in effect: "The difference between Judge Douglas and myself is that he does not feel slavery is a moral wrong. I do." Popu-

> Weaver personifies (those) rhetoricians who have focused their attention almost exclusively on the relationship between rhetoric and ethics.

lar sovereignty, therefore, represented to Weaver an argument from circumstance. To oppose this expedient policy for moral reasons, on the other hand, is to rely on first principles or the essential nature of things.

The final chapter in *Ethics of Rhetoric* also deserves special attention. The theme is "ultimate words" called "god" and "devil" terms. These are the words that rhetors use for the purpose of expressing values. A "god" term embraces a universal value that is generally regarded as good or desirable. Most Americans, for example, associate a favorable connotation with such positive words as "progress," "science," "fact," "modern," "democracy," "freedom," and "justice." They tend to view as unfavorable, however, such terms as "reactionary," "un-American," "fascist," and "communist." What places the use of ultimate terms in the sphere of ethics is the frequent tendency to employ such words in an irrational manner. Our language thus becomes, in the opinion of Weaver, a "perverse shibboleth."[27]

The essay which follows is perhaps Weaver's most mature statement as a rhetorical theorist. Weaver reminds us here that the object of rhetoric "is the whole man" and the office of rhetoric "is advising men." Moreover, he gives us his hierarchy ranking of arguments, ranging from circumstance (the lowest) and progressing upward through cause to effect, similitude or analogy, to definition (the highest). The full sweep of Weaver's claim that "language is sermonic" is seen in his eloquent concluding passage which states:

Finally, we must never lose sight of the order of values as the ultimate sanction of rhetoric. No one can live a life of direction and purpose without some scheme of values. As rhetoric confronts us with choices involving values, the rhetorician is a preacher to us, noble if he tries to direct our passion toward noble ends and base if he uses our passion to confuse and degrade us.[28]

Notes

1. Donald K. Smith, *Man Speaking: A Rhetoric of Public Speech* (New York: Dodd, Mead and Company, 1969), p. 228.

2. Thomas R. Nilsen, *Ethics of Speech Communication,* 1st ed. (New York: Bobbs-Merrill Company, 1966), p. 10.

3. Karl Wallace, "The Substance of Rhetoric: Good Reasons," in Richard L. Johannesen (ed.), *Contemporary Theories of Rhetoric: Selected Readings* (New York: Harper and Row, 1971), p. 360.

4. *Ibid.,* p. 368.

5. Richard Weaver, "Language Is Sermonic," in Richard L. Johannesen, Rennard Strickland, and Ralph Eubanks (eds.), *Language is Sermonic: Richard M. Weaver on the Nature of Rhetoric* (Baton Rouge, Louisiana: Louisiana State University Press, 1970), p. 179.

6. Richard Murphy, "Preface to an Ethics of Rhetoric," in Donald C. Bryant (ed.), *The Rhetorical Idiom* (New York: Russell and Russell Company, 1966), p. 140.

7. Wayne L. Minnick, "The Ethics of Persuasion," in Johannesen (ed.), *Ethics and Persuasion: Selected Readings* (New York: Random House, 1967), p. 38.

8. Donald C. Bryant and Karl Wallace, "Ethics of Persuasion," in *Fundamentals of Public Speaking* (New York: Appleton-Century Crofts, 1960), p. 293.

9. Robert L. Scott (ed.), *The Speaker's Reader: Concepts in Communication.* (Glenview, Ill.: Scott, Foresman and Company, 1969), p. 22.

10. Lawerence J. Flynn, "The Aristotelian Basis for the Ethics of Speaking," in Johannesen (ed.), *Ethics and Persuasion,* p. 121.

11. *Ibid.,* pp. 121–123.

12. James C. McCroskey, An *Introduction to Rhetorical Communication,* 2nd ed. (Englewood Cliffs, New Jersey: Prentice-Hall, Inc., 1972), p. 270.

13. Edward Rogge, "Evaluating the Ethics of a Speaker in a Democracy," in Johannesen (ed.), *Ethics and Persuasion,* p. 91.

14. Karl Wallace, "An Ethical Basis of Communication," in Goodwin F. Berquist (ed.), *Speeches for Illustration and Example* (Chicago, Ill.: Scott, Foresman and Company, 1965), p. 188.

15. *Ibid.,* p. 190.

16. Thomas Nilsen, "Free Speech, Persuasion, and the Democratic Process," in Johannesen (ed.), *Ethics and Persuasion,* p. 74.

17. Franklyn S. Haiman, "Democratic Ethics and the Hidden Persuaders," in Johannesen (ed.), *Ethics and Persuasion*, p. 62.

18. Ralph Eubanks and Virgil Baker, "Toward an Axiology of Rhetoric," in Johannesen (ed.), *Contemporary Theories of Rhetoric*, p. 346.

19. *Ibid.*, p. 347.

20. Ch. Perelman and L. Oblrechts-Tyteca, *The New Rhetoric: A Treatise on Argumentation* (London: University of Notre Dame Press, 1971), p. 75.

21. *Ibid.*

22. Marie Hochmuth Nichols, "The Criticism of Rhetoric," in *History and Criticism of American Public Address,* III (New York: McGraw-Hill, 1954), p. 16.

23. *Ibid.*, p. 17.

24. Barnet Baskerville, "Emerson as a Critic of Oratory," *Southern Speech Journal,* XVIII (September 1952), pp. 150–162.

25. Richard Weaver, *The Ethics of Rhetoric* (Chicago: Henry Regnery Company, 1970), p. 17.

26. *Ibid.*, p. 86.

27. *Ibid.*, p. 232.

28. Weaver, "Language is Sermonic," op. cit., p. 179.

Language Is Sermonic

Richard M. Weaver

Our age has witnessed the decline of a number of subjects that once enjoyed prestige and general esteem, but no subject, I believe, has suffered more amazingly in this respect than rhetoric. When one recalls that a century ago rhetoric was regarded as the most important humanistic discipline taught in our colleges—when one recalls this fact and contrasts it with the very different situation prevailing today—he is forced to see that a great shift of valuation has taken place. In those days, in the not-so-distant Nineteenth Century, to be a professor of rhetoric, one had to be *somebody*. This was a teaching task that was thought to call for ample and varied resources, and it was recognized as addressing itself to the most important of all ends, the persuading of human beings to adopt right attitudes and act in response to them. That was no assignment for the plodding sort of professor. That sort of teacher might do a middling job with subject matter courses, where the main object is to impart information, but the teacher of rhetoric had to be a person of gifts and imagination who could illustrate, as the need arose, how to make words even in prose take on wings. I remind you of the chairs of rhetoric that still survive in title in some of our older universities. And I should add, to develop the full picture, that literature was then viewed as a subject which practically anyone could teach. No special gift, other than perhaps industry, was needed to relate facts about authors and periods. That was held to be rather pedestrian work. But the instructor in rhetoric was expected to be a man of stature. Today, I scarcely need point out, the situation has been exactly reversed. Today it is the teacher of literature who passes through a long period of training, who is supposed to possess the mysteries of a learned craft, and who is placed by his very speciality on a height of eminence. His knowledge of the intricacies of Shakespeare or Keats or Joyce and his sophistication in the critical doctrines that have been developed bring him the esteem of the academy. We must recognize in all fairness that the elaboration of critical techniques and special approaches has made the teaching of literature a somewhat more demanding profession, although some think that it has gone in that direction beyond the point of diminishing returns. Still, this is not enough

Reprinted from *Language Is Sermonic* by R.L. Johannesen, R. Strickland, R.T. Eubanks, eds., (Baton Rouge: Louisiana State University Press, 1970). Reprinted with permission of the editors.

to account for the relegation of rhetoric. The change has gone so far that now it is discouraging to survey the handling of this study in our colleges and universities. With a few honorable exceptions it is given to just about anybody who will take it. The "inferior, unlearned, mechanical, merely instrumental members of the profession"—to recall a phrase of a great master of rhetoric, Edmund Burke—have in their keeping what was once assigned to the leaders. Beginners, part-time teachers, graduate students, faculty wives, and various fringe people, are now the instructional staff of an art which was once supposed to require outstanding gifts and mature experience. (We must note that at the same time the course itself has been allowed to decline from one dealing philosophically with the problems of expression to one which tries to bring below par students up to the level of accepted usage.) Indeed, the wheel of fortune would seem to have turned for rhetoric; what was once at the top is now at the bottom, and because of its low estate, people begin to wonder on what terms it can survive at all.

We are not faced here, however, with the wheel of fortune; we are faced with something that has come over the minds of men. Changes that come over the minds of men are not inscrutable, but have at some point their identifiable causes. In this case we have to deal with the most potent of cultural causes, an alteration of man's image of man. Something has happened in the recent past to our concept of what man is; a decision was made to look upon him in a new light, and from this decision new bases of evaluation have proceeded, which affect the public reputation of rhetoric. This changed concept of man is best described by the word "scientistic," a term which denotes the application of scientific assumptions to subjects which are not wholly comprised of naturalistic phenomena. Much of this is a familiar tale, but to understand the effect of the change, we need to recall that the great success of scientific or positivistic thinking in the Nineteenth Century induced a belief that nothing was beyond the scope of its method. Science, and its offspring applied science, were doing so much to alter and, it was thought, to improve the material conditions of the world, that a next step with the same process seemed in order. Why should not science turn its apparatus upon man, whom all the revelations of religion and the speculations of philosophy seemed still to have left an enigma, with the promise of much better result? It came to be believed increasingly that

to think validly was to think scientifically, and that subject matters made no difference.

Now the method of scientific investigation is, as T.H. Huxley reminded us in a lecture which does great credit to him as a rhetorician, merely the method of logic. Induction and deduction and causal inference applied to the phenomena of nature yielded the results with which science was changing the landscape and revolutionizing the modes of industry. From this datum it was an easy inference that men ought increasingly to become scientists, and again, it was a simple derivative from this notion that man at his best is a logic machine, or at any rate an austerely unemotional thinker. Furthermore, carried in the train of this conception was the thought, not often expressed of course, that things would be better if men did not give in so far to being human in the humanistic sense. In the shadow of the victories of science, his humanism fell into progressive disparagement. Just what comprises humanism is not a simple matter for analysis. Rationality is an indispensable part to be sure, yet humanity includes emotionality, or the capacity to feel and suffer, to know pleasure, and it includes the capacity for aesthetic satisfaction, and, what can be only suggested, a yearning to be in relation with something infinite. This last is his religious passion, or his aspiration to feel significant and to have a sense of belonging in a world that is productive of much frustration. These at least are the properties of humanity. Well, man had been human for some thousands of years, and where had it gotten him? Those who looked forward to a scientific Utopia were inclined to think that his humanness had been a drag on his progress; human qualities were weaknesses, except for that special quality of rationality, which might be expected to redeem him.

However curious it may appear, this notion gained that man should live down his humanity and make himself a more efficient source of those logical inferences upon which a scientifically accurate understanding of the world depends. As the impulse spread, it was the emotional and subjective components of his being that chiefly came under criticism, for reasons that have just been indicated. Emotion and logic or science do not consort; the latter must be objective, faithful to what is out there in the public domain and conformable to the processes of reason. Whenever emotion is allowed to put in an oar, it gets the boat off true course. Therefore emotion is a liability.

Under the force of this narrow reasoning, it was natural that rhetoric should pass from a status in which it was regarded as of questionable worth to a still lower one in which it was positively condemned. For the most obvious truth about rhetoric is that its object is the whole man. It presents its arguments first to the rational part of man, because rhetorical discourses, if they are honestly conceived, always have a basis in reasoning. Logical argument is the plot, as it were, of any speech or composition that is designed to persuade. Yet it is the very characterizing feature of rhetoric that it goes beyond this and appeals to other parts of man's constitution, especially to his nature as a pathetic being, that is, a being feeling and suffering. A speech intended to persuade achieves little unless it take into account how men are reacting subjectively to their hopes and fears and their special circumstances. The fact that Aristotle devotes a large proportion of his *Rhetoric* to how men feel about different situations and actions is an evidence of how prominently these considerations bulked even in the eyes of a master theorist.

Yet there is one further fact, more decisive than any of these, to prove that rhetoric is addressed to man in his humanity. Every speech which is designed to move is directed to a special audience in its unique situation. (We could not except even those radio appeals to "the world." Their audience has a unique place in time.) Here is but a way of pointing out that rhetoric is intended for historical man, or for man as conditioned by history. It is part of the *conditio humana* that we live at particular times and in particular places. These are productive of special or unique urgencies, which the speaker has got to recognize and to estimate. Hence, just as man from the point of view of rhetoric is not purely a thinking machine, or a mere seat of rationality, so he is not a creature abstracted from time and place. If science deals with the abstract and the universal, rhetoric is near the other end, dealing in significant part with the particular and the concrete. It would be the height of wishful thinking to say that this ought not be so. As long as man is born into history, he will be feeling and responding to historical pressures. All of these reasons combine to show why rhetoric should be considered the most humanistic of the humanities. It is directed to that part of our being which is not merely rational, for it supplements the rational approach. And it is directed to individual men in their individual situations, so that by the very definitions of the terms here involved, it takes into account what science deliberately, to satisfy its own purposes, leaves out. There is consequently no need for wonder

that, in an age that has been influenced to distrust and disregard what is characteristically human, rhetoric should be a prime target of attack. If it is a weakness to harbor feelings, and if furthermore it is a weakness to be caught up in historical situations, then rhetoric is construable as a dealer in weaknesses. That man is in this condition religion, philosophy, and literature have been teaching for thousands of years. Criticism of it from the standpoint of a scientistic Utopia is the new departure.

The incompleteness of the image of man as a creature who should make use of reason only can be demonstrated in another way. It is a truism that logic is a subject without a subject matter. That is to say, logic is a set of rules and devices which are equally applicable whatever the data. As the science of the forms of reasoning, it is a means of interpreting and utilizing the subject matters of the various fields which do have their proper contents. Facts from science or history or literature, for example, may serve in the establishment of an inductive generalization. Similar facts may be fed into a syllogism. Logic is merely the mechanism for organizing the data of other provinces of knowledge. Now it follows from this truth that if a man could convert himself into a pure logic machine or thinking machine, he would have no special relation to any body of knowledge. All would be grist for his mill, as the phrase goes. He would have no inclination, no partiality, no particular affection. His mind would work upon one thing as indifferently as upon another. He would be an eviscerated creature or a depassioned one, standing in the same relationship to the realities of the world as the thinking technique stands to the data on which it is employed. He would be a thinking robot, a concept which horrifies us precisely because the robot has nothing to think about.

A confirmation of this truth lies in the fact that rhetoric can never be reduced to symbology. Logic is increasingly becoming "symbolic logic"; that is its tendency. But rhetoric always comes to us in well-fleshed words, and that is because it must deal with the world, the thickness, stubbornness, and power of it.[1]

Everybody recognizes that there is thus a formal logic. A number of eminent authorities have written of rhetoric as if it were formal in the same sense and degree. Formal rhetoric would be a set of rules and devices for persuading anybody about anything. If one desires a certain response, one uses a certain device, or "trick" as the enemies of the art would put it.

The set of appeals that rhetoric provides is analogized with the forms of thought that logic prescribes. Rhetoric conceived in this fashion has an adaptability and virtuosity equal to those of logic.

But the comparison overlooks something, for at one point we encounter a significant difference. Rhetoric has a relationship to the world which logic does not have and which forces the rhetorician to keep an eye upon reality as well as upon the character and situation of his audience. The truth of this is seen when we begin to examine the nature of the traditional "topics." The topics were first formulated by Aristotle and were later treated also by Cicero and Quintilian and by many subsequent writers on the subject of persuasion.

They are a set of "places" or "regions" where one can go to find the substance for persuasive argument. Cicero defines a topic as "the seat of an argument." In function they are sources of content for speeches that are designed to influence. Aristotle listed a considerable number of them, but for our purposes they can be categorized very broadly. In reading or interpreting the world of reality, we make use of four very general ideas. The first three are usually expressed, in the language of philosophy, as being, cause, and relationship. The fourth, which stands apart from these because it is an external source, is testimony and authority.

One way to interpret a subject is to define its nature—to describe the fixed features of its being. Definition is an attempt to capture essence. When we speak of the nature of a thing, we speak of something we expect to persist. Definitions accordingly deal with fundamental and unchanging properties.

Another way to interpret a subject is to place it in a cause-and-effect relationship. The process of interpretation is then to affirm it as the cause of some effect or as the effect of some cause. And the attitudes of those who are listening will be affected according to whether or not they agree with our cause-and-effect analysis.

A third way to interpret a subject is in terms of relationships of similarity and dissimilarity. We say that it is like something which we know in fuller detail, or that it is unlike that thing in important respects. From such a comparison conclusions regarding the subject itself can be drawn. This is a very common form of argument, by which probabilities can be established. And since probabilities are all we have to go on in many questions of this life, it must be accounted a usable means of persuasion.

The fourth category, the one removed from the others by the fact of its being an external source, deals not with the evidence directly but accepts it on the credit of testimony or authority. If we are not in position to see or examine, but can procure the deposition of some one who is, the deposition may become the substance of our argument. We can slip it into a syllogism just as we would a defined term. The same is true of general statements which come from quarters of great authority or prestige. If a proposition is backed by some weighty authority, like the Bible, or can be associated with a great name, people may be expected to respond to it in accordance with the veneration they have for these sources. In this way evidence coming from the outside is used to influence attitudes or conduct.

Now we see that in all these cases the listener is being asked not simply to follow a valid reasoning form but to respond to some presentation of reality. He is being asked to agree with the speaker's interpretation of the world that is. If the definition being offered is a true one, he is expected to recognize this and to say, at least inwardly, "Yes, that is the way the thing is." If the exposition of cause-and-effect relationship is true, he may be expected to concur that X is the cause of such a consequence or that such a consequence has its cause in X. And according to whether this is a good or a bad cause or a good or a bad consequence, he is disposed to preserve or remove the cause, and so on. If he is impressed with the similarity drawn between two things, he is as a result more likely to accept a policy which involves treating something in the same way in which its analogue is treated. He has been influenced by a relationship of comparability. And finally, if he has been confronted with testimony or authority from sources he respects, he will receive this as a reliable, if secondary, kind of information about reality. In these four ways he has been persuaded to read the world as the speaker reads it.

At this point, however, I must anticipate an objection. The retort might be made: "These are extremely formal categories you are enumerating. I fail to see how they are any less general or less indifferently applicable than the formal categories of logic. After all, definitions and so on can be offered of anything. You still have not succeeded in making rhetoric a substantive study."

In replying, I must turn here to what should be called the office of rhetoric. Rhetoric seen in the whole conspectus of its function is an art of emphasis embodying an order of desire. Rhetoric is advisory; it has the office of advising men with reference to an independent order of goods and with reference to their particular situation as it relates to these. The honest rhetorician (therefore) has two things in mind: a vision of how matters should go ideally and ethically and a consideration of the special circumstances of his auditors. Toward both of these he has a responsibility.

I shall take up first how his responsibility to the order of the goods or to the hierarchy of realities may determine his use of the topics.

When we think of rhetoric as one of the arts of civil society (and it must be a free society, since the scope for rhetoric is limited and the employment of it constrained under a despotism) we see that the rhetorician is faced with a choice of means in appealing to those whom he can prevail upon to listen to him. If he is at all philosophical, it must occur to him to ask whether there is a standard by which the sources of persuasion can be ranked. In a phrase, is there a preferred order of them, so that, in a scale of ethics, it is nobler to make use of one sort of appeal than another? This is of course a question independent of circumstantial matters, yet a fundamental one. We all react to some rhetoric as "untruthful" or "unfair" or "cheap," and this very feeling is evidence of the truth that it is possible to use a better or a worse style of appeal. What is the measure of the better style? Obviously this question cannot be answered at all in the absence of some conviction about the nature and destiny of man. Rhetoric inevitably impinges upon morality and politics; and if it is one of the means by which we endeavor to improve the character and the lot of men, we have to think of its methods and sources in relation to a scheme of values.

To focus the problem a little more sharply, when one is asking men to cooperate with him in thinking this or doing that, when is he asking in the name of the highest reality, which is the same as saying, when is he asking in the name of their highest good?

> The honest rhetorician (therefore) has two things in mind: a vision of how matters should go ideally and ethically and a consideration of the special circumstances of his auditors. Toward both of these he has a responsibility.

> he is making the highest order of appeal when he is basing his case on definition or the nature of the thing.

Naturally, when the speaker replies to this question, he is going to express his philosophy, or more precisely, his metaphysics. My personal reply would be that he is making the highest order of appeal when he is basing his case on definition or the nature of the thing. I confess that this goes back to a very primitive metaphysics, which holds that the highest reality is being, not becoming. It is a quasi-religious metaphysics, if you will, because it ascribes to the highest reality qualities of stasis, immutability, eternal perdurance—qualities that in Western civilization are usually expressed in the language of theism. That which is perfect does not change; that which has to change is less perfect. Therefore, if it is possible to determine unchanging essences or qualities and to speak in terms of these, one is appealing to what is most real in so doing. From another point of view, this is but getting people to see what is most permanent in existence, or what transcends the world of change and accident. The realm of essence is the realm above the flux of phenomena, and definitions are of essences and genera.

I may have expressed this view in somewhat abstruse language in order to place it philosophically, yet the practice I am referring to is everyday enough, as a simple illustration will make plain. If a speaker should define man as a creature with an indefeasible right to freedom and should upon this base an argument that a certain man or group of men are entitled to freedom, he would be arguing from definition. Freedom is an unchanging attribute of his subject; it can accordingly be predicated of whatever falls within the genus man. Stipulative definitions are of the ideal, and in this fact lies the reason for placing them at the top of the hierarchy. If the real progress of man is toward knowledge of ideal truth, it follows that this is an appeal to his highest capacity—his capacity to apprehend what exists absolutely.

The next ranking I offer tentatively, but it seems to me to be relationship or similitude and its subvarieties. I have a consistent impression that the broad resource of analogy, metaphor, and figuration is favored by those of a poetic and imaginative cast of mind. We make use of analogy or comparison when the available knowledge of the subject permits only probable proof. Analogy is reasoning from something we know to something we do not know in one step; hence there is no universal ground for predication. Yet behind every analogy lurks the possibility of a general term. The general term is never established as such, for that would change the argument to one of deductive reasoning with a universal or distributed middle. The user of analogy is hinting at an essence which cannot at the moment be produced. Or, he may be using an indirect approach for reason of tact; analogies not infrequently do lead to generalizations; and he may be employing this approach because he is respectful of his audience and desires them to use their insight.

I mentioned a moment earlier that this type of argument seems to be preferred by those of a poetic or non-literal sort of mind. That fact suggests yet another possibility, which I offer still more diffidently, asking your indulgence if it seems to border on the whimsical. The explanation would be that the cosmos is one vast system of analogy, so that our profoundest intuitions of it are made in the form of comparisons. To affirm that something is like something else is to begin to talk about the unitariness of creation. Everything is like everything else somehow, so that we have a ladder of similitude mounting up to the final one-ness—to something like a unity in godhead. Furthermore, there is about this source of argument a kind of decent reticence, a recognition of the unknown along with the known. There is a recognition that the unknown may be continuous with the known, so that man is moving about in a world only partly realized, yet real in all its parts. This is the mood of poetry and mystery, but further adumbration of it I leave to those more gifted than I.

Cause and effect appears in this scale to be a less exalted source of argument, though we all have to use it because we are historical men. Here I must recall the methaphysical ground of this organization and point out that it operates in the realm of becoming. Causes are causes having effect and effects are resulting from causes. To associate this source of argument with its habitual users, I must note that it is heard most commonly from those who are characteristically pragmatic in their way of thinking. It is not unusual today to find a lengthy piece of journalism or an entire political speech which is nothing but a series of arguments from consequence—completely devoid of reference to principle or defined ideas. We rightly recognize these as sensational types of appeal. Those who are partial to arguments based on effect are under a temptation to play too much upon the fears of their audience by stressing the awful nature of some consequence or by exaggerating the power of some cause. Modern advertising is prolific in this kind of abuse. There is likewise a temptation to appeal to prudential considerations only in a passage where things are featured as happening or threatening to happen.

An even less admirable subvariety of this source is the appeal to circumstance, which is the least philosophical of all the topics of argument. Circumstance is an allowable source when we don't know anything else to plead, in which case we say, "There is nothing else to be done about it." Of all the arguments, it admits of the least perspicaciousness. An example of this which we hear nowadays with great regularity is: "We must adapt ourselves to a fast-changing world." This is pure argument from circumstance. It does not pretend, even, to offer a cause-and-effect explanation. If it did, the first part would tell us why we must adapt ourselves to a fast-changing world; and the second would tell us the result of our doing so. The usually heard formulation does neither. Such argument is preeminently lacking in understanding or what the Greeks called *dianoia*. It simply cites a brute circumstance and says, "Step lively." Actually, this argument amounts to a surrender of reason. Maybe it expresses an instinctive feeling that in this situation reason is powerless. Either you change fast or you get crushed. But surely it would be a counsel of desperation to try only this argument in a world suffering from aimlessness and threatened with destruction.

Generally speaking, cause and effect is a lower-order source of argument because it deals in the realm of the phenomenal, and the phenomenal is easily converted into the sensational. Sensational excitements always run the risk of arousing those excesses which we deplore as sentimentality or brutality.

Arguments based on testimony and authority, utilizing external sources, have to be judged in a different way. Actually, they are the other sources seen through other eyes. The question of their ranking involves the more general question of the status of authority. Today there is a wide-spread notion that all authority is presumptuous. ("Authority is authoritarian" seems to be the root idea); consequently it is held improper to try to influence anyone by the prestige of great names or of sanctioned pronouncements. This is a presumption itself, by which every man is presumed to be his own competent judge in all matters. But since that is a manifest impossibility, and is becoming a greater impossibility all the time, as the world piles up bodies of specialized knowledge which no one person can hope to command, arguments based on authority are certainly not going to disappear. The sound maxim is that an argument based on authority is as good as the authority. What we should hope for is a new and discriminating attitude toward what is authoritative, and I would like to see some source recognized as having moral authority. This hope will have to wait upon the recovery of a more stable order of values and the recognition of qualities in persons. Speaking most generally, arguments from authority are ethically good when they are deferential toward real hierarchy.

With that we may sum up the rhetorical speaker's obligation toward the ideal, apart from particular determinations. If one accepts the possibility of this or any other ranking, one has to concede that rhetoric is not merely formal; it is realistic. It is not a playing with counters; its impulses come from insights into actuality. Its topic matter is existential, not hypothetical. It involves more than mere demonstration because it involves choice. Its assertions have ontological claims.

Now I return to the second responsibility, which is imposed by the fact that the rhetorician is concerned with definite questions. These are questions having histories, and history is always concrete. This means that the speaker or writer has got to have a rhetorical perception of what his audience needs or will receive or respond to. He takes into account the reality of man's composite being and his tendency to be swayed by sentiment. He estimates the pressures of the particular situation in which his auditors are found. In the eyes of those who look sourly upon the art, he is a man probing for weaknesses which he means to exploit.

But here we must recur to the principle that rhetoric comprehensively considered is an art of emphasis. The definite situation confronts him with a second standard of choice. In view of the receptivity of his audience, which of the topics shall he choose to stress, and how? If he concludes that definition should be the appeal, he tries to express the nature of the thing in a compelling way. If he feels that a cause-and-effect demonstration would stand the greatest chance to impress, he tries to make this linkage so manifest that his hearers will see an inevitability in it. And so on with the other topics, which will be so emphasized or magnified as to produce the response of assent.

Along with this process of amplification, the ancients recognized two qualities of rhetorical discourse which have the effect of impressing an audience with the reality or urgency of a topic. In Greek these appear as *energia* and *enargia,* both of which may be translated "actuality," though the first has to do with liveliness or animation of action and the second with vividness of scene. The speaker now indulges in actualization to the minds' eyes of his hearers.

The practice itself has given rise to a good deal of misunderstanding, which it would be well to remove. We know that one of the conventional criticisms of rhetoric is that the practitioner of it takes advantage of his hearers by playing upon their feelings and imaginations. He overstresses the importance of his topics by puffing them up, dwelling on them in great detail, using an excess of imagery or of modifiers evoking the senses, and so on. He goes beyond what is fair, the critics often allege, by this actualization of a scene about which the audience ought to be thinking rationally. Since this criticism has a serious basis, I am going to offer an illustration before making the reply. Here is a passage from Daniel Webster's famous speech for the prosecution in the trial of John Francis Knapp. Webster is actualizing for the jury the scene of the murder as he has constructed it from circumstantial evidence.

The deed was executed with a degree of steadiness and self-possession equal to the wickedness with which it was planned. The circumstances now clearly in evidence spread out the scene before us. Deep sleep had fallen upon the destined victim and all beneath his roof. A healthful old man, to whom sleep was sweet, the first sound slumbers of the night held him in their soft but strong embrace. The assassin enters, through a window already prepared, into an unoccupied apartment. With noiseless foot he paces the lonely hall, half-lighted by the moon; he winds up the ascent of the stairs, and reaches the door of the chamber. Of this, he moves the lock by soft and continued pressure, till it turns on its hinges without noise; and he enters, and beholds the victim before him. The room is uncommonly open to the admission of light. The face of the innocent sleeper is turned from the murderer, and the beams of the moon, resting on the gray locks of the aged temple, show him where to strike. The fatal blow is given! and the victim passes, without a struggle or a motion, from the repose of sleep to the repose of death! It is the assassin's purpose to make sure work; and he plies the dagger, though it is obvious that life has been destroyed by the blow of the bludgeon. He even raises the aged arm, that he may not fail in his aim at the heart, and replaces it again over the wound of the poniard! To finish the picture, he explores the wrist for the pulse! He feels for it, and ascertains that it beats no longer! It is accomplished. The deed is done. He retreats, retraces his steps to the window, passes out through it as he came in, and escapes. He has done the murder. No eye has seen him, no ear has heard him. The secret is his own, and it is safe!

By depicting the scene in this fullness of detail, Webster is making it vivid, and "vivid" means "living." There are those who object on general grounds to this sort of dramatization; it is too affecting to the emotions. Beyond a doubt, whenever the rhetorician actualizes an event in this manner, he is making it mean something to the emotional part of us, but that part is involved whenever we are deliberating about goodness and badness. On this subject there is a very wise reminder in Bishop Whately's *Elements of Rhetoric:* "When feelings are strongly excited, they are not necessarily overexcited; it may be that they are only brought to the state which the occasion fully justifies, or even that they fall short of this." Let us think of the situation in which Webster was acting. After all, there is the possibility, or even the likelihood that the murder was committed in this fashion, and that the indicted Knapp deserved the conviction he got. Suppose the audience had remained cold and unmoved. There is the victim's side to consider and the interest of society in protecting life. We should not forget that Webster's "actualization" is in the service of these. Our attitude toward what is just or right or noble and their opposites is not a bloodless calculation, but a feeling for and against. As Whately indicates, the speaker who arouses feeling may only be arousing it to the right pitch and channeling it in the right direction.

To re-affirm the general contention: the rhetorician who practices "amplification" is not thereby misleading his audience, because we are all men of limited capacity and sensitivity and imagination. We all need to have things pointed out to us, things stressed in our interest. The very task of the rhetorician is to determine what feature of a question is most exigent and to use the power of language to make it appear so. A speaker who dwells insistently upon some aspect of a case may no more be hoodwinking me than a policeman or a doctor when he advises against a certain course of action by pointing out its nature or its consequences. He *should* be in a position to know somewhat better than I do.

It is strongly to be suspected that this charge against rhetoric comes not only from the distorted image that makes man a merely rationalistic being, but also from the dogma of an uncritical equalitarianism. The notion of equality has insinuated itself so far that it appears sometimes as a feeling, to which I would apply the name "sentimental plebeianism," that no man is better or wiser than another, and hence that it is usurpation for one person to undertake to instruct or admonish another. This preposterous (and we could add, wholly unscientific judgment, since our differences are manifold and provable) is propagated in subtle ways by our institutions of publicity and the perverse art of demagogic politics. Common sense replies that any individual who advises a friend or speaks up in meeting is exercising a kind of leadership, which may be justified by superior virtue, knowledge, or personal insight.

The fact that leadership is a human necessity is proof that rhetoric as the attempt through language to make one's point of view prevail grows out of the nature of man. It is not a reflection of any past phase of social development, or any social institution, or any fashion, or any passing vice. When all factors have been considered, it will be seen that men are born rhetoricians, though some are born small ones and others greater, and some cultivate the native gift by study and training, whereas some neglect it. Men are such because they are born into history, with an endowment of passion and a sense of the *ought.* There is ever some discrepancy, however slight, between the situation man is in and the situation he would like to realize. His life is therefore characterized by movement toward goals. It is largely the power of rhetoric which influences and governs that movement.

For the same set of reasons, rhetoric is cognate with language. Ever since I first heard the idea mentioned seriously it impressed me as impossible and even ridiculous that the utterances of men could be neutral. Such study as I have been able to give the subject over the years has confirmed that feeling and has led me to believe that what is sometimes held up as a desideratum—expression purged of all tendency—rests upon an initial misconception of the nature of language.

The condition essential to see is that every use of speech, oral and written, exhibits an attitude, and an attitude implies an act. "Thy speech betrayeth thee" is aphoristically true if we take it as saying, "Your speech reveals your disposition," first by what you choose to say, then by the amount you decide to say, and so on down through the resources of linguistic elaboration and intonation. All rhetoric is a rhetoric of motives, as Kenneth Burke saw fit to indicate in the title of his book. At the low end of the scale, one may be doing nothing more than making sounds to express exuberance. But if at the other end one sits down to compose a *Critique of the Pure Reason,* one has the motive of refuting other philosophers' account of the constitution of being and of substituting one's own, for an interest which may be universal, but which nonetheless proceeds from the will to alter something.

Does this mean that it is impossible to be objective about anything? Does it mean that one is "rhetorical" in declaring that a straight line is the shortest distance between two points? Not in the sense in which the objection is usually raised. There are degrees of objectivity, and there are various disciplines which have their own rules for expressing their laws or their content in the most effective manner for their purpose. But even this expression can be seen as enclosed in a rhetorical intention. Put in another way, an utterance is capable of rhetorical function and aspect. If one looks widely enough, one can discover its rhetorical dimension, to put it in still another way. The scientist has some interest in setting forth the formulation of some recurrent feature of the physical world, although his own sense of motive may be lost in a general feeling that science is a good thing because it helps progress along.[2]

In short, as long as man is a creature responding to purpose, his linguistic expression will be a carrier of tendency. Where the modern semanticists got off on the wrong foot in their effort to refurbish language lay in the curious supposition that language could and should be outwardly determined. They

were positivists operating in the linguistic field. Yet if there is anything that is going to keep on defying positivistic correlation, it is this subjectively born, intimate, and value-laden vehicle which we call language. Language is a system of imputation, by which values and percepts are first framed in the mind and are then imputed to things. This is not an irresponsible imputation; it does not imply, say, that no two people can look at the same clock face and report the same time. The qualities or properties have to be in the things, but they are not in the things in the form in which they are framed by the mind. This much I think we can learn from the great realist-nominalist controversy of the Middle Ages and from the little that contemporary semantics has been able to add to our knowledge. Language was created by the imagination for the purposes of man, but it may have objective reference—just how we cannot say until we are in possession of a more complete metaphysics and epistemology.

Now a system of imputation involves the use of predicates, as when we say, "Sugar is sweet" or "Business is good." Modern positivism and relativism, however, have gone virtually to the point of denying the validity of all conceptual predication. Occasionally at Chicago I purposely needle a class by expressing a general concept in a casual way, whereupon usually I am sternly reminded by some member brought up in the best relativist tradition that "You can't generalize that way." The same view can be encountered in eminent quarters. Justice Oliver Wendell Holmes was fond of saying that the chief end of man is to frame general propositions and that no general proposition is worth a damn. In the first of these general propositions the Justice was right, in the sense that men cannot get along without categorizing their apprehensions of reality. In the second he was wrong because, although a great jurist, he was not philosopher enough to think the matter through. Positivism and relativism may have rendered a certain service as devil's advocates if they have caused us to be more careful about our concepts and our predicates, yet their position in net forms is untenable. The battle against general propositions was lost from the beginning, for just as surely as man is a symbol-using animal (and a symbol transcends the thing symbolized), he is a classifying animal. The morality lies in the application of the predicate.

Language, which is thus predicative, is for the same cause sermonic. We are all of us preachers in private or public capacities. We have no sooner uttered words than we have given impulse to other people to look at the world, or some small part of it, in our way. Thus caught up in a great web of inter-communication and inter-influence, we speak as rhetoricians affecting one another for good or ill. That is why I must agree with Quintilian that the true orator is the good man, skilled in speaking—good in his formed character and right in his ethical philosophy. When to this he adds fertility in invention and skill in the arts of language, he is entitled to that leadership which tradition accords him.

If rhetoric is to be saved from the neglect and even the disrepute which I was deploring at the beginning of this lecture, these primary truths will have to be recovered until they are a part of our active consciousness. They are, in summation, that man is not nor ever can be nor ever should be a depersonalized thinking machine. His feeling is the activity in him most closely related to what used to be called his soul. To appeal to his feeling therefore is not necessarily an insult; it can be a way to honor him, by recognizing him in the fullness of his being. Even in those situations where the appeal is a kind of strategy, it but recognizes that men—all men—are historically conditioned.

> As rhetoric confronts us with choices involving values, the rhetorician is a preacher to us, noble if he tries to direct our passion toward noble ends and base if he uses our passion to confuse and degrade us.

Rhetoric must be viewed formally as operating at that point where literature and politics meet, or where literary values and political urgencies can be brought together. The rhetorician makes use of the moving power of literary presentation to induce in his hearers an attitude or decision which is political in the very broadest sense. Perhaps this explains why the successful user of rhetoric is sometimes in bad grace with both camps. For the literary people he is too "practical"; and for the more practical political people he is too "flowery." But there is nothing illegitimate about what he undertakes to do, any more than it would be illegitimate to make use of the timeless principles of aesthetics in the constructing of a public building. Finally, we must never lose sight of the order of values as the ultimate sanction of rhetoric. No one can live a life of direction and purpose without some scheme of values. As rhetoric confronts us with choices involving values, the rhetorician is a preacher to us, noble if he tries to direct our passion toward noble ends and base if he uses our passion to confuse and degrade us. Since all utterance influences us in one or the other of these directions, it is important that the direction be the right one, and it is better if this lay preacher is a master of his art.

Notes

1. I might add that a number of years ago the Mathematics Staff of the College at the University of Chicago made a wager with the English Staff that they could write the Declaration of Independence in mathematical language. They must have had later and better thoughts about this, for we never saw the mathematical rendition.
2. If I have asked confusion by referring to "rhetoricians" and "rhetorical speakers," and to other men as if they were all non-rhetoricians, while insisting that all language has its rhetorical aspect, let me clarify the terms. By "rhetorician" I mean the deliberate rhetor: the man who understands the nature and aim and requirements of persuasive expression and who uses them more or less consciously according to the approved rules of the art. The other, who by his membership in the family of language users, must be a rhetorician of sorts, is an empirical and adventitious one; he does not know enough to keep invention, arrangement, and style working for him. The rhetorician of my reference is thus the educated speaker; the other is an untaught amateur.

Kenneth Burke's Theory of Dramatistic Rhetoric

By common consent Kenneth Burke ranks as the foremost rhetorician in the twentieth century. Not since Bacon and Vico has a single author been able to roam so freely and authoritatively over the literature of the humanities and the social and behavioral sciences in order to construct a rhetorical system. From the philosophers, poets, theologians, and social scientists, Burke derives materials that are woven into his theories. He is as much at home with Sigmund Freud, Karl Marx, and Charles Darwin as he is with Plato, Aristotle, Isocrates, Cicero, Milton, Keats, Hume, and Kant. When we heard him speak at a conference sponsored by the Department of English at Ohio State University in the Spring of 1975, and later at the Speech Communication Association convention in Washington, D.C., in December, 1977, we were impressed with the broad range of his intellect and his talent for brilliant impromptu retorts. His advanced years seem to have sharpened his critical skills.

The legacy Burke has left to communication theory and literary criticism is remarkable in its conception and execution. Here are but a few of the terms he has used which are now an essential part of the rhetoric of Western thought:

1. dramatism;
2. pentad (act, agency, agent, scene, and purpose);
3. identification;
4. consubstantiality;
5. motives; and

6. magic.

As a model of criticism the "pentad" had perhaps surpassed neo-Aristotelianism as a type of methodology to examine rhetorical transactions in the 1970s. And the term "identification" has enhanced our understanding of ethical proof, rhetorical stance, and audience analysis and adaptation. But it is the concept of "motives" which most appropriately explains Burke's principal contribution to the vocabulary of what might be called a "new rhetoric."

In its most common use, a motive today is frequently labeled as the *cause* of an action. Thus, one's motive for attending college may perhaps be the belief that a college diploma will guarantee a good job in the future. Burke does not ascribe this meaning to "motive," however. Rather, he uses "motive" as a label for *completed action.* "From this viewpoint," Leonard Hawes tells us, "language frequently is used to label behavior after it has been enacted. Language fits and adjusts behavior to a symbolically created world."[1]

More than most of his contemporaries, Burke best personifies the sociological thrust that typifies modern rhetoric. In his two volumes, The *Grammar of Motives* and *The Rhetoric of Motives,* he employs the phrase "human relations" at least twelve times. This accounts for his great concern with the problem of division or estrangement that separates men. Thus he introduced the notion of "identification" as a potential unifying force that has the power to cope with

> By common consent Kenneth Burke ranks as the foremost rhetorician in the twentieth century.

"the state of Babel after the Fall."[2] His statement, "I was a farm boy myself," is disarming in its simplicity. Yet it tells a speaker far more than the need to identify with a farm audience. It also reminds him of the persistent challenge to become "consubstantial" so as to remove division.

Notwithstanding Burke's provocative insights and memorable phrases, his works are often marred by intricate details, obscure allusions, troubling digressions, and occasional contradictions. As a result, he is hard to read and comprehend. We cannot easily summarize Burke's major theories up through 1952 without duplicating what has already been done by those who knew him well. We have chosen, therefore, to reproduce Marie Nichols' classic essay, "Kenneth Burke and the 'New Rhetoric.'"[3] Burke is quoted as saying that this monograph is the best analysis of his rhetorical ideas appearing to date.

Notes

1. Leonard C. Hawes, *Pragmatics of Analoguing: Theory and Model Construction in Communication,* (Reading, Massachusetts: Addison-Wesley Publishing Company, 1975), p. 48.

2. Burke, p. 547.
3. *Quarterly Journal of Speech,* XXXVIII (April 1952), pp. 133–144.

Kenneth Burke and the "New Rhetoric"

Marie Hochmuth Nichols

"We do not flatter ourselves that any one book can contribute much to counteract the torrents of ill will into which so many of our contemporaries have so avidly and sanctimoniously plunged," observes Kenneth Burke in introducing his latest book, *A Rhetoric of Motives,* but "the more strident our journalists, politicians, and alas! even many of our churchmen become, the more convinced we are that books should be written for tolerance and contemplation."[1] Burke has offered all his writings to these ends.

Burke's first work, *Counter-Statement,* published in 1931, was hailed as a work of "revolutionary importance," presenting "in essence, a new view of rhetoric."[2] Since that time, he has written a succession of books either centrally or peripherally concerned with rhetoric: *Permanence and Change,* 1935; *Attitudes toward History,* 1937; *The Philosophy of Literary Form,* 1941; *A Grammar of Motives,* 1945; and his latest, *A Rhetoric of Motives,* 1950. An unfinished work entitled *A Symbolic of Motives* further indicates his concern with the problem of language.

Sometimes thought to be "one of the few truly speculative thinkers of our time,"[3] and "unquestionably the most brilliant and suggestive critic now writing in America,"[4] Burke deserves to be related to the great tradition of rhetoric.

Although we propose to examine particularly *A Rhetoric of Motives* we shall range freely over all his works in order to discover his principles. We propose to find first the point of departure and orientation from which he approaches rhetoric; next to examine his general concept of rhetoric; then to seek his method for the analysis of motivation; and finally, to discover his application of principles to specific literary works.

In 1931, in *Counter-Statement,* Burke noted, "The reader of modern prose is ever on guard against 'rhetoric,' yet the word, by lexicographer's definition,

---

Reprinted from the *Quarterly Journal of Speech,* 38 (April 1952), 133–144. Reprinted with the permission of the author and editor of Q.J.S.

refers but to 'the use of language in such a way as to produce a desired impression upon the reader or hearer.'"[5] Hence, accepting the lexicographer's definition, he concluded that "effective literature could be nothing else but rhetoric."[6] In truth, "Eloquence is simply the end of *art,* and is thus its essence."[7]

As a literary critic, representing a minority view, Burke has persisted in his concern with rhetoric, believing that "rhetorical analysis throws light on literary texts and human relations generally."[8] Although Burke is primarily concerned with literature "as art,"[9] he gives no narrow interpretation to the conception of literature. He means simply works "designed for the express purpose of arousing emotions,"[10] going so far as to say, "But sometimes literature so designed fails to arouse emotions—and words said purely by way of explanation may have an unintended emotional effect of considerable magnitude."[11] Thus a discussion of "effectiveness" in literature "should be able to include unintended effects as well as intended ones."[12] By literature we mean written or spoken words."[13]

As has been observed, the breadth of Burke's concepts results "in a similar embracing of trash of every description. . . . For purposes of analysis or illustration Burke draws as readily on a popular movie, a radio quiz program, a *Herald Tribune* news item about the National Association of Manufacturers, or a Carter Glass speech on gold as on Sophocles or Shakespeare. Those things are a kind of poetry too, full of symbolic and rhetorical ingredients, and if they are bad poetry, it is a bad poetry of vital significance in our lives."[14]

Sometimes calling himself a pragmatist, sometimes a sociological critic, Burke believes that literature is designed to "do something"[15] for the writer and the reader or hearer. "Art is a means of communication. As such it is certainly designed to elicit a 'response' of some sort."[16] The most relevant observations are to be made about literature when it is considered as the embodiment of an "act,"[17] or as "symbolic action."[18] Words must be thought of as "acts upon a scene,"[19] and a "symbolic act" is the *"dancing of an attitude,"*[20] or incipient action. Critical and imaginative works are "answers to questions posed by the situation in which they arose." Not merely "answers," they are *strategic* answers," or *stylized* answers."[21] Hence, a literary work is essentially a "strategy for *encompassing a situation."*[22] And, as Burke observes, another name for strategies might be *attitudes."*[23] The United States Constitution, e.g., must be thought of as the *"answer"* or *"rejoinder"* to "assertions current in the situation in which it arose."[24]

Although Burke distinguishes between literature "for the express purpose of arousing emotions" and "literature for use," the distinction is flexible enough to permit him to see even in such a poem as Milton's *Samson Agonistes,* "moralistic prophecy" and thus to class it as "also a kind of 'literature for use,' use at one remove. . . ."[25]

In further support of his comprehensive notion of art is his conception that since "pure art makes for acceptance," it tends to "become a social menace in so far as it assists us in tolerating the intolerable."[26] Therefore, "under conditions of competitive capitalism there must necessarily be a large *corrective* or *propaganda* element in art."[27] Art must have a "hortatory function, an element of suasion or inducement of the educational variety; it must be partially *forensic."*[28]

Burke thus approaches the subject of rhetoric through a comprehensive view of art in general. And it is this indirect approach that enables him to present what he believes to be a "New Rhetoric."[29] In part, he has as his object only to "rediscover rhetorical elements that had become obscured when rhetoric as a term fell into disuse, and other specialized disciplines such as esthetics, anthropology, psychoanalysis, and sociology came to the fore (so that esthetics sought to outlaw rhetoric, while the other sciences. . . took over, each in its own terms, the rich rhetorical elements that esthetics would ban).[30]

II

Sometimes thought to be "intuitive" and "idiosyncratic"[31] in his general theories, Burke might be expected to be so in his theory of rhetoric. "Strongly influenced by anthropological inquiries,"[32] and finding Freud "suggestive almost to the point of bewilderment,"[33] Burke, essentially a classicist in his theory of rhetoric, has given the subject its most searching analysis in modern times.

According to Burke, "Rhetoric [comprises] both the use of persuasive resources (*rhetorica utens,* as with the Phillipics of Demosthenes) and the *study* of them (*rhetorica docens,* as with Aristotle's treatise on the 'art' of Rhetoric).[34] The "basic function of rhetoric" is the "use of words by human agents to form attitudes or to induce actions in other human agents. . . ."[35] It is *"rooted in an essential function of language itself, a function that is wholly realistic, and is continually born anew; the use of language as a symbolic means of inducing cooperation in beings that by nature respond to symbols"*[36] The basis of rhetoric lies in "generic divisiveness which, being common to all men, is a universal fact about them, prior to any divisiveness caused by social classes." "Out of this emerge the motives for linguistic persuasion. Then, *secondarily,* we get the motives peculiar to particular economic situations. In parturition begins the centrality of the nervous system. The different nervous systems, through language and the ways of production, erect various communities of interests and insights, social communities varying in nature and scope. And out of the division and the community arises the 'universal' rhetorical situation."[37]

Burke devotes 131 pages to a discussion of traditional principles of rhetoric, reviewing Aristotle, Cicero, Quintilian, St. Augustine, the Mediaevalists, and such more recent writers as De Quincey, De Gourmont, Bentham, Marx, Veblen, Freud, Mannheim, Mead, Richards, and others,[38] noting the "wide range of meanings already associated with rhetoric, in ancient texts. . . ."[39] Thus he comes upon the concept of rhetoric as "persuasion"; the nature of rhetoric as "addressed" to an audience for a particular purpose; rhetoric as the art of "proving opposites"; rhetoric as an "appeal to emotions and prejudices"; rhetoric as "agonistic"; as an art of gaining "advantage"; rhetoric as "demonstration"; rhetoric as the verbal "counterpart" of dialectic; rhetoric, in the Stoic usage, as opposed to dialectic; rhetoric in the Marxist sense of persuasion "grounded in dialectic." Whereas he finds that these meanings are "often not consistent with one another, or even flatly at odds,"[40] he believes that they can all be derived from "persuasion" as the "Edenic" term, from which they have all "Babylonically" split, while persuasion, in turn "involves communication by the signs of consubstantiality, the appeal of *identification.*"[41] As the "simplest case of persuasion," he notes that "You persuade a man only insofar as you can talk his language by speech, gesture, tonality, order, image, attitude, idea, *identifying* your ways with his."[42]

In using *identification* as his key term, Burke notes, "Traditionally, the key term for rhetoric is not 'identification,' but 'persuasion.' . . . Our treatment, in terms of identification, is decidedly not meant as a substitute for the sound traditional approach. Rather, . . . it is but an accessory to the standard lore."[43] He had noted that "when we come upon such aspects of persuasion as are found in 'mystification,' courtship, and the 'magic' of class relationships, the reader will see why the classical notion of clear persuasive intent is not an accurate fit, for describing the ways in which the members of a group promote social cohesion by acting rhetorically upon themselves and one another."[44] Burke is completely aware that he is not introducing a totally new concept, observing that Aristotle had long ago commented, "It is not hard. . . to praise Athenians among Athenians,"[45] and that one persuades by "identifying" one's ways with those of his audience.[46] In an observation of W.C. Blum, Burke found additional support for his emphasis on *identification* as a key concept. "In identification lies the source of dedications and enslavements, in fact of cooperation."[47] As for the precise relationship between identification and persuasion as ends of rhetoric, Burke concludes, "we might well keep it in mind that a speaker persuades an audience by the use of stylistic identifications; his act of persuasion may be for the purpose of causing the audience to identify itself with the speaker's interests; and the speaker draws on identification of interests to establish rapport between himself and his audience. So, there is no chance of our keeping apart the meanings of persuasion, identification ('consubstantiality') and communication (the nature of rhetoric as 'addressed'). But, in given instances, one or another of these elements may serve best for extending a line of analysis in some particular direction."[48] "All told, persuasion ranges from the bluntest quest of advantage, as in sales promotion or propaganda, through courtship, social etiquette, education, and the sermon to a 'pure' form that delights in the process of appeal for itself alone, without ulterior purpose. And identification ranges from the politician who, addressing an audience of farmers, says, 'I was a farm boy myself,' through the mysteries of social status, to the mystic's devout identification with the source of all being."[49] The difference between the "old" rhetoric and the "new" rhetoric may be summed up in this manner: whereas the key term for the "old" rhetoric was *persuasion* and its stress was upon deliberate design, the key term for the "new" rhetoric is *identification* and this may include partially "unconscious" factors in its appeal. Identification, at its simplest level, may be a deliberate device, or a means, as when a speaker identifies his interests with those of his audience. But *identification* can also be an "end," as "when people earnestly yearn to identify themselves with some group or other." They are thus not necessarily acted upon by a conscious external agent, but may act upon themselves to this end. Identification "includes the realm of transcendence."[50]

Burke affirms the significance of *identification* as a key concept because men are at odds with one another, or because there is "division." "Identification is compensatory to division. If men were not apart from one another, there would be no need for the rhetorician to proclaim their unity. If men were wholly and truly of one substance, absolute communication would be of man's very essence."[51] In pure identification there would be no strife. Likewise, there would be no strife in absolute separateness, since opponents can join battle only through a mediatory ground that makes their communication possible, thus providing the first condition necessary for their interchange of blows. But put identification and division ambiguously together. . . and you have the characteristic invitation to rhetoric. Here is a major reason why rhetoric, according to Aristotle, 'proves opposites.'[52]

As a philosopher and metaphysician Burke is impelled to give a philosophic treatment to the concept of unity or identity by an analysis of the nature of *substance* in general. In this respect he makes his most basic contribution to a philosophy of rhetoric. "Metaphysically, a thing is identified by its *properties*,"[53] he observes. "To call a man a friend or brother is to proclaim him consubstantial with oneself, one's values or purposes. To call a man a bastard is to attack him by attacking his whole line, his 'authorship,' his 'principle' or 'motive' (as expressed in terms of the familial). An epithet assigns substance doubly, for in stating the character of the object it. . . contains an implicit program of action with regard to the object, thus serving as motive."[54]

According to Burke, language of all things "is most public, most collective, in its substance."[55] Aware that modern thinkers have been skeptical about the utility of a doctrine of substance,[56] he nevertheless recalls that "substance, in the old philosophies, was an *act;* and a way of life is an *acting-together;* and in acting together, men have common sensations, concepts, images, ideas, attitudes that make them *consubstantial*."[57] "A doctrine of *consubstantiality* . . . may be necessary to any way of life."[58] Like Kant, Burke regards substance as a "necessary form of the mind." Instead

> Burke affirms the significance of *identification* as a key concept because men are at odds with one another, or because there is "division."

of trying to exclude a doctrine of substance, he restores it to a central position and throws critical light upon it.

In so far as rhetoric is concerned, the "ambiguity of substance" affords a major resource. "What handier linguistic resource could a rhetorician want than an ambiguity whereby he can say 'The state of affairs is substantially such-and-such,' instead of having to say 'The state of affairs *is* and/or *is not* such-and-such."[59]

The "commonplaces" or "topics" of Aristotle's *Rhetoric* are a "quick survey of opinion" of "things that people generally consider persuasive." As such, they are means of proclaiming *substantial* unity with an audience and are clearly instances of identification.[60] In truth, *identification* is "hardly other than a name for the function of sociality."[61] Likewise, the many tropes and figures, and rhetorical form in the large as treated by the ancients are to be considered as modes of identification.[62] They are the "signs" by which the speaker identifies himself with the reader or hearer. "In its simplest manifestation, style is ingratiation."[63] It is an attempt to "gain favor by the hypnotic or suggestive process of 'saying the right thing.'"[64] Burke discusses form in general as "the psychology of the audience,"[65] the "arousing and fulfillment of desires."[66] The exordium of a Greek oration is an instance of "conventional"[67] form, a form which is expected by the audience and therefore satisfies it. Other recognizable types of form are "syllogistic progression," "repetitive" form, and "minor or incidental" forms which include such devices as the metaphor, apostrophe, series, reversal, etc.[68] The proliferation and the variety of formal devices make a work eloquent.[69]

Reviewing *A Rhetoric of Motives,* Thomas W. Copeland observed, "It gradually appears that there is no form of action of men upon each other (or of individuals on themselves) which is really outside of rhetoric. But if so, we should certainly ask whether rhetoric as a term has any defining value."[70] The observation is probably not fair, for Burke does give rhetoric a defining value in terms of persuasion, identification, and address or communication to an audience of some sort, despite his observation, "Wherever there is persuasion, there is rhetoric. And wherever there is 'meaning' there is 'persuasion.'"[71]

It is true that in his effort to show "how a rhetorical motive is often present where it is not usually recognized, or thought to belong,"[72] Burke either points out linkages which have not been commonly stressed, or widens the scope of rhetoric. A twentieth-century orientation in social-psychological theory thus enables him to note that we may with "more accuracy speak of persuasion 'to attitude,' rather than persuasion to out-and-out action." For persuasion "involves choice, will; it is directed to a man only insofar as he is *free.*" In so far as men "*must* do something, rhetoric is unnecessary, its work being done by the nature of things, though often these necessities are not of natural origin, but come from necessities imposed by man-made conditions,"[73] such as dictatorships or near-dictatorships. His notion of persuasion to "attitude" does not alter his generally classical view of rhetoric, for as he points out, in "Cicero and Augustine there is a shift between the words 'move' (*movere*) and 'bend' (*flectere*) to name the ultimate function of rhetoric." And he merely finds that this shift "corresponds to a distinction between act and attitude (attitude being an incipient act, a leaning or inclination)."[74] His notion of persuasion to "attitude" enables him to point out a linkage with poetry: "Thus the notion of persuasion to *attitude* would permit the application of rhetorical terms to purely *poetic* structures; the study of lyrical devices might be classed under the head of rhetoric, when these devices are considered for their power to induce or communicate states of mind to readers, even though the kinds of assent evoked have no overt, practical outcome."[75]

In his reading of classical texts, he had noted a stress "upon *teaching* as an 'office' of rhetoric." Such an observation enables him to link the fields of rhetoric and semantics. He concludes that "once you treat instruction as an aim of rhetoric you introduce a principle that can widen the scope of rhetoric beyond persuasion. It is on the way to include also works on the theory and practice of exposition, description, *communication* in general. Thus, finally, out of this principle, you can derive contemporary 'semantics' as an aspect of rhetoric."[76]

As he persists in "tracking down" the function of the term *rhetoric,* Burke notes an ingredient of rhetoric "lurking in such anthropologist's terms as 'magic' and 'witchcraft,'"[77] and concludes that one "comes closer to the true state of affairs if one treats the socializing aspects of magic as a 'primitive rhet-

oric' than if one sees modern rhetoric simply as a 'survival of primitive magic.'"[78] Whereas he does not believe that the term *rhetoric* is a "substitute" for such terms as *magic, witchcraft, socialization,* or *communication,* the term *rhetoric* "designates a *function* . . . present in the areas variously covered by those other terms."[79] Thus, one can place within the scope of rhetoric "all those statements by anthropologists, ethnologists, individual and social psychologists, and the like, that bear upon the *persuasive* aspects of language, the function of language as *addressed,* as direct or roundabout appeal to real or ideal audiences, without or within."[80] All these disciplines have made "good contributions to the New Rhetoric."[81]

In "individual psychology," particularly the Freudian concern with the neuroses of individual patients, "there is a strongly rhetorical ingredient."[82] Burke asks the question, "Indeed, what could be more profoundly rhetorical than Freud's notion of a dream that attains expression by stylistic subterfuges designed to evade the inhibitions of a moralistic censor? What is this but the exact analogue of the rhetorical devices of literature under political or theocratic censorship? The *ego* with its *id* confronts the *superego* much as an orator would confront a somewhat alien audience, whose susceptibilities he must flatter as a necessary step toward persuasion. The Freudian psyche is quite a parliament, with conflicting interests expressed in ways variously designed to take the claims of rival factions into account."[83]

By considering the individual self as "audience" Burke brings morals and ethics into the realm of rhetoric. He notes that "a modern 'post-Christian' rhetoric must also concern itself with the thought that, under the heading of appeal to audiences, would also be included any ideas or images privately addressed to the individual self for moralistic or incantatory purposes. For you become your own audience, in some respects a very lax one, in some respects very exacting, when you become involved in psychologically stylistic subterfuges for presenting your own case to yourself in sympathetic terms (and even terms that seem harsh can often be found on closer scrutiny to be flattering, as with neurotics who visit sufferings upon themselves in the name of very high-powered motives which, whatever this discomfiture, feed pride)." Therefore, the "individual person, striving to form himself in accordance with the communicative norms that match the cooperative ways of his society, is by the same token concerned with the rhetoric of identification."[84]

By considering style as essentially a mode of "ingratiation" or as a technique by which one gives the signs of identification and consubstantiality, Burke finds a rhetorical motive in clothes, pastoral, courtship, and the like.[85]

Burke links dialectics with rhetoric through a definition of dialectics in "its most general sense" as "linguistic transformation"[86] and through an analysis of three different levels of language, or linguistic terminology.[87] Grammatically, he discusses the subject from the point of view of linguistic merger and division, polarity, and transcendence, being aware that there are "other definitions of dialectics:"[88] "reasoning from opinion"; "the discovery of truth by the give and take of converse and redefinition"; "the art of disputation"; "the processes of 'interaction' between the verbal and the non-verbal"; "the competition of cooperation or the cooperation of competition"; "the spinning of terms out of terms"; "the internal dialogue of thought"; "any development. . . got by the interplay of various factors that mutually modify one another, and may be thought of as voices in a dialogue or roles in a play, with each voice or role in its partiality contributing to the development of the whole"; "the placement of one thought or thing in terms of its opposite"; "the progressive or successive development and reconciliation of opposites"; and "so putting questions to nature that nature can give unequivocal answer."[89] He considers all of these definitions as "variants or special applications of the functions"[90] of linguistic transformation conceived in terms of "Merger and division," "The three Major Pairs: action-passion, mind-body, being-nothing," and "Transcendence."[91]

Burke devotes 150 pages to the treatment of the dialectics of persuasion in the *Rhetoric,*[92] in addition to extensive treatment of it on the grammatical level.[93] Linguistic terminology is considered variously persuasive in its Positive, Dialectical, and Ultimate levels or orders.[94] "A positive term is most unambiguously itself when it names a visible and tangible thing which can be located in time and place."[95] Dialectical terms "have no such strict location."[96] Thus terms like "Elizabethanism" or "capitalism" having no positive referent may be called "dialectical."[97] Often called "polar" terms,[98] they require an "opposite"[99] to define them and are on the level of "action," "principles," "ideas."[100] In an "ultimate order" of terminology, there is a "guiding idea" or "unitary principle."[101]

From the point of view of rhetoric, Burke believes that the "difference between a merely 'dialec-

tical' confronting of parliamentary conflict and an 'ultimate' treatment of it would reside in this: The 'dialectical' order would leave the competing voices in a jangling relation with one another (a conflict solved *faute de mieux* by 'horsetrading'); but the 'ultimate' order would place these competing voices themselves in a *hierarchy,* or *sequence,* or *evaluating series,* so that, in some way, we went by a fixed and reasoned progression from one of these to another, the members of the entire group being arranged *developmentally* with relation to one another."[102] To Burke "much of the *rhetorical* strength in the Marxist dialectic comes from the fact that it is 'ultimate' in its order,"[103] for a "spokesman for the proletariat can think of himself as representing not only the interests of that class alone, but the grand design of the entire historical sequence. . . ."[104]

In his concept of a "pure persuasion," Burke seems to be extending the area of rhetoric beyond its usual scope. As a metaphysician he attempts to carry the process of rhetorical appeal to its ultimate limits. He admits that what he means by "pure persuasion" in the "absolute sense" exists nowhere, but believes that it can be present as a motivational ingredient in any rhetoric, no matter how "advantage-seeking such a rhetoric may be."[105] Pure persuasion involves the saying of something, not for an extraverbal advantage to be got by the saying, but because of a satisfaction intrinsic to the saving. It summons because it likes the feel of a summons. It would be nonplused if the summons were answered. It attacks because it revels in the sheer syllables of vituperation. It would be horrified if, each time it finds a way of saying, 'Be damned,' it really did send a soul to rot in hell. It intuitively says, 'This is so,' purely and simply because this is so."[106] With such a concept Burke finds himself at the "borders of metaphysics, or perhaps better 'metarhetoric'. . . ."[107]

III

Of great significance to the rhetorician is Burke's consideration of the general problem of motivation. Concerned with the problem of motivation in literary strategy,[108] he nevertheless intends that his observations be considered pertinent to the social sphere in general.[109] He had observed that people's conduct has been explained by an "endless variety of theories: ethnological, geographical, sociological, physiological, historical, endocrinological, economic, anatomical, mystical, pathological, and so on."[110] The assigning of motives, he concludes, is a "matter of *appeal*,"[111] and this depends upon one's general orientation. "A motive is not some fixed thing, like a table, which one can go to and look at. It is a term of interpretation, and being such it will naturally take its place within the framework of our *Weltanschauung* as a whole."[112] "To explain one's conduct by the vocabulary of motives current among one's group is about as self-deceptive as giving the area of a field in the accepted terms of measurement. One is simply interpreting with the only vocabulary he knows. One is stating his orientation, which involves a vocabulary of ought and ought-not, with attendant vocabulary of praiseworthy and blame-worthy."[113] "We discern situational patterns by means of the particular vocabulary of the cultural group into which we are born."[114] Motives are "distinctly linguistic products."[115]

To Burke, the subject of motivation is a "philosophic one, not ultimately to be solved in terms of empirical science."[116] A motive is a "shorthand" term for "situation."[117] One may discuss motives on three levels, rhetorical, symbolic, and grammatical.[118] One is on the "grammatical" level when he concerns himself with the problem of the "intrinsic," or the problem of "substance."[119] "Men's conception of motive . . . is integrally related to their conception of substance. Hence, to deal with problems of motive is to deal with problems of substance."[120]

On the "grammatical" level Burke gives his most profound treatment of the problem of motivation. Strongly allied with the classicists throughout all his works in both his ideas and his methodology, Burke shows indebtedness to Aristotle for his treatment of motivation. Taking a clue from Aristotle's consideration of the "circumstances" of an action,[121] Burke concludes that "In a founded statement about motives, you must have some word that names the *act* (names what took place, in thought or deed), and another that names the *scene* (the background of the act, the situation in which it occurred); also, you must indicate what person or kind of person *(agent)* performed the act, what means or instruments he used *(agency),* and the *purpose.*"[122] Act, Scene, Agent, Agency, Purpose become the "pentad" for pondering the problem of human motivation.[123] Among these various terms grammatical "ratios" prevail which have rhetorical implications. One might illustrate by saying that, for instance, between scene and act a logic prevails which indicates that a certain quality of scene calls for an analogous quality of act. Hence, if a situation is said to be of a cer-

tain nature, a corresponding attitude toward it is implied. Burke explains by pointing to such an instance as that employed by a speaker who, in discussing Roosevelt's war-time power exhorted that Roosevelt should be granted "unusual powers" because the country was in an "unusual international situation." The scene-act "ratio" may be applied in two ways. "It can be applied deterministically in statements that a certain policy *had* to be adopted in a certain situation, or it may be applied in hortatory statements to the effect that a certain policy *should* be adopted in conformity with the situation."[124] These ratios are "principles of determination."[125] The pentad would allow for ten such ratios: scene-act, scene-agent, scene-agency, scene-purpose, act-purpose, act-agent, act-agency, agent-purpose, agent-agency, and agency-purpose.[126] Political commentators now generally use *situation* as their synonym for *scene,* "though often without any clear concept of its function as a statement about motives."[127]

Burke draws his key terms for the study of motivation from the analysis of drama. Being developed from the analysis of drama, his pentad "treats language and thought primarily as modes of action."[128] His method for handling motivation is designed to contrast with the methodology of the physical sciences which considers the subject of motivation in mechanistic terms of "flat cause-and-effect or stimulus-and-response."[129] Physicalist terminologies are proper to non-verbalizing entities, but man as a species should be approached through his specific trait, his use of symbols. Burke opposes the reduction of the human realm to terms that lack sufficient "coordinates"; he does not, however, question the fitness of physicalist terminologists for treating the physical realm. According to Burke, "Philosophy, like common sense, must think of human motivation dramatistically, in terms of action and its ends."[130] "Language being essentially human, we should view human relations in terms of the linguistic instrument."[131] His "vocabulary" or "set of coordinates" serves "for the integration of all phenomena studied by the *social* sciences."[132] It also serves as a "perspective for the analysis of history which is a 'dramatic' process. . . ."[133]

One may wonder with Charles Morris whether "an analysis of man through his language provides us with a full account of human motives."[134] One strongly feels the absence of insights into motivation deriving from the psychologists and scientists.

IV

Burke is not only philosopher and theorist; he has applied his critical principles practically to a great number of literary works. Of these, three are of particular interest to the rhetorician. In two instances, Burke attempts to explain the communicative relationship between the writer and his audience. Taking the speech of Antony from Shakespeare's *Julius Caesar,*[135] Burke examines the speech from "the standpoint of the rhetorician, who is concerned with a work's processes of appeal."[136] A similar operation is performed on a scene from *Twelfth Night.*[137]

Undoubtedly one of his most straightforward attempts at analysis of a work of "literature for use," occurs in an essay on "The Rhetoric of Hitler's 'Battle'"[138] The main ideal of criticism, as I conceive it," Burke has observed, "is to use all that there is to use."[139] "If there is any slogan that should reign among critical precepts, it is that 'circumstances alter occasions.'"[140] Considering *Mein Kampf* as "the well of Nazi magic,"[141] Burke brings his knowledge of sociology and anthropology to bear in order to "discover what kind of 'medicine' this medicine-man has concocted, that we may know, with greater accuracy, exactly what to guard against, if we are to forestall the concocting of similar medicine in America."[142] He considers Hitler's "centralizing hub of *ideas*"[143] and his selection of Munich as a "mecca geographically located"[144] as methods of recruiting followers "from among many discordant and divergent bands. . . ."[145] He examines the symbol of the "international Jew"[146] as that "of a *common enemy,*"[147] the "'medicinal' appeal of the Jew as scapegoat. . . ."[148]

His knowledge of psychoanalysis is useful in the analysis of the "sexual symbolism" that runs through the book: "Germany in dispersion is the 'dehorned Siegfried.' The masses are 'feminine.' As such, they desire to be led by a dominating male. This male, as orator, woos them—and, when he has won them, he commands them. The rival male, the villainous Jew, would on the contrary 'seduce' them. If he succeeds, he poisons their blood by intermingling with them. Whereupon, by purely associative connections of ideas, we are moved into attacks upon syphilis, prostitution, incest, and other similar misfortunes, which are introduced as a kind of 'musical' argument when he is on the subject of 'blood poisoning' by inter-

marriage or, in its 'spiritual' equivalent, by the infection of 'Jewish' ideas. . . ."[149]

His knowledge of history and religion is employed to show that the *"materialization"* of a religious pattern is "one terrifically effective weapon. . . in a period where religion has been progressively weakened by many centuries of capitalist materialism."[150]

Conventional rhetorical knowledge leads him to call attention to the "power of endless repetition"[151]; the appeal of a sense of "community"[152]; the appeal of security resulting from "a world view" for a people who had previously seen the world only "piecemeal";[153] and the appeal of Hitler's "inner voice"[154] which served as a technique of leader-people "identification."[155]

Burke's analysis is comprehensive and penetrating. It stands as a superb example of the fruitfulness of a method of comprehensive rhetorical analysis which goes far beyond conventional patterns.

CONCLUSION

Burke is difficult and often confusing. He cannot be understood by casual reading of his various volumes. In part the difficulty arises from the numerous vocabularies he employs. His words in isolation are usually simple enough, but he often uses them in new contexts. To read one of his volumes independently, without regard to the chronology of publication, makes the problem of comprehension even more difficult because of the specialized meanings attached to various words and phrases.

Burke is often criticized for "obscurity" in his writings. The charge may be justified. However, some of the difficulty of comprehension arises from the compactness of his writing, the uniqueness of his organizational patterns, the penetration of his thought, and the breadth of his endeavor. "In books like the *Grammar* and the *Rhetoric,*" observed Malcolm Cowley, "we begin to see the outlines of a philosophical system on the grand scale. . . . Already it has its own methodology (called 'dramatism'), its own esthetics (based on the principle that works of art are symbolic actions), its logic and dialectics, its ethics (or picture of the good life) and even its metaphysics, which Burke prefers to describe as metarhetoric."[156]

One cannot possibly compress the whole of Burke's thought into an article. The most that one can

> Burke is difficult and often confusing.

achieve is to signify his importance as a theorist and critic and to suggest the broad outlines of his work. Years of study and contemplation of the general idea of effectiveness in language have equipped him to deal competently with the subject of rhetoric from its beginning as a specialized discipline to the present time. To his thorough knowledge of classical tradition he has added rich insights gained from serious study of anthropology, sociology, history, psychology, philosophy, and the whole body of humane letters. With such equipment, he has become the most profound student of rhetoric now writing in America.

Notes

1. Kenneth Burke, *A Rhetoric of Motives* (New York: Prentice-Hall, Inc., 1950), p. xv. Reprinted with permission.
2. Isidor Schneider, "A New View of Rhetoric," *New York Herald Tribune Books,* VIII (December 13, 1931), p. 4.
3. Malcolm Cowley, "Prolegomena to Kenneth Burke," *The New Republic,* CXXI (June 5, 1950), pp. 18, 19.
4. W. H. Auden, "A Grammar of Assent," *The New Republic,* CV (July 14, 1941), p. 59.
5. *Counter-Statement* (New York, 1931), p. 265.
6. *Ibid.*
7. *Ibid.,* p. 53.
8. *A Rhetoric of Motives,* pp. xiv, xv.
9. *Counter-Statement,* p. 156.
10. *Ibid.*
11. *Ibid.*
12. *Ibid.*
13. *Ibid.*
14. Stanley Edgar Hyman, *The Armed Vision* (New York, 1948), pp. 386, 387.
15. *The Philosophy of Literary Form* (Louisiana, 1941), p. 89.
16. *Ibid.,* pp. 235, 236.
17. *Ibid.,* p. 89.
18. *Ibid.,* p. 8.
19. *Ibid.,* p. vii.
20. *Ibid.,* p. 9.
21. *Ibid.,* p. 1.
22. *Ibid.,* p. 109.
23. *Ibid.,* p. 297.
24. *Ibid.,* p. 109.
25. *A Rhetoric of Motives,* p. 5.
26. *The Philosophy of Literary Form,* p. 321.
27. *Ibid.*
28. *Ibid.*
29. *A Rhetoric of Motives,* p. 40.
30. *Ibid.,* pp. xiii, 40.
31. *The Philosophy of Literary Form,* p. 68.
32. *A Rhetoric of Motives,* p. 40.
33. *The Philosophy of Literary Form,* p. 258.
34. *A Rhetoric of Motives,* p. 36.
35. *Ibid.,* p. 41.
36. *Ibid.,* p. 43.
37. *Ibid.,* p. 146.
38. *Ibid.,* pp. 49–180.
39. *Ibid.,* p. 61.
40. *Ibid.,* pp. 61, 62.
41. *Ibid.,* p. 62.
42. *Ibid.,* p. 55.
43. *Ibid.,* p. xiv.
44. *Ibid.*
45. *Ibid.,* p. 55.
46. *Ibid.*
47. *Ibid.,* p. xiv.
48. *Ibid.,* p. 46.
49. *Ibid.,* p. xiv.
50. Kenneth Burke, "Rhetoric—Old and New," *The Journal of General Education,* V (April 1951), p. 203.
51. *A Rhetoric of Motives,* p. 22.
52. *Ibid.,* p. 25.
53. *Ibid.,* p. 23.
54. *A Grammar of Motives* (New York, 1945), p. 57. For discussion of *substance* as a concept, see, *ibid.,* pp. 21–58; Aristotle, *Categoriae,* tr. by E. M. Edghill, *The Works of Aristotle,* ed. by W. D. Ross, I, Ch. 5; Aristotle, *Metaphysics,* tr. by W. D. Ross, Book, 8, 1017b, 10; Spinoza, *The Ethics,* in *The Chief Works of Benedict De Spinoza,* tr. by R. H. M. Elwes (London 1901), Rev. ed., II, pp. 45 ff; John Locke, *An Essay Concerning Human Understanding* (London 1760), 15th ed., I, Bk. II, Chs. XXIII, XXIV.
55. *The Philosophy of Literary Form,* p. 44.
56. *A Rhetoric of Motives,* p. 21.
57. *Ibid.*
58. *Ibid.*
59. *A Grammar of Motives,* pp. 51, 52.
60. *A Rhetoric of Motives,* pp. 56, 57.
61. *Attitudes toward History* (New York, 1937), II. p. 144.
62. *A Rhetoric of Motives,* p. 59.
63. *Permanence and Change* (New York, 1935), p. 71.

64. *Ibid.*
65. *Counter-Statement,* pp. 38–57.
66. *Ibid.,* p. 157.
67. *Ibid.,* p. 159.
68. *Ibid.,* pp. 157–161.
69. *Ibid.,* pp. 209–211.
70. Thomas W. Copeland, "Critics at Work," *The Yale Review,* XL (Autumn 1950), pp. 167–169.
71. *A Rhetoric of Motives,* p. 172.
72. *Ibid.,* p. xiii.
73. *Ibid.,* p. 50.
74. *Ibid.*
75. *Ibid.*
76. *Ibid.,* p. 77.
77. *Ibid.,* p. 44.
78. *Ibid.,* p. 43.
79. *Ibid.,* p. 44.
80. *Ibid.,* pp. 43–44.
81. *Ibid.,* p. 40.
82. *Ibid.,* p. 37.
83. *Ibid.,* pp. 37, 38.
84. *Ibid.,* pp. 38, 39.
85. *Ibid.,* pp. 115–127; see also, p. xiv.
86. *A Grammar of Motives,* p. 402.
87. *A Rhetoric of Motives,* p. 183.
88. *A Grammar of Motives,* pp. 402, 403.
89. *Ibid.,* p. 403.
90. *Ibid.*
91. *Ibid.,* p. 402.
92. *A Rhetoric of Motives,* pp. 183–333.
93. *A Grammar of Motives,* pp. 323–443.
94. *A Rhetoric of Motives,* p. 183.
95. *Ibid.*
96. *Ibid.,* p. 184.
97. *Ibid.*
98. *Ibid.*
99. The *Philosophy of Literary Form,* n. 26, p. 109.
100. *A Rhetoric of Motives,* p. 184.
101. *Ibid.,* p. 187.
102. *Ibid.*
103. *Ibid.,* p. 190.
104. *Ibid.,* pp. 190, 191.
105. *Ibid.,* p. 269.
106. *Ibid.*
107. *Ibid.,* p. 267.
108. *The Philosophy of Literary Forms,* n. 26, p. 109.
109. *Ibid.,* p. 105.
110. *Permanence and Change,* p. 47.
111. *Ibid.,* p. 38.
112. *Ibid.*
113. *Ibid.,* p. 33.
114. *Ibid.,* p. 52.
115. *Ibid.*
116. *A Grammar of Motives,* p. xxiii.
117. *Permanence and Change,* p. 44.
118. *A Grammar of Motives,* p. 465.
119. *Ibid.*
120. *Ibid.,* p. 337.
121. *Ethica Nicomachea,* tr. by W.D. Ross, III, i, p. 16.
122. *A Grammar of Motives,* p. xv.
123. *Ibid.*
124. *Ibid.,* p. 13.
125. *Ibid.,* p. 15.
126. *Ibid.*
127. *Ibid.,* p. 13.
128. *Ibid.,* p. xxii.
129. *The Philosophy of Literary Form,* pp. 103, 106.
130. *A Grammar of Motives,* pp. 55, 56.
131. *Ibid.,* p. 317.
132. *The Philosophy of Literary Form,* p. 105.
133. *Ibid.,* p. 317.
134. Charles Morris, "The Strategy of Kenneth Burke," *The Nation,* CLXIII (July 27, 1946), p. 106.
135. "Antony in Behalf of the Play," *Philosophy of Literary Form,* pp. 329–343.
136. *Ibid.,* p. 330.
137. "Trial Translation" (From *Twelfth Night*), *ibid.,* pp. 344–349.
138. *Ibid.,* pp. 191–220.
139. *Ibid.,* p. 23.
140. *Ibid.*
141. *Ibid.,* p. 192.
142. *Ibid.,* p. 191.
143. *Ibid.,* p. 192.
144. *Ibid.*
145. *Ibid.*
146. *Ibid.,* p. 194.
147. *Ibid.,* p. 193.
148. *Ibid.,* p. 195.
149. *Ibid.*
150. *Ibid.,* p. 194
151. *Ibid.,* p. 217.
152. *Ibid.*
153. *Ibid.,* p. 218.
154. *Ibid.,* p. 207.
155. *Ibid.*
156. Malcolm Cowley, "Prolegomena to Kenneth Burke," *The New Republic,* CXXII (June 5, 1950), pp. 18, 19.

SUMMARY

In developing the preceding essay, Dr. Nichols became the first major scholar in rhetoric to alert her colleagues to the significance of Burke. The question which now must be asked is, to what extent has Burke reaffirmed, extended, or altered his rhetorical philosophy in the past quarter century? To answer this query, we will examine Burke's representative works and speeches which were produced following the appearance of the Nichols essay.

At the heart of Burke's present, as well as past, theory of rhetoric is his notion of dramatism. In his 1968 monograph on dramatism,[1] which he now calls his most effective treatment of the subject,[2] he both reinforces and extends his earlier views. "Dramatism," he says, is "the study of human relations and motives" by means of "a methodical inquiry into cycles or clusters of terms and their functions."[3] Still crucial to his system of dramatism are his "five children," as he affectionately calls them—Act, Agent, Scene, Agency, and Purpose.[4] But he hints that a sixth element might be added, that of Attitude.[5]

Since the central term is "act," Burke continues to use this element as a peg upon which to hang his theory. The "act," he suggests, is "a terministic center from which. . .a whole universe of terms is derived."[6] Observe, for instance, how the other four elements of the pentad radiate from the notion of "act." An "act" takes place only when there is an "agent" who operates in a "scene" or situation, and employs an "agency" or means in order to accomplish a particular "purpose." If any one of these elements is missing, an "act" has not been consummated.

Whenever we isolate any two parts of the pentad and examine their relationships to each other, we are using what Burke calls "ratios." A "purpose-agency ratio," for example, is present when we focus on the selection of means or on adapting means to an end. These ratios are useful in explaining or justifying acts. Thus an "agent-act ratio" comes into play when we attempt to relate "a man's character and the character of his behavior." A "scene-act ratio" pertains to the relationship of an act to the situation in which it

> At the heart of Burke's present, as well as past, theory of rhetoric is his notion of dramatism. Still crucial to his system of dramatism are his "five children," as he affectionately calls them—Act, Agent, Scene, Agency, and Purpose.

occurs. In many instances, Burke adds, an "agent-act ratio" may exist in conjunction with a "scene-act ratio."[7] We may illustrate this principle by recalling the behavior (act) of John Dean (agent) during the Watergate Hearings (scene).

Of overriding concern to Burke is the distinction he draws between "sheer motion" and symbolic action. He touches briefly on this theme in the essay on dramatism, by articulating three propositions:

1. "There can be no action without motion."
2. "There can be motion without action."
3. "Action is not reducible to terms of motion."[8]

By 1977, he had decided that this topic would be his principal subject for his Speech Communication Association presentation.[9] Stressing his preference for dramatism over behaviorism because the latter does not distinguish between motion and action, Burke set forth what he perceived to be the difference. The physical world, located in the realm of matter, is limited to motion. Thus when the sun rises, or the tide rolls in, or the air conditioning unit regulates the temperature, we have motion but not action. For action not only embraces motion but is grounded in symbolism—one of man's greatest contributions to life. What we have then is a "motion-action pair" resting on two different points of a continuum.

In explaining this key aspect of dramatism, Burke gives discomfort to those who make large claims regarding the communication capacity of animals. Man alone, he argues, can both "use symbols and be reflexive." Cicero, for example, could deliver eloquent orations in the Roman Forum, and then retire to his study to write rhetorical treatises influenced, in part, by his speaking experiences. Dogs, by contrast, know how to bark but cannot discourse on the nature of barking. To strengthen his claim, Burke next argues that to remove mankind from the earth would be to leave behind a world comprised only of motion; for with the disappearance of man would come the elimination of all vestiges of symbolic action. Language, he concludes, becomes a reality-based form of action by transcending motion.[10]

Also vital to an understanding of Burke's theory of dramatism is his analysis of order—a concept that relates both to commands and hierarchical arrangements. Concerned here with the principle of the "negative" as a "linguistic invention," he suggests that whereas "scientism" deals with such statements as "it is not," dramatism stresses hortatory appeals contained in the idiom of "thou shalt nots."[11] The energy crisis during the winter of 1978 is useful in illustrating this distinction between scientism and dramatism, and to highlight the concept of order as command. Scientists claimed the existence of an energy shortage due to the prolonged coal strike and severe weather. In effect, they were saying, *"there is not enough mined coal to last throughout the winter."* This, in turn, prompted Governor James Rhodes of Ohio to proclaim an order asserting that governmental agencies *"shall not"* use more energy than fifty percent of the normal output. A dramatistic order of this type, phrased in the language of the negative, required obedience on the part of such state officials as the President of Ohio State University. Order, it is clear, is tied in closely with hierarchy. The governor as the top official in the state is able to communicate his orders downward, knowing in advance that in time of emergency he has the power to enforce his commands.

Included in a "dramatistic analysis of order" is a consideration of the principles of "sacrifice," "victimage," and "scapegoatism." Whenever a person receives an order calling for some kind of sacrifice, observes Burke, "the sacrificial principle is intrinsic in the nature of the order." Similarly the notion of victimage as seen in the idea of scapegoat is characteristic of the "human congregation." The following statements emphasize these principles:

1. "If order, then guilt; if guilt, then need for redemption; but any such 'payment' is victimage."
2. "If action, then drama; if drama, then conflict; if conflict, then victimage."[12]

The significance of these claims becomes evident when we realize that, in Burke's view, "life is drama"—a fact which stems from symbolic action and features the elements of "order," "guilt," "conflict," and "victimage."

It is further helpful to see that the culmination of the process described in the above claim is "victimage" or the associative concept of "scapegoatism." This principle can be demonstrated by alluding to the areas of religion and politics. In the book of Genesis in the Old Testament, God issued an order to Abraham commanding him to offer his son Isaac as a sacrifice. In dramatistic terms, this resulted in a feeling of guilt which Abraham had to allay through the redemptive influence of obedience that subsequently led to the experience of victimage. Scapegoatism or victimage in politics implies the rhetorical strategies of "antithesis," "substitution," and "identification." Political leaders engaged in campaigns, for example, make use of antithesis or substitution by urging the adoption of policies which represent what they are against; and "establish identification in terms of an enemy shared in common . . . ."[13] In the 1968 presidential primary campaign, George Wallace of Alabama exemplified this technique. Repeatedly he came out against federal intervention in state rights, judicial leniency toward criminals, war protesters, and free speech advocates. As he did so, he described the common enemy as bureaucrats, civil rights marchers, and "draft dodgers" who failed to uphold law and order as spelled out in the Constitution and Bill of Rights.

Burke's definition of man likewise finds its roots in his theory of dramatism. "Man," he asserts, "is the symbol-using, symbol-misusing, and symbol-making animal."[14] Notwithstanding the fact he shares the common experience of birth with other animals, man is unique in his compelling need for a detailed "system of speech." Indeed, every "aspect of reality" he comes to know "is on the side of language" or symbolic action.[15]

"Man," secondly, "is an inventor of the negative." He has devised his theory of religion and morals in terms of the negative; and he has opted to define a thing or an idea from the perspective of what it is not. As a result, God, who epitomizes the highest level of being, is described as "immortal" (*not* mortal), "infinite" (*not* finite), and "impassive" (*not* passive). In a similar vein, the seemingly positive idea of "freedom" can only fully be explained by employing the language of the negative. A person who is free, for instance, is not restrained, *"not* bound," *"not* under obligation or necessity," *"not* dependent," *"not* affected by a given condition or circumstance," *"not* inhibited," or *"not* committed."

Thirdly, man, continues Burke, is "separated from his natural condition by instruments of his own making." That he has the capacity and will to create and use tools to make tasks easier in time of peace and war there can be little question. These tools, in turn, function as instruments which work their way into our language transactions. Although the end result may be a positive achievement overall, it tends to move man away from the basic nature he was endowed with at birth.[16]

Finally, man "is goaded by the spirit of hierarchy." This compulsion for a "sense of order" has made man "rotten with perfection," causing him to seek the ideal or ultimate language in a given situation so as to express the most appropriate attitudes and motives. It is this penchant for hierarchy and perfection, Burke notes, that led Castiglione in his *Book of the Courtier* to recommend the practice of resting on one knee when in the presence of a sovereign in order to show deference, and on both knees when communicating with God.[17] Burke could have added that this desire to use a hierarchical language form has set one standard for telling the truth in a normal conversational situation and another for stating it before a court of law. In the latter case we are often required to take an oath with our hand on the Bible as a means of improving our chances of reaching perfection in our language.

If dramatism has helped forge Burke's ideas on man as language-maker and language-user, it has also shaped his views on language in general which, as we have seen, is the essence of symbolic action. "There are four realms to which words may refer," he tells us in *The Rhetoric of Religion.* These are the "natural," the "sociopolitical," the "logological" ("words about words"), and the "supernatural." Words used to depict things, "material operations," "physiological conditions," or "animality" are part of the natural realm. Terms used to describe "social relations," "laws," "moral obligations," right and wrong, good and bad, justice and injustice are in the political realm. Words used to designate God, though sometimes borrowed from the other three realms, are in the celestial or supernatural sphere. Since God by nature is an "ineffable" being who cannot be fully described, it behooves us to detail what he represents in an analogical manner. Hence, we speak "of God's 'powerful arm' (a physical analogy), or of God as 'lord' or 'father' (a sociopolitical analogy), or of God as the 'word' (a linguistic analogy)."[18]

As words interact with each other in the four realms, they have relationships with things. Expressing this relatedness in the form of a simile, Burke observes that "words are to the nonverbal things they name as Spirit is to Matter."[19] Although there is a "communion" between the symbol and the "symbolized" or between the thing and its name, the word, in reality, "transcends" its referent.

In a provocative essay entitled, "What are the Signs of What?," Burke cautions his readers not to be overly committed to the traditional notion that "words are the signs of things."[20] He then proceeds to ask us to consider reversing the idea by saying that "things are the signs of words." This perspective requires us to focus on the possibilities inherent in the process of "entitling." The words we use to label or entitle the subject in a particular sentence, for example, will provide an insight supporting the claim that "things are the signs of words." Burke illustrates this idea by citing the phrase, "a man walking down the street." Upon reading these words, we have all kinds of potential images, not the least of which are the following: a tall, short, thin, fat, erect, or stooped man; a brisk, slow, or loping walk; a wide, narrow, two way, cement, or curbed street. In such an instance, with its multiple images, we have, suggests Burke, three different possibilities for entitling this nonverbal circumstance. We may call it a "man-situation," a "walk-situation," or a "street situation."[21] The entitlement we choose affects the relationship between things and words that appear in the sentence or phrase.

Burke further asserts that "the thing (is) a visible, tangible sign of the essence or spirit contained in the word itself. For you can't see a meaning. . . ." Conversely, since we can see a bicycle (a thing), it is easy to define this mode of transportation by pointing to it. In this sense, the bicycle as thing typifies "the genius that resides in words."[22]

One of the most important and useful ideas in Burke's general theory of language usage is his description of what he calls "terministic screens." His use of this term "screen" is borrowed from the field of photography. Let us assume, he says, that we take several pictures of an object, each with a different

> One of the most important and useful ideas in Burke's general theory of language usage is his description of what he calls "terministic screens." His use of this term "screen" is borrowed from the field of photography.

type of color filter. Under such circumstances, the finished product we see will vary according to the filter used. Likewise this is what happens when we employ language. For "the nature of our terms (or terministic screens) affects the nature of our observations, in the sense that the terms direct the attention to one field rather than to another."[23] The Holy Bible, Burke points out, begins with a reference to God in the first sentence, while Darwin's *Origin of Species* ignores the term. Consequently, the terministic screens used in these two works direct our attention to a particular point of view which affects the nature of our communication transactions in the areas of theology and in the natural sciences.

There are many examples that come to mind which tend to give credence to Burke's discussion of terministic screens. The debate on miracles, analyzed in the British period, reveals how Hume and Campbell were strongly influenced by the terministic screens they employed. A similar result would doubtless occur if a cross section of university students were asked to explain what "God" or "Christ" meant to them. Those who respond by relying on the terministic screens of "deity" and "trinity" would perhaps direct our attention to the miracles of the "Virgin Birth," the "Resurrection," and the "Ascension." Others who opt for the phrase, "one of the Biblical prophets," would tend to use a terministic screen that relegates "Christ" to the level of a "good man" on a par with Mahomet or Gandhi. A striking example encountered by one of the authors occurred during the Senate Select Committee Hearings on Watergate in the summer and autumn of 1973. The research team, of which he was a part, interviewed members of the Select Committee and the press covering the event, as well as a sample of the residents of Columbus, Ohio. Each interviewee was asked the question: "Do you view the Watergate event as a 'caper,' a 'crime,' a 'conspiracy,' or a 'crisis?'" We found that the choice of one of these four words, or terministic screens, by the respondent, directed our attention to the degree of seriousness he or she associated with Watergate.

Up to this point we have summarized Burke's latest views on dramatism. Rather than replace or substantially alter his earlier ideas Burke, in the past twenty-five years, has reinforced and enlarged them. Taken as a whole, Burke's dramatistic theory center-

> "Wherever there is persuasion, there is rhetoric. And wherever there is 'meaning' there is persuasion."

ing on language as symbolic action has had a profound influence on contemporary rhetoric and criticism. We would like to emphasize two of his most far-reaching accomplishments in the generation of new perspectives in rhetorical theory, and then show how he has advanced our knowledge of rhetorical criticism.

We are indebted to Burke as a rhetorical theorist, first of all, because of his compelling description of the rhetoric-reality pair. In the current age, many contemporary commentators, including political leaders and mass media analysts, have sought to disassociate rhetoric from reality. Tauntingly they suggest in a moment of crisis that "what is needed is action, not rhetoric." Through an effective associative technique drawn from his system of dramatism, Burke brings rhetoric and reality together. We quoted him earlier as saying: Rhetoric "is rooted in an essential function of language itself, a function that is wholly realistic, and is continually born anew; the use of language as a symbolic means of inducing cooperation in beings that by nature use symbols."[24] For a human being to use symbols, he further urges, "is in essence not magical but realistic." Rhetoric, in short, is not a polar term for action or reality. In fact, it is equated with the only type of genuine action known to man—symbolic action.

Burke's second great contribution as a rhetorical theorist is his bold attempt to extend the range of rhetoric. In our previous discussion of the Elocutionary Movement and our allusion to the stylistic rhetoricians who were a part of the British period, we used the word "truncators" to signify the tendency to limit the focus of rhetoric to a single canon. Unlike these reductionists, Burke has moved in an opposite direction, encompassing the role of expansionist. Moreover, unlike Aristotle who tended to separate rhetoric from poetics, Burke has gone in the direction of combining the two fields under a single rubric. He was able to do this because of his belief in the principle: "Wherever there is persuasion, there is rhetoric. And wherever there is 'meaning' there is persuasion."[25] Both rhetoric and poetics, moreover, use the same three language forms: "progressive," "repetitive," and "conventional."[26]

This expansionist view of rhetoric prompted Burke, additionally, to incorporate non-verbal elements into his theory of communication. He was thus able to say: ". . . we could observe that even the medical equipment of a doctor's office is not to be judged purely for its diagnostic usefulness, but also has a function in the *rhetoric* of medicine. Whatever it is as apparatus, it also appeals to imagery. . . ."[27] This philosophy enabled him further to regard clothes as a rhetorical form.

Another interesting dimension of Burke's broad-scope view regarding the parameters of rhetoric is his often overlooked notion of "administrative rhetoric." Deriving his inspiration for this concept by reading Machiavelli's *The Prince,* Burke details ways in which a rhetor communicates a message largely through nonverbal action that is nevertheless symbolic.[28] By attending a function, signing a document or petition, visiting a colleague in the hospital, going to the funeral of an acquaintance, or shaking the hand of an adversary, an administrator delivers an unspoken message depicting concern and friendship. Numerous political leaders, particularly presidents, have taken advantage of the persuasive power associated with administrative rhetoric. Here are but a few mid-twentieth-century examples: Richard Nixon's good will mission to Communist China; Gerald Ford's presentation of awards in the Rose Garden of the White House; and Jimmy Carter's walk from the Capitol to the White House on Inaugural Day. What makes the idea of administrative rhetoric an appeal-

ing strategy to Burke is its tendency to produce identification. The process of doing, taking place in a scene requiring a symbolic response, and having as its purpose to remove division allows the designated observer or interpreter to see a good relationship between the agent and the act.

But Burke's pioneering contributions are not limited to rhetorical theory; he also has provided us with brilliant insights into rhetorical, literary, sociological, and philosophical criticism. His interest in symbolic action has led him to remind all critics to start with the work itself.[29] This practice permits the critic to distinguish between facts, inferences, and proof; to look for shifting attitudes within the study; to search for recurring terms or phrases; and to ferret out the "universe of discourse." The worth of the critique, he concludes, is directly proportional to its reliance on and conformity to identifiable "critical principles."[30]

Burke's belief in the idea that "life is drama" spawned the creation of his pentad—a fresh methodological approach to criticism which presents the modern student with a viable alternative to neo-Aristotelianism. The pentad, which may be used either implicitly or explicitly, gives to the critic an instrument for assessing a rhetorical event. It functions equally well as a tool for analyzing a specified rhetorical work, a particular speaker or writer, a rhetorical campaign, or a social movement.

--------------------------------------- **Notes** ---------------------------------------

1. "Dramatism," *The International Encyclopedia of the Social Sciences,* David L. Sills, ed., Vol. 7, pp. 445–451. Copyright 1968 by Macmillan Publishing Co., Inc.
2. Interview with Kenneth Burke, Washington, D.C., December 2, 1977. The interview was conducted by Larry Hugenberg.
3. "Dramatism," p. 445.
4. Lecture on "Non-Symbolic Motion and Symbolic Action," SCA Convention, Washington, D.C., December 1, 1977.
5. "Dramatism," p. 446.
6. *Ibid.,* p. 446.
7. *Ibid.*
8. *Ibid.,* p. 447.
9. Lecture on "Non-Symbolic Motion and Symbolic Action."
10. *Ibid.*
11. "Dramatism," p. 450.
12. *Ibid.*
13. *Ibid.,* p. 451.
14. Kenneth Burke, "Mind, Body, and the Unconscious," in *Language as Symbolic Action* (Berkeley, California: University of California Press, *1966*), p. 63. Also see "Definition of Man," in *ibid.,* pp. 3–9.
15. Lecture on "Non-Symbolic Motion and Symbolic Action."
16. *Ibid.,* pp. 13–15.
17. *Ibid.,* pp. 15–16.
18. *The Rhetoric of Religion* (Berkeley, 1970), pp. 14–15.
19. *Ibid.,* p. 16.
20. *Language as Symbolic Action,* p. 360.
21. *Ibid.,* p. 361.
22. *Ibid.,* p. 373.

23. "Terministic Screens," in *ibid.*, p. 46.
24. Kenneth Burke, *A Grammar of Motives and A Rhetoric of Motives* (Cleveland, Ohio, 1962), p. 567. Later in the same volume, Burke observes: "The use of symbols to induce action in beings that normally communicate by symbols is essentially realistic in the most practical and pragmatic sense of the term." p. 686.
25. *Ibid.*, p. 696.
26. Kenneth Burke, "Rhetoric and Poetics," in *Language as Symbolic Action*, p. 305.
27. *A Grammar of Motives and a Rhetoric of Motives*, p. 695.
28. *Language as Symbolic Action*, pp. 301–302. Also see *A Grammar of Motives and A Rhetoric of Motives*, pp. 682–690.
29. Kenneth Burke, "Colloquium on Walt Whitman," The Ohio State University, February 24, 1975. Malcolm Cowley was the other member of the Colloquium.
30. Kenneth Burke, "The Principle of Composition," in *Terms for Order* (Bloomington, Indiana, 1964), pp. 194–195. Also see essay on "Fact, Inference, and Proof in the Analysis of Literary Symbolism," in *ibid.*, pp. 145–172.

To see further the utility of the pentad as a method of rhetorical criticism, let us examine briefly how it may be applied to a communication event involving numerous agents. The event was the celebrated "March on Washington, D.C.," August 28, 1963. Here is an outline sketching a procedure that might be followed:

I. Act
   A. Civil Rights demonstration in Washington, D.C., August 28, 1963.
   B. The marching of 200,000 demonstrators who had come from all over the country.
II. Agents
   A. Martin Luther King, Jr. and other Civil Rights leaders.
   B. Representative liberal members from Congress, including Senator Hubert Humphrey.
III. Agency
   A. Music
      1. Songs by Peter, Paul and Mary; Marian Anderson; Bob Dylan, etc.
      2. Demonstrators singing, "We Shall Overcome."
   B. Unison Chants: "1, 2, 3 Freedom!"
   C. Martin Luther King's "I Have a Dream Speech."
   D. Channeling of the Act through the mass media.
IV. Scene
   A. General political and social unrest caused by racial discrimination.
   B. Centennial Anniversary of the Emancipation Proclamation.
   C. Washington, D.C. natives and tourists encouraged to stay at home or in hotels to avoid possible incidents.
   D. The setting at the Monument Grounds and Lincoln Memorial.
V. Purpose
   A. To heighten the American consciousness regarding human rights.
   B. To secure passage of pending civil rights legislation.

In this outline we have preferred to call the Act the demonstration itself. The flexibility of the pentad, however, would permit numerous other possibilities for labeling the Act. The "I Have a Dream Speech," for example, could be entitled the Act, thereby making King the Agent and the speech content and style the Agency. The Scene and Purpose could remain unchanged; or the Scene could be narrowed in scope.

In 1967, Burke was asked to present a condensed version of his principal ideas on "Dramatism" by the editors of the *International Encyclopedia of the Social Sciences*. Notwithstanding the fact that a number of the points in this essay have been highlighted in the preceding pages, we feel that it is important to reprint this brief and insightful study in its entirety so that the reader will see how Burke constructs arguments and utilizes language to describe an essential aspect of his rhetorical philosophy.

Dramatism

Kenneth Burke

Dramatism is a method of analysis and a corresponding critique of terminology designed to show that the most direct route to the study of human relations and human motives is via a methodical inquiry into cycles or clusters of terms and their functions.

The dramatistic approach is implicit in the key term "act." "Act" is thus a terministic center from which many related considerations can be shown to "radiate," as though it were a "god-term" from which a whole universe of terms is derived. The dramatistic study of language comes to a focus in a philosophy of language (and of "symbolicity" in general); the latter provides the basis for a general conception of man and of human relations. The present article will consider primarily the dramatistic concern with the resources, limitations, and paradoxes of terminology, particularly in connection with the imputing of motives.

THE DRAMATISTIC APPROACH TO ACTION

Dramatism centers in observations of this sort: for there to be an *act,* there must be an *agent.* Similarly, there must be a *scene* in which the agent acts. To act in a scene, the agent must employ some means, or *agency.* And it can be called an act in the full sense of the term only if it involves a *purpose* (that is, if a support happens to give way and one falls, such motion on the agent's part is not an act, but an accident). These five terms (act, scene, agent, agency, purpose) have been labeled the dramatistic pentad; the aim of calling attention to them in this way is to show how the functions which they designate operate in the imputing of motives (Burke [1945–1950] 1962, Introduction). The pattern is incipiently a hexad when viewed in connection with the different but complementary analysis of *attitude* (as an ambiguous term for *incipient* action) undertaken by George Herbert Mead (1938) and by I.A. Richards (1959).

Later we shall consider the question whether the key terms of dramatism are literal or metaphorical. In the meantime, other important things about the terms themselves should be noted.

Obviously, for instance, the concept of scene can be widened or narrowed (conceived of in terms of varying "scope" or circumference). Thus, an agent's behavior ("act") might be thought of as taking place against a polytheistic background; or the overall scene may be thought of as grounded in one god; or the circumference of the situation can be narrowed to naturalistic limits, as in Darwinism; or it can be localized in such terms as "Western civilization," "Elizabethanism," "capitalism," "D day," "10 Downing Street," "on this train ride," and so on, endlessly. Any change of the circumference in terms of which an act is viewed implies a corresponding change in one's view of the quality of the act's motivation. Such a loose yet compelling correspondence between act and scene is called a "scene-act ratio" (Burke [1945–1950] 1962, pp. 1–7).

All the terms are capable of similar relationships. A "purpose-agency ratio," for instance, would concern the logic of "means selecting," the relation of means to ends (as the Supreme Court might decide that an emergency measure is constitutional because it was taken in an emergency situation). An "agent-act ratio" would reflect the correspondence between a man's character and the character of his behavior (as, in a drama, the principles of formal consistency require that each member of the dramatis personae act in character, though such correspondences in art can have a perfection not often found in life). In actual practice, such ratios are used sometimes to explain an act and sometimes to *justify* it (ibid., pp. 15–20). Such correlations are not strict, but analogical. Thus, by "scene-act ratio" is meant a proposition such as: Though agent and act are necessarily different in many of their attributes, some notable element of one is implicitly or analogously present in the other.

David Hume's *An Inquiry Concerning Human Understanding* (first published in 1748) throws a serviceable light upon the dramatistic "ratios." His treatise begins with the observation that "moral philosophy, or the science of human nature, may be treated after two different manners." One of these "considers man chiefly as born for action." The other would "consider man in the light of a reasonable rather than an active being, and endeavor to form his understanding more than cultivate his manners" ([1748] 1952, p. 451). Here, in essence, is the distinction between a dramatistic approach in terms of *action* and an approach in terms of *knowledge*. For, as a "reasonable being," Hume says, man "receives from science" his proper food and nourishment. But man "is a sociable, no less than a reasonable being. . . . Man is also an active being; and from that disposition, as well as from the various necessities of human life, must submit to business and occupation" (*ibid.*, p. 452).

Insofar as men's actions are to be interpreted in terms of the circumstances in which they are acting, their behavior would fall under the heading of a "scene-act ratio." But insofar as their acts reveal their different characters, their behavior would fall under the heading of an "agent-act ratio." For instance, in a time of great crisis, such as a shipwreck, the conduct of all persons involved in that crisis could be expected to manifest in some way the motivating influence of the crisis. Yet, within such a "scene-act ratio" there would be a range of "agent-act ratios," insofar as one man was "proved" to be cowardly, another bold, another resourceful, and so on.

Talcott Parsons, in one of his earlier works, has analytically unfolded, for sociological purposes, much the same set of terministic functions that is here being called dramatistic (owing to their nature as implied in the idea of an "act"). Thus, in dealing with "the unit of action systems," Parsons writes:

An "act" involves logically the following: (1) It implies an agent, an "actor." (2) For purposes of definition the act must have an "end," a future state of affairs toward which the process of action is oriented. (3) It must be initiated in a

"situation" of which the trends of development differ in one or more important respects from the state of affairs to which the action is oriented, the end. This situation is in turn analyzable into two elements: those over which the actor has no control, that is which he cannot alter, or prevent from being altered, in conformity with his end, and those over which he has such control. The former may be termed the "conditions" of action, the latter the "means." Finally (4) there is inherent in the conception of this unit, in its analytical uses, a certain mode of relationship between these elements. That is, in the choice of alternative means to the end, in so far as the situation allows alternatives, there is a "non-native orientation" of actions. (1937, p. 44)

Aristotle, from whom Aquinas got his definition of God as "pure act," gives us much the same lineup when enumerating the circumstances about which we may be ignorant, with corresponding inability to act voluntarily:

A man may be ignorant, then, of who he is, what he is doing, what or whom he is acting on, and sometimes also what (e.g. what instrument) he is doing it with, and to what end (e.g. he may think his act will conduce to some one's safety), and how he is doing it (e.g. whether gently or violently). (Nichomachean Ethics 1111a5)

This pattern became fixed in the medieval questions: *quis* (agent), *quid* (act), *ubi* (scene defined as place), *quibus auxiliis* (agency), *cur* (purpose), *quo modo* (manner, "attitude"), *quando* (scene defined temporally).

THE NATURE OF SYMBOLIC ACTION

Within the practically limitless range of scenes (or motivating situations) in terms of which human action can be defined and studied, there is one overall dramatistic distinction as regards the widening or narrowing of circumference. This is the distinction between "action" and "sheer motion." "Action," is a term for the kind of behavior possible to a typically symbol-using animal (such as man) in contrast with the extra-symbolic or nonsymbolic operations of nature.

Whatever terministic paradoxes we may encounter en route (and the dramatistic view of terminology leads one to expect them on the grounds that language is primarily a species of action, or expression of attitudes, rather than an instrument of definition), there is the self-evident distinction between symbol and *symbolized* (in the sense that the *word* "tree" is categorically distinguishable from the *thing* tree). Whatever may be the ultimate confusions that result from man's intrinsic involvement with "symbolicity" as a necessary part of his nature, one can at least *begin* with this sufficiently clear distinction between a "thing" and its name.

The distinction is generalized in dramatism as one between "sheer motion" and "action." It involves an empirical shift of circumference in the sense that although man's ability to speak depends upon the existence of speechless nature, the existence of speechless nature does not depend upon man's ability to speak. The relation between these two distinct terministic realms can be summed up in three propositions:

1. There can be no action without motion—that is, even the "symbolic action" of pure thought requires corresponding motions of the brain.
2. There can be motion without action. (For instance, the motions of the tides, of sunlight, of growth and decay.)
3. Action is not reducible to terms of motion. For instance, the "essence" or "meaning" of a sentence is not reducible to its sheer physical existence as sounds in the air or marks on the page, although material motions of some sort are necessary for the production, transmission, and reception of the sentence. As has been said by Talcott Parsons:

Certainly the situation of action includes parts of what is called in common-sense terms the physical environment and the biological organism . . . these elements of the situation of action are capable of analysis in terms of the physical and biological sciences, and the phenomena in question are subject to analysis in terms of the units in use in those sciences. Thus a bridge may, with perfect truth, be said to consist of atoms of iron, a small amount of carbon, etc., and their constituent electrons, protons, neutrons and the like. Must the student of action, then, become a physicist, chemist, biologist in order to understand his subject? In a sense this is true, but for purposes of the theory

of action it is not necessary or desirable to carry such analyses as far as science in general is capable of doing. A limit is set by the frame of reference with which the student of action is working. That is, he is interested in phenomena with an aspect not reducible to action terms only in so far as they impinge on the schema of action in a relevant way—in the role of conditions or means. . . . For the purposes of the theory of action the smallest conceivable concrete unit is the unit act, and while it is in turn analyzable into the elements to which reference has been made—end, means, conditions and guiding norms—further analysis of the phenomena of which these are in turn aspects is relevant to the theory of action only in so far as the units arrived at can be referred to as constituting such elements of a unit act or a system of them. (1937, pp. 47–48)

Is Dramatism Merely Metaphorical?

Although such prototypically dramatistic usages as "all the world's a stage" are clearly metaphors, the situation looks quite otherwise when approached from another point of view. For instance, a physical scientist's relation to the materials involved in the study of motion differs in quality from his relation to his colleagues. He would never think of "petitioning" the objects of his experiment or "arguing with them," as he would with persons whom he asks to collaborate with him or to judge the results of his experiment. Implicit in these two relations is the distinction between the sheer motion of things and the actions of persons.

In this sense, man is defined literally as an animal characterized by his special aptitude for "symbolic action," which is itself a literal term. And from there on, drama is employed, not as a metaphor but as a fixed form that helps us discover what the implications of the terms "act" and "person" *really are*. Once we choose a generalized term for what people do, it is certainly as literal to say that "people act" as it is to say that they "but move like mere things."

Dramatism and the Social System

Strictly speaking, then, dramatism is a theory of terminology. In this respect a nomenclature could be called dramatistic only if it were specifically designed to talk, at one remove, about the cycle of terms implicit in the idea of an act. But in a wider sense any study of human relations in terms of "action" could to that extent be called dramatistic. A major difficulty in delimiting the field of reference derives from the fact that common-sense vocabularies of motives are spontaneously personalistic, hence innately given to drama-laden terms. And the turn from the naïve to the speculative is marked by such "action words" as *tao, karma, dike, hodos,* islam (to designate a submissive *attitude*), all of which are clearly dramatistic when contrasted with their terminological ideals proper to the natural sciences (Burke [1945–1950] 1962, p. 15).

The dramatistic nature of the Bible is proclaimed in the verb *(bara)* of the opening sentence that designates God's creative act; and the series of fiats that follows identifies such action with the principle of symbolicity ("the Word"). Both Plato's philosophy of the Good as ultimate motive and Aristotle's potentiality-actuality pair would obviously belong here, as would the strategic accountancy of active and passive in Spinozas *Ethics* (Burke [1945–1950] 1962, pp. 146–152). The modern sociological concern with "values" as motives does not differ in principle from Aristotle's list of persuasive "topics" in his *Rhetoric*. One need not look very closely at Lucretius' atomism to discern the personality in those willful particles. Contemporary theories of role-taking would obviously fall within this looser usage, as indicated on its face by the term itself. Rhetorical studies of political exhortation meet the same test, as do typical news reports of people's actions, predicaments, and expressions. Most historiography would be similarly classed, insofar as its modes of systematization and generalization can be called a scientifically documented species of storytelling. And humanistic criticism (of either ethical or aesthetic sorts) usually embodies, in the broad sense, a dramatistic attitude toward questions of personality. Shifts in the locus and scope of a terminology's circumference allow for countless subdivisions, ranging from words like "transaction," "exchange," "competition," and "cooperation," or the maneuvers studied in the obviously dramalike situations of game theories, down to the endless individual verbs designed to narrate specifically what some one person did, or said, or thought at some one time. Thus Duncan (1962) has explicitly applied a dramatistic nomenclature to hierarchy and the sociology of comedy. Similarly, Golfman (1956) has characterized his study of "'impression management" as "dramaturgical."

Does Dramatism Have a Scientific Use?

If the dramatistic nature of terms for human motives is made obvious in Burke's pentad (act, scene, agent, agency, purpose), is this element radically eliminated if we but introduce a *synonym* for each of those terms? Have we, for instance, effectively dodged the dramatistic "logic" if instead of "act" we say "response," instead of "scene" we say "situation" or "stimulus," instead of "agent" we say "subject" or "the specimen under observation in this case," instead of "agency" we say "implementation," and instead of "purpose" we use some term like "target"? Or to what extent has reduction *wholly* taken place when the dramatistic grammar of "active," "passive," and "reflexive" gets for its analogues, in the realm of sheer motion, "effectors," "receptors" (output, input), and "feedback," respectively? Might we have here but a *truncated* terminology of action, rather than a terminology intrinsically nondramatistic? Such issues are not resolved by a dramatistic perspective; but they are systematically brought up for consideration.

A dramatistic analysis of nomenclature can make clear the paradoxical ways in which even systematically generated "theories of action" can culminate in kinds of observation best described by analogy with mechanistic models. The resultant of many disparate acts cannot itself be considered an act in the same purposive sense that characterizes each one of such acts (just as the movement of the stock market in its totality is not "personal" in the sense of the myriad decisions made by each of the variously minded traders). Thus, a systematic analysis of interactions among a society of agents whose individual acts variously reinforce and counter one another may best be carried out in terms of concepts of "equilibrium" and "disequilibrium" borrowed from the terminology of mechanics.

In this regard it should also be noted that although equilibrium theories are usually interpreted as intrinsically adapted only to an upholding of the *status quo,* according to the dramatistic perspective this need not be the case. A work such as Albert Mathiez's *The French Revolution* (1922–1927) could be viewed as the expression of an *anima naturaliter dramatistica* in that it traces step by step an ironic development whereby a succession of unintentionally wrong moves led to unwanted results. If one viewed this whole disorderly sequence as itself a species of order, then each of the stages in its advance could be interpreted as if "designed" to stabilize, in constantly changing circumstances, the underlying pattern of conditions favorable to the eventual outcome (namely, the kind of equilibrium that could be maintained only by a series of progressive developments leading into, through, and beyond the Terror).

Though a drama is a mode of symbolic action so designed that an audience might be induced to "act symbolically" in sympathy with it, insofar as the drama serves this function it may be studied as a "perfect mechanism" composed of parts moving in mutual adjustment to one another like clockwork. The paradox is not unlike that which happened in metaphysics when a mystical view of the world as a manifestation of God's purposes prepared the way for mechanistic views, since the perfect representation of such a "design" seemed to be a machine in perfect order.

This brings up the further consideration that mechanical models might best be analyzed, not as downright antidramatistic, but as fragments of the dramatistic. For whatever humanist critics might say about the "dehumanizing" effects of the machine, it is a characteristically *human* invention, conceived by the perfecting of some human aptitudes and the elimination of others (thus in effect being not inhuman, but man's powerful "caricature" of himself—a kind of mighty homunculus).

If, on the other hand, it is held that a dramatistic nomenclature is to be avoided in any form as categorically inappropriate to a science of social relations, then a systematic study of symbolic action could at least be of use in helping to reveal any hitherto undetected traces of dramatistic thinking that might still survive. For otherwise the old Adam of human symbolicity, whereby man still persists in thinking of himself as a *personal agent capable of acting,* may lurk in a symbol system undetected (a tendency revealed in the fact that the distinction between "action" and "sheer motion" so readily gets lost, as with a term like *kinesis* in Aristotle or the shift between the mechanistic connotations of "equilibrium" and the histrionic connotations of "equilibrist"). Similarly, since pragmatist terminologies lay great stress upon "agencies" (means) and since all machines have a kind of built-in purpose, any nomenclature conceived along the lines of pragmatist instrumentalism offers a halfway house between teleology and sheer aimless motion.

At one point dramatism as a critique of terminology is necessarily at odds with dramatism as applied for specifically scientific purposes. This has been made clear in an article by Wrong (1961), who charges that although "modern sociology after all originated as a protest against the partial views of man contained in such doctrines as utilitarianism, classical economics, social Darwinism, and vulgar Marxism," it risks contributing to "the creation of yet another reified abstraction in socialized man, the status-seeker of our contemporary sociologists" (p. 190). He grants that "such an image of man is . . . valuable for limited purposes," but only "so long as it is not taken for the whole truth" (p. 190). He offers various corrections, among them a stress upon "role-playing" and upon "forces in man that are resistant to socialization," such as certain "biological" and "psychological" factors—even though some sociologists might promptly see "the specter of 'biological determinism'" (p. 191) and others might complain that already there is "too much 'psychologism' in contemporary sociology" (p. 192).

Viewed from the standpoint of dramatism as a critique of terminology, Wrong's article suggests two notable problems. Insofar as any science has a nomenclature especially adapted to its particular field of study, the extension of its *special* terms to provide a definition of man *in general* would necessarily oversociologize, overbiologize, overpsychologize, or overphysicize, etc., its subject; or the definition would have to be corrected by the addition of elements from other specialized nomenclatures (thereby producing a kind of amalgam that would lie outside the strict methodic confines of any specialized scientific discipline). A dramatistic view of this situation suggests that an overall definition of man would be not strictly "scientific," but philosophical.

Similarly, the dramatistic concept of a scene-act ratio aims to admonish against an overly positivist view of descriptive terms, or "empirical data," as regards an account of the conditions that men are thought to confront at a given time in history. For insofar as such a grammatical function does figure in our thoughts about motives and purpose, in the choice and scope of the terms that are used for characterizing a given situation dramatism would discern implicit corresponding attitudes and programs of action. If the principle of the scene-act ratio always figures in some form, it follows that one could not possibly select descriptive terms in which policies of some sort are not more or less clearly inherent. In the selection of terms for describing a scene, one automatically prescribes the range of acts that will seem reasonable, implicit, or necessary in that situation.

DRAMATISTIC ANALYSES OF ORDER

Following a lead from Bergson (1907, especially chapter 4), dramatism is devoted to a stress upon the all-importance of the negative as a specifically linguistic invention. But whereas Bergson's fertile chapter on "the idea of nothing" centers in the propositional negative ("It is not"), the dramatistic emphasis focuses attention upon the "moralistic" or "hortatory" negative ("Thou shalt not"). Burke (1961, pp. 183–196) has applied this principle of negativity to a cycle of terms implicit in the idea of "order," in keeping with the fact that "order," being a polar term, implies a corresponding idea of "disorder," while these terms in turn involve ideas of "obedience" or "disobedience" to the "authority" implicit in "order" (with further terministic radiations, such as the attitude of "humility" that leads to the act of obedience or the attitude of "pride" that leads to the act of disobedience, these in turn involving ideas of guidance or temptation, reward or punishment, and so on).

On the side of order, or control, there are the variants of faith and reason (faith to the extent that one accepts a given command, proscription, or statement as authoritative; reason to the extent that one's acceptance is contingent upon such proofs as are established by a methodic weighing of doubts and rebuttals). On the side of disorder there are the temptations of the senses and the imagination. The senses can function as temptations to the extent that the prescribed order does not wholly gratify our impulses (whether they are natural or a by-product of the very order that requires their control). Similarly, the imagination falls on the side of disorder insofar as it encourages interests inimical to the given order, though it is serviceable to order if used as a deterrent by picturing the risks of disorder-or, in other words, if it is kept "under the control of reason."

Midway between the two slopes of order and disorder (technically the realm where one can say yes or no to a thou-shalt-not) there is an area of indeterminacy often called the will. Ontologically, action is treated as a function of the will. But logologically the situation is reversed: the idea of the will is viewed as derivable from the idea of an act.

From ideas of the will there follow in turn ideas of grace, or an intrinsic ability to make proper choices (though such an aptitude can be impaired by various factors), and sacrifice (insofar as any choices involve the "mortification" of some desires). The dramatistic perspective thus rounds out the pattern in accordance with the notion that insofar as a given order involves sacrifices of some sort, the sacrificial principle is intrinsic to the nature of order. Hence, since substitution is a prime resource available to symbol systems, the sacrificial principle comes to ultimate fulfillment in vicarious sacrifice, which is variously rationalized, and can be viewed accordingly as a way to some kind of ultimate rewards.

By tracing and analyzing such terms, a dramatistic analysis shows how the negativistic principle of guilt implicit in the nature of order combines with the principles of thoroughness (or "perfection") and substitution that are characteristic of symbol systems in such a way that the sacrificial principle of victimage (the "scapegoat") is intrinsic to human congregation. The intricate line of exposition might be summed up thus: If order, then guilt; if guilt, then need for redemption; but any such "payment" is victimage. Or: If action, then drama; if drama, then conflict; if conflict, then victimage.

Adapting theology ("words about God",) to secular, empirical purposes ("words about words"), dramatistic analysis stresses the perennial vitality of the scapegoat principle, explaining why it fits so disastrously well into the "logologic" of man's symbolic resources. It aims to show why, just as the two primary and sometimes conflicting functions of religion (solace and control) worked together in the doctrines of Christianity, we should expect to find their analogues in any society. Dramatism, as so conceived, asks not how the sacrificial motives revealed in the institutions of magic and religion might be eliminated in a scientific culture, but what new forms they take (Burke [1945–1950] 1962, pp. 406–408).

This view of vicarious victimage extends the range of those manifestations far beyond the areas ordinarily so labeled. Besides extreme instances like Hitlerite genocide, or the symbolic "cleansings" sought in wars, uprisings, and heated political campaigns, victimage would include psychogenic illness, social exclusiveness (the malaise of the "hierarchal psychosis"), "beatnik" art, rabid partisanship in sports, the excessive pollution of air and streams, the "bulldozer mentality" that rips into natural conditions without qualms, the many enterprises that keep men busy destroying in the name of progress or profit the ecological balance on which, in the last analysis, our eventual well-being depends, and so on.

The strongly terministic, or logological, emphasis of dramatism would view the scapegoat principle not primarily as a survival from earlier eras, but as a device natural to language here and now. Aristotle, in the third book of his *Rhetoric* (chapter 10), particularly stresses the stylistic importance of antithesis as a means of persuasion (as when a policy is recommended in terms of what it is *against*). In this spirit dramatism would look upon the scapegoat (or the principle of vicarious victimage) as but a special case of antithesis, combined with another major resource of symbol systems, namely, substitution.

In the polemics of politics, the use of the scapegoat to establish identification in terms of an enemy shared in common is also said to have the notable rhetorical advantage that the candidate who presents himself as a spokesman for "us" can prod his audience to consider local ills primarily in terms of alien figures viewed as the outstanding causes of those ills. In accord with this emphasis, when analyzing the rhetorical tactics of *Mein Kampf,* Burke (1922–1961) lays particular stress upon Hitler's use

of such deflections to provide a "noneconomic interpretation of economic ills."

While recognizing the amenities of property and holding that "mine-ownness" or "our-ownness" in some form or other is an inevitable aspect of human congregation, dramatistic analysis also contends that property in any form sets the conditions for conflict (and hence culminates in some sort of victimage). It is pointed out that the recent great advances in the development of technological power require a corresponding extension in the realm of negativity (the "thou-shalt-nots" of control). Thus, the strikingly "positive" nature of such resources (as described in terms of "sheer motion") is viewed dramatistically as deceptive; for they may seem too simply like "promises," whereas in being *powers* they are properties, and all properties are *problem,* since powers are bones of contention (Burke 1960).

A dramatistic view of human motives thus culminates in the ironic admonition that perversions of the sacrificial principle (purgation by scapegoat, congregation by segregation) are the constant temptation of human societies, whose orders are built by a kind of animal exceptionally adept in the ways of symbolic action (Burke [1941] 1957, pp. 87–113).

Bibliography

Benne, Kenneth D. 1964, From Polarization to Paradox. Pages 216–247 in Leland P. Bradford, Jack R. Gibb, and Kenneth D. Benne (editors), *T-Group Theory and Laboratory Method: Innovation in Reeducation.* New York: Wiley.

Bergson, Henri, (1907) 1944, *Creative Evolution.* New York: Modern Library. First published in French.

Burke, Kenneth, (1922–1961) 1964, *Perspectives by Incongruity* and *Terms for Order.* Edited by Stanley Edgar Hyman. Bloomington: Indiana Univ. Press. Two representative collections of readings from Burke's works. Each collection is also available separately in paperback from the same publisher.

Burke, Kenneth, (1937) 1959, *Attitudes Toward History.* 2d ed., rev. Los Altos, Calif.: Hermes.

Burke, Kenneth, (1941) 1957, *The Philosophy of Literary Form: Studies in Symbolic Action.* Rev. ed., abridged by the author. New York: Vintage. The Louisiana State University Press reprinted the unabridged edition in 1967.

Burke, Kenneth, (1945–1950) 1962, *A Grammar of Motives* and *A Rhetoric of Motives.* Cleveland: World.

Burke, Kenneth, 1955, Linguistic Approach to Problems of Education. Pages 259–303 in National Society for the Study of Education, Committee on Modern Philosophies and Education, *Modern Philosophies and Education.* Edited by Nelson B. Henry. National Society for the Study of Education Yearbook 54, Part 1. Univ. of Chicago Press.

Burke, Kenneth, 1960, Motion, Action, Words. *Teachers College Record* 62:244–249.

Burke, Kenneth, 1961, *The Rhetoric of Religion: Studies in Logology.* Boston: Beacon.

Burke, Kenneth, 1966, *Language as Symbolic Action: Essays on Life, Literature, and Method.* Berkeley: Univ. of California Press.

Duncan, Hugh D., 1962, *Communication and Social Order.* Totowa, N.J.: Bedminster Press.

Goffman, Erving, (1956) 1959, *The Presentation of Self in Everyday Life.* Garden City, N.Y.: Doubleday.

Hume, David, (1748) 1952, An Inquiry Concerning Human Understanding. Pages 451–509 in *Great Books of the Western World.* Volume 35: Locke, Berkeley, Hume. Chicago: Benton.

Mathiez, Albert, (1922–1927) 1962, *The French Revolution.* New York: Russell. First published in French in three volumes. A paperback edition was published in 1964 by Grosset and Dunlap.

Mead, George Herbert, 1938. *The Philosophy of the Act.* Univ. of Chicago Press. Consists almost entirely of unpublished papers which Mead left at his death in 1931.

Parsons, Talcott, 1937, *The Structure of Social Action: A Study in Social Theory With Special Reference to a Group of Recent European Writers.* New York: McGraw-Hill.

Richards, Ivor A, (1959) 1961, *Principles of Literary Criticism.* New York: Harcourt.

Rueckert, William H., 1963, *Kenneth Burke and the Drama of Human Relations.* Minneapolis: Univ. of Minnesota Press.

Wrong, Dennis H, 1961, The Oversocialized Conception of Man in Modern Sociology. *American Sociological Review* 26: pp. 183–193.

SUMMARY

Burke, as we can see from the discussion in this chapter, is a many-faceted theorist who combines important elements of "old" and "new" rhetoric. His remarkable grasp of the literature of the humanities and the social and behavioral sciences, reinforced by a talent for penetrating critical insights, has placed him far above his contemporaries. You may recall that in 1952, Marie Nichols concluded her essay on Burke with these words: ". . . he has become the most profound student of rhetoric now writing in America." It is an important tribute to Burke that Dr. Nichols, twenty-five years later, said to us in Detroit in the Spring of 1977, that Burke, in her opinion, is still the greatest rhetorician and critic in America today.

Stephen Toulmin on the Nature of Argument

In the preceding chapters on contemporary rhetorical theory, we have described some of the leading aspects of rhetoric as meaning, rhetoric as motives, and rhetoric as values. While all of these trends have their origin in earlier writings, the approach used by the authors we have cited is sufficiently unique to qualify their works as a form of "new rhetoric." Yet to be analyzed is another developing trend which is rapidly gaining adherents. Representatives of this school of thought tend to view rhetoric as a way of knowing. They, like their counterparts in the British period, may be classified as modern epistemologists.

Among the first communication theorists in mid-twentieth century America to catch the significance of this emerging trend was Robert Scott in his 1967 essay, "On Viewing Rhetoric as Epistemic."[1] In this seminal study, Scott takes issue with the notion that the purpose of rhetoric is to "make the truth effective in practical affairs." Even if one assumes the existence of truth, Scott argues in the following passage, there are serious problems which arise:

Accepting the notion that truth exists, may be known, and if communicated leads logically to the position that there should be only two modes of discourse: a neutral presenting of data among equals and a persuasive leading to inferiors by the capable. The attitude with which this position may be espoused can vary from benevolent to cynical, but it is certainly undemocratic. Still the contemporary rhetorician is prone to accept the assumption to say, in effect, "My art is simply one which is useful in making the truth effective in practical affairs," scarcely conscious of the irony inherent in his statement.[2]

Surely, adds Scott, rhetoric serves a more significant function. The significant function suggested by Scott and other authors to be considered in this chapter is grounded in the process of knowing resulting from argument. Although the linking of rhetoric with argument dates back to Whately, what makes this contemporary emphasis unique is its stress on knowing rather than on persuading.

Douglas Ehninger and Wayne Brockriede began to make the above link evident in their volume, *Decision by Debate*. Influenced by the philosophy of Stephen Toulmin, these scholars describe debate as a critical and cooperative instrument of investigation. Here are a few of their conclusions: "(a) the end and method of debate are critical; (b) debate is an instrument of investigation rather than of propagation; (c) debate is a cooperative rather than competitive enterprise."[3] This viewpoint seeks to reclaim the hitherto lost or subverted epistemological dimension of the art of rhetoric. As Scott has noted: "If debate is critical inquiry, then it is not simply an effort to make a preconceived position effective."[4]

Quite clearly, then, when rhetoric is defined so as to include the argumentative process, a way of knowing emerges. Through the critical interaction of arguments wherein rhetors "seek" and listeners "judge" what they hear, knowledge is generated, tested, and acted upon. Observe how Carroll Arnold identifies this perspective with the teachings of the "new rhetoricians" who rely on "practical experience."

The new rhetoricians contend that subjecting itineraries of attempts to conclude probabilisticly to the judgments of others is a way of coming to know. The view seems supportable from practical experience. Rhetorical situations do seem to entail tacit understandings that the rhetors are "seeking" and the respondents "judging," not just responding autonomically. And if the rhetor is tested as he acts rhetorically, he can learn from his audience's judgment—unless he ignores their judgments, which would be a denial that communication was rhetorical.[5]

As a way of knowing, rhetoric does not simply seek to proclaim "truth"; rather, it becomes a means for generating understanding. What does this position imply, then, concerning the nature of "truth?" Scott answers this inquiry in this way:

What these statements do suggest is that truth is not prior and immutable but is contingent. Insofar as we can say that there is truth in human affairs, it is in time; it can be the result of a process of interaction at a given moment. Thus rhetoric may be viewed not as a matter of giving effectiveness to truth but of creating truth.[6]

Strongly supporting the position of Scott is that held by Richard Rieke who says:

> As a way of knowing, rhetoric does not simply seek to proclaim "truth"; rather, it becomes a means for generating understanding.

From these materials I will conclude that rhetoric is inextricably involved in the generation of knowledge; not merely a way of knowing, but involved in all ways of knowing. To be more specific, the division of the world into the realm of the absolute and that of the contingent may be rejected totally. All knowledge will be viewed as contingent, and rhetoric, the rationale of the contingent, will be recognized as essential to all knowledge—scientific, humanistic, or whatever.[7]

Truth viewed from this perspective, then, is something created by the rhetorical process which, in turn, is situation- or context-bound. Men interlocked and interacting critically in the rhetorical dimension arrive at the "truth" for a given people, at a given time in their history, within given situational or environmental factors. And so, a priori truth is not possible within the philosophical framework proposed by the contemporary rhetorical epistemologists. In commenting on this point, Scott observes:

The direction of analysis from Toulmin through Ehninger and Brockriede, leads to the conclusion that there is no possibility in matters relevant to human interaction to determine truth in any a priori way, that truth can arise only from cooperative critical inquiry. Men may have recourse to some universal ideas in which they are willing to affirm their faith, but these must enter into the contingencies of time and place and will not give rise to products which are certain.[8]

Man's quest for universals is thus a rhetorical process. For men interacting in a critical and cooperative attitude discover knowledge together.

It would appear, therefore, that rhetoric as a way of knowing established for itself the goal of gaining adherence of minds regarding the facts of a particular discipline or field of inquiry. A communicator and communicatee thus should reach an intellectual agreement only after they have engaged in rhetorical transactions presented against a background of strong reasoning and compelling evidence. Within this argumentative environment, discovery occupies a position equal to or surpassing that of persuasion. The ensuing statement by Arnold capsulizes this view:

For most of the writers I am calling a "new school," manipulating symbolic devices for the purpose of gaining one's own or someone else's adherence is essential to the very process of coming to know. And manipulation of verbal devices is also an indispensable way of testing what one thinks he, himself, knows. Rhetorical activity thus becomes not persuasive alone but an activity of ideational discovery.[9]

The "moment by moment" discovery of knowledge, as emphasized by the "new school" rhetoricians, is doubtless a creative, exciting endeavor founded on the inherent rhetorical attribute of all men and women.

STEPHEN TOULMIN

The two rhetoricians who best exemplify the trend being described in the next two chapters are Stephen Toulmin and Chaim Perelman who have much in common as students of argument. Toulmin is an English philosopher whose intellectual specialties are logic and the philosophy of science. Perelman is a Belgian philosopher and lawyer who is well known on the Continent for his works on logic and practical argument. Both have borrowed ideas from law and jurisprudence and applied them to rhetoric. It is our purpose now to probe more deeply into their theories so as to gain a fuller appreciation of the relationship between rhetoric and knowing.

Toulmin's Uses of Argument

Stephen Toulmin's *Uses of Argument* was first published in 1958. Perhaps the most noted contribution made by his text to rhetorical theory is the Toulmin model of argument which consists of the following elements: claim, warrant, data, qualifier, rebuttal, and backing. This model is considered in the essay immediately following. Before examining it in detail, however, we need to provide a background or frame of reference into Toulmin's thought.

Toulmin is dissatisfied with formal syllogistic-based logic. Believing that the syllogism does not necessarily *advance* knowledge and that formal logical systems fail to represent adequately the human reasoning process, Toulmin provides a rationale for his inquiry. In effect, Toulmin is critical of formal logic because it is *not* a way of knowing. Toulmin then sets out to formalize a model of argument which corresponds to the "rational process," characteristic of human decision-making. "We shall aim," he says, "to characterize what may be called 'the rational process,' the procedures and categories by using which claims-in-general can be argued for and settled."[10]

Toulmin begins his inquiry by turning his attention to "fields of argument." Here the author introduces the concepts of "field invariant" and "field dependent" arguments.

What things about the modes in which we assess arguments, the standards by reference to which we assess them and the manner in which we qualify our conclusions about them, are the same regardless of field (field-invariant), and which of them vary as we move from arguments in one field to arguments in another (field-dependent)? How far, for instance, can one compare the standards of argument relevant in a court of law with those relevant when judging a paper in the Proceedings of the Royal Society,

or those relevant to a mathematical proof or a prediction about the composition of a tennis team?[11]

When comparing and analyzing arguments it is necessary to discern if each argument is field-invariant or dependent, according to Toulmin. That is, the context which surrounds an argument—its field—determines the nature—stringency and looseness—of the said argument. On this point, Toulmin explains: "Two arguments will be said to belong to the same field when the data and conclusions in each of the two arguments are respectively, of the same logical type; they will be said to come from different fields when the backing or the conclusions in each of the two arguments are not of the same logical type."[12] Obviously, arguments within the same field can be compared. Arguments from different fields, however, must be carefully scrutinized, for comparisons are difficult, if not impossible, to make. Whereas formal logic attempts to judge all arguments from its established categories, Toulmin advocates judgment based on the fields in which they reside. "Indeed," observes Toulmin, "whether questions about comparative stringency can even be asked about arguments from different fields may be worth questioning."[13]

Relating these ideas to arguments found in the courtrooms, Toulmin states: "So it can be asked about law cases, as about arguments in general, how far their form and the canons relevant for their criticism are invariant—the same for cases of all types—and how far they are dependent upon the type of case under consideration."[14]

Toulmin's criticism of logic is more profound than time and space permit us to consider here. His dissatisfaction with the science of formal logic, however, is partially evident even in the above quoted statements. Toulmin claims that we must recognize the powerful influence inherent in the fields surrounding arguments and that the application of formal logic *rules* to field-dependent arguments is questionable at best. As a way of knowing, rhetoric cannot be restricted to formal rules and regulations. As a way of knowing, argument must not be restrained, but must *advance* knowledge.

With this background, Toulmin begins his search for those stages of any justificatory argument "to see how far these stages can be found alike in the case of arguments taken from many different fields."[15] Herein, Toulmin implies that there is indeed a "rational form" or model of argument which follows a similar course regardless of the argument's field. The claim-data-warrant-reservation-backing-qualifier model is Toulmin's answer.

We need at this point to mention the concept of "probability" which Toulmin builds into his system—a concept which serves to differentiate his model from formal logic. The model is characterized by its inclusion of probability terms which, in turn, serve to *qualify* the argument under consideration. Such statements serve to protect the universality and absoluteness of the argument. As he notes:

> *Our probability-terms come to serve, therefore, not only to qualify assertions, promises and evaluations themselves, but also as an indication of the strength of the backing which we have for the assertion, evaluation or whatever. It is the quality of the evidence or argument at the speaker's disposal which determines what sort of qualifier he is entitled to include in his statements. . . .* [16]

In sum, the Toulmin model of argument is a dynamic model which highlights the *movement* of the rhetor's reasoning. As such, Toulmin claims his model is more realistic and representative of the rational process involved in decision-making—that is, the Toulmin model is *epistemic.* Accordingly, Toulmin argues that, "a radical re-ordering of logical theory is needed in order to bring it more nearly into line with critical practice. . . ."[17]

An analysis of Toulmin's views, particularly his model of argument, was first introduced to American students by Ehninger and Brockriede in 1960. So effectively have the authors caught the essence of Toulmin's rhetorical philosophy that we are reprinting the essay here as a summary statement and application of *Uses of Argument.* We do so with the understanding that Brockriede and Ehninger have since modified some of their positions. See the 2nd. ed. of *Decision by Debate* (New York. Harper and Row, 1977).

Notes

1. Robert Scott, "On Viewing Rhetoric as Epistemic," *Central States Speech Journal,* XVIII (Feb. 1967), pp. 9–17.
2. *Ibid.,* p. 10.
3. Douglas Ehninger and Wayne Brockriede, *Decision By Debate* (New York: Dodd, Mead and Company, 1972), p. 16.
4. Scott, op. cit. p. 13.
5. Carroll C. Arnold, "Inventio and Pronunciatio in a 'New Rhetoric'"; unpublished paper, abstract, Central States Speech Association Convention, 1972. p. 12.
6. Scott, op. cit., p. 13.
7. Richard D. Rieke, "Rhetorical Perspectives in Modern Epistemology," unpublished paper, abstract, Speech Communication Association Convention, 1974. p. 1.
8. Scott, op. cit., p. 14.
9. Arnold, op. cit. p. 4.
10. Stephen E. Toulmin, *The Uses of Argument* (Cambridge: Cambridge University Press, 1958), p. 7.
11. *Ibid.,* p. 15.
12. *Ibid.,* p. 14.
13. *Ibid.,* p. 15.
14. *Ibid.,* p. 16.
15. *Ibid.,* p. 17.
16. *Ibid.,* pp. 90–91.
17. *Ibid.,* p. 253.

Toulmin on Argument: An Interpretation and Application

Wayne E. Brockriede and Douglas Ehninger

During the period 1917–1932 several books, a series of articles, and many Letters to the Editor of *QJS* gave serious attention to exploring the nature of argument as it is characteristically employed in rhetorical proofs.[1] Since that time, however, students of public address have shown comparatively little interest in the subject, leaving to philosophers, psychologists, and sociologists the principal contributions which have more recently been made toward an improved understanding of argument.[2]

Among the contributions offered by "outsiders" to our field, one in particular deserves more attention than it has so far received from rhetoricians. We refer to some of the formulations of the English logician Stephen Toulmin in his *The Uses of Argument,* published in 1958.[3]

Toulmin's analysis and terminology are important to the Rhetorician for two different but related reasons. First, they provide an appropriate structural model by means of which rhetorical arguments may be laid out for analysis and criticism; and, second, they suggest a system for classifying artistic proofs which employs argument as a central and unifying construct. Let us consider these propositions in order.

1

As described by Toulmin, an argument is *movement* from accepted *data,* through a *warrant,* to a *claim.*

Data (D) answer the question, "What have you got to go on?" Thus *data* correspond to materials of fact or opinion which in our textbooks are commonly called *evidence.* Data may report historical or contemporary events, take the form of a statistical compilation or of citations from authority, or they may consist of one or more general declarative sentences established by a prior proof of an artistic nature. Without data clearly present or strongly implied, an argument has no informative or substantive component, no factual point of departure.

Claim (C) is the term Toulmin applies to what we normally speak of as a *conclusion.* It is the explicit appeal produced by the argument, and is always of a potentially controversial nature. A claim may stand as the final proposition in an argument, or it may be an intermediate statement which serves as data for a subsequent inference.

Data and claim taken together represent the specific contention advanced by an argument, and therefore constitute what may be regarded as its *main proof line;* the usual order is *data* first, and then *claim.* In this sequence the *claim* contains or implies "therefore." When the order is reversed, the *claim* contains or implies "because."

Warrant (W) is the operational name Toulmin gives to that part of an argument which authorizes the mental "leap" involved in advancing from data to claim. As distinguished from data which answer the question "What have you got to go on," the warrant answers the question "How do you get there." Its function is to *carry* the accepted data to the doubted or disbelieved proposition which constitutes the claim, thereby certifying this claim as true or acceptable.

The relations existing among these three basic components of an argument, Toulmin suggests, may

Wayne Brockriede was a Professor of Communication, California State University, Fullerton. Douglas Ehninger was Professor of Speech and Dramatic Art, University of Iowa.
Reprinted from the *Quarterly Journal of Speech,* 46 (February 1960) 44–53 with the permission of the authors and editor, *Quarterly Journal of Speech.*

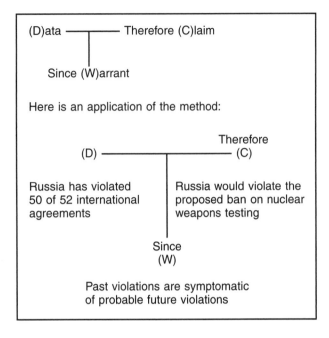

Here is an application of the method:

We may illustrate the model as follows:

Other nations which had such a record of violations continued such action/Expert X states that nations which have been chronic violators nearly always continued such acts/etc.

be represented diagrammatically, as shown on the following page.

In addition to the three indispensable elements of *data, claim,* and *warrant,* Toulmin recognizes a second triad of components, any or all of which may, but need not necessarily, be present in an argument. These he calls (1) *backing,* (2) *rebuttal,* and (3) *qualifier.*

Backing (B) consists of credentials designed to certify the assumption expressed in the warrant. Such credentials may consist of a single item, or of an entire argument in itself complete with data and claim. Backing must be introduced when readers or listeners are not willing to accept a warrant at its face value.

The rebuttal (R) performs the function of a safety valve or escape hatch, and is, as a rule, appended to claim statement. It recognizes certain conditions under which the claim will not hold good or will hold good only in a qualified and restricted way. By limiting the area to which the claim may legitimately be applied, the rebuttal anticipates certain objections which might otherwise be advanced against the argument.

The function of the qualifier (Q) is to register the degree of force which the maker believes is his claim to possess. The qualification may be expressed by a quantifying term such as "possibly," "probably," "to the five percent level of confidence," etc., or it may make specific reference to an anticipated refutation. When the author of a claim regards it as incontrovertible no qualifier is appended.

These additional elements may be superimposed on the first diagram, as shown in the next column.

2

With Toulmin's structural model now set forth, let us inquire into its suitability as a means of describing and testing arguments. Let us compare Toulmin's method with the analysis offered in traditional logic, the logic commonly used as a basic theory of argumentation in current textbooks. We conceive of arguments in the customary fashion as (1) deriving from probable causes and signs, (2) proceeding more often by relational than implicative principles, (3) emphasizing material as well as formal validity, (4) employing premises which are often contestable, and (5) eventuating in claims which are by nature contingent and variable.

The superiority of the Toulmin model in describing and testing arguments may be claimed for seven reasons:

1. Whereas traditional logic is characteristically concerned with *warrant-using* arguments (i.e.,

arguments in which the validity of the assumption underlying the inference "leap" is uncontested), Toulmin's model specifically provides for *warrant-establishing* arguments (i.e., arguments in which the validity of the assumption underlying the inference must be established—through backing—as part of the proof pattern itself).[4]

2. Whereas traditional logic, based as it is upon the general principle of implication, always treats proof more or less as a matter of classification or compartmentalization, Toulmin's analysis stresses the inferential and relational nature of argument, providing a context within which all factors—both formal and material—bearing upon a disputed claim may be organized into a series of discrete steps.

3. Whereas in traditional logic, arguments are specifically designed to produce universal propositions, Toulmin's second triad of backing, rebuttal, and qualifier provide, within the framework of his basic structural model, for the establishment of claims which are no more than probable. The model directs attention to the ways in which each of these additional elements may operate to limit or condition a claim.

> Toulmin's model lays an argument out in such a way that each step may be examined critically.

4. Whereas traditional logic, with its governing principle of implication, necessarily results in an essentially static conception of argument, Toulmin by emphasizing *movement* from data, through warrant, to claim, produces a conception of argument as dynamic. From his structural model we derive a picture of arguments "working" to establish and certify claims, and as a result of his functional terminology we are able to understand the role each part of an argument plays in this process.

5. Whereas the models based on the traditional analysis—enthymeme, example, and the like—often suppress a step in proof, Toulmin's model lays an argument out in such a way that each step may be examined critically.

6. Whereas in the traditional analysis the division of arguments into premises and conclusions (as in the syllogism, for example) often tends to obscure deficiencies in proof, Toulmin's model assigns each part of an argument a specific geo-

graphical or spatial position in relation to the others, thus rendering it more likely that weak points will be detected.

7. Whereas traditional logic is imperfectly equipped to deal with the problem of material validity, Toulmin makes such validity an integral part of his system, indicating clearly the role which factual elements play in producing acceptable claims.

In short, without denying that Toulmin's formulations are open to serious criticism at several points[5]—and allowing for any peculiarities in our interpretations of the character of traditional logic—one conclusion emerges. Toulmin has provided a structural model which promises to be of greater use in laying out rhetorical arguments for dissection and testing than the methods of traditional logic. For although most teachers and writers in the field of argumentation have discussed the syllogism in general terms, they have made no serious attempt to explore the complexities of the moods and figures of the syllogism, nor have they been very successful in applying the terms and principles of traditional logic to the arguments of real controversies. Toulmin's model provides a practical replacement.

3

Our second proposition is that Toulmin's structural model and the vocabulary he has developed to describe it are suggestive of a system for classifying artistic proofs, using argument (defined as *movement* from data through warrant, to claim) as a unifying construct.[6]

In extending Toulmin's analysis to develop a simplified classification of arguments, we may begin by restating in Toulmin's terms the traditional difference between *inartistic* and *artistic* proof. Thus, conceiving of an argument as a movement by means of which accepted data are carried through a certifying warrant to a controversial claim, we may say that in some cases the data themselves are conclusive. They approach the claim without aid from a warrant—are tantamount to the claim in the sense that to accept them is automatically to endorse the claim they are designed to support. In such cases the proof may be regarded as *inartistic*. In another class of arguments, however, the situation is quite different. Here the data are not immediately conclusive, so that the role of the warrant in carrying them to the claim becomes of crucial importance. In this sort of argument the proof is directly dependent upon the inventive powers of the arguer and may be regarded as *artistic.*

If, then, the warrant is the crucial element in an artistic proof, and if its function is to carry the data to the claim, we may classify artistic arguments by recognizing the possible routes which the warrant may travel in performing its function.

So far as rhetorical proofs are concerned, as men have for centuries recognized, these routes are three in number: (1) an arguer may carry data to claim by means of an assumption concerning the relationship existing among phenomena in the external world; (2) by means of an assumption concerning the quality of the source from which the data are derived; and (3) by means of an assumption concerning the inner drives, values, or aspirations which impel the behavior of those persons to whom the argument is addressed.

Arguments of the first sort (traditionally called *logical*) may be called *substantive;* those of the second sort (traditionally called *ethical*) may be described as *authoritative;* and those of the third sort (traditionally called *pathetic*)as *motivational.*

SUBSTANTIVE ARGUMENTS

The warrant of a substantive argument reflects an assumption concerning the way in which things are related in the world about us. Although other orderings are possible, one commonly recognized, and the one used here, is six-fold. Phenomena may be related as cause to effect (or as effect to cause), as attribute to substance, as some to more, as intrinsically similar, as bearing common relations, or as more to some. Upon the first of these relationships is based what is commonly called argument from *cause;* on the second, argument from sign; on the third, argument from *generalization;* and the fourth, argument from *parallel case;* on the fifth, argument from *analogy;* and on the sixth, argument from *classification.*

Cause

In argument from cause the data consist of one or more accepted facts about a person, object, event, or condition. The warrant attributes to these facts a creative or generative power and specifies the nature of the effect they will produce. The claim relates these

results to the person, object, event, or condition named in the data. Here is an illustration, from cause to effect:

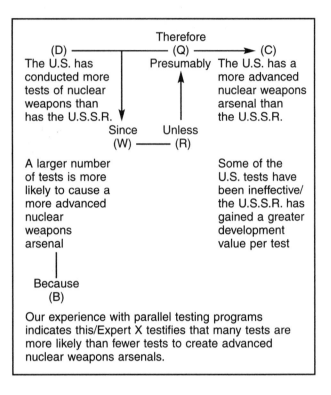

When the reasoning process is reversed and the argument is from effect to cause, the data again consist of one or more facts about a person, object, event, or condition; the warrant asserts that a particular causal force is sufficient to have accounted for these facts; and the claim relates the cause to the person, object, event, or condition named in the data.

Sign

In argument from sign the data consist of clues or symptoms. The warrant interprets the meaning or significance of these symptoms. The claim affirms that some person, object, event, or condition possesses the attributes of which the clues have been declared symptomatic. Our first example concerning Russia's violation of international agreements illustrates the argument from sign.

Generalization

In argument from generalization the data consist of information about a number of persons, objects, events, or conditions, taken as constituting a representative and adequate sample of a given class of phenomena. The warrant assumes that what is true of the items constituting the sample will also be true of additional members of the class not represented in the sample. The claim makes explicit the assumption embodied in the warrant. The form can be diagrammed so:

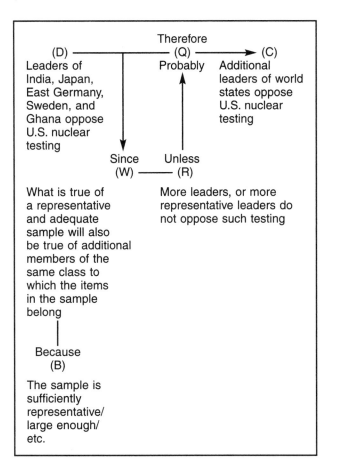

Parallel Case

In argument from parallel case the data consist of one or more statements about a single object, event, or condition. The warrant asserts that the instance reported in the data bears an essential similarity to a second instance in the same category. The claim affirms about the new instance what has already been accepted concerning the first. Following is an illustration.

In argument from parallel cases a rebuttal will be required in either of two situations: (1) if another parallel case bears a stronger similarity to the case under consideration; or (2) if in spite of some essential similarities an essential dissimilarity negates or reduces the force of the warrant. The example illustrates the second of these possibilities.

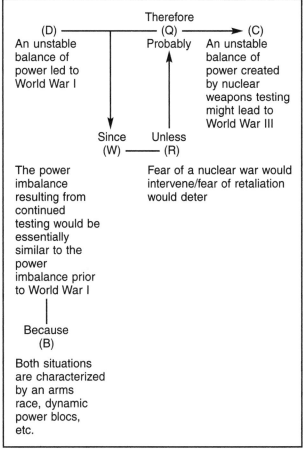

Analogy

In argument from analogy the data report that a relationship of a certain nature exists between two items. The warrant assumes that a similar relationship exists between a second pair of items. The claim makes explicit the relationship assumed in the warrant. Whereas the argument from parallel case assumes a resemblance between two *cases*, the analogy assumes only a similarity of *relationship*. Analogy may be illustrated as shown on the following page.

In most cases the analogical relation expressed in an argument from analogy will require a strongly qualifying "possibly."

Classification

In argument from classification the statement of the data is a generalized conclusion about known members of a class of persons, objects, events, or conditions. The warrant assumes that what is true of the items reported in the data will also be true of a hitherto unexamined item which is known (or thought) to fall within the class there described. The claim then transfers the general statement which has been

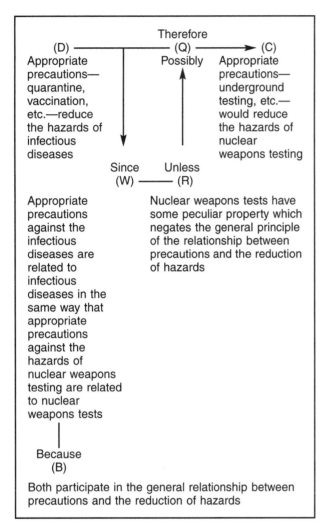

made in the data to the particular item under consideration. As illustrated, the form would appear:

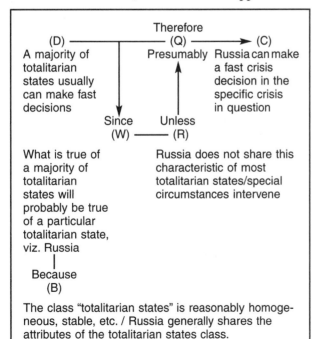

Two kinds of reservations may be applicable in an argument from classification: (1) a class member may not share the particular attribute cited in the data, although it does share enough other attributes to deserve delineation as a member of the class; and (2) special circumstances may prevent a specific class member from sharing at some particular time or place the attributes general to the class.

Authoritative Arguments

In authoritative arguments the data consist of one or more factual reports or statements of opinion. The warrant affirms the reliability of the source from which these are derived. The claim reiterates the statement which appeared in the data, as now certified by the warrant. An illustration follows:

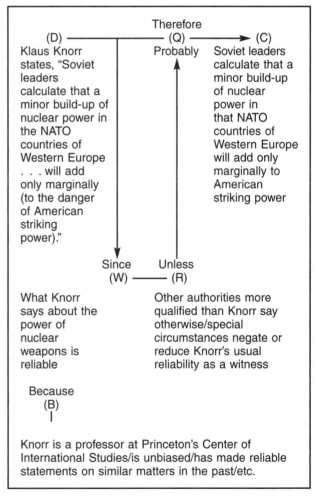

The structure and function of an authoritative argument remains basically the same when the source of the data is the speaker or writer himself. The data is carried to claim status by the same sort of assumption embodied in the warrant. We may infer a claim from what Knorr says about nuclear weapons whether he is himself the speaker, or whether another speaker is quoting what Knorr has said. Thus the *ethos* of a speaker may be studied by means of the Toulmin structure under the heading of authoritative argument.

Motivational Arguments

In motivational arguments the data consist of one or more statements which may have been established as claims in a previous argument or series of arguments. The warrant provides a motive for accepting the claim by associating it with some inner drive, value, desire, emotion, or aspiration, or with a combination of such forces. The claim as so warranted is that the person, object, event, or condition referred to in the data should be accepted as valuable or rejected as worthless or that the policy there described should or should not be adopted, or the action there named should or should not be performed. Illustrated, the form would appear:

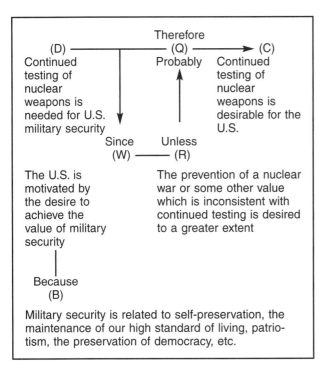

4

We have exhibited the structural unity of the three modes of artistic proof by showing how they may be reduced to a single invariant pattern using argument as a unifying construct. Let us as a final step explore this unity further by inquiring how artistic proofs, so reduced, may conveniently be correlated with the

various types of disputable questions and the claims appropriate to each.

Let us begin by recognizing the four categories into which disputable questions have customarily been classified: (1) Whether something is? (2) What it is? (3) Of what worth it is? (4) What course of action should be pursued? The first of these queries gives rise to a question of fact, and is to be answered by what can be called a *designative claim;* the second, to a question of definition, to be answered by a *definitive claim;* the third, to a question of value, to be answered by an *evaluative claim;* and the fourth, to a question of *policy,* to be answered by an *advocative claim.*

Supposing, then, that an arguer is confronted with a question of fact, calling for a designative claim; or a question of policy, calling for an advocative claim, etc., what types of argument would be available to him as means of substantiating his claim statement? Upon the basis of the formulations developed in earlier sections of this paper, it is possible to supply rather precise answers.

Designative Claims

A designative claim, appropriate to answering a question of fact, will be found supportable by any of the six forms of substantive argument, or by authoritative argument, but not by motivational argument. That is, whether something exists or is so, may be determined: (1) by isolating its cause or its effect (argument from cause); (2) by reasoning from the presence of symptoms to the claim that a substance exists or is so (argument from sign); (3) by inferring that because some members of a given class exist or are so, more members of the same class also exist or are so (argument from generalization); (4) by inferring because one item exists or is so, that a closely similar item exists or is so (argument from parallel case); (5) by reasoning that D exists or is so because it stands in the same relation to C that B does to A, when C, B, and A are known to exist or to be so (argument from analogy); and (6) by concluding that an unexamined item known or thought to fail within a given class exists or is so because all known members of the class exist or are so (argument from classification). Moreover, we may argue that something exists or is so because a reputable authority declares this to be the case. Motivational argument, on the other hand, may not be critically employed in designative claims, because values, desires, and feelings are irrelevant where questions of fact are concerned.

Definitive Claims

The possibilities for establishing definitive claims are more limited. Only two of the forms of substantive argument and authoritative argument are applicable. We may support a claim as to what something is: (1) by comparing it with a closely similar phenomenon (argument from parallel case); or (2) by reasoning that because it stands in the same relation to C as B does to A it will be analogous to C, where the nature of C, B, and A are known (argument from analogy). In addition, we may support a definition or interpretation by citing an acceptable authority. Among the substantive arguments, cause, sign, generalization, and classification are inapplicable; and once again motivational argument is irrelevant since emotions, wishes, and values cannot legitimately determine the nature of phenomena.

Evaluative Claims

Evaluative claims may be supported be generalization, parallel case, analogy, and classification, and by authoritative and motivational arguments. By generalization a class of phenomena may be declared valuable or worthless on the ground that a typical and adequate sample of the members of that class is so. By classification, in contrast, we infer from the worth of known members of a class the probable worth of some previously unexamined item known or thought to belong to that class. By parallel case, we infer goodness or badness from the quality of an item closely similar. By analogy, however, we infer value on the basis of a ratio of resemblances rather than a direct parallel. In authoritative argument our qualitative judgment is authorized by a recognized expert. In motivational argument, however, an item is assigned a value in accordance with its usefulness in satisfying human drives, needs, and aspirations. Arguments from cause and sign, on the other hand, are inapplicable.

Advocative Claims

Advocative claims may legitimately be established in only four ways. We may argue that some policy should be adopted or some action undertaken because a closely similar policy or action has brought desirable results in the past (argument from parallel case). We may support a proposed policy or action because it bears the same relation to C that B does to A, where B is known to have brought desirable results (argument from analogy). Or, of course, we may support our claim by testimony (authoritative argument), or by associating it with men's wishes, values, and aspirations (motivational argument).

This analysis concerning the types of arguments applicable to various sorts of claims may be summarized in tabular form:

	Designative	Definitive	Evaluative	Advocative
Substantive				
A. Cause	X			
B. Sign	X			
C. Generalization	X		X	
D. Parallel Case	X	X	X	X
E. Analogy	X	X	X	X
F. Classification	X		X	
Authoritative	X	X	X	X
Motivational			X	X

The world of argument is vast, one seemingly without end. Arguments arise in one realm, are resolved, and appear and reappear in others; and new arguments appear. If one assumes some rationality among men, a system of logical treatment of argument is imperative. The traditional logical system of syllogisms, of enthymemes, of middles distributed and undistributed, may have had its attraction in medieval times. The inadequacies of such a logic, however, have been described by experts; for example, see J.S. Mill on the syllogism and *peririo principii*.[7] The modern search has been for a method which would have some application in the dynamics of contemporary affairs.

Toulmin has supplied us with a contemporary methodology, which in many respects makes the traditional unnecessary. The basic theory has herein been amplified, some extensions have been made, and illustrations of workability have been supplied. All this is not meant to be the end, but rather the beginning of an inquiry into a new, contemporary, dynamic, and usable logic for argument.

Notes

1. E.g., such books as James M. O'Neill, Craven Laycock, and Robert L. Scales, *Argumentation and Debate* (New York, 1917); William T. Foster, *Argumentation and Debating* (Boston, 1917); and A. Craig Baird, *Public Discussion and Debate* (Boston, 1928); such articles as Mary Yost, "Argument from the Point of View of Sociology," *QJS*, III (1917); pp. 109–24; Charles H. Woolbert, "The Place of Logic in a System of Persuasion," *QJS*, IV, (1918), pp. 19–39; Gladys Murphy Graham, "Logic and Argumentation," *QJS*, X (1924), pp. 350–363; William E. Utterback, "Aristotle's Contribution to the Psychology of Argument," *QJS*, XI (1925), pp. 218–225; Herbert A. Wichelns, "Analysis and Synthesis in Argumentation," *QJS*, XI (1925), pp. 266–272; and Edward Z. Rowell, "Prolegomena to Argumentation," *QJS*, XVIII (1932), pp. 1–13, 224–248, 381–405, 585–606; such Letters to the Editor as those by Utterback, XI (1925), pp. 175-177, Wichelns, XI (1925), pp. 286–288; Ralph C. Ringwalt, XII (1926), pp. 66–68; and Graham, XII (1925), pp. 196–197.

2. See, for example, Mortimer Adler, *Dialectic* (New York, 1927); Paul Edwards, *The Logic of Moral Discourse* (Glencoe, Ill, 1955); Carl I. Hovland, Irving L. Janis, and Harold W. Kelley, *Communication and Persuasion* (New Haven, Conn., 1953); Chaim Perelman, *Traite de l'argumentation,* 2 vols. (Padis, 1958), and *La nouvelle rhetorique* (Paris, 1952); and John Cohen, "Subjective Probability," *Scientific American,* MCMVII (1957), pp. 128–38.

3. (Cambridge, Cambridge University Press). See especially the third of the five essays in the book. *Cf.* J.C. Cooley, "On Mr. Toulmin's Revolution in Logic," *The Journal of Philosophy,* LVI (1959), pp. 297–319.

4. In traditional logic only the epicheirema provides comparable backing for premises.

5. It may be charged that his structural model is merely "a syllogism lying on its side," that it makes little or no provision to insure the formal validity of claims, etc.

6. Our suggestion as to the structural unity of artistic proofs is by no means novel. The ancients regularly spoke of *pathetic* and *ethical* enthymemes, and envisioned the *topoi* as applicable beyond the *pistis.* (See in this connection James H. McBurney, "The Place of the Enthymeme in Rhetorical Theory," *SM,* III [1936], p. 63.) At the same time, however, it must be recognized that especially since the advent of the faculty psychology of the seventeenth and eighteenth centuries, rhetorical thought has been profoundly and persistently influenced by the doctrine of a dichotomy between pathetic and logical appeals. (For significant efforts to combat this doctrine see Charle H. Woolbert, "Conviction and Persuasion: Some Considerations of Theory," *QJS,* III (1917), pp. 249–264; Mary Yost, "Argument from the Point of View of Sociology," *QJS,* III [1917], pp. 109–124; and W. Norwood Brigance, "Can We Redefine the James-Winans Theory of Persuasion?" *QJS,* XXI [1935], pp. 19–26.)

7. *A System of Logic,* I, chap. 3, Sec. 2.

TOULMIN'S HUMAN *UNDERSTANDING,* VOLUME I

As a companion volume to *Uses of Argument,* Toulmin wrote a follow-up study in 1972, entitled *Human Understanding.*[1] Since the principal theme in this work is "the collective use and evolution of concepts," Toulmin continues his campaign to show how argument is a way of knowing. Our purpose in this section is to depict how argument rests on a continuum at a mid-point between absolutism on the one hand and relativism on the other. To see how argument is the primary force responsible for conceptual change or the generation of new knowledge, let us first examine the principal characteristics of absolutism and relativism as summarized and criticized by Toulmin.

Absolutism

The absolutists, according to Toulmin, are enamored with the formal logician's approach which upholds the value of a "logical systematicity" that features a "quasi-mathematical" method capable of producing "eternal principles." The absolutist is concerned with the "acceptability of propositions" based upon the criteria of correctness, incorrectness, form, and validity. Similarly, he views as authoritative that which is coherent, consistent, and properly entailed. Thus he imposes "from outside, on all milieus alike, an abstract and ideal set of formal criteria, defined in terms of a universal, quasi-mathematical 'logical system'. . . ."[2]

Toulmin discards absolutism as a satisfactory means of explaining conceptual change on the grounds that it is "static" and "stereotyped." Additionally, it is unable to bridge the gap between theory and practice. Obsessed with an unusually narrow view of rationality as logicality, the absolutist, in short, all too frequently lacks the desire or the flexibility to modify a strongly held position even when countering evidence may demand a revision.

Relativism

The contrary notion of relativism grew out of an opposition to absolutism. Proponents of this rapidly developing perspective on conceptual change, Toulmin points out, reject outright the premise that knowledge can be universal in nature. Borrowing from the field of Anthropology, the relativist makes such claims as these: (1) individuals should determine what is binding on themselves in a given situation involving moral issues; (2) a meaningful world view can only emanate from a particular "historico-cultural context"; (3) what is to be accepted as knowledge is dependent on the culture; and (4) a rational judgment is limited to the social milieu in which it is being rendered.

It is instructive to observe that while relativism differs from absolutism in the area of universality of knowledge, it shares a similar devotion to logical systematicity. A hierarchical order utilizing logical relations moves from "relative presuppositions" to "absolute presuppositions" which are binding in a particular "historico-cultural milieu." Both relativism and absolutism, therefore, subscribe to a rationality that is equated with logicality.

As in the case of absolutism, Toulmin argues that relativism is an inappropriate description of how knowledge is to be generated or understood. Its greatest weakness is its tendency to resist the application of viable intellectual concepts from one milieu to another. It also offers an inadequate explanation of how it is possible to move in a hierarchical order from relative to universal or absolute presuppositions.

Argument and Conceptual Change

From the above two polar views, Toulmin places argument on a middle point on the continuum, demonstrating how conceptual change or knowledge generation is the result of practical reasoning. Argument, he asserts, is an intellectual enterprise or a form of ecology in which claims are addressed to "conceptual populations" for the end of creating new disciplinary insights and beliefs. It makes use of "meta-statements" rather than formal claims, and is adaptive and nonstereotyped in its procedures. Be-

TOULMIN'S CONCEPTUAL CHANGE CONTINUUM MODEL		
Absolutism	**Argument**	**Relativism**
Logical Systematicity	Intellectual Enterprise	Logical systematicity
Quasi-mathematical	Ecological	Hierarchical Order
Rationality	"Meta-statements"	Absolute
Logicality	Modifiability	Presuppositions
Predictability	Reasonableness	Relative
Evaluative Criteria for	Evaluative Criteria for	Presuppositions
Assessing General Principles	Assessing General Principles	Logically
Correctness	Applicability	Historical
Coherency	Relevance	Evaluative Criteria for
Consistency	Adaptability	Assessing General
Entailment	Justification	Principles
Generalizability	Generalizability	Applicability
Universality (All cultures)	Within Cultures	Relevance
Eternality (Not limited to	Across Cultures	Generalizability
time)	Dynamic/Developing	Culture Dependent
Static	Non-stereotyped	Time bound
Stereotyped	↓	Non-transferable
	CONCEPTUAL CHANGE	

cause argument deals with probable or contingent propositions, its conclusions are tentative and modifiable. Thus when faced with new experiences and data, the rhetor is obligated to reconsider, revise, refine, or reinterpret an earlier position. Modification, therefore, becomes a moral duty when the circumstances demand it. Finally, an argument is assessed as convincing when it is applicable to the situation at hand, when it produces a result that is "better" than the status quo can offer, when it is relevant, and when it is capable of justification.

This stress on reasonableness instead of on strict rationality and on contingency rather than on formal validity puts argument in direct conflict with absolutism. In addition, in assuming that thoughtful "comparisons can meaningfully be drawn between concepts and judgements operative within different milieus,"[3] the arguer accomplishes what the relativist says is undesirable, if not impossible.

The relationship of argument, as described by Toulmin, to absolutism and relativism is summarized under the heading: "Conceptual Change Continuum Model." Although argument in a particular instance may move slightly toward the left or toward the right on the scale, it always remains close to the center point.

Three important implications may be derived from Toulmin's notion of argument as the principal cause of conceptual change. Of considerable significance, first of all, is the impact of these views on the interpretation of rhetoric as a way of knowing. The essence of his volume *Human Understanding* is the thesis that our collective use of concepts in any discipline or field of study is the direct result of a method of practical reasoning or intellectual enterprise that meets the test of reasonableness. In developing this idea, Toulmin says, in effect, that we know the worth of a person's theories by the quality of his arguments. He puts it this way in his analysis:

We shall do well . . . to consider a man's practical ideals of intellectual method in light of his theoretical ideas about intellectual activities and higher mental functions. By making explicit the arguments underlying his conceptual ambitions and dissatisfactions, we bring to light his own epistemic self-portrait: *the particular picture of human beings as active intelli-*

gences which governs his stance towards the objects of human understanding. The general problem of human understanding is, in fact, to draw an epistemic self-portrait which is both well-rounded and trustworthy; which is effective because its theoretical base is realistic, and which is realistic because its practical applications are effective.[4]

From this description, it would appear, rhetoric is an epistemic activity which is realistic, practical, and influential.

A second implication that stems from Toulmin's theory of argument and its impact on human understanding is the parallel that exists with jurisprudence. The model of reasoning employed by lawyers and judges also occupies a midpoint between absolutism and relativism. Using precedents as a starting point in courts of law, the jurisprudential speaker asks such questions as the following: (1) Is a particular precedent applicable to the present situation? or (2) should the precedent in this instance be overturned in light of the changing social circumstances? Quite clearly, then, a precedent can never be viewed as permanent or static. Nor is the legal speaker prevented from taking the practice of one jurisdiction and showing its relevance for another. In demonstrating how his theory of practical reasoning and the common-law tradition come together, Toulmin says:

Rationality . . . has its own "courts" in which all clear-headed men with suitable experience are qualified to act as judges or jurors. Within different cultures and epochs, reasoning may operate according to different methods and principles, so that different milieus represent the parallel "jurisdictions" of rationality. But they do so out of a shared concern with common "rational enterprises," just as parallel legal jurisdictions do with their common judicial enterprise. . . .[5]

Jurisprudence as the ideal model of argument, therefore, uses the evaluative criteria of applicability, adaptability, and relevance. Moreover, it is a dynamic and developing process.

A third inference that can be drawn be examining Toulmin's ideas on the nature and influence of

> This stress on reasonableness instead of on strict rationality and on contingency rather than on formal validity puts argument in direct conflict with absolutism.

argument, as explained in *Human Understanding,* is his partiality for an evolutionary interpretation of conceptual change. By its very essence, argument or practical reasoning, with its emphasis on modification and refinement, is a slow method. For a "conceptual population" to alter its view of a widely held theory or scholarly procedure, members participating in the intellectual enterprise engage in deliberation until a consensus is reached. This consensus, in turn, represents the adoption of a new idea or belief.

Toulmin's dedication to evolution as an explanatory theory led him to question any analysis of conceptual change that gave the appearance of subscribing to a revolutionary perspective. For this reason he devotes twenty-five pages in *Human Understanding* to a brilliant refutation of Thomas Kuhn's highly acclaimed volume *The Structure of Scientific Revolutions.* Toulmin counters Kuhn's claims by first demonstrating what he perceives to be the meaning of a genuine scientific revolution. It is, he asserts, a "complete change" in which "one fundamental paradigm" is displaced by another. He then adds:

> *Newthink . . . sweeps aside Oldthink entirely; so much so that, in the nature of the case, the reasons for replacing Oldthink by Newthink can be explained in the language of neither system. Like men committed to different constellations of absolute presuppositions, a Newthinker and an Oldthinker have no common vocabulary for comparing the rational claims of their respective theoretical positions.*[6]

The primary objection, then, to such an interpretation of conceptual change is Toulmin's conviction that it is virtually impossible for knowledge to follow a path of "radical discontinuity," causing a complete break with the past. Instead, he argues, knowledge is created in an evolutionary manner in which ideas become a natural outgrowth of all that has gone before. The most that Toulmin is willing to concede is that on occasion a conceptual change may move slightly on the continuum toward the revolutionary perspective.

In subsequent university and convention program lectures, Toulmin continually has refined the ideas discussed here. Moreover, these central points also have been reaffirmed in private conversations with the authors.[7]

> Toulmin's dedication to evolution as an explanatory theory led him to question any analysis of conceptual change that gave the appearance of subscribing to a revolutionary perspective.

Notes

1. (Princeton: Princeton University Press, 1972).
2. *Ibid.,* p. 486.
3. *Ibid.,* p. 493.
4. *Ibid.,* p. 3.
5. *Ibid.,* p. 95.
6. *Ibid.,* p. 102.
7. It is of interest to note that Volume II of *Human Understanding* was scheduled to be published in 1983. To date, however, it has not appeared.

Summary

Because of Toulmin's overriding significance as a theorist in the area of argument and as a major force in the trend we have called "rhetoric as a way of knowing," we were anxious to see if his ideas had changed since he wrote the volume on *Human Understanding.* As a result we requested a copy of one of his most recent monographs for use in this edition. After informing us that almost all of his writings are in book form, he agreed to let us reprint the manuscript of the lecture he delivered at the University of Michigan in October, 1982. Entitled "Logic and the Criticism of Arguments," this perceptive and provocative essay, as you will see, contains an insightful history of the past and present and an important guideline for future action. Before we present this study for your analysis, we would like to pinpoint several crucial aspects pertaining to Toulmin's background statements and central claims.

First the author still strongly adheres to the belief that in all human affairs we engage in argument for the purpose of establishing and evaluating claims that are probable in nature and for the end of generating knowledge. Secondly, he has coined a new phrase, "substantive logic," to describe the essence of practical reasoning. Thirdly, in this lecture Toulmin freely uses, and identifies with, the term rhetoric. In his earlier works alluded to in this chapter—*The Uses of Argument and Human Understanding*—the concept of rhetoric does not appear. By contrast he now acknowledges his indebtedness to Aristotle and Hermagoras who were the primary motivating forces for setting the rhetorical tradition into motion. Observe, for instance, this statement: "Only in retrospect is it apparent that—even though sleepwalkingly—I had rediscovered the topics of (Aristotle's) *Topics,* which were expelled from the agenda of philosophy in the years around 1900."

Since we predict that this lecture will become a landmark study in the rhetoric of Western thought, we submit the outline, below, summarizing what Toulmin perceives to be the essential characteristics of substantive logic and formal logic.

Notwithstanding the fact that, as the following chart shows, substantive logic or rhetoric is in many ways distinct from formal logic or analytical reasoning, Toulmin recognizes the worth of both approaches because of their mutual interest in establishing a method for the criticism of arguments. Consequently, he makes a vital plea for a collaborative effort between the philosophers, mathematicians, and logicians who use the analytical method, and the lawyers, biological and social scientists, and physicians who rely on the topical and functional method. Thus the two ways of helping us make a rational exposition and criticism of arguments are to be viewed not as natural enemies but as complementary endeavors. Toulmin's call for a rapprochement between the formal and informal logicians, he feels, will go far toward achieving the goal of enhancing our understanding of the nature and potential of argument so that our "human interchanges" will be "substantively adequate."

FORMAL AND SUBSTANTIVE LOGIC CHART	
Formal Logic	**Substantive Logic**

Nature and Goals
  Analytical
    Rational Exposition and Criticism of
      Arguments
    Generation of Knowledge
Leading Advocates
  Plato   Frege
  Descartes   Russell
  Kant
Representative Users
  Mathematicians
  Astronomers
  Formal Logicians
Argumentation Field
  Invariant
  General
Level of Reliability
  Certainty
  Exact Statements
Type of Argumentative Technique
  Retrospective
	Nature and Goals
	  Topical and Functional
	    Rational Exposition and Criticism of Arguments
	    Generation of Knowledge
	Leading Advocates
	  Aristotle Hume
	  Hermagoras Toulmin
	  Cicero
	Representative Users
	  Biological Scientists
	  Social Scientists
	  Physicians
	  Lawyers
	Argumentation Field
	  Dependent
	  Situational
	  Specific
	Level of Reliability
	  Probability
	  Opinions
	Type of Argumentation Techique
	  Prospective

(Continued)

FORMAL AND SUBSTANTIVE LOGIC CHART *(Continued)*	
Formal Logic	**Substantive Logic**
Essential Vocabulary Elements	Essential Vocabulary Elements
Premise	Grounds
Conclusion	Claim
Entailment	Warrant
Necessity	Support
Principle of Inference	Qualifier
Episteme (Formal Mathematical Theory)	*Doxai* (Opinions)
Criteria for Evaluating Arguments	Criteria for Evaluating Arguments
Right/Wrong	Relevant/Irrelevant
Correct/Incorrect	Strong/Weak
Valid/Invalid	Reasonable/Unreasonable
Consistent/Contradictory	Sound/Unsound
Coherent/Incoherent	Appropriate/Inappropriate
	Solid/Groundless
	Warranted/Unwarranted

Logic and the Criticism of Arguments

Stephen Toulmin

I

My purpose in this lecture is to share a problem with you. It is a problem that I have found significant in all my own work, so I shall first present it in autobiographical terms. But it is one that also has a good deal of intellectual history behind it—it took me some twenty-five years to realize just how much—and I shall reconstruct some of this for you. (In thinking the lecture through, for reasons I will come back to later on, I was tempted to call it, "A Funny Thing happened to Logic on the way to the Academy.") If I am right about the solution of this problem, that has serious implications for the intellectual agenda of professional philosophy, and also for the goals and methods of general education. So I shall add some remarks about the ways in which (if I am right) we should be teaching students to approach questions about "logic," "method" or "argumenta-tion," call it what you will: that is, about the rational exposition and criticism of the arguments that face them in different fields of academic study and professional work.

First, a slice of life, to indicate how this problem became a problem for me personally. From the start, my curiosity drew me toward the subject of "rationality." Even when the central focus of my interests was still physics, what I most wanted to find out was, how it could ever be more "rational" to accept one overall scientific theory, cosmology or natural philosophy rather than another: If intelligent fish learned to do science, I asked myself, must they in the long run end up with the same body of ideas as human beings? (That was, of course, an epistemological not an ichthyological question!) So when, at the end of World War II, I returned to Cambridge as a philosophy graduate student, my central interest

"Logic and the Ciritcism of Arguments" by Dr. Stephen Toulmin. Reprinted by permission of the author.

was already what it has been ever since: viz., *rationality.*

Almost at once, I ran up against a difficulty. My questions were: How the reasons we rely on in different kinds of research, inquiry and decision *function,* and, How these *functional* differences affect the ways in which arguments and beliefs are to be judged in one field rather than another. (My Ph.D. thesis, *Reason in Ethics,* compared and contrasted our ways of reasoning about scientific and moral issues.) But the current fashion in both logic and analytical philosophy was, I found, to focus exclusively on *formal* aspects of argument: in particular, on questions about "validity," "necessity," and "entailment." As a result, I was aware of a discontinuity every time my reading or thinking crossed the frontier between science and philosophy; ideas that I could present in one set of terms to people in one academic subculture had to be wholly restated if they were to be acceptable on the other side of the border.

By now, of course, I realize that this discontinuity is the one that David Hume speaks about in his *Treatise of Human Nature,* when he tells us how modes of reasoning that remained convincing to him, so long as he stayed in his Study, appeared strained and ridiculous the moment he went off to the Club, had a good dinner, and sat down to play backgammon and chat with his friends. His deepest philosophical convictions proved unintelligible to those friends: worse, to lay ears, the philosophical terms he used in framing them sounded merely cynical.

So, my chief purpose in writing *The Uses of Argument,* in the late 1950s, was to relate traditional philosophical paradoxes to the standing contrast between "substantive" and "formal" aspects of reasoning and argument. By construing issues of substance or function in terms drawn from formal logic (I argued) philosophers had come to view all substantial arguments as involving "logical" gulfs, and so as justifying "rational" doubts. But, given only a little care in keeping formal and functional aspects of argument clear in our minds, we could steer safely past those paradoxes.

What happened? Peter Strawson brushed my book aside in *The Listener,* and a great hush fell upon my colleagues in England. After that, I assumed that the book would (in Hume's words) "fall stillborn from the press", so I was a little surprised when it continued to sell in worthwhile numbers: it took me some time to find out why. Worse, my graduate adviser at Cambridge, Richard Braithwaite, was deeply pained by the book, and barely spoke to me

for twenty years; while one of my colleagues at Leeds, Peter Alexander, described it as "Toulmin's *anti*-logic book." This last description took my breath away then, as it does today; but I can best explain the reasons why if I shift gears, and talk now about the history of this whole issue.

II

I start where we always have to start, in Classical Athens. The Greek words *logos* and *logikos* were then—and still are—general words, meaning "reason" and "reasonable." When the first philosophers framed their definition of "knowledge" as "a belief accompanied by a *logos,*" they meant only "a belief with good enough reason for it"; and the problem that presented itself for their consideration was, quite simply, "What kinds of things *counted as* good enough reasons to raise beliefs to the level of knowledge?"

The two most creative classical philosophers approached the problem of "good reasons"—as all others—with very different temperaments and interests; and their answers dealt with it on correspondingly different levels. Plato, as always, approached it with the theoretical interests of a mathematical physicist, and in the spirit of a utopian. In thinking about theoretical issues (he argued) we should not be content with pragmatic half measures, but should aim at an *ideal* solution; and, so long as we keep this goal in mind, we cannot be satisfied with anything less than "exact" knowledge. The astronomer aims at developing a mathematical model of the planetary system, to which the actual appearances and motions of heavenly bodies will approximate more or less exactly. . . . And Bully for him! At one and the same time, the resulting body of ideas is both an *intrinsically intelligible* conceptual system, and an *extrinsically relevant* account of the astronomical facts.

Aristotle approached the same problem with the scientific interests of a systematic biologist, and in the realistic spirit of a craftsman. Rather than demand a single kind of "reasons" in all areas of experience (he retorted) we should consider the specific demands of each current task; and, so long as we keep that requirement in mind, we shall not be led astray by the misleading models of astronomy and geometry. People working in different fields rightly use different methods to deal with their problems: the demands of theoretical astronomy, for instance, are no guide to the methods of argument appropriate to field zoology, political organization, or the moral problems of everyday life.

As a result, the two men had quite different ideas about "rational criticism." For Plato, learning to criticize arguments was the same in all fields: it demanded a grasp of mathematics. (The best preparation for Political Theory, in his eyes, was to learn formal geometry; as, today, some people suggest that all politicians should learn econometrics.) But, for Aristotle, the task was polymorphous: it demanded that the critic understand not only how problems and arguments in one field *resemble* those in another, but also how they *differ.*

Plato's line cut *between* different fields: Aristotle's cut *within* each such field. For Plato, theories set out in abstract mathematical form were always preferable to ones framed in everyday language. Colloquial language is a feeble instrument, and opinions couched in it are inherently unreliable: the modern terms for putting the same criticism of qualitative theories are "anecdotal" and "folklore."

Hence, Plato's insistence that only *episteme* qualifies as true knowledge, while all *doxai* are to be set aside as unreliable appearances. Hence, too, his scorn for the Sophists, whom he ridiculed for arguing about "mere opinions," about whose formal justification they were ignorant, and did not trouble to inquire. It did not matter to him that some *doxai* could be given stronger *substantive* support—nonmathematical reasons—than others: the Sophists showed their basic shallowness by failing to insist on mathematical reasons at all cost.

For Aristotle, by contrast, the practical issue was, How to choose *among* opinions: i.e., how to tell (say) biological, moral or political views that are supported by the relevant substantive reasons, from those that lack the appropriate foundations, and are therefore baseless. So, for Aristotle, the scope of "logic" (the theory and practice of rational criticism) could not be only *formal and universal:* what he called "analytics." It had also to include a *functional and specific* part, which was the subject matter of "topics." Keep that reference in mind, for we shall come back to it: just how long is it (we may ask) since British or American professional philosophers last took a serious look at Aristotle's *Topics?*

III

Properly understood, then, the two men's approaches were complementary, not in conflict. As always, Plato was utopian. Calling for the use of exact, mathematical theories, wherever available, is fine as a counsel of

perfection. But, as a counsel of practicality, we cannot let this mathematical ideal distract us from the immediate Aristotelian task of assembling the best rounded body of substantive opinions open to us.

As a matter of history, unfortunately, this point was not clearly understood. The idea grew up that Plato's ideal, formal goal provided a basis for criticizing actual, substantive views. So, the threefold distinction between formal mathematical theory *(episteme),* substantively well-founded opinions (good *doxai*) and baseless opinions (bad *doxai*), collapsed into a twofold division between, on the one hand, *episteme* (which is a Good Thing) and, on the other hand, *doxai* (which are all, equally, Bad Things).

Am I falling, here, into the language of that caricature of English History, *1066 and All That?* I do so without any apology. For at this point there developed a corrupt tradition, not merely within philosophy itself, but also in the history of philosophy; and the resulting caricature of the actual historical debate was as crude, in its own way, as anything the authors of *1066* could ever dream up. In the canonical account to which I myself was introduced, for instance, Ancient Philosophy went downhill after Aristotle, and there ensued the Dark Ages of Philosophy, which were finally enlightened only by the genius of René Descartes. As *1066* would have put it, Descartes was "a Good Thing." However, the improvement did not last: after Kant, the argument went downhill again, until the arrival of Gottlob Frege, who was also "a Good Thing."

At this point, let me interject two points. Firstly: both Descartes and Frege were unambiguously on the Platonizing side of the fence. Descartes never disguised his scorn for subjects that do not lend themselves to mathematical treatment. In his eyes, for example, history is no better than foreign travel: it may broaden the mind, but it cannot deepen the understanding. As for Frege, the aim of his *Foundations of Arithmetic* (he declared) was "to strip away the historical and psychological accretions" which had veiled "*number* in its pure form" from "the eye of the mind." So, the caricature of history with which I was presented was one in which all the major heroes—and I might add Henry Sidgwick, Bertrand Russell and G.E. Moore—shared a preference for the analytical examination of concepts and theories, and disregarded the topical heritage of Aristotle and his successors.

Secondly, one can in fact give an alternative historical account, which keeps a fairer balance between the two approaches. This second account eliminates the notion that serious philosophy somehow vanished during the Dark Ages. (That, as Peter Brown has taught us, is a virtue in itself; the "Dark Ages" are an invention of 18th-century rationalist ideologues like Edward Gibbon, who refused to take seriously ideas and periods they did not feel at home in.) But the second account also gives center stage to a series of figures whom philosophers of my kind never read, and may not even have heard of (e.g., Hermagoras) while it attributes fresh importance to others, whom we have heard of, but do not think of primarily as philosophers: for example, Cicero, Boethius and Adam Smith.

Mention Hermagoras of Temnos in an academic conversation today, and—chances are—the only response will be: "Who he?" Until recently, I confess, I was equally ignorant of the reasons why, for centuries, Hermagoras was seen as a major constructive figure in the debate about logic, rationality and practical reasoning. Here, let me just say this much; that, in the last two centuries B.C., no one did more than Hermagoras to build up a systematic analysis of substantive arguments along the lines sketched in Aristotle's *Topics, Nichomachean Ethics, Rhetoric,* and *Politics.* As one example: anyone who goes through Law School today is introduced to the idea that a "case" is defined in terms of its *elements*—the types of factors and considerations that have to be covered, if you are to specify a genuine "case" at all. This idea was first formulated in Hermagoras' analysis of argumentation; and, alongside the valid forms of the syllogism—"Barbara, Celarent. . ." and the rest— all students going through the Medieval Schools memorized a Latin hexameter which summarized Hermagoras' "elements":

Quis, quid, ubi, quibus auxiliis, cur, quomodo, quando? That is to say:
"Who did what? Where? With what help? Why? In what manner? And when?"

If Plato gave the Sophists a bad name, he left one group even worse off: the Rhetoricians. Sophists were condemned for wandering in a jungle of "mere opinions" unguided by any ideal of mathematical proof: Rhetoricians were despised for the graver sin of substituting the psychological arts of *persuasion* for the mathematical techniques of *proof.* And, since it was Hermagoras who founded the Rhetorical tradition, it is perhaps no surprise that right minded modern philosophers consistently ignore him.

Here again, however, we face the same old slander. Plato's attack on the Sophists equated all "mere opinions," and rejected them all as irremediable. So, honest Sophists—who used the best available methods of "dispute resolution" to arbitrate or mediate substantive controversies—were tarred with the same brush as Quacks and Hucksters who engaged in no such honest trade. Rhetoricians suffered the same fate. The honest ones, who attempted to use and to teach *sound* arguments were damned as mercilessly as the rabble rousing ones, who were only interested in dominating their hearers.

This, of course, obscures the fact that in all the serious professions—Law, Science, Medicine and the rest—procedures of *substantive* argumentation are passed on from Master to Pupil in ways that *show* the differences between "sound" procedures and "shaky" ones, "good" arguments and "bad" ones, "warranted" and "unwarranted" inferences, "solid" and "groundless" conclusions. If these things can be taught, then should we not also be able to spell out explicitly what they involve? (Every Law School teacher does just this, when he discusses the admissibility of evidence, initial presumptions, standards of proof and so on.) Plato's example thus blackened *all* "rhetoric" as dishonest, in the same way and for the same reasons that *all* substantive arguments and opinions were dismissed as misleading "sophistry": conversely, Aristotle's example indicated that *sound and honest* substantive arguments differ from plausible ranting quite as much as *either* of them differs from a Euclidean proof.

To digress a moment, let me offer a tidbit to lovers of the English language. Looking into the history of moral reasoning, I turned up the *Oxford English Dictionary* entry for the word, "casuistry." Now, you can always learn something new from the *O.E.D.!* Here, it points out that there is a family of words ending in "-ry" which refer to the *dishonest* use of techniques. We are all familiar with (e.g.) *wizardry, harlotry* and *Popery; sophistry* and *casuistry* refer to the dishonest use of the sophist's and casuist's arts, and thus are two more examples; *oratory* is a marginal case; while *chemistry* and *dentistry* definitely do not belong to the same family! (It is no accident that the first recorded use of the word "casuistry" is taken from Alexander Pope's 1725 *Essay on Man,* which was written after Pascal damned the Jesuit casuists in the *Provincial Letters,* and so gave *all* "case morality" the same kind of Bad Name that Plato had given *all* the Sophists and Rhetoricians.)

IV

Enough of ancient history: I am nearly ready to state my central thesis. But, first, let me briefly remind you what has happened to logic in the 20th century. When Gottlob Frege and Bertrand Russell embarked on their logical innovations at the turn of the century, they used the term "logic" to mean just what the term "analytics" had meant to Aristotle. Ever since Frege and Russell, therefore, philosophers have discussed logic, not as "the art and theory of rational criticism" (with both a formal part, or analytics, and a functional part, i.e. a "topics"), but as a field which is *purely formal.* For their purposes, the functional issues might as well not exist; or, if they do, they are certainly not part of the business of *logic.* As a result, logicians in the 20th century have drawn narrower boundaries around their subject than any of their predecessors: not just narrower than Aristotle, but also narrower than respected 18th and 19th-century figures like Adam Smith and William Whewell.

This new Platonizing approach to logic has even generated its own version of the libel on the Sophists. For fifty years and more, philosophers read Frege's arguments as expelling all but formal issues from their subject. Empiricism and positivism became "logical" empiricism and positivism: any attempt to broaden the agenda of philosophy was condemned for committing, either the *genetic* fallacy, of appealing to irrelevant historical facts, or else the fallacy of *psychologism,* of asking, "How do people reason?," instead of, "How is it logical for them to reason?" So, all the substantive questions which Rhetoricians and Sophists had asked—questions about the procedures lawyers, scientists and others *in fact* use in arguing—were relegated to the philosophical slagheaps of history and psychology.

By the time I wrote *The Uses of Argument,* in the mid 1950s, then, logic had been completely identified with "analytics," and Aristotle's *Topics* was totally forgotten: so much so that, when I wrote the book nobody realized that it bore the same relation to the *Topics* that Russell and Frege's work bore to traditional "analytic" and "syllogistic." Only in retrospect is it apparent that—even though sleepwalkingly—I had rediscovered the topics of the *Topics,* which were expelled from the agenda of philosophy in the years around 1900.

What I have just said is not precise. It is not wholly true that the "functional" aspects of practical argumentation were *totally* forgotten, and that *no-*body recognized my book for what it was. Given its reception by my British colleagues, the book went on selling surprisingly well; and it was only when I visited the United States that I found out who was buying it. Then, I met people from Departments of Speech and Communication up and down the country, who told me that they used it as a text on rhetoric and argumentation. So, the study of practical reasoning was kept alive after all; but this was done only *outside* the Departments of Philosophy, under the wing of Speech or English, or at Schools of Law.

V

Only during the last ten years have philosophers seriously begun to reclaim some parts at least of "practical reasoning," through the rise of the "informal logic" movement, based at the University of Windsor in Canada. Yet, up to now, this movement has been exposed to a serious professional handicap. In the eyes of the philosophical elite, its goals seem to be educational, not intellectual: it is viewed merely as devising soft options for weaker students—ways of teaching Intro Logic to those who lack the intellectual power to tackle (say) Irving Copi's introduction to *real* logic. But that impression is a sad misunderstanding. Behind the practical programs of the informal logic movement lie some definite doctrines and theses, which I must now attempt to state.

First, then: Philosophers can legitimately investigate all relevant aspects of the "rational criticism" of arguments. This means that whatever is needed in order to show how "well founded" opinions are distinguished from "baseless" ones, or "sound" and "reasonable" arguments from "shaky" or "dogmatic" ones is the proper concern of *philosophy,* and can not be banished into the *psychological* realm of "mere" rhetoric.

Secondly: The theory and techniques of rational criticism must be approached from two complementary directions, *formal* and *functional.* On the one hand, we can use the word "argument" for a string of propositions, which may be written on the blackboard or thought about in the abstract; and we can examine the formal relations—of consistency and inconsistency, entailment and contradiction—by which these propositions are (or are not) knitted into a logical fabric. (It would be foolish to deny that this "formal" aspect of rational criticism is one legitimate and well established part of the subject: all I want to do is show its proper role.) On the other hand, we can instead use the word "argument" for the stating of a substantively disputed position, followed by an exploring of possible consequences, an exchanging of evidence, and a sound (or unsound) resolving of the dispute. In our second sense an "argument" is not a *string of propositions* which may (or may not) be formally consistent: rather, it is a *human interchange* which is (or is not) substantively adequate.

The traditional jargon of "logical structure" tempts one to compare these two approaches to rational criticism with anatomy and physiology, respectively. Formal logic then tells us how the propositions in any argument "hang together" in an articulated intellectual skeleton: functional analysis tells us how it is that the elements of some arguments successfully "work" together—as legal or scientific or common sense arguments—while others "fail to work." This analogy is certainly picturesque, but it is not the most helpful one we can find, and I want here to offer you another comparison, which seems to me more illuminating.

Think of the parts which accountants and business planners, respectively, play in a commercial enterprise. Accountants put together a balance sheet of *last* year's activities, make sure it is complete and coherent, and tell us how we did at that time: planners survey, present and appraise possible directions for next year's activities, and aim to strike a reasonable balance between the business's needs, ambitions and hopes. On the one hand, a thriving business requires good accountants: nobody can formulate a sound policy for next year, who is unclear about how things worked out last year. A *formally* adequate past balance sheet is thus a precondition of *functionally* successful policies for the future. On the other hand, it is by now a truism that accountants make good servants but bad masters; or, to put the same point in American idiom, good advisers but bad executives. For, despite fashionable talk about "the bottom line," judgments about future policy never turn on matters of formal consistency alone: such judgments always involve, also, essential elements of "priority" and "decision."

The *critical* question now is:

Was the chosen policy arrived at in an open, timely and reasonable manner, after a full consideration of the strengths and weaknesses of other possible courses of action?

Clearly, one of the arts which Graduate Schools of Business try to teach is the art of meeting just this demand—that all decisions be open, timely and reasonable, and be based on a full consideration of available estimates about the likely outcomes of alternative policies.

And yet, I would now ask: Is this "critical question" just a matter for Business Schools to deal with? Surely, the issue can be broadened, by asking, for instance:

What general kinds *of considerations and arguments are relevant and reasonable, when arriving at (or defending) business policies, rather than (say) judicial rulings, or scientific explanations?*

The critical question about business policy is, thus, a specific example of the more general critical question about "practical reasoning," which Aristotle first framed in his *topical* works, and which was subsequently pursued by writers and teachers in the "rhetorical" tradition. To state this more general question as concisely as I can:

What are the forums of discussion, rules of procedure, techniques of argument, criteria of relevance, standards of proof, and practical implications, that serve the special purposes of the different enterprises within which "argumentation" and "reasoning together" go on?

Evidently, the differences between the proceedings involved in devising and carrying through a scientific experiment, putting a law case through the Courts, or formulating and arriving at a business decision—to mention only three "rational activities"—are more than *formal* differences. It is not just a matter of the one using "syllogisms," another (say) "enthymemes": instead, we need to understand the *substance* of debate in each area.

The relations between the formal and functional analyses of an argument thus resemble the relations between business planners and accountants: In criticism of actual arguments, the role of formal logic is "intellectual accountancy": the ability to use notions like consistency and contradiction is indispensable to the rational thinker, in the same way that the ability to read a balance sheet is indispensable to a business planner. But, once again, formal logicians can tell us if our *last* arguments were coherent, and can reconstruct them so as to show what assumptions they relied on; but deciding how to reason *next* time is by no means a formal matter. Scrutinizing and checking the formal relations between the propositions embodied in earlier arguments is a *retrospective* technique: the considerations it involves are formal ones, and are of the same kind whatever the topic of the particular argument. But understanding what kinds of arguments have a reliable, well-established place in science, law or business planning is a *prospective* art: there, the considerations that carry weight depend on the purposes and procedures of the particular enterprise.

VI

Do not *mishear* the point I am making. I am not just saying that *pro*spective arguments are "inductive" or "evaluative" rather than "deductive." That ho-hum formula is well intentioned, but misleading, for two reasons. In the first place, there is no virtue in limiting "deduction." In colloquial usage, *deduce* is synonymous with *infer*: it does not have a purely mathematical or formal meaning. So understood, the term "deductive inference" is tautologous. Any argument whatever can be set out in deductive form, if we only state its assumptions as extra premises; and this is often worth doing, since we may recognize what exactly those assumptions were, only after they are made explicit.

In the second place, resorting to such terms of logical art as "induction" and "inductive inference" tends to confuse several very different distinctions. To begin with, we can distinguish between arguments in substantive disciplines (e.g. physics) and arguments within pure mathematics (e.g. in geometry): this is important, when we ask what kinds of *backing* support the general warrants governing arguments of each kind. (Experimental proof is clearly relevant in physics, but not in the "purer" parts of mathematics.) But scientific and legal arguments can be, and are, set out in deductive form as often as arguments in pure geometry or set theory, so that cannot be the crucial issue.

Again, we can distinguish between arguments which appeal to established principles, without challenging them, and arguments which are designed to probe and refine those principles. But we can draw that distinction with equal force in all fields, so that is evidently not the issue. Nor is either of these distinctions (in turn) identical with the distinction from which we began, between retrospective and prospective arguments.

No, the very term "induction" was introduced to disguise the *functional* analysis of arguments as a

new kind of *formal* art. To reinforce that interpretation, recall how the logical empiricists insisted on separating the *justification* of scientific opinions (the topic for "inductive logic") from the *discovery* of those opinions: to them, "discovery meant the processes by which we *happen* on our opinions, and they relegated it to "psychology." This move simply repeated the Platonist rejection of all "mere opinions." Yet surely (we may reply) some ways of "happening on" substantive opinions are more *reasonable* than others, and so open to philosophical analysis? Not, apparently, for the logical empiricists: they damn all discovery alike with a single breath, as Plato damned all the opinions of the Sophists: "reasonable" procedures are to be told from ones that are "off the wall", only by the formal procedures of inductive logic. So much, then, for Nero Wolfe, who tries to put Sherlock Holmes right on "deduction" and "induction": like the social and behavioral scientists, he has read too many elementary logic texts, and gets himself into the same pickle that they do!

VII

It is time to state these points in more constructive terms. For this purpose, let me present three theses.

(1) The rational criticism of arguments involves two distinct arts: one "analytical," the other "topical."

> *The techniques of the first art are concerned with the question, "Am I arguing rightly (or impeccably)?—i.e. Am I avoiding formal inconsistencies, and other errors of intellectual accountancy?*
>
> *Those of the second are concerned with the question, "Are these the* right *(or relevant) arguments to use when dealing with this kind of problem, in this situation?"—i.e., Are they of a kind appropriate to the substantive demands of the problem and situation?*

The art of reasoning "rightly" is one concern of *formal logic,* with the help of which we recognize internal contradictions and similar formal errors. But the art of identifying and explaining the nature and mode of operation of "right" arguments is a field for which professional philosophers today no longer have a name. Historically, it was called by a dozen different names—among others, *topics, argumentation, rhetoric, organon,* and *method.* Today, this art is coming to be known as "informal" logic; but there are disadvantages to this *negative* name, which defines its scope only by what it is not, viz. "formal." To make its actual scope and significance clearer, I would for myself prefer a more positive name, such as *substantive* logic.

(2) The two arts quite properly employ distinct vocabularies. Far from these vocabularies having a significant overlap, it is well to keep them distinct; for, once again, the *arguments* to which they are addressed are not "arguments" in the same sense. The formal connections in a string of propositions are *strong or weak,* in the sense of "valid" or "invalid"; and a string of propositions is an "argument" in my first sense. The substantive support which an attorney or scientist gives a claim, by producing the particular grounds he does, in the forum and at the time he does, is *strong or weak,* in the sense of "sound" or "shaky"; and, by stating his case as he does, each man presents an "argument" in my second, human interaction sense.

Terms Used in the Language of Formal Logic
premise
conclusion
entailment
principle of inference
valid
invalid
necessary
contradictory

Terms Used in the Language of Substantive Logic
grounds
claim
support
sound
skaky
presumably
unfounded

There are just a few, very general terms that have a use in both these arts: for example, the term "fallacy." In thinking about these borderline issues, however, it becomes doubly prudent to keep in mind the differences between formal and substantive criticism. For instance, people writing introductory logic texts are sometimes tempted to equate the term "fallacious" with the term "invalid"; and this confuses the elementary student, by suggesting that fallacies are typically formal blunders, rather than (as they more often are) errors of substance. Scientific arguments may successfully use theoretical "models," just as legal arguments successfully use theoretical "interpretations." Yet, in both fields, arguments are also sometimes rejected, as appealing to "false analogies"; and, formally speaking, both the successful and the fallacious arguments are quite similar. What mark fallacious analogies off from fruitful models and theories, in practice, are matter of *substance:* e.g., the fact that the "theory" or "model" in question is *warranted* by deeper underlying principles, whereas by contrast the corresponding appeals to "mere analogy" are "unwarranted."

(3) The art of criticizing arguments on "topical" rather than "analytical" grounds is one in which (as Aristotle insisted from the outset) the central issues can be faced, and formulated, only if we address ourselves to *the nature of the case:* i.e., to the general demands of the problems currently under consideration, and the "forums" that are available for resolving them.

In Aristotelian usage, such issues are issues of *prudence.* In legal contexts, they overlap into *juris*prudence: there, they are concerned with the "standards of proof" required in judicial proceedings of different kinds, the "rules of evidence" relevant in different branches of law, and the demands of "due process" that govern the conduct of different sorts of cases. As at earlier stages in the field of rhetoric and practical reasoning, lawyers today continue to pay more explicit attention to their methods of arguing than professionals in many other fields; so they have much clearer ideas than (say) scientists or physicians about the substantive tests which must be satisfied, if legal arguments are to serve the goals of the legal enterprise.

Does this mean that the "topical" aspects of legal reasoning can be understood only by trained lawyers? The answer to that question is not entirely obvious. We might equally ask, Can the corresponding aspects of medical and scientific reasoning be understood only by trained physicians and scientists? Just so long as such issues are treated as extensions of formal logic, it can be argued that they are philosophical not professional; but, if we view them rather as matters of substance, it is less clear that philosophers can monopolize them. Indeed, there has been a lively debate between those philosophers of science such as Popper and Lakatos, who still insist on the right to lay down methodological "statute law" to working scientists, and those others, like Polanyi and myself, who see scientific methods of argumentation as requiring more of a "common law" analysis.

While some detailed points of method in both law and science may be too refined for any but professionals, the *general pattern* of reasoning in both fields is quite intelligible to lay people as well. Logicians and philosophers also have something of their own to contribute, to the extent that the substantive merits and defects of disciplinary reasoning is discussed (as in Aristotle's *Topics*) on a *comparative* basis. In what respects, for instance, do "theories" play the same kinds of part in law as in science? To what extent are appeals to authority admissible or fallacious in different fields of reasoning on the same occasions, and for the same reasons? And on what conditions can arguments about questions of "causation" in medicine be assimilated to those about "causality" in pure science?

None of those questions is "proper to" law or science or medicine taken alone: still, none of them can be answered by someone who has no knowledge whatever (however general) of how people in fact think, argue and resolve problems in those fields. In short, the topical criticism of legal, scientific and other technical arguments can become the substantive mode of inquiry it needs to be, only if the discussion of practical reasoning is made into a collaborative debate: one in which philosophers are prepared to listen to lawyers, scientists and others, instead of merely lecturing them! Parts of the resulting debate may be somewhat technical: e.g. statistical analyses of the design of experiments, or jurisprudential discussions of the minuter rules of evidence. But a common framework of analysis, at least, covers the whole territory of practical argumentation; and the outcome of such a collaborative analysis would do for us, in our own day, just the kinds of things that Aristotle, Hermagoras and the medieval rhetoricians aimed at in earlier times.

VIII

To close, let me speak briefly about the philosophical and educational implications of the positions for which I have been arguing here. First, let me say something about the current controversy over the *rationality* of scientific argument, between Karl Popper and Paul Feyerabend.

(1) I hinted earlier that, since the 17th century, a revival of the Platonist approach to argumentation has led professional philosophers to expel all the functional aspects of "rationality" from consideration; to equate "rationality" with "logicality"; and to look for *formal* criteria to judge the "rationality" of all arguments.

One glance at the Popper-Feyerabend dispute confirms this reading of the matter. Both men assume that the arguments by which scientists arrive at novel discoveries can be genuinely "rational," only if they satisfy certain formal conditions, at least of a weak enough kind. Otherwise, such discoveries will merely be the products of good fortune, chance, irrational speculation, or pure intuition. Popper, for his part, still assumes that we can state such formal conditions in advance; and that scientific knowledge can thus be elevated—however hypothetically and fallibly—to the status of *episteme:* only so can he be satisfied that the procedures of science are truly "rational."

Underlining the Platonist element in his position, Popper asserts that scientific knowledge is essentially concerned with a Third World of *eternal entities,* which are neither "physical objects," nor "psychological thoughts" in the scientists' heads. By contrast, Feyerabend believes that no such conditions can be found, still less imposed on the work of actual scientists; while Popper's "Third World" is for him a reactionary myth. But, instead of arguing that it was a mistake to look for such formal conditions of rationality, Feyerabend strikes a disillusioned pose, and concludes (in the spirit of Nietzsche) that science can make progress, only if scientists deliberately reject all method in favor of an irrational "scientific anarchism."

Here, Karl Popper once again plays the part of the Utopian: to be a scientist one must believe in the invisible Third World, and only a scientist who shares that belief is truly "rational." Paul Feyerabend defines a counterposition, but states it in the same terms: only, because (in his eyes) the Third World can have no practical relevance to the actual work of science, he calls on us to give up the idea that science is rational as a comfortable illusion. Both men take it for granted that we know what demands "rationality" makes of science, *in advance of* looking to see how the arguments of science function in actual practice. Neither of them has the patience to wait for a first-hand examination of "the nature of the case" to clarify our ideas about what kind of thing "scientific rationality" could in practice be. For both of them, Aristotle, Hermagoras and the rhetoricians wrote in vain.

(2) Finally, let me turn to the educational implications of my argument. Any revival of "substantive logic," "rhetoric," "practical reasoning," or "theory of argumentation" (call it what you will) requires both philosophers, and those whose work the philosophers reflect on—lawyers and physicians, scientists and critics—to "modify their present claims to full disciplinary autonomy. The substantive analysis of practical argumentation is worthwhile only if it is *collaborative,* with philosophers and practitioners working together to establish, firstly, how reasons function in all these different fields of work, secondly, what are the accepted procedures and forums for the resulting arguments and, lastly, what standards are available for judging the "success" and "failure" of work in one field or another.

The differences between the ways we interpret issues, in one field or another, are *ineliminable,* and also *functional.* They cannot be explained away by formal devices: e.g., by inventing separate formal systems of alethic, deontic, or epistemic logic for every purpose and field. Practical argumentation has both field invariant and field dependent features.

Some topical terms (e.g. "grounds" and "warrants") have a use in most fields of argument; more specialized terms (e.g. numerical "probability") are relevant only in very few fields. In between, a middle category of terms of topical analysis—"kind" and "degree," "fallacy" and "analogy," "cause" and "definition"—apply in varying ways as we move from one field to another. These are the notions which philosophers and practitioners can master fully only by pooling their efforts.

I do not wholly despair of this kind of collaboration; though I am not starry eyed about the prospects, either. It is manageable enough within an institution like the University of Chicago, which has an established network of interdepartmental committees devoted to multidisciplinary investigations. Still, my hope and fears for the subject are best symbolized by the contrast between two undergraduate colleges, both of which I know rather well. One college is committed to interdepartmental teaching; so, when the philosophers tried adapting the analysis set out in *The Uses of Argument,* so as to teach the criticism of reasoning alongside the techniques of formal logic, they met with no obstacles from the other departments. Quite the reverse: after a while, they even had students coming back to them, to report that they were still using the methods they had learned during that course, in writing essays and reports in their other academic subjects, also.

The other college is among the most distinguished colleges in New England. It was notable among those colleges for having long had a Department of Speech, which operated alongside the Philosophy Department without serious competition or friction. A few years ago, the Speech Department offered to make a greater contribution to the undergraduate curriculum, by expanding its courses on the criticism of reasoning; though, in this way, it risked trespassing onto the territory of the philosophers, who already had a high-powered Intro course on the elements of formal logic.

Was this not a God-sent opportunity for the departments to get together, and collaborate on a course covering *both* formal logic and substantive criticism in a uniquely comprehensive way? One might have thought so but what happened was quite different. Faced with financial stringencies, the philosophers argued that speech is not an academically serious subject; and, in the ensuing politics, the Department of Speech was *closed down!*

Chaim Perelman on Practical Reasoning

Remarkably close to the ideas on argument established by Toulmin are those articulated by Chaim Perelman, the Belgian philosopher whose major concern in the last few years has been rhetoric. Disturbed by his philosopher-colleagues' tendency to push aside approaches to knowledge that yield less reliable information than that produced by formal logic, Perelman reminds us that philosophers, in reality, function as rhetors. It is practical argument, not formal reasoning, he asserts, which is the required tool for disseminating ideas.

Most of Perelman's rhetorical writing emphasizes the distinction that must be drawn between practical and demonstrative reasoning. The former type, for example, does not deal with questions of "truth and falsehood." Perelman explains this claim, according to his friend and colleague Guy Haarscher, by noting that "in practical life, we can and must always give 'good reasons,' allowing us to persuade the others (and first to persuade ourselves) that a choice is preferable to another." But it must be remembered that "these good reasons have never the force and constraining character of a demonstration: they are more fragile, less absolute, more 'modest.' " As a result, "we are never absolutely sure of the validity of our choices, which means that we can *learn* by dialoguing with others."[1]

Much of what Perelman has to say on this subject is found in his *New Rhetoric: A Treatise on Argument,* which was co-authored with L. Olbrechts-Tyteca.[2] At first glance it would appear that Perelman is little more than a modern classicist who seems content to cite the works of Aristotle, Cicero, and Quintilian. That he relies on them freely there

can be no doubt. Aristotle is applauded for his psychological insights on the nature of various age groups and emotions, for his meaningful suggestions regarding persuasive strategies, and for recognizing that rhetoric is rooted in probability. Additionally, Perelman is one of the few authors in the contemporary period who has adapted Aristotelian theories on commonplaces and lines of argument. This seeming partiality for classical doctrines has led some recent scholars in communication to describe Perelman as a twentieth-century Aristotelian.

But Perelman, in our opinion, is far more than a classicist. In several very important respects he has departed significantly from ancient teachings. With Whately, he concludes that argumentation goes beyond the oral statement. Written documents may be as much a part of rhetoric as interpersonal communication or public address. Not only does Perelman broaden the scope of rhetoric and argumentation, he also introduces an innovative vocabulary that opens up fresh perspectives. These are but a few of the terms he uses which have gained wide circulation: universal audience, quasi-logical arguments, starting points, rule of justice, communion, presence, and dissociation of concepts.

A universal audience, according to Perelman, is that audience, either immediate or long range, which is comprised of rational men and women. These are the people who know how to judge and test the strength or weakness of an argument by applying the criterion of "experience." What the universal audience looks for in responding to a speaker is an "affirmation of that which corresponds to an objective fact, of that which constitutes a true and even necessary assertion."[3] When an advocate receives agreement from this audience, he has helped produce an adherence of minds concerning values. Thus he has successfully participated in rhetoric as a knowing process.

The concept of the universal audience, which is perhaps the most controversial and misunderstood idea advanced by Perelman, drew its inspiration from the writings of Aristotle, St. Thomas Aquinas, and Immanuel Kant. A point worth noting is the fact that it "is a construct of the speaker that stresses an ideal rather than a material reality, and is appropriate for a given historical milieu."[4] In keeping with Perelman's description of this claim, the following arguments may be offered:

1. The primary challenge facing the rhetor is to construct in his mind an ideal audience that, while not achieving complete reality, at least approaches it.
2. The arguer, in constructing an ideal audience, must regard himself as an incarnation of the audience.
3. (One should) include in the imaginary audience reflective persons who are able to transcend their particular biases, value systems, political and religious beliefs, and, to a certain extent, cultural heritage.[5]

An important implication of the idea of the universal audience is its potential for "the development of a rhetorical criticism model that features the significance of an artistic standard of evaluation which gives priority to universal values rather than to the criterion of effectiveness."[6]

Since the universal audience described by Perelman is a construct of the speaker that stresses an ideal rather than a material reality, it is difficult to find effective examples in which rhetors have developed arguments to appeal to such an audience. It is far more characteristic to speak to people as they are rather than address them as they are capable of becoming. There are, however, representative cases, both historical and contemporary, where a speaker achieved this high ideal. Socrates' speech in Plato's "Apology," for instance, is a compelling illustration of how the discourse presented at his trial was directed toward the universal audience. If Socrates' speech epitomizes the essence of philosophical dis-

course based on the notion of the universal audience, Senator John F. Kennedy's address to the Greater Houston Ministerial Association in 1960 teaches us how a political communicator can approach a similar level of rhetorical excellence when arguments utilizing universal values become the guiding force. Standing before a largely hostile and skeptical audience comprised of three hundred protestant ministers and three hundred other spectators, Kennedy started with the premise that both he and his listeners were to be incarnations of the universal audience. It was his purpose, therefore, to use this occasion as a means of generating new knowledge on the controversial issue of church and state. To do so, as we shall now note, he sought, to give the audience "better versions of themselves."

Kennedy's initial task was to summarize his career-long beliefs that the separation of church and state is a sacred political doctrine, and that religious tolerance is a fundamental right guaranteed by the Constitution. In the arguments that followed, Kennedy developed moving appeals consistent with Perelman's overall philosophy of rhetoric. Since Protestants, Catholics, and Jews, he asserted, fought and died side by side at the Alamo and in World War II, they should be accorded the same rights and privileges.

Kennedy next challenged his listeners to transcend their fears and prejudices by using reasons that meet the critical tests of soundness and relevance:

> *I ask you tonight to follow in that tradition, to judge me on the basis of fourteen years in Congress—on my declared stands against an ambassador to the Vatican, against unconstitutional aid to parochial schools, and against any boycott of the public schools (which I attended myself—instead of judging me on the basis of these pamphlets and publications we have all seen that carefully select quotations out of context from the statements of Catholic Church leaders, usually in other countries . . . and rarely relevant to any situations here. . . .*[7]

Near the end of the speech, Kennedy, adhering to moral values reminiscent of those expressed by Socrates, affirmed his belief that effectiveness must be subservient to responsibility. "I do not intend to

A universal audience, according to Perelman, is that audience, either immediate or long range, which is comprised of rational men and women.

disavow either my views or my church in order to win this election. If I should lose on real issues, I shall return to my seat in the Senate, satisfied that I tried my best and was fairly judged." This appeal to Perelman's notion of the universal audience demonstrates that a political speaker, like his counterpart in philosophy, has the capacity to use an elevated discourse that speaks to our better nature.

The use of the phrase "quasi-logical" is not an example of accidental or deliberate jargon. To Perelman, these words suggest the very nature of practical argument as contrasted with formal reasoning. Quasi-logical arguments imply a non-formal structure and a special method of reasoning associated with "reality." What makes Perelman's discussion of these ideas so intriguing is not the fact that he necessarily covers new ground, but rather the terminology and explanation employed. He is perhaps the first author to label specific types of argument with such suggestive terms as "reciprocity," "transitivity," "sacrifice," "waste," and "direction." Moreover, he gives a new perspective to ethos by analyzing the relationship between "the person and his acts," and between "model and anti-model."

> A student of the rhetoric of Western thought (therefore) may assume the role of advocate by attempting to dissociate rhetoric from appearance, and then associate it with reality.

Three other notions developed by Perelman are also integral concepts in his rhetorical system. The first he calls "the starting point of argument." There is little chance, he states, for an advocate to promote an adherence of minds unless the listeners are in agreement at the outset with respect to facts, truths, presumptions, and values. The second notion—designated "the rule of justice"—"requires giving identical treatment to beings or situations of the same kind."[8] In Perelman's own view, the third idea we wish to stress here—dissociation of concepts—may be the most important single principle in his theory of argumentation. This dissociation process or break-

ing of connecting links "is always prompted by the desire to remove an incompatibility arising out of the confrontation of one proposition with others, whether one is dealing with norms, facts, or truths."[9] Let us assume, for example, that there is a philosophical pair which may be diagrammed as follows:

$$\frac{\text{appearance}}{\text{reality}}$$

You may recall that the sophists had a tendency to identify rhetoric with appearance rather than with reality. A student of the rhetoric of Western thought, therefore, may assume the role of advocate by attempting to dissociate rhetoric from appearance, and then associate it with reality.

In another instance a political leader may wish to separate himself from the office he holds in order to preserve the reality inherent in the office. In the famous encounter between President Harry Truman and General Douglas MacArthur during the Korean War, Truman advised MacArthur that he did not care what the general thought of the president as a man, but he demanded that the office he occupied be honored. An embattled Richard Nixon sought to do the same thing in the midst of the Watergate controversy.

The foregoing discussion is but a brief overview of some of the leading concepts appearing in *The New Rhetoric*. Hopefully, it will point out Perelman's belief that the use of argument for the purpose of knowing is a sound method for advancing understanding. Since it is difficult to abstract a particular portion of *The New Rhetoric* and still maintain the thrust of the work, we are including the following essay which pulls together all of the salient features of Perelman's theories. To read it in its entirety is to gain a thorough grasp of Perelman's system of rhetorical thought.

Notes

1. Guy Haarscher, "Preface," in Mieczyslaw Maneli, *Perelman's New Rhetoric as Philosophy and Methodology for the Next Century* (Dordrecht, Boston, and London: Kluwer Academic Publishers, 1994), ix–x.

2. Ch. Perelman and L. Olbrechts-Tyteca, *The New Rhetoric: A Treatise on Argumentation* (Notre Dame: University of Notre Dame Press, 1969).

3. *Ibid.,* pp. 31–32.

4. James L. Golden, "The Universal Audience Revisited," in Golden and Joseph J. Pilotta, eds., *Practical Reasoning in Human Affairs* (Dordrecht. D. Reidel Publishing Co., 1986), p. 289.

5. *Ibid.,* pp. 290–91.

6. *Ibid.,* p. 292.

7. The text of the speech appears in Theodore H. White, *The Making of the President 1960* (New York. Atheneum Publishers, 1961), pp. 391–93.

8. *Practical Reasoning,* p. 218.

9. *Ibid.,* p. 413.

The New Rhetoric: A Theory of Practical Reasoning

Chaim Perelman

The Loss of a Humanistic Tradition

The last two years of secondary education in Belgium used to be called traditionally "Poetry" and "Rhetoric." I still remember that, over forty years ago, I had to study the "Elements of Rhetoric" for a final high-school examination, and I learned more or less by heart the contents of a small manual, the first part of which concerned the syllogism and the second the figures of style. Later, in the university, I took a course of logic which covered, among other things, the analysis of the syllogism. I then learned that logic is a formal discipline that studies the structure of hypothetico-deductive reasoning. Since then I have often wondered what link a professor of rhetoric could possibly discover between the syllogism and the figures of style with their exotic names that are so difficult to remember.

Lack of clarity concerning the idea of rhetoric is also apparent in the article on the subject in the *Encyclopaedia Britannica,* where rhetoric is defined as "the use of language as an art based on a body of organized knowledge." But what does this mean? The technique or art of language in general, or only that of literary prose as distinct from poetry? Must rhetoric be conceived of as the art of oratory—that is, as the art of public speaking? The author of the article notes that for Aristotle rhetoric is the art of persuasion. We are further told that the orator's purpose, according to Cicero's definition, is to instruct, to move, and to please. Quintilian sums up this view in his lapidary style as *ars bene dicendi,* the art of speaking well. This phrase can refer either to the efficacy, or the morality, or the beauty of a speech, this ambiguity being both an advantage and a drawback.

For those of us who have been educated in a time when rhetoric has ceased to play an essential part in education, the idea of rhetoric has been definitely associated with the "flowers of rhetoric"—the name used for the figures of style with their learned and incomprehensible names. This tradition is represented by two French authors, Cesar Chesneau, sieur Dumarsais, and Pierre Fontanier, who provided the basic texts for teaching what was taken for rhetoric in the eighteenth and nineteenth centuries. The work of Dumarsais, which first appeared in 1730 and enjoyed an enormous success, is entitled *Concerning tropes or the different ways in which one word* can *be taken in a language.*[1] Fontanier's book, reprinted in 1968 under the title *The figures of discourse,* unites in one volume two works, which appeared respectively in 1821 and 1827, under the titles *A classical manual for the study of tropes* and *Figures other than tropes.*[2]

These works are the outcome of what might be called the stylistic tradition of rhetoric, which was started by Omer Talon, the friend of Petrus Ramus, in his two books on rhetoric published in 1572. The extraordinary influence of Ramus hindered, and to a

Translated from the French by E. Griffin-Collart and O. Bird. Reprinted from *Great Ideas Today* (Chicago: Encyclopedia Britannica, Inc., 1970). Reprinted with permission of the editors of *Great Ideas Today.*

large extent actually destroyed, the tradition of classical rhetoric that had been developed over the course of twenty centuries and with which are associated the names of such writers as Aristotle, Cicero, Quintilian, and St. Augustine.

For the ancients, rhetoric was the theory of persuasive discourse and included five parts: *inventio, dispositio, elocutio, memoria,* and *actio.* The first part dealt with the art of finding the materials of discourse, especially arguments, by using common or specific *loci*—the *topoi* studied in works which, following Aristotle's example, were called *Topics.*[3] The second part gave advice on the purposive arrangement or order of discourse, the *method,* as the Renaissance humanists called it. The third part dealt mainly with style, the choice of terms and phrases; the fourth with the art of memorizing the speech; while the fifth concerned the art of delivering it.

Ramus also worked for the reform of logic and dialectic along the lines laid down by Rodolphus Agricola in his *De inventione dialectica* (1479) and by the humanists who followed him in seeking to break away from scholastic formalism by restoring the union of eloquence and philosophy advocated by Cicero. This reform consisted essentially in rejecting the classical opposition between science and opinion that had led Aristotle to draw a distinction between analytical and dialectical reasoning—the former dealing with necessary reasonings, the latter with probable ones. Analytical reasoning is the concern of Aristotle's *Analytics,*[4] dialectical reasoning that of the *Topics, On Sophistical Refutations,* and the *Rhetoric.*[5]

Against this distinction, this is what Ramus has to say in his *Dialectic:*

> *Aristotle, or more precisely the exponents of Aristotle's theories, thought that there are two arts of discussion and reasoning, one applying to science and called Logic, the other dealing with opinion and called Dialectic. In this—with all due respect to such great masters—they were greatly mistaken. Indeed these two names, Dialectic and Logic, generally mean the very same thing, like the words* dialegesthai *and* logizesthai *from which they are derived and descended, that is, dispute or reason. . . . Furthermore, although things known are either necessary and scientific, or contingent and a matter of opinion, just as our sight can perceive all colors, both unchanging and change-*

> *able, in the same way the art of knowing, that is Dialectic or Logic, is one and the same doctrine of reasoning well about anything whatsoever. . . .*[6]

As a result of this rejection, Ramus unites in his *Dialectic* what Aristotle had separated. He divides his work into two parts, one concerning invention, the other judgment. Further, he includes in dialectic parts that were formerly regarded as belonging to rhetoric the theory of invention or *loci* and that of disposition, called *method.* Memory is considered as merely a reflection of these first two parts, and rhetoric—the "art of speaking well," of "eloquent and ornate language"—includes the study of tropes, of figures of style, and of oratorical delivery, all of which are considered as of lesser importance.

Thus was born the tradition of modern rhetoric, better called stylistic, as the study of techniques of unusual expression. For Fontanier, as we have seen, rhetoric is reduced to the study of figures of style, which he defines as "the more or less remarkable traits and forms, the phrases with a more or less happy turn, by which the expression of ideas, thoughts, and feelings removes the discourse more or less far away from what would have been its simple, common expression."[7]

Rhetoric, on this conception, is essentially an art of expression and more especially, of literary conventionalized expression; it is an art of style. So it is still regarded by Jean Paulban in his book *Les fleurs de Tarbes ou la terreur dans les lettres* (1941, but published first as articles in 1936).

The same view of rhetoric was taken in Italy during the Renaissance, despite the success of humanism. Inspired by the Ciceronian ideal of the union of philosophy with eloquence, humanists such as Lorenzo Valla sought to unite dialectic and rhetoric. But they gave definite primacy to rhetoric, thus expressing their revolt against scholastic formalism.

This humanistic tradition continued for over a century and finally produced in the *De principiis* by Mario Nizolio (1553) its most significant work from a philosophical point of view. Less than ten years later, however, in 1562, Francesco Patrizi published in his *Rhetoric* the most violent attack upon this discipline, to which he denied any philosophical interest whatsoever. Giambattista Vico's reaction came late and produced no immediate result. Rhetoric became a wholly formal discipline—any living ideas that it contained being included in Aesthetics.

Germany is one country where classical rhetoric has continued to be carefully studied, especially by scholars such as Friedrich Blass, Wilhelm Kroll, and Friedrich Solmsen, who devoted most of their lives to this study. Yet, even so, rhetoric has been regarded only as the theory of literary prose. Heinrich Lausberg has produced a most remarkable work which is the best tool in existence for the study of rhetorical terminology and the structure of discourse, and yet in the author's own eyes it is only a contribution to the study of literary language and tradition.[8]

The old tradition of rhetoric has been kept longest in Great Britain—it is still very much alive among Scots jurists—thanks to the importance of psychology in the empiricism of Bacon, Locke, and Hume, and to the influence of the Scottish philosophy of common sense. This tradition, in which the theory of invention is reduced to a minimum and interest is focused on the persuasive aspect of discourse, is represented by such original works as George Campbell's *The Philosophy of Rhetoric* (1776) and Richard Whately's *Elements of Rhetoric* (1828). In this work, Whately, who was a logician, deals with argumentative composition in general and the art of establishing the truth of a proposition so as to convince others, rhetoric being reduced to "a purely managerial or supervisory science."[9] His disciple, the future Cardinal John Henry Newman, applied Whately's ideas to the problems of faith in his *Grammar of Assent* (1870). This outlook still consists in seeing in rhetoric only a theory of expression. It was the view adopted by Ivor Armstrong Richards in his *Principles of Literary Criticism* (published in 1924) and in his *Philosophy of Rhetoric* (1936).

While in Europe rhetoric has been reduced to stylistics and literary criticism, becoming merely a part of the study of literature insofar as it was taught at all, in the United States the appearance of a speech profession brought about a unique development.

Samuel Silas Curry, in a book entitled *The Province of Expression* (1891), was the first to emphasize spoken discourse and its delivery, rather than the composition of literary prose, and to claim autonomy for speech as opposed to written composition. "Expression," as he understood it, did not mean the way in which ideas and feelings are expressed in a literary form, but instead the manner in which they are communicated by means of an art of "delivery." Concern for this element, apparently one of lesser importance, clearly reveals a renewed interest in the audience, and this interest helped to promote the creation of a new "speech profession," separate from the teaching of English and of English literature. Under the influence of William James, James Albert Winans published a volume entitled *Public Speaking* (1915) that firmly established a union between professors of speech and those of psychology. With the cooperation of specialists in ancient and medieval rhetoric, such as Charles S. Baldwin, Harry Caplan, Lane Cooper, Everett Lee Hunt, and Richard McKeon, the whole tradition of classical rhetoric has been retraced. This study has been continued and further developed in the works of Wilbur Samuel Howell, Donald C. Bryant, Karl R. Wallace, Walter J. Ong, Lloyd F. Bitzer, Douglas Ehninger, and Marie K. Hochmuth. The work of these scholars—the titles of which can be found in the Bibliography that has been regularly published by the *Quarterly Journal of Speech* since 1915—constitutes a unique achievement which is as yet too little known outside the United States.[10]

> There is nothing of philosophical interest in a rhetoric that has turned into an art of expression, whether literary or verbal.

AN ORNAMENTAL OR A PRACTICAL ART?

There is nothing of philosophical interest in a rhetoric that has turned into an art of expression, whether literary or verbal.[11] Hence it is not surprising that the term is missing entirely from both Andre Lalande's *Vocabulaire technique et critique de la philosophic* and the recent American *Encyclopedia of Philosophy* (1967). In the Western tradition, "Rhetoric" has frequently been identified with verbalism and an empty, unnatural, stilted mode of expression. Rhetoric then becomes the symbol of the most outdated elements in the education of the old regime, the elements that were the most formal, most useless and most opposed to the needs of an equalitarian, progressive democracy.

This view of rhetoric as declamation—ostentatious and artificial discourse—is not a new one. The same view was taken of the rhetoric of the Roman Empire. Once serious matters, both political and judiciary, had been withdrawn from its influence, rhetoric became perforce limited to school exercises, to set speeches treating either a theme of the past or an imaginary situation, but, in any case, one without any real bearing. Serious people, especially the Stoics, made fun of it. Thus Epictetus declares: "But this faculty of speaking and of ornamenting words, if there is indeed any such peculiar faculty, what else does it do, when there happens to be discourse about a thing, than to ornament the words and arrange them as hairdressers do the hair?"[12]

Aristotle would have disagreed with this conception of rhetoric as an ornamental art bearing the same relation to prose as poetics does to verse. For Aristotle, rhetoric is a practical discipline that aims, not at producing a work of art, but at exerting through speech a persuasive action on an audience. Unfortunately, however, those responsible for the confusion between the two have been able to appeal to Aristotle's own authority because of the misleading analysis he gave of the epideictic or ceremonial form of oratory.

In his *Rhetoric* Aristotle distinguishes three genres of oratory: deliberative, forensic, and ceremonial. "Political speaking," he writes, "urges us either to do or not to do something: one of these two courses is always taken by private counsellors, as well as by men who address public assemblies. Forensic speaking either attacks or defends somebody: one or other of these two things must always be done by the parties in a case. The ceremonial oratory of display either praises or censures somebody." But whereas the audience is supposed to act as a judge and make a decision concerning either the future (deliberative genre) or the past (forensic genre), in the case of an epideictic discourse the task of the audience consists in judging, not about the matter of discourse, but about the orator's skill.[13] In political and forensic discourse the subject of the discourse is itself under discussion, and the orator aims at persuading the audience to take part in deciding the matter, but in epideictic discourse the subject—such as, for example, the praise of soldiers who have died for their country—is not at all a matter of debate. Such set speeches were often delivered before large assemblies, as at the Olympic Games, where competition between orators provided a welcome complement to the athletic contests. On such occasions, the only decision that the audience was called upon to make concerned the talent of the orator, by awarding the crown to the victor.

One might well ask how an oratorical genre can be defined by its literary imitation. We know that Cicero, after having lost the suit, rewrote his *Pro Milone* and published it as a literary work. He hoped that by artistically improving the speech, which had failed to convince Milo's judges, he might gain the approbation of lovers of literature. Are those who read this speech long after its practical bearing has disappeared any more than spectators? In that case, all discourses automatically become literature once they cease to exert a persuasive effect, and there is no particular reason to distinguish different genres of oratory. Yet it can be maintained, on the contrary, that the epideictic genre is not only important but essential from an educational point of view, since it too has an effective and distinctive part to play—that, namely, of bringing about a consensus in the minds of the audience regarding the values that are celebrated in the speech.

The moralists rightly satirize the view of epideictic oratory as spectacle. La Bruyère writes derisively of those who "are so deeply moved and touched by Theodorus's sermon that they resolve in their hearts that it is even more beautiful than the last one he preached." And Bossuet, fearful lest the real point of a sermon be missed, exclaims: "You should now be convinced that preachers of the Gospel do not ascend into pulpits to utter empty speeches to be listened to for amusement."[14]

Bossuet here is following St. Augustine's precepts concerning sacred discourse as set forth in the fourth book of his work *On Christian Doctrine*. The orator is not content if his listener merely accepts the truth of his words and praises his eloquence, because he wants his full assent:

If the truths taught are such that to believe or to know them is enough, to give one's assent implies nothing more than to confess that they are true. When, however, the truth taught is one that must be carried into practice, and that is taught for the very purpose of being practised, it is useless to be persuaded of the truth of what is said, if it be not so learnt as to be practised. The eloquent divine, then, when he is urging a practical truth, must not only teach so as to give instruction, and please so as to keep up the attention, but he must also sway the mind so as to subdue the will.

The listener will be persuaded, Augustine also claims,

> *if he be drawn by your promises, and awed by your threats; if he reject what you condemn, and embrace what you commend; if he grieve when you heap up objects for grief, and rejoice when you point out an object for joy; if he pity those whom you present to him as objects of pity, and shrink from those whom you set before him as men to be feared and shunned.*[15]

The orator's aim in the epideictic genre is not just to gain a passive adherence from his audience but to provoke the action wished for or, at least, to awaken a disposition so to act. This is achieved by forming a community of minds, which Kenneth Burke, who is well aware of the importance of this genre, calls *identification*. As he writes, rhetoric "is rooted in an essential function of language itself, a function that is wholly realistic and is continually born anew; the use of language as a symbolic means of inducing cooperation in beings that by nature respond to symbols."[16] In fact, any persuasive discourse seeks to have an effect on an audience, although the audience may consist of only one person and the discourse be an inward deliberation.

The distinction of the different genres of oratory is highly artificial, as the study of a speech shows. Mark Antony's famous speech in Shakespeare's *Julius Caesar* opens with a funeral eulogy,[17] a typical case of epideictic discourse, and ends by provoking a riot that is clearly political. Its goal is to intensify an adherence to values, to create a disposition to act, and finally to bring people to act. Seen in such perspective, rhetoric becomes a subject of great philosophical interest.

THINKING ABOUT VALUES

In 1945, when I published my first study of justice,[18] I was completely ignorant of the importance of rhetoric. This study, undertaken in the spirit of logical empiricism, succeeded in showing that *formal justice* is a principle of action, according to which beings of one and the same essential category must be treated in the same way.[19] The application of this principle to actual situations, however, requires criteria to indicate which categories are relevant and how their members should be treated, and such decisions involve a recourse to judgments of value. But on posi-

tive methods I could not see how such judgments could have any foundation or justification. Indeed, as I entirely accepted the principle that one cannot draw an "ought" from an "is"—a judgment of value from a judgment of fact—I was led inevitably to the conclusion that if justice consists in the systematic implementation of certain value judgments, it does not rest on any rational foundation: "As for the value that is the foundation of the nonnative system, we cannot subject it to any rational criterion: it is utterly arbitrary and logically indeterminate. . . . The idea of value is, in effect, incompatible both with formal necessity and with experiential universality. There is no value which is not logically arbitrary."[20]

I was deeply dissatisfied with this conclusion, however interesting the analysis, since the philosophical inquiry, carried on within the limits of logical empiricism, could not provide an ideal of practical reason, that is, the establishment of rules and models for reasonable action. By admitting the soundness of Hume's analysis, I found myself in a situation similar to Kant's. If Hume is right in maintaining that empiricism cannot provide a basis for either science or morals, must we not then look to other than empirical methods to justify them? Similarly, if experience and calculation, combined according to the precepts of logical empiricism, leave no place for practical reason and do not enable us to justify our decisions and choices, must we not seek other techniques of reasoning for that purpose? In other words, is there a logic of value judgments that makes it possible for us to reason about values instead of making them depend solely on irrational choices, based on interest, passion, prejudice, and myth? Recent history has shown abundantly the sad excesses to which such an attitude can lead.

Critical investigation of the philosophical literature yielded no satisfactory results. The French logician Edmond Goblot, in his work *La logique des jugements de valeur*,[21] restricted his analysis to derived or instrumental value judgments, that is, to those judgments that use values as a means to already accepted ends, or as obstacles to their attainment. The ends themselves, however, could not be subjected to deliberation unless they were transformed into instrumental values, but such a transformation only pushes further hack the problem of ultimate ends.

We thus seem to be faced with two extreme attitudes, neither of which is acceptable: subjectivism, which, as far as values are concerned, leads to skepticism for lack of an intersubjective criterion; or an absolutism founded on intuitionism. In the latter case, judgments of value are assimilated to judgments of a reality that is *sui generis*. In other words, must we choose between A.J. Ayer's view in *Language, Truth, and Logic* and G.E. Moore's view in *Principia Ethica?* Both seem to give a distorted notion of the actual process of deliberation that leads to decision making in practical fields such as politics, law, and morals.

Then too, I agreed with the criticisms made by various types of existentialism against both positivist empiricism and rationalistic idealism, but I could find no satisfaction in their justification of action by purely subjective projects or commitments.

I could see but one way to solve the dilemma to which most currents of contemporary philosophy had led. Instead of working out *a priori* possible structures for a logic of value judgments, might we not do better to follow the method adopted by the German logician Gottlob Frege, who, to cast new light on logic, decided to analyze the reasoning used by mathematicians? Could we not undertake, in the same way, an extensive inquiry into the manner in which the most diverse authors in all fields do in fact reason about values? By analyzing political discourse, the reasons given by judges, the reasoning of moralists, the daily discussions carried on in deliberating about making a choice or reaching a decision or nominating a person, we might be able to trace the actual logic of value judgments which seems continually to elude the grasp of specialists in the theory of knowledge.

For almost ten years Mme L. Olbrechts-Tyteca and I conducted such an inquiry and analysis. We obtained results that neither of us had ever expected. Without either knowing or wishing it, we had rediscovered a part of Aristotelian logic that had been long forgotten or, at any rate, ignored and despised. It was the part dealing with dialectical reasoning, as distinguished from demonstrative reasoning—called by Aristotle *analytics*—which is analyzed at length in the *Rhetoric, Topics,* and *On Sophistical Refutations.* We called this new, or revived, branch of study, devoted to the analysis of informal reasoning, *The New Rhetoric.*[22]

> The new rhetoric is a theory of argumentation.

ARGUMENTATION AND DEMONSTRATION

The new rhetoric is a theory of argumentation. But the specific part that is played by argumentation could not be fully understood until the modern theory of demonstration—to which it is complementary—had been developed. In its contemporary form, demonstration is a calculation made in accordance with rules that have been laid down beforehand. No recourse is allowed to evidence or to any intuition other than that of the senses. The only requirement is the ability to distinguish signs and to perform operations according to rules. A demonstration is regarded as correct or incorrect according as it conforms, or fails to conform, to the rules. A conclusion is held to be demonstrated if it can be reached by means of a series of correct operations starting from premises accepted as axioms. Whether these axioms be considered as evident, necessary, true, or hypothetical, the relation between them and the demonstrated theorems remains unchanged. To pass from a correct inference to the truth or to the computable probability of the conclusion, one must admit both the truth of the premises and the coherence of the axiomatic system.

The acceptance of these assumptions compels us to abandon pure formalism and to accept certain conventions and to admit the reality of certain models or structures. According to the classical theory of demonstration, which is rejected by formalism, the validity of the deductive method was guaranteed by intuition or evidence—by the natural light of reason. But if we reject such a foundation, we are not compelled to accept formalism. It is still insufficient, since we need good reasons to accept the premises from which we start, and these reasons can be good only for a mind capable of judging them. However, once we have accepted the framework of a formal system and know that it is free from ambiguity, then the demonstrations that can be made within it are compelling and impersonal; in fact, their validity is capable of being controlled mechanically. It is this specific character of formal demonstration that distinguishes it from dialectical reasoning founded on opinion and concerned with contingent realities. Ramus failed to see this distinction and confused the two by using a faulty analogy with the sight of moving and unmoving colors.[23] It is sometimes possible, by resorting to prior arrangements and conventions, to transform an argument into a demonstration of a more or less probablistic character. It remains true, nonetheless, that we must distinguish carefully between the two types of reasoning if we want to understand properly how they are related.

An argumentation is always addressed by a person called the orator—whether by speech or in writing—to an audience of listeners or readers. It aims at obtaining or reinforcing the adherence of the audience to some thesis, assent to which is hoped for. The new rhetoric, like the old, seeks to persuade or convince, to obtain an adherence which may be *theoretical* to start with, although it may eventually, be manifested through a disposition to act, or *practical,* as provoking either immediate action, the making of a decision, or a commitment to act.

Thus argumentation, unlike demonstration, presupposes a meeting of minds: the will on the part of the orator to persuade and not to compel or command, and a disposition on the part of the audience to listen. Such mutual goodwill must not only be general but must also apply to the particular question at issue; it must not be forgotten that all argumentation aims somehow at modifying an existing state of affairs. This is why every society possesses institutions to further discussion between competent persons and to prevent others. Not everybody can start debating about anything whatever, no matter where. To be a man people listen to is a precious quality and is still more necessary as a preliminary condition for an efficacious argumentation.

In some cases there are detailed rules drawn up for establishing this contact before a question can be debated. The main purpose of procedure in civil and criminal law is to ensure a balanced unfolding of the judicial debate. Even in matters where there are no explicit rules for discussion, there are still customs and habits that cannot be disregarded without sufficient reason.

Argumentation also presupposes a means of communicating, a common language. The use of it in a given situation, however, may admit of variation according to the position of the interlocutors. Sometimes only certain persons are entitled to ask questions or to conduct the debate.

> argumentation, unlike demonstration, presupposes a meeting of minds: the will on the part of the orator to persuade and not to compel or command, and a disposition on the part of the audience to listen.

From these specifications it is apparent that the new rhetoric cannot tolerate the more or less conventional, and even arbitrary, limitations traditionally imposed upon classical rhetoric. For Aristotle, the similarity between rhetoric and dialectic was all-important.[24] According to him, they differ only in that dialectic provides us with techniques of discussion for a common search for truth, while rhetoric teaches how to conduct a debate in which various points of view are expressed and the decision is left up to the audience. This distinction shows why dialectic has been traditionally considered as a serious matter by philosophers, whereas rhetoric has been regarded with contempt. Truth, it was held, presided over a dialectical discussion, and the interlocutors had to reach agreement about it by themselves, whereas rhetoric taught only how to present a point of view—that is to say, a partial aspect of the question—and the decision of the issue was left up to a third person.[25]

It should be noted, however, that for Plato dialectic alone does not attain to metaphysical truth. The latter requires an intuition for which dialectic can only pave the way by eliminating untenable hypotheses.[26] However, truth is the keynote for dialectic, which seeks to get as close to the truth as possible through the discursive method. The rhetorician, on the other hand, is described as trying to outdo his rivals in debate, and, if his judges are gross and ignorant, the triumph of the orator who shows the greatest skill in flattery will by no means always be the victory of the best cause. Plato emphasizes this point strongly in the *Gorgias,* where he shows that the demagogue, to achieve victory, will not hesitate to use techniques unworthy of a philosopher. This criticism gains justification from Aristotle's observation, based evidently on Athenian practice, that it belongs to rhetoric "to deal with such matters as we deliberate upon without arts or systems to guide us, in the hearing of persons who cannot take in at a glance a complicated argument, or follow a long chain of reasoning."[27]

For the new rhetoric, however, argumentation has a wider scope as nonformal reasoning that aims at obtaining or reinforcing the adherence of an audience. It is manifest in discussion as well as in debate, and it matters not whether the aim be the search for truth or the triumph of a cause, and the audience may have any degree of competence. The reason that rhetoric has been deemed unworthy of the philosopher's efforts is not because dialectic employs a technique of questions and answers while rhetoric proceeds by speeches from opposing sides.[28] It is not this but rather the idea of the unicity of truth that has disqualified rhetoric in the Western philosophical tradition. Thus Descartes declares: "Whenever two men come to opposite decisions about the same matter one of them at least must certainly be wrong, and apparently there is not even one of them who knows; for if the reasoning of the second was sound and clear he would be able so to lay it before the other as finally to succeed in convincing *his* understanding also."[29] Both Descartes and Plato hold this idea because of their rejection of opinion, which is variable, and their adoption of an ideal of science based on the model of geometry and mathematical reasoning—the very model according to which the world was supposed to have been created. *Dum Deus calculat, fit mundus* (While God calculates, the world is created) is the conviction not only of Leibniz but of all rationalists.

Things are very different within a tradition that follows a juridical, rather than a mathematical, model. Thus in the tradition of the Talmud, for example, it is accepted that opposed positions can be equally reasonable; one of them does not have to be right. Indeed, "in the Talmud two schools of Biblical interpretation are in constant opposition, the school of Hillel and that of Shammai. Rabbi Abba relates that, bothered by these contradictory interpretations of the sacred text, Rabbi Samuel addresses himself to heaven in order to know who speaks the truth. A voice from above answers him that these two theses both expressed the word of the Living God."[30]

So too, for Plato, the subject of discussion is always one for which men possess no techniques for reaching agreement immediately:

Suppose for example that you and I, my good friend [Socrates remarks to Euthyphro], differ about a number; so differences of this sort make us enemies and set us at variance with one another? Do we not go at once to arithmetic, and put an end to them by a sum? . . . Or suppose that we differ about magnitudes, do we not quickly end the differences by measur-

ing? . . . And we end a controversy about heavy and light by resorting to a weighing machine? . . . But what differences are there which cannot be thus decided, and which therefore make us angry and set us at enmity with one another? I dare say the answer does not occur to you at the moment, and therefore I will suggest that these enmities arise when the matters of difference are the just and unjust, good and evil, honourable and dishonourable.[31]

When agreement can easily be reached by means of calculation, measuring, or weighing, when a result can be either demonstrated or verified, nobody would think of resorting to dialectical discussion. The latter concerns only what cannot be so decided and, especially, disagreements about values. In fact, in matters of opinion, it is often the case that neither rhetoric nor dialectic can reconcile all the positions that are taken.

Such is exactly how matters stand in philosophy. The philosopher's appeal to reason gives no guarantee whatever that everyone will agree with his point of view. Different philosophies present different points of view, and it is significant that a historian of pre-Socratic philosophy has been able to show that the different points of view can be regarded as antilogics or discourses on opposite sides, in that an antithesis is opposed in each case to a thesis.[32] One might even wonder with Alexandre Kojeve, the late expert in Hegelian philosophy, whether Hegelian dialectic did not have its origin, not in Platonic dialectic, but rather in the development of philosophical systems that can be opposed as thesis to antithesis, followed by a synthesis of the two. The process is similar to a lawsuit in which the judge identifies the elements he regards as valid in the claims of the opposed parties. For Kant as well as for Hegel, opinions are supposed to be excluded from philosophy, which aims at rationality. But to explain the divergencies that are systematically encountered in the history of philosophy, we need only call these opinions the natural illusions of reason as submitted to the tribunal of critical reason (as in Kant) or successive moments in the progress of reason toward Absolute Spirit (as in Hegel).

To reconcile philosophic claims to rationality with the plurality of philosophic systems, we must recognize that the appeal to reason must be identified not as an appeal to a single truth but instead as an appeal for the adherence of an audience, which can be thought of, after the manner of Kant's categorical imperative, as encompassing all reasonable and competent men. The characteristic aspect of philosophical controversy and of the history of philosophy can only be understood if the appeal to reason is conceived as an appeal to an ideal audience—which I call the universal audience—whether embodied in God,[33] in all reasonable and competent men, in the man deliberating or in an elite.[34] Instead of identifying philosophy with a science, which, on the positivist ideal, could make only analytical judgments, both indisputable and empty, we would do better to abandon the ideal of an apodictic philosophy. We would then have to admit that in the discharge of his specific task, the philosopher has at his disposal only an argumentation that he can endeavor to make as reasonable and systematic as possible without ever being able to make it absolutely compelling or a demonstrative proof. Besides, it is highly unlikely that any reasoning from which we could draw reasons for acting could be conducted under the sign of truth, for these reasons must enable us to justify our actions and decisions. Thus, indirectly, the analysis of philosophical reasoning brings us back to views that are familiar in existentialism.

Audiences display an infinite variety in both extension and competence: in extent, from the audience consisting of a single subject engaged in inward deliberation up to the universal audience; and in competence, from those who know only *loci* up to the specialists who have acquired their knowledge only through a long and painstaking preparation. By thus generalizing the idea of the audience, we can ward off Plato's attack against the rhetoricians for showing greater concern for success than for the truth. To this criticism we can reply that the techniques suited for persuading a crowd in a public place would not be convincing to a better educated and more critical audience, and that the worth of an argumentation is not measured solely by its efficacy but also by the quality of the audience at which it is aimed. Consequently, the idea of a rational argumentation cannot be defined *in abstracto,* since it depends on the historically grounded conception of the universal audience.

The part played by the audience in rhetoric is crucially important, because all argumentation, in aiming to persuade, must be adapted to the audience and, hence, based on beliefs accepted by the audience with such conviction that the rest of the discourse can be securely based upon it. Where this is not the case, one must reinforce adherence to these starting points by means of all available rhetorical techniques before attempting to join the controverted points to them. Indeed, the orator who builds his discourse on premises not accepted by the audience commits a classical fallacy in argumentation—a *petitio principii.* This is not a mistake in formal logic, since formally any proposition implies itself, but it is a mistake in argumentation, because the orator begs the question by presupposing the existence of an adherence that does not exist and to the obtaining of which his efforts should be directed. The objects of agreement on which the orator can build his argument are various. On the one hand, there are facts, truths, and presumptions; on the other, values, hierarchies, and *loci* of the preferable.[35]

Facts and truths can be characterized as objects that are already agreed to by the universal audience, and, hence, there is no need to increase the intensity of adherence to them. If we presuppose the coherence of reality and of our truths taken as a whole, there cannot be any conflict between facts or truths on which we would be called to make a decision. What happens when such a conflict seems to occur is that the incompatible element loses its status and becomes either an illusory fact or an apparent truth, unless we can eliminate the incompatibility by showing that the two apparently incompatible truths apply to different fields. We shall return to this argumentative method later when dealing with the dissociation of ideas.

Presumptions are opinions which need not be proved, although adherence to them can be either reinforced, if necessary, or suppressed by proving the opposite. Legal procedure makes abundant use of presumptions, for which it has worked out refined definitions and elaborate rules for their use.

Values are appealed to in order to influence our choices of action. They supply reasons for preferring one type of behavior to another, although not all would necessarily accept them as good reasons. Indeed, most values are particular in that they are accepted only by a particular group. The values that are called universal can be regarded in so many different ways that their universality is better considered as only an aspiration for agreement, since it disappears as soon as one tries to apply one such value to a concrete situation. For argumentation, it is useful to distinguish concrete values, such as one's country, from abstract values, such as justice and truth. It is characteristic of values that they can become the center of conflict without thereby ceasing to be values. This fact explains how real sacrifice is possible, the object renounced being by no means a mere appearance. For this reason, the effort to reinforce adherence to values is never superfluous. Such an effort is undertaken in epideictic discourse, and, in general, all education also endeavors to make certain values preferred to others.

After values, we find that accepted hierarchies play a part in argumentation. Such, for example, are the superiority of men over animals and of adults over children. We also find double hierarchies as in the case in which we rank behavior in accordance with an accepted ranking of the agents. For this reason, such a statement as "You are behaving like a beast" is pejorative, whereas an exhortation to "act like a man" calls for more laudable behavior.

Among all the *loci* studied by Aristotle in his *Topics,* we shall consider only those examined in the third book, which we shall call *loci of the preferable.* They are very general propositions, which can serve, at need, to justify values or hierarchies, but which also have as a special characteristic the ability to evaluate complementary aspects of reality. To *loci of quantity,* such as "That which is more lasting is worth more than that which is less so" or "A thing useful for a large number of persons is worth more than one useful for a smaller number," we can oppose *loci of quality,* which set value upon the unique, the irremediable, the opportune, the rare—that is, to what is exceptional instead of to what is normal. By the use of these loci, it is possible to describe the difference between the classical and the romantic spirit.[36]

While it establishes a framework for all nonformal reasoning, whatever its nature, its subject, or audience, the new rhetoric does not pretend to supply a list of all the *loci* and common opinions which can serve as starting points for argumentation. It is sufficient to stress that, in all cases, the orator must know the opinion of his audience on all the questions he intends to deal with, the type of arguments and reasons which seem relevant with regard to both subject and audience, what they are likely to consider as a strong or weak argument, and what might arouse them, as well as what would leave them indifferent.

Quintilian, in his *Institutes of Oratory,* points out the advantage of a public-school education for future orators: it puts them on a par and in fellowship with their audience. This advice is sound as regards argumentation on matters requiring no special knowledge. Otherwise, however, it is indispensable for holding an audience to have had a preliminary initiation into the body of ideas to be discussed.

In discussion with a single person or a small group, the establishment of a starting point is very different from before a large group. The particular opinions and convictions needed may have already been expressed previously, and the orator has no reason to believe that his interlocutors have changed their minds. Or he can use the technique of question and answer to set the premises of his argument on firm ground. Socrates proceeded in this way, taking the interlocutor's assent as a sign of the truth of the accepted thesis. Thus, Socrates says to Callicles in the *Gorgias:*

> *If you agree with me in an argument about any point, that point will have been sufficiently tested by us, and will not require to be submitted to any further test. For you could not have agreed with me, either from lack of knowledge or from superfluity of modesty, nor yet from a desire to deceive me, for you are my friend, as you tell me yourself. And therefore when you and I are agreed, the result will be the attainment of perfect truth.*[37]

It is obvious that such a dialogue is out of the question when one is addressing a numerous assembly. In this case, the discourse must take as premises the presumptions that the orator has learned the audience will accept.[38]

CREATING "PRESENCE"

What an audience accepts forms a body of opinion, convictions, and commitments that is both vast and indeterminate. From this body, the orator must select certain elements on which he focuses attention by endowing them, as it were, with a "presence." This does not mean that the elements left out are entirely ignored, but they are pushed into the background. Such a choice implicitly sets a value on some aspects of reality rather than others. Recall the lovely Chinese story told by Meng-Tseu: "A king sees an ox on its way to sacrifice. He is moved to pity for it and orders that a sheep be used in its place. He confesses he did so because he could see the ox, but not the sheep."[39]

Things present, things near to us in space and time, act directly on our sensibility. The orator's endeavors often consist, however, in bringing to mind things that are not immediately present. Bacon was well aware of this function of eloquence:

> *The affection beholdeth merely the present; reason beholdeth the future and sum of time. And therefore the present filling the imagination more, reason is commonly vanquished; but after that force of eloquence and persuasion hath made things future and remote appear as present, then upon the revolt of the imagination reason prevaileth.*[40]

To make, "things future and remote appear as present," that is, to create presence, calls for special efforts of presentation. For this purpose all kinds of literary techniques and a number of rhetorical figures have been developed. *Hypotyposis* or *demonstratio,* for example, is defined as a figure "which sets things out in such a way that the matter seems to unfold, and the thing to happen, before our very eyes."[41] Obviously, such a figure is highly important as a persuasive factor. In fact, if their argumentative role is disregarded, the study of figures is a useless pastime, a search for strange names for rather farfetched and affected turns of speech. Other figures, such as *repetition, anaphora, amplification, congerie, metabole, pseudo direct discourse, enallage,* are all various means of increasing the feeling of presence in the audience.[42]

In his description of facts, truths, and values, the orator must employ language that takes into account the classification and valuations implicit in the audience's acceptance of them. For placing his discourse at the level of generality that he considers best adapted to his purpose and his audience, he has at hand a whole arsenal of linguistic categories—substantives, adjectives, verbs, adverbs—and a vocabulary and phrasing that enable him, under the guise of a descriptive narrative, to stress the main elements and indicate which are merely secondary.

In the selection of data and the interpretation and presentation of them, the orator is subject to the accusation of partiality. Indeed, there is no proof that his presentation has not been distorted by a tendentious vision of things. Hence, in law, the legal counsel must reply to the attorney general, while the judge forms an opinion and renders his decision only after hearing both parties. Although his judgment may appear more balanced, it cannot achieve perfect objectivity—which can only be an ideal. Even with the elimination of tendentious views and or errors, one does not thereby reach a perfectly just decision.

So too in scientific or technical discourse, where the orator's freedom of choice is less because he cannot depart, with special reason, from the accepted terminology, value judgments are implicit, and their justification resides in the theories, classifications, and methodology that gave birth to the technical terminology. The idea that science consists of nothing but a body of timeless, objective truths has been increasingly challenged in recent years.[43]

THE STRUCTURE OF ARGUMENT

Nonformal argument consists, not of a chain of ideas of which some are derived from others according to accepted rules of inference, but rather of a web formed from all the arguments and all the reasons that combine to achieve the desired result. The purpose of the discourse in general is to bring the audience to the conclusions offered by the orator, starting from premises that they already accept—which is the case unless the orator has been guilty of a *petitio principii.* The argumentative process consists in establishing a link by which acceptance, or adherence, is passed from one element to another, and this end can be reached either by leaving the various elements of the discourse unchanged and associated as they are or by making a dissociation of ideas.

We shall now consider the various types of association and of dissociation that the orator has at his command. To simplify classification, we have grouped the processes of association into three classes: quasi-logical arguments, arguments based upon the structure of the real, and arguments that start from particular cases that are then either generalized or transposed from one sphere of reality to another.[44]

QUASI-LOGICAL ARGUMENTS

These arguments are similar to the formal structures of logic and mathematics. In fact, men apparently first came to an understanding of purely formal proof by submitting quasi-logical arguments, such as many of the *loci* listed in Aristotle's *Topics,* to an analysis that yielded precision and formalization. There is a difference of paramount importance between an argument and a formal proof. Instead of using a natural language in which the same word can be used with different meanings, a logical calculus employs an artificial language so constructed that one sign can have only one meaning. In logic, the principle of identity designates a tautology, an indisputable but empty truth, whatever its formulation. But this is not the case in ordinary language. When I say "Business is business," or "Boys will be boys," or "War is war," those hearing the words give preference, not to the univocity of the statement, but to its significant character. They will never take the statements as tautologies, which would make them meaningless, but will look for different plausible interpretations of the same term that will render the whole statement both meaningful and acceptable. Similarly, when faced with a statement that is formally a contradiction—"When two persons do the same thing it is not the same thing," or "We step and we do not step into the same river,"—we look for an interpretation that eliminates the incoherence.

To understand an orator, we must make the effort required to render his discourse coherent and meaningful. This effort requires goodwill and respect for the person who speaks and for what he says. The techniques of formalization make calculation possible, and, as a result, the correctness of the reasoning is capable of mechanical control. This result is not obtained without a certain linguistic rigidity. The language of mathematics is not used for poetry any more than it is used for diplomacy.

Because of its adaptability, ordinary language can always avoid purely formal contradictions. Yet it is not free from incompatibilities, as, for instance, when two norms are recommended which cannot both apply to the same situation. Thus, telling a child not to lie and to obey his parents lays one open to ridicule if the child asks, "What must I do if my father orders me to lie?" When such an antinomy occurs, one seeks for qualifications or amendments—and recommends the primacy of one norm over the other or points out that there are exceptions to the rule. Theoretically, the most elegant way of eliminating an incompatibility is to have recourse to a dissociation of concepts—but of this, more later. Incompatibility is an important element in Socratic irony. By exposing the incompatibility of the answers given to his insidious questions, Socrates compels his interlocutor to abandon certain commonly accepted opinions.

Definitions play a very different role in argumentation from the one they have in a formal system. There they are mostly abbreviations. But in argumentation they determine the choice of one particular meaning over others—sometimes by establishing a relation between an old term and a new one. Definition is regarded as a rhetorical figure—the oratorical definition—when it aims, not at clarifying

the meaning of an idea, but at stressing aspects that will produce the persuasive effect that is sought. It is a figure relating to choice: the selection of facts brought to the fore in the definition is unusual because the *definiens* is not serving the purpose of giving the meaning of a term.[45]

Analysis that aims at dividing a concept into all its parts and interpretation that aims at elucidating a text without bringing anything new to it are also quasi-logical arguments and call to mind the principle of identity. This method can give way to figures of speech called *aggregation* and *interpretation* when they serve some purpose other than clarification and tend to reinforce the feeling of presence.[46]

These few examples make it clear that expressions are called figures of style when they display a fixed structure that is easily recognizable and are used for a purpose different from their normal one—this new purpose being mainly one of persuasion. If the figure is so closely interwoven into the argumentation that it appears to be an expression suited to the occasion, it is regarded as an argumentative figure, and its unusual character will often escape notice.

Some reasoning processes—unlike definition or analysis, which aim at complete identification—are content with a partial reduction, that is, with an identification of the main elements. We have an example of this in the rule of justice that equals should be treated equally. If the agents and situations were identical, the application of the rule would take the form of an exact demonstration. As this is never the case, however, a decision will have to be taken about whether the differences are to be disregarded. This is why the recourse to precedent in legal matters is not a completely impersonal procedure but always requires the intervention of a judge.

Arguments of reciprocity are those that claim the same treatment for the antecedent as for the consequent of a relation—buyers-sellers, spectators-actors, etc. These arguments presuppose that the relation is symmetrical. Unreasonable use of them is apt to have comic results, such as the following story, known to have made Kant laugh:

At Surat, an Englishman is pouring out a bottle of ale which is foaming freely. He asks an Indian who is amazed at the sight what it is that he finds so strange. "What bothers me," replies the native, "isn't what is coming out of the bottle, but how you got it in there in the first place."

Other quasi-logical arguments take the transitivity of a relation for granted, even though it is only probable: "My friends' friends are my friends." Still other arguments apply to all kinds of other relations such as that between part and whole or between parts, relations of division, comparison, probability. They are clearly distinct from exact demonstration, since, in each case, complementary, nonformal hypotheses are necessary to render the argument compelling.[47]

APPEAL TO THE REAL

Arguments based on the structure of reality can be divided into two groups according as they establish associations of succession or of coexistence.

Among relations of succession, that of causality plays an essential role. Thus we may be attempting to find the causes of an effect, the means to an end, the consequences of a fact, or to judge an action or a rule by the consequences that it has. This last process might be called the pragmatic argument, since it is typical of utilitarianism in morals and of pragmaticism in general.[48]

Arguments establishing relations of coexistence are based on the link that unites a person to his actions. When generalized, this argument establishes the relation between the essence and the act, a relation of paramount importance in the social sciences. From this model have come the classification of periods of history (Antiquity, the Middle Ages), all literary classifications (classicism, romanticism), styles (Gothic, baroque), economic or political systems (feudalism, capitalism, fascism), and institutions (marriage, the church).[49] Rhetoric, conceived as the theory of argumentation, provides a guidance for the understanding both of the manner in which these categories were constituted and of the reasons for doing so. It helps us grasp the advantages and the disadvantages of using them and provides an insight into the value judgments that were present, explicitly or implicitly, when they took shape. The specificity of the social sciences can be best understood by considering the methodological reasons justifying the constitution of their categories—Max Weber's *Ideal-typus.*

Thanks to the relations of coexistence, we are also able to gain an understanding of the argument from authority in all its shapes as well as an appreciation of the persuasive role of ethos in argumentation, since the discourse can be regarded as an act on the orator's part.[50]

ESTABLISHING THE REAL

Arguments attempting to establish the structure of reality are first arguments by example, illustration, and model; second, arguments by analogy.

The example leads to the formulation of a rule through generalization from a particular case or through putting a new case on the same footing as an older one. Illustration aims at achieving presence for a rule by illustrating it with a concrete case. The argument from a model justifies an action by showing that it conforms to a model. One should also mention the argument from an antimodel; for example, the drunken Helot to whom the Spartans referred as a foil to show their sons how they should not behave.

In the various religions, God and all divine or quasi-divine persons are obviously preeminent models for their believers. Christian morality can be defined as the imitation of Christ, whereas Buddhist morality consists in imitating Buddha. The models that a culture proposes to its members for imitation provide a convenient way of characterizing it.[51]

The argument from analogy is extremely important in nonformal reasoning. Starting from a relation between two terms A and B, which we call the *theme* since it provides the proper subject matter of the discourse, we can by analogy present its structure or establish its value by relating it to the terms C and D, which constitute the *phoros* of the analogy, so that A is to B as C is to D. Analogy, which derives its name from the Greek word for proportion, is nevertheless different from mathematical proportion. In the latter the characteristic relation of equality is symmetrical, whereas the *phoros* called upon to clarify the structure or establish the value of the *theme* must, as a rule, be better known than the *theme*. When Heraclitus says that in the eyes of God man is as childish as a child is in the eyes of an adult, it is impossible to change the *phoros* for the *theme,* and vice versa, unless the audience is one that knows the relationship

> Arguments attempting to establish the structure of reality are first arguments by example, illustration, and model; second, arguments by analogy.

between God and man better than that between a child and an adult. It is also worth noting that when man is identified with *adult,* the analogy reduces to three terms, the middle one being repeated twice: *C* is to *B* as *B* is to *A.* This technique of argumentation is typical of Plato, Plotinus, and all those who establish hierarchies within reality.

Within the natural sciences the use of analogy is mainly heuristic, and the intent is ultimately to eliminate the analogy and replace it with a formula of a mathematical type. Things are different, however, in the social sciences and in philosophy, where the whole body of facts under study only offers reasons for or against a particular analogical vision of things.[52] This is one of the differences to which Wilhelm Dilthey refers when he claims that the natural sciences aim at explaining, whereas the human sciences seek for understanding.

The metaphor is the figure of style corresponding to the argument from analogy. It consists of a condensed analogy in which one term of the *theme* is associated with one term of the *phoros.* Thus "the morning of life" is a metaphor that summarizes the analogy: Morning is to day what youth is to life. Of course, in the case of a good many metaphors, the reconstruction of the complete analogy is neither easy nor unambiguous. When Berkeley, in his *Dialogues,*[53] speaks of "an ocean of false learning," there are various ways to supply the missing terms of the analogy, each one of which stresses a different relation unexpressed in the metaphor.

The use of analogies and metaphors best reveals the creative and literary aspects of argumentation. For some audiences their use should be avoided as much as possible, whereas for others the lack of them may make the discourse appear too technical and too difficult to follow. Specialists tend to hold analogies in suspicion and use them only to initiate students into their discipline. Scientific popularization makes extensive use of analogy, and only from time to time will the audience be reminded of the danger of identification of *theme* and *phoros.*[54]

THE DISSOCIATION OF IDEAS

Besides argumentative associations, we must also make room for the dissociation of ideas, the study of which is too often neglected by the rhetorical tradition. Dissociation is the classical solution for incompatibilities that call for an alteration of conventional ways of thinking. Philosophers, by using dissocia-

tion, often depart from common sense and form a vision of reality that is free from the contradictions of opinion.[55] The whole of the great metaphysical tradition, from Parmenides to our own day, displays a succession of dissociations where, in each case, reality is opposed to appearance.

Normally, reality is perceived through appearances that are taken as signs referring to it. When, however, appearances are incompatible—an oar in water looks broken but feels straight to the touch—we must admit, if we are to have a coherent picture of reality, that some appearances are illusory and may lead us to error regarding the real. One is thus brought to the construction of a conception of reality that at the same time is capable of being used as a criterion for judging appearances. Whatever is conformable to it is given value, whereas whatever is opposed is denied value and is considered a mere appearance.

Any idea can be subjected to a similar dissociation. To real justice we can oppose apparent justice and with real democracy contrast apparent democracy, or formal or nominal democracy, or quasi-democracy, or even "democracy" (in quotes). What is thus referred to as apparent is usually what the audience would normally call justice, democracy, etc. It only becomes apparent after the criterion of real justice or real democracy has been applied to it and reveals the error concealed under the name. The dissociation results in a depreciation of what had until then been an accepted value and in its replacement by another conception to which is accorded the original value. To effect such a depreciation, one will need a conception that can be shown to be valuable, relevant, as well as incompatible with the common use of the same notion.

We may call "philosophical pairs" all sets of notions that are formed on the model of the "appearance-reality" pair. The use of such pairs makes clear how philosophical ideas are developed and also shows how they cannot be dissociated from the process of giving or denying value that is typical of all ontologies. One thus comes to see the importance of argumentative devices in the development of thought, and especially of philosophy.[56]

INTERACTION OF ARGUMENTS

An argumentation is ordinarily a spoken or written discourse, of variable length, that combines a great number of arguments with the aim of winning the adherence of an audience to one or more theses. These arguments interact within the minds of the audience, reinforcing or weakening each other. They also interact with the arguments of the opponents as well as with those that arise spontaneously in the minds of the audience. This situation gives rise to a number of theoretical questions.

Are there limits, for example, to the number of arguments that can be usefully accumulated? Does the choice of arguments and the scope of the argumentation raise special problems? What is a weak or an irrelevant argument? What is the effect of a weak argument on the whole argumentation? Are there any criteria for assessing the strength or relevance of an argument? Are such matters relative to the audience, or can they be determined objectively?

We have no general answer to such questions. The answer seems to depend on the field of study and on the philosophy that controls its organization. In any case, they are questions that have seldom been raised and that never have received a satisfactory answer. Before any satisfactory answer can be given, it will be necessary to make many detailed studies in the various disciplines, taking account of the most varied audiences.

Once our arguments have been formulated, does it make any difference what order they are presented in? Should one start, or finish, with strong arguments, or do both by putting the weaker arguments in the middle—the so-called Nestorian order? This way of presenting the problem implies that the force of an argument is independent of its place in the discourse. Yet, in fact, the opposite seems to be true, for what appears as a weak argument to one audience often appears as a strong argument to another, depending on whether the presuppositions rejected by one audience are accepted by the other. Should we present our arguments then in the order that lends them the greatest force? If so, there should be a special technique devoted to the organization of a discourse.

Such a technique would have to point out that an exordium is all-important in some cases, while in others it is entirely superfluous. Sometimes the objections of one's opponent ought to be anticipated beforehand and refuted, whereas in other cases it is better to let the objections arise spontaneously lest one appear to be tearing down straw men.[57]

In all such matters it seems unlikely that any hard-and-fast rules can be laid down, since one must take account of the particular character of the audience, of its evolution during the debate, and of the fact that habits and procedures that prove good in one sphere are no good in another. A general rhetoric cannot be fixed by precepts and rules laid down once and for all. But it must be able to adapt itself to the most varied circumstances, matters, and audiences.

REASON AND RHETORIC

The birth of a new period of culture is marked by an eruption of original ideas and a neglect of methodological concerns and of academic classifications and divisions. Ideas are used with various meanings that the future will distinguish and disentangle. The fundamental ideas of Greek philosophy offer a good example of this process. One of the richest and most confused of all is that expressed by the term *logos,* which means among other things: word, reason, discourse, reasoning, calculation, and all that was later to become the subject of logic and the expression of reason. Reason was opposed to desire and the passions, being regarded as the faculty that ought to govern human behavior in the name of truth and wisdom. The operation of *logos* takes effect either through long speeches or through questions and answers, thus giving rise to the distinction noted above between rhetoric and dialectic, even before logic was established as an autonomous discipline.

Aristotle's discovery of the syllogism and his development of the theory of demonstrative science raised the problem of the relation of syllogistic—the first formal logic—with dialectic and rhetoric. Can any and every form of reasoning be expressed syllogistically? Aristotle is often thought to have aimed at such a result, at least for deductive reasoning, since he was well aware that inductive reasoning and argument by example are entirely different from deduction. He knew too that the dialectical reasoning characteristic of discussion, and essentially critical in purpose, differed widely from demonstrative reasoning deducing from principles the conclusions of a science. Yet he was content to locate the difference in the kind of premises used in the two cases. In analytical, or demonstrative, reasoning, the premises, according to Aristotle, are true and ultimate, or else derived from such premises, whereas in dialectical reasoning the premises consist of generally accepted opinions. The nature of reasoning in both cases was held to be the same, consisting in drawing conclusions from propositions posited as premises.[58]

Rhetoric, on the other hand, was supposed to use syllogisms in a peculiar way, by leaving some premises unexpressed and so transforming them into enthymemes. The orator, as Aristotle saw, could not be said to use regular syllogisms; hence, his reasoning was said to consist of abbreviated syllogisms and of arguments from example, corresponding to induction.

What are we to think of this reduction to two forms of reasoning of all the wide variety of arguments that men use in their discussions and in pleading a cause or justifying an action? Yet, since the time of Aristotle, logic has confined its study to deductive and inductive reasoning, as though any argument differing from these was due to the variety of its content and not to its form. As a result, an argument that cannot be reduced to canonical form is regarded as logically valueless. What then about reasoning from analogy? What about the *a fortiori* argument? Must we, in using such arguments, always be able to introduce a fictive unexpressed major premise, so as to make them conform to the syllogism?

It can be shown that the practical ressorting involved in choice or decision making can always be expressed in the form of theoretical reasoning by introducing additional premises. But what is gained by such a move? The reasoning by which new premises are introduced is merely concealed, and resort to these premises appears entirely arbitrary, although in reality it too is the outcome of a decision that can be justified only in an argumentative, and not in a demonstrative, manner.[59]

At first sight, it appears that the main difference between rhetoric and dialectic, according to Aristotle, is that the latter employs impersonal techniques of reasoning, whereas rhetoric relies on the orator's *ethos* (or character) and on the manner in which he appeals to the passions of his audience (or *pathos*).[60,61] For Aristotle, however, the *logos* or use of reasoning is the main thing, and he criticizes those authors before him, who laid the emphasis upon oratorical devices designed to arouse the passion. Thus he writes:

If the rules for trials which are now laid down in some states—especially in well-governed states—were applied everywhere, such people would have nothing to say. All men, no doubt, think that the laws should prescribe such rules, but some, as in the court of Areopagus, give practical effect to their thoughts and forbid talk about non-essentials. This is sound law and custom. It is not right to pervert the judge by moving him to anger or envy or pity—one might as well warp a carpenter's rule before using it.

For this reason, after a long discussion devoted to the role of passion in oratorical art, he concludes:

As a matter of fact, it [rhetoric] is a branch of dialectic and similar to it, as we said at the outset.[62]

To sum up, it appears that Aristotle's conception, which is essentially empirical and based on the analysis of the material he had at his disposal, distinguishes dialectic from rhetoric only by the type of audience and, especially, by the nature of the questions examined in practice. His precepts are easy to understand when we keep in mind that he was thinking primarily of the debates held before assemblies of citizens gathered together either to deliberate on political or legal matters or to celebrate some public ceremony. There is no reason, however, why we should not also consider theoretical and, especially, philosophical questions expounded in unbroken discourse. In this case, the techniques Aristotle would have presumably recommended would be those he himself used in his own work, following the golden rule that he laid down in his *Nicomachean Ethics,* that the method used for the examination and exposition of each particular subject must be appropriate to the matter, whatever its manner of presentation.[63]

After Aristotle, dialectic became identified with logic as a technique of reasoning, due to the influence of the Stoics. As a result, rhetoric came to be regarded as concerned only with the irrational parts of our being, whether will, the passions, imagination, or the faculty for aesthetic pleasure. Those who, like Seneca and Epictetus, believed that the philosopher's role was to bring man to submit to reason were opposed to rhetoric, even when they used it, in the name of philosophy. Those like Cicero, on the other hand, who thought that in order to induce man to submit to reason one had to have recourse to rhetoric, recommended the union of philosophy and eloquence. The thinkers of the Renaissance followed suit, such as Valla, and Bacon too, who expected rhetoric to act on the imagination to secure the triumph of reason.

The more rationalist thinkers, like Ramus, as we have already noted, considered rhetoric as merely an ornament and insisted on a separation of form and content, the latter alone being thought worthy of a philosopher's attention. Descartes adopted the same conception and reinforced it. He regarded the geometrical method as the only method fit for the sciences as well as for philosophy and opposed rhetoric as exerting an action upon the will contrary to reason—thus adopting the position of the Stoics but with a different methodological justification. But to make room for eloquence within this scheme, we need only deny that reason possesses a monopoly of the approved way of influencing the will. Thus, Pascal, while professing a rationalism in a Cartesian manner, does not hesitate to declare that the truths that are most significant for him—that is, the truths of faith—have to be received by the heart before they can be accepted by reason:

We all know that opinions are admitted into the soul through two entrances, which are its chief powers, understanding and will. The more natural entrance is the understanding, for we should never agree to anything but demonstrated truths, but the more usual entrance, although against nature, is the will; for all men whatsoever are almost always led into belief not because a thing is proved but because it is pleasing. This way is low, unworthy, and foreign to our nature. Therefore everybody disavows it. Each of us professes to give his belief and even his love only where he knows it is deserved.

I am not speaking here of divine truths, which I am far from bringing under the art of persuasion, for they are infinitely above nature. God alone can put them into the soul, and in whatever way He pleases. I know He has willed they should enter into the mind from the heart and not into the heart from the mind, that He might make humble that proud power of reason . . .[64]

To persuade about divine matters, grace is necessary; it will make us love that which religion orders us to love. Yet it is also Pascal's intention to conduce to this result by his eloquence, although he has to admit that he can lay down the precepts of this eloquence only in a very general way:

It is apparent that, no matter what we wish to persuade of, we must consider the person concerned, whose mind and heart we must know,

what principles he admits, what things he loves, and then observe in the thing in question what relations it has to these admitted principles or these objects of delight. So that the art of persuasion consists as much in knowing how to please as in knowing how to convince, so much more do men follow caprice than reason.

Now of these two, the art of convincing and the art of pleasing, I shall confine myself here to the rules of the first, and to them only in the case where the principles have been granted and are held to unwaveringly; otherwise I do not know whether there would be an art for adjusting the proofs to the inconstancy of our caprices.

But the art of pleasing is incomparably more difficult, more subtle, more useful, and more wonderful, and therefore if I do not deal with it, it is because I am not able. Indeed I feel myself so unequal to its regulation that I believe it to be a thing impossible.

Not that I do not believe there are as certain rules for pleasing as for demonstrating, and that whoever should be able perfectly to know and to practise them would be as certain to succeed in making himself loved by kings and by every kind of person as in demonstrating the elements of geometry to those who have imagination enough to grasp the hypotheses. But I consider, and it is perhaps my weakness that leads me to think so, that it is impossible to lay hold of the rules.[65]

Pascal's reaction here with regard to formal rules of rhetoric already heralds romanticism with its reverence for the great orator's genius. But before romanticism held sway, associationist psychology developed in eighteenth-century England. According to the thinkers of this school, feeling, not reason, determines man's behavior, and books on rhetoric were written based on this psychology. The best known of these is Campbell's *The Philosophy of Rhetoric*, noted above.[66] Fifty years later, Whately, following Bacon's lead, defined the subject of logic and of rhetoric as follows:

I remarked in treating of that Science [Logic], that Reasoning may be considered as applicable to two purposes, which I ventured to designate respectively by the terms "Inferring" and "Proving," i.e., the ascertainment of the truth by investigation and the establishment of it to the satisfaction of another; *and I there re-marked that Bacon, in his* Organon, *has laid down rules for the conduct of the former of these processes, and that the latter belongs to the province of Rhetoric; and it was added, that to* infer, *is to be regarded as the proper office of the Philosopher, or the Judge;—to* prove, *of the Advocate.*[67]

This conception, while stressing the social importance of rhetoric, makes it a negligible factor for the philosopher. This tendency increases under the influence of Kant and of the German idealists, who boasted of removing all matters of opinion from philosophy, for which only apodictic truths are of any importance.

The relation between the idea that we form of reason and the role assigned to rhetoric is of sufficient importance to deserve studies of all the great thinkers who have said anything about the matter—studies similar to those of Bacon by Prof. Karl Wallace and of Ramus by Prof. Walter J. Ong.[68] In what follows, I would like to sketch how the positivist climate of logical empiricism makes possible a new, or renovated, conception of rhetoric.

Within the perspective of neopositivism, the rational is restricted to what experience and formal logic enable us to verify and demonstrate. As a result, the vast sphere of all that is concerned with action—except for the choice of the most adequate means to reach a designated end—is turned over to the irrational. The very idea of a reasonable decision has no meaning and cannot even be defined satisfactorily with respect to the *whole* action in which it occurs. Logical empiricism has at its disposal no technique of justification except one founded on the theory of probability. But why should one prefer one action to another? Only because it is more efficacious? How can one choose between the various ends that one can aim at? If quantitative measures are the only ones that can be taken into account, the only reasonable decision would seem to be one that is in conformity with utilitarian calculations. If so, all ends would be reduced to a single one of pleasure or utility, and all conflicts of values would be dismissed as based on futile ideologies.

Now if one is not prepared to accept such a limitation to a monism of values in the world of action and would reject such a reduction on the ground that

the irreducibility of many values is the basis of our freedom and of our spiritual life; if one considers how justification takes place in the most varied spheres—in politics, morals, law, the social sciences, and, above all, in philosophy—it seems obvious that our intellectual tools cannot all be reduced to formal logic, even when that is enlarged by a theory for the control of induction and the choice of the most efficacious techniques. In this situation, we are compelled to develop a theory of argumentation as an indispensable tool for practical reason.

In such a theory, as we have seen, argumentation is made relative to the adherence of minds, that is, to an audience, whether an individual deliberating or mankind as addressed by the philosopher in his appeal to reason. Whately's distinction between logic, as supplying rules of reasoning for the judge, and rhetoric, providing precepts for the counsel, falls to the ground as being without foundation. Indeed, the counsel's speech that aims at convincing the judge cannot rest on any different kind of reasoning than that which the judge uses himself. The judge, having heard both parties, will be better informed and able to compare the arguments on both sides, but his judgment will contain a justification in no way different in kind from that of the counsel's argumentation. Indeed, the ideal counsel's speech is precisely one that provides the judge with all the information that he needs to state the grounds for his decision.

If rhetoric is regarded as complementary to formal logic and argumentation as complementary to demonstrative proof, it becomes of paramount importance in philosophy, since no philosophic discourse can develop without resorting to it. This became clear when, under the influence of logical empiricism, all philosophy that could not be reduced to calculation was considered as nonsense and of no worth. Philosophy, as a consequence, lost its status in contemporary culture. This situation can be changed only by developing a philosophy and a methodology of the reasonable. For if the rational is restricted to the field of calculation, measuring, and weighing, the reasonable is left with the vast field of all that is not amenable to quantitative and formal techniques. This field, which Plato and Aristotle began to explore by means of dialectical and rhetorical devices, lies open for investigation by the new rhetoric.

─────────────────────────── **Notes** ───────────────────────────

1. Dumarsais, *Des tropes ou des différents sens dans lesquels on peut prendre un même mot dans une même langue* (1818; reprint ed., Geneva: Slatkine Reprints, 1967).

2. Pierre Fontanier, *Les figures du discours,* ed. Gerard Genette (Paris: Flammarion, 1968).

3. **GBWW,* Vol. 8, pp. 139–223.

4. †*GBWW,* Vol. 8, pp. 37–137.

5. ‡*GBWW,* Vol. 8, pp. 139–253; Vol. 9, pp. 585–675.

6. Petrus Ramus, *Dialectic,* 1576 edition, pp. 3–4; also in the critical edition of *Dialectique,* 1555, ed. Michel Dassonville (Geneva: Librairie Droz, 1964), p. 62. Cf. Walter J. Ong, *Ramus: Method, and the Decay of Dialogue* (Cambridge, Mass.: Harvard University Press, 1958).

7. Fontanier, *Les figures du discourse,* p. 64. *See also* J. Dubois, F. Edeline, J.M. Klinkenberg, P. Minguet, F. Pire, and H. Trinon, *Rhetorique generale* (Paris: Larousse, 1970).

8. Heinrich Lausberg, *Handbuch der literarischen Rhetorik,* 2 vols. (Munich: M. Hueber, 1960).

9. Douglas Ehninger, ed., Whately's *Elements of Rhetoric* (Carbondale: Southern Illinois University Press, 1963), pp. xx–xxvii.

10. Robert T. Oliver and Marvin G. Bauer, ed., *Reestablishing the Speech Profession: The First Fifty Years* (New York: Speech Association of the Eastern States, 1959). *See also* Frederick W. Haberman and James W. Cleary, eds., *Rhetoric and Public Address: A Bibliography, 1947–1961* (Madison: University of Wisconsin Press, 1964). Prof. Carroll C. Arnold of Pennsylvania State University has graciously supplied me the following information: "The statement about the bibliography in *Quarterly Journal of Speech* is not quite correct. The 'Bibliography of Rhetoric and Public Address' first appeared in the *Quarterly Journal of Speech* in 1947 and was published there annually to 1951. From 1952 through 1969, the bibliography was annually published in *Speech Monographs.* As it happens the bibliography will cease to be published in a *Monographs* and, beginning with this year, 1970, will be published in a *Bibliographical Annual,* published by the Speech Association of America. As far as I know, this bibliography remains the only multilingual listing of works (admittedly incomplete) on rhetoric published in the United States."

11. See Vasile Florescu, "Retorica si reabilitarcea ei in filozofia contemporanea" [Rhetoric and its rehabilitation in contemporary philosophy] in *Studii de istorie a filozofiei universale,* published by the Institute of Philosophy of the Academy of the Socialist Republic of Rumania (Bucharest, 1969), pp. 9–82.

12. *Discourses* 11.23; *GBWW,* Vol. 12, pp. 170–171.

13. *Rhetoric* I. 1358b 1–13; *GWBB,* Vol. 9, p. 598.

14. Ch. Perelman and L. Olbrechts-Tyteca, *The New Rhetoric,* trans. John Wilkinson and Purcell Weaver (Notre Dame, Ind.: University of Notre Dame Press, 1969), p. 50. French edition: *La nouvelle rhetorique* (Paris: Presses universitaires de France, 1958).

15. *On Christian Doctrine* IV. 13, 12; *GBWW,* Vol. 18, p. 684.

16. Kenneth Burke, A *Rhetoric of Motives* (New York: Prentice-Hail, 1950), p. 43.

17. Act II, scene ii; GBWW, Vol. 26, pp. 584ff.

18. Ch. Perelman, *The Idea of Justice and the Problem of Argument,* trans. John Petrie (New York Humanities Press, 1963), pp. 1–60.

19. *Ibid., p. 16.*

20. *Ibid.,* pp. 56–57.

21. Edmond Goblot, *La logique des jugements de valeur* (Paris: Colin, 1927).

22. Perelman and Olbrechts-Tyteca, *The New Rhetoric, See also* Olbrechts-Tyteca, "Rencontre avec la rhetorique," in *La theorie de l'argumentation,* Centre Nationale de Recherches de Logique (Louvain: Editions Nauwelaerts, 1963), 1, pp. 3–18 (reproduces nos. 21–24 of *Logique et Analyse*).

23. This identification is faulty, as dialectical reasoning can no more than commonplaces *(topoi)* be reduced to formal calculation. Cf. Otto Bird, "The Tradition of the Logical Topics: Aristotle to Ockham," *Journal of the History of Ideas* 23 (1962): pp. 307–23.

24. See *Rhetoric* I. 135a 1–6, 1355a 35–37, 1355b 8–10, 1356a 30–35, 1356b 36, 1356b 37–38; *GBWW,* Vol. 9, pp. 593–96.

25. Plato, *Republic* I 348a–b; *GBWW,* Vol. 7, p. 306.

26. *Republic* 511; *GBWW,* Vol. 7, p. 387. *Seventh Letter* 344b; *GBWW,* Vol. 7, p. 810.

27. Rhetoric I. 1357a 1–4; *GBWW,* Vol. 9, p. 596.

28. Plato, *Cratylus* 390c; *GBWW,* Vol. 7, pp. 88–89. *Theaetetus* 167d; *GBWW,* Vol. 7, p. 526.

29. *Rules for the Direction of the Mind; GBWW,* Vol. 31, p. 2.

30. *Babylonian Talmud, Seder Mo'ed 2, 'Erubin 136* (ed. Epstein). Cf. Ch. Perelman, "What the Philosopher May Learn from the Study of Law," *Natural Law Forum* 11 (1966): pp. 3–4; idem, "Desaccord et rationalite des decisions," in *Droit, morale et philosophie* (Paris: Librairie generale de droit et de jurisprudence, 1968), pp. 103–10.

31. *Euthyphro 7; GBWW,* Vol. 7, pp. 193–94.

32. See Clemence Ramnoux, "Le developpement antilogique des ecoles grecques avant Socrate," in *La dialectique* (Paris: Presses universitaires de France, 1969), pp. 40–47.

33. Plato, *Phaedrus* 273c; *GBWW,* Vol., 7, p. 138.

34. Perelman and Olbrechts-Tyteca, *The New Rhetoric,* §§ 6–9.

35. *Ibid.,* §§ 15–27.

36. Ch. Perelman and L. Olbrechts-Tyteca, "Classicisme et Romantisme dans l'argumentation," *Revue Internationale de Philosophie,* 1958, pp. 47–57.

37. Plato. *Gorgias* 487 d-e; *GBWW,* Vol. 7, p. 273.

38. Perelman and Olbrechts-Tyteca, *The New Rhetoric,* p. 104.

39. *Ibid.,* p. 116.

40. *Advancement of Learning,* Bk. II, xviii, 4; *GBWW,* Vol. 30, p. 67.

41. *Rhetorica ad Herennium* 4. 68.

42. Perelman and Olbrechts-Tyteca, *The New Rhetoric,* § 42.

43. To mention only a few works besides Thomas Kuhn's *The Structure of Scientific Revolutions* (Chicago, Ill.: University of Chicago Press, 1962), there is Michael Polanyi's fascinating work significantly entitled *Personal Knowledge* (London Routledge & Kegan Paul, 1958). The social, persuasive, nay, the rhetorical aspect, of scientific methodology was stressed by the physicist John Ziman in his brilliant book *Public Knowledge* (London: Cambridge University Press, 1968). The latter is dedicated to the Late Norwood Russell Hanson, whose *Patterns of Discovery* (London: Cambridge University Press, 1958), and *The Concept of the Positron* (London: Cambridge University Press, 1963), gave much weight to the new ideas.

44. Perelman and Olbrechts-Tyteca, *The New Rhetoric,* §§ 45–88.

45. *Ibid.,* pp. 172–73.

46. *Ibid.,* p. 176.

47. *Ibid.,* § 45–49.

48. See J.S. Mill. *Utilitarianism: GBWW,* Vol. 43, pp. 443ff.

49. Ch. Perelman, ed., *Les categories en histoire* (Brussels: Editions de l'Institut de Sociologie, 1969).

50. Perelman and Olbrechts-Tyteca, *The New Rhetoric,* §§60–74.

51. *Ibid.,* §§78–81.

52. Ch. Perelman, "Analogie et metaphore en science, poesie, et philosophie," *Revue Internationale de Philosophie,* 1969, pp. 3–15; *see also* Hans Blumenberg, *Paradigmen zu einer Metaphorologie* (Bonn: H. Bouvier, 1960), and Enzo Melandri, *La lines e il circolo: Studio logico-filosofico sull'analogia* (Bologna: Il Mulino, 1968).

53. George Berkeley, *Works,* 2 vols. (London, 1843), 2: p. 259.

54. Perelman and Olbrechts-Tyteca, *The New Rhetoric,* §§82–88.

55. Ch. Perelman, "Le reel commun et le reel philosophique," in *Etudes sur l'histoire de la philosophie, en hommage a Martial Gueroult* (Paris: Fischbacher, 1964), pp. 127–38.

56. Perelman and Olbrechts-Tyteca, *The New Rhetoric,* §§89–92.

57. *Ibid.,* §§97–105.

58. *Topics* I. 100a 25–32; *GBWW,* Vol. 8, p. 143.

59. Ch. Perelman, "Le raisonnement pratique," in *Contemporary Philosophy,* ed. Raymond Klibansky (Florence: La Nuova Italia, 1968-), 1: pp. 168–78.

60. *Rhetoric* I. 1356a 5–18; *GBWW,* Vol. 9, p. 595.

61. *See* Paul I. Rosenthal, "The Concept of Ethos and the Structure of Persuasion," *Speech Monographs,* 1966, pp. 114–26.

62. *Rhetoric* I. 1354a pp. 19–27, 1356a pp. 30–31: *GBWW,* Vol. 9, pp. 593, 395–96.

63. *Ethics* I. 1094b 12–27; *GBWW,* Vol. 9, pp. 339–40.

64. On *Geometrical Demonstration; GBWW,* Vol. 33, p. 440.

65. *Ibid.,* p. 441.

66. Cf. V.M. Bevilacqua, "Philosophical Origins of George Campbell's Philosophy of Rhetoric," *Speech Monographs,* 1965, pp. 1–12; and Lloyd F. Bitzer, "Hume's Philosophy in George Campbell's Philosophy of Rhetoric," *Philosophy and Rhetoric,* 1969, pp. 139–66.

67. Whately, *Elements of Rhetoric* (1828), pp. 6–7.

68. Karl Wallace, *Francis Bacon on Communication and Rhetoric* (Chapel-Hill: University of North Carolina Press, 1943); and Ong, *Ramus: Method, and the Decay of Dialogue.*

Summary

Since completing his book and essay on his interpretation of a "new rhetoric," Perelman has been active in the past decade in presenting his theories to European and American audiences. To summarize his recent works would require more space than is available for our present purposes. We are convinced, however, that no discussion of Perelman's generative ideas is complete without at least a brief analysis of his study on "The Rational and the Reasonable."[1] First presented as a lecture at an International Symposium held at the University of Ottawa in October, 1977, this paper has been reprinted and cited both by Perelman and by other authors.

What Perelman attempts to do in his provocative analysis is of great value to students of rhetoric who have a strong interest in argument and are inclined to subscribe to the trend of rhetoric as a way of knowing. The primary thrust of his position is that the terms "reasonable" and "rational," while similar in some respects, are not interchangeable concepts. To clarify this point he makes the following claim. It is meaningful, he suggests, to say "rational decision" or "rational deduction" and to refer to a compromise as "reasonable." But it is unacceptable to say "reasonable decision," "reasonable deduction," or "rational compromise."

Next Perelman delineates the characteristics of both concepts, concluding that the notion of reasonable is a fundamental requirement of practical argument. The term rational he equates with a mathematical model or an immutable divine standard. Thus the degree of certitude is on the level of an *a priori* self-evident truth similar to what Kant called a Categorical Imperative. Because it demands the same type of high level certainty for all social milieus throughout time, rationality meets the test of formal validity,

> The term reasonable (on the other hand) is related to what takes place in practical human affairs, including courts of law. A reasonable man, in Perelman's view, adopts a legal reasoning model that utilizes contingent propositions and an audience-centered perspective.

logical coherence, purposefulness, and predictability. The fact that rationality is responsive only to those claims which have a certitude approximating that of mathematics, divine standards, or natural law insulates it from such presumably extraneous forces as education, culture, experience, dialogue, and time.

The term reasonable, on the other hand, is related to what takes place in practical human affairs, including courts of law. A reasonable man, in Perelman's view, adopts a legal reasoning model that utilizes contingent propositions and an audience-centered perspective.

His principal concern is not with logical coherence, formal validity, or a slavish devotion to precedents, but with what is fair, equitable, and just in a particular situation or analogous circumstance. As a result he assesses the worth of an argument or a legal decision by asking these questions: (1) Does it conform to the principle of common sense? (2) Is it consistent with prevailing societal values and beliefs? (3) Will it produce a socially useful consequence? (4) Is it practical, realistic, and relevant? Finally, the concept of reasonableness, unlike that of rationality, is shaped by education, culture, experience, dialogue, and time.

To see more clearly the distinctions which Perelman has drawn between the rational and the reasonable, we have prepared the foregoing chart highlighting the special features of each.

Notwithstanding the fact that Perelman's distinctions regarding what is rational and reasonable may at first glance appear arbitrary and overdrawn, they nevertheless are useful in understanding his theory of practical reasoning. Perelman, like Toulmin, has taught us to view the argumentative process as a practical and realistic endeavor which not only seeks to gain an adherence of minds but seeks to expand our knowledge.

1. Chaim Perelman, *The New Rhetoric and the Humanities* (Dordrecht, Holland: D. Reidel Publishing Company, 1979), pp. 117–123.

PERELMAN'S THEORY OF THE RATIONAL AND THE REASONABLE	
Rational	**Reasonable**

Degree of Certitude
  Mathematical Model
  Immutable Divine Standards
  A priori Self-evident Truths
  Natural Law
  Kantian Categorical Imperative
	Degree of Certitude
	  Legal Reasoning Model
	  Contingent Propositions
	  Acceptability by Audience

Criteria for Evaluating Decisions and Arguments
  Formal Validity
  Logical Coherence
  Purposefulness
  Conformity to Precedents
	Criteria for Evaluating Decisions and Arguments
	  Equitable and Fair
	  Conformity to Common Sense
	  Consistent with Societal Beliefs and Values
	  Practical, Realistic, Relevant
	  Socially Useful Consequences

Applicability
  Individual Level
  Universal Level
  All Social Milieus
	Applicability
	  Situational Level
	  Analogous Circumstances

Unresponsive to Education, Culture, Experience, Dialogue, Time	Responsive to Education, Culture, Experience, Dialogue, Time

Emerging European Perspectives on Rhetoric

In the preceding chapters on contemporary rhetorical thought, we have sought to provide an overview of the major communication perspectives advanced by representative scholars from the United States, Canada, Great Britain, and Belgium. Such authors as Burke, Richards, McLuhan, Perelman, Toulmin, and Weaver, as observed in this section, have had a profound influence on current thinking during the past several decades. They by no means, however, are the only significant theorists in the last half of the twentieth century who have turned their attention to at least some of the important aspects of rhetorical theory. Of these numerous writers who have done so, four European scholars stand out as major synthesizers and innovators of Western thought. All have in their own way contributed significantly to our understanding of the nature and potentialities of rhetoric. They are the Italian humanist Ernesto Grassi, the French philosopher and historian Michel Foucault, the German critical theorist Jurgen Habermas and Michel Meyer, the Belgian philosopher and rhetorician.[1] It will be our purpose in this chapter not to discuss their broad-ranging theories as a whole, but to highlight some of their most crucial ideas that have relevance for contemporary students of rhetoric.

Our analysis will begin with Grassi whose primary intellectual concern is rhetoric as grounded in the philosophy of humanism.

ERNESTO GRASSI

Grassi relies heavily, as we shall see, upon the writings of such authors as Plato, Aristotle, Cicero, and Quintilian. But the principal source and inspiration for his ideas are the works of Giambattista Vico and the Italian humanists. Grassi, however, is far more

than a summarizer or synthesizer of the contributions of others. Instead, as we are now ready to note, he takes their premises and through his own observations of life and sense of values is able to apply them to contemporary rhetorical situations. What gives freshness and an enduring thrust to Grassi's approach is the vocabulary he uses and the arguments he develops to show that rhetoric is essential to the doing of philosophy and science; and, as a result, is on a comparable level as a worthy field of study.

In examining the principal elements of Grassi's perspectives on rhetoric, we will divide our discussion into two parts: (1) an analysis of his views on the general nature of rhetoric; and (2) a consideration of three essential faculties that are available to the rhetor who is interested in a humanistic-based theory of communication.

The Nature of Rhetoric

An important starting point in gaining an understanding of Grassi's description of the nature of rhetoric is to summarize the distinction he draws between critical or rational discourse and topical discourse. In making this differentiation, he takes the side of Vico who, as earlier pointed out, developed his stance as a response to Descartes' critical method. What Vico and Grassi find unacceptable in a strictly rationalistic approach is its emphasis on truth derived from logical demonstration; its rejection of probable knowledge; its dismissal of history, metaphysics, and politics; its relegation of rhetoric to a non-philosophical and non-scientific category; and its tendency to ignore human problems as a legitimate field of study for scientific inquiry.[2]

Topical philosophy, on the other hand, is an initial step in a relevant scientific investigation. As in the case of Vico, Grassi equates the canon of invention with the topical method. Through this process the rhetor creates arguments that generate hypotheses which must be tested in the subsequent phases of any scientific analysis. When viewed from this vantage point, topics, which ultimately lead to a discovery of first principles, take priority over pure rationalism.[3]

Grassi's enthusiasm for Vico's notion of topical philosophy, with its stress on probability, verisimilitudes, and creativity; and his distrust of the Cartesian doctrine of truth and certainty, with its focus on mathematical logic, helped form his concept of the nature of rhetoric. A human being, he concluded, cannot be expected to respond to rational appeals alone. All persons have affective as well as cognitive components in their nature which are related to the emotions. It follows, therefore, that unless the passions are stirred, genuine persuasion will not occur.[4]

On this point Plato served as a model to Grassi. In the third speech delivered in the *Phaedrus,* for example, Socrates made it clear that arguments based on strong reasoning must be reinforced by those designed to arouse the emotions and elevate the soul. Thus in keeping with Plato's intention the reader of this dialogue on true rhetoric can experience the feeling of eros or love as a powerful motivating force.[5]

In detailing approvingly Plato's strong interest in uniting content and form, knowledge and the passions, Grassi had in mind another purpose—to place rhetoric on an equal plane with that of philosophy. Whereas philosophy sets for itself the goal of stimulating the intellect, he argues, rhetoric seeks to appeal to the whole person.[6] In extending this idea, Grassi follows a pattern similar to that which we noted in Weaver's essay on the "Phaedrus and the Nature of Rhetoric." We recall that Weaver sought to show that the three speeches set forth in this dialogue represent addresses that may be called specimens of evil, neuter, and noble rhetoric respectively. Grassi, as can be seen from the ensuing excerpt drawn from his essay on "Rhetoric

> Grassi's enthusiasm for Vico's notion of topical philosophy, with its stress on probability, verisimilitudes, and creativity; and his distrust of the Cartesian doctrine of truth and certainty, with its focus on mathematical logic, helped form his concept of the nature of rhetoric.

> Three Primary Faculties of True Rhetoric
> ■ *ingenium*
> ■ work
> ■ metaphor

and Philosophy," uses a different vocabulary to reach a similar conclusion concerning what he perceives to be three types of discourse:

> *To sum up, we are forced to distinguish between three kinds of speech: (1) The* external, 'rhetorical speech,' *in the common meaning of the expression, which only refers to images because they affect the passions. But since these images do not stem from insight, they remain an object of opinion. This is the case of the purely emotive, false speech: 'rhetoric' in the usual negative sense. (2) The* speech which arises exclusively from a rational proceeding. *It is true that this is of a demonstrative character but it cannot have a rhetorical effect, because purely rational arguments do not attain to the passions, i.e., 'theoretical' speech in the usual sense. (3) The* true rhetorical speech. *This springs from the* archai, *non-deducible moving, and indicative, due to its original images. The original speech is that of the wise man, of the* sophos *who is not only* episthetai *but the man who with insight leads, guides, and attracts.*[7]

In demonstrating that meaningful rhetoric contains a happy blending of eloquence and wisdom, of rational and emotional appeals, Grassi is also striving to illustrate that "true philosophy is rhetoric and . . . true rhetoric is philosophy, a philosophy which does not need an 'external' rhetoric to convince, and a rhetoric that does not need an 'external' content of verity."[8] What he is arguing for, in short, is the adoption of a type of rhetoric that is both epistemic and persuasive. At the point where this occurs rhetoric and philosophy become one.

Three Primary Faculties of True Rhetoric

The preceding discussion suggests the broad outline used by Grassi to sketch the general nature of his theory of rhetoric. In order to understand more fully how a rhetor may achieve this high level discourse, we need to shift our focus to three vitally significant faculties that are crucial parts of "true rhetorical speech." Influenced by Cicero and Vico in particular and the renaissance scholars in general, Grassi labels two of these faculties *ingenium* and work. The third concept, which is a more traditional one, he refers to as metaphor. Quite clearly these three faculties, as will be seen, are interrelated and integrated elements which depend upon each other for their effectiveness. Despite the fact that they are interdependent and often overlap, we will analyze each as a separate notion that performs a special task in a rhetorical enterprise.

Ingenium

Of the three faculties we are ready to discuss, *ingenium* appears to be the most important; for it is the concept which forms the foundation of the other two and, in effect, constitutes the essence of the humanistic tradition. Since Cicero was the first western author who dealt with *ingenium* in depth, Grassi uses him as a point of departure, praising him as he does so for his Latin originality. What Cicero saw when he contemplated nature, Grassi observes, was a mysterious notion which can never reveal itself fully to a human being. Those who lack discernment, therefore, are incapable of rising above sensory data or experiences—a condition which significantly limits their knowledge and understanding. To offset this fact, one needs to possess the necessary virtues to exercise *ingenium*. This suggests an ability to "catch sight of relationships of *similitudes* among things. . . ."[9] When this is realized, a person has succeeded in transcending a sensory awareness and in constructing "a world of his own."[10] In holding such a favorable attitude toward the idea *of ingenium*, Grassi argues, Cicero came to believe that rhetoric assumes a position of primacy: in helping an individual cope with the complexities of nature.

Cicero's ideas on *ingenium* as a central aspect of rhetoric had a noticeable influence on the thinking of Renaissance scholars. Not the least of these was Gracian—a Spanish philosopher and critic. To Gracian *ingenium* is an "act of insight," a process which reveals divinity, and a "sphere of acuteness and wit" which enables one to "decipher the world" through the power of recognizing resemblances between objects."[11]

Additionally, as in the case of his ideas on rhetoric in general, Grassi found Vico's description of *in-genium* to have special significance because of its connection with topical philosophy. By contrasting *ingenium* with rational reasoning, Vico was able to point out that genius as a faculty of comprehension is prior to a system of deduction which is unable to go beyond original premises. To put it another way, "the ingenious faculty assumes the important function of supplying arguments which the rational process itself" cannot discover.[12]

The ideas expressed by Cicero, Gracian, and Vico led Grassi to conclude that *ingenium* is the major source responsible for our image of the world. Moreover it is this faculty which gives purpose and direction to a speaker's use of *inventio* which, in turn, enables him/her to demonstrate creativity in uniting diverse as well as similar aspects of nature.[13]

Work

If *ingenium* is the virtue that enables a rhetor to create and establish the climate for shared meaning through discourse, the domain of work, according to Grassi, is the energizing force which helps make this possible. The function of work is to fulfill human needs by stimulating the development of language and by bringing about the transfer of meaning. Work, in sum, is the activity that gives birth and thrust to human history and society.[14] Perceived in this light, it is an important handmaiden of *ingenium*.

Metaphor

In our discussion of the first two faculties, we have seen that ingenium is a creative talent that enables one to see similitudes in nature and to apply work in an imaginative manner for the purpose of assisting human beings to fulfill their desire to gain new knowledge. The principal method by which this can be done is in the use of language—primarily the metaphor. The humanistic tradition, Grassi forcefully argues, emphasizes the limitations of a "purely rational" language which seeks to prove the validity and reliability of a proposition by using objective language that crosses the boundaries of time. Such language, he adds, is non-rhetorical and, therefore, nonpersuasive.[15]

In making the above claims, Grassi's purpose is not to show that rational thought and language have no utility for one who seeks a deeper appreciation of the intricacies of nature; rather his aim is to demonstrate that there is an initial step that is necessary in the production of knowledge. That step consists of the utilization of analogical or metaphorical language "whereby the soul transfers meaning to appearances."[16] Since imagistic statements outline "the basis or framework of rational argument," they come "before and provide that which deduction can never discover."[17]

Grassi reminds us that the metaphor, which has its roots in the classical period and finds eloquent expression in the form of parables and allegories in the Old and New Testaments, gains its strength through the process of "showing" or revealing important relationships in nature. Convinced that the essence of rhetoric is persuasion and that the metaphor is a powerful instrument to stimulate a reader or hearer, Grassi uses the catch phrase "poet as orator." As a practitioner in the art of using symbols in a graphic manner, the poet relies on "figurative expressions" that convey impressions of "color, sounds, smells, tangibles" which open the doors to the mind.[18]

The fact that poetry often utilizes fantasy and occasionally takes the form of "divine madness" in no way diminishes its effectiveness or soundness as a legitimate rhetorical genre. For the poetorator performs a highly valuable function. By using words that are vivid images revealing relationships, he/she "calls the human world into being," and, therefore, provides "the possibility of mankind liberating itself from the immediate structures of nature."[19]

> metaphor, which has its roots in the classical period and finds eloquent expression in the form of parables and allegories in the Old and New Testaments, gains its strength through the process of "showing" or revealing important relationships in nature.

Grassi, it is clear, has detailed a theory of rhetoric that is humanistic in its outlook. Quite clearly much of what he says is not new. As an admirer of Plato, Cicero, Quintilian, Vico, and a group of Renaissance authors, he makes extensive use of their ideas in forging his own philosophy. His contributions, nevertheless, are significant. In recognizing the oratorical function of the poet, he reaffirms in a telling way the relevance of Blair's practice of combining rhetoric and belles lettres, and in Burke's belief that rhetoric and poetics share similar forms. In addition, by stressing the need to appeal to the whole person in order to produce persuasion that is value-laden, he lends force to Weaver's refutation of those semanticists who in their attempt to reduce language to a scientific expression depreciate the worth of tropes as a stylistic form. Similarly in stating that rhetorical language precedes the articulation of rational claims, he gives fresh emphasis to the current trend we have described as "rhetoric as a way of knowing." With Toulmin and Perelman he is stating anew that rhetoric's principal ally is informal or practical reasoning that strives to generate understanding and gain an adherence of minds.

Jurgen Habermas

As we move now to a consideration of some of the leading perspectives on rhetoric developed by Habermas, we will be confronted with a scholar whose range of knowledge is broad and whose critical skills are sufficiently well honed to enable him to help us glimpse the nature of a rhetoric of the future.

Habermas has been appropriately described as "the most promising latter-day descendant of what has come to be known as the 'Frankfurt School' of social theory."[20] Along with other members of this group, he is a Marxist whose non-orthodox perspective prompts him to attempt to modify Marxism in order to help this world view become more relevant in contemporary society. Since he is motivated by a desire to "reunite theory and practice in the twentieth-century world," he has achieved the important status of a "grand theorist."[21] Perceiving natural science as an inadequate means of studying human behavior, he focuses on communication and informal reasoning as areas of study which are central to his philosophy.[22] And herein lies his significance to contemporary students of rhetoric.

Habermas' ideas on rhetoric fall neatly within several carefully delineated categories which move in an order of progression that gives his thoughts strong unity, coherence, and emphasis. Thus we will adhere to the following pattern that seems to characterize his writings on communication theory. First we will discuss briefly his overall ideas on communicative competence or, as he describes it, universal pragmatics. Next we will analyze how competence is achieved through speech act utterances and soundly conceived arguments. Our final step will strive to demonstrate how a level of communicative competence which epitomizes the effective use of speech acts and persuasive reasons has the potential to produce an ideal speech situation. What we will note as our discussion proceeds is that each of these concepts is closely integrated with the others.

Communication Competence or Universal Pragmatics

In introducing his first theme, Habermas notes: "I have proposed the name Universal Pragmatics for the research program aimed at reconstructing the universal basis of speech."[23] Within this context the word "universal" refers to that type of communication practiced in normal speech. Unlike distorted communication patterns, normal speech conforms to public, "intersubjectively recognized rules" in which "the communicated meanings are identical for all members of the language community."[24] Any person engaged in normal speech is aware of the distinction between a "subject and object" and can "differentiate between outer and inner speech and separate the private from the public word."[25]

Normal speech occurs, moreover, when a speaker takes cognizance of the fact that as conversation takes place, he/she not only focuses on the propositional subject at hand but on the self. This type of discourse, therefore, combines communication on an object with "a metacommunication on the level of intersubjectivity."[26] Unless it can be assumed by a participant in a rhetorical setting that each speaker is a competent communicator who has knowledge of the topic, an awareness of the role of self, and an interest in shared meaning, there is no opportunity for the fulfillment of rational communication goals. It is for this reason that Habermas, influenced in part by Freud's ideas on psychoanalysis, spends so much time discussing the nature of distorted communication.

Even though we will now discuss speech act utterances and argumentation theory and practices as separate units, it should be remembered that they play a fundamental role in Habermas' theory of communication competence or Universal Pragmatics.

> Habermas notes: "I have proposed the name Universal Pragmatics for the research program aimed at reconstructing the universal basis of speech." Within this context the word "universal" refers to that type of communication practiced in normal speech.

Speech Act Utterances

We were first introduced to the notion of speech act theory in the section on Rhetoric as Meaning. Some of the ideas discussed in that chapter, particularly those advanced by the linguistic philosophers Austin and Searle, serve as a basis or a launching point for Habermas' analysis of speech utterances. But, as in the case of most of Habermas' summaries and formulations, he utilizes his talent as a critic to modify some of the basic beliefs that have influenced him. In keeping with this practice, he points out the limitations as well as the strengths of Austin and Searle, and then extends some of their main ideas with the help of a fresh vocabulary that is uniquely his own.

"A general theory of speech actions," according to Habermas, "would thus describe exactly that fundamental system of rules that adult subjects master to the extent that they can fulfill the conditions for a happy employment of sentences and utterances."[27] These rules, for the most part, center on the dual problem of normative expectations as they pertain to the meaning of the content of a message and the successful forming of an intended relationship between the speaker and the listener.[28]

Habermas adheres to a traditional approach in drawing a distinction between locutionary and illocutionary speech acts. The first of these components, which is concerned with propositional content, is of little long range interest to him. Here he is satisfied to say that such action "says something" by expressing "states of affairs." The major criterion used to evaluate a locutionary act is comprehensibility. This suggests that in assessing the effectiveness of this type of utterance, the following question must be answered: "Is the content of the proposition clear?"

Where Habermas places his greatest emphasis is on the illocutionary component which features performative or action-centered utterances. These statements may contain, for example, a promise, request, command, assertion, or avowal on the part of the speaker; and they generally make use of the first person pronoun. The following typical illustration is listed by Habermas: "I hereby promise you (command you, confess to you) that p . . . ."[29] Such claims, in short, constitute an offer that presumably will be carried out at a specified time within a specific situation. If the author of the utterance appears to be sincere and if the content of the message makes a reasonable appeal, the illocutionary or persuasive force is strengthened.

One of Habermas' most original contributions to speech act theory is his five-fold classification of performative acts. The terms he uses to describe these acts are "imperatives," "constatives," "regulatives," "expressives," and "communicatives." "Imperatives" or "perlocutions" are used when a speaker, who has come to believe that a particular action is needed in order to bring about a desired state in the future, attempts to persuade a specific listener to take on this challenge. This expression of a will is designed to influence another person in an objective manner. The end goal of this strategic action is to produce success.[30]

The purpose of "constatives" is to explain the meaning contained in a statement. As Habermas puts it: "Constative speech acts . . . not only embody knowledge," they "represent it,"[31] and they do so by stating, asserting, describing, and explaining. Whether or not "constatives" are viewed as productive depends on the degree of understanding reached and conformity of the claim to the criterion of truth.[32]

In contrast to the first two speech act components, "regulatives" operate within the sphere of accepted moral standards. A speaker who utilizes this act may issue a command or use such words as "forbid," "allow," or "warn" in an effort to establish a relationship with another person and to implement a moral or legal rule. The ensuing criteria are used to measure the worth of this type of statement: (1) To what extent does an act conform to a normative regulation; and (2) How desirable is the norm itself.[33] Notwithstanding the fact that "regulatives" are concerned with the generation of a shared meaning among participants who, it is hoped, will have a mutually respectful relationship with each other, these speech acts gain their distinctive quality by focusing primarily on "what ought to be."[34]

The term "expressives" is used by Habermas to depict a fourth category of speech acts. This form of statement has as its major purpose the revelation of a speaker's self—his/her subjective thoughts concerning a personal experience involving an emotional attitude, the interpretation of a desire or need, or the commitment to a value. In this sense, as Habermas observes, it represents a dramaturgical action that embodies "a knowledge of the agent's own subjectivity." If such self-representation is to be taken seriously, it must meet the test of "truthfulness."[35]

The final speech act that is rhetorically significant, according to Habermas, is labeled "communicatives." This concept appears to be more comprehensive than are the other four types because of the fact that they perform some of the functions of regulative speech acts. Through the activity of "questioning and answering, addressing, objecting, admitting, and the like," for instance, they "serve the organization of speech, its arrangement into themes and contributions, the distribution of conversational roles," and "the regulation of turn-taking in conversation."[36] But, as Habermas is careful to point out, "communicatives" should be treated "as a separate class because of *their reflexive relation to the process of communication.*" This reflexivity empowers "communicatives" to include within their scope such argumentative utterances as "affirming," "denying," "assuring," and "confirming."[37]

The foregoing analysis has sought to show how Habermas took the ideas of Austin and Searle, and then modified, refined, and extended them by creating a fresh vocabulary and by instituting an instructive classification system. More importantly for our purposes in this chapter, his discussion of speech act theory is vitally relevant for the development of his ideas on communication competence. It is further significant to note that speech act theory as detailed here lays the groundwork for Habermas' philosophy of argument.

Theory of Argument

To see how Habermas' theory of argument unfolds and to understand the crucial part that it plays in his discussion of communication competence, we will begin this section with a brief description of the importance of argumentation and then proceed to a consideration of the analytical aspects of argumentative speech, the nature of validity claims, and the notion of truth.

Habermas makes the point that all speech act utterances have as an end to achieve an agreement that is based on good reasons. This means that whenever an expression is articulated by a rhetor, the reasons for delivering it should be evident to the hearer. To highlight this position, Habermas makes the following claim: "Thus the rationality proper to the communicative practice of everyday life points to the practice of argumentation as the court of appeal."[38] This statement, which is strikingly similar to the belief of Toulmin—a scholar whose ideas have doubtless influenced Habermas' thinking—sets the stage for the additional claim that an argument is a systematic expression that "contains reason or grounds that are connected. . . with the *validity claim*" of a problematic utterance.[39]

A final point concerning Habermas' description of the importance of argumentation is his conviction, shared by both Toulmin and Perelman, that a rhetor engaged in the presentation of reasons in supporting a position must be willing to expose his claims to criticism by others. It follows, therefore, that if the criticism is perceived as sound, the original claim should be altered so as to gain an adherence of minds. Viewed from this perspective, "argumentation," it seems clear, "plays an important role in learning processes."[40]

Habermas is more innovative as he next moves to a consideration of the three aspects of argumentative speech. These he defines as "process," "procedures," and "product." Since the latter two aspects are not basically rhetorical, we will touch on these first, and then amplify the central concept of "'process."

all speech act utterances have as an end to achieve an agreement that is based on good reasons.

When we treat argumentation as a "procedure," states Habermas, we are focusing on an interaction method that is "subject to specific rules." The communication genre that is used here is dialectic which tends to be outside of rhetoric because of its preoccupation with a "ritualized competition" and "pragmatic procedures of argumentation."[41]

Similarly non-rhetorical is argumentation that is concerned with "product." Such argumentation is designed "to produce cogent arguments that are convincing in virtue of their intrinsic properties and with which validity claims can be redeemed or rejected."[42] This type of reasoning falls within the realm of logic, and has as its ends to reach a level of validity that is certain.

We are now prepared to see how argument as "process" is rhetorical and, at the same time, crucial to Habermas' belief that it is a cornerstone to achieving communication competence. A "process" view

suggests that argumentation, which is informal and practical in nature, is based on contingent statements that must be negotiated between the rhetor and the listener. This perspective exemplifies a reflective enterprise that excludes the use of force and stresses the value of a cooperative search for knowledge.[43]

In his development of the "process" view of argument, Habermas introduces Perelman's notion of the universal audience. This form of argument, he says, implies the existence of a universal audience that, it is hoped, will give its assent to a particular utterance. If it does, the soundness of the argument has been upheld even by the most insightful hearer.[44]

Two other elements of Habermas' treatment of argument are essential aspects of his theory of practical reasoning. They are his ideas on the nature of validity and truth. To be valid a claim, he asserts, should be comprehensible, truthful, right, and appropriate. For the purpose of illustrating how these criteria work, let us examine the following seven statements which are similar to the ones used by Habermas in his work on *Reason and the Rationalization of Society:*

1. The Washington Redskins are a certainty for winning the Super Bowl in January, 2001.
2. AIDS may be caused by intravenous needles and by sexual intercourse.
3. The best way to reduce the federal government budget deficit is to raise personal income taxes.
4. Universities should make greater efforts to recruit minority students.
5. A student is entitled to see letters of recommendation that are in his/her file.
6. The movie *Cry for Freedom* spends too little time in discussing the role played by black South Africans in their struggle for human rights.
7. A whale is a mammal.

In each of these instances, the hearer, according to Habermas, is confronted with three choices: to agree, to disagree, or to abstain. Statements 1, 2, and 3—which deal with prediction, explanation, and efficacy respectively—are to be evaluated from the standpoint of truth. Utterances 4 and 5, which contain an admonition and an expression of justification, are to be tested by the standard of normative rightness. Claim 6 is a value judgment that is to be measured against the criterion of appropriateness. Finally, statement 7 is expected to meet the dual test of truth and comprehensibility.[45]

In view of the fact that the notion of truth is so vital in assessing the soundness of a speech act utterance that sets forth an argument, it is desirable at this juncture for us to see more clearly the stance Habermas takes on this subject. He upholds the premise that truth is not something which necessarily conforms to scientific verifiability. Nor does it consist of a relationship between an individual and the external world. It is instead a shared conclusion that is reached through the process of sound reasoning. Since it refers to an agreement resulting from the use of warrants, it may be described as "a consensus theory of truth."[46]

One critic has observed that "Habermas' theory of truth has been quite widely influential in the philosophical literature, and leads directly to his concept of the ideal speech situation."[47] This latter theme, which will now be analyzed, is the ultimate point in a philosophy that emphasizes communication competence.

Ideal Speech Situation

What has been said thus far about Habermas' ideas on the subject of communication competence or Universal Pragmatics, speech act theory, and argument as "process" are essential elements of his famous concept of the ideal speech situation. This speech situation, first of all, presupposes the existence of a normal, rather than distorted, communication pattern by each of the participants. Each person taking part in a conversation is expected to use symbols that are to be understood in a comparable manner by all of those who are present.

Secondly, an ideal speech situation is one in which each participant has full freedom to make use of the five types of speech act utterances. That is, the speaker has the privilege of using "imperatives" for the purpose of influencing, in an objective manner, the will of another; of using "constatives" to explain what a statement means; of using "regulatives" to establish an interpersonal relationship concerning a moral code; of using "expressives" to reveal his/her

> Habermas upholds the premise that truth is not something which necessarily conforms to scientific verifiability. Nor does it consist of a relationship between an individual and the external world. It is instead a shared conclusion that is reached through the process of sound reasoning.

subjective thought or identity; and of using "communicatives" not only to regulate such matters as turn-taking but to assure, affirm, or deny.

An ideal speech situation, thirdly, suggests the need to make certain that all of the speech act utterances fulfill the requirements of sound reasoning. This includes the four validity tests of comprehensibility, truthfulness, rightness, and appropriateness. Of similar importance it embraces the notion that when one develops an argumentative claim, the position that is being advanced is open to criticism by others with the expectation that the claim may have to be modified.

The ideal speech situation, then, is one that features the following elements: (1) each person participating in a rhetorical situation has the freedom to express his/her ideas openly and to critique the utterances of others; (2) the concepts of force and power, which are inclined to inhibit the contributions of lower status discussants, are to be eliminated; (3) arguments primarily based on an appeal to tradition, because of their tendency to superimpose the past on the present, are to be exposed; and (4) truth is to be obtained by gaining a consensus or an adherence of minds.

Not a few critics have tried to suggest that Habermas' ideal speech situation, like Perelman's notion of the universal audience which Habermas endorses, is an "arbitrarily constructed ideal" that can never be achieved in a real life setting. This view, we feel, would not disturb Habermas. For what he is arguing is that if all the speakers engaged in a dialogue presuppose the presence of an ideal speech situation, the quality of the discourse will be significantly improved.[48]

As we think about a rhetoric of the future, we are convinced that Habermas' theories will play a fundamental role. His abiding belief that communication competence resulting from an instructive and persuasive use of speech act utterances and sound reasoning, occurring within an ideal speech situation, place him in the forefront of those who are interested in the theme of how rhetoric may perform the task of producing knowledge.

MICHEL FOUCAULT

The third European scholar to be considered in this chapter, Michel Foucault, is unlike any of the authors we have analyzed in this volume. He has not developed, for example, a well organized theory of rhetoric or system of argumentation; nor do his numerous works contain, except in an incidental way, any references to the ideas of the leading rhetoricians of Western thought. Yet despite this approach, Foucault is an important figure for any student interested in a rhetoric of the future.

Some observers have ranked Foucault as a "grand theorist";[49] others have described him as "the thinker who wedded philosophy and history and in so doing developed a dazzling critique of modern civilization."[50] These tributes are consistent with the enthusiasm shown by the educated populace who have read his works. Translations of his writings have appeared in sixteen different languages. Moreover, between the period from 1966 to 1984, the *Social Sciences Citation Index* and the *Arts and Humanities Citation Index* contain 4,385 references to his journal articles alone. Overall, he ranks twenty-fourth among the sixty most heavily cited authors in the field of the Arts and Humanities in the twentieth century.[51]

What is present in the works of Foucault which account for his current popularity and influence? More specifically for our purposes, what does he say about the subject of communication theory that warrants his inclusion in this textbook on rhetorical theory? The answer to these queries, we hope, will be made clear as we summarize some of Foucault's major perspectives on language and discourse. Our analysis will center on three main themes which tend to be treated, with varying degrees of emphasis, in most of his works. They are as follows: (1) his theory of *epistemes* or discursive formations; (2) his archaeological/genealogical method of inquiry; and (3) his notion of power. It will soon be evident that these three subjects will be united under Foucault's strong concern for language structure and usage.[52]

Epistemes or Discursive Formations

As a historian Foucault is interested in knowing what constitutes knowledge in a given period in history. He seeks to ascertain this by examining the nature of the discourse that is used which proves to be acceptable to society at the time of its utterance. This discourse "is made up of a limited number of state-ments for which a group of conditions can be defined," and it features "particular modes of existence."[53] When these statements or groups of signs adhere to a consistent, repeatable pattern and employ similar rules, they may be classified as *epistemes* or discursive formations which represent the shared knowledge of an historical era.

What Foucault is suggesting is that the expression of knowledge is an articulation of propositional statements that conform to widely accepted rules. Often, however, these rules of discourse, while operative, "are not rules which individuals consciously follow."[54] But even though the rules may be only on a subconscious level, they nevertheless are the dominant influence in the making of knowledge claims.

To study a particular discursive formation, therefore, a theorist needs to ask specific questions designed to discover the rules that undergird the statements that are employed. The following sample of questions listed by Philip illustrates the types of interrogatives that are relevant for an understanding of Foucault's position:

1. What rules permit certain statements to be made?
2. What rules order these statements?
3. What rules permit us to identify some statements as true and some as false?
4. What rules allow the construction of a. . .classificatory system?
5. What rules are revealed when an object of discourse is modified or transformed?
6. What rules allow us to identify certain individuals as authors?[55]

To these might be added two other questions raised by Foucault: (1) What rules give a discourse "value and practical application as scientific discourse?" (2) Why "is it that one particular statement appeared rather than another?"[56] Such questions, it should be noted, "provide necessary pre-conditions for the formation of statements."[57]

Throughout Foucault's writings answers to the foregoing rule-related questions may be found. Our end here, however, is not to discuss each of these queries but to analyze two or three that are uniquely important. We will phrase them as follows: (1) What rules allow specific statements to be made, while other possible statements are excluded or silenced? (2) What rules enable us to determine whether or not a statement may be viewed as true or false? (3) What rules make it possible to decide who or what an author is? A discussion of these questions, it is hoped, will give us a clearer understanding of what is involved in the concept of an *episteme* or discursive formation.

Foucault's answer to the first question above, dealing with the making and the prohibiting of certain statements, has far reaching significance for a student of contemporary rhetorical theory. For in his discussion of the "rules of exclusion," whereby possible knowledge claims are not permitted to be expressed, he is covering ground that all of the authors we have analyzed to date have left largely unexplored. He does so with the rationale that what is excluded or silenced may be as important as what is accepted as knowledge.

Foucault's career-long interest in the subjects of madness or insanity and of sexuality, which he felt were taboos in discourse for centuries, doubtless played a part in motivating him to examine the "rules of exclusion." In his "Discourse on Language," he tells us that every society has a system of rules for controlling what is to be said and for disseminating what is to be regarded as knowledge. This control may take the form of exclusion or prohibition. "We know perfectly well," he notes, "that we are not free to say just anything, that we simply cannot speak of anything, when we like, or where we like . . . ."[58] This prohibition may extend to objects, to rituals, or to specific subjects.

But exclusion is not limited to external rules; it may also involve internal rules that govern "the principles of classification, ordering and distribution."[59] Finally, there are rules of exclusion which prevent certain people from entering discourse if they are perceived as lacking specific qualifications or as failing to meet a series of preconditions. One of the implications of Foucault's notion of the "rules of exclusion" is that when one studies an *episteme* that existed in any period, it is desirable to know how certain possibilities for discourse were never realized.

Foucault appears to be on more controversial ground when he seeks to answer the question about the truth and the falsity of a claim. The rule which he embraces is a discourse-centered one in which he argues that truth is what is accepted as being true within a discursive formation. He held that since there can be no perfect relationship between a symbol and its referent, and since the human sciences can be traced back primarily to nonrational origins, then truth is at all times dependent upon discourse.[60] One critic expresses the following strong reservations about what he concludes is a relativistic theory of truth: "If what Foucault says is true then truth is always relative to discourse; there cannot be any statements which are true in all discourses, nor can there be any statements which are true for all discourses. . . ."[61]

In his discussion of the third question, which focuses on the rules characterizing the nature of an author, Foucault is both innovative and insightful. The title of his provocative essay on this subject is "What Is an Author?" In providing an answer to his own question, Foucault refutes the traditional view that an author automatically holds a superior position to that of the text. The argument that he propounds instead is that the author is a product of the discursive formation that is prevalent. Thus the role and function of an author vary from period to period according to the dominant *episteme* that is in operation. This means that at times it is necessary to identify an author; at other times the name is suppressed or pushed aside. All that counts in such instances are the meanings inherent in the statements or propositions that are uttered.

There are two other problems, Foucault adds, associated with the idea of elevating the status of an author. First, an author's published works only reveal what was stated for public consumption. They do not give a full picture of all his/her ideas. For instance, they do not show what was said in conversations, or in unpublished writings, or in marginal notations on manuscripts—all of which are also fundamental aspects of the author's philosophy or beliefs.

Secondly, Foucault points out, author one is not author two. Many authors of the first type, such as creators of novels or another communication genre,

> For in his discussion of the "rules of exclusion," whereby possible knowledge claims are not permitted to be expressed, Foucault is covering ground that all of the authors we have analyzed to date have left largely unexplored. He does so with the rationale that what is excluded or silenced may be as important as what is accepted as knowledge.

may develop an approach that is worthy of emulation. But in the end this level of writer is never more than the author of a particular text. The second type author, however, performs a more vital function. It is one who initiates a new discursive practice that has the power to generate a completely different kind of discourse that will be influential over a long period of time. Included in this category are Freud and Marx whose works "established the endless possibility of discourse."[62]

Our task in examining the nature and role of an author, therefore, is to discover the rules that account for the author's function and position in a specific discourse. What Foucault most earnestly wished to happen in the future is the initiation of a culture in which we do not need to raise questions about the identity of an author or the nature of the self revelation through language. Instead of wondering who is speaking, our attention should be centered on the more important questions such as these:

- What are the modes of existence of this discourse?
- Where does it come from; how is it circulated; what controls it?
- Who can fulfill these diverse functions of the subject?
- What placements are determined for possible subjects (authors)?[63]

It seems clear that by upgrading the value of the content of discourse and by depreciating the worth of an author's role in the production of discourse, Foucault offers a compelling challenge to the traditional theory of ethos or ethical proof as an essential factor in rhetoric.

The Archaeological/Genealogical Method of Inquiry

Foucault gave two names to his method of inquiry for examining the discursive formations of a historical era. He used the words "archaeological" and "genealogical." These metaphors were carefully chosen so that they could depict in a graphic manner the nature of his investigative procedure. Just as an archaeologist digs into the earth in order to discover physical artifacts that shed light on a particular age, Foucault's archaeologist is one who similarly follows a path of descent in an effort to unearth the rules responsible for a discursive formation.

Before we make the slight distinction that may be drawn with respect to the meaning of the terms genealogy and archaeology, let us see in a general way what the method entails. Earlier we noted Foucault's concern about how a particular discursive formation tended to present a limited view of the possibilities for knowledge within a historical period. This occurred for the most part, as we have seen, because of the "rules of exclusion" or the practice of silencing certain potential statements that could have been made. As a result, history has passed on to us a unitary view of what knowledge was at a given time. All too often it was a view based on fragments and presumed continuities of thought which failed to take into consideration the notion of discontinuity.

Archaeology, in sum, is a special method of research which seeks "to emancipate historical knowledges" that have been suppressed or ignored; to give a history to sentiments and instincts that have been motivating; and to cast doubt on traditional conclusions that have been presented with unchallenged finality. In the doing of its work, archaeology would give attention to local as well as to more widely circulated claims. As Foucault elaborates on this point, he draws a distinction between the related terms of archaeology and genealogy:

> Foucault gave two names to his method of inquiry for examining the discursive formations of a historical era. He used the words "archaeological" and "genealogical."

Archaeology would be the appropriate methodology of this analysis of local discursivities, and genealogy would be the tactics whereby, on the basis of the descriptions of these local discursivities, the subjected knowledges which were thus released would be brought into play.[64]

It is highly instructive to observe that this method of inquiry, from Foucault's perspective, is not merely an exercise in recreating a more accurate picture of the past. It also serves the essential function of gaining an access to knowledge that might be used in a tactical way for the benefit of members of society today—especially that group of people who have been excluded from participating in discourse on a subject that is of significance to them.

Foucault applies his archaeological/genealogical method in his most influential book *The Order of*

Things.[65] His research on the period beginning with the sixteenth century and extending to the current period led him to conclude that there were four eras that exemplify well-delineated *epistemes.* He identifies them as the pre-Classical era (approximately 1500 to 1620 or 1630); the Classical period (about 1630 to 1775 or 1780); the Modern age (roughly 1800 to 1950); and the Contemporary era (from 1950 to the present). A brief summary of the first two *epistemes* will be given here for the purpose of seeing how the archaeological method does its work. Regrettably, Foucault did not develop the *episteme* that has been paramount in the last four decades.

Foucault argues that the pre-Classical *episteme* derived force from the single theme of resemblance. Consequently, all of the statements that were accepted as knowledge in this era were grounded in the unifying notion of comparisons or similitudes. Man, nature, the stars, and the divine, for example, were merely reflections of each other. The world, according to this view, "must fold in upon itself, duplicate itself, or form a chain with itself so that things can resemble one another."[66]

Gradually, Foucault asserts, scholars in the seventeenth century began to see the inherent limitations of this *episteme.* They came eventually to believe that knowledge based on resemblances was incapable of enlarging our understanding. Indeed, a statement expressing a so-called knowledge claim did no more than affirm what was already recognized as being true. Among the first to see this major shortcoming, observes Foucault, was Francis Bacon whose concept of the fallacies of the idols—Tribe, Cave, Marketplace, and Theatre—was a critique of resemblances. Since the idols as conceived by Bacon were errors in perception, those who were led astray by these faulty judgments tended to see resemblances where resemblances did not exist.

Later when Descartes also saw weaknesses in the pre-Classical interpretation of resemblances, he joined Bacon and other scientific thinkers in initiating a discontinuity that ushered in a new discursive formation that Foucault describes as Classical. This episteme drew heavily upon reasoning, representation, and order, and remained dominant until the end of the eighteenth century.[67]

> Power produces that which is judged to be knowledge and truth.

Power

The last element to be analyzed in our brief description of Foucault's principal perspectives on discourse is the subject of power. As one whose most active years occurred in the volatile decade of the 1960s, Foucault saw power from many different angles. He saw it as an apparatus of the state, as a means of influence enforced by the judicial system, and as an economic function which, in the view of many Marxist scholars, had a relationship to production and domination. These personal observations, in conjunction with his indepth studies of the past, turned him in a different direction as he sought to discover the role that power played in the development and perpetuation of a discursive formation, and in the eventual creation of a discontinuity that resulted in the initiation of a new *episteme.*

Foucault's probes led him to infer that power focuses on social relations and persuasive strategies. Commenting on this point, Philip notes: "Foucault (in the latter part of his career) sees power as a relationship between individuals where one agent acts in a manner which affects another's actions."[68] Individuals, according to this interpretation, serve the dual function of being the targets of power and the exercisers of it. "Because of this, power relations are always potentially unstable and potentially reversible—I may limit your choice of actions, but your actions may equally limit mine."[69]

If power utilizes persuasive strategies in order to influence the actions of others, what is its relationship to knowledge and truth? Foucault's answer to this question is unequivocal. Power produces that which is judged to be knowledge and truth. A practitioner is able to do this by stimulating a hearer to put his/her received knowledge into use in such a way that further knowledge may be generated. An ethical issue arises, Foucault implies, from this concept of power. If one persuades another to adopt a particular claim, ordering, or classification that is only partial in scope, then we may be endorsing a discursive formation that has excluded vital points of view. Although the resulting formation will constitute what is regarded as truth at a given moment in history, it will be flawed.[70]

Because power makes use of persuasion that affects social relations, thereby determining what is to be viewed as knowledge and truth, Foucault draws this conclusion:

> *The longer I continue, the more it seems to me that the formation of discourses and the genealogy of knowledge need to be analysed, not in terms of consciousness, modes of perception and forms of ideology, but in terms of tactics and strategies of power.*[71]

As can be readily seen, many of Foucalt's ideas challenge some of the basic assumptions that have been made by other rhetoricians and by historians. Regardless of what we think about the merits of some of his most provocative claims, he has presented to us a challenge that we cannot easily ignore. In effect, he is saying that if we want a viable rhetoric of the future, we need to reexamine the past again and again to see what possibilities we have overlooked, or what potentially rich ideas have been silenced or excluded. Equally important, he has outlined an archaeological method of inquiry that may serve as a guide in performing this task.

MICHEL MEYER

During the past decade Michel Meyer, Professor of Rhetoric and Philosophy at the University of Brussels, has emerged as a major European scholar in the field of nonformal or practical reasoning. Influenced in part by his mentor and colleague Chaim Perelman, and drawing upon his experiences as founder and director of the European Center for the Study of Argument, and as editor of two international journals, he has written extensively on the role that questioning plays in the rhetorical process.

In dealing with this largely neglected theme, Meyer seeks to devise a new theory of argument that he calls "problematology." Our purpose in this section is to highlight the important elements of this approach. In order to provide a necessary orientation for our analysis, however, we will summarize at the outset what Meyer perceives to be a current crisis in the area of rhetoric. We will then show how his philosophy of problematology is an attempt to respond to the question.

> **Two Major Causes of Depreciation of Rhetoric**
> ■ Failure to understand and appreciate the decisive role that questioning must play in discourse
> ■ Excessive reliance on the propositional model

The Nature and Causes of the Current Crisis in Rhetoric

Meyer's theory of discourse begins with the premise that rhetoric as a field of study, despite its enormous promise, has not fulfilled its potential; and, as a result, its value has been seriously depreciated. Rhetoric, he tells us, all too often is viewed as "the poor child. . .handicapped of reason."[72] With its undue concern for persuading an audience to adopt a particular attitude or action, rhetoric has in many instances become a manipulative enterprise which employs the device of seduction to achieve its goal.[73] Additionally, rhetoric as it is frequently taught is treated as a separate discipline from its natural ally, poetics. The end result emanating from these problems is a truncated art that commands far less respect than it deserves.

The depreciation of rhetoric, according to Meyer, has been largely due to two important factors. The first is a failure to understand and appreciate the decisive role that questioning must play in discourse. Questioning, to Meyer, is "the fundamental reality of the human mind, to which all other intellectual powers are connected."[74] Thus it is "the basic principle of thought itself, the philosophical principle *par excellence.*"[75] Whenever we engage in discourse, Meyer further suggests, we are speaking or writing for the purpose of responding to a question that is in our mind. It may be said, therefore, that the use of language is always concerned with "the resolution of a question."[76]

A second contributing factor responsible for rhetoric's devaluation is an excessive reliance on the propositional model. The practice of debating propositions rather than questions moves us out of the area of rhetoric, which deals with probability, into the field of logic that strives to ascertain "the truth of assertions."[77] Propositionalism, in sum, is counterproductive to the student of rhetoric because it operates on the principle that alternatives involving a question should be eliminated. It says in effect that "if A is the case, not-A is necessarily excluded."[78] It should be remembered, Meyer concludes, that since rhetoric is a problem-centered and not truth-oriented field of study, a continued reliance on the propositional model will permanently relegate rhetoric, with its emphasis on a probabilistic form of argumentation, to a debased position.

In developing his ideas on the extent of the crisis in rhetoric, Meyer places the primary blame on some of the major Greek authors and practitioners. Plato, Aristotle, and the sophists, he noted, weakened rhetoric by giving precedence to answers over questions. His arguments containing this charge may be found in his essay on "Dialectic and Questioning: Socrates and Plato."[79] In this study, Meyer partitions Plato's works into three periods—the early, the middle, and the later dialogues. In doing so, he demonstrates that Plato progressively moved from an interest in questioning to an overriding concern with providing answers. This change in Plato's original position, as we shall see, profoundly influenced Aristotle.

Despite the occasional limitations in his approach, Socrates in the early dialogues of Plato set standards for questioning and answering that were not adequately met in the subsequent dialogues and in Aristotle's *Rhetoric* and *Topica*. Observe, for instance, the recognizable pattern Socrates used. He wanted each disputant to take turns both as a questioner and as a respondent. This practice made it possible for the interlocutors to function as equals. Under such circumstances, no participant could assume the role of ultimate authority. Socrates, in Meyer's opinion, is to be praised during this period for ensuring "the problematic character of the discourse." But at the same time his method fell short because it did not "advance knowledge" beyond the level of "non-knowledge."

In his middle and later dialogues, Plato showed a steadily increased interest in answering which, in turn, led to a diminished emphasis on questioning. Motivated by a desire to do away with problematicity in the middle dialogues, Plato began to move from his belief that dialectic should be "a question and answer process." His concern now is "what makes an answer an answer"; or what constitutes justification. By thus emphasizing the value of propositions, "all the previous allusions to questioning" disappear.

Plato, in the later dialogues, took an additional step in reducing the role of questioning in his rhetorical system. Questioning thus is tied in with the ontological concept of recollection. Instead of generating new knowledge, a question merely triggers an answer which "reveals an already-there toward which the mind returns." In other words, "recollec-

tion makes us aware that what has been learned and what one knows were concealed in our memory without our knowing it."

Aristotle, Meyer argues, gave further impetus to Plato's tendency to permit answers to take priority over questions. His ideas on the syllogism, on justification, and on dialectic were a natural outgrowth of Plato's philosophy. So, too, was his strongly-held view that "rhetoric is a propositional process . . . ." Indeed, he was willing to claim that a question is a proposition put into interrogative form.[80]

Finally, in the classical era, the sophists, asserts Meyer, contributed significantly to the decline of questioning and the ensuing depreciation of rhetoric as a moral force in a democratic society. A sophist is inclined to raise a question, not for the purpose of eliciting knowledge, but for establishing a rhetorical situation that allows him to display his expertise. The questioner assumes the inferior position of pupil whose task is to help the "Master-Sophist" have an opportunity to supply an answer that is presumed to be certain at the moment of utterance.[81] Unfortunately, the sophist may offer a completely different answer to the same question in another rhetorical setting.

But Plato, Aristotle, and the sophists were not alone in producing a crisis in rhetoric by downplaying the importance of questioning. To this list of enemies of questioning, Meyer affirms, must be added the name of Déscartes. At first glance, Déscartes' inclusion does not seem warranted because of his commitment to a belief in the significance of radical questioning. Meyer makes the point, however, that even Déscartes' concept of doubt is "a propositional attitude." For to say that one doubts is tantamount to affirming a proposition.[82]

It is against the background of this perceived crisis caused primarily by the substitution of propositionalism, with its stress on truth-values, for questioning grounded in probability that Meyer proceeds to articulate a system of rhetoric designed to eliminate or ameliorate the current weaknesses in discourse theory resulting from the death of questioning instigated by Plato.

Toward a Problematological Theory of Rhetoric

The Question-Answer Pair

To elevate rhetoric to its legitimate place as a relevant and productive enterprise, a theory of problematology based on the question approach, Meyer believes, must be the guiding principle. This type of emphasis, first of all, should include an understanding of the question-answer pair. Meyer defines a question as that which "can be solved and eliminated thereafter."[83] To be meaningful a question must have a solution, and be clearly distinguished from its counterpart the answer. This distinction is described by Meyer as "the *problematological difference* because it enables us to provide answers about questioning and still maintain the questioning process."[84] It should also be observed that whenever we are confronted with alternative choices in our attempt to solve a problem, it is "the question itself" which "constitutes the issue. . . ."[85]

A question, Meyer reminds us, may be expressed in several ways including "imperative" and "interrogative" forms. The type of form we select indicates the kind of cooperation or action we expect from the listener. When we say to a dinner companion, for instance, "Will you please pass the salt?", we are using an interrogative structure expressing a desire for cooperation. But since such a question is not designed to elicit a "verbal solution," it has no epistemic purpose. The same is true when we ask someone: "Would you please shut the door?" Another example of a question expressed interrogatively is the following request: "What time is it?" Here the speaker states a problem and makes it explicit that he wishes to find a solution to the query that has been raised.[86]

But a question specifying a problem may also be phrased in a declarative manner. This may be illustrated by a speaker's assertion that "it is nice outside." Such a declaration states an opinion on a problem involving the issue of the weather.[87]

In other instances, an interrogative form may be employed as a means of expressing a "hidden affirmation." To ask "Is he dishonest?" is equivalent to declaring that the particular person under discussion is in fact dishonest.[88]

Meyer further advises us to consider these two statements delivered by two political candidates running for office:

> To elevate rhetoric to its legitimate place as a relevant and productive enterprise, a theory of problematology based on the question approach (Meyer believes) must be the guiding principle.

> In view of the fact that problematological answers represent only partial solutions to a problem, the questioning process is kept open. As other questions are then raised, "new presuppositions" are added "to the existing theory."

1. "No, my rival John is not a crook!"; and
2. "There are good police officers in my opponent's hometown."

In the first statement, the speaker's denial that his rival is a "crook" actually suggests that it is appropriate to ask a question dealing with his honesty. And for one to say in the second instance that "there are good police officers in my opponent's hometown" is to "call into question the efficiency of the whole police department."[89]

A question, in sum, is a statement of a problem that requires a solution; an expression of an idea that is rooted in probability; and a language form that may utilize either an interrogative or declarative structure.

The second element of the language pair is the answer. In describing the first of two types of answers that are available to a rhetor, Meyer again uses the most crucial term in his theory of discourse—problematological. Such an answer, as its designation implies, does not seek to offer a final solution to a problem. It is aimed instead at analysis and enquiry. "In general, when human beings search for meaning, as philosophers and rhetors are wont to do, they proceed by a method of successive enquiry." They begin their research process by asking a question, "not to find the ultimate meaning of a term, but to establish a premise, provide data, learn information, or set the ground for further questions."[90]

In view of the fact that problematological answers represent only partial solutions to a problem, the questioning process is kept open. As other questions are then raised, "new presuppositions" are added "to the existing theory."[91] This ongoing procedure not only has a special relevance for science but for rhetoric as well. "Every speech act," Meyer notes, "is then an answer, since the locutor discusses it in order to respond to some problem: if he expresses it, it is problematological."[92]

The word "apocritical" is used to describe the second type of answer. Unlike a problematological response that tends to maintain openness regarding the ultimate resolution of a question, an apocritical answer is neither tentative nor partial. Meyer draws the following distinction: "When we resort to language in order to express our problems as such, we answer problematologically. When we want to stipulate their solution, we answer apocritically (from *apokrisis*, which means 'answer' in Greek)."[93]

Of these two answers, both of which may be necessary depending on the nature of the rhetorical situation, Meyer shows a strong preference for problematological statements. This conviction is derived from the premise that an apocritical answer generally ignores or suppresses the questions that constitute a problem that should be carefully explored. By failing to "mention the questions that they solve," and by conforming closely to the propositional model, these answers are partly responsible for producing the current crisis in philosophy and rhetoric.[94]

A final consideration that should be noted in our description of the language pair is the dynamic relationship that exists between questions and answers. As Meyer has observed, a problematological approach ensures us that since "questions and answers succeed one another," they "constantly interact in time." When we contrast this dynamic quality with the "logically distinct" and "static" nature that characterizes "topographical" questions and answers often preferred by scientists, we have a clearer understanding of why he identifies problematology with rhetoric.[95]

Meaning, Context, and Reference

A problematological-based theory of rhetoric, secondly, must give special attention to the elements of meaning, context, and reference. Meaning, Meyer informs us, is integrally related to the question-answer pair. As a listener hears a claim and determines its link to an explicit or implicit question that needs to be solved, meaning is generated.[96]

Quite clearly, however, sentences may not be viewed as isolated utterances. They are part of a context that enables us to determine the link that binds questions and answers together, thereby creating meaning. The context gives the listener or reader the necessary background to understand the dynamics of the rhetorical situation and the rhetor's possible intent. To make the element of context more compelling, Meyer asks us to examine the following three statements:

1. "John stopped beating his wife."
2. "Peter is not there."
3. "Close the door please!"

In each of these cases if we lack knowledge of the context, there is no way to assess the meaning. But, on the other hand, if we were present in the situation in which these assertions were made, we would grasp the meaning because of our ability to see the implied question undergirding the statement. To hear someone say, for example, that "John stopped beating his wife" is to know through the context that it is an answer to the question. "Has John stopped beating his wife?" The context also informs us that the assertion "Peter is not there" is a response to the question "whether Peter was there." Finally, when a person observes in our presence "Close the door," we are aware immediately that "the speaker's problem is that he wants a certain door to be closed."[97]

The importance of context to meaning in a rhetorical situation is, according to Meyer, easily seen and affirmed. "In brief," he summarizes, "the context of discourse includes (a) a speaker who writes or speaks, (b) a listener, (c) knowledge and belief, and more particularly, awareness of knowledge, and belief in believing."[98] But the significance of context is greatly diminished in the area of science. This reduced role is caused by the fact that the "theoretical exposition" associated with science has little, or no, connection with context.[99]

Reference, which is closely related to meaning and context, is, as Meyer puts it, a by-product of the question-answer process. It is thus important to recall that "an answer is rarely explicit and direct to the question to which it is paired in discourse." Instead, we may say that an answer "is referential to another question, the one to which it corresponds most directly in an enquiry series."[100] Reference assumes a position of considerable importance because it reveals "the interrogative relation between man and reality," and because it upholds the idea that "to judge is to respond to an interrogation."[101] It is incumbent on the reader or listener, therefore, to know as precisely as possible the question to which an answer refers.

Problematology and Argumentation

Finally, problematology, as it relates to rhetoric, features a theory of argumentation that fulfills four basic requirements. It uses as a starting point a recognition of the fact that practical reasoning deals not with truth or certainty, but with probability. Meyer is consistent with Toulmin and Perelman in his belief that practical argumentation adheres to a nonformal pattern of reasoning. Consequently, he also supports their claim that rhetoric has no place for formal logic which features rigorously constructed arguments that offer no possibility for challenge. But Meyer covers new ground in delineating the strong relationship between argumentation and questioning. "What is an argument," he asks, "but an opinion on a question?"[102] A distinctive feature of rhetoric, Meyer maintains, is its emphasis on problematicity, which tolerates opposing judgments on a particular question. By accepting the equivocal notion that there may be multiple answers to the same question, it says in effect that even though a response may appear to be convincing, additional discussion of a problem may be both appropriate and necessary.[103] What makes this possible is that an answer "can express questions afresh, while it was meant to solve one specific problem."[104] This concept may be illustrated by the following statement: "It is one o'clock." Not only does this assertion present an answer to the question pertaining to the time at a given moment, but it also may be a response to this question: "Is it time for lunch?" By allowing alternative answers to a particular question, and by accepting the premise that "an answer to some question" may in fact be "an answer to another question," a theory of argumentation derived from problematology maintains its nonformal nature.[105]

A second aspect of this type of argumentation is its stress on the importance of involving the audience in the decision-making process regarding an issue under discussion. Persuasion viewed from a problematological perspective, Meyer argues, succeeds in providing answers to questions that concern a target audience.[106]

The most convincing type of argument that may be presented, according to Meyer, is one that permits listeners to draw their own conclusions. In this connection, Meyer points out, "the force of an argument varies directly with the freedom left to the addressed individual." Thus an argument imposed on an audience has much less power than one that the listeners are "free to reject."[107] Consider, for instance, the fol-

> The most convincing type of argument that may be presented (according to Meyer) is one that permits listeners to draw their own conclusions.

lowing situation in which A says to B: "Is not John dishonest?" In such a case, A is more convincing if he elicits the answer from B because B has the privilege to take an opposing position if he or she desires. Since audience members are free to infer their own conclusions with respect to a question, they become equal partners in the dialogue.

In the third place, a theory of argumentation, as discussed here, highlights the significance of utilizing reasoning for the purpose of generating knowledge. Since questions are problems that need to be addressed, and since all participants in a discourse have an equal opportunity both to raise and answer questions, the rhetorical situation is an ideal setting for promoting the acquisition of knowledge. Although the locutor and the communicatee together may enhance their understanding when considering a particular argument, it is possible for the questioner only (either the speaker or the listener) to make a discovery. To clarify this contention, Meyer uses as an example the ensuing assertion: "King Richard is a lion." Already aware that Richard was a courageous king, historians, for example, do not gain new insights from this metaphor. Nevertheless, the statement may represent new information for the speaker and the audience. In recognizing the epistemic as well as the persuasive function of language, Meyer has contributed importantly to the interpretation of rhetoric as a way of knowing.

Meyer has added in the last few years a fourth basic premise to his philosophical/rhetorical theory of argument which may be stated as follows: There is a reciprocal relationship between problematology and the nature and utility of the passions. This theme is developed at length in his volume on *Philosophy and the Passions*[108] which is perhaps the most comprehensive analysis of passionality in western literature.

Disturbed by the fact that the two most distinguished philosopher-rhetoricians in the contemporary era—Chaim Perelman and Stephen Toulmin—tended to ignore the powerful role that passions play in argumentation and persuasion, Meyer strove in the above work to correct this oversight. Reason and passionality, he argued, should not be perceived as opposing forces or as belonging to different intellectual categories. Rather they should be treated as complementary elements which reinforce each other.

The rationale for this inference is derived from the fact that "the human condition is one and indivisible. . . ." This suggests that a person's instincts and desires are integrally related to judgments, beliefs, and actions. It should be remembered, therefore, that "rhetoric and passionality are intimate associates." What he is calling for in making this claim, in sum, is a passionate type of reasoning based upon a "logic of consequences."

It is against this backdrop that the theory of problematology may be regarded as innovative and instructive. It "enables us to understand better the passions, as answers to others, to ourselves, to problems, to situations and also as ways of expressing those problems rather than merely solving them." When passions are perceived in this light, therefore, they may be considered as "behavioral modes of problem-solving and problem-expression." This perspective, in short, is a reaffirmation of the question-answer pair.

Up to this point we have seen how arguments may be found in those rhetorical situations involving interpersonal and public discourse. But Meyer's theory of problematology is also built upon the notion that arguments abound in literary texts as well. So important is the study of literature in developing his ideas that he includes in most of his works sections on this topic. In his volume on *Meaning and Reading,* which we have alluded to on a number of occasions, he uses as his subtitle, "A Philosophical Essay on Language and Literature"; and labels three of his chapters: "The Rhetoric of Textuality," "The Nature of Literariness," and "The Interpretative Process." His rationale for providing this emphasis is his belief that literary and nonliterary texts are both rhetorical in nature since they share a concern for "problems and solutions."[109] As in the case of oral discourse, he asserts, "the rhetorical nature of fiction stems from the fact that alternatives are open, and sometimes deliberately left open."[110] By taking this stance, it is only natural for him to conclude that there should be no "scission between poetics and rhetoric."[111]

Meyer, in brief, has taught us about the interrogativity of the mind and the value of understanding the question-answer pair; the influential role of meaning, context, and reference; the severe limitations of the propositional model; and the problematological basis of argumentation and the desirability of having the listener infer his or her solution to the problem at hand. Moreover, by example he has demonstrated the worth of applying contemporary principles of thought in a reexamination of the works of such celebrated authors as Plato, Aristotle, and Déscartes. In a similar vein, he has reminded us, as Kenneth Burke earlier had done, that rhetoric and poetics share comparable features and must, therefore, be viewed as a unified whole.

> Meyer, (in brief) has taught us about the interrogativity of the mind and the value of understanding the question-answer pair;

Overall, Meyer has shown that rhetoric is a dynamic, developing enterprise that deserves a prominent place in a democratic society.[112] His works, too, continue to be produced at a rapid rate, each extending his theory of problematology. We have in our library, for example, four volumes published since we first discussed his philosophy in the 5th edition of *The Rhetoric of Western Thought*[113] Because of these accomplishments Meyer's theory of problematology, with its vocabulary of fresh and provocative terms, serves as a fitting summary of the resurging interest in rhetoric on the European Continent.

Notes

1. We would like to congratulate Sonya K. Foss, Karen A. Foss, and Robert Trapp for their inclusion of chapters on Grassi, Foucault, and Habermas in their volume entitled: *Contemporary Perspectives on Rhetoric* (Prospect Heights, Ill., 1985).

2. Ernesto Grassi, "Critical Philosophy or Topical Philosophy?", in George Tagliacozzo and Hayden V. White, eds., *Giambattista Vico: An International Symposium* (Baltimore: The Johns Hopkins University Press, 1969), pp. 39–44.

3. "Critical Philosophy or Topical Philosophy?", pp. 45–49.

4. Grassi, "Rhetoric and Philosophy," *Philosophy and Rhetoric,* 9 (1976), pp. 208–209.

5. "Rhetoric and Philosophy," pp. 210–212.

6. *Ibid.*, p. 214.
7. *Ibid.*
8. *Ibid.*
9. Grassi, *Rhetoric as Philosophy: The Humanist Tradition* (University Park: The Pennsylvania State University Press, 1980). Hereafter cited as *Rhetoric as Philosophy.*
10. *Rhetoric as Philosophy,* p. 10.
11. *Rhetoric as Philosophy,* p. 16.
12. Grassi, "The Priority of Common Sense and Imagination: Vico's Philosophical Relevance Today," in George Tagliacozzo, Michael Mooney, and Donald P. Verene, eds. *Vico and Contemporary Thought* (Atlantic Highlands, N.J.: Humanities Press, 1976), p. 172.
13. *Rhetoric as Philosophy,* p. 51.
14. See *Rhetoric as Philosophy,* pp. 86, 100; and "The Priority of Common Sense," pp. 174–183.
15. *Rhetoric as Philosophy,* p. 96.
16. *Rhetoric as Philosophy,* p. 100.
17. *Rhetoric as Philosophy,* p. 97.
18. *Rhetoric as Philosophy,* p. 113.
19. *Rhetoric as Philosophy,* p. 75.
20. Anthony Giddens, "Jurgen Habermas," in Quentin Skinner, ed., *The Return of Grand Theory in the Human Sciences* (Cambridge: Cambridge University Press, 1985), p. 124.
21. Giddens, p. 123.
22. See Thomas McCarthy's "Introduction," in Jurgen Habermas, *Communication and the Evolution of Society* (Boston: Beacon Press, 1979), p. xvii.
23. *Communication and the Evolution of Society,* p. 5.
24. Habermas, "Toward a Theory of Communicative Competence," *Recent Sociology,* No. 2, Hans Peter Dreitzel, ed. (London: Collier-MacMillan, 1970), p. 122.
25. *Ibid*
26. *Ibid.*, p. 143.
27. Habermas, *Communication and the Evolution of Society,* p. 26.
28. *Communication and the Evolution of Society,* p. 35.
29. Habermas, *Reason and the Rationalization of Society,* p. 289.
30. *Reason and the Rationalization of Society,* pp. 325, 329.
31. *Reason and the Rationalization of Society,* p. 333. On this point McCarthy notes: "The employment of constatives makes possible the distinction between a public world (being, that which really is) and a public world (appearance)." "A Theory of Communicative Competence," *Phil. Soc. Sci.* 3 (1973), p. 138.
32. *Reason and the Rationalization of Society,* p. 329.
33. *Reason and the Rationalization of Society,* p. 334.
34. McCarthy, "A Theory of Communicative Competence," p. 138.
35. *Reason and the Rationalization of Society,* pp. 326, 329, and 334.
36. *Reason and the Rationalization of Society,* p. 326.
37. *Reason and the Rationalization of Society,* p. 326.
38. *Reason and the Rationalization of Society,* pp. 17–18.
39. *Reason and the Rationalization of Society,* p. 18.
40. *Ibid.*
41. *Reason and the Rationalization of Society,* p. 26.
42. *Reason and the Rationalization of Society,* p. 25.
43. *Ibid.*
44. *Reason and the Rationalization of Society,* p. 26.
45. See *Reason and the Rationalization of Society,* pp. 36–40.
46. McCarthy, "A Theory of Communicative Competence," p. 141.
47. Giddens, 130.
48. For an excellent analysis of Habermas' ideas on the ideal speech situation, see Giddens, p. 131, and McCarthy, "A Theory of Communicative Competence," pp. 137–148.
49. See Mark Philip, "Michel Foucault," in *The Return of Grand Theory in the Human Sciences.*
50. J.G. Merquior, *Foucault* (Berkeley: University of California Press, 1985), p. 16.
51. See Allan Megill, "The Reception of Foucault by Historians," *Journal of the History of Ideas,* XLVIII (Jan.-Mar., 1987), pp. 135–141.
52. See "Preface" of Donald F. Bouchard, ed., *Language, Counter-Memory, Practice* (Ithaca: Cornell University Press, 1977).
53. Foucault, *The Archaeology of Knowledge* (New York: Pantheon Books, 1972), p. 117.

54. Philip, 70. Also see Foucault's "Foreward to the English Translation of *The Order of Things*" (New York: Vintage Books, 1970).

55. Philip, pp. 69–70.

56. *The Archaeology of Knowledge,* p. 27.

57. Philip, p. 69.

58. *The Archaeology of Knowledge,* p. 216.

59. *The Archaeology of Knowledge,* p. 220.

60. In his essay on Nietzsche, he observed: "Truth is undoubtedly the sort of error that cannot be refuted because it was hardened into an unalterable form in the long baking process of history." "Nietzsche, Genealogy, History," in *Language, Counter-Memory, Practice,* p. 144.

61. Philip, p. 70.

62. "What is an Author?", in Bouchard, pp. 131–136. Foucault also makes the following interesting point: "A study of Galileo's works would alter our knowledge of the history, but not the science of mechanics; whereas, a reexamination of the books of Freud or Marx can transform our understanding of psychoanalysis or Marxism." "What is an Author?", p. 136.

63. "What is an Author?", p. 138.

64. *Power/Knowledge,* Colin Gordon, ed. (New York: Pantheon Books, 1980), p. 87.

65. Merquior calls this work Foucault's "masterpiece." *Foucault,* p. 35.

66. *The Order of Things,* pp. 25–26.

67. See in particular the chapter on "Representing," *The Order of Things,* pp. 46–77.

68. Philip, p. 74. Foucault noted: "In reality, power means relations, a more-or-less organized, hierarchical coordinated cluster of relations," *Power/Knowledge,* p. 199.

69. Philip, p. 75.

70. Consider, for example, the following statement describing the end of the pre-Classical *episteme:* "And it was also in the nature of things that the knowledge of the sixteenth century should leave behind it the distorted memory of a muddled and disordered body of learning in which all the things in the world could be linked indiscriminately to men's experiences, traditions, or credulities." *The Order of Things,* p. 51.

71. *Power/Knowledge,* p. 77.

72. *Langue Française.* 79 (Septembre 1988), p. 3.

73. See Michel Meyer, "Problematology and Rhetoric," in James L. Golden and Joseph J. Pilotta, eds, *Practical Reasoning in Human Affairs: Studies in Honor of Chaim Perelman* (Dordrecht: D. Reidel Publishing Company, 1986), p. 147; and *Meaning and Reading* (Amsterdam/Philadelphia: John Benjamins Publishing Company, 1983), pp. 72–73.

74. *Langue Française,* 52 (Decembre 1981), p. 3.

75. *De La Problematologie* (Brussells: Pierre Mardaga, 1986), p. 11.

76. *Meaning and Reading* p. 3.

77. "Problematology and Rhetoric," p. 37.

78. "The Problematological Turn," *Questioning Exchange,* 2 (May 1988), p. 166.

79. *American Philosophical Quarterly,* 17 (October 1980), pp. 281–89. Similar comments are found in his other writings. See in particular Section 3 in the introduction to his volume *Aristotle's Rhétorique* (Librairie Generale, 1991), pp. 11–17.

80. Also see "Problematology and Rhetoric," p. 148.

81. "Dialectic and Questioning," p. 283.

82. "The Problematological Turn," p. 167.

83. "Problematology and Rhetoric," p. 129.

84. Ibid., p. 131. Also see the essay, "Argumentation in Light of a Theory of Questioning," *Philosophy and Rhetoric* 15 (Spring 1982), p. 81.

85. "Argumentation in Light of a Theory of Questioning," p. 84.

86. "Science as a Questioning Process: A Prospect for a New Type of Rationality," *Revue Internationale de Philosophie* (Trente-Quatrième année, 1980), p. 141.

87. "Argumentation in Light of a Theory of Questioning," p. 82.

88. *Ibid.,* p. 83.

89. "Problematology and Rhetoric," p. 139.

90. James L. Golden and David L. Jamison, "Meyer's Theory of Problematology," *Questioning Exchange,* 2 (1988), p. 155.

91. "Science as a Questioning Process," p. 65.

92. *Ibid.,* p. 69.

93. *Meaning and Reading,* p. 26.

94. *Ibid.,* p. 54.

95. "Science as a Questioning Process," p. 58.

96. "Argumentation in Light of a Theory of Questioning," pp. 70, 92.

97. "Science as a Questioning Process," p. 71.

98. "La conception problématologique du Language," in *Langue Française,* p. 81.

99. "Argumentation in Light of a Theory of Questioning," p. 87.

100. "Meyer's Theory of Problematology," p. 158.
101. "Argumentation in Light of a Theory of Questioning," p. 92.
102. *Ibid.,* p. 100.
103. "Problematology and Rhetoric," p. 137.
104. *Meaning and Reading,* p. 69.
105. *Ibid.,* p. 73.
106. "Problematology and Rhetoric," p. 135.
107. *Ibid.*
108. *Le Philosophe Et Les Passions* (Librairie Générale Française, 1991)
109. See *Meaning and Reading,* p. 80; and "Problematology and Rhetoric," p. 146.
110. "Problematology and Rhetoric," p. 147.
111. *Ibid.*
112. For further insights on Meyer's contribution to argumentation theory and on the heuristic value of his problematological model, see the following essays: David L. Jamison, "Michel Meyer's Philosophy of Problematology: Toward a New Theory of Argument," *Argumentation,* 5 (February 1991), pp. 57–68; and James L. Golden, "An Application of Michel Meyer's Theory of Problematology to David Hume's *Dialogues Concerning Natural Religion*", ibid., pp. 69–89.
113. These publications are as follows: *Questions De Rhetorique* (Librairie Générale Française, 1993); *Rhetoric, Language, and Reason* (University Park, PA: The Pennsylvania State University Press, 1994); *De l'Insolence* (Paris: Bernard Grasset, 1995); and an English translation of *Problematology* by David Jamison (Chicago: University of Chicago Press, 1995).

Protest Rhetoric, Social Movements, and Moral Exclusion of the American Indian

During the 1930s, '40s, and '50s, it was fashionable for American scholars in the field of rhetorical criticism to evaluate the past persuasive efforts of a *single speaker.* Or, more narrowly, to assess some aspect of an individual's speaking upon a single important issue of the day. Following the lead of historians and literary scholars, rhetorical critics typically focused their attention on figures from the past, or as some would have it, those who were "safely dead." It was generally assumed at the time that one could not possibly be objective about events happening in her/his own day.

Such figure studies served a purpose but most observers would agree they had serious shortcomings. They did not help us understand the diverse role persuasion plays in an historical campaign or social movement, let alone one happening in our own day. They neglected to appraise the effect of multiple advocates or to explore their interactions with one another. Usually they centered attention upon oral messages alone, to the neglect of written ones designed to influence others. Clearly a new, broader approach was needed if we were to comprehend the complexities of other changes in the nature of American society.

In all likelihood, the social turmoil of America in the sixties—the war in Vietnam, the civil rights struggle, and the campaign for women's rights—heightened the interest of rhetorical critics in movement rhetoric and new approaches to its study. In the present chapter, our aim is to show how a group of rhetors, acting as members of a large social or political unit, engage in discourse as representatives of a collectivity or a campaign. The first half of this dis-

cussion will focus on protest rhetoric and social movements, and the second on a case study of an important dimension of a presidential campaign.

PROTEST RHETORIC AND SOCIAL MOVEMENTS

Persuasive discourse which accompanies any significant social movement is unique in several respects. This essay explores the rhetorical dimensions of social protest rhetoric by examining the definitions, characteristics, strategies, and themes of this genre.

The rhetoric of social agitation or protest is perhaps one of the oldest forms of discourse known to man. Here is a rhetorical genre primarily concerned with altering social relationships among people, groups, and power centers or "establishments." Here is a rhetoric which is truly persuasive. As Bitzer observes:

A work of rhetoric is pragmatic; it comes into existence for the sake of something beyond itself; it functions ultimately to produce action or change in the world; it performs some task. In short, rhetoric is a mode of altering reality, not by the direct application of energy to objects, but by the creation of discourse which changes reality through the mediation of thought and action.[1]

The history of mankind abounds with individuals and groups who at one time or another engaged in some form of verbal protest. The ancient prophet

Amos, Martin Luther, Martin Luther King, Jr., the Berrigans, Billy James Hargis, and Carl McIntire are a few well-known religious agitators. Joseph Stalin, Gandhi, Fidel Castro, Samuel Adams, and Tom Hayden frequently agitated in the political realm. Thousands of individuals could be easily included here. All had one general goal in mind: to alter the power relationship dimension between individuals and/or between individuals and "establishments."

If a realignment of power relationships is the major objective of a social movement, what factors account for or justify the formation of the movement? An inquiry into the causes of a social movement is not the objective of this essay for such an investigation lies in the realm of the sociologist rather than of the rhetorical critic. However, it should be obvious that the *general cause* of any reform movement can be traced to a growing feeling of *dissatisfaction* with the "status quo" on the part of a group or segment of society. Members of the movement often feel "put down," oppressed, or abused by the power holders. Charles Lomas summarizes: "Neither rhetorical nor activist agitation can hope to succeed even partially unless social and political conditions are favorable to the initiation and growth of the movement. There must be clear evidence of *injustice or apparent injustice* deeply affecting the well being of those who compose the audience."[2] When such a feeling takes hold in the disciple's ranks, a generalized attitude of *unrest* is fostered. Furthermore, if the established powers fail to deal with this dissatisfaction an organization of the frustrated or disfranchised begins. Thus, a movement is born. A strategy for change emerges. The establishment is challenged. The "haves" are confronted publicly by the "have nots."

> *The "have nots" picture themselves as radically divided from traditional society, questioning not simply the limitations of its benevolence but more fundamentally its purposes and modes of operation. Whether they experience deprivation as poverty, or lack of political power, or disaffection from traditional values, the "have not" leaders and theorists challenge existing institutions.*[3]

Thus, a social movement is dependent on a generalized feeling of unrest which is then translated into a call for change. Furthermore, the agitator's demands for change must be met by resistance from the estab-

> a social movement is dependent on a generalized feeling of unrest which is then translated into a call for change.

lishment. The interaction of an urgent call for change "falling on deaf ears" results in an emotionally charged climate—a potentially explosive situation. "On the part of the established ruling groups," says Lomas, "there must be massive *resistance to change.* This resistance may be motivated by high principles, by apathy, by self-interest, or by fear. . . ."[4]

As stated previously, this essay is not concerned with a thorough examination of the *causes* of human protest. Rather, our prime focus is the *rhetorical dimension* of agitation. Our discussion begins with a consideration of definition.

Scholars from the speech-communication field have examined protest discourse and defined their focus in slightly different formulations. For instance, Bowers and Ochs discuss the phenomenon of *agitation* discourse. "Agitation exists when (1) people outside the normal decision making establishment (2) advocate significant social change and (3) encounter a degree of resistance within the establishment such as to require more than the normal discursive means of persuasion."[5] Accordingly, agitation occurs when "powerless" individuals demand "significant change" and find that their efforts are actively resisted by the establishment. Mary McEdwards continues this emphasis. "Agitative language belongs to a particular type of rhetoric whose end is movement away from the *status quo.* Some may argue that all rhetoric has this same end. However, the rhetoric we call *agitation* evokes extreme movement away from the *status quo*—usually a complete reversal of existing conditions or situations.[6] Bowers, Ochs, and McEdwards, then, consider the discourse of social protest as those rhetorical efforts concerned with "significant social change," or a movement away from the status quo. Lomas discusses "agitation" in a similar fashion. "Agitation may be defined as a persistent and uncompromising statement and restatement of grievances through all available communication channels, with the aim of creating public opinion favorable to a change in some condition."[7] Robert Browne labels this genre the rhetoric of *discontinuity* because it is aimed at social *change*—not at maintaining the status quo, "keeping the existing political system going," or maintaining "continuity between groups, classes, generations."[8]

Paul Brandes considers the rhetoric of social protest and formulates a definition of the rhetoric of *revolt* which moves beyond the discourse of agitation or discontinuity discussed above. "Revolt rhetoric," according to Brandes, "openly advocates lawlessness. The Old Regime is not to be modified peacefully. It is to be amended by force. Not until there is an open call for lawlessness can the rhetoric of revolt be said to have begun."[9] Hence, Brandes has described a discourse which advocates lawlessness and force rather than mere social change as characteristic of agitation. The rhetoric of revolt advocates a complete upheaval of existing institutions.

Perhaps the most suitable perspective for our immediate purposes is to view the discourse accompanying a social protest as a continuum rhetoric. Anchoring the "conservative" extremity is the rhetoric of agitation. We define agitation discourse as that rhetoric which (1) is uttered by "frustrated" individuals either inside or outside the power-holding elite, (2) calls for a "significant social change" in the system, and (3) encounters resistance from the establishment such as to require its advocates to go beyond the "acceptable" or approved channels of communication—a definition obviously influenced by Bowers, Ochs, Browne, and McEdwards. In other words, if the establishment fails to respond to the change demanded by the "discontented," a movement may emerge which finds it necessary to go beyond and outside the normal channels of communication to accomplish its goals. This, then, is the rhetoric of agitation. At the other extreme of the continuum is the rhetoric of revolt. Here is discourse which openly calls for a total revolution or overthrow of the existing power centers. Individuals in this camp are not satisfied with mere "significant" social change. They demand a complete and total upheaval: revolution. Between these poles are those forms of discourse which call for change in society or a part of the social system—a call which differs only in intensity and extremism. Herbert Simons recognizes this diversity in radicalism characteristic of protest discourse when he discusses the variety of rhetorical strategies available to leaders of any movement. "Along a continuum from the sweet and reasonable to the violently revolutionary, one may identify *moderate, intermediate, and militant* types of strategies, each with its own appropriate tactics and styles."[10]

All reform movements, then, engage in protest discourse which helps initiate, organize, and sustain a unified effort where energy is directed toward an "enemy" or establishment. The protestors' use and misuse of language in the form of demands makes their rhetoric the major vehicle for change in the en-suing power struggle. Ernest Bormann discusses the importance of rhetoric for any reform movement.

A reform movement . . . requires organization to succeed. A chaotic impulse may influence events by blindly striking out or by surfacing in unusual unexpected violence like black rioting in the cities in the 1960s, but a reform movement requires more than the impulse. In addition to a program of action, an ideology, and administrative skills, an organization requires meetings that provide interaction among the members until leadership emerges. Spokesmen must then establish channels of communication so they can indoctrinate people into the party line, encourage them in adversity, and inform them in times of triumph. Most important for our concerns is that among the leadership of any successful reform movement there must be rhetoricians who provide both the insider and outsider with a meaningful interpretation of the movement.[11]

Thus, basic to any reform movement is the rhetorician or, as Eric Hoffer calls him, the "Man of Words."

Mass movements do not usually rise until the prevailing order has been discredited. This discrediting is not an automatic result of the blunders and abuses of those in power, but the deliberate work of men of words with a grievance. . . . The preliminary work of undermining existing institutions, of familiarizing the masses with the idea of change, and of creating a receptivity to a new faith, can be done only by men who are, first and foremost, talkers or writers and are recognized as such by all.[12]

Any social movement, then, requires a man of words who manages the "language." These are the rhetoricians who weave a discourse which captures the urgent feelings and desires of the movement. The success of the movement in realizing its goals is partly, if not wholly, dependent on the designated man of words. His importance, Hoffer suggests in the ensuing paragraph, cannot be underestimated:

To sum up, the militant man of words prepares the ground for the rise of a mass movement: (1) by discrediting prevailing creeds and institutions and detaching from them the allegiance of the people; (2) by indirectly creating a hunger for faith in the hearts of those who cannot live without it, so that when the new faith is preached it finds an eager response among the disillusioned masses; (3) by furnishing the doctrine and the slogans of the new faith; (4) by undermining the convictions of the 'better people'—those who can get along without faith—so that when the new fanaticism makes its appearance they are without the capacity to resist it.[13]

In sum, the man of words vocalizes the discontent and demands of the movement. He works with the leaders and rhetorically portrays a symbolic reality which attracts, maintains, and molds workers into an efficiently organized unit. He attempts to secure adoption of the movement's product or program by the larger structure or establishment. In so doing, the man of words must be prepared to react rhetorically to the resistance generated by the establishment.[14]

> the man of words vocalizes the discontent and demands of the movement.

Several symbolic strategies are available to the rhetoricians or men of words. For instance, in discussing the rhetoric of the black revolution, Arthur Smith conceptualizes four major language strategies: vilification, objectification, mythication and legitimation.

Vilification

Since a major task of the rhetorician is to "interpret reality" to those both inside and outside the fellowship, the man of words begins by denouncing the leader of the "establishment" which in turn becomes the defined target for the movement's energies. Smith labels this strategy vilification or "the agitator's use of language to degrade an opponent's person, actions, or ideas."[15] The strategy of vilification results in the *naming* of the opposition's *leadership*. So, the "devil" is personified and identified for all to see.

> Smith's Four Major Language Strategies
> ■ vilification
> ■ objectification
> ■ mythication
> ■ legitimation

Objectification

A second rhetorical strategy related to vilification is "objectification."

*It is the agitator's use of language to direct the grievances of a particular group toward another collective body such as an institution, nation, political party, or race. Related to, but dif-*ferent from vilification, objectification uses similar devices of sarcasm and low humor while attacking an ill-defined body. Both strategies direct attention to the opposition; however, objectification strives to channel all of the frustrations of a group onto a single ill-defined body.[16]

The "enemy" is now publicly noted. "The agitator is concerned with showing that a certain race, party, or secret collection of men is responsible for all of the misfortune that befalls the agitator's votarists. The solution is simple: we must get rid of them."[17]

Mythification

Smith notes a further strategy calling it "mythication."

Employing language that suggests the sanction of supra-rational forces, the agitator creates a spiritual dynamism for his movement. Seizing on what is probably the rationale for black hope, the agitator often attempts to use religious symbolism in an effort to demonstrate the righteousness of his cause.[18]

Besides religious symbolism, agitators in the black movement have also employed the sanction of history. According to Smith, "The black rhetor wants to demonstrate that his agitation is sanctioned by history because great agitators have sought to establish justice, create equality, and build dignity."[19]

Legitimation

A final strategy discussed by Smith is that of "legitimation" or the use of language to answer the arguments and resistance of the opponent.

Finally, the rhetor of black revolution makes use of legitimation, insofar as it is the use of language to answer the opposition, it is a refutative strategy. But it is more than an argumentative rebuttal to an opponent; it is a psychological weapon. In legitimation, the black revolutionist seeks to explain, vindicate, and justify the activists involved in the movement.[20]

Thus, Smith considers these four as major strategies found in black revolutionary discourse. These same tactics, however, can be identified in almost any movement's rhetoric. Smith concludes:

He (the black revolutionary) endeavors to degrade and stigmatize the opposition with the strategies of vilification and objectification; and he attempts to unify and defend his followers with mythication and legitimation. Even though these strategies are not necessarily found in all agitational rhetoric in the same degree, they always occur at some point in an agitational campaign waged with intensity and persistence.[21]

Complementing Smith's categories, Robert Scott and Donald Smith list four major rhetorical strategies or themes involved in social confrontations: we are already dead; we can be reborn; we have the stomach for the fight, you don't; we are united and understand.[22] Thus, in their function as rhetoricians, the men of words will often develop one or all of the above general themes which are then directed at the "establishment" as the primary audience.

First, in order to help unify the movement, the rhetorician must foster a feeling of frustration and powerlessness among the disciples. So, the "we are already dead" theme emerges. "In the world as it is," state Scott and Smith, "we do not count. We make no difference. We are not persons. . . . Some radicals take oaths, changing their names, considering themselves as dead, without families, until the revolution succeeds. It is difficult to cow a dead orphan."[23]

But, precisely because the disciples are already dead—worthless human beings—they have the potential to be reborn—to have a second chance. Scott and Smith summarize:

Having accepted the evaluation of what is, agreeing to be the most worthless of things, we can be reborn. We have nothing to hang on to. No old identity to stop us from identifying with a new world, no matter how horrifying the prospect may seem at the outset; and a new world will certainly be born of the fire we shall create.[24]

Thus, through his rhetoric, the man of words attempts to prove to the faithful followers of the movement that they are worthless and because of this, they can be born anew. Language and arguments are tailored for this purpose. Next, the theme of stamina

for the struggle usually emerges: we have the stomach for the fight, you don't. "We can strike to kill for the old world is not ours but one in which we are already dead, in which killing injures us not, but provides us with the chance of rebirth."[25] With their dignity stripped and nothing to lose in their battle with the "establishment," the theme emerges which stresses the unity of the "brotherhood": we are united and understand. Scott and Smith explain:

We are united in a sense of a past dead and a present that is valuable only to turn into a future free of your degrading domination. We have accepted our past as past by willing our future. Since you must cling to the past, you have no future and cannot even understand.[26]

Thus, the authors have identified four general rhetorical themes characteristic of the discourse surrounding any radical reform. These are strategies which surface as the movement approaches the "revolt" extreme of our continuum.

The man of words, then, has as his chief duty the construction of a unique *symbolic world*. Klapp observes:

Man not only constructs objects but also builds his own symbolic world. These worlds vary (or are indemonstrably identical) for each individual and cultural group. Yet a frame of reference that is collectively constructed *allows members to coordinate their behavior in ways which would never be possible without such common understandings.*

Humans are continually constructing images of the present, images of the future, and images of the past—and tying them together and sharing them by symbols. This is the reality to which they respond. In brief, reality is what you make it.[27]

Within the perimeters of the protestors' symbolic world, the movement's rhetorician lists the causes of dissatisfaction, discredits the "enemy," helps unify and mold the ensuing organization, helps define the goals and objectives of the movement and interprets them to the disciples and the rest of the world. Above all, the man of words is an "explainer" and an interpreter of "reality." He occupies a unique and powerful place within the movement. No reform effort can succeed without him.

In conclusion, the rhetoric of social protest is a demanding and urgent rhetoric aimed at (a) unifying and molding an organized effort from the powerless disciples and (b) concerned with symbolically destroying the establishment in an effort to initiate the desired change. The rhetorical themes inherent in this discourse are geared toward this two pronged symbolic attack.

Social protest rhetoric is a necessary ingredient for any social movement. Let us now turn attention to social movements focusing our discussion on the environmental movement.

Stewart, Smith and Denton define a social movement as "an organized, uninstitutionalized, and significantly large collectivity that emerges to bring about or to resist a program for change in societal norms and values, operates primarily through persuasive strategies, and encounters opposition in what becomes a moral struggle."[28] The persuasive strategies referred to in this definition might include those highlighted in the previous pages. A quick glance at American history reveals that social movements have played significant roles in the life of this country. William Lloyd Garrison, Wendell Phillips, Frederick Douglass, and other advocates in the abolitionist movement, for example, fought to free the slaves; Elizabeth Cady Stanton, Lucretia Mott, and backers of the suffragette movement sought women's right to vote; Dr. Martin Luther King, Jr., Roy Wilkins, Jesse Jackson, and supporters of civil rights movement rallied for equal rights including the right to vote; Gloria Steinem, Bela Abzug, and other women's movement adherents continue the struggle for women's rights and equality.

Movements generally are made up of various philosophical and tactical perspectives represented by disparate individuals and organizations. For instance, the civil rights movement was energized by the NAACP, Southern Christian Leadership Conference, Black Panthers, Student Nonviolent Coordinating Committee, Black Muslims, Malcolm X, Bobby Seale, and Eldridge Cleaver, to name a few. Each differed in the approach taken to conceptualize and explain the problem. Likewise, these advocates disagreed on such matters as philosophy, strategy, and tactics; however, each had a degree of allegiance to the common goal of the movement.

> "Persuasion is a communication process by which a social movement seeks through the use of verbal and nonverbal symbols to affect the perceptions of audiences and thus to bring about desired changes in ways of thinking, feeling, and/or acting."

Despite a movement's ability to accommodate a range of opinion, a certain level of organization must be apparent. Structures need to be in place and spokespersons identifiable. Just as important, philosophies, tactics, and goals must evolve together with the various organizations' leadership and membership.

A social movement is also an uninstitutionalized collectivity, according to the definition presented earlier. This means that the movement stands outside of the existing power structure. In most cases, this suggests that the movement challenges the political establishment from a distance, with a position clearly removed from that held by the institution confronted. This challenge is generally one that "proposes or opposes change in societal norms, values, or both."[29] In other words, the movement attempts to compel existing institutions to move from their present position on an issue. In the case of civil rights, the movement was successful in forcing the legislative power structure to enact civil rights legislation—to change from its previously-held position on racial matters.

Oftentimes the change proposed is "moral in tone" as the movement may cast its goals in terms of "right" or "wrong," moral principles, righteousness, or ethical beliefs. In one way or another, the movement proclaims: "Our goal is just and right."

As an uninstitutionalized collectivity, advocating change from the way things are now done, any legitimate movement will encounter opposition from the status quo. This becomes more of a reality as the movement grows in popularity and impetus. As noted earlier, the movement must be significantly large in scope, "The word 'significant' means large enough—in geographical area, time, events, and participants— to carry out the program of the movement."[30] Not surprisingly, as more voices clamor for change, opposition from the established power structure mounts.

The final characteristic of a movement mentioned in the above definition, is the pervasiveness of persuasion. "Persuasion is a communication process by which a social movement seeks through the use of verbal and nonverbal symbols to affect the perceptions of audiences and thus to bring about desired changes in ways of thinking, feeling, and/or acting."[31] Although persuasion is not the only tactic available for the movement (for example coercion and bargaining are also possible), it is the major means by which the movement accomplishes its goals. With this overview, let us examine the rhetoric of a movement in more detail.

The Environmental Movement

For the last two decades or so, more and more organizations and individuals have become involved in attempting to solve what has been called, the environmental "crisis." Perhaps Earth Day I held in April 1970 was the "coming out party" for various environmentally-concerned groups. In time, there arose such a significant number of converts standing outside the establishment demanding social change that the power structure was forced to recognize and deal with them. In the meantime, loose organizational structures emerged, alliances between groups and individuals were solidified, and a sort of moral crusade was launched that employed persuasion as a major tactic. Today, given the definition offered at the outset of this chapter, we can readily identify an environmental movement.

The environmental movement is a worldwide phenomenon. The remainder of this chapter considers this movement by utilizing the American Greens as a case study. First, however, we must consider a brief history of the movement in America, a few of its representative voices, and its international flavor before we highlight the American Greens.

Rhetorical Stance and the Environmental Movement

In America, anxiety about the environment originally was voiced by the "conservationists" who became disturbed over land and resource use during the westward expansion and industrialization of our country. Recognizing that more and more land was being farmed and turned into ranches and that natural resources were being taken from the earth in complete disregard for the environment to fuel the speedy expansion process, the conservationists spoke out.

> In America, anxiety about the environment originally was voiced by the "conservationists" who became disturbed over land and resource use during the westward expansion and industrialization of our country.

President Theodore Roosevelt, an environmentally-concerned president, appointed Gifford Pinchot, his chief conservationist, to oversee land and resource use in an expanding America. Pinchot's attitude toward natural resources and that of the conservationists in general can be summed up as a "wise use" philosophy or the belief that the resources of the earth are here to serve humankind. Thus, unlimited logging, grazing, farming, and mining were fitting activities, provided no particular area was "overused." Stoltz summarizes:

> *For the conservationists, nature was a place: 1) of abundant harvestable resources; 2) bountiful enough for all to get what they want; 3) to be saved for the future, but not at the expense of the current generation; and 4) a "land of many uses" . . . that included, among others, recreation, spiritual rejuvenation and solitude; 5) to serve humankind, providing "the greatest good to the greatest number."[32]*

This "wise use" philosophy eventually was challenged by the "preservationists" who believed that the land and its resources were not simply there for humankind's use. On the contrary, land needed to be preserved, not exploited. Henry David Thoreau, Ralph Waldo Emerson, and John Muir were among the first advocates of the preservationist position. Perhaps John Muir is today the best-known member of this school of thought. Muir, a Scottish immigrant, settled first in Wisconsin, moving to California in 1868. Working as a shepherd in the Yosemite Valley literally changed his life. Here he was introduced to the grandeur and splendor of the natural wilderness and consequently began questioning the "wise use" philosophy of that splendor. Muir summarizes:

> *Nature's object in making animals and plants might possibly be first of all the happiness of each one of them, not the creation of all for the happiness of one. Why ought man to value himself as more than an infinitely small composing unit of the one great unit of creation? . . . The universe would be incomplete without man; but*

it would also be incomplete without the smallest transmicroscopic creature.[33]

Clearly, for Muir, humankind was *not* the center of the universe; all of nature must be appreciated. So, he loudly condemned the industrialization and westward expansion process that showed a willful disregard for the resources of the earth. A spiritual bond with the land and a reverence for all living things was at the heart of Muir's thinking. In 1892, Muir founded the Sierra Club to champion his preservationist position.

Borrelli summarizes the conservationist-preservationist schism:

The conservation/preservation split reflects far more than disagreement over humanity's responsibility toward the land: it is rooted in fundamentally different perceptions of humankind and nature. Roosevelt and Pinchot shared an anthropocentric world view, in which man is the measure of creation. Muir's world view was biocentric; man is but one form of life, one part of creation.[34]

In 1962 Rachel Carson published Silent Spring wherein she eloquently condemned human carelessness, greed, and irresponsibility in environmental matters. By documenting the health hazards of environmental pollution and pesticide use, and discussing problems that accompany overpopulation. Carson immediately seized the attention of the country and the world. Of all the alarms raised. Carson's was by far the most eloquent and far-reaching.

In the past three decades, other voices have joined the environmental debate so that today an abundant number of philosophical positions can be found. As can be imagined, the dialogue has moved far beyond the conservationist-preservationist stage. For the purposes of this chapter, we have isolated four leading voices in the environmental movement: the bioregionalists, the social ecologists, the deep ecologists, and the radical activists. A discussion of these four schools of thought follows beginning with the bioregionalists.

Bioregionalists

The bioregionalists share a key assumption with the social ecologists, deep ecologists, and activists when

they set forth a critique of the modern industrial system.

The planet is on the road to, perhaps on the verge of, global ecocide and that survival depends not merely on checking the abuses of the industrial system, not merely on abandoning its excesses, but on nothing less than abandoning industrial culture itself. In its place must come a culture that, by contrast, is rooted in the natural world, in harmony with natural systems and capacities and developed according to the natural configurations of the earth and its inherent life forms.[35]

To address this environmental crisis, the bioregionalists focus on "bioregions," or places "defined by . . . life forms, . . . topography, and . . . biota. . . . a region governed by nature, not legislature."[36] In sum, bioregionalists seek to know the land and learn its lore, to develop the potential of each place within sound ecological guidelines, liberating both humans and the bioregion in the process. Focusing on regional and local concerns, bioregionalists tackle inherent problems and develop potentials. Following is an illustration of bioregional thinking:

> Leading Voices in the Environmental Movement
> ■ Bioregionalists
> ■ Social ecologists
> ■ Deep ecologists
> ■ Radical activists

My own home state, Maine, could serve as an example here. We are a colony, occupied territory. Occupation is the imposition of rule by aliens. Aliens. Foreign to the soil. Two thirds of the state [is] owned by multinational timber companies, and the multinational food companies, the military, the tourists who fill cottages and second homes for a few months and then leave them vacant. . . . And the politicians supporting this occupation, basing our economy on it. The cities get newspapers and toilet paper, we get clear cuts, dirty rivers, and air, massive aerial spray programs, Reyes syndrome, more rivers dammed, wastes dumped, nuclear power. The caribou move north, the eagles and whales become impediments to progress, hardwoods are considered weeds and sprayed, the lakes and ponds die from acid rain. . . . Local politics, state, national, global politics should be informed by bioregional voices. There is need for coordina-

tion, for a unity of ecological politics, a politics which focuses on the quality of life, within the context of global responsibility.[37]

Social Ecologists

The second major voice in the environmental dialogue is that of the social ecologists. Murray Bookchin, associated with the Institute for Social Ecology, has written, among other works, *The Ecology of Freedom: The Emergence and Dissolution of Hierarchy.* Herein, Bookchin expresses the social ecologist's position on social hierarchies. In brief, any form of hierarchy—where one person or species dominates another—is to be opposed as they are unnatural. These human inventions create artificial and unnecessary divisions in the world. Accordingly, Bookchin claims that science and technology have fragmented humanity into "hierarchies, classes, state institutions, gender, and ethnic division."[38]

Hierarchies, classes, and states warp the creative powers of humanity. They decide whether humanity's ecological creativity will be placed in the service of life or in the service of power and privilege. Whether humanity will be irrevocably separated from the world of life by hierarchal society, or brought together with life by an ecological society depends on our understanding of the origins, development, and, above all, the scope of hierarchy—the extent to which it penetrates our daily lives, divides us into age group against age group, gender against gender, man against man, and yields absorption of the social and political into the all-pervasive State. The conflicts within a divided humanity, structured around domination, inevitably lead to conflicts with nature. The ecological crisis with its embattled division between humanity and nature stems, above all, from division between human and human.[39]

Deep Ecologists

A third force in the rhetoric of the environmental movement is the deep ecology school of thought. When compared to all other voices in the movement, deep ecologists stress a more spiritual approach to the earth. "We believe . . . . that we may not need something new, but need to reawaken something very, old, to reawaken our understanding of Earth

wisdom. In the broadest sense, we need to accept the invitation to the dance—the dance of unity of humans, plants, animals, the earth."[40]

Among the fundamental tenets of deep ecology are:

- The well-being and flourishing of human and nonhuman Life on Earth have value in themselves. . . . These values are independent of the usefulness of the nonhuman world for human purposes.
- Richness and diversity of life forms contribute to the realization of these values and are also values in themselves.
- Humans have no right to reduce this richness and diversity except to satisfy *vital* needs.
- Present human interference with the nonhuman world is excessive, and the situation is rapidly worsening.
- Policies must therefore be changed. These policies affect basic economic, technological, and ideological structures. The resulting state of affairs will be deeply different from the present.[41]

Radical Activists

A fourth philosophical voice in the environmental movement is that raised by the more radical activists. This position argues for direct and immediate action in defense of nature. The most publicized representative of this school is the group Earth First!, which stands "for the more radical proposition that the natural world should be preserved *for its own sake,* not for the sake of any real or imagined benefits to humanity."[42] Dave Foremen, founder of Earth First!, proclaimed in a 1987 speech:

Wilderness is the essence of everything we're after. We aren't an environmental group. Environmental groups worry about environmental health hazards to human beings, they worry about clean air and water for the benefit of people and ask us why we're so wrapped up in something as irrelevant and tangential and elitist as wilderness. Well, I can tell you a wolf or a redwood or a grizzly bear doesn't think wilderness is elitist. Wilderness is the essence of everything. It's the real world.[43]

To carry out this philosophical stance, followers of Earth First! has been linked to a program of "ecotage" that involves such activities as posting human blockades in front of logging equipment, tree sitting, tree spiking, and other acts of sabotage meant to halt logging and other forms of human encroachment on the ecosystem. However, it is often not enough to deter human progress and development. Indeed, these radical activists often advocate the dismantling of such monuments to human development as dams and electrical power plants—in effect to return nature to its original state insofar as possible. So unlike the previous positions discussed, the radicals act on their convictions—often seeing themselves as warriors for nature and the wilderness.

The four approaches to understanding the environment discussed above share some of the same values and ideas. Bioregionalists feature the local region, social ecologists stress the exploitation resulting from hierarchal thinking, deep ecologists highlight a spiritual oneness with the earth, and the activists advocate direct action. It should be noted that the above positions are far richer than described here. As our immediate purpose is not to detail each but to provide a context for better understanding the rhetoric of the American Greens, interested students may wish to pursue on their own the authors alluded to in the summaries. However, it should be apparent that the bioregionalists, social ecologists, deep ecologists, and activists differ markedly from their forerunners—the conservationists and preservationists.

The above philosophical positions (perhaps with the exception of the radical activists) provide impetus to corresponding rhetorical stances that can be discerned in most mainstream environmental groups. Bioregionalists, deep ecologists, and social ecologists can be found in the Sierra Club, for instance. They can also be found pushing their agendas in organizations such as the World Wildlife Fund, Greenpeace, and the National Audubon Society, Defenders of the Wildlife, Wilderness Society, and Friends of the Earth, to name only a few. Since many of these are international in scope, environmental rhetoric reaches a good portion of the world's citizens.

International Green Political Parties

It is significant to note that environmental concerns are not confined to American borders. For instance, organized groups began forming in Europe about the time John Muir was active.

The first conservation groups were formed by the late 1860s in most Northern European countries responding to the waves of industrialization. The 1920s saw another rise in in-

terest in conservation and other environmental issues. But not before the 1960s did environmental questions become the subject of broader social movements seeking fundamental change.[44]

Now that we have discussed the leading rhetorical stances in the contemporary environmental movement, we are prepared to consider the numerous organizations comprising the global "green movement." As noted, environmental groups such as Greenpeace are active throughout the world today. For the remainder of this discussion, however, we will narrow our focus to those environmental organizations known as "green parties." Roughly defined, these are *active political parties* that are attempting to induce social change through the political process. Whereas groups such as Greenpeace and the Sierra Club are uninstitutionalized, green parties are part of a "system." Therefore, their approach to change is limited to the parameters of their national political system. Advantages as well as disadvantages can result from such relationships.

Concerns with the state of the environment have been voiced worldwide by green parties in several European countries including Belgium (Ecolo and Agalev), Italy (Liste Verdi), Great Britain (the Green Party), Austria (Green Union and Alternative List), Denmark (de Gronne), Finland (Vihreat), France (Les Verts), Luxembourg (Greng Alternative), Sweden (Miljopartiet de Grona). Switzerland (Greens), and Ireland (Green Alliance). In addition, smaller green-related parties exist in Greece, Spain, and Hungary.

Although there is not an organized European Green Party, various groups subscribing to green fundamentals have been successful in their respective national elections. "Green candidates have been elected to the national parliaments of Switzerland, first appearing in 1979; Belgium (1981); Finland, Portugal, and West Germany (1983); Luxembourg (1984); Austria (1986); Italy (1987); Sweden (1988); and the Netherlands (1989)."[45]

In general, the above green parties are grass roots organizations that attempt to be sensitive to the needs and desires of the ordinary citizen. They are decentralized and structured to facilitate discussion and debate at all levels. Muller-Rommel summarizes their political positions:

Most green parties follow an ideology that consists of strong concerns with equal rights (es-

pecially for minorities), strong ecological and antinuclear power thinking, solidarity with the Third World. . . . Among others, green parties stand for peace through unilateral disarmament and a nuclear-free Europe; protection of the natural environment through the introduction of transnational pollution controls and more generally an effective environmental policy directed against an unquestioned commitment to economic growth. Green parties advocate an alternative life-style through less emphasis on material goods, more individualism, self-realization, and self-determination.[46]

Perhaps the most well-known and successful green party is Die Grünen—the German Greens. Formally begun in January 1980, the German Greens trace their political roots to such disparate groups as left-wing liberals and pacifists as well as those working in the areas of peace, human rights, women's rights, the Third World, and the movement against nuclear energy. Expressing allegiance to a grassroots, democratic, decentralized party organization, the German Greens have constructed a biocentric party philosophy that stresses the theme of exploitation.

Human life is enmeshed in the circuits of the ecosystem: we intervene in it by our actions and this reacts back on us. . . . In particular an ecological policy implies all-round rejection of an economy based on exploitation and the uncontrolled pillage of natural wealth and raw materials, as well as refraining from destructive intervention in the circuits of the natural ecosystem. It is our conviction that the exploitation of both nature and human beings must be countered by human beings, in order to repel an acute and serious threat to life.[47]

Moving from these premises, the 1990 party platform of the Greens covers such topics as threats to the atmosphere (ozone layer depletion), exhausting of fossil fuels for energy, climatic change (droughts, hurricanes, floods, warming of the oceans), contamination of soil and water, death of the forests, environmental damage caused by chemicals (fertilizers, pesticides), genetic technology, and waste treatment.

The German Greens have been successful in attracting public support. Today, Greens sit in town councils, state parliaments, and the federal legisla-

ture. Their voices are being heard and their influence is being felt in legislation and policy decisions on local, state, and federal levels. In essence, the Greens have become institutionalized in that they are now part of the system. However, philosophically and pragmatically they do not consider themselves members of the establishment. Even so, organized green parties represent that wing of the environmental movement willing to become institutionalized, thereby attempting to affect change from within the system.

The European Green Coordination (EGC) is the organizational structure of national green parties in Europe. Founded in 1984 by five Western European green parties, the group today consists of twenty-four members and two observer-parties from Western as well as Eastern Europe. "Its original purpose, according to current EGC political secretary Leo Cox (Agalev Flanders, Belgium) and EGC co-secretary Paolo Bergamaschi (Federazione dei Verdi, Italy), was 'to stimulate the process of Green Parties coming into being in Europe through the exchange of information and political ideas, and through supporting each others' campaigns.'"[48] With the political readjustment occurring in Eastern Europe and the former Soviet Union and the formation of the European Community, the Greens today are pushing for a "'Europe of Regions,' with ecologically self-reliant and democratically oriented communities and regions becoming the base for society. The Greens also advocate a delegation of power from the nation-state to the supra-national level, so that minimum (but not maximum) pan-European agreements on environment, human rights, and security/disarmament could be enforced."[49]

A "green influence" has been leveraged in the European Parliament through an organization called the Green Alternative European Link (GRAEL), which originally included representatives from the West German Greens, the Dutch Groen-Progressief Akkoord, the Belgium green party Agalev, the Democrazia Proletaria in Italy, and the Basque Party of Spain. In their Paris Declaration of 28 April 1984, GRAEL lists its central focus as a "commitment to a new, neutral decentralized Europe made up of self-administering regions, each maintaining its own cultural individuality. . . ."[50] To this end, GRAEL claims,

We are against the deployment of nuclear missiles in Eastern and Western Europe. We are in

favor of complete disarmament and the dissolution of military and power blocs. We are in favor of a no-compromise policy on the environment so as to safeguard the ecological balance. We are against pollution of the air, the water, and the soil and against the destruction of nature and the countryside through reckless urbanization.[51]

The latest European Parliament elections held in June of 1989 saw the Greens improve their position in the 518 member body winning a total of 39 seats. Of these 39, four are representatives from Belgium, two from Holland, three from Spain, one from Portugal, nine from France, one from Ireland, four from Denmark, seven from Italy, and eight from Germany. Even though the green voice is gaining strength in the EC Parliament, it still represents a minority opinion as revealed in the breakdown of the current Parliament: Socialists (181), Communist (41), Independent (15), Christian Democrats (123), Liberal Democrats (44), European Democratic Alliance (19), Conservatives (34), and the Right (22). Thus, a "green" rhetoric has had some success in Europe. However, it has not fared as well in America.

American Greens

Murray Bookchin, prominent philosopher and founder of the highly-respected social ecology position in the American environmentalist dialogue, recognized the significance of the West German Greens as early as 1983 when he wrote:

What the German Greens have done for us, however, is not to enter the German parliament. They have shown us how to raise and broaden the real issues of peace. *They have turned these issues into questions of social reconstruction, not only social protest. They have offered alternatives to the ills of our times, not merely lamented them. And perhaps most importantly, they have linked armaments, ecology, sexism, lifestyle, community, direct action, and decentralization into an increasingly coherent and well-focused program—a comprehensive outlook for Germans that Europeans, and hopefully Americans, will emulate, modify, debate, or complete.*[52]

The initial formal attempt at a national organization of American Greens occurred in May of 1984 when the North American Bioregional Congress convened. In August of the same year, the Green Committees of Correspondence was founded and a national clearinghouse established in Kansas City. As local green committees developed, regional confederations were organized as well as interregional committees. The American Greens have met three times in national conventions to discuss their future direction and organization. In June 1989, over 200 delegates attended a Green convention in Eugene, Oregon. Although several resolutions were passed, perhaps the most important outcome of the conference was the decision not to form a national political party, but rather to remain active as a pressure group. At this juncture in their history, the American Greens believed that, given the realities of the two-party system in the United States, the likelihood of launching a viable formal political party was not promising. This same thinking prevailed at the 1990 convention held at Boulder, Colorado.

However, during the 1991 gathering in Elkins, West Virginia, delegates decided the time had come to move the Greens toward an active, alternative political party. To this end, the process for final revisions of the party's platform was begun and a ratification process established. A committee of Greens called SPAKA (Strategy and Policy Approaches in Key Areas) has been coordinating the platform ratification process—a complex democratic process that solicits input from local green groups. In addition, fund-raising issues were discussed and the relationship of state green parties to a national party was hammered out. Also, delegates at the Elkins gathering passed a Green Action Plan that advocated three national actions for 1992: Detroit Summer (a pilot program to rebuild the inner city), 500 Years of Resistance and Dignity (a project to celebrate cultural diversity, not conquest and imperialism that was brought about by Columbus's "discovery" of America), and Earth/Sun Day 1992 (a program pushing alternative energy sources).

To date there are over 160 local green groups in ten bioregional congresses across the country: Pacific Northwest, Far West, Northern Plains/Wild Rockies, Southwest/Southern Rockies, Upper Great Lakes, Prairie, Upper Mississippi and Ohio, Deep South, Northeast, and Mid-Atlantic. Newsletters and an extensive series of "Green Working Papers" circulate throughout these various groups.

One could consider the Greens the most successful third political party in America as they claim 27 elected offices nationwide. The Green Party of Alaska became the first Green Party in the country with permanent ballot access and claims the first Green mayor in the United States—in Cordova, Alaska. The Green Party of California became the second to be granted permanent ballot access and the Greens of Hawaii are not far behind. Other states are making similar efforts. In addition, Greens sit on local town councils in several parts of the country—especially New England.

Still in their formative stages, American Greens have yet to display the political influence attained nationally by the German Greens, and internationally, by European Greens. Outside of the few elected local officials in small towns, American Greens largely have been absent from the state and national political scenes. However, as an organizational structure becomes clarified and a coherent national program articulated. American Greens intend to enter the political process as a viable alternative to the established Democrats and Republicans.

While actively pursuing local, state, and national issues, American Greens are in the process of defining themselves. The Green Committees of Correspondence have published a statement that presents an overview of the Green philosophy:

What makes Green politics different is its holistic, ecological outlook. It recognizes the deep interconnection of all life and social processes; and neither social nor environmental problems can be solved in isolation from each other.

Green politics recognizes that the attempt to dominate nature is connected to and has grown historically in tandem with the domination of human by human: men over women, the mature over the young and old, some ethnic groups over others, some nations over others, landowners over the landless, corporate owners over the propertyless, bureaucrats over clients, professional politicians over citizens. There is no solution to the ecological crisis that fails to uproot human domination in all its forms.

In a culture that orders all things and beings around hierarchical rankings of inferior and superior, nature is reduced to a resource to be exploited instead of a living partner in a cooperative ecological community.[53]

When the Green Committees of Correspondence were formed in August 1984, a list of ten key values was adopted. Revised over the years, these values express the core of the Green philosophy: ecological wisdom, grassroots democracy, social justice, nonviolence, decentralization, community-based economics, postpatriarchal values, respect for diversity, personal and global responsibility, and a future focus.

One of the more active groups in America is the New Hampshire and Vermont Greens who have published a statement of principles. Among these are:

Ecological Humanism: Greens hold that human liberation and ecological harmony are inextricably interwound and connected. They seek to build a society based on human liberty, equality, and solidarity, living in ecological harmony with nature. They are striving to create a world where each individual is free to develop his or her full potential because every person enjoys basic political, economic, and individual human rights.

Non-nuclear, Home-based, Democratic Defense: Greens call for immediate unilateral nuclear disarmament combined with nonprovocative, home-based defense by both voluntary conventionally armed militia and nonviolent social defense. . . . They demand the dismantling of all nuclear weapons, the recall of all armed forces from stations abroad, and the use of the 97% of the American military budget now devoted to nuclear blackmail and foreign intervention for social and ecological reconstruction. Greens hold that only such measures can create the conditions for a peace that is durable because it is just, democratic, and ecologically sustainable.

Nonaligned Democratic Internationalism: Greens support human rights according to one universal criterion of freedom, without regard for national boundaries and military blocs, in complete independence from both blocs of the Cold War. They actively solidarize our movement with nonaligned peace, ecology, democracy, workers, and national liberation movements in every country. . . .[54]

The Program of the Green Party USA originally published in August 1991 is a fairly comprehensive document that discusses policies in the following areas: agriculture and food, the arts, biological diversity and animal liberation, community, direct action, economics, education, energy, foreign and military policy, forestry, health, indigenous people, land use, waste management, peace and nonviolence, politics, social justice, spirituality, and technology.

To provide the reader with a feeling for their rhetoric, consider the following ideas on economics that are developed in the program. These ideas are premised on (1) a biocentric view of the world—a conviction that the earth, by definition, cannot be owned, but instead must be cared for—and (2) the exploitative tendency of the American economic system which uses people as well as the earth's resources in its drive for growth, profits, and economic expansion.

We . . . note the following goals for a Green economy:

to align our economic systems with natural ecologies in a sustainable way that does not ultimately degrade or deplete the Earth;

to supply an ecologically sustainable level of food, shelter, health services, and education to meet the basic economic needs of each person on the planet;

to reduce alienation due to economic systems by providing meaningful and rewarding work and increasing leisure for all;

to reduce coercion and oppression from economic structures by, for example, encouraging workplace democracy and employee ownership;

to eliminate harassment, unequal opportunity for advancement, and pay differentials based on sex, age, race, ethnicity, sexual orientation, religion, and physical or mental abilities;

to restructure our patterns of income distribution to reflect the wealth created by those outside the formal monetary economy, such as parents, housekeepers, community volunteers, and so on. . . .[55]

The formation of a Left Green Network has led to an important voice in the green dialogue that feels that the mainstream American Greens have been too conservative and compromising in their thinking. In their "Call for a Left Green Network" this statement is found: "We hold the concept of 'Green' to be explicitly radical, inherently anticapitalistic, and completely wedded to the New Left's commitment to participatory democracy. We believe the Green movement should carry forward the antihierarchical and antiauthoritarian themes of the New Left, while advancing a socialecological perspective as the basis for a new independent political movement."[56] The

Left Greens are quite direct in their condemnation of the capitalistic economic system, compared to most American Greens. Certainly their radical economic stance will serve to differentiate their message from the others and establish their credibility with the "New" Left.

The Left Greens' approach regarding nonaligned internationalism is similar to that published by the Committees of Correspondence noted above:

Left Greens support human rights according to one universal criterion—freedom—without regard for national boundaries or the military blocs of the cold war. They actively solidarize with nonaligned peace, ecology, democracy, worker, feminist, antiracist, antimilitarist, and anti-imperialist movements in every country. . . . Left Greens demand that every nuclear power initiate immediate unilateral nuclear disarmament and conversion to nonprovocative, home-based defense based on both voluntary conventionally-armed militia and nonviolent social defense. . . . Left Greens demand that every country recall all armed forces from stations abroad and use the savings from military spending for social and ecological reconstruction. Only such measures can create a just, democratic, and ecologically sustainable condition necessary for a durable peace.[57]

It is apparent that American Greens share several core beliefs with European Greens. Among these are the holistic approach to ecological understanding wherein the state of the environment is a part of a vast web in which elements such as economic systems, arms control, peace strategies, and human relations dynamically interact. The themes of exploitation and domination are also interwoven throughout their thinking. In sum, what many European Greens have accomplished and the American Greens are struggling with is the movement from single-issue ecology stances characteristic of many environmental groups to a position that frames environmental concerns within a broader, more realistic perspective. As noted by Bookchin,

We have not reached this broad, unified, and increasingly coherent level of social concern. We are too focused on trying to deal with each issue as though it can be separated from the others which loom over us. We suffer from a

bad American habit of "setting priorities" rather than establishing connections in a coherent and programmatic way.[58]

The key for creating a flourishing "green" rhetoric, then, will be to establish these connections and formulate them into an intelligible, comprehensive political agenda in which peace is inextricably bound to the environment and wherein eco-peace becomes a valid concept.

Consider how peace issues interlock with ecological issues. It is the domination of human by human as it is ultimately expressed in war, weaponry, and the Patton-image of the combative male that gave rise to the very notion of dominating nature. . . . On the other hand, the abolition of war against nature with its all-consuming fever of domination has its roots in a sensibility of peace—of peace between human and human. Ecology and peace are united by the grammar, vocabulary, and sensibility of a respect for life as a whole, be it life in human society or in the more general web of life we call the biosphere.[59]

The Greens' message of eco-peace that is philosophically challenging, politically bold, and intellectually sophisticated poses problems for the "green" rhetorician.

Rhetorical Obstacles to a Successful Green Discourse

It is plain from the above discussion that a convincing "green" rhetoric must carefully connect ecological and peace issues by demonstrating that the state of the world's environment is interdependent with the state of world peace. In making this rhetorical bridge, concerns such as disarmament, the exploitation of the environment by an economic system powered by growth, the denunciation of munitions manufacturers and arms traders, world food production, health care, citizens' rights, energy, safe water supplies, animal protection, education, and so forth must be woven into a holistic world view that is appealing to the audience. In brief, a compelling "green" rhetoric must feature the eco-peace concept and its concern with all manner of exploitation in a compelling rhetorical vision.

In this regard, a chief task for the "green" rhetorician is to broaden the issues and carefully establish a systems mindset in which the interdepend-

ency of these issues is made obvious. Salzman summarizes the mainstream American Green strategy, underscoring its complexity:

The Green critique . . . precedes from specifics to the general, from the concrete problems that exist thence to appropriate and appropriate-scale solutions and programs. . . the Green analysis says that by specifically and programmatically addressing the specific problems of the destruction of Nature, an appropriate social analysis and critique, and then a program, can be developed that not only resolves the problem at hand but, by the nature of this broad social critique, necessarily gives rise to a restructuring (or replacement) of existing institutions.[60]

A "green" rhetoric offers complexity and advocates a sustained examination of all phases of contemporary life. Thus, a major hurdle is the establishment of a systems approach—an intellectual scheme that posits eco-peace as the solidifying element.

Second, a "green" rhetoric must successfully reorient its audience's conception of time. The world is presently one in which individuals seek both quick solutions to problems and immediate gratification. Both political and economic systems are short-range oriented. But, the complexity of the environmental/peace problem demands a sustained, arduous effort in which long-range planning (rather than short-range rewards) is paramount. A systems perspective takes the long view in which the interaction of multiple elements (such as natural resources) and processes (such as military spending) is thoroughly analyzed and comprehensive plans formed so the problems (not merely a symptom or two) truly can be solved. The Greens, then, must deal with perceptions of time by instilling in the audience a sense of long-range effort and planning.

A further obstacle facing "green" rhetoricians is convincing the audience that the capitalistic economic system is a major villain in the ecopeace system—that economic exploitation, the abuse of nature and humans alike are intertwined. The economic critique must be handled deftly—especially in the United States where "capitalism," "consumerism," and "materialism" are far from derogatory concepts. In criticizing the economic system, a "green" rhetoric forces every worker within that system to scrutinize his or her values. Just how far individuals living in a capitalistic, materialistic state are willing to buy into a "green" critique remains to be seen. In essence, the Greens are asking people to give up their present economic lifestyle; thus, clearly conceived and articulated alternatives to the present consumption-oriented society must be a part of the Green's rhetoric if they hope to win converts. So, the American Greens focus their critique on capitalism. It needs to be noted, however, that they are also critical of state-controlled economic systems. To their way of thinking, any economic system geared toward growth at the expense of human and natural resources must be rejected and replaced by an ecologically-sensitive system.

In summary, a "green" rhetoric is a radical rhetoric in the purest sense of the word. It challenges the basic social and mate-

> a "green" rhetoric is a radical rhetoric in the purest sense of the word. It challenges the basic social and material bases of contemporary society. It advocates more than substantive social change. A complete overhaul of the economic and political power structures is called for, not mere reform.

rial bases of contemporary society. It advocates more than substantive social change. A complete overhaul of the economic and political power structures is called for, not mere reform. It seeks to alter forever existing social and economic relationships and to supplant society's dominant values with an entirely new way of life. As Stewart has noted, a successful social movement must transform perceptions of history and alter perceptions of society and prescribe courses of action while mobilizing for action and sustaining the movement.[61] If the "green" rhetoricians are successful at the above tasks and can link quality-of-life issues with ecopeace, the Greens might one day become a truly global force.

Notes

1. Lloyd F. Bitzer, "The Rhetorical Situation," in Douglas Ehninger, ed., *Contemporary Rhetoric: A Reader's Coursebook* (Glenview, Illinois: Scott, Foresman and Company, 1972), p. 41.

2. Charles Lomas, *The Agitator in American Society* (Englewood Cliffs: New Jersey: Prentice-Hall, Inc., 1968), p. 8.

3. Robert L. Scott and Donald K. Smith, "The Rhetoric of Confrontation," in Ehninger, op. cit., p. 182.

4. Lomas, op. cit., p. 8.

5. John W. Bowers and Donovan J. Ochs, *The Rhetoric of Agitation and Control* (Reading, Massachusetts: Addison-Wesley Publishing Company, 1971), p. 4.

6. Mary G. McEdwards, "Agitative Rhetoric: Its Nature and Effect," in J. Jeffery Auer, ed., *The Rhetoric of Our Times* (New York: Appleton-Century-Crofts, 1969), p. 7.

7. Lomas, op. cit., p. 2.

8. Robert M. Browne, "Response to Edward P.J. Corbett: The Rhetoric of the Open Hand and the Rhetoric of the Closed Fist," in Ehninger, op. cit., pp. 211–215.

9. Paul D. Brandes, *The Rhetoric of Revolt* (Englewood Cliffs, New Jersey: Prentice-Hall, Inc., 1971), p. 3.

10. Herbert W. Simons, "Requirements, Problems, and Strategies: A Theory of Persuasion for Social Movements," in Ehninger, op. cit., p. 195.

11. Ernest G. Bormann, ed., *Forerunners of Black Power* (Englewood Cliffs, New Jersey: Prentice-Hall. Inc., 1971), p. 17.

12. Eric Hoffer, *The True Believer: Thoughts on the Nature of Mass Movements* (New York: Harper and Row, 1951), p. 119.

13. *Ibid.*, p. 128.

14. Simons, op. cit., pp. 191–192.

15. Arthur Smith, *Rhetoric of Black Revolution* (Boston: Allyn and Bacon, Inc., 1969), p. 26.

16. *Ibid.*, p. 29.

17. *Ibid.*

18. *Ibid.*, p. 34.

19. *Ibid.*, p. 36.

20. *Ibid.*, p. 40.

21. *Ibid.*, pp. 41–42.

22. Scott and Smith, op. cit., pp. 185–186.

23. *Ibid.*, p. 185.

24. *Ibid.*

25. *Ibid.*, pp. 185–186.

26. *Ibid.*, p. 186.

27. Orrin E. Klapp, *Currents of Unrest: An Introduction to Collective Behavior* (New York: Holt, Rinehart and Winston, Inc., 1972), p. 91.

28. Charles J. Stewart, Craig Alien Smith, Robert E. Denton, Jr., *Persuasion and Social Movements.* 2nd ed. (Prospect Heights, Illinois: Waveland Press, 1989), p. 17.

29. *Ibid.*, p. 9.

30. *Ibid.*, p. 8.

31. *Ibid.*, p. 14.

32. P.G. Stoltz, "Contaminating Presentationism: The Beginning of the End." Paper delivered at the Speech Communication Association Convention, New Orleans, 3 November 1988, p. 11.

33. Patrick Carr, ed., *The Sierra Club: A Guide.* (San Francisco: Sierra Club, 1989), p. 5.

34. Peter Borrelli, "The Ecophilosophers." *Amicus Journal* (Spring 1988): p. 32.

35. Kirkpatrick Sale, "Bioregionalism: A Sense of Place." *The Nation* (12 October 1985), p. 336.

36. *Ibid.*

37. Gary Lawless, "The Bioregional Voice and the Green Movement." South Harpswell, Maine: Green Working Papers, n.d., p. 2.

38. Murray Bookchin, *The Modern Crisis* (Philadelphia: New Society Publishers, 1986), p. 53.

39. Murray Bookchin, *Remaking Society: Pathways to a Green Future* (Boston: South End Press, 1990), p. 72.

40. Bill Devall and George Sessions, *Deep Ecology: Living as if it Mattered* (Salt Lake City: Peregrine Smith Books, 1985), p. ix.

41. *Ibid.*, p. 70.

42. Christopher Manes, *Green Rage: Radical Environmentalism and the Unmaking of Civilization* (Boston: Little, Brown and Company, 1990), p. 71.

43. *Ibid.*, p. 72.

44. Wolfgang Rudig, "Peace and Ecology Movements in Western Europe." *West European Politics.* 11 (January 1988), p. 27.

45. Michael Renner, "Europe's Green Tide." *World Watch* (January/February 1990), p. 25.

46. Ferdinand Muller-Rommel, ed., *New Politics in Western Europe: the Rise and Success of Green Parties and Alternative Lists* (Bolder: Westview Press, 1989), p. 8.

47. Die Grünen, "Programme of the German Green Party." (East Haven, CT: Long River Books/Inland Book Company, 1985). p. 7.

48. Mike Finestein, "The European Greens Coordination." *GreenLetter in Search of Greener Times,* vol. 7, no. 2 (1991). p. 36.

49. *Ibid.*, p. 37.

50. GRAEL, "Rainbow Politics." (Brussels: Rainbow Group, Green-Alternative European Link in the European Parliament, 1988), p. 7.

51. GRAEL, p. 7.

52. Bookchin, Murray, "The American Peace Movement: A Green Perspective," Burlington, VT: Green Program Project, Discussion Paper no. 1., p. 1.

53. Green Committees of Correspondence," Green Politics Growing at the Grassroots," Kansas City, MO: Green Committees of Correspondence Clearinghouse, p. 2.

54. New Hampshire and Vermont Greens, "Principles," White River Junction, VT, p. 1.

55. The Greens/Green Party USA, "The Green Program," Camden, NJ: Prompt Press, 1991, pp. 8–9.

56. Left Green Network, "Call for a Left Green Network." West Lebanon, New Hampshire, August 1988.

57. "Call for a Left Green Network."

58. Bookchin, op. cit., p. 1.

59. Ibid.

60. Salzman, Loma, "Is the Left-Green Network Really Green?" *Green Synthesis,* June 1989, p. 11.

61. Stewart, Charles. "A Functional Perspective on the Study of Social Movements," *Central States Speech Journal* (Winter 1980), pp. 298–305.

Moral Exclusion and the American Indian

The major rhetorical focus of this volume has been on language. However, it is imperative to keep in mind that rhetoric is not limited to language. For example, stereotypes or image construction by the popular culture have rhetorical implications and dimensions. The following essay examines the role that negative stereotypes have played in the history of a people and highlights the link between that stereotype and the social policies society has set in place to deal with that people. In brief, the rhetorical implications of stereotypes have human consequences that can not be ignored.

There are many paths to liberation. Some are violent; others peaceful. Some remain within the "system"; others stray outside. All struggles for liberation or self-determination, however, are framed by the historical, social, economic, and political realities in which they are embedded. For example, sometimes the liberation of a people is best sought through revolution—the overthrow of the power structure—because circumstances dictate such extreme measures. In other contexts, liberation may be attained by separating from the dominant culture, or through the passage of human rights legislation or by manipulating public opinion through nonviolent, direct action.

No matter the path, those strategizing for liberation must do so within the confines of their unique historical situation. Tactics for combating oppression must be grounded in the realities of the moment. One factor in contemporary American society that has become increasingly crucial in the last few decades of this century is the power of the mass media. This means, among other things, that those battling for self-determination must carefully study the mass media to discern how the oppressor is manipulating the media to maintain power. Jewell speaks to this point: "While the function of all institutions is to maintain the status quo through the cultural transmission of norms, values, belief systems and behaviors, the mass media are the main instru-

ments by which societal institutions undertake and complete this process of perpetuating the social order" (Jewell 86). In addition, those struggling for liberation need to think carefully about how the media can be engaged as a political tool for their cause. In this regard, two questions that revolve around media representations of the oppressed require study: How are the oppressed depicted in mainstream media? Who controls these depictions?

Using the American Indian as a case study, this essay argues that in American society today any oppressed minority striving for liberation must struggle also to control its image. Since the images spun out by the media have a powerful effect on public opinion, freedom fighters must ensure that favorable images are constructed and broadcast. Gaining favorable images, in turn, means wrestling control of those images from media conglomerates that presently perpetuate them. For as long as the oppressor controls the images, public opinion and (more importantly) social policies that stem from that opinion can be manipulated to the detriment of the oppressed. "The role that the mass media play in proliferating cultural images that define the extent to which various segments of the population are entitled to social policies that will improve their access to, and acquisition of, societal resources cannot be overemphasized" (Jewell 18).

Writing in 1992 about the power of media images in relation to African Americans, bell hooks stated, "opening a magazine or book, turning on the television set, watching a film, or looking at photographs in public spaces, we are most likely to see images of black people that reinforce and reinscribe white supremacy" (hooks 1). Continuing, "there is a direct and abiding connection between the maintenance of white supremacist patriarchy in this society and the institutionalization via the mass media of specific images, representations of race, of blackness that support and maintain the oppression, exploitation, and overall domination of all black people" (2).

Given this situation, hooks argues that "unless we transform images of blackness, of black people, our ways of looking and our ways of being seen, we cannot make radical interventions that will fundamentally alter our situation" (7).

The parallel with American Indians is apparent. Like African Americans, American Indians must be conscious of the way they are portrayed by the media. Historically, that portrayal (from their perspective) has been negative in that it has supported white supremacy and justified actions and social policies directed toward them. To make our case, this essay begins with a brief history of the American Indian from a social policy perspective and moves to a consideration of how Indians have been portrayed throughout history.

SOCIAL POLICY HISTORY

When the early settlers and explorers came to these shores, they landed on a continent inhabited by millions of people—some 12–13 million within the boarders of the current United States. A question in the minds of the Europeans soon arose: what should be done with the indigenous peoples? For five-hundred years the Europeans and their descendants have offered numerous answers to this question which to this day

> From approximately 1500 to 1900, the removal of the savage was a dominant theme that relied on the Manifest Destiny doctrine for justification.

has not been satisfactorily resolved. Following is a brief review of a few of the major policy decisions that have been made in response to the above question.

As more and more settlers arrived on this continent, the demand for land increased. Unwilling to leave their homelands, the Indians presented a formidable obstacle to the Europeans. So, the first answer to the above question was "removal." From approximately 1500 to 1900, the removal of the savage was a dominant theme that relied on the Manifest Destiny doctrine for justification. Sometimes referred to as the "400 Year War," three main removal tactics were tried: warfare, relocation, and genocide.

The use of physical force was the initial major removal tactic and early history is replete with hundreds of settler-Indian battles. A very few of the more notable skirmishes include the Powhatan War, Little Turtle War, Tecumseh's Rebellion, Black

Hawk War, Sand Creek Massacre, Battle of Little Big Horn, and the Battle of Wounded Knee. Literally volumes have been written on these and other bloody encounters and every school child has some understanding of white-Indian confrontations; albeit that understanding may be distorted. Nonetheless, dramatic clashes and fights to the death were typical removal tactics.

Besides physical annihilation, forced relocation was a tactic employed during the removal phase. Here, Indians were physically forced to leave their homelands and relocate further West. The most noted relocation was the 1838 Trail of Tears when the Cherokee Nation was forced at gunpoint to march some 800 miles from their homes in Georgia to Oklahoma Territory in the dead of winter. A lack of supplies and warm clothing coupled with harsh weather led to the death of some 25% or 4,000 of the marchers. About this time, the Choctaws, Chickasaws, Creeks, and Seminoles were also marched from their ancestral lands.

A third tactic that served to remove the Indians from their lands was the introduction of European diseases to the natives. Lacking natural immunity, Indians died in the tens of thousands when exposed to European diseases—especially smallpox. Documentation exists claiming that in more than a few cases, diseases were spread intentionally. For instance, Sir Jeffrey Amherst who was commander-in-chief of the British forces in 1763 sent small pox infected blankets to the Ottawas in hopes of wiping them out thus saving British lives. (Stiffarm and Lane 34)

By 1900 (the end of this four hundred year removal phase) the native population stood at approximately 237,000. Down from an estimated 13 million in 1500, that represents about a 98% loss in population.

In the late 1800s the U.S. government abandoned its removal philosophy and switched to another strategy: forced assimilation. This was basically an attempt to compel the Indians to accept European values and blend into mainstream society. One tactic used was the boarding school concept. Here, native children were taken from their homes and sent to boarding schools in the East where many lived from the age of 6 to 18. In these schools, they were taught the standard European curriculum and were forbidden to wear their native dress or speak their native language. They were taught job skills and often forced to work on nearby farms. The Puritan work ethic, Christianity, and appreciation for European culture were all hammered into susceptible minds. The Carlisle School in Pennsylvania was probably the most well known boarding school.

In order to break up tribal lands and instill a sense of private property and land ownership in the Indians, legislation such as the Dawes Allotment Act (1887) was passed. Indian lands were divided into 160 acre plots and awarded to qualified Indians. They were given title to the lands in hopes that they would turn into land owners and farmers—thus good capitalists. The Dawes Act as well as other legislation attempted to instill a European economic mind set. Dr. Merrill Gates, President of Amherst College at the time, sums up: "To bring the Indians out of savagery into citizenship . . . we need to awaken in him wants. In his dull savagery, he must be touched by the wings of the divine angel of discontent. . . . Discontent with the tepee and the Indian camp . . . is needed to get the Indian out of the blanket and into trousers—trousers with a pocket in them, and with a pocket that aches to be filled with dollars" (Mander 276).

Through the sale of their land and fraud, Native Americans lost some 60% of their tribal land base as a result of the Dawes Act. Some scholars claim that Dawes was perhaps the greatest single blow to the American Indian for it broke up their fundamental collective or communal land use philosophy.

Forced assimilation was also attempted through the passage of the 1934 Indian Reorganization Act which essentially replaced traditional Indian forms of governance with Bureau of Indian Affairs puppet governments and elected tribal councils. The Indian Citizenship Act (1924) unilaterally conferred U.S. citizenship to all Indians thus attempting to legally force them into the mainstream. Other important social policies enacted during the assimilation phase included the Major Crimes Act (1885), Indian Claims Act (1946), the Termination Act (1953), the Relocation Act (1956), and the American Indian Re-

> In the late 1800s the U.S. government abandoned its removal philosophy and switched to another strategy: forced assimilation. This was basically an attempt to compel the Indians to accept European values and blend into mainstream society.

ligious Freedom Act (1978). In one way or other, these acts were attempts to force the Indians into the European value system.

Throughout the years, social policies in the form of various court rulings often have worked against the American Indian. Lyng v. Northwest Indian Cemetery Protective Association (1988) and the 1990 "Peyote Case" (Employment Division, Department of Human Resources of Oregon v. Smith), and the ongoing Leonard Peltier case which began in 1977 are just three examples of court cases that have had negative impacts on the self-determination efforts of American Indians.

Nor should we think that social policy abuses exist only in this nation's ancient past. Indeed, they continue today. From 1972–76, for instance, the Indian Health Service was involved in the involuntary sterilization of young Indian women. It is estimated that approximately 12,000 tubal ligations and hysterectomies were unknowingly performed on mothers shortly after childbirth during this time (Larson and Dillingham).

As we look over the history of American Indians in this country, it is painfully clear that they have been subjected to decades of mistreatment at the hands of whites. Social policies have been enacted that have led to their murder, relocation, removal, oppression and demoralization. Furthermore, these unjust social policies have rarely been criticized by the white majority. One reason there has been little public outcry toward the treatment of the Indians is that historically, in the public's mind, the Indian has been perceived as not being equal to the European. The images and the stereotypes that have been constructed over the centuries have contributed to this fact. So, when we ask ourselves "how was all this injustice via social policies possible?" we have to look first at the images and stereotypes that paralleled and offered justification for the social policies.

AMERICAN INDIAN IMAGES

Examination of the historical evidence regarding the early European explorers' perceptions of the indigenous peoples of the new world reveals a variety of opinion. The writings of Christopher Columbus were perhaps the first attempts at constructing Native American images.

The people of this island and of all the other islands which I have found and of which I have information, all go naked, men and women, as their mothers bore them, although some of the women cover a single place with the leaf of a plant or with a net of cotton which they make for that purpose. . . . they are so guileless and so generous with all that they possess, that no one would believe it who has not seen it. They refuse nothing that they possess, if it be asked of them; on the contrary, they invite one to share it and display as much love as if they would give their hearts. . . .

They do not hold any creed nor are they idolaters; but they all believe that power and good are in the heavens and were very firmly convinced that I, with these ships and men, came from the heavens, and in this belief they everywhere received me after they had mastered their fear. This belief is not the result of ignorance for they are, on the contrary, of a very acute intelligence and they are men who navigate all those seas, so that it is amazing how good an account they give of everything. . . .

In all these islands, it seems to me that all men are content with one woman, and to their chief or king they give as many as twenty. It appears to me that the women work more than do the men. I have not been able to learn if they hold private property; it seemed to me to be that all took a share in whatever any one had, especially of eatable things (Berkhofer 6).

For the most part, the early accounts by Columbus portrayed the natives as a noble people living in harmony with nature. "In the beginning, the people who heard Columbus' accounts said, 'Aha, these Indians are people who inhabit the Garden of Eden.' . . . The first round of arguments, then, was to glorify nature, to glorify Indians as they appeared in the European imagination" (Mohawk 440). Columbus and others laid the foundation for the "good" Indian—the Indian as the noble, innocent child of God image. One of the many implications of this image is that innocent children are in need of guidance—spiritual, economic, social, and political. They are not capable of "civilization" independently, but require help from the European. So, for those who desired to

make the Indian a subject in a European colony, the image was a ready-made justification.

Amerigo Vespucci offers a different image of the indigenous peoples on the new continent. Writing in 1504–1505 he stated,

They live together without king, without government, and each is his own master. They marry as many wives as they please; and son cohabits with mother, brother with sister, male cousin with female, and any man with the first woman he meets. They dissolve their marriages as often as they please, and observe no sort of law with respect to them. Beyond the fact that they have no church, no religion and not idolaters, what can I say? . . . . The nations wage war upon one another without art or order. The elder by means of certain harangues of theirs bend the youths to their will and inflame them to wars in which they cruelly kill one another, and those whom they bring home captives from war they preserve, not to spare their lives, but that they may be slain for food; for they eat one another, the victors the vanquished, and among other kinds of meat human flesh is a common article of diet with them. Nay be assured of this fact because the father has already been seen to eat children and wife, and I knew a man who I spoke to who was reputed to have eaten more than three hundred human bodies. And I remained twenty-seven days in a certain city where I saw salted human flesh suspended from beams between houses, just as with us it is the custom to hang bacon and pork. I say further: they themselves wonder why we do not eat our enemies and do not use as food their flesh which they say is most savory (Berkhofer 8–9).

Vespucci's writings which portrayed the Indian as uncivilized and without moral principles helped construct the image of the "bad" Indian—the less than human, wild, heathen.

Writing in 1612, Captain John Smith picked up on the negative portrayal of the natives referring to them as savages: "They (the Indians) are inconstant in everything, but what fear constraineth them to keep. Crafty, timorous, quick of apprehension and very ingenious, some are of disposition fearful, some bold, most cautious, all savage" (Churchill, *Fantasies* 20).

In the early 1600s, Alexander Whitaker added to the negative image of the Indian:

Let the miserable condition of these naked slaves of the devil move you to compassion toward them. They acknowledge that there is a great God, but they know him not. . . . wherefore they serve the devil for fear, after a most base manner. . . . They live naked of body, as if the shame of their sinne deserved no covering. . . . They esteem it a virtue to lie, deceive, steal. . . . if this be their life, what think you shall become of them after death, but to be partakers with the devil and his angels in hell for evermore (Churchill, Fantasies 21).

Reflecting on the incident some twenty years after the Puritans attacked and massacred the Pequots in Connecticut and Rhode Island in 1636, Edward Johnson penned, "The Lord in his mercy toward his poor churches having thus destroyed these bloody barbarous Indians, he returns his people safely to their vessels, where they take account of their prisoners" (Churchill, *Fantasies* 21–22). Thus, thanks were given to the Christian God who helped the Puritans annihilate the savages. Images, such as those constructed by Johnson provided a theological rationale for the early colonists' behavior.

Through the writings of these men and others, the Indian was constructed in the minds of the Europeans as an uncivilized animal—an untamed savage who had little respect for human life. The Spanish, French, and English all contributed to this image through their journals, letters, sermons, and art. In time, this "bad" Indian image was picked up and refined in the theater, poetry, novels, short stories, film, and television. "Thus for generations it was taught that darker-skinned peoples were prone to savagery and violence, were incapable of self-governance, and were in need of the White man's uplifting rule" (Parenti 13).

Image construction was enhanced when Americans and Europeans were treated to live exhibitions and wild West shows. Buffalo Bill Cody's extravaganza, organized in 1883, was a traveling rodeo and theatrical company that enacted famous Indian battles for audiences throughout Europe and America. In addition, early settlers were known to kidnap a few Indians and transport them back to England for exhibition.

To the spectators of these "exhibits," Indians personified "savagery." They were depicted as "cruel, barbarous and most treacherous." They were thought to be cannibals, "being most furious in their rage and merciless . . . not being content to kill and take away life, but delight to torment men in the most bloody manner . . . flaying some alive with the shells of fishes, cutting off the members and joints of others by piecemeal and broiling on the coals, eating the collops of their flesh in their sight whilst they live" (Takaki 31).

In both instances, audiences were "treated" to living savages. Images were further entrenched.

Through sermons, word of mouth, journals, exhibitions, and writings, the early settlers were slowly constructing images that served to exclude the Indians from the dominant culture. The Indians, first viewed as a threat, were later seen as obstacles to the material self-interest of the settlers when Westward expansion commenced. Here, the negative stereotype served to rationalize the conquest of the Indians. In time, the stereotype was used to justify the privileged status of the whites to ensure their presence at the top of the social hierarchy.

Whether intended or not, a particularly effective way of spreading the negative image was through fiction. One story that evolved in the late 1600s and continued for 300 years in various forms was the captivity narrative. Although the details varied from author to author, the basic plot of the narrative remained constant: (a) beautiful, young, innocent white woman; (b) is captured by the wild savages; (c) falls in love with a handsome Indian; (d) is rescued and returns to her European ways or she refuses rescue and remains with her lover. A variation of the captivity narrative is found in the often repeated Pocahontas myth which continues to contribute American Indian images—especially those of females. Through literature and film, Pocahontas has been firmly established in the American psyche as a beautiful, slender, loving heroine who risks her life to save John Smith. Even though it is debatable that the incident occurred (Smith first told the story some seventeen years after it allegedly happened), Pocahontas, Indian Princess, has become part of our un-

> the Indian was constructed in the minds of the Europeans as an uncivilized animal—an untamed savage who had little respect for human life.

derstanding of the American Indian. The recent Disney animation continues to perpetuate an image that many American Indians find offensive.

> Disney productions and Pocahontas fans have no idea of the damage this film will inflict on the self-image and esteem of Aboriginal children. What does it tell our kids? That White men are stronger, braver smarter, more industrious and better looking than Indian men. And that Aboriginal women have no loyalty (will turn on their own people) and are fulcrums of their people's demise. With the image of Pocahontas reaching icon status among our children, it will traumatize our daughters' self-images and pervert the perspectives of our sons (Stevenson).

It is not the intention of this essay to provide a comprehensive review of the development of Indian images in American society. Others have done this admirably (cf. Berkhofer). Suffice it to note that through the years, Indian images have included the "brutal savage-warrior," the "noble red man" or "innocent child of God," the "loyal sidekick," the "Indian Princess," and the "drunkin, lazy Injun." Individuals such as Cotton Mather, George Catlin, Henry Wadsworth Longfellow, Nelson Baker, James Fenimore Cooper, Francis Parkman, and Frederic Remington among others played significant roles in the construction of Indian images in our early history.

More recently, American Indian images have been propagated as mascots and nicknames of sports teams: Florida State Seminoles, Washington Red Skins, Kansas City Chiefs, Cleveland Indians, Atlanta Braves to name a few. Images of a buck toothed, grinning Chief Wahoo and of fans performing the Tomahawk Chop remind us that not much has changed over the years. These logos, mascots, and fan rituals do nothing to enhance a positive American Indian identity.

In film and television, John Wayne, Kevin Costner and Tonto have contributed unfavorable images. Examining films since 1925, Churchill claims that Native Americans are "habitually presented to mass audiences in a one-dimensional manner, devoid of

recognizable human motivations and emotions, thoroughly and systematically dehumanized (Churchill, *Indians* 79)." Josephy continues,

> For many, the moving pictures, [and] television. . . . have firmly established a stereotype as the true portrait of all Indians: the dour, stoic, warbonneted Plains Indian. He is a warrior, he has no humor unless it is that of an incongruous and farcical type, and his language is full of "hows," "ughs," and words that end in "um." Only rarely in the popular media of communications is it hinted that the Indians, too, were, and are, all kinds of real, living persons like any others and that they included peace-loving wise men, mothers who cried for the safety of their children, young men who sang songs of love and courted maidens, dullards, statesmen, cowards, and patriots (Josephy 8)

In his study of Native American portrayals in film, Leuthold raises another important image issue:

> In film, the lives and problems of contemporary Native Americans are ignored in favor of the readily identifiable nineteenth-century Indian. It is almost as if Indians and the popular understanding of them were frozen in time a century ago. . . . By fixing the image of Indians in the past, Hollywood overlooks the complexity of contemporary native realities. (161)

Agreeing with this line of thought, Churchill writes,

> North American indigenous peoples have been reduced in terms of cultural identity within the popular consciousness—through a combination of movie treatments, television programming and distortive literature—to a point where the general public perceives them as extinct for all practical intents and purposes. Given that they no longer exist, that which was theirs—whether land and the resources on and beneath it, or their heritage—can now be said, without pangs of guilt, to belong to those who displaced and ultimately supplanted them. Such is one function of cinematic stereotyping within North

America's   advanced   colonial   system.
(Churchill, Fantasies *239)*

In summary, contemporary media portrayals of American Indians are not positive. They are presented as warrior-braves in sports and as dehumanized, extinct beings in film. The realities of contemporary Native life are ignored. In essence, these images of American Indians continue to offer justification for social policy decisions. This is not to say that the images have directly caused social policy decisions although that argument could be made. It is to say, however, that these stereotypes have been important factors in the process that can be labeled "moral exclusion."

> contemporary media portrayals of American Indians are not positive. They are presented as warrior-braves in sports and as dehumanized, extinct beings in film.

MORAL EXCLUSION

Susan Opotow writes about the concept of moral exclusion—a concept that helps frame this essay. Moral exclusion, according to Opotow, "occurs when individuals or groups are perceived as *outside the boundary in which moral values, rules, and considerations of fairness apply*" (Opotow "Moral Exclusion" 1). By definition, all groups erect boundaries which delineate who is "in" as well as who is "out." The importance of these boundaries is that "moral values, rules, and considerations of fairness apply only to those within this boundary for fairness, called our 'scope of justice' or 'moral community'" (3). American history is replete with groups that have been morally excluded from the mainstream, dominant society. Once excluded, the rationale for unfair and unjust treatment is in place. For instance, women, Irish and Jewish immigrants, and African Americans have all at one time or other found themselves defined as outsiders—outside the arena where moral behavior and justice prevail. As outsiders, they found themselves oppressed by the dominant group; the moral values applicable to the majority were not bestowed upon the minority.

> A requisite of effectual moral exclusion, because it provides the all important justification for the process, is the construction of the excluded group as an entity something less than human. In other words, the excluded must be redefined as unequal to, lower than, or beneath the dominant society; that is, dehumanized.

Once a group is defined as outside the moral community and that definition embedded in the psyche of the dominant group, the consequences can be calamitous. "Those who are morally excluded are perceived as nonentities, expendable or undeserving; consequently, harming them appears acceptable, appropriate, or just." (1) So, the morally excluded can be and often are subjected to discrimination, racism, and sexism. The denial of human rights, oppression, and, in extreme cases, genocide can result. There is a connection, then, between social policy (for example Jim Crow segregation laws) and being morally excluded. Since the oppressed are viewed as nonentities and expendable, the dominant group can forge social policies, procedures, and laws geared toward the excluded that it would never apply to itself. Hence, the foundation of the oppressor-oppressed relationship is laid. As Opotow summarizes, "Examples of moral exclusion . . . follow a similar progression: perceived *conflicts of interest* give rise to *groups categorizations;* conflict of interest and categorization contribute to *moral justifications for unjust procedures,* which can themselves be injurious and which permit other *harmful outcomes* to ensue" (Opotow, "Determining" 174).

A requisite of effectual moral exclusion, because it provides the all important justification for the process, is the construction of the excluded group as an entity something less than human. In other words, the excluded must be redefined as unequal to, lower than, or beneath the dominant society; that is, dehumanized. "One of the first important acts of an oppressor is to redefine the oppressed victims he intends to jail or eradicate so that they will be looked upon as creatures warranting suppression and in some cases separation and annihilation. I say 'creatures' because the redefinition usually implies a dehumanization of the individual" (Bosmajian 197). Once dehumanized, it is but a short step to total domination or eradication of the excluded. Ward Churchill's brilliant essay, "In the Matter of Julius Streicher," highlights the role played by editor and cartoonist Streicher in the dehumanizing of the Jew that paved the way for the "extermination" of the Jews who had become "creatures," "rats," and "vermin" in the minds of a good part of the German populace (Churchill, *Indians* 73–87).

To help dehumanize the excluded, negative stereotypes are fabricated by the ruling group. These stereotypes can be perpetuated through folk tales, journals, poems, novels, biographies, histories, cartoons, television, advertisements, and film to name a few media. But no matter what form they take or what medium is used, stereotypes are a key component in the moral exclusion process for they serve to dehumanize the oppressed group. Once dehumanized, the rationale is in place to exclude the group from the moral community of the dominant society which is no longer obligated to treat the excluded within its established rule system. The values, norms, and laws of the dominant society do not apply to the excluded. In a very real sense, then, all excluded groups (by nature of being defined outside the bounds of the moral community) are oppressed.

Stereotypes, labels attached to categories of people which serve to explain them, are powerful dehumanizing agents pivotal to the process of moral exclusion. These categories are significant because they construct behavioral, cognitive, personality, and often physical traits of the stereotyped (Hummert and Shaner). Once stereotyped, the individual is lost—he or she is lumped into a category thus sharing the traits common to all its members. When an individual is stereotyped, those outside the category have a "handle"—they "know" how the stereotyped behave and think—what they value and look like. One of the numerous unfortunate results of being stereotyped is that the individual is explained and interpreted as a member of the larger category. Individual traits are overlooked. When this occurs, accurate portrayal of any member within the category is impossible. In short, stereotypes are misleading. This is especially true of Indian stereotypes.

A second unfortunate result occurs when the stereotype is internalized by the members of the categorized group. If members,

internalize prevailing stereotypes about their group . . . they come to believe that they themselves are inadequate and unqualified, and thus they blame themselves for their failures, even

when they are clearly the victims of discrimination. Stereotypes are not merely broad generalizations we impose on others; they are ways of seeing . . . that we internalize and use to define and limit ourselves and our expectations (Rothenberg 321).

So, while stereotypes are inaccurate and simplified generalizations, they are fundamental to the moral exclusion process. When internalized, believed, and acted upon by members of the stereotyped group, these images further serve to oppress. This internalization of the negative stereotypes phenomenon somewhat explains the excessive rates of alcoholism and domestic violence characteristic of the Native American community today.

AMERICAN INDIAN REALITIES

How does the above help shed light on our understanding of the treatment of the American Indian throughout our history? Briefly, the American Indian has been—almost from first contact—morally excluded from American society. Over the years, this exclusion has been driven by negative stereotypes which serve to dehumanize. Within this context, Chief Wahoo of the Cleveland Indians and Pocahontas of Disney fame are not simply amoral, entertaining and harmless cartoons. To the American Indian, they are images integral to the dehumanization process which has excluded them from American society. They are political instruments wielded by the oppressor asserting the boundary between "us" and "them." As Ward Churchill says when discussing the negative Indian stereotypes in American literature,

Viewed in this way, treatment of the American Indian in the arena of American literature must be seen as part and parcel of the Anglo-American conquest of the North American continent. How else could general Euroamericans have been massively conditioned to accept, on their behalf, a system or policy of non-stop expropriation and genocide of the native population throughout U.S. history? The dehumanizing aspects of the stereotyping of American Indians in American literature may be seen as an historical requirement of an imperial process. (Churchill, Fantasies 28–29)

To understand more fully the moral exclusion of the American Indian, it is helpful to discuss briefly reasons why certain groups are singled out for exclusion. According to Staub, one explanation for morally excluding the "other" is grounded in "the fact that people often dislike, fear, and feel threatened by other people's way of life, beliefs, and values that are substantially different from their own. These differences threaten people's beliefs in the goodness of their own identity and group, and their comprehension of reality" (Staub 52). A second reason offered by Staub revolves around the self-interest of the dominant group.

> *At times a group in power or a majority may protect or seek to enhance its power and wealth by partially or wholly excluding some group from their moral universe. . . . Exclusion makes possible discrimination in education or employment, restriction of civil rights, persecution that leads to intimidation, and a progression that ultimately can end in mass murder (56).*

Material self-interest, then, can lead to excluding others from the group. In this regard, the "exclusion serves to protect an elevated self-concept and maintain one's existing view of reality, which justifies a privileged status" (57). In sum, the dominant group or oppressor subjugates others because it fears them and feels threatened, or it is seeking to expand its power and wealth at the expense of the other, while protecting its privileged status. One could easily argue that in the cases of women, blacks, and American Indians all of these reasons were/are operative.

The first reason for excluding others mentioned by Staub—that people who are perceived as different threaten one's identity—was certainly in the minds of the earliest explorers who set foot on this continent and met the Indian face-to-face for the first time. Surely, these strange talking, curiously dressed, peculiarly behaving "beings" were a threat to the "sophisticated" and "cultured" Europeans. The colonists began to erect the boundary: "According to Sir Walter Raleigh, Indians had 'their eyes in their shoulders, and their mouths in the middle of their breasts.' In *Nova Brittania,* published in 1609, Richard Johnson described the Indians in Virginia as 'wild and savage people,' living 'like herds of deer in a forest'" (Takaki 31).

A second reason a dominant group will exclude others from its moral community revolves around the issue of power. Herein, the ruling group seeks to expand its power or wealth at the expense of the excluded. Certainly this has been the case with American Indians throughout our history. The whites wanted the land and resources to enhance their power and wealth. The Indians occupied the land and had to be removed. Thus, they had to be excluded from the dominant society in order to rationalize warfare, forced marches, genocide, and oppressive legislation. When Article I, Section 2 of the United States Constitution was written, the fate of the indigenous population was sealed. "Once the Indians were successfully defined as governmental nonentities, no more justification was needed to drive them off their lands and to force them into migration and eventual death" (Bosmajian 202). With the stroke of a pen, they were formally and legally excluded from their homeland. Power was seized by the whites.

> Throughout history, negative images and stereotypes have plagued American Indians playing a central role in excluding them from mainstream society. The harsh and often unjust treatment through social policies designed to exploit them, while simultaneously enhancing the power of white society, is explained in part by their being morally excluded.

CONCLUSION

Throughout history, negative images and stereotypes have plagued American Indians playing a central role in excluding them from mainstream society. The harsh and often unjust treatment through social policies designed to exploit them, while simultaneously enhancing the power of white society, is explained in part by their being morally excluded. What guidance does framing the American Indian situation in the above perspective suggest in their ongoing struggle for liberation?

Foremost, it is critical that American Indians gain control over their representations. Negative images need to be corrected and counteracted. Responsible images must be manufactured for at least two reasons. First, it is important to amend the misleading and inaccurate perceptions presently accepted by the dominant society. Negative images must be replaced by positive, realistic portraits. When American Indians are perceived accurately and their history told truthfully, they will gain not only the attention but also the respect of white society. At this point, the possibility will exist to commence a meaningful dialogue between the two parties which is based on equality and fact. Out of this dialogue, perhaps solutions could be discovered.

Second, and just as important as the first, control over images is significant for the impact it has on Indian self-perceptions. Paula Allen speaks to the significance of image control regarding Native American women.

Image casting and image control constitute the central process that American Indian women must come to terms with, for on that control rests our sense of self, our claim to a past and to a future that we define and that we build. Images of Indians in the media and educational materials profoundly influence how we act, how we relate to the world and to each other, and how we value ourselves. . . . Evidently while Americans and people all over the world have been led into a deep and unquestioned belief that American Indians are cruel savages, a number of American Indian men have been equally deluded into internalizing that image and acting on it. Media images, literary images, and artistic images, particularly those embedded in popular culture, must be changed before Indian women will see much relief from the violence that destroys so many lives (45).

Images have consequences. This is why the racist Chief Wahoo and the romanticized Pocahontas must be confronted. Media conglomerates and the entertainment industries must be accountable for the part they have played and continue to play in the oppression of the American Indian.

In the early pages of this essay, bell hooks was quoted regarding media images of blackness. Reworking her quote from a Native American perspective her thoughts become: "There is a direct and abiding connection between the maintenance of white supremacist patriarchy in this society and the institutionalization via the mass media of specific images, representation of race, of Native Americans, that support and maintain the oppression, exploitation, and overall domination of the American Indian. Unless we transform these images we cannot make the radical interventions that will fundamentally alter the situation." In essence, American Indians must tell their story in their own way. When this comes to pass, they will be on a road to liberation.

Bibliography

Allen, Paula."Angry Women Are Building." in Margaret Anderson and Patricia Hill Collins. *Race, Class, and Gender.* Belmont, California: Wadsworth Publishing, 1993: 42–46.

Berkhofer, Robert. *The White Man's Indian: Images of the American Indian from Columbus to the Present.* New York: Knopf, 1978.

Bosmajian, Haig. "Defining the 'American Indian': A Case Study in the Language of Suppression." in Gary Goshgarian, ed., *Exploring Language.* Boston: Little Brown and Co., 1977.

Churchill, Ward. *Fantasies of the Master Race: Literature, Cinema and the Colonization of American Indians.* Monroe, Maine: Common Courage Press, 1992.

———. "In the Matter of Julius Streicher," in *Indians Are Us?: Culture and Genocide in Native North America.* Monroe, Maine: Common Courage Press, 1994: 73–87.

Dillingham, Brint. "American Indian Women and IHS Sterilization Practices," *American Indian Journal,* January 1977.

hooks, bell. *Black Looks: Race and Representation.* Boston: South End Press, 1992.

Hummert, Mary and Shaner, Jayne. "Patronizing Speech to the Elderly As a Function of Stereotyping," *Communication Studies* 45 (1994): 45–158.

Jewell, Sue K. *From Mammy to Miss America and Beyond: Cultural Images and the Shaping of US Social Policy.* New York: Routledge, 1993.

Josephy, Alvin M. *The Indian Heritage of America.* New York: Knopf, 1968.

Larson, Janet. "And Then There Were None," *The Christian Century,* January 26, 1977: 61–63.

Leuthold, Steven. "Native American Responses to the Western." *American Indian Culture and Research Journal.* 19 (1995): 153–189.

Mander, Jerry. *In the Absence of the Sacred: the Failure of Technology and the Survival of the Indian Nations.* San Francisco: Sierra Books, 1991.

Mohawk, John. "Looking for Columbus," in *The State of Native America: Genocide, Colonization, and Resistance,* M. Annette Jaimes, ed., Boston: South End Press, 1992.

Opotow, Susan. "Moral Exclusion and Injustice: An Introduction." *Journal of Social Issues* 46 (1990): 1–20.

———. "Deterring Moral Exclusion," *Journal of Social Issues* 46 (1990): 173–182.

Parenti, Michael. *Make-Believe Media: the Politics of Entertainment.* New York: St. Martin's Press, 1992.

Rothenberg, Paula. *Race, Class & Gender in the United States.* New York: St. Martin's Press, 1992.

Staub, Ervin. "Moral Exclusion, Personal Goal Theory, and Extreme Destructiveness." *Journal of Social Issues* 46 (1990): 47–64.

Stevenson, Winona. "Commentary." CBC Radio Canada, June 23, 1995.

Stiffarm, Lenore and Lane, Phil. "The Demography of Native North America: A Question of Indian Survival." in Annette Jaimes, ed. *The State of Native America.* Boston: South End Press, 1992: 23–53.

Takaki, Ronald. *A Different Mirror: A History of Multicultural America.* New York: Little Brown and Co., 1993.

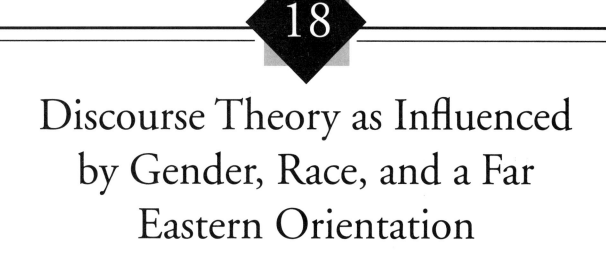

Discourse Theory as Influenced by Gender, Race, and a Far Eastern Orientation

Throughout the preceding chapters of this volume, our principal emphasis has focused on the writings of white American and European male rhetoricians, all of whom have exerted a major influence in forging perspectives on discourse theory. We feel it is appropriate in this chapter, therefore, to discuss some of the significant contributions that women, African Americans, and Far Eastern scholars have made to western rhetorical thought. To help us meet this challenge, we have asked several authorities, whose personal experiences and research activities have given them creative insights into each of these areas, to provide us with essays that might serve as a starting point for enhancing our understanding of these neglected fields of study.

The first of these essays, written by Beth Waggenspack,[1] is entitled "Women's Role in Rhetorical Traditions." The second study, authored by Melbourne S. Cummings and Jack L. Daniel,[2] discusses the theme "The Study of African American Rhetoric." The final work, produced by Roichi Okabe,[3] describes representative "Cultural Assumptions of East and West: Japan and the United States."

Our first study which deals with "Women's Role in Rhetorical Traditions" moves chronologically through history. Along the way we are introduced to women leaders whose writings, until recently, have been largely unknown or ignored. We learn, for example, that Aspasia, who lived in the 5th century, B.C., was a popular rhetorician and speech writer admired by Socrates, quoted by Plato, and sought after for help by aspiring public speakers. Next we are told how Christine de Pisan (1364–1430) and Mary Astell (1666–1731) produced books for the goal of elevating the status of women by educating them concerning principles of discourse. Through their rhetorically-centered writings, they became respected scholars during the early and late phases of the Renaissance Era. This description is followed by an analysis of the teachings of Mary Wollstonecraft (1759–1797), depicted by many observers as "the founding mother of feminism." One of her enduring concerns, as we will note, was the need for women to strengthen their reasoning ability.

In her treatment of a group of 19th-century advocates, including Elizabeth Cady Stanton and Susan B. Anthony, Professor Waggenspack has drawn upon her extensive researches in this field to show how their speeches, dialogues, books, newspaper columns, and leadership functions on behalf of women's rights helped lay the foundation for the development of modern social protest and movement practices. The final portion of this essay demonstrates how a group of prominent female rhetorical scholars have identified special features of women's philosophy and practice of discourse, and called for further probes into the nature of this communication genre. But while doing so, Professor Waggenspack reminds us, these authors have continued their interest in nongender related research as well.

If rhetoric goes beyond persuasion, if it is viewed as an attempt to understand how people construct the worlds in which they live and how those worlds make sense to them, than we need to study how rhetoric affects all people—men and women. The following essay revisits feminist rhetoric about which the writer wrote so meaningfully five years ago.

Notes

1. Professor Waggenspack is a member of the Department of Communication Studies at Virginia Polytechnic Institute and State University.
2. Professor Cummings is Chair of the Department of Human Communication Studies at Howard University; and Professor Daniel is Associate Provost at the University of Pittsburgh. We are indebted to Professor Lyndrey A. Niles for granting us permission to reprint this essay which appears in his recently published volume African American Rhetoric (Dubuque: Kendall/Hunt Publishers, 1995).
3. Professor Okabe is a faculty member and current Vice President of Academic Affairs at Nanzan University in Nagoya, Japan.

Women's Role in Rhetorical Traditions

Beth Waggenspack

For centuries, the traditional myth has been that "man" is the sole originator of rhetorical theory and practice, and rhetorical history has been written as the province of men. Communication theorists and practitioners (male) discounted women's ability to participate in public discourse or its creation and damned or demeaned the "effeminate" style of communication. Women encountered profound resistance to their efforts to change these conditions because rhetorical action of any sort was, as defined by biological, social, cultural, and religious tenets, a masculine activity. After all, the argument was, women were created to conceive children, not ideas. It was thought that females could not hold their own in speaking because they supplanted thinking with feeling, data with drama, reasoning with emotion, arguing with empathizing.

In his *Politics*, Aristotle legitimized the assumption that women are biologically unsuited for political activity and also saw silence and modesty as virtues befitting a woman. Others suggested that conception, gestation, and birth robbed women of eloquence. It was felt that women sacrificed their womanhood and risked their reproductive capacity through public speech. Speakers were expected to take stands, initiate action, assert expertise; women were thought to be retiring and modest, had indirect influence, and possessed no expertise or authority. They were thought naturally incapable of reasoning, not driven by competition or ambition.

Activities requiring competition or winning others over were thought to "unsex" women. Speakers had to be expert and authoritative; women were submissive. Speakers ventured into the public domain of courts, legislature, pulpits, or lecture platforms; women's domain was domestic. By banning women from education and citizenship, by barring them from the pulpit, the jury, the legal bench and the government, society encouraged women to be seen but not heard.

As Karlyn Kohrs Campbell noted,

Men have an ancient and honorable rhetorical history. Their speeches and writings, from antiquity to the present, are studied and analyzed by historians and rhetoricians. Public persuasion has been a conscious part of the Western male's heritage from ancient Greece to the present. This is not an insignificant matter. For centuries, the ability to persuade others has been a part of Western man's standard of excellence in many areas, even of citizenship itself. Moreover, speaking and writing eloquently has long been the goal of the humanistic tradition in education.

Women have no parallel rhetorical history. Indeed, for much of their history women have been prohibited from speaking, a prohibition reinforced by such powerful cultural authorities as Homer, Aristotle, and Scripture.[1]

Recent articles[2] attempt to reconcile the exclusion of women from the rhetorical heritage; they have led attacks on decades of misrepresentation of woman's role. Women have not been mere onlookers; rather, they have played an integral part in the development of our rhetorical traditions, both as rhetorical theorists and rhetorical figures.

Traces of women's presence and perspective are preserved in works from Plato and numerous sophists, dramatists, historians and writers. Aristotle alludes to priestesses and women speakers, including Cleobulina of Rhodes, whom he reports was renowned as a public speaker and counselor to her father the king. In the seventeenth century, spurred by a growing interest in France in learned women, Gilles Menage wrote his *History of Women Philosophers,* compiling a catalogue identifying women philosophers of antiquity and providing sources of information about them. By this time, some women, instead of arguing about the nature of woman and of her inferiority or equality to man, quietly developed their talents, pursued their intellectual interests, and manifested their competence in conversation or in writing or both. In this age of the salons, women with intellectual interests invited celebrities and scholars of their time to regular gatherings in their homes. The reading of poetry and plays, parlor games, dancing and music all served as part of the entertainment, but the principal attraction was conversation. Women began to write of their experiences and ideas. The eighteenth and nineteenth centuries' rise of the female women's rights advocates and anti-slavery orators and women's gradual admission into higher education impelled them in to the public domain. Contemporary insights into how language structures our perceptions, expresses our experiences, and communicates knowledge within communities owe much to female epistemologists.

Women's contribution to rhetorical thought and practice, like other aspects of women's experience, has only begun to be retrieved and investigated. Although Plato had acknowledged that a woman could be a philosopher, the popular impression seems to be

that there were at best few women rhetoricians. Apparently, selecting whom in rhetorical history to involve and whom to omit remains a quandary for those studying the field. Over the years our discipline has chosen to advance a core group of known rhetoricians, and as a result, the exclusion of other rhetoricians has resulted in a lack of awareness that different choices and perspectives are available for inclusion. One aspect of our history demonstrates the result of such selectivity: the history of Western rhetorical theory is overwhelmingly male.

It is an unfortunate consequence that knowing so little about this aspect of our past, about what women have thought and how their ideas have been forwarded, means that our education has been truncated. Yet that is also the theme that sounds throughout the rhetorical thought and practice of many of the women introduced here: the lack of education diminishes all people's intellectual development. Reconstructing the tradition of women in communication is an ongoing process, one that reflects inquiries into how women have contributed to rhetorical theory and how they have used rhetoric to reflect their vision of themselves and their age.

> Aspasia's intellectual specialty was philosophy and political discussion, and she had great skill as a teacher of sophistic rhetoric. She was the only female member of the Periclean circle, consisting of some of the most important sophists of the day, including Xenophon, Alcibiades, Phidias, and Anaxagoras.

THE CLASSICAL ERA

The early history of rhetoric reflects the vast difficulties encountered by woman as we attempt to reconstruct her roles in the rhetorical front lines. Questions of woman's existence, of her impact, and of her teaching abound, for there is no written record left by woman. She lived during a time when women were devalued for their intellect and admonished for going beyond severely prescribed roles. Perhaps it is with Aspasia, a teacher of sophistic rhetoric who overcame great social and cultural odds because of her gender, that the examination of woman's role in rhetorical theory and history should begin.

Aspasia of Miletus (ca. 470–410 B.C.)

Aspasia began her life in Athens as Pericles of Athens's a *hetaera,* a professional companion and mistress educated more than respectable women and expected to accompany men on occasions where intelligent conversation with a women was appreciated but wives were not welcome. Aspasia's intellectual specialty was philosophy and political discussion, and she had great skill as a teacher of sophistic rhetoric. She was the only female member of the Periclean circle, consisting of some of the most important sophists of the day, including Xenophon, Alcibiades, Phidias, and Anaxagoras. Plato mentions her as having taught philosophy to Pericles and to the young Socrates. Jarratt and Ong call Aspasia "perhaps the first female orator in the Western tradition."[3]

As Jarratt and Ong note, the reconstruction of Aspasia is difficult. None of her own legacy remains because she left nothing in writing, although philosophers of her time and after wrote about her. A number of Socrates' disciples included her in their works on him (keep in mind that what we know of Socrates is based on the work of these same disciples: Aeschines of Sphettus, Xenophon, Antisthenes, and Plato). In most of the Socratic discourses dealing with her, Socrates is usually her mouthpiece, recounting his conversations with her to his students.[4] In his *Life of Pericles* Plutarch noted that Socrates visited with Aspasia often, both alone and with others. Cicero recorded a dialogue called "Aspasia" by Aeschines, one of Socrates' pupils. Her teaching talents were mentioned by authorities ranging from Plato (*Menexenus*) to Plutarch (*Twelve Lives*) to Athenaeus (*Deipnosophistae*); the first two go so far as to credit her with instructing Pericles, the founder of Athenian democracy. It has been suggested that she deserves credit for ghost writing Pericles' speeches, including his classic "funeral Oration,"[5] considered by many to be one of the greatest speeches of antiquity. Aspasia has been credited with teaching Socrates rhetoric and instructing Athenian women in home making. Athenaeus records that Socrates and Aspasia enjoyed a strong friendship and says that while Socrates' "soul was deep, he laboured with lighter pains when he visited the house of Aspasia."[6] Suidas in *Aspasia* and the commentator on Aristophanes' work *The Acharnians* called her a wise woman and "mistress of eloquence."[7] Athenaeus in Book 5 cites several of her verses. Yet she also had enemies: Aristophanes called her a whore and spread the rumor that she was largely responsible for the Peloponnesian war because of her demands of vengeance over the theft of two of her slave women.

Plato discusses Aspasia in his dialogue on sophistic rhetoric, the *Menexenus;* in fact, she is one of only two female characters in all of Plato's dialogues. The *Menexenus* consists of an entire funeral oration said to be composed by Aspasia and reported by Socrates.[8] Framing the oration is a dialogue between Socrates and Menexenus concerning who will be chosen to deliver that year's ritual state funeral oration for men who have died in battle. Menexenus asks Socrates whether he would be able to respond to such a challenge, and Socrates replies, "That I should be able to speak is no great wonder, Menexenus, considering that I have an excellent mistress in the art of rhetoric—she who has made so many good speakers, and one who was the best among all the Hellenes—Pericles, the son of Xanthippus." Socrates then relates that he "heard Aspasia composing a funeral oration about these very dead. For she had been told, as you were saying, that the Athenians were going to choose a speaker, and she repeated to me the sort of speech which he should deliver, partly improvising and partly from previous thought, putting together fragments of the funeral oration which Pericles spoke, but which, as I believe, she composed." After the speech, Menexenus was awed that "Aspasia, who is only a woman, should be able to compose such a speech." Here Socrates hints that perhaps he was the actual composer, but he never recants anything said about Aspasia. The funeral oration is an ironic tale of Athens' military blunders and provides an unflattering image of the "triumphant" warrior city-state. Plato used the oration as a sharp attack on the current use of oratory for its detrimental influence in contemporary political life; it fooled the hearts and minds of Athenians, who were won over or kept loyal and centered on the value of Athens and its acts of war.[9]

In the *Menexus* of Plato, it is revealed that many Athenians associated with Aspasia because of her instruction in the art of speaking. Aspasia was skilled in the use of the Socratic method, where students would generate arguments on contradictory propositions. This rhetorical training created a climate where a speaker did not just repeat or embellish the already accepted public view but would question, analyze, and imagine differences. Aspasia used another common practice: she generated a speech out of common topics arranged with some spontaneity for the occasion and purpose at hand. To prepare, small groups working with an accomplished rhetorician would listen to and memorize speeches composed by the teacher and then would practice composing or delivering speeches among themselves.

Aeschines of Sphettus, as reported by Menage, recounts a dialogue describing Aspasia as an exemplar of effective inductive reasoning. More specifically, Cicero in *De Inventione*, gives the following account of an incident showing how Aspasia reasoned with Xenephon's wife and with Xenephon himself:

"Please tell me, madam, if your neighbor had a better gold ornament than you have, would you prefer that one or your own?" "That one," she replied. "Well, now, if she had a better husband than you have, would you prefer your husband or hers?" At this the woman blushed. "I wish you would tell me Xenophon," she said, "If your neighbor had a better horse than yours, would you prefer your horse or his?" "His," was the answer. "Now, if he had a better wife than you have, would you prefer yours or his?" And at this X, too, was himself silent. Then Aspasia, "Since both of you have failed to tell me the only thing I wished to hear, I myself will tell you what you both are thinking. Then, you, madam, wish to have the best husband, and you, X, desire above all things to have the finest wife. Therefore, unless you can contrive that there be no better man or finer woman on earth you will certainly always be in dire want of what you consider best, namely, that you be the husband of the very best of wives, and that she be wedded to the very best of men."[10]

Aspasia's accomplishments in the earliest foundations of rhetorical theory began with her interest in politics, although citizenship was denied her. Her education, movement, and rights were severely circumscribed by her culture and times. Yet her expertise as a sophist utilizing the Socratic method and expertise in manipulating principles of reasoning and oratory established her as an important role player within the intellectual tradition of the philosophers and rhetoricians in the lively intellectual atmosphere of fifth-century Athens.

WOMEN'S RHETORIC AND RENAISSANCE HUMANISM

Rhetoric, as we have seen, underwent a decline during the middle ages, but that trend was reversed during the Renaissance, primarily because of the rise of humanism. For some, this concept means the ideal state where human intellect reigns supreme; for others, it is a historical episode where new educational materials were discovered. Nevertheless, one common denominator that marks humanism is a keen interest in the classical texts, and the rediscovered rhetorical works' interest in eloquence. These texts were marked by the harmonious union of wisdom and style whose aim was to guide people toward virtue, not to mislead them for the sake of winning the day. Humanists also believed that knowledge ought to serve practical ends; education should instruct not only the intellect but also the will. The theme of education gained strength in the arguments of several impassioned women; their views on the place of rhetoric in daily lives reflects the "faculty psychology" school of thought.

Christine dePisan (ca. 1364–1430)

In the early 15th Century, Frenchwoman Christine dePisan instructed medieval women on the practical and philosophical aspects of persuasion; her stated objective was to offer schooling in the means of achieving honor and virtue through lessons that would demonstrate humility, diligence, and moral rectitude, of which all women were capable. Women were to gain eloquence and the persuasive skills made necessary by their public and private roles. These educated women would become worthy residents of the City of Ladies, dePisan's allegorical refuge for women whose good lives refuted stereotypes of weakness and immorality. Her works "struck a responsive chord in a culture beginning to rediscover the value of classical philosophy and humanistic ideals."[11] Her books, particularly, *The Book of the City of Ladies* and *The Treasure of the City of Ladies,* were a rhetoric for women reflecting the changes from the late Medieval period into the early Renaissance. By providing secular examples of womanly virtues, dePisan directed women to discover meaning and achieve worthy acts in their lives while reversing the misrepresentation of women popular during this time. Women could develop their minds and still achieve a good afterlife. In essence, dePisan presents instruction in how woman's intellect and words could empower her gender.

> Rhetoric, underwent a decline during the middle ages, but that trend was reversed during the Renaissance, primarily because of the rise of humanism.

RHETORICA · XXIII

Plate from *Die Tarocchi. Zwei italienische Kupferstichfolgen aus dem XV. Jahrhundert* (Cassirer, 1910: Berlin). Ascribed to the painter Mantegna.

Christine dePisan left 41 known pieces of poetry and prose, written over a thirty-year career; she was perhaps Europe's first professional woman writer. Royalty commissioned her prose, and following her death many authors acknowledged her intellectual influence. Her desire to instruct other women was derived from her life-long struggles to avoid the penury of being a widow and the disrespect for womanhood in the existing culture and social order. Her *Vision of Christine* (1405) autobiographically reveals that dePisan was completely unprepared to work to support her household upon her husband's death, so she turned to a scholarly life of study and writing, partly because no other means of livelihood were open to her. She wrote in French vernacular, rather than in Latin, the language that had previously been unavailable to most women. Her allegorical women possessed strengths to speak authoritatively; they established a feminine ethos complete with authority and integrity. They were used to battle common stereotypes that demeaned women and reduced their ability to argue.

One of dePisan's earliest public arguments on behalf of woman was over the immorality promoted by a popular ballad, *The Romance of the Rose*. Begun around 1230 by Guillaume deLorns and finished in 1280 by Jean de Meun, this popular piece described a lady's seduction by her lover. The ballad defended three much-admired principles of the times: love is a wonderful kind of suffering; love between husband and wife cannot exist because of the demands of the marriage contract; and virtue increases through devotion to a lover. In 1401, dePisan argued that the ballad subverted public morality, extolled carnal acts, and incited licentious conduct while it also promoted myths about feminine virtue. dePisan's arguments established her as a well-spoken intellectual who could argue effectively.

The Book of the City of Ladies constructed an imaginary city from the biographies of virtuous women, while *The Treasure* prepared them for life in this community. These two works serve to empower women in public and private matters; Redfern asserts that "Her most important lesson is that women's success depends on their ability to manage and mediate by speaking and writing effectively."[12] *The Book of the City of Ladies* introduces the reader to three allegorical women role models who appear to a despondent Christine, revealing themselves as God's daughters. They represent the most important virtues for woman's success: Reason, Rectitude, and Justice. As the Three Virtues answer Christine's questions, their female voices offer examples and opinions that present the truths about women in order to contradict the negative, narrow stereotypes in existence. Each story of virtuous feminine behavior recounted by the Virtues represents a building block in the walled city of words: all honorable women will be invited to this city, where they will be protected from unjust verbal attacks.

The Treasure focused on woman's contemporary lifestyle, both in public and private. dePisan champions chastity and honor, promotes accomplishing good works, and warns against the deadly sins. The Virtues remind woman that her primary concern should be "to account to God, for her life in comparison to the life everlasting is only a short time."[13] *The Treasure* is divided into advice for the three aspects of social hierarchy: princesses and other noblewomen; the women who serve them; and all other women (wives, artisans, widows, servants, prostitutes, peasants). In *The Treasure,* other virtues are introduced, including Prudence, Sobriety, and Chastity, which symbolize feminine morality.

Redfern says that dePisan "directed women to speak and write for the good of society, and to affirm the best of themselves and their accomplishments in the world."[14] dePisan advocated deliberative, epideictic, and forensic rhetoric for women, believing that they are the peacemakers, the givers of praise and blame, and the decision-makers. For example, she said a woman needed discourse skills because she may be called to mediate disputes: "She will speak to her husband well and wisely, calling other wise persons if necessary, and will very humbly petition him on behalf of the people. She will show the reasons, which she will understand thoroughly"[15] "She will urge the people, her husband and his council to consider this matter (war) carefully before undertaking it, in view of the evil which could result from it. It would be much better to think of some more suitable way to reach agreement."[16] Books 2 and 3 provide more insight into the use of practical rhetoric: widows should be able to defend themselves in court; women must know how to make others feel comfortable and to calm quarrels; merchant wives should be able to conduct commerce.

In essence, *The Treasure* is a woman's guide to the practical use of rhetoric. In dePisan's time, the ancient rules of oral persuasion had been translated into rules that extended into letters and conversations. Women were instructed in all forms of discourse, both written and oral, both public and private. dePisan also demonstrated her rhetorical strategies through use of reasoned argument. Reason, her first allegorical virtue figure, displays a familiarity with Plato, Aristotle and Augustine. Rectitude reminds women to "say and uphold the truth." She notes that God "endowed women with the faculty of speech" so that they should not fear speaking in public. dePisan utilizes Augustine, for example, in giving advice on how the noble lady may achieve a love of God; using a saint for advice on how the noble woman could reach the good afterlife is a strategy of

medieval scholastics.[17] She refers to Seneca's advice to speak kindly to those of a lower class, reminding the reader of the classics. The book advises woman on her obligations as daughter and wife while encouraging the development of the mind.

The contemporary concern over "empowerment" has roots in dePisan's work. dePisan argued for the equal cultural importance of woman and gave the most practical advice on how to work within the social status quo, achieving power through the manipulation of words. Eloquence and persuasive skill had a place both in public and private affairs. As Willard noted, she presented her female audience with models of successful rhetoric and with herself as the model rhetor.[18]

Mary Astell (1666–1731)

Astell, celebrated as one of the earliest English protofeminists, was well known and highly regarded in her own day for making a mark on her times in the struggle for woman's education and for her attacks on a patriarchal society. For rhetorical studies, her importance lies in Astell's mastery of the art of eloquence; she was a practitioner who demonstrated that women have the ability to participate in rhetorical activities. Astell grew up in Newcastle as part of a royalist coal merchant family, conservative in political and religious affiliation. Her father died when she was young, which threw the family into debt, leaving Astell no dowry. Because she was a gentlewoman, her class would not allow menial work, for young girls of her class were expected to marry well and bring a dowry. Astell had no such opportunity. In 1688, Astell moved to London to seek her fortune in writing; Lady Elizabeth Hastings became her patron, and from early 1690 to 1709, Mary Astell published six books and two pamphlets, as well as a record of correspondence.

The oppressed women of whom Astell wrote were economically privileged, and her feminism is not politically motivated but rather represents a firm assertion of woman's right to privacy, contemplation, and an identity. She insisted there were differences between the sexes but philosophically believed that the soul and intellect have no gender. She was guided by principles of the naturalness of human reason; women, as human beings, she argued, are endowed with reason and they could become fully competent by using the knowledge they already have.

In Astell's view, women were capable of engaging in rhetorical activity except for public speaking, which she assumed was inappropriate for them. Women could and should join in debate on philosophy and politics, write poems and handbooks, fiction and plays, letters to their friends, and pamphlets (which were a feature of the day). In the salons of the Renaissance and in the 17th and 18th centuries, women perfected the art of conversation through literary breakfasts and evening conversation parties, and it was here that their intellect could be engaged.

A Serious Proposal to the Ladies for the Advancement of Their True and Greatest Interest (1694) was her first book that established Astell's reputation. The book went through five editions by 1701. In her day, she was renowned for her eloquence; John Evelyn refers to her writing as "sublime."[19] John Norris spoke of her "moving Strains of the most natural and powerful Oratory."[20] The book recounts her horror of the waste of time, intelligence, and talents of most women. *Serious Proposal* appeared at a time when "conduct books" were popular: these recorded information on tradition-bound duties of a wife, mother, and source of comfort and pleasure to men. There was wide dissemination of these books through boarding schools, private tutorial programs, from mother to daughter. Deluna says conduct books essentially sold "traditional female roles on an unprecedented scale."[21] At this time, misogynists were also very active; they satired women as irredeemably vain, proud, and ignorant. Astell repeatedly opposed the satirists' claim that women are ignorant. To believe this claim, she states, is to argue that women lack the souls which would allow them to develop intellectual agility, and to deny women, "wou'd be as unphilosophical as it is unmannerly."[22] At another point she reflected on the difficulty of women escaping the predictable consequences of having been "taught to be Proud and Petulant, Delicate and Fantastic, Humorous and Inconstant."[23] What is remarkable, she declares, is not that "all Women are not wise and good" but that "there are any so."[24] Astell reflected the teachings of faculty psychology as she asserted the naturalness of intellectual activity:

> *As Nature teaches us logic, so does it instruct us in Rhetoric much better than Rules of Art, which if they are good ones are nothing else but those Judicious Observations which Men of Sense have drawn from nature, and which all who reflect on the Operations of their own Minds will find out 'emselves. (sic) The common Precepts*

> *of Rhetoric may teach us how to reduce Ingenious ways of speaking to a certain Rule, but they do not teach us how to Invent them, this is Nature's work and she does it best.*[25]

Astell proposed that there should be established a "Protestant Nunnery" or all female college, an academic religious retreat where women who could or would not marry could take refuge in a life of holiness and service, leading a life of philosophical reflection, educating children and doing good among the poor; in essence establishing a separate community to create a communal life of the mind (similar to dePisan's figurative withdrawal for women in to a safe "City of Ladies"). Such a community would help these women achieve the goal of salvation. On this point she asked: "Can Ignorance be a fit preparative for Heaven? Isn't likely that she whose Understanding has been busied about nothing but froth and trifles, shou'd be capable of delighting her self in noble and sublime Truths."[26] Those who left the group to marry would have been prepared by their education there to nurture their own children.[27]

The eloquence of Astell's arguments began with her selection of audience, as she first addresses the women of the upper class, the ladies who were so concerned with their appearance. She told them that intellectual exertion had the power to dignify them more than their shallow pursuit of physical beauty or social amusement. Astell says that her desire is "to improve your Charms and heighten your value, to fix that Beauty, to make it lasting and permanent, which Nature with all the helps of Art cannot secure."[28] Astell believed that a trained mind and understanding heart surpass physical attractiveness, and she appealed to her readers on the basis that these attributes will attract favorable attention. A secondary audience is comprised of parents, who are reminded that the cost of sending their unmarried daughters to such an institution is lower than the dowry needed for an acceptable marriage, or that suspect suitors would be kept away. She was employing methods centered in faculty psychology: the soul "always Wills according as she understands, so that if she understands amiss, she Wills amiss."[29] Astell also encouraged the socially concerned to promote the training of competent teachers who will educate manners and morals of the next generation. Her argument consisted of a fifty-page analysis of the problems facing women. She then offered a solution, described its potential benefits, and answered some of the possible objections through refutation. As she did so, she employed the "moderate style" of language, using few metaphors.

According to Astell, nature is the guiding principle for arrangement, eloquence, grammar and spelling. Astell urged women to use their natural good sense of language: "Those who speak true grammar, unless they're very careless cannot write false, since they need only peruse what they've writ and consider whether they wou'd express themselves thus in Conversation."[30] She also asserted that women have certain natural advantages over men in rhetoric, especially in the art of conversation, which she believed comes naturally to women; this is extremely important because it guides correctness and good writing style. "Nature does for the most part furnish 'em with such a Musical Tone, Perswasive Air and Winning Address as renders their Discourse sufficiently agreeable in Private Conversation."[31] Then, echoing the views of Cicero and Quintilian, she said, "I have made no distinction in what has been said between Speaking and Writing, because tho they are talents which do not always meet, yet there is no material difference between 'em. They Write best perhaps who do't with the gentile and easy air of Conversation; and they Talk best who mingle Solidity of Thought with th' agreeableness of a ready Wit."[32] Conversation was the foundation of all. Astell also believed that women's ethos gave them a rhetorical advantage. She said that it was "to little purpose to Think well and speak well, unless we live well."[33] Part of that ethos was Christian morality: "The way to be good Orators is to be good Christians."[34] In essence, by applying Christian principles to the practice of communication, they would overcome the deficiencies of their education.

Deluna has observed that *Serious Proposal* catapulted Astell to celebrity status as a woman's advocate. This volume revolutionized the conduct book genre instructing ladies how they should behave. In keeping with this concept, Astell repeatedly enjoined women to reject frivolous pursuits in favor of the pleasures of philosophy. She used the generic, familiar signposts of conduct books regarding beauty, for example, in these words: "Your Glass will not do you half so much service as a serious reflection of your own Mind. Virtue has certainly the most attractive Air, and Wisdom the most graceful and becoming Mien: Let these attend you, and your Carriage will be always well compos'd, and ev'ry thing you do will carry its Charm with it."[35] Her proposed ver-

bal strategies capitalize on the concept of mind over body, devaluing the notions of female excellence found in the day's beauty manuals and replacing them with superior ideals of women's spiritual edification through the study of philosophy. Whereas the typical woman's guide of the time linked religious piety to such domestic virtues as wifely subservience and good housekeeping, Astell made the connection between holy living and philosophic meditation.[36] Sutherland suggests that "the principle of caring" was another one of *Serious Proposal's* most important features.[37] While Astell championed the use of Christian morality as a guide to women's practice of rhetoric, hers was not an original idea. Astell recommended tenderness to the feelings of the audience, avoiding for them the pain of humiliation and a distaste for confrontation. This theme of caring and concern is echoed in many twentieth-century studies of women's rhetoric.

Astell's *A Serious Proposal to the Ladies Part II Wherein A Method is Offer'd for the Improvement of their Minds* (1697) provided a detailed discussion of her earlier proposal. Ch. 1 ("Of the Mutual Relation Between Ignorance and Vice, and Knowledge and Purity") deals with the relationship between knowledge and virtue, essentially building Astell's goodwill; this first chapter refuted the common belief that silent women were the most pure. Astell attempted to show that the training of the mind and voice promoted morality by developing the understanding, which (according to 17th-century faculty psychology) should control the passions and direct the will. Women, therefore, should develop their rationality, which alone can promote moral behavior. Her attempts here are to clarify and teach, rather than to persuade. The retreat would allow women to escape unhappy marriages and to reflect on a self rather than on clothes and adornments while enjoying female company and finding renewed strength in traditional religious commitment. Ch. 2 discusses avoiding slothfulness, selfishness, and pride, as well as the elimination of prejudices arising from authority, education, and custom. Astell promotes the exercise of the power of reason and speech. She takes it for granted that thinking belongs to logic rather than rhetoric, in the tradition of Ramus and Déscartes. Cartesian philosophy fostered an introspective psychology, a consciousness of self that was important for the "rescue" of women. Astell boldly proclaimed the thesis that God had given all humans the same intellectual potential and that only circumstances precluded women from exercising their rational faculties[38] She even provided six rules for clear thinking, obviously derived in part from Déscartes' four rules (from his *Discourse on Method*).

ASTELL'S SIX RULES FOR CLEAR THINKING

1. We should in the first place Acquaint our selfves thoroughly with the State of the Question, have a Distinct Notion of our Subject, whatever it be, and of the Termes (sic) we make use of, knowing precisely what it is we drive at: that so we may in the second

2. Cut off all needless Ideas and whatever has not a necessary Connexion to the matter under Consideration.

3. To conduct our Thought by Order, beginning with the most Simple and Easie Objects, and ascending as by Degrees to the Knowlege of the more Compos'd

4. Not to leave any part of our Subject unexamin'd. . . . To this rule belongs that of Dividing the Subject of our Meditations into as many parts as we can, and shall be requisite to Understand it perfectly.

5. We must Always keep our Subject Directly in our Eye, and Closely pursue it through our Progress.

6. To judge no further than we Perceive, and not to take any thing for Truth which we do not evidently know to be so[39].

In sum, Astell placed great emphasis on clarity, exactness, and method. Ch. 3 instructs on how to improve the understanding, and Ch. 4 educates the reader on the regulation of the will and passions.

Some Reflections Upon Marriage, Occasion'd by the Duke and Duchess of Mazarine's Case; Which is Also Consider'd (1700) is a satirical work, where the unmarried Astell spoke for the women who where tyrannized and oppressed by marriage. It emphasized the delusions of courtship, argued against blind obedience to husbands, and suggested taking refuge in virtue. The book's genesis was the death of the notorious Duchess of Mazarin, who had endured psychological and physical tyranny at the hands of her in-

sane husband before escaping to England, where she led a decadent life. Her scandalous life was seen by Astell as a demonstration of the necessity of giving women the rights to education, as well as a recognition of the plight of many in abusive marriages. She asserted that married women were no better than slaves. She argued for a woman to be educated to understand the risks involved in marriage, such as a husband who merely wants the woman's money, her wit, or her beauty. This book is an example more of the grand style; Astell's metaphors are menacing, representing marriage at best as not being that of conquest but as capture. For example, she noted, "It were endless to reckon up the diverse stratagems Men use to catch their Prey, their different ways of insinuating which vary with the Circumwstances (sic) and the Ladies Temper. But how unfairly, how basely soever they processd, when the Prey is once caught it passes for lawful Prize."[40] This book contains a defense of women's rationality; Astell associates reason with the power of speech by pointing out that men have always complained that women speak too much rather than too little. Therefore, it follows that you could not question the fact that women are endowed with reason, and if their reasoning powers were inferior to men's it was because of a lack of exercise.

> As long as rhetoric was based on knowledge of the Latin language, which then opened doors to classical history, philosophy, and literature, women were excluded from improving their intellect.

What is very important to remember, besides Astell's eloquence, is her insistence upon the right of women to participate in a rhetorical tradition from which they had been excluded; women were ignorant of the classics and could not learn Latin because they were excluded from such instruction. She insists that custom, not nature, produced inferior women and called for a collective female audience that could recognize its common interests. As long as rhetoric was based on knowledge of the Latin language, which then opened doors to classical history, philosophy, and literature, women were excluded from improving their intellect.[41]

Mary Wollstonecraft (1759–97)

Known by many as the founding mother of feminism (as though woman's rhetorical history began with her) Mary Wollstonecraft challenged 18th-century cultural norms by arguing for rights of women, exposing the irrationality of arguments and assumptions used to debase and exclude women. A proponent of the natural rights philosophy, she believed in the principles of individualism, the universal capacity for reason, and political democracy. Wollstonecraft espoused the enlightenment conviction that reason would lead the way to a progressively better social order, free of the superstitions that had in the past limited people. Wollstonecraft is generally recognized as the first to insist that women's nature was basically the same as men's: free, rational, and independent, and that like men, a woman's first duty was to be a rational creature.

Ironically, Wollstonecraft's *Vindication of the Rights of Woman,* her extended argument that advocated the supremacy of reason in guiding human affairs, was censured by a torrent of abuse directed less at the ideas than at their writer. Writing at the time of the French Revolution, she urged the liberals of her day, compatriots in the overthrow of decadent aristocratic privilege, that the rights of man (that is, citizenship) should be extended to women. Contemporary conservatives such as Horace Walpole (who called her a "hyena in petticoats") found the idea of women's rights to be unnatural; more importantly, many feminists in the eighteenth century also called her work tainted, mostly because of Wollstonecraft's abandonment of conventional morality. She had had a long and unhappy love affair, a child born out of wedlock, and several desperate suicide attempts. These affronts to prevailing virtues made Wollstonecraft a pariah, one whose detractors claimed that she advocated hedonism as part of women's rights. She was invoked occasionally by Abigail Adams, Elizabeth Cady Stanton, and Virginia Woolf, but for the most part the early women's rights campaigns ignored their indebtedness to Wollstonecraft's early work.

Like many women of her century, it was a financial prod that started Wollstonecraft on the path to a writing career. Her first published work was a collection of essays called *Thoughts on the Education of Daughters* (1786), written in order to meet the rent coming due on the building she used for her boarding school. In 1789, she wrote *A Vindication of the Rights of Man, in a Letter to the Right Honourable Edmund Burke,* a scathing rejection of Burke's acceptance of social injustices. Her pamphlet, though weakly organized, is powerful in its appeal to political and human sentiments. Leading journals took note of her response and swept her into center stage in political debates of the day.

Her best-known book, *A Vindication of the Rights of Woman* (1792), was written in response to Talleyrand's *A Report on Public Instruction,* which laid out his proposals for national education under the new French constitution. Central to Wollstonecraft's response was Talleyrand's proposal that French girls be educated with their brothers in public schools only to age eight and after that, to remain at home. Wollstonecraft urged him to revise his educational plan and not bar women from their democratic rights. *Vindication* advanced a theory of human sexuality that places imperatives of woman's education, the beginning point for woman's ultimate civic and political emancipation. Stylistically, the book was given to exaggeration by taking exceptional abuses as though they typified the experiences of all women. In Wollstonecraft's view, all differences are rooted in the social environment and could be eradicated by changes in that environment. She professed "a profound conviction that the neglected education of my fellow-creatures is the grand source of the misery I deplore; and that women are rendered weak and wretched by a variety of concurring causes, originating from one hasty conclusion."[42] She professed her desire "to persuade women to endeavour to acquire strength, both of mind and body, and to convince them that the soft-phrases, susceptibility of heart, delicacy of sentiment, and refinement of taste, are almost synonymous with epithets of weaknesses."[43]

Wollstonecraft argued that men had violated natural laws by marginalizing women and had created and shaped cultural conditions that victimized all society. For example, *Vindication* says that "reason has been perplexed and involved in error" because it is confined to male experience and "built on partial experience and on narrow views."[44] She argues that "for man and woman, Truth, if I understand the meaning of the word, must be the same,"[45] rather than the false truth that men put forward about women, which justifies their own superiority and power. Wollstonecraft's writing relies primarily on personal experience *as a woman* for evidence; she asserts that in a male-dominated society, such evidence has little currency. She knew that her arguments were outside male experience, yet she defiantly asserted the validity of women's personal experiences.

Like her contemporaries and earlier philosophers of social problems, Wollstonecraft felt that both cause and solution were in education: ignorance, poverty, prejudice, and sin all came in the absence of knowledge and could be solved by the spread of education. All differences, whether racial, sexual, or social class, were rooted in the social environment. Her belief in education as the cure-all for human ignorance and corruption came directly from confidence in the human cognitive faculty. Reason, if properly cultivated through education, could set men and women free. Her expectation was that free inquiry would be the path to truth. She believed that the educational system had deprived women of the knowledge and skills which would allow them to behave rationally. She developed the following premise: If morality is a consequence of rationality, and education is one of the ways to cultivate virtue through rationality, then women are deprived of those natural rights. She claimed that the educational system and writers such as Rousseau . . . "have contributed to render women more artificial, weak characters, than they would otherwise have been; and consequently more useless members of society."[46]

Wollstonecraft suggested that coed day schools should be established by the government for children ages five to nine; here, students would study science, reading, writing, mathematics, and philosophy; she also recommended the use of the Socratic dialogue in teaching elements of religion, history, and politics. As children grew older, children would be separated in terms of their future destiny (mechanical trades, millinery, etc.) but the sexes would still be taught together. They would still be exposed to subjects that would maintain their active minds: literary pursuits, philosophy and reasoning, scientific subjects, politics, and morality. While it may seem that Wollstonecraft was arguing merely for changes in the educational system, her ultimate goal was woman's independence. She crafted an argument providing extensive supporting evidence, statements of problems, and proposals for solutions. Wollstonecraft believed that education would improve women's position and character, but what distinguished her was her commitment to the kind of education that would narrow the moral and intellectual distance between men and women.

Much of her time was spent discussing the deficiencies of male reasoning. She wonders why it is that men are in a position to decide what is valid and what is not: "Who made man the exclusive judge," she asks, "if women partake with him the gift of reason?"[47] She ponders by what authority do men judge what is best for women? Why is the term "women's

reason" virtually a derogatory one? She asserts that men are tyrants who have excluded women without having a voice, and thus reason has been "perplexed and involved in error"[48] because it is confined to the narrow views of male experience. Male reasoning justifies their supposed superiority, which is a false truth; women's experience, which is qualitatively different, is based on different assumptions which can give rise to different truths. Chapter 5, for example, demonstrates the flawed assumptions by which men justified their power over women. Wollstonecraft also employed the stratagem of allowing men to speak for themselves in order to refute their so-called logic. She quoted extensively from the male authorities and then commented critically on their case. Rousseau and his theories on women's education provided her with some of the most successful evidence for her analysis of the corruption of male reasoning. She noted Rousseau's claim that "the first and most important qualification in a woman is good nature or sweetness of temper: formed to obey a being so imperfect as man, often full of vices and always full of faults, she ought to learn even to suffer injustice."[49] Wollstonecraft archly pointed out the illogic of this patriarchal explanation for men's violence against women: it is women's fault. "The perverseness and ill nature of the woman only serve to aggravate their own misfortunes and the misconduct of their husbands."[50] She listed all the qualities men think desirable in a woman (further making use of Rousseau): passivity, weakness, lassitude and dependency, frivolity, and a dislike of serious pursuit. Then Wollstonecraft dissected the list, asking if these qualities are natural. If so, then women should be left alone to allow them to develop, rather than having rigid discipline forced on them to limit these qualities. Her critique of the inadequacies of the assumptions with which males began and her disregard for their limited frames of reference (where women are held responsible for the ills of the world which men control) exposed the absurdities of the world.

Wollstonecraft created a legacy of arguments and demands that retain value and force. She understood that women would continue to be perceived as abnormal while the limited experience of men was treated as the sum total of human experience. She was one of a long line of women who understood the significance of male power to name the world and to say what is and what is not important, valuable and logical. Most enduring is her argument that the position of women in a given culture is not natural but is produced by that culture. This legacy would be expanded upon by later generations of women orators and writers.

WOMEN EMERGE AS SPEAKERS: NINETEENTH-CENTURY TRANSFORMATIONS OF WOMEN'S ROLE IN THE PUBLIC ARENA

During the 1830s and 40s, American women began to form networks of local all-women's organizations to remedy what they perceived to be their wider moral obligations, from the care of indigents and education of orphans to the elimination of prostitution. In the context of these organizations, they were more able to express profound resentment of the social and economic power that men had over them. For example, New York moral reform societies denounced male debauchery to the legislature, where they petitioned for a law making the sexual seduction of any unmarried, chaste female a crime. This type of influence on the legislature gave impetus to even greater crusades. The National Female Anti-Slavery Society was formed in 1833; it was the first effort by an organized women's society to attack a political question from a public forum. Women abolitionists asserted that they had a particular obligation in the cause because slavery was a threat to the moral character of society. Slavery encompassed questions of religion, philanthropy, political economy, commerce, and education. Initially they observed the proprieties by meeting separately from men, but antislavery activity brought women into conflict with established centers of power, leading them beyond the "woman's sphere" way of conceiving their social role.

Concurrent with this budding public political activism and the emergence of new social movements came the hard-won admittance of females into higher education institutions, where gradually women were provided with institutionalized, formal training in rhetoric. Following Oberlin College's admission of women in 1835, they were grudgingly permitted to have rhetorical preparation in elocution,

> During the 1830s and 40s, American women began to form networks of local all-women's organizations to remedy what they perceived to be their wider moral obligations, from the care of indigents and education of orphans to the elimination of prostitution.

composition, criticism, and argument. Lucy Stone and Antoinette Brown helped to organize the first women's debating society there, for women were banned from public speaking in their rhetoric classroom because of its "mixed audience" status. The creation of the Seven Sisters colleges, founded exclusively for women (Barnard College, 1889; Bryn Mawr College, 1889; Mount Holyoke College, 1888; Radcliffe College, 1879; Smith College, 1875; Vassar College, 1865; and Wellesley College, 1875) required rhetoric courses, instructing students in logic, delivery, and the articulation of ideas. As an extension of their collegiate work, the women of the Seven Sisters colleges formed extracurricular groups, often called debating or literary societies, in which they practiced their rhetorical skills.[51] Many of the early women writers and orators who promoted social change over the next century had their rhetorical roots in these colleges.

With the advent of these educational and social transformations, women began to participate more widely in the public platforms that would transfigure what were previously perceived as personal grievances into massed political consciousness. By making public their demands for equal citizenship, women were able to collectively argue against their oppression, rather than each arguing individual cases. The public address platforms and developing journalistic outlets available to women allowed them to challenge beliefs and express opinions on topics of equality, immigration, education, suffrage, abolition, temperance, and a host of other issues. Woman's rhetoric blossomed in national and international movements of social change.

Social movements aren't born overnight. They ferment in societies which ignore or downplay problems. Potential audiences for change must be gathered and persuaded of the needs for those important alterations in society's fundamental assumptions. Early leaders must dramatize society's imperfections, must discredit those in power, and must set the stage for change. As a movement gathers momentum and more people begin to recognize concerns over perceived wrongs, leaders must begin to organize members and create a framework of ideas and demands, meet with resistance, and present the issues in public campaigns to raise consciousness with the larger audience. With time, movements must deal with competing ideologies and coalitions, attempt to diversify in issues, and keep a unified front. The rhetorical demands change from early visions of sweeping reform that usually employ more strident or impassioned arguments to the use of rhetoric that is more composed and restrained, focusing on maintaining successes and identifying new issues.[52]

The movement campaigns that were embraced in nineteenth-century America were marked by pragmatic concerns: they were more concerned with discovering and implementing practical means of social improvement than with dealing with the root causes of the problems. Reform was comprehensive in scope; reformers, confident in their abilities, attacked on several fronts, so one could work simultaneously on temperance, on prison reform, and on sensible dress for women with equal fervor. In addition, reform was largely regional, centering in the North and West; the South was relatively untouched. Since one reform usually snowballed into another, Southerners could not risk opening the door to even one, for fear of granting inroads to abolitionism. Further, until the mid-nineteenth century, reform movements were largely apolitical, doing their work from outside partisan political frameworks. Religious evangelism gave reform campaigns their earliest bases of support; revivalists believed that people were perfectible and that social reform was a moral imperative because people's sins resulted in social evils.

The agency chosen to accomplish reform was the voluntary association, consisting of like-minded individuals who organized community groups, published journals, organized speakers' bureaus, held conventions, and grew into powerful governmental lobbies. Women figured prominently in many of these organizations, even though their subordinate role denied them the speaker's platform. Yet out of the efforts by women to speak for abolition and temperance came a desire and a means for them to take a more active part in public affairs. As their home lives improved, they had time to read tracts, discuss issues, and attend approved public meetings.

Our attention to woman's role in developing rhetorical traditions will center on a few leading American advocates to see how they used rhetoric to reflect their vision of themselves and their age, and how this rhetoric marked the beginning of women's public political and social activism on a national campaign scale.

Frances Wright (1795–1852)

Like Wollstonecraft, Frances Wright believed that girls and boys should be educated in the same way and at the same schools. She was a particularly caustic critic of the domestic institutions that structured women's lives, advocating "free and voluntary affection" as an alternative to monogamous marriage and a childrearing system based on state-run coeducational boarding schools to replace families. She fueled the American debate on woman's proper "sphere" by articulating ideas of egalitarianism, secularism, and sexual freedom, which she believed were the basis on which a woman's true position should be established.

"It was as a lecturer—a female lecturer—that Fanny Wright made her greatest impact on the United States," according to Gurko. "She was the first woman to speak in public here, and this as much as her radical ideas created a sensation."[53] Wright's July 4, 1828, oration in New Harmony, IN is traditionally acknowledged to be the first public speech by a woman in America. The range and richness of ideas promoted in writing and on the lecture circuit by Frances Wright were matched only by the outrage she created as she flaunted just about every precept laid down for decorous behavior in women of her times. The Biblical prohibition against women speaking in public was universally enforced and accepted in the early nineteenth century. Thus, when the Scottish radical Frances Wright toured the eastern United States in 1829 and addressed mixed audiences with a message combining antislavery with anticlerical attitudes, the shock waves were great. She spoke on education for women, birth control, married women's property rights, unions, birth control, and the clergy to what were probably the first mixed audiences. As an example of her speaking prowess, in one lecture she said, "Until women assume the place in society which good sense and good feeling alike assign to them, human improvement must advance but feebly."[54] Wright argued that men were themselves degraded by the inferiority imposed on women. Every relationship to which woman was a party, including friendship, marriage, or parenthood, suffered as long as she was regarded and treated as a lesser human being. *The History of Woman Suffrage* acknowledges the pioneering contribution she made:

"Her radical ideas on theology, slavery, and the social degradation of women, now generally accepted by the best minds of the age, were then denounced by both press and pulpit, and maintained by her at the risk of her life."[55] She was one of the first public campaigners for women's rights.

Margaret Fuller (1810–1850)

Urbanski calls Fuller "the most important woman of the Nineteenth century"[56] for her multitude of roles as literary critic, first editor of the *Dial,* precursor nurse to both Florence Nightingale and Clara Barton, foreign correspondent of the daily *New York Tribune,* and author of numerous works, including *Woman in the Nineteenth Century,* the intellectual foundation of the feminist movement. Kolodny suggests that through her educational efforts, Fuller was trying to fashion a set of rhetorical strategies appropriate to the emerging feminist consciousness of her era.

Acutely aware from a young age of the narrow education which women received, she set up two important educational programs for women outside the institutions controlled by men. Fuller's Greene Street School utilized Richard Whatley's *Elements of Rhetoric* (which was essentially an introductory manual presenting a set of procedures for argumentative composition). In August, 1839, she informed Sophia Ripley that she taught girls there "to bear their part, to question, to define, to state and examine their opinions."[57]

Fuller had read Plato's dialogues to prepare herself for her other innovation, women's "conversations" whose purpose was to allow participants to throw off "the garb of modesty" in order to "openly state their impressions and consent to learn by blundering."[58] Women paid $20 to attend a three-month series of conversations on a wide range of topics ranging from philosophy to mythology to the arts. These conversations were the precursors to twentieth-century consciousness-raising groups, which have been credited with providing impetus and forums for the feminist movement's rebirth in the 1960's. In Whately's terms, Fuller could be said to have used the dialogue as a pedagogical device incorporating his ideas of "rational conversation." (Whately noted that in conversation, a person attempts to convey thoughts in several ways). Unfortunately, with the exception of Caroline Healey Dall's transcription of ten conversations in 1841, there is no detailed written record remaining of the conversa-

tions, and this series was unusual because ten men, including Ralph Waldo Emerson, were also permitted to attend. Rossi says that "Fuller provided an important circle of Boston women with skill in public speaking, in defending their viewpoints, in marshaling their evidence."[59] Fuller's familiarity with literature and philosophy, her adeptness in several languages, her training and teaching in formal rhetoric, and her admiration of the early women platform speakers provided her with a strong base from which to help women make the transition from the private to the public realm.

Woman in the Nineteenth Century was an attempt to provide a symbolic framework in which women's existence could be made meaningful: it is a panorama of women and their lives, with a subtext which argues for their equality. In a patriarchal society where women's existence and reality are systematically denied, made invisible, and consigned to the realm of non-data, Fuller posits that men have created myths to give lesser substance and significance to women's lives. Throughout the book there are references to individual women, to female writers and characters, all introduced to serve as models and to make women's cultural presence visible and real.

Fuller's analysis ranges across a huge spectrum of issues, and her theoretical framework remains constant: it is men who are in charge of what we know, and the result is that we know only what is convenient and enhancing for them. She questioned existing hierarchies: no human being can own or have rights over other human beings. No amount of rationalization about chivalry or protection could justify the restrictions society placed on women or eliminate the hypocrisy when they are exploited. She points out that women are held in such low esteem (despite social protestations to the contrary) that any woman who is admired by a man is inclined to be labeled as "above her sex."[60] Fuller pinpoints one of the fundamental features of patriarchy: men have claimed for themselves the qualities they perceive as positive and imposed on women the qualities they regard as negative and which they seek to avoid. With little concern for the evidence, men have appropriated attributes such as creative energy and intellectual accomplishment, but women (despite the obstacles) demonstrate that they also possess the same qualities. How do men overcome this contradiction, asks Fuller? They refuse to admit that their definitions of maleness are inadequate but instead, treat the woman as unusual, as atypical of her sex.

"She has a masculine mind" they would say.[61] By presenting this argument, male ownership of creativity and intellectuality is not challenged, nor is the male definition of woman challenged; instead, the woman getting this "compliment" is expected to accept as flattering the notion that she is a pseudo-male. Fuller suggests this contradiction places this woman into a limbo between both genders; males may find this arrangement logical and satisfactory, but Fuller (and by extension, all women) does not.

Once men stipulate via definition that women don't possess these prestigious qualities, they then go to great lengths to ensure that their beliefs come true: Fuller notes that men often discourage women with school boy brag, "Girls can't do that: girls can't play ball!"[62] She concludes that men feel the need to define women as a being made for men partly because of vanity, partly because of power. It is the need for power "for each wishes to be lord in a little world, to be at least superior over one"[63] that distinguishes men from women. Men engage in the intimidation of women by a variety of means so that women cannot move out of that narrow space men have decreed is woman's natural sphere. Nature, says Fuller, plays no part in it: it is force that keeps woman in her place.[64]

Fuller's style is characteristic of its time and place; she freely mixes Latin and English words, circles around the same point over and over to provide different illustrations of it, asks questions of her reader, and uses complex sentences. Fuller apparently was concerned about "the gap between her conversational talents and her writing abilities,"[65] yet she explained this style by saying that she wanted to leave no room for doubt in her use of repetition. She utilized analogies, anecdotes, and myths extensively as she created a frame of reference for women. Critics said that the book was loosely arranged and read more like a long talk rather than a treatise. She wrote graphically about women's sexual lives, social preference for sons over daughters, prostitution, and other scandalous topics, risking the charge of using language "offensive to delicacy."[66]

As a woman speaking for women, she needed to put forward a treatise that would not simply replicate male strategies; she wanted women to find their own voice. Kolodny notes Fuller's extensive use of Whately's principles, however. Fuller attempted to use the syllogism that shifted the burden of proof to the opponent when responding to the presumption in favor of existing institutions. For example, she said

that men see only their own needs and do not look at both sides; so women must stop asking them and being influenced by them. She used Whately's recommendations for the use of testimony and cross-examination of adversaries, argument from analogies, and drawing a conclusion from a single instance and inferring to a large class. For example, she presented a vignette of the father who would not educate his daughter, which illustrates an instance of a male who does not always act in women's best interest. Because men view woman as made for man and because men are bound by habit to this thought, they can never speak for woman or act in her best interests: this is a clear cause-effect argument, which Whately believed would give the greatest satisfaction to the candid mind. From her own observations and newspaper reports of the female lectures of the day, she concluded that "women who speak in public, if they have a moral power, invariably subdue the prejudices of their hearers."[67]

Elizabeth Cady Stanton (1815–1902) and Susan B. Anthony (1820–1906)

In the half century since Wollstonecraft, the debate over sexual egalitarianism had shifted politics. Frances Wright had recognized the importance of political organization, but she did not demand that women be enfranchised. But the emergence and partnership of two very different women whose insistence on building a movement based primarily on the leadership of women, separate from the leadership of abolitionist men and radical Republican politicians, laid the new foundation for woman's rhetorical power.

Elizabeth Cady Stanton and Susan B. Anthony are the two women most widely acclaimed for their lifelong leadership of the 19th-century women's rights movement, yet their writings and speeches have been difficult to access except for a few speeches reprinted in anthologies until recently. The two projected a public image of unity, teamwork, and a collaboration so close they seemed to merge into one.[68] However, they were two separate identities, not infrequently in conflict, often stressing different aspects of a problem. Their half-century collaboration found the pair complementing each other's abilities. Anthony was the stimulus mobilizing Cady Stanton to work, and together they wrote addresses and essays for causes ranging from temperance to women's rights. Cady Stanton reminisced: "We forged resolutions, protests, appeals, petitions, agricultural reports, and constitutional arguments; for we made it a matter of conscience to accept every invitation to speak on every question, in order to maintain woman's right to do so."[69] She also commented on the relationship, noting:

It has been said, by those who know me best, that I forged the thunderbolts and she in the early days fired them. In thought and sympathy we were one, and in the division of labor we exactly complemented each other. I am the better writer, she the better critic. She supplied the facts and statistics, I the philosophy and rhetoric, and together, we have made arguments that have stood unshaken through the storms of long years; arguments that no one has answered.[70]

Elizabeth Cady Stanton's visionary leadership during the movement's early phases, marked by her controversial insistence on including the demand for

From the archives of the Seneca Falls Historical Society.

Elizabeth Cady Stanton and Susan B. Anthony are the two women most widely acclaimed for their lifelong leadership of the 19th-century women's rights movement, yet their writings and speeches have been difficult to access except for a few speeches reprinted in anthologies until recently.

woman suffrage, was firmly rooted in traditional American values. She argued that the suffrage demand was the key that transformed personal grievances into political consciousness. She was instrumental in convening the first Woman's Rights Convention at Seneca Falls, NY in July 1848. It was her idea to adapt the Declaration of Independence for use as a women's rights manifesto, and she assembled the list of grievances designed to prove that "the history of mankind is the history of repeated injuries and usurpations on the part of man toward woman."[71] The Declaration of Sentiments bore many hallmarks of Cady Stanton's rhetoric: it was shaped by a powerful, eloquent conviction of men's absolute tyranny over women; it was rooted in a document of great significance which the audience revered; it demanded full equality and true freedom as woman's natural rights.[72] In it, Cady Stanton argued that political equality was the key to women's overthrow of male despotism. Women had an "inalienable right to the elective franchise." From this flowed men's ability to pass laws that deprived women of control over property and wages, subjected them to the authority of their husbands in marriage, deprived them of their children in case of divorce. She understood that law played a major role in setting men over women. By demanding political power, women could struggle collectively against their degradation, rather than each against her father or husband.

By itself, the initial woman's rights convention did not physically reach many advocates, and a meeting of 300 people in a small New York town was not ordinarily a national event; but news of it spread. Reports were widely published and the proceedings were ridiculed by the press and denounced by the clergy. The venomous attacks gave the meeting a publicity boost that no one had dreamed of. Typical of press statements was one editorial that called the convention "the most shocking and unnatural incident ever recorded in the history of womanity."[73] Cady Stanton noted in her diary:

No words could express our astonishment on finding that what seemed to us so timely, so rational, and so sacred, should be the subject for sarcasm and ridicule to the entire press of the nation . . . so pronounced was the popular voice against us, in the parlor, press, and pulpit, that most of the ladies who had attended the convention and signed the declaration, one by one, withdrew their names and influence, and joined our persecutors.[74]

The shock waves created by the Seneca Falls and later conventions attracted the attention of a young Quaker teacher, Susan Brownell Anthony, whose reform activities and alliance with Cady Stanton were to have a marked effect on the progress of Cady Stanton's rhetoric and of American feminism. It is Anthony who should be credited with building a national women's coalition, for the early conventions were spontaneously conceived and loosely affiliated. It took Anthony's administrative genius to create the national organization.

When the two met in May 1851 at an antislavery convention in Seneca Falls, Anthony was more curious about rather than sympathetic to Cady Stanton's woman's rights ideas. Susan B. Anthony had suffered through reproaches to keep silent at earlier temperance meetings, and such treatment aroused her zeal. She called for a Woman's State Temperance Convention to be held in Rochester in April, 1852. Cady Stanton saw temperance as a stepping-stone to woman's rights, and she used the opportunity to broach previously ignored topics. While temperance advocates believed that liquor was the cause of family problems, Cady Stanton dissented, saying that only when women could own their wages, hold property, and be legally recognized guardians of their children would they be able to protect the family. Anthony's conversion from moral reform to political reform began with this meeting, and the internal fight over the platform solidified their comradeship. The effect of their partnership on Cady Stanton was enormous: "In turning the intense earnestness and religious enthusiasm of this great-souled woman into this channel, I soon felt the power of my convert goading me forward to more untiring work."[75]

The women shared a common idealism and complementary differences in style and focus on women's oppression. Together, they extended the assertion of women's natural rights into programmatic attacks on women's major economic and sexual grievances, expanding the early demands for woman's suffrage into a more multifaceted feminism. Anthony concentrated her attention on the economic needs of women, trying to integrate feminist and trade union goals. Elizabeth Cady Stanton, following in Fanny Wright's utopian tradition, concentrated her attacks on the sexual oppression of women, arguing for self-sovereignty, or woman's control over her own body. Susan B. Anthony focused more strictly on suffrage, asserting that voting was the answer to nearly all social problems, while Cady Stanton linked women's issues to a widely based program of political reform and attacks on religious fundamentalism. For example, Cady Stanton advocated easier divorce laws, an end to prostitution, and redress for wives against the excesses of violent or drunken husbands. Anthony was the organizer, Stanton the stylist. Anthony supplied facts and statistics, and Stanton put them together. Elizabeth Cady Stanton's power came as a political orator possessing a passionate and militant character of thought. Anthony's contribution was as an organizer with the ability to draw out women's anger and commitment to change.

Cady Stanton possessed argumentative skills for public and private debate, which she developed and exploited as a lyceum speaker, social reform critic and women's rights advocate. At the 1869 Woman Suffrage Convention, Grace Greenwood in the *Philadelphia Press* described Cady Stanton:

Of all their speakers, she seemed to me to have the most weight. Her speeches are models of composition, clear, compact, elegant and logical. She makes her points with peculiar sharpness and certainty, and there is no denying or dodging her conclusions . . . (She is) now impassioned, now playful, now witty, now pathetic. Mrs. Stanton has the best arts of the politician and the training of the jurist, added to the fiery, unresting spirit of the reformer. She has a rare talent for affairs, management, and mastership. Yet she is in an eminent degree womanly, having an almost regal pride of sex.[76]

Anthony's effectiveness as an orator was less. She presented a staid and austere image, and her greater strengths lay in her logical precision in placing arguments, lobbying skills, and ability to organize others.

The major thrust of their argumentative positions revolved around four essential societal assumptions:

1. The sphere argument, which insisted that anatomy is destiny;
2. The theological argument, which asserted God's divine limitations on woman and her subservience to man;

3. The domestic argument, which said that woman's role as mother and wife was paramount and that her sole duty was to the family;
4. The legal argument, which claimed that woman needed special judicial or political protection.

In attacking each of these fundamental assumptions, Cady Stanton and Anthony were faced with the challenge of altering society's mistaken ideas into a newly conceptualized belief. They had to convince listeners that their dominant beliefs were based on inconsistencies, false notions, and outmoded customs. In order to create such arguments, Cady Stanton and Anthony grounded them in principles that formed the basis of American democracy: freedom, no taxation without representation, and the desire to achieve autonomy. They espoused the natural rights philosophy of the American Enlightenment, and they believed that false notions could be changed through society's political, religious, legal, and cultural realignment. There was no justification for denying women the freedoms that Nature promised, because woman possessed the same natural abilities as man. All restrictions or presumed disabilities were artificial or misguided.

One way that Anthony and Cady Stanton forwarded their multifaceted ideas was through their radical newspaper, *The Revolution,* first issued on January 8, 1868, with Cady Stanton as senior editor and primary author of most columns, providing her with free reign for the wide range of her ideas. Parker Pillsbury (1809–1898), a Massachusetts reformer and former editor of the Anti-Slavery Standard, served as co-editor. Anthony was office manager and accountant, and her psychological and financial involvement with the paper can be seen as she personally assumed its entire debt upon its demise. The newspaper, with the masthead motto "Principle, not Policy; Justice, not Favors; Men, their rights and nothing more; Women, their rights and nothing less," was indeed devoted more to principle than to policy. It reported on issues such as the status of women tailors, divorce reform, Colorado suffrage, infanticide, prostitution, conditions of prisons and tenements, temperance, and the defeat of the Fifteenth Amendment. It also served as a clearinghouse for information on suffrage lectures, meetings, and conventions, as well as publishing essays, poetry stories, and reviews by leading American and international writers (including serialization of Wollstonecraft's *Vindication of the Rights of Women*).

Cady Stanton, in a letter defending the paper's name on December 28, 1869, wrote to Anthony:

The establishing of woman on her rightful throne is the greatest revolution the world has ever known or will know. . . . A journal called the Rosebud might answer for those who come with kid gloves and perfumes to lay immortal wreaths on the monument . . . but for us . . . there is no name like The Revolution.[77]

Their rhetoric displayed a wide range of rhetorical strategies. They were especially adept in using extensive testimony and precedent, vivid imagery, extended metaphor and analogy, humor and irony. They developed compelling narratives replete with imagery that evoked emotions ranging from despair to elation. They gently (but sometimes sarcastically) juxtaposed truth and reality with false beliefs by citing examples of the conditions woman was forced to endure. Together, they displayed a unique ability to draw from wide-ranging sources in legal, religious, political, and literary arenas. They painted a bold and comprehensive portrait of woman's condition.

Anthony personified the quest for political and social reform in her times; from her earliest public speeches for temperance and abolition through fifty years of woman's rights, she was one of the most zealous advocates of social change in U.S. history. She lectured, toured, organized, lobbied, testified before congressional committees, petitioned, wrote letters and articles. By her own estimate, she averaged between 75 and 100 lectures a year from 1852–97. Anthony's interest in the woman wage-earner helped to broaden the scope of nineteenth-century feminism, for what she wanted for working women was what working men had been demanding for themselves: equal opportunity to compete for wealth and advancement. Her speech "Homes of Single Women" described a new generation of self-supporting women who had achieved economic and personal independence.

Placed in the spotlight by government persecution for her suffrage convictions (her arrest on federal charges represented an extraordinary response to "illegal voting"), Anthony spoke about 40 times in the county in which she was to be tried, speaking about the legal and Constitutional issues involved in her case. Her "Constitutional Argument" speech used as its framework questions of Constitutional law but also communicated the sense of the larger political struggle involved with women's suffrage.

Anthony's argument was that suffrage was a right of citizenship and that all persons, women as well as men, were citizens; thus, women's disfranchisement was merely a matter of prejudice and precedent and not Constitutional law. Her theme was of inalienable natural rights irrespective of sex, She said,

> *It was we, the people, not we the white male citizens, nor we, the male citizens, but we, the whole people who formed this Union. We formed it not to give the blessings of liberty but to secure them; not to the half of ourselves and the half of our posterity, but to the whole people—women as well as men. It is downright mockery to talk to women of their enjoyment of the blessings of liberty while they are denied the only means of securing them provided by this democratic-republican government—the ballot.*[78]

The latter decades of the nineteenth century saw tremendous expansion in women's reform activities. There was growth in socially conscious, all-female organizations, and the dilemma for suffragists became how to relate their concerns for sexual equality and political power to this proliferation of organized public concern over temperance, education, and labor concerns. Anthony maintained her organization presence, attempting to create coalitions that would unify reform-minded women around the demand for the vote. Cady Stanton wanted more comprehensive political unity and challenged women whenever she thought they were being too conservative on any issue.

Cady Stanton believed that effective social change could come only through total autonomy and self-reliance. Once women were freed from encumbering social, moral, legal, and religious traditions, she felt they could then achieve their true potential. She demanded that people be treated as individuals without regard for the incidental relations of life such as mother or father, wife or husband. In order to be free, she felt, people had to be released from all forms of superstition, custom, and bondage. According to Judith Nies, Cady Stanton once told an inquisitive reporter to put this down in capital letters: "SELF-DEVELOPMENT IS A HIGHER DUTY THAN SELF-SACRIFICE. The thing which most retards and militates against woman's self-develop-

ment is self-sacrifice."[79] This is not to say that Cady Stanton only believed in the individual. She viewed society as interconnected, an organic whole that was bettered when the rights of one were improved. But unless the individual was permitted to achieve all due freedoms and self-sovereignty, the good of society was diminished.

She was not always successful. Indeed, some of her arguments angered, embarrassed, and alienated even her allies. In a life centered around controversial issues, Elizabeth Cady Stanton regularly found herself to be the notorious cause of more conflict. She advocated dress reform with her adoption of the Bloomer costume, which freed women from encumbering skirts by dressing them in pants. She called for marriage reform, saying that religious and social hypocrisy were more evil than divorce. She wanted sweeping reforms in education. Cady Stanton was impatient with slow-moving progress and often proceeded into new territory without thought about the consequences. She charged ahead, fearlessly confronting society's perceptions of woman's duties and roles wherever she encountered them: in the church, the court, the workplace, the immigration station, the schools, and the home. For example, she posited that the degradation of women came from an aristocracy of sex that man had dictatorially created. Her rhetoric emphasized the detrimental effects on woman's physical, legal, religious, moral, economic, and intellectual development that male-dominated society had created and maintained. This aristocracy of sex was harmful to all of society, because it promoted rape, prostitution, discrimination, and oppression as well as the moral disintegration of society. Such a patriarchal dictatorship, she claimed, would eventually cause the downfall of society. It directly opposed the shining ideals upon which the nation had been founded. Cady Stanton's speeches, like her wide-ranging intellect, occasionally took off on contradictory paths. One time she would assert that men and women were equal; the next she would articulate woman's inherent superiority over man. Although she was a staunch supporter of education for all, she later turned to educated suffrage as a right, portraying the uneducated as undeserving of the elective franchise.

> The latter decades of the nineteenth century saw tremendous expansion in women's reform activities.

In the meantime, Anthony was busy organizing meetings, developing labor groups, and facilitating dialogue among the many women's rights societies springing up. One of Anthony's more dramatic gestures in delivering the suffrage message occurred July 4, 1876, during Philadelphia ceremonies celebrating the centennial of the Declaration of Independence. Denied a place on the program, Anthony and several accomplices sneaked in, distributed copies of a "Declaration of Rights for Women" which she and Matilda Joslyn Gage had composed. In the shadow of the Liberty Bell, Anthony then read the Declaration, saying "We ask justice, we ask equality, we ask that all the civil and political rights that belong to citizens of the United States be guaranteed to us and our daughters forever."[80]

Cady Stanton's final public speech was a departure from her typical "radical" suffrage rhetoric. Widowed and at an age when many older people become dependent, Cady Stanton had become increasingly self-reliant. She supported herself by writing and speaking, hailed by newspapers as "the Grand Old Woman of America;" politically, she remained an eminent philosopher now aloof from organizational clashes. She proclaimed her total independence from all others by synthesizing her feminist ideology in 1892 in "The Solitude of Self," the culmination of her philosophy, a summary of her principles, crusades, and self-discovery. Campbell calls it a masterpiece of rhetorical literature, "a manifesto for humanistic feminism and lyric expression of the experience of human life."[81] Her ideology demanded woman's complete self-reliance in physical, social, political, legal, and emotional spheres. She argued that women had to be independent and take responsibility for all aspects of their lives.

One of Cady Stanton's last outrageous acts was a potent published attack on the bondage under which the Church kept women. The publication of *The Woman's Bible* in 1895 exposed her to public ridicule and outrage.[82] Its object was to make women aware of derogatory theological doctrines that libeled and subjugated women. She used this platform to attack the accepted interpretations of scripture; she felt that traditional church teachings were hostile to women. In its introduction, she said:

The canon and civil law, church and state, priests and legislators, all political parties and religious denominations have alike taught that woman was made after man, of man, and for man, an inferior being, subject to man. Creeds, codes, Scriptures, and statutes are all based on this idea. The fashions, forms, ceremonies and customs of society, church ordinances and discipline all grow out of this idea.[83]

Under the facade of biblical scholarship, she convened a board of scholarly women to make a thorough revision of the Bible in order to discover what woman's status had been under the original Hebrew and Christian religions. Because all the Bible's revised versions had been written by men, Cady Stanton reasoned that it was likely that males had misinterpreted scripture in their own favor; why not have a more accurate revision by women? Published in two parts, the work served to show discrepancies in interpretations, or areas where she felt women had been slighted. For instance, she demonstrated that while in one passage in Genesis, the "rib" story dominated; in another passage, Adam and Eve came into being at the same time. While *The Woman's Bible* is still interesting to read, Cady Stanton's sarcastic tone and obvious animosity toward traditional religion made her seem irreverent. To a society that didn't question the doctrine that the accepted Bible was the direct word of God, this work must have appeared as heresy. In fact, many of the interpretations Cady Stanton made are widely accepted today.[84]

What was the effect of the pair on the role of women in rhetoric? Cady Stanton's spoken oratory and far-flung writing have been largely ignored by rhetorical historians and critics, due partly to ignorance and partly because of the traditional male dominance of the study of American public address. Her multitudinous contributions to the foundation, formation of arguments, and generation of the broad women's rights movement have been overshadowed by those of the less controversial Susan B. Anthony, although Anthony herself admitted that most of her public addresses came from Cady Stanton's pen. Even feminists have ignored many of her contributions, perhaps due to the controversial or radical nature of some of her arguments, or to unfamiliarity with the wide range of historical documents that await further exploration. Anthony, on the other hand, has been recognized as a major propagandist for women's rights. Her intense devotion to social reform has been recognized in many ways, most particularly in the Nineteenth Amendment, often called the "Anthony Amendment," which granted women the right to vote and was added to the Constitution in

August, 1920. In truth, their partnership weathered distance, animosity, setbacks, and discord. They were searching and visionary in thought, forceful in their actions, indomitable in their dedication to women's emancipation from all types of oppression. Elizabeth Cady Stanton and Susan B. Anthony were each a dominant rhetorical figure in American society for over fifty years. Their visionary foresight, coupled with their public campaigns for a variety of political and social issues, set the course for the contemporary women's movement.

> The nineteenth-century orators discussed in this section were highly persuasive communicators who dedicated their public careers to the challenge of elevating women's role in American society.

The nineteenth-century orators discussed in this section were highly persuasive communicators who dedicated their public careers to the challenge of elevating women's role in American society. As they did so, they often relied on Plato's theory of dialectic, Blair's teachings on rhetoric and polite literature, and, most of all, Whately's principles of argument. But their most significant contribution to the history of American rhetorical theory and public address were the insights they provided to students of contemporary discourse on the subjects of social protest and movements, and on political campaigns. Motivated, as we have seen, by a compelling desire to promote personal welfare and the public good, they came down hard on the side of justice and equality. By teaching us how to organize collectivities, and by utilizing multiple communication channels—the stump, the lyceum, newspaper columns, books, informal conversational settings, and mass demonstrations—to convey their message, they produced a representative anecdote which highlighted the nature and persuasive power that can be generated in a rhetorical campaign and protest movement.

> Susanne K. Langer posited a most useful conception of language; she considered symbolism to be the key issue that underlies all human knowing and understanding.

INTO THE 21ST CENTURY: REDISCOVERY AND REBIRTH

The recent history of woman's role in rhetorical theory and practice has seen the emergence of new questions about what constitutes a "feminist perspective" in communication research, as well as questions of what constitutes rhetoric. These questions focus on such inquiries as how communication constructs our gender system and about how gender informs communication. As we will see, they challenge rhetorical research by suggesting new methodologies, data, and perspectives for analysis.

For example, contemporary feminist theories might question analyses that judge the effectiveness of persuasion by examining it, success or effect, suggesting instead that an examination of the process is a better measure of effectiveness. Scholars who theorize about the nature of language may have to account for differences in the way that men and women perceive symbols. Several contemporary rhetorical theorists question the basic assumptions of rhetorical theory as they examine differences in communication styles and practices. Recognizing the limitations of a lack of historical perspective, let us examine the contributions of some of the women making a mark on how rhetoric is explored.

Susanne K. Langer (1896–1985)

One of the most important topics in philosophy of the past century has been the relationship between language and meaning. Susanne K. Langer posited a most useful conception of language; she considered symbolism to be the key issue that underlies all human knowing and understanding. According to Langer, all animal life is dominated by feeling, but human feeling includes the additional ability to conceive of objects in their absence via symbols and language. Language doesn't just communicate; it creates symbols that construct our reality. Langer demonstrated the primacy of symbols to knowledge and to represent meaning as constructed within the individual and the cultural. All knowledge is based in the community's symbols, and all symbols (including myth, ritual, science, and art) are equally valuable. Langer's axiomatic work, *Philosophy in a New Key,* developed and popularized a vision of language as structuring our perceptions, giving expression to our experiences, and developing and communicating knowledge within a culture. At its essence, the "new key" is that logic doesn't rule rhetoric and that symbols serve in a socially unifying role.

Langer uses the term **sign** as a stimulus that signals the presence of something else, corresponding closely with the actual signified object. In this way, clouds may be a sign of rain, a red light means cross traffic, and a frown is often associated with displeasure. A **symbol** is more complex, for "symbols are not proxy of their objects but are vehicles for the conception of objects."[85] Symbols allow someone to think about something apart from its immediate presence. Langer calls the symbol "an instrument of thought"[86] because it allows human beings to share meaning.

Humans have a capacity to use symbols and a basic need to symbolize apart from the practical necessities of living. The symbol-making process is a continuous function in humans, basic like sleeping and eating, and human behavior can largely be explained in terms of meeting their symbolic needs. As Langer describes it, there is both a logical and psychological sense of symbolic meaning. The logical meaning is the relationship between the symbol and its referent, and the psychological in the relationship between the symbol and its user.

The real significance of language is not in words, but in discourse. Words name things, but "before terms are built into propositions, they assert nothing, preclude nothing, say nothing."[87] Grammatical structure ties words together, playing an important symbolic role. A **proposition** is a complex symbol that presents a picture of something. For example, the word "game" brings to mind a conception, but its combination with other words in a proposition provides a unified picture: "The football game went into overtime when the final play resulted in a tie." It is through language that we become human, because this is how we think and communicate.

Symbols work by communicating a common **concept,** which Langer defines as the general idea, pattern, or form embodied by the symbol. A concept is the common meaning shared among communicators. This symbolic form has been developed through history by society's needs and communal attitudes and evolves into a uniform belief. But each communicator also has a private image or meaning, which fills in details of that common picture; this private

meaning is the person's **conception.** Meaning consists of the person's conception and the universal concept. For example, Dr. Seuss's stories are filled with symbols. The **concept** of *The Lorax,* for example, consists of the reader's shared, commonly recognized images and rhyming words: characters such as the Truffula Trees and the Once-ler; the ritual of rhyming text; the narrative history of how and why the Lorax went away. The conception involves the reader's private meanings attributed to the text, including the symbols of deforestation, environmental pollution, and the loss of endangered species. Thus, meaning is achieved through a collaboration between the expressive, feeling, subjective self and the common community's stable interpretations or structures.

Three other terms are important in understanding Langer's framework. **Signification** is the meaning of a sign, the one-to-one relationship between sign and object, such as between a stop light and cross traffic. **Denotation** is the relationship between the symbol and its object through the person's conception (private meaning). The **Connotation** of a symbol is the direct relationship between the symbol and the conception; it includes personal feelings and associations attached to the symbol. For example, the denotation of the symbol "game" is the relationship that occurs only in your mind as you think of the game scenario. Even when the football game isn't happening, you can imagine and "experience" it because of the relationship between the symbol and the conception: the word's connotation.

Langer says that people possess a built-in tendency to abstract, a crucial human function that is the essence of rationality. She defines **abstraction** as a process of forming a general conception from a variety of concrete experiences. It is the process of leaving out details in conceiving of an object, event, or situation in general terms. For example the word "game" brings to mind a conception that is incomplete, because it leaves details out. The more abstract the symbol, the more sketchy is the conception. A "game" might be called a contest, a competition, a sport, a pastime, an amusement; each term leaves out more details in the conception.

According to Langer, two important types of symbols are language and ritual. **Language symbols** are discursive, involving the combination of smaller language units into larger ones. Individual word meanings are combined into larger concepts, sentences, and larger blocks of discourse. Langer suggests that thought represents discursive symbolism.

Ritual symbols are presentational; such forms may not have distinct meanings, and their meaning is understood only through the whole. A wedding ceremony or commencement exercise illustrate this idea. For Langer, feeling represents presentational symbolism. She asserts that both forms are rational and that some of the most important human experiences are best communicated through presentational forms such as art and music. As she notes,

> *The continual pursuit of meanings—wider, clearer, more negotiable, more articulate meanings—is philosophy. It permeates all mental life; sometimes in conscious form of metaphysical thought, sometimes in the free confident manipulation of established ideas to derive their more precise, detailed implications, and sometimes—in the greatest creative periods—in the form of passionate mythical, ritual, and devotional expression.*[88]

Langer places meaning at the center of a complex, diverse social system. As noted by Lyon, "Langer located individual expression within the social contexts of shared ethics, and argued that discourse is formed by the sensory experience we share. Meaning comes into being through the symbols constructed by both the speaker and the hearer, and the speaker and the hearer are unified through social activity."[89]

Karen A. Foss and Sonja K. Foss

Foss and Foss have taken the lead in examining new rhetorical perspectives that are emerging, including questions about the nature of rhetoric and appropriate frameworks for understanding how rhetoric operates to create understanding. One of their more recent essays demonstrated that a feminist perspective to rhetoric has not been fully incorporated into mainstream communication studies. This feminist perspective challenges communication research through its use of methodologies that allow women to speak in their own voices, rather than through the traditional lenses of more traditional paradigms. At its essence, a feminist perspective is a research position that begins with assumption that the division of the world by gender is critical.

A feminist perspective differs from others in several ways, including the choice of data to analyze and the techniques and goals for that analysis. Foss and Foss see gender as a critical component of all di-

mensions of culture; the critic must understand gender as a basic, fundamental category of analysis. Gender functions as a lens through which all other perceptions pass. In this view, gender is not seen as biological but rather as a social construction. The feminist perspective questions frameworks where traditional gender roles are taken for granted and thus have little impact on experience or on the research process. The primary goal of the feminist perspective is the development of theory that challenges common assumptions of the culture, raises fundamental questions about social life, and fosters reconsideration of what has been taken for granted.[90] It requires the reconceptualization of the gender construct by building on assumptions different from those research frameworks biased toward men. Through this traditional, male-biased social construction of reality, women's experiences are subordinated. The implications of this subordination for both women and men constitute the focus of feminist inquiry.[91]

Foss and Foss explain how the feminist perspective shares methodological principles with new paradigm scholarship. Taking this label from Kuhn's (1970) work on how paradigm shifts occur in the scientific community, so-called new-paradigm scholars challenge beliefs and practices of sciences in explaining people and their behavior. New paradigms (including a feminist perspective) share five fundamental assumptions that distinguish them from old paradigms. They emphasize whole rather than parts, process rather than structure, knowledge as a process of interconnection rather than hierarchy, approximate descriptions rather than absolute truth, and cooperation rather than competition[92] At the same time, it is important to remember that the objectives of research of a feminist perspective and other new paradigms are different: feminism focuses on the deconstruction of gender.

As Foss and Foss note, a feminist perspective challenges existing research frameworks by considering women's perceptions, meanings, and experiences as appropriate and important data for analysis. Feminist inquiry incorporates the values and qualities that characterize women's experiences: interdependence, emotionality, a sense of self-questioning, fusion of the public and private, wholeness, the egalitarian use of power, a focus on process rather than product, multiplicity, and paradox.[93] Another way the feminist perspective challenges traditional rhetorical analysis is in the creation of new rules for how knowledge is created: feminist scholars seek to change the rules for the construction of knowledge so they reflect women's experiences and incorporate women's values, such as self-questioning. Robert suggested examples of such different types of knowledge: ". . .what if the masculinist world view, which has depended on a logic of time lines, is also erroneous? What if the most fundamental error is the search for monocausation? What if the search for simplistic orderliness is, itself, the common problem?"[94] The final challenge in a feminist perspective is that it recommends basic social changes be undertaken to more inclusively incorporate human behavior in all its forms.

Foss and Foss point out several methodological assumptions that distinguish the feminist perspective.[95] The first assumption, **Wholeness,** asserts that the properties of parts only can be understood in relation to the dynamics of the whole; so ultimately there are no parts. For example, attention to wholeness would encourage a researcher seeking to understand a family to study the communication not only of the parent to child but also of all family members to each other. Similarly, in studying a trial, rather than examining only the relationship of attorneys to clients and jury, all of the participants (including the judge, the courtroom audience, and the witnesses, for example) are essential to understanding the dynamics of the event. **Process,** the second assumption, states that structure is inseparable from process. The process by which something comes to be seen is more important than the fixed elements of its structure. A focus on process would suggest, for example, that researchers should not study a phenomenon such as "women's role in organizations alone but should also examine the process by which those roles are constructed."[96] The third assumption, **Interconnectedness of knowledge,** asserts that knowledge is a process of lateral interconnection that isn't necessarily explained by a linear, systematic progression. Rather than hierarchically attempting to define knowledge, feminism operates more from a network metaphor. For example, scholars who study media effects have generally built knowledge hierarchically, based upon and incorporating the findings of the previous studies, using a selected instrument that measures those effects. If a researcher were to approach the same topic laterally, she may generate an alternative conception of effects and study them from a different starting point. As another illustration, consider the differences one would find in

studying an organization if, instead of looking at the organizational chart and examining downward communication flow, one analyzed the networks developed *among* the various aspects of the organization. In **Approximation,** the traditional Cartesian notion of the certainty of scientific knowledge (old paradigm) is replaced by an understanding that knowledge is a process of construction; knowledge is limited, approximate, and relative. Rather than saying absolutely and with certainty that "we know," we can at best say that we have provided one perspective on a topic. This concept of "perspective" is "to say that a person has a particular way of interpreting that phenomenon;"[97] a perspective represents one set of conceptual lenses that affect the way that we interpret a phenomenon. It acknowledges that there may be other ways of seeing and explaining the phenomenon. Finally, **Cooperation** suggests that implicit in the old paradigm is that a researcher must stand apart from subjects and data in order to dominate/control them. A feminist perspective suggests cooperation rather than competition and abandoning notions of superiority over the world.

As Foss and Foss note, this feminist view provides a research perspective that asserts that gender is a significant aspect in our explanations of the world and that it must be used as an essential category of analysis. Thus, feminist scholars (both men and women) would attempt to examine and change the conception of gender as it is created and maintained in communication. The feminist perspective offers another means of answering research questions, such as how do women's vocabulary, values, experiences, rituals, and narratives help make sense of women's experiences, and how does their communication contribute to the construction of conceptions of gender. It has been argued that the development of a feminist perspective in rhetorical theory may facilitate the discovery of lost or forgotten rhetorical works, or of women's discourse that has been devalued, disregarded, or destroyed. A feminist perspective allows researchers to value and to study communication that has been ignored or discounted in traditional rhetorical theory. As Dobris notes,

When rhetorical theory accounts for gender by acknowledging the validity of female experience, the entire philosophy of rhetoric may be altered profoundly. When we ask, "What does 'rhetoric' mean for women" we find that 2,000 years of philosophy and theory may not reflect women's experience.[98](153)

Kathleen Hall Jamieson

Kathleen Hall Jamieson, Dean at the Annenberg School for Communication of the University of Pennsylvania, well-known as a political communication analyst, has written extensively on the transformation of political communication. She has provided insight as a critic of genre studies, noting the power of conventions, traditions, and prior rhetoric to mold and constrain rhetorical action. Jamieson reminds us that rhetorical acts are born into a symbolic context as well as a historical/political one.[99]

With Karlyn Kohrs Campbell (who will be discussed next) she has developed a generic perspective applied to the major types of presidential discourse, "which emphasizes continuity within change and treats recurrence as evidence that symbolic institutional needs are at least as powerful as the force of events in shaping the rhetoric of any historical period."[100] The range of her topics extends from presidential speechmaking to political advertising, from the overall packaging of the presidency to what she and Campbell together term "the rhetorical presidency." She has said that her desire is to understand Who is elected and how that occurs; at a time when voters are searching beyond promises for signs of a candidate's character, public address

> rhetorical acts are born into a symbolic context as well as a historical/political one.

has assumed an increasingly important role, for the contradiction between words and actions is central to voters' decisions.

Jamieson's *Packaging the Presidency: A History and Criticism of Presidential Campaign Advertising* (1984) examined presidential campaigns through the perspective provided by their advertising. Focusing on presidential elections from 1952 through 1980 (and later updated through 1988), Jamieson explains the history of presidential advertising and examines how candidates shape and are shaped by their ads. She also attempts to posit how advertising has affected the political process by a thorough analysis of many types of political ads, including personal testimony ads, pseudo-documentary ads, attack ads, and broadcast speech ads. Jamieson asserts that ads can enable a candidate to create and build name recognition, set the election's agenda, and argue the relevance of issues to our lives. The ability of ads to personalize the candidate have in turn led to an increased saliency of issues in the public's minds.

Jamieson also argues that ads can define the nature of the presidency by legitimizing attributes that a president should have.

Jamieson's book *Eloquence in an Electronic Age* (1988) attempts to "search out eloquence's new incarnations and ultimately asks whether they can and should mesh with the ancient art."[101] She says that the book is about political eloquence: what constitutes it, how it has evolved, and the talents and techniques that differentiate those who aspire to it. Moreover, she asks and attempts to answer a crucial question: "Has television changed our concept of eloquence, altered its audience's receptivity to eloquence, or functioned as the scapegoat blamed for destroying something it never laid electrons on?"[102]

Jamieson asserts that public address holds an ignoble place in our society, partly because it is no longer the only means of influencing a mass public, partly because of a lack of seriousness accorded to it by the media, partly because the audience now expects more of a "hit and run" approach where a single support is expected to sustain a claim, partly because of a decline in the number of civic occasions where speakers can present their messages, and partly because we have come to rely upon a visual medium requiring different techniques. Jamieson traces the evolution of eloquence, from "the old eloquence of fire and sword" to an "intimate disclosive art bent on conciliation, not conquest."[103]

One of the more intriguing ideas that Jamieson posits in this work is the distinction between "manly" and "effeminate" speech and how those styles work in contemporary mediated political discourse. She reveals that the Romans distinguished between a revered manly style and a reviled effeminate style. By the late 19th century the scientific style was considered manly because it was presumably driven by reason; thus the manly style was thought to be factual, analytic, organized, and impersonal. Jamieson suggests that because it was presumably driven by emotion, womanly speech was thought to be personal, excessive, disorganized, and unduly ornamental.[104] Manly speech style has been described as impersonal, rational, direct, and data-based. Womanly speech created disorder; manly speech called for order. Womanly speech corrupted an audience by inviting it to judge on deceptive premises; manly speech invited sober decisions. The world was civilized by manly speech and contaminated by effeminate speech. As a result, the proper place for effeminate discourse was limited to the parlor or the corrupt government. In addition, past traditions suggested that the high pitch of woman's voice was seen as symptomatic of excessive emotionalism. If language is the dress of thought, then a manly style is sharp-witted; effeminate style is merely ornamental.

However, Jamieson points out that where women's public speech traditionally has been suspect, and their silence has been golden, these traditionally condemned forms of speech are ideally suited to effectiveness in an electronic age. The traditional male style, is, in McLuhan's terms, too hot for the cool medium of television. The ability to comfortably express feelings is an asset on television. "Women are more inclined than men to verbally indicate emotion"[105] Females have an advantage in communicating emotion by expressive faces and gestures and general skill in deciphering the nonverbal cues of others.[106] A manly style impedes one's ability to disclose private information, but because the mass media concentrate on and enlarge differences between the private and public self of public figures, a comfort with expressing rather than camouflaging self (or at the minimum an ability to feign disclosure) is useful for a politician. That utility benefits females, according to Jamieson. In addition, she notes that "television favors a conciliatory style over a combative one."[107] Where women tend to cooperate, men tend to compete. "Whether in public or private communication, men are more comfortable than women in a combative 'debate' style."[108] She provides examples of how in political ads, women usually stress their strengths rather than counteract their weaknesses. In addition, because the broadcast media invite an intimate style, conversational and narrational skills also give an advantage to women.[109]

Television also prizes the narrative skills traditional to women, the family's storytellers, the ones who pass on the common wisdom and history from generation to generation. This talent for capturing ideas and lessons in brief dramatic narratives is cultivated by bedtime stories and gossip-telling. Television invites a personal, self-disclosing style that draws public discourse out of a private self and reduces the complex world to dramatic narratives.[110] In an extended example of how political speechmaking has moved from memorable words and eloquent ideas to dramatic, digestive, visual moments, Jamieson develops an extended analysis of Ronald Reagan, the so-called "Great Communicator." She asserts that his success was at least partially attributable to his use of the effeminate style, his use of self-disclosive narratives immunized him from political attacks, and his ability to make claims defying traditional logic by visual assertions. She says that Reagan employed a self-disclosive, narrative persona that pioneered a revolution in political communication. Rather than substantiate his claims in statistics, Reagan preferred to lodge them in stories. "Better than any modern president, Reagan translated words into memorable tele-visual pictures."[111] He was able to evoke common visual experiences and reduce complex issues to dramatic narratives, and his effectiveness resulted in his use of a style once condemned as rhetorically effeminate.

Campbell and Jamieson's *Deeds Done in Words* (1990) offers a generic framework to critique types of presidential discourse, hoping to discover the character of presidential rhetoric that has been developed, sustained, and altered through time by the nature of the presidency as an institution. Jamieson and Campbell attempt to explore the link between rhetoric and the institution of the presidency: discourse that marks beginnings and endings of the presidency, genres that preserve the presidency and adapt it to changing conditions, and genres that carry forward policy initiatives. How do genres enable discourse to accommodate the institutional need for stability and change. They note recognizable forms of discourse that give the presidency a sense of stability: the inaugural, where the president is invested with the office; pardoning rhetoric that asserts that the president is the final voice in determining justice for the public good; veto messages that place the president in the legislative role; war rhetoric that legitimizes the role of commander in chief. As Jamieson and Campbell note, "These words are deeds; in their speaking, the presidency is constituted and reconstituted."[112] They suggest that presidents are provided a symbolic repertoire through which they assert the fundamental continuity of the presidency, while making changes as circumstances require them. They also assert that presidents produce discourse that reaffirms their place in the leadership succession. Finally, the rhetorical genre of the presidency offers precedent to the less eloquent and transcendence to the adept. In other words, the genres available to the president create a distinct identity for the presidency as an institution, while setting rhetorical boundaries for its occupants.[113]

Kathleen Hall Jamieson, one of today's leading political analysts, has provided students of rhetoric with a growing body of work on the genre of political communication. Her critical insights and thorough historical tracking, as well as insider intelligence from actual campaigns, allow the reader to better understand the power of the ballot; political communication in general affirms our belief that votes can make a difference in changing society.

Karlyn Kohrs Campbell

Karlyn Kohrs Campbell, Professor of Speech Communication at the University of Minnesota, was earlier recognized for her groundbreaking work on the genre of presidential communication. But in addition to her work in formulating generic criticism, Campbell has added an important dimension to our knowledge of women's discourse. Her two-volume set, *Man Cannot Speak for Her* (1989), analyzed and anthologized the discourse that appeared at critical moments of the women's movement. This discourse represents particular issues and groups within the early movement, including African-American women's discourse. Campbell offers the work to "call into question what has become the canon of public address in the United States, a canon that excluded virtually all works by women."[114] At the heart of her groundbreaking work, Campbell calls for a reexamination of U.S. rhetorical literature to examine artistic excellence in speaking from the population that has been largely excluded from traditional anthologies studying the history of rhetoric. She reminds the reader that "rhetorical invention is rarely originality of argument, but rather the selection and adaptation of materials to the occasion, the purpose, and the audience. . . . The relationship between rhetoric and feminism is pertinent to all facets of this study. . . ."[115]

The two volumes focus on the central women's movement in its early stages rather than examining its branches. Faced with a daunting task, recognizing the lack of historical artifacts and the lack of room to discuss less nationally known speakers, Campbell finds the women she anthologizes a remarkable group virtually unique in rhetorical history because they had been denied the right to the platform. She suggests that women strategically adopted a "feminine style" to cope with the conflicting demands of the podium: they had to meet the requirements of speakers, demonstrating expertise, authority and rationality in order to show competence and make themselves credible to the audience. In doing that, speakers were likely to be judged masculine and unwomanly. Thus, they had to develop strategies that would bridge that gap.

In her construction of the feminine style, Campbell notes that women of this time (deprived of formal education and confined to a home) learned the crafts of housewifery and motherhood from other women. Learning to adapt to variation is essential to mastery of a craft, and the highly skilled craftsperson is alert to variation, aware of alternative strategic choices, and able to read cues related to specific conditions. If rhetoric is a craft, then it produces discourse with certain characteristics.[116] Campbell uses the craft metaphor as she develops her image of the "feminine style." It is personal in tone (crafts are learned from a mentor), relies heavily on personal experience, anecdotes, and other examples; is structured inductively (crafts are learned bit by bit, from which a whole emerges); and invites audience participation, including testing generalizations against the audience's experiences. Audience members are addressed as peers, with recognition of their authority based on experience. A speaker must make efforts to create identification with audience experiences. Campbell says that the goal of such rhetoric is empowerment, the process of persuading listeners that they can be agents of change in the world?[117] According to Campbell, early woman's rights rhetoric always had at least two dimensions: presentation of their grievances and justification of woman's right to function in the public sphere,[118] and her anthologies chronicle the evolution of those arguments. She recognizes that the feminine style was suitable to women because of the societal expectations for female speakers and their audiences, because it was less aggressive and authoritative, more cooperative and affirming.

> Kathleen Hall Jamieson, one of today's leading political analysts, has provided students of rhetoric with a growing body of work on the genre of political communication.

Campbell's "rescue of the works of great women speakers from the oblivion to which most have been consigned" is an important contribution to western rhetorical history. Her attempts to revise rhetorical history present a carefully documented narrative that exposes the manner in which male experiences have been made to symbolize all of rhetoric. Campbell alerts us to the prodigious past that women held in public address in the United States, starting in the early 1800's.

CONCLUSION

In 1928 Professor Arthur M. Schlesinger took historians to task for their neglect in presenting women's role in society, when he said "If the silence of the historians is to mean anything, it would appear that one-half of our population have been negligible factors in our country's history." In recent years, great progress has been made in excavating and reclaiming the history of women in the rhetorical tradition. Gender studies have analyzed famous women speakers in political, social, and religious domains; theorists have posited the dif-

> Campbell's "rescue of the works of great women speakers from the oblivion to which most have been consigned" is an important contribution to western rhetorical history.

ferences in female and male linguistic and thinking styles; and researchers have considered gender differences in many aspects of communication, offering philosophical perspectives of the very nature of rhetoric. Yet there continues to be an argument made against feminist research in communication, based upon the assertion that communication studies operates from a position of gender neutrality; hence women are included in disciplinary practices. The dilemma is this: since research strategies are formulated by human experiences, we can expect differing scholarly choices depending on the gender orientation of the researcher. It is likely that women and men will have different perceptions of relevant questions, data collection techniques, subject selection, data interpretation, and the relationship between researcher and researched. The share of women in the process of rhetorical history, theory, and practice needs to be brought into better balance. This chapter can take only a limited step toward filling that gap.

Notes

---

1. K.K. Campbell, *Man Cannot Speak for Her: A Critical Study of Early Feminist Rhetoric, Vol. 1* (NY: Greenwood Press, 1989), 1.
2. See for example, K. Carter and C. Spitzack, *Doing Research on Women's Communication: Perspectives on Theory and Method* (Norwood, NJ: Ablex, 1989).
3. S. Jarratt and R. Ong, "Aspasia: Rhetoric, Gender, and Colonial Ideology," in *Reclaiming Rhetorica: Women in the Rhetorical Tradition*, A. Lunsford, ed. (Pittsburgh, University of Pittsburgh Press, 1995), 22.
4. A. C. Carlson, "Aspasia of Miletus: How One Woman Disappeared from the History of Rhetoric." *Women's Studies in Communication* 17(1) (Spring 94), 32.
5. Carlson, 29.
6. Menage, 6.
7. Menage, 6.

8. Plato, The Menexenus, in *Dialogues of Plato*, tr. B. Jowett (NY: Random House, 1937), para 235–249.
9. The reaction to this dialogue among nineteenth-century scholars initially was to claim that the dialogue was spurious, that Plato didn't write it, although Aristotle twice quoted from it in his Rhetoric and attributed it to Plato. Others called it completely satirical, although Cicero in *De Oratore* claimed that Athenians devoted a day annually to public recitation of this speech. Carlson suggests that this dialogue demonstrated Plato's habit of ridiculing a famous practitioner of rhetoric; remember, Gorgias was the butt of the dialogue by that name, and Lysias' speech in the *Phaedrus* is displayed as defective both as philosophy and rhetoric. In the Menexenus, Plato selected a rhetorician with a reputation for funeral orations and proceeded to ridicule her.

10. Cicero, *De Inventione,* trans. H. Hubbell (Cambridge, Mass.: Harvard University Press, 1962), 51.

11. J.R. Redfern, "Cristine dePisan and the Treasure of the City of Ladies: A Medieval Rhetorician and Her Rhetoric," in *Reclaiming Rhetorica,* 75.

12. Redfern, 74.

13. C. dePisan, *The Treasure of the City of Ladies: or, The Book of the Three Virtues,* trans. Sarah Lawson (Harmondsworth: Penguin, 1985), Book 1, 47.

14. Redfern, 91.

15. dePisan, 80.

16. dePisan, 51.

17. Redfern, 74.

18. C. Willard, "The 'three virtues' of Christine de Pisan." *Journal of the History of Ideas* 27 no. 3 (1966), 433.

19. R. Perry, "Mary Astell and the Feminist Critique of Possessive Individualism," *Eighteenth Century Studies,* 78.

20. Perry, 79.

21. D.N. Deluna, "Mary Astell: England's First Feminist Literary Critic." *Women's Studies,* vol. 22 (1993), 236.

22. M. Astell, *A Serious Proposal to the Ladies for the Advancement of Their True and Greatest Interest by a Lover of Her Sex* (London, 1694), 154.

23. Astell, *Serious Proposal,* 144.

24. *Serious proposal,* 142.

25. *Serious Proposal,* 175.

26. *Serious Proposal,* 154.

27. Sutherland notes that this type of proposal had been tried but such communities aroused suspicion in the authorities for suspicion of being in sympathy with the Catholic church. C.M. Sutherland, "Outside the Rhetorical Tradition: Mary Astell's Advice to Women in Seventeenth Century England." *Rhetorica* 9 (Spring 1991), 149.

28. *Serious Proposal,* 53.

29. *Serious Proposal,* 64.

30. *Serious Proposal,* 194.

31. *Serious Proposal,* 192.

32. *Serious Proposal,* 192.

33. *Serious Proposal,* 201.

34. *Serious Proposal,* 189.

35. *Serious Proposal,* 140.

36. Deluna, 238.

37. Sutherland, 113.

38. *Serious Proposal,* Part 1, p. 29.

39. *Serious Proposal,* Part 2, pp. 143–49.

40. M. Astell, Mary, *Some Reflections Upon Marriage, Occasion'd by the Duke and Duchess of Mazarine's Case, Which is Also consider'd* (London, 1700), 70.

41. NOTE: It is interesting to note a historical perplexity: Richard Steele's *The Ladies Library* includes an entire chapter on Ignorance, which includes two selections taken from *A Serious Proposal,* with no recognition of its true author, Astell. Those parts Steele deemed unacceptable were excluded, including a call for women's independence from men and for the religious community. Yet the rationale for *The Ladies Library* was that women should think and act responsibly, that women have a duty to read serious literature, and that they should lead an active intellectual life.

42. M. Wollstonecraft, *A Vindication of the Rights of Woman,* in *The Works of Mary Wollstonecraft,* vol. 5, M. Butler and J. Todd, eds. (NY: Washington Square, 1989) 42.

43. Wollstonecraft, 42.

44. Wollstonecraft, 92.

45. Wollstonecraft, 139.

46. Wollstonecraft, 101.

47. Wollstonecraft, 87.

48. Wollstonecraft, 92.

49. Wollstonecraft, 105.

50. Wollstonecraft, 179.

51. K. Conway, "Woman Suffrage and the History of Rhetoric at the Seven Sisters Colleges, 1865–1919," in *Reclaiming Rhetorica,* 204.

52. For a general discussion of the role of rhetoric in social movements, see, for example, C. Stewart, C. Smith, and R. Denton, *Persuasion and Social Movements,* third ed. (Prospect Heights, IL: Waveland, 1994).

53. M. Gurko, *The Ladies of Seneca Falls: The Birth of the Woman's Rights Movement* (NY: MacMillan, 1974), 32.

54. E. Hahn, *Once Upon a Pedestal* (NY: Thomas Y. Crowell Company, 1974), 48.

55. E.C. Stanton, S.B. Anthony, and M.J. Gage, eds. *History of Woman Suffrage,* vol. 1 (NY: Fowler and Wells, 1881), 35.

56. M. Urbanski, *Margaret Fuller's "Women in the Nineteenth Century: A Literary Study of Form and Content, of Sources and Influence* (Westport, CT: Greenwood Press, 1980), 3.

57. R.N. Hudspeth, ed. *The Letters of Margaret Fuller, vol. 1* (Ithaca: Cornell University Press, 1983–84), 86.

58. Hudspeth 2:86–89.

59. A. Rossi, ed., *The Feminist Perspective: From Adams to de Beauvoir* (NY: Bantam Books 1974), 149.

60. M. Fuller, *Woman in the Nineteenth Century* (NY: Norton, 1971), 30.

61. Fuller, 30.

62. Fuller, 33.

63. Fuller, 32.

64. Critics of the times responded typically like the following: "The restraints which Miss Fuller complains of as hindering women are the restraints which Nature has imposed."

65. Kolodny, 140.

66. Kolodny, 138.

67. Fuller, 98.

68. In 1868 Theodore Tilton described the Cady Stanton-Anthony alliance in the following manner: "Mrs. Stanton is a fine writer, but a poor executant; Miss Anthony is a thorough manager, but a poor writer. . . neither has any selfish ambition for celebrity; but each view with the other in a noble enthusiasm for the cause to which they are devoting their lives. These two women have. . . been diligent forgers of all manners of projectiles, from fireworks to thunderbolts, and have hurled them with unexpected explosion into the midst of all manner of educational, reformatory, religious, and political assemblies. I know of no two more pertinacious incendiaries in the whole country. In fact, this noise-making twain are the two sticks of a drum, keeping up what Daniel Webster called "The rub-a-dub of agitation." T. Stanton and H. Stanton Blatch, eds., *Elizabeth Cady Stanton as Revealed in Her Letters, Diary, and Reminiscences,* vol. 1 (NY: Harper and Brothers, 1922), 154.

69. Stanton and Stanton Blatch, 154.

70. B. Waggenspack, *The Search for Self-Sovereignty: The Oratory of Elizabeth Cady Stanton* (Westport, CT: Greenwood, 1989), 25.

71. *Women's Rights Conventions: Seneca Falls & Rochester, 1848.* (NY: Arno Press, 1969), 6.

72. Cady Stanton had been educated in a comprehensive curriculum at the Troy Seminary, which was considered an intellectual mecca of the times. She had a grounding in physiology, higher mathematics, Greek, Latin, French, music, criticism, religious and moral instruction, chemistry, domestic science, and elocution, utilizing Blair's *Lectures on Rhetoric and Belles Lettres.* Waggenspack, 11.

73. Stanton and Blatch, 148.

74. Waggenspack, 22.

75. E. Dubois, ed., *Elizabeth Cady Stanton, Susan B. Anthony: Correspondence, Writings, Speeches* (NY: Schocken Books, 1981), 17.

76. Stanton and Blatch, 1.

77. Stanton and Blatch, 123.

78. Dubois, *Correspondence,* 154.

79. Waggenspack, 90.

80. Dubois, *Correspondence,* 176.

81. K.K. Campbell, "Elizabeth Cady Stanton," in B. Dully and H. Ryan, eds. *American Orators Before 1900* (Westport, CT: Greenwood Press, 1987), 346.

82. Although the authorship is credited to both Cady Stanton and "The Revising Committee," most of *The Woman's Bible* was written by Cady Stanton. She bought cheap bibles, cut out negative parts which referred to women, pasted them on blank paper, and wrote her commentaries.

83. E.C. Stanton and the Revising Committee, *The Woman's Bible,* vol. 1 (New York: 1895), iv.

84. Public reaction to *The Woman's Bible* was marked by dismay and scandal. It rapidly became a best seller, went through seven printings in one year and was translated into many languages. Churches rang with the sermons of clergy condemning the work, calling it a travesty of the Scriptures. Libraries limited its access, keeping it for reference only and denying it circulation. The conservatives in the National American Woman Suffrage Association opposed any association with it; in fact a resolution of censure at the convention that year was offered to deny any connection with the work. Anthony gave an eloquent plea against censure, but the resolution passed. Cady Stanton wanted Anthony to resign in protest, but Anthony didn't want to leave the association. The partnership was once again strained by this difference in strategies and goals. In addition, as if in retaliation against the NAWSA, Cady Stanton's next edition of *The Woman's Bible* had the censure resolution appended to it. Whenever possible, she reminded the public of her roles as

founder and president of the organization. However, to the mainstream attempting to maintain the movement's successes, she had become an embarrassment.

85. S.K. Langer, *Philosophy in a New Key* (Cambridge, Mass: Harvard University Press, 1942), 61.
86. Langer 63.
87. Langer, 67.
88. Langer, 293–294.
89. A. Lyon, "Susanne K. Langer: Mother and Midwife at the Rebirth of Rhetoric," in *Reclaiming Rhetorica,* 276.
90. K. Gergen, *Toward transformation in Social Knowledge* (NY: Springer-Verlag, 1982), 67.
91. K. Foss and S. Foss, "The Status of Research on Women and Communication," *Communication Quarterly* 31 (1983), 195–204.
92. F. Capra, The concept of paradigm and paradigm shift. ReVision, volume 9 (1986), 11–12.
93. See, for example, A. Schaef, *Women's Reality: An Emerging Female System in the White Male Society* (Minneapolis: Winston, 1981).
94. J. Roberts, *Beyond Intellectual Sexism: A New Woman, a New Reality* (NY: David McKay Robert, 1976) 46.
95. Foss and Foss, 70.
96. Foss and Foss, 70.
97. S.K. Foss, K. A. Foss, and R. Trapp, *Contemporary Perspectives on Rhetoric* (Prospect Heights, IL: Waveland, 1985), 14.
98. Foss and Foss, 153.
99. K.K. Campbell and K.H. Jamieson, eds., *Form And Genre: Shaping Rhetorical Action* (Falls Church, VA: SCA, 1982), 17.
100. K.K. Campbell and K.H. Jamieson, *Deeds Done in Words: Presidential Rhetoric and the Genres of Governance* (Chicago: University of Chicago Press, 1990), 8.
101. K.H. Jamieson, *Eloquence in an Electronic Age: The Transformation of Political Speechmaking* (NY: Oxford University Press, 1988), ix.
102. Jamieson, x.
103. Jamieson, x.
104. Jamieson, 76.
105. D. Dosser, Balswick, J. and Halverson, C. "Male Inexpressiveness and Relationships," *Journal of Social and Personal Relationships* 3 (1986), 251.
106. J. Hall, *Nonverbal Sex Differences* (Baltimore: Johns Hopkins University Press, 1984), 143.
107. Jamieson, 82.
108. Jamieson, 100.
109. Jamieson, 83.
110. Jamieson, 84.
111. Jamieson, 119.
112. Jamieson, 214.
113. Jamieson, 214.
114. Campbell, *Man Cannot Speak,* 9.
115. Campbell, 9.
116. Campbell, 13.
117. Campbell, 13.
118. Campbell, 14.

Our second essay to be reprinted in this chapter was completed in 1995 and published in a volume produced by Lindrey Niles. The two authors—Melbourne Cummings and Jack Daniel—have devoted much of their professional career studying "African American Rhetoric," which is the title of this article. This comprehensive research effort makes use of 113 footnote listings, fourteen of which are from their own writings, and contains a thirteen-page bibliography of the research they have undertaken in order to present their analysis.

In highlighting what the authors call a "state of the art" in Black communication research, they have organized their study under these four principal headings: (1) "African American Rhetorical Stud-ies"; (2) "Social-Psychological Responses to Oppression"; (3) "Anthropological Studies"; and (4) "Afrocentric Perspectives." As you read this essay, observe the amount of information that can be gained concerning "theories, methodologies, and literature of African American Communication." Also note the emphasis on "Black communication similarities," and on "the multi-linguistic nature of the African Diaspora" (the scattering and dispersal of a significant ethnic group). We feel, in sum, that this critical survey is not only useful for understanding "African American Rhetoric" but also for gaining an appreciation of the potential this field offers for additional research.

The Study of African American Rhetoric

Melbourne S. Cummings and Jack L. Daniel

INTRODUCTION

This article reviews theories, methodologies, and literature of African American communication. It also discusses the multidisplinary nature of the study of Black communication, including dyadic and small-group interactions, significant speech events, and folklore. Linguistic, literary, and aesthetic phenomena are occasionally used to gain insights, but they are not of primary concern. This restriction is a matter of focus as opposed to the perceived nature of things. Our review of Black communication literature includes studies from various disciplines, including African and African Diaspora studies, anthropology, literature, psychology, and speech communication. Not only is a multidisciplinary approach essential for a comprehensive analysis of Black communication, but it is also the case that the actual relevant literature is spread across various disciplines.

"Black" is used here to refer to people of African descent. Black communication refers to communication whose key defining characteristics stem from African cultural influences. If Black is to define the communication, then it must have functional African roots. The emphasis also acknowledges the tremendous varieties of Black communication, given both the multilinguistic nature of the African Diaspora and the complex interactions between African and European cultures. The authors recognize that "African American" is the preferred term to "Black"; however, to use the latter term is to deny other people of African descent their role in this communication phenomena. Therefore, both terms will be utilized.

More than 800 African languages, various European and Asian languages, and innumerable pidgins and creoles await students of African communication.[1] Throughout the African Diaspora, Black communication complexities are further expanded by (1) demographic factors, such as education, income, sex, and religion, (2) political, economic, social, and psychological consequences of colonialism and racism, as practiced by different Europeans over time in various geographical settings, and (3) creative, that is, new uses of languages throughout the Diaspora. No amount of cultural chauvinism can deny African cultural continuities around the world. Given the many linguistic codes that are used in Black communication, it follows that the ethnography of Black communication is an equally diverse and complex matter. Ethnography deals with the "situations and uses, the patterns and functions, of speaking as an activity in its own right."[2] By "ethnography" we mean what Dell H. Hymes describes as "what a child internalizes about speaking, beyond rules of grammar and a dictionary, while becoming a full-fledged member of its speech community."[3] Roger Abrahams' "men of words," those who are good at using words effectively, can still be found throughout the Diaspora.[4] However, the social conventions governing Black English-speaking "men of words" vary from New York City to Chicago to Trinidad-Tobago, and Nevis. New York City men of words, without prior knowledge of the Nevis men of words' rhetorical conventions, would simply be lost at a Nevis "tea meeting."[5] In spite of the seemingly formidable number of Black communication combinations and permutations, we hold that there are common Black communication elements—at least we cannot meaningfully speak of Black communication without identifying the common elements of it.

Melbourne S. Cummings is professor and chair of the Department of Human Communication Studies at Howard University in Washington, D.C.
Jack L. Daniel is Associate Provost, University of Pittsburgh, Pittsburgh, Pa.

A major purpose of this article is to present and discuss theories of Black communication similarities. Theory is used here in the descriptive and generative senses, i.e, descriptions of Black communication processes, which can be used to generate further empirical research. More specifically, we will focus on that theory which seeks to provide explanations of Black communication similarities throughout the African Diaspora. This ordering of attention is based on the idea that the real differences within Black communication and between it and other kinds of communication can be best established once we know the similarities with Black communication. For example:

Only to the extent that physical objects share such attributes as length, weight, and volume and to the extent that these attributes can be abstracted and quantified, can comparison among them be made on anything other than an intuitive basis. The same holds true for subjective culture.[6]

While it was decided to focus on theories of Black communication similarities, we were mindful of the need to present a state of the art. Hence, this article begins with a review of communication scholarship that does not focus on establishing Black communication similarities throughout the African Diaspora. This scholarship consists of published works on African American public address, e.g, collections of African American political speeches, collections of African American speeches plus introductory analytic essays, and descriptive articles on African American speakers' strategies, tactics, styles, and audience effects.

The second body of reviewed literature deals with Black communication similarities, but it is based on similarities resulting more from colonialism, racism, and other oppressive conditions instead of African cultural continuities. While these studies occasionally consider African cultural survivals, such survivals are treated as more a function of oppression as opposed to the survival of strong, intrinsically important cultural traits. An example of this second body of literature is the perception of "Black English features" as marks of oppression that sur-

vived not because of West African linguistic dominance, but because American slaves were not given formal education, and their modern contemporaries received less than adequate education in segregated urban schools. A major stream of this literature consists of social-psychological reactions to racism, such as the positive symbolic value of "European" versus the negative symbolic value of "African".

Frantz Fanon, in explaining the European's fixed concept of the Negro, noted that when he met a Russian or German who spoke bad French, he would give the European information via gestures but would never once forget that the Russian or German had a language and a country of his own.[7] Fanon also observed that "when it comes to the case of the Negro, nothing of the kind. He has no culture, no civilization, no long historical past. This may be the reason for the strivings of contemporary Negroes: to prove the existence of a black civilization to the white world at all costs."[8]

It could be said that concerns with results of European and African cultural interactions have stimulated most of the academic work in Black communication. The essential issue has been a focus on African humanity with antagonists seeking to deny Africans admission to the human species or, at best, admitting them to an inferior order, and protagonists seeking to demonstrate things ranging from superior African human sensibilities to the continuity of primary African cultural concerns (cultural focus) throughout the Diaspora. The conceptual foundation for the cultural continuities studies was established by the work of Melville J. Herskovits.

Herskovits' seminal work *The Myth of the Negro Past* set forth the concepts of "syncretism" (based on Arthur Ramos' work), "retention and reinterpretation," and "cultural focus."[9] Syncretism entails a merging of cultures, such as in the case of faithful Black Brazilian Catholics whose saints consist of African deities. Retention and reinterpretation refer "not to the question of what Africanisms were carried over in unaltered forms, but how, in the contact of Africans with Europeans and American Indians, cultural accommodation and cultural integration had been achieved."[10] Cultural focus is defined as that aspect of culture which a group stresses or is of greatest interest to them. When given the freedom to choose, the cultural focus consists of the cultural phenomenon which is held "more tenaciously than those of other aspects" of their culture.[11] For African people there is a demonstrable case for spiritual phenomena constituting their cultural focus. Given Herskovits' conceptual framework, referenced above, and our concern with theories of similarities, we might say that we are concerned with black communication theory which attempts to identify African cultural focus, and African retentions and reinterpretations.

The third body of literature reviewed here covers anthropological field studies which attempt to map a given black community's prevailing communication patterns and characteristics, or detail a specific communication phenomenon. Examples of such studies would include a field study of logic and rhetoric among a given African group, or a field study of the form and function of riddles in a given African American population.

The fourth body of literature, Afrocentric perspectives, consists of work which seeks to define black communication in terms of African cultural focus, African world view, or some other summary concept of traditional African culture, and conduct black communication research from the cultural vantage points of the African cultural focus or world view. A case in point would be the study of religious influences on black communication throughout the African Diaspora.

AFRICAN AMERICAN RHETORICAL STUDIES

One of the first voids that had to be filled in African American rhetorical communication studies was the lack of significant numbers and representative examples of African American speakers in traditional communication texts and courses. Over and over again, students had been taught the historical developments of America and the world as they related to Whites. Countless numbers of landmark white American speeches had been assigned to them for

critical evaluation. Yet there was a reluctance to acquaint students with black orators other than Frederick Douglass and Booker T. Washington. Students of the 1960's were curious about the identity of black speakers other than Douglass and Washington. Indeed these two speakers represented only a limited facet of black protest rhetoric. There were others who marshaled effective arguments, disagreed with the Washington and Douglass strategies, had followers of their own, and had solutions that were vastly different from the "acceptable" solutions of these two well-known rhetorical figures.

As of the early 1960's, a number of scholars had studied African American speeches for historical and sociological purposes. However, few had shown interest in these speakers for rhetorical study. Prior to this time, only one comprehensive text existed that chronicled African American speakers, significant African American speech events, and gave a cursory assessment of the effects of the speeches on the various audiences: Carter G. Woodson's *Negro Orators and Their Orations*.[12] Aside from its limited rhetorical use, the book was also limited by its concentration on early African American historical figures. Moreover, *Negro Orators and Their Orations* enjoyed such initial popularity that a copy of it from the local library was almost impossible to find. With the virtual deluge of African American speech anthologies, this problem was significantly reduced.

> One of the first voids that had to be filled in African American rhetorical communication studies was the lack of significant numbers and representative examples of African American speakers in traditional communication texts and courses.

Some of the notable speech texts that appeared in response to the Black student demands of the late 60's and early 70's were Marcus Boulware's *The Oratory of Negro Leaders: 1900–1960*,[13] Daniel O'Neil's *Speeches by Black Americans*,[14] James Golden and Richard Rieke's *The Rhetoric of Black Americans*,[15] Jamye C. and McDonald Williams' *The Negro Speaks: The Rhetoric of Contemporary Black Leaders*,[16] Molefi Asante (Arthur L. Smith) and Stephen Robb's *The Voice of Black Rhetoric*,[17] and Robert L. Scott and Wayne Brockriede's *The Rhetoric of Black Power*.[18] But these texts still left a void in rhetorical data about people of African descent.

These African American speech anthologies focus, for the most part, on the historical development and contributions of African Americans through oratory. They were meant to demonstrate the existence of a variety of black speaking styles, viewpoints, and strategies. They were also very helpful in determining the extent to which classical and modern, European and Euro-American, rhetorical theories could be useful in analyzing Black speakers and their speeches. Some of the authors ventured to discuss the differences in makeup, style, and character of the Black speaker and his/her audience but, on the whole, attention was given to the same general criteria for criticism used for mainstream speakers, i.e., strategies, modes of proof, appeals, and so on. It was almost as if the author's intentions were to show how similar African American speakers were to whites, that the only major difference existing between them was in their viewpoints, their way of looking at problems affecting African American people.

In addition to the above speech communication texts, several historical collections of speeches emerged, e.g., *Philosophy and Opinions of Marcus Garvey,*[19] *W.E.B. DuBois Speaks,*[20] and *The Black Panthers Speak.*[21] As with *Negro Orators and Their Orations,* these texts do not contain critical analyses of the speeches. One text which did provide critical analysis was *Black Preaching*[22] by Henry H. Mitchell.

Henry H. Mitchell recognized that Black preaching is by its very nature oblivious of the rules and requirements of the majority culture; that the very process of reducing it to writing may cause some to question the terms and forms which are not always characteristic of Black culture. He describes Black preaching as a dialogue.[23] Mitchell describes Black preaching style as follows:

1. Nothing in the communication process is certain or fixed;
2. Individuality is celebrated;
3. Musical tones or chants are used;
4. Intonation is often used;
5. Rhythm pervades the dialogue;
6. Repetition and call-response are frequently employed;
7. The preacher role-plays;
8. Slow delivery rates are the mode;
9. Stammers and hesitations are suspense builders;
10. Aphorisms and other clever phrases are fairly common.

Molefi Asante's (Smith) book, *Rhetoric of Black Revolution,* is another work that not only provided a basis for the critical evaluation of African American speech events, but also set down ideas for the beginning theoretical framework for Black rhetorical discourse. It was the first communication text to address the issue of revolutionary themes permeating all types of Black rhetorical acts, including songs, literature, sermons, etc., and the issue of the common thread of oppression that makes Black communication in Africa and the Diaspora similar.[24]

Mitchell's seminal work on black preaching and his subsequent work *Black Belief a*and Asante's *Rhetoric of Black Revolution* establish much of the Black cultural foundation for a viable critical framework.[25] However, there are few other major rhetorical studies whose primary function is to provide an exegesis based on Black cultural norms and concerns.

To be sure, current historical critical methods that consider more than the speech, audience, and occasion are useful tools for the Black communication critic.[26] Similarly, the notion of movement studies is useful.[27] The point here is that these tools and conceptualizations do not take into consideration Black ethnography of speaking, i.e., how and why Blacks use the word in rhetorical discourse. Moreover, the researcher's time frames are too restricted, for in attempting to obtain manageable historical periods, they overlook broader concerns that unite seemingly disparate movements such as the civil rights movement, the Black power movement, the Black nationalist movement, etc. Unless we are able to understand the common sociopolitical circumstances, common Black responses to those circumstances, and common aspects of Black subjective culture, we will not be able to define *Black* rhetoric, note internal differences within and between Africa, the Caribbean, and the Americas, nor explain the significant differences between Black communication and non-Black communication. There are also some practical problems that await the Black rhetorical critic.

> Efforts to produce a representative body of African American public address have been made difficult because of the oral tradition, and circumstances which reinforced the fact that many Black speeches of significance were not written or electronically recorded.

Efforts to produce a representative body of African American public address have been made difficult because of the oral tradition, and circumstances which reinforced the fact that many Black speeches of significance were not written or electronically recorded. Researchers must search relentlessly for speeches alluded to in minutes of meetings, memoirs of speakers and their families, and brief newspaper accounts.

There have been countless impassioned speakers who spoke without notes, and who left no permanent records. Some had a capable person on hand to at least report the essence of the message. This person could have been a newspaper reporter, a member of the family, or a friend. Where this was the case, accounts can sometimes be found in local newspapers or in old family letters and papers. However, if the local newspaper carried the speech, and if the speech were delivered some decades ago, it is likely that the newspaper is out of business. Or, worse still, a fire may have destroyed all the papers. The same could be the case with the family. After tracking down which descendant has possession of the old family trunks containing important papers and heirlooms, the researcher may find that the owner may have only recently discarded the papers since they had been of no use to anybody.[28]

It is possible that many of the most historically and rhetorically significant Black American speeches were made without the benefit of written manuscripts or recording devices. As eloquent, spellbinding, and memorable as some of these speeches were, the speakers seldom wrote them down for posterity. Because of their degraded positions in society, Black rhetors spoke to achieve immediate responses of great consequences as opposed to being concerned with making historical records. Moreover, the agitational nature of many Black speeches led to partial, slanted, and distorted accounts that seldom reached a mass audience. Herein lies one of the greatest problems for researchers of African American rhetoric: the knowledge that some of the greatest and most representative speeches were made without even a partial manuscript that could attest to the speaker's subject, the speech's motivational appeal, what part it or the speaker played in influencing action or other people, and the like.

In addition to the absence of historical Black rhetorical data, many of the rhetorical studies do very little to enhance the Black experience, for the studies are either conventionally academic, tradition-

ally biased, or even purposely distorted to degrade Blacks and to misinform and mislead future researchers. Consequently, Black rhetorical researchers are faced not only with the task of discovering and placing Black orators into the discipline, but also of establishing basic facts, reevaluating previous conclusions, and validating fundamental methods and procedures for critically judging a speech and the speaking situation.

An example of the need for redefinition and reevaluation is in the very basics of the discipline. Traditionally, a speech is defined as an uninterrupted discourse. By this definition we can see one reason why Black speakers and Black speech events were hardly ever considered for rhetorical texts. Critics were unable to assess the event, the speech, or the speaker-audience relationships. Certainly those Blacks who were a part of the audience at a Black Baptist church, observing and participating in the constant call and response feedback surrounding a traditional revival meeting sermon by a dynamic preacher, would not have said that the minister considered the "noise" from the audience to be an interruption or that it in any way frustrated him/her. On the contrary, if the minister got no response, s/he would have found it difficult to go on.

Redefining what is considered a speech and reassessing criteria for evaluation are no small tasks for the speech critic. Indeed the very concept of rhetoric is called into question. Rhetorical systems are culturally determined. Until we come to grips with what is essentially Black (African) about Black communication, we cannot develop a culturally valid African rhetorical criticism.

Several articles, dissertations, and theses[29] have addressed the same general issues and reflected the concerns and general research directions of the books discussed above. Using various methodologies, they discussed the communicators' accounts and reactions to the contemporary and historical world that Black people have found themselves a part of. They showed that, throughout the Diaspora, and Africa itself, Black speakers have been concerned with the making and sustaining of a viable protest against injustice.[30]

Most of the Black communication articles are rhetorical case studies. An important outcome of this is that one can observe the styles, tactics, themes, audiences, etc., common to a wide range of Black speakers. The studies show how dramatically similar many of the speeches are, regardless of the speakers' place of origin, and that the concerns for injustice, economic security, decent housing and education are the same whether the speakers come from the slums of the United States, the villages of Africa, or the shantytowns of the Caribbean. These studies, however, share some of the same problems as the other research in Black communication. They are interesting and frequently provocative, but, on the whole, fairly uncreative in terms of defining the essence of Black communication.[31]

In some notable instances,[32] critics of Black rhetoric are coming to grips with the phenomenon that has been largely ignored by authors and editors of most books on Black communication. These critics have used existing critical methodologies, engaged in much analytical probing, and have developed generative questions concerning the fundamental nature of Black communication, i.e., what sets it apart and makes it unique from other systems of rhetoric.[33] What most of these researchers have found is that, as opposed to merely studying Black rhetoric within the traditional frameworks of rhetorical criticism, the whole history of Black people, their culture, and their experiences have to be dealt with before a critical assessment of Black speeches can be made.

The deluge of books and articles from the seventies sets the record straight in terms of the potential numbers of outstanding Black speakers and their contributions to society. These studies also indicated both the values and the limitations of using European and Euro-American based critical methods to evaluate Black speakers and their discourse. However, several other major problems still remain for the Black American rhetorical critic. Specifically, there is a tremendous void to be filled in terms of historical comparative data, there is the need to map the ethnography of Black communication, and there is the need to develop culturally valid theories of, and supporting data on, Black communication. One area in which there is more functional accounting of Black communication is what we have termed "social-psychological responses to oppression."

> Colonialism, slavery, and racism all sought to reduce and/or deny the African's human status.

SOCIAL-PSYCHOLOGICAL RESPONSES TO OPPRESSION

Colonialism, slavery, and racism all sought to reduce and/or deny the African's human status. Human status is intertwined with language to the extent that "a change in language can transform our appreciation of the cosmos."[34] It is little wonder then that dehumanization efforts include attacks on the victim's language and uses of language, and that many liberation efforts focus on revised language uses, e.g., redefining such concepts as Black, Negro, and African. Indeed, one can look at modes of oppression and Black responses to them in order to account for some aspects of Black communication since the colonial experiences.

An essay by Richard W. Thomas presents an account of the processes through which Black cultural phenomena are shaped and maintained.[35] More specifically, Thomas proves a "social-history theory of Black class and culture formation" which holds that, in America,

from the initial period of Black enslavement to the end of the Civil War . . . two strands of Black cultural formation developed. The major strand was obviously born from slavery, which Blauner calls "the first great source of Black culture." . . . But Blauner ignored the minor strand, the quasi-assimilationist marginal free Black culture.

. . . The two major and minor strands of cultural formation were based on the same organic ethos: freedom from slavery in the South and the protracted struggle against racial oppression in the North . . . Notwithstanding the unifying force of a shared ethos, the communities, spatially and situationally distinct, developed two separate cultural traditions.[36]

Thomas maintained that the major strand of Black southern culture produced the oral stream—rich and expressive music, folklore, dance, and folk religion. The minor strand of northern free Blacks produced a literary tradition—Black newspapers, reading and writing clubs, debate and political struggle, and, at its peak, the Harlem Renaissance. Whereas the northern strand of Blacks produced novels about mulattos and their middle-class aspirations, the southern strand preserved and produced work songs, gospels, hollers, and blues. Moreover, Thomas argued that "the Black cultural core products such as soul music, dance, street corner fellowship, soul food, Black English, etc., have not historically been and are presently not the culture of all Black people.[37] Instead, he argues that they are the property of the lowest, most oppressed Black class.

After a detailed discussion of his theoretical premises, Thomas arrived at the "paradoxical conclusion that traditional Black culture is dependent in most cases on oppressive conditions, and it seems to decline considerably when its creators undergo assimilation into the dominant ethnic variant of white culture."[38] Perhaps the matter would not be perceived as being so paradoxical if Thomas had remembered his own analysis of the historical-political conditions of Africans in America. Efforts to dehumanize are efforts to destroy culture. Basic reinforcement theory can explain the shedding of Black culture in exchange for pieces of the American pie. African culture does not drop dead in the face of European culture. One merely needs to examine the cultural behavior of White American athletes in sports where Blacks are dominant in order to see otherwise. The essential point here, however, is that Thomas viewed the survival of Black communication and other core Black cultural phenomena as more a matter of responses to differential oppression as opposed to domineering African cultural influences.

In support of the notion that traditional Black cultural phenomena are found more among the oppressed people, we take note of the following:

1. Most of the studies on Black American phenomena such as toasts, sounding, playing the dozens, folk poetry, shuckin' and jivin', and the like, are based on lower-class inner-city Blacks from places such as New York, Chicago, Philadelphia, and other eastern cities. We also note that such studies are based primarily on lower-class Black men who inhabit the bars, pool rooms, street corners, and prisons.[39]

2. While Black English features can be found throughout all Black social classes, we note that such features occur more regularly among lower-class, poorly educated, innercity, urban American Blacks and lower-class, southern American Blacks; and much more linguistic switching occurs among educated and middle-class Black Americans. We also note that in the Caribbean it

is the lower class which still makes primary use of pidgins, creoles, patois, etc., while the more educated and affluent Blacks make increasing use of the colonizers' languages.[40]

3. Throughout the African Diaspora, particularly in America, much attention has been paid to the rhetorical styles of Black religious leaders. In fact, cases have been made for the Black spiritual leaders being the masters of Black rhetorical nuances. It is very clear, however, that the much talked about call-response, for example, is a lower-class phenomenon. Indeed, some Blacks develop hostile attitudes toward Black traditional religious practices as they increase in education and social class.[41]

4. The various Caribbean religions which preserve more of African culture than other sectors of those societies, e.g., Yoruba oral literature in Cuba (Olofin, Obatala, Oyo and their oral literature), are peopled more by the lower classes. As Africans become more intellectually developed, that is, adopt Western intellectual equipment, we also note a decline in traditional modes of behavior.[42]

5. Collectors of Caribbean and Black American folklore almost invariably go to the rural and lower social classes, i.e., the least economically and culturally assimilated.

As Zora Neale Hurston (1969) commented on folklore collecting: Folklore is not as easy to collect as it sounds. The best source is where there are the least outside influences and these people, being usually under-privileged, are the shyest."[43] At the Second Caribbean Scholars' Conference, Mervyn C. Alleyne described the social and political communication difficulties that developed between the Black elite and the Black masses as a result of oppressive experiences.

Alleyne noted that in Haiti, Surinam, Jamaica, and elsewhere, the masses spoke languages that were significantly different from the elite's use of French, Dutch and English.[44] The masses developed West African-based grammars with European vocabularies. It is interesting to note that Alleyne attributed the masses' language to "the insufficiency of learning conditions."[45] As a result, polarized linguistic habits signal major differences and tremendous social conflict centers around language differences. "We" and "they" come to mean creole versus French, Dutch, or English. Marxist protesters write in creole languages. Nationalist movements make use of creoles. In St. Lucia, some elites who do not speak the French creole will do so: "1) when addressing domestics and other menial workers, and 2) when it is desired to display very popular and democratic ideals."[46] Some elites are insulted when they are addressed in creole. Creole is also relegated to the vehicle for expressing profanity, telling obscene jokes, proverbs, and in general, for handling the more intimate forms of communication such as ceremonies and rituals.[47] In sum, in Africa and throughout the diaspora, language differences forged out of oppressive circumstances serve to socially polarize Blacks within given areas, and, simultaneously, the lower-class, "disrespected," "uneducated" communication forms are the ones with the greatest Black cultural significance.

Frantz Fanon, in *Black Skin, White Masks,* presented a penetrating analysis of the psychological, political, and cultural problems that stem from former speakers of Wolof, Mandingo, etc. who want to be French and English.[48] In *The Wretched of the Earth,* however, Fanon described yet another aspect of how oppressive circumstances have shaped and given substance to Black communication. Colonialism, by negating national reality, makes possible cultural obliteration.[49] At first, the native intellectual criticizes his own national culture. With the downfall of colonial rule and other international events, new tensions develop.[50] The intellectual then begins to produce a new literature.

This literature at first chooses to confine itself to the tragic and poetic style, but later on novels, short stories and essays are attempted. It is as if a kind of internal organization or law of expression existed which wills that poetic expression become less frequent in proportion as the objectives and the methods of the struggle for liberation become more precise. Themes are completely altered, in fact, we find less and less of bitter, hopeless recrimination and less also of that violent, resounding, florid writing which on the whole serves to reassure the occupying power. The colonialists have in former times encouraged these modes of expression and made their existence possible. Stinging denunciations, the exposing of distressing conditions and passions which find their outlet in expression are in fact assimilated by the occupying power in a cathartic process. To aid such

processes is in a certain sense to avoid their dramatization and to clear the atmosphere.[51]

By describing the uses of discourse in liberation struggles, Fanon continues to show how oppressed circumstances give form and content to Black communication. The oral literature of combat changes as follows:

On another level, the oral tradition—stories, epics, and songs of the people—which formerly were filed away as set pieces are now beginning to change. The storytellers who used to relate inert episodes now bring them alive and introduce into them modifications which are increasingly fundamental. There is a tendency to bring conflicts up to date and to modernize the kinds of struggle which the stories evoke, together with the names of heroes and the types of weapons. The method of allusion is more and more widely used. The formula "This all happened long ago" is substituted by that of "What we are going to speak of happened somewhere else, but it might well have happened here today, and it might happen tomorrow." The example of Algeria is significant in this context. From 1952–1953 on, the storytellers, who were before that time stereotyped and tedious to listen to, completely overturned their traditional methods of storytelling and the contents of their tales. Their public, which was formerly scattered, became compact. The epic, with its typified categories, reappeared. . . . Colonialism made no mistake when from 1955 on it proceeded to arrest these storytellers systematically.[52]

Fanon maintained that the intellectual's discourse goes through three distinct stages as be moves toward national liberation. First, the native intellectual communicates in ways to demonstrate that s/he has "assimilated the culture of the occupying power."[53] After the first phase of "unqualified assimilation," the disturbed native begins to reflect on childhood memories, old legends, and in short, who s/he really is and from whence s/he came.[54] After gathering his/her esteem, s/he turns to the "fighting phase", and revolutionary discourse is produced to awaken the people.[55] One could easily apply Fanon's three stages to the discourse of African Americans as they have waged struggles in America—from Phyllis Wheatley to Langston Hughes to LeRoi Jones.

Relying on Fanon's work, David Llorens used the typologies of "the fellah, the chosen ones and the guardian" to describe communication patterns in America.[56] The fellah is the most downtrodden African American, and his/her concerns were voiced through the likes of Malcolm X. Chosen ones are the nonfellah, learned African Americans who work for the guardian who is the White person.[57] Chosen ones will talk "of things being soulful, nitty-gritty, and funky—but they will unfailingly avoid this ethnic behavior wherever the atmosphere suggests that their 'place' might be jeopardized."[58] Chosen ones are embarrassed when fellahs act like fellahs at the wrong time or place. Fellahs are the "holy rollers", and fellahs "tell it like it tis."[59]

Malcolm X spoke of "house niggers" and "field niggers". Sapphire, Caldonia, Peaches, and other Black women types have been identified in African American music and literature. "Uncle Toms", "bad niggers", "militants", "coons", "mammies", and "mulattos" have been depicted in American movies and television. All of these types have their identifying communication trademarks. The point here is that these types and their discourse are largely a function of oppression. In this sense, much of Black communication may be thought of as marks of oppression.

A careful study of African American literature, and Black literature in general, will reveal that among other things, it is a literature which (1) depicts Black people's oppressed conditions, (2) protests the nature of Black oppression, (3) attacks the sources of oppression, (4) offers liberation strategies, and (5) seeks to reclaim and affirm Black identity. The same can be said of the most studied Black rhetorical figures, e.g., Malcolm X, Marcus Garvey, and Martin Luther King, Jr. Indeed, high points in literature and rhetorical discourse are marked by phenomena such as the Harlem Renaissance and Martin Luther King, Jr.'s "I Have a Dream" address.

An examination of recent Caribbean and African literature will reveal a considerable number of novels, plays, and poems addressed to the themes of (1) cultural disintegration, integration, and assimilation, (2) protests against colonial-

Martin Luther King. Jr. Copyright Washington Post; Reprinted by permission of D.C. Public Library.

ism, racism, imperialism, and capitalism, and (3) explanations and advocacy of liberation strategies. There have been more than a few instances of Caribbean and African scholars and activists debating the uses of European oppressor languages versus creoles and African languages in Black oral and written discourse. In America, many Blacks have held forth on the theme "The English Language is My Enemy."[60]

> While we have gone to considerable length to articulate Black communication as a function of oppression, we hasten to add that we by no means view oppression as the key determinant of Black communication.

While we have gone to considerable length to articulate Black communication as a function of oppression, we hasten to add that we by no means view oppression as the key determinant of Black communication. Moreover, we are mindful that this focus on oppression's results can be very misleading. There are still some who wish to believe that slavery destroyed all major aspects of African culture in the "New World". This is not our view. Finally, and most importantly, the focus on oppression's results ignores those Black communication modes and characteristics which were developed prior to colonialism and still exist throughout the African diaspora, e.g., dance, the role of tonality compared with syntax, uses of indirection, the value of style given an emphasis on tradition, and the uses of rhythm in discourse.

ANTHROPOLOGICAL STUDIES

Afro-American Anthropology: Contemporary Perspectives, edited by Norman E. Whitten, Jr., and John Szwed, provides excellent illustrations of what has been termed "anthropological perspectives" on Black communication.[61] Representative articles are "Cultural and Linguistic Ambiguity in a West Indian Village", "Toward an Ethnography of Black American Speech Behavior", "Patterns of Performance in the British West Indies", and "The Homogeneity of African—Afro-American Musical Style."[62] While the editors acknowledge that "Afro-American anthropology is not a distinctive sub-discipline," they do seek to bring anthropological theories and methods to bear "on some of the persistent problems in African American research—problems of family, kinship, ethnicity, and economics; of bilingualism and code switching."[63]

Karl Risman, in 1960–61, conducted field research on the island of Antigua, West Indies. He focused on Herskovits' observation that "certain norms of behavior, of reticence and discretion, of respect and acceptance rather than confrontation, were closely related to an indirect and ambiguous mode of expression and reaction."[64] "Indirection" was developed as a summary term reflecting social norms of discretion and avoidance of direct confrontation. As a consequence of such a social norm, Antiguans use indirect modes of reprisal. Multiple meanings of words become commonplace. Cultural duality develops whereby words have both European and African connotations, e.g., the word for sweet potato is a noun to indicate the vegetable and, with a slightly different pronunciation, it sounds like "come go home" and' "Congo home."[65] Even the use of creole is manipulated to indicate high and low status, relaxed as opposed to formal social situations, and confrontation versus nonconfrontation. Creole is used for the purposes of relaxation, playfully "going on ignorant," cursing, expressing anger to another person, and to indicate that one is genuine.[66]

Roger Abrahams' study of performance patterns in the British West Indies is an anthropological study designed in response to Herskovits' "call for a re-

examination of material in terms of similarities and differences on a regional basis."[67] Focusing on the "men of words," Abrahams studied the acclaim given to men who were good at using words, their patterns of performances, and the ways in which they interact with their audiences. Abrahams observed that (1) in the United States, the men of words hold forth in bars, pool rooms, and at special events such as wakes, weddings, and Christmas; (2) in Tobago, the men of words perform at Bongs (wakes), Thanksgiving parties, and as the central figures in a Carnival "mas"; and (3) in Nevis, a more conflict-oriented, virtuoso type man of words holds forth at special times such as Christmas and tea meetings.[68] Abrahams indicated that such men of words' performance patterns might be a "deep structure that assumes many shapes in different regional environments."[69]

Pursuing the need to empirically document claims about the homogeneity of African and African American expressive behavior, Alan Lomax developed a rating system—cantometrics—for rating song performance in Africa, Western Europe, and the New World.[70]

Applying his rating system to "2500 plus songs from 233 cultures." (George Murdock's Ethnographic Atlas), Lomax came up with the following results:

1. The extraordinary homogeneity of African song style is the result of the almost universal use by the African of the highly cohesive, complexly integrated song model. Black Africans synchronize their motor and their vocal acts more tightly than the people of other culture regions.
2. This relaxed, repetitive, cohesive, multileveled, yet leader-oriented style is distinctly African. . . . It is both a source and symbol of African cultural homogeneity.
3. Afro-Americans exhibit clear European folk song influences. However, Afro-American style is ". . . cantometrically identical with the core AFRICAN GARDENER style," i.e., a style ". . . prominently in most of West and Equatorial Africa. The main Afro-American song, the old spiritual, is derived from the primary African song style."[71]

Continuing with the attempts to account for the cultural patterning of speech events, Ethel M. Albert conducted a field study of how the Central African Burundi define rhetoric, logic, and poetics.[72] Citing

Rundi speech characteristics that are common to Mediterranean and African cultures, Albert indicated the following:

1. Practical and esthetic values take precedence over logical criteria in all but a few cases of communication situations.
2. Reliance upon appeals to the emotions as the chief technique of rhetoric is taken for granted as right and natural and indeed the whole ground of its utility.
3. There are no reservations about the desirability of flattery, untruths, taking advantage of weakness of character of profiting from others' misfortunes.[73]

Ethel Albert made a careful analysis of what might be termed Rundi world view or ethnophilosophy and its impact on discourse. More specifically, she studied world view factors, such as the hierarchical order in the universe and society, and its influence on the following:

1. Speech training according to caste, age, and sex
2. Forms of petition (gifts and favors)
3. Formulas for visiting (formal and informal)
4. Rules of precedence and good speech manners
5. Respect patterns and role relativism
6. Formulas of politeness

Albert also studied ethnoepistemological values such as "ubgenge", which applies to the intellectual-verbal management of significant life situations, and "umuschingantahe", i.e., slow, well-chosen words and figures of speech, attentive to others, and god with logic.[74]

Finally, she observed the social use of discretion and falsehood, "The man who tells no lies cannot feed his children, "the aesthetic hierarchy of speech forms, i.e., everyday descriptive discourse at the bottom, public address at the midpoint, and oral literature at the top, and the use of indirection, allusion, gesture, and idioms.[75] Albert's study is extremely valuable as a case study in the cultural patterning of speech. Other valuable studies can be found among African folklore research.

James Boyd Christensen studied the role of proverbs in Fante culture.[76] Although Christensen's fieldwork took place around the central coastal area of Ghana, he maintained that much of his work could be extended to include the approximately two mil-

lion Akan people, which includes the Fante. Utilizing elders as informants, Christensen collected proverbs during conversations, proverb-quoting contests, and requests to present proverbs. He then analyzed the collected proverbs in terms of their roles in judicial proceedings, indicators of clan responsibility and cooperation, the role and significance of Fante elders, responsibilities and relationships between the chief and the state, child rearing, entertainment, and the communication of proper behavior and values.[77]

An extremely useful work on African folklore is a volume edited by Richard M. Dorson.[78] Dorson has a very good introductory essay in which he traces the history of folklore as a concept; discusses the scholarly utility of the terms "folklore", "oral literature", and "verbal art"; and discusses the oral-literature approach to folklore, folklore and anthropology, folklore and oral history, and folklore as an end in itself.[79] The volume contains African and American scholars' field studies on storytellers, tales, proverbs, riddles, oral history, poetry, and drama from various parts of Africa.

Although there is considerably less material in terms of critical analysis, Harold Courlander's *A Treasury of Afro-American Folklore* would make a fair companion volume for Dorson's *African Folklore*.[80] Following the introductory essay, on "Africa's Mark in the Western Hemisphere", Courlander presents material such as Yoruba legends riddles, West Indian calypso, Jamaican games and songs, and American spirituals, plantation proverbs, and religious practices.

A number of field studies have taken place in African American urban settings. Thomas Kochman's *Rappin' and Stylin' Out: Communication in Urban Black America* is an edited volume designed to "illuminate the communicative habits and expressive life-style of urban Black Americans."[81] Using linguistic, sociolinguistic, and ethnographic techniques, the authors discuss topics such as the use of time, nonverbal behavior, motion and feeling through music, audience behavior, soul language, inversion, street talk, signifying, the dozens, and so on. Examples of other African American field studies are Ulf Hannerz' Washington, D.C., study entitled, "Gossip, Networks and Culture in A Black American Ghetto", and *Soulside,* and Bruce Jackson's *Narrative Poetry from Black Oral Tradition*.[82] In the late seventies, Linda Wharton completed a doctoral dissertation on African American children's singing games and Lorna Shaw completed a dissertation in

1992 at Howard University on the Jamaican *Kumina Dynamics: An Expression of Orature.*[83]

The anthropological field studies take Black communication beyond that which developed out of oppressive situations. Moreover, the field studies get at the ways in which various Black cultures define and make use of communication. Through systematic field studies, it is hoped that we will be better able to articulate the salient features of African-derived communication. Two major problems in the development of this area have emerged as: (1) the absence of significant numbers of cultural anthropologists, sociolinguists, oral historians, and speech communication persons to work in the area, and (2) the lack of historical and comparative data necessary for establishing trends, patterns, generalizations, and theories about Black communication.

Earlier, it was stipulated that communication must have African roots if it is to be classified as Black communication. Anthropological field studies are essential for conducting studies seeking to establish the African genesis of communication and its continuities throughout the diaspora. For example, one could conduct field studies of children's singing games in Nigeria, Jamaica, and Pittsburgh, Pennsylvania, in an effort to ascertain similarities and differences in the games' structures, rules, role clothing, outcomes, rewards and socioeducational functions. In short, one could take any alleged Black communication cultural focus, conduct ethnographic field studies along the African continuum, and, in this way, begin to establish the body of empirical data that is essential for generating theories and models of Black communication.

> An Afrocentric perspective holds that the whole history and culture of Black people constitute the proper internal frame of reference for giving explanations and critical assessments of Black communication.

AFROCENTRIC PERSPECTIVES

We recognize that some people of African descent use symbolic discourse in ways hardly distinguishable from users of European and Asiatic languages. The contention here is that the African-ness of the communication is derived from African roots. When African roots no longer exist, then we are talking about a Black person's use of language as opposed to Black or African communication.

An Afrocentric perspective holds that the whole history and culture of Black people constitute the proper internal frame of reference for giving explanations and critical assessments of Black communication. While descriptive and comparative studies are eventually needed, an accounting for and criticism of Black communication should proceed from an understanding of how Black people view realities and organize their world, i.e., their metaphysics, philosophy, cosmology, etymology, religion, ontology, and psychology. Consider the case of Black rhetorical criticism.

Black rhetoric, with its concentration on Nommo, rhythmical patterns, audience assertiveness, and so on, cannot be dealt with by simply applying the conventional Euro-American tools of rhetorical criticism. Molefi Asante, in two early 1970's landmark articles, recognized that new African-based methods must be explored and instituted before effective critical judgments might be made.[84] Asante's seminal work set forth the most comprehensive and definitive philosophical statement on the subject of Afrocentricity that has been made.[85] The focal point of these works can be summarized by quoting the first sentence of the article "Markings of an African Concept of Rhetoric": "Any interpretation of African rhetoric must begin to dispense with the notion that Europe is teacher and Africa is pupil".[86] Africa now becomes central as we assess Black communication; the standards by which we evaluate are African; the traditions we hold up as models are African. The values, the customs, the way of life, are not to be put aside, but embraced. The drum, dance, song, and poetry become some of the primary genres that must be examined. Style, rhythm, creativity, spontaneity, call-response, "become primary tactics for study. If one is to engage in the criticism of African (or Black) communication from an Afrocentric point of view, one has to understand more than the structures of Black people's songs, dances, and other discourse. It means that one must also come to grips with the primary assumptions that make up the traditional African world view;[87] that is, the researcher has to understand the primary, underlying religious-philosophical assumptions which are integrated into a traditional African world view.[88] Subsequently, as Asante argued during his beginning research on Afrocentricity, specific criteria should be developed for the evaluation of Black communication, taking into account its uniquely mother-African distinctiveness.[89]

Jack L. Daniel has devoted most of his Black communication research concerns to the African-derived nature of Black communication. He has urged, as follows, that researchers go beyond simply establishing communication correlations throughout the Diaspora.

While answering the question of African survivals is of extreme importance for improving our understanding of Black communication, merely trying to correlate external behaviors found in Africa, (the Caribbean) and America will not suffice. While it is important for the investigator to describe observable behavior, the fact of the matter is that the investigator is still in the realm of description and not explanation. Explanation of a given African survival can only be obtained when the investigator can apply his understanding of the African attitude of mind that produces the described behavior.[90]

Pursuing this line of thinking, Jack Daniel and Geneva Smitherman provided an analysis of the call-response phenomenon based on its functional relationship to what they termed the "traditional African world view." After noting some salient features of this world view, such as unity between spiritual and material, centrality of religion, and time as participation in events, they account for call-response as a basic, African-derived, and African American Church-maintained communication tactic that "seeks to synthesize 'speakers' and 'listeners' in a unified movement.[91] This same mode of analysis has been followed by Paul Carter Harrison and Oliver Jackson.[92]

First in *The Drama of Nommo* and subsequently in *Kuntu Drama*, Harrison uses traditional African cosmology and related dramatic performances to account for African American communication.[93] Relying on Jahnheinz Jahn's *Muntu* and Oliver Jackson's exposition of the survival of traditional African cosmology in America, Harrison focuses on Black people's (Muntu) uses of the Word (Nommo) in dramatic situations by the Kuntu forces of Song, Dance, and Drum.[94] Jackson points out that "the most powerful and far-reaching manifestation of intelligence is

the collective religious ceremony, in which collective power summons and brings the forces of the ancestors, the forces of their sons, and the forces of God."[95] One such ceremony, along the African continuum, is a Jamaican ritualistic ceremony invoking the spirits of ancestors and is called the Kumina. This ceremony was analyzed as a manifestation of the concept of orature, a term describing the oral tradition of Black culture. In this religious ritual, the believers communicate with ancestors for the purpose of receiving information that they use to direct their personal and community life. Another ceremony, is Kuntu Drama, i.e., "a drama that has as its ultimate purpose to reveal and invoke the reality of the particular mode that it has ritualized.[96] He also notes that 'the play is the ritualized context of reality. The ritual confirms the mode: it is a living incantation that focuses power to invoke and release beneficent power to the audience.'"[97] According to Harrison, the event is the thing, not the play.

Harrison's summary of Kuntu Drama highlights much of what is articulated as an Afrocentric perspective.

Despite economic considerations, there is a future for the black theatre when we begin to accept Africa as the antecedent reference to our contemporary American folk styles. It is the source that gives expression to our walk/dance, talk/song, and provides rhythm/silence at the Sunday chicken dinner table, urban/rural: all of it must be attended in a manner which creates the strongest reality of our power to summon the dynamics of black life into harmonious relationships with the mode.[98]

All this describes what is now called *orature*, a term used by Micere Mugo and Ngugi wa Thiong at the World Congress on Communication and Development in Africa and the African Diaspora held in Nairobi, Kenya in 1981 and later discussed in Molefi Asante's *The Afrocentric Idea* and detailed in the dissertation by Lorna Shaw in 1990.[99]

Other examples of efforts to gain understanding of Black people's life via African people's world view and their discourse can be found among a few historians. Two historical documents are of importance in viewing discourse from the cultural vantage points of African Americans. Arguing that "separate black national culture has always been American, however much it has drawn on African origins or reflected the distinct development of African American people," Eugene D. Genovese nevertheless uses the slaves' discourse to show their contributions to the development of Black national consciousness and American nationality as a whole.[100] Genovese's data sources consist primarily of archives. A parallel work and one of great interest to communications is Leonard Levin's *Black Culture and Black Consciousness*.[101] Levine summed up his work on early African American folk thought as follows:

> *It focuses upon the orally transmitted expressive culture of Afro-Americans in the United States during the century that stretched from the antebellum era to the end of the 1940's, and is primarily concerned with two major questions: What were the contours of slave folk thought on the eve of emancipation and what were the effects of freedom upon that thought?*[102]

Levine relied heavily on "songs, folktales, proverbs, aphorisms, jokes, verbal games and the long narrative oral poems known in African American cultures as 'toasts'."[103] He dealt with questions such as those related to the impact of West African beliefs on the African American spirituals, and he arrived at summary descriptions that remind one of the earlier works cited as reflecting on Afrocentric perspectives, e.g., "spirituals born during and after slavery were the product of an 'improvisational communal consciousness.'"[104] Through similar works covering different time periods and geography, we should be able to determine the African aspects of Black communication. Of particular importance is the need for studies in Africa.

One might assume that there were a significant number of Afrocentric communication studies in Africa. This in not the case, primarily because of the absence of written records. If one could allow himself/herself the time for field research, however, s/he would find that verbal art and criticism in Africa are as old as speech itself. The traditional forms of rhetoric in Africa utilize various rhetorical forms such as proverbs, idioms, repetitions, songs denoting different aspects of life's cycles, fables, and myths. There are the village oracles or griots whose jobs are to set the standards for oral presentations and to comment on what others say and do. They, in their rhetorical criticism, make life more comprehensible. They are the creators as well as the critics of rhetoric. Not much has been done, however, to put on permanent record most of these traditional theories and criti-

cisms of rhetoric, although a beginning is being made. This is one reason why one has to spend time studying this medium in its very basic forms. One has to experience it to know and understand its existence.

Several African scholars, including Soyinka, p'bitek, Awoonor, Achebe, and Iyasare, are studying or have studied folk media in their various manifestations, including rhetorical criticism.[105] But most of the great orators of Africa have not been studied; their rhetoric is in the realm of oral tradition. Even modern African orators like Nkrumah, Kenyatta, and Nyerere have not come under close scrutiny by rhetorical critics, although they have been the frequent subjects of scholars. Perhaps when speech scholars find them interesting enough to do critical evaluations, then more of their tradition, culture, and world view will be known.

The Afrocentric rhetorical criticism which has been done in Africa by Africans is that which has been written in a political/cultural/literary vein by writers such as Ali Mazrui *(The Trial of Christopher Okigbo)*, Wole Soyinka *(The Interpreters)*, Kofi Awoonor *(This Earth, My Brother)*, Ayi Kewi Armah *(Fragments)*, Gabriel Okara *(The Voice)*, Chinua Achebe *(Things Fall Apart)*, Alechi Amada *(The Concubines)*, Ngugi wa Thiongo *(The River Between, Petals of Blood)*, Okot p'bitek *(Song of Lawino, Song of Ocol, Song of the Prisoner)*, and other African writers who have represented the epitome of Afrocentric communication.[106] Though they write in the languages of the colonizers, their messages are taken from traditional African content and forms. Their writings constitute Afrocentric criticism because they explore, explain, and criticize traditions, as well as social, political, cultural, and economic movements and values from an African mind-set. They know the traditions; they have lived and experienced the ways of life they discuss; they understand the dynamics of the philosophies, the African world view.

G. Awooner Williams, acting as critic for his own communication as well as other African writers writing from the vantage point of tradition, speaks of the richness of his culture when he says: "I should take my unique. . .sensibility. . .from the tradition that feeds my language. . .because in my language there is a lot of poetry, a lot of old literary art—even though not written."[107]

European and American critics, usually not understanding the purpose and intent of authors like those listed above, have harshly criticized them.

First, they criticized them for using languages (French and English) that were not their own, and then for using art forms (novels and poetry) and thought patterns that were also alien.

Solomon Iyasere took issue with the criticisms, for he too recognized that any critical evaluation of Black communication should be based on a "culture-sensitive approach, informed by an intelligent understanding of the traditional background [for] this will prove more responsive to the unique nativisms of African communicators."[108] To assess a work by foreign standards leads to a mutilation of the message and robs the communication of its vitality.[109]

There are quite a number of African American and Caribbean rhetorical/cultural critics who speak from the point of view similar to those that were mentioned from Africa. Molefi Asante, Jack L. Daniel, Deborah Atwater, Paul Carter Harrison, Lorna Shaw, Keith Warner, Cecil Cone, Mark McPhail, Ronald Jackson, and Carlos Morrison, to name a few. These authors' works provide culturally valid sets of philosophical principles from which knowledge of the functionally derived modes of communication such as dance, drum, song, and a dynamic interactive style may be learned. They also discuss the underlying religious-philosophical assumptions on which the traditional African world view is based and on which an understanding of the synthesis into oneness of speaker, audience, and event is manifested. An excellent example of this is Leonard Barrett's *Soul Force,* in which he extensively discusses African survivals in the form of dance, drum, song, proverbs, ways of talking, and lifestyles in the Caribbean and America.[110] Articles by Fela Sowande and Olive Lewin in the book *Black Communication: Dimensions of Research and Instruction* discuss the African world view and its relationship to communication in Africa and Jamaica.[111] The book *African Myths and Tales* by Susan Feldman is also a good resource book for achieving an understanding of the African world view through folk culture.[112]

The point made initially concerning developing viable theoretical bases for evaluating African-based communication becomes even more fundamental when we search the literature and discover what scholars of traditional African culture have found about the pervasiveness of Africa in the entire Black world. No area and no group of people were left unaffected. It is, therefore, culturally invalid to do an effective critical evaluation of any aspect of verbal and nonverbal communication as it relates to the Black world without beginning with the influences of Africa.

Given our review of Black communication literature, we offer the following list of Black communication research needs:

BLACK COMMUNICATION RESEARCH NEEDS

1. There is a great need for field studies that account for traditional and modern Africans' (throughout the African diaspora) ways of viewing the cosmos, and how these views help to shape their uses of discourse. Stated differently, we need to determine the philosophical first principles of Black rhetoric and the ethnography of Black communication. Subsequently, there is a need for cross cultural studies that demonstrate the differences and similarities between Black communication and other major cultures' world views and systems of communication.

2. There need to be comparative empirical studies of specific Black communication genres throughout the African diaspora among at least two non-African cultural groups. Alan Lomax's study of Black musical style is a case in point.

3. Proceeding according to geography—Africa, Caribbean, and the Americas, as well as within each major area—there is a need to study the impact of factors such as age, education, caste, social class, and religion on specific aspects of Black communication. One might, for example, study the ways in which Black American call-response behavior and related attitudes vary according to age, education, sex, class, and religion.

4. The predominance of an oral culture, and the fact that Black people, as with all people, are in cultural transition, suggest the need for collection and preservation studies. Throughout the diaspora, the folkloric items (orature), public addresses of Black culturally defined significant speakers, and other modes of Black communication need to be collected and preserved in archives. Current archives need to be validly and reliably categorized and researchers need to be informed of how to access them.

5. The complex relationships between racism, colonialism, oppression in general, and Black peo-

ple's use of language are yet to be fully explored. In addition to the need to systematically study these relationships, these data need to be put to use in liberation struggles. The problem of colonial languages versus African languages and African expression of the colonial languages is still replete with psychological, political, and economic ramifications. Can the Black person ever be culturally and psychologically free if s/he does not master his/her words?

6. Black communication researchers must develop appropriate theoretical and conceptual foundations and corresponding methodologies for the study of African centered communication. There is a clear absence of theories and methodologies that are demonstrated required alternatives to existing theories and methodologies and that account for Afrocentric communication free of external cultural oppression as well as that where oppression has occurred.

The Black communication research needs are such that teams of African and Diaspora scholars are needed to pursue joint research efforts if a body of data is to be systematically produced in a reasonable period of time. The multiplicity of languages, the variations in historical and cultural experiences, the paucity of data in all areas, and the urgent need for data demand international team efforts.

> The Black communication research needs are such that teams of African and Diaspora scholars are needed to pursue joint research efforts if a body of data is to be systematically produced in a reasonable period of time.

Notes

1. Joseph H. Greenberg, "African Languages," in *Peoples and Cultures of Africa,* edited by Elliot P. Skinner (Garden City: Doubleday/Natural History Press, 1973), pp. 71–80.

2. Dell H. Hymes, "The Ethnography of Speaking," in *Readings in the Sociology of Language,* edited by Joshua Fishman (The Hague: Mouton, 1968), p. 101.

3. *Ibid.*

4. Roger D. Abrahams, "Patterns of Performance in the British West Indies," in *Afro-American Anthropology: Contemporary Perspectives,* edited by Norman E Whitten, Jr., and John Szwed (New York: The Free Press, 1970), pp. 163–180.

5. *Ibid.,* pp. 171–176.

6. Charles E. Osgood, William H. May, and Murray S. Miron, *Cross-Cultural Universals of Affective Meaning* (Urbana: University of Illinois Press, 1975), p. 4.

7. Frantz Fanon, *Black Skin, White Mask* (New York: Grove Press, 1982), p. 34.

8. *Ibid.*

9. Melville J. Herskovits, *The Myth of the Negro Past* (Boston: Beacon Press, 1958), p. xxii.

10. *Ibid.,* p. xxiii

11. *Ibid.,* p. xxvi

12. Carter G. Woodson, *Negro Orators and Their Orations* (1925) reprint (New York: Russell Press, 1968).

13. Marcus Boulware, *The Oratory of Negro Leaders 1900–1968* (Westport: Negro Universities Press, 1969).

14. Daniel O'Neill, editor, *Speeches by Black Americans* (Encino: Dickerson Press, 1971).

15. James Golden and Richard Rieke, *The Rhetoric of Black Americans* (Columbus: Merrill Press, 1971).

16. Jamye C. Williams and McDonald Williams, *The Negro Speaks: The Rhetoric of Contemporary Black Leaders* (New York: Noble Press, 1970).

17. Arthur L. Smith and Stephen Robb, *The Voice of Black Rhetoric: Selections* (Boston: Allyn and Bacon, 1971).

18. Robert L. Scott and Wayne Brockriede, editors, *The Rhetoric of Black Power* (New York: Harper and Row, 1969).

19. Amy Jacques-Garvey, *Philosophy and Opinions of Marcus Garvey* (New York: Atheneum, 1969).

20. Phillip S. Foner, editor, *W.E.B. DuBois Speaks* (New York: Pathfinder Press, 1970).

21. Phillip S. Foner, editor, *The Black Panther Speaks* (New York: Lippincott, 1970).

22. Henry H. Mitchell, *Black Preaching* (Philadelphia: J.B. Lippincott, 1970).

23. *Ibid.,* p. 13.

24. Arthur L. Smith (Molefi Asante), *Rhetoric of Black Revolution* (Boston: Allyn and Bacon, 1969).

25. Henry H. Mitchell, *Black Belief* (New York: Harper and Row, 1975).

26. Arthur L. Smith (Molefi Asante), "Theoretical and Research Issues in Black Communication," in *Black Communication Dimensions of Research and Instruction,* edited by Jack L. Daniel (New York: Speech Communication Association, 1974), p. 136.

27. Leland Griffin, "The Rhetoric of Historical Movements," *Quarterly Journal of Speech* 38 (April 1952), pp. 184–188.

28. Melbourne S. Cummings, "Problems of Researching Black Rhetoric," *Journal of Black Studies* 2 (June 1972), pp. 503–508.

29. Bart Bardley, "Negro Speakers in Congress, 1869–1875," *Southern Speech Journal* 12 (4) (May 1953), pp. 216–225.
Thomas Benson, "Rhetoric and Autobiography: The Case of Malcolm X," *Quarterly Journal of Speech* 60 (1) (February 1974), pp. 1–13.
Wayne Brockriede and Robert L. Scott, "Stokely Carmichael: Two Speeches on Black Power," *Central State Speech Journal* 19 (1) (Spring 1968), pp. 3–13.
Parke G. Burgess, "The Rhetoric of Black Power: A Moral Demand," *Quarterly Journal of Speech* 54 (2) (April 1968), pp. 122–133.
Thomas R. Cheatham, "The Rhetorical Structure of the Abolitionist Movement Within the Baptist Church: 1833–1845," unpublished Ph.D. thesis (Indiana: Purdue University, 1969).
Melbourne S. Cummings, "The Rhetoric of Bishop Henry McNeal Turner, Leading Advocate in the African Emigration Movement, 1866–1907," unpublished Ph.D. thesis (Los Angeles: University of California, 1972).
Jack L. Daniel, "Black Folk and Speech Education," *Speech Teacher* 9 (2) (March 1970), pp. 123–129.
Robert C. Dick, "Rhetoric of the Negro-Antebellum Protest Movement," unpublished Ph.D. thesis (California: Stanford University, 1969).

Gerald Fulkerson, Exile as Emergence: Frederick Douglass in Great Britain: 1845–1848," *Quarterly Journal of Speech,* 60 (7) (October 1974), pp. 1–13.
Thomas E. Harris and Patrick C. Kennicott, "Booker T. Washington: A Study of Conciliatory Rhetoric," *Southern Speech Journal* 37 (Fall 1971), pp. 47–59.
John Illo, "The Rhetoric of Malcolm X," *The Columbia University Forum* 9 (Spring 1966), pp. 5–12.
Andrew King, "Booker T. Washington and the Myth of Heroic Materialism", *Quarterly Journal of Speech* 60 (3) (October 1974).
Arthur L. Smith (Molefi Asante), "Henry Highland Garnet: Black Revolutionary in Sheep's Vestments," *Central State Speech Journal* 21 (2) (Summer 1970), pp. 4–14.
John H. Thurber and John L. Petelle, "The Negro Pulpit and Civil Rights," *Central State Speech Journal* 19 (4) (1968), p. 273–278.

30. Arthur L Smith (Moleii Asante), ed., "The Rhetoric of Psychical and Physical Emigration," in *Language, Communication, and Rhetoric in Black America* (New York: Harper and Row, 1972).

31. Arthur L. Smith (Molefi Asante), "Theoretical and Research Issues in Black Communication," p. 136.

32. Jack L. Daniel and Geneva Smitherman, "How I Got Over: Communication Dynamics in the Black Community," *Quarterly Journal of Speech* 62 (February 1976), pp. 26–39.
Arthur L. Smith, "Toward the Making of an African Concept of Rhetoric," in *Language, Communication, and Rhetoric in Black America* (New York: Harper and Row, 1972).
Dorthy Pennington, "Temporality Among Black Americans: Implications for Intercultural Communications," Unpublished Ph.D. dissertation (University of Kansas, 1974).
Linda E. Wharton, "Curriculum Development in Black Communication: The Design of an Introductory Course," unpublished Masters thesis (Pennsylvania: University of Pittsburgh, 1975).

33. *Ibid.,* specifically, Pennington, Smith (Asante), and Daniel and Smitherman.

34. John B. Carroll, ed., *Language, Thought and Reality: Selected Writings of Benjamin Lee Whorf* (Cambridge: MIT Press, 1966), p. 263.

35. "Richard W. Thomas, "Working-class and Lower-class Origins of Black Culture: Class

Formation and the Division of Black Cultural Labor," *Minority Voices* 1 (Fall 1977), pp. 81–99.

36. *Ibid.,* pp. 88–89.

37. *Ibid.,* p. 81.

38. *Ibid.,* p. 89.

39. Bruce Jackson, *Narrative Poetry From Black Oral Tradition* (Cambridge: Harvard University Press, 1974), p. viii.

40. Frantz Fanon, *Black Skin, White Masks,* pp. 17–40.

41. Alan Dundes, ed., *Mother Wit From the Laughing Barrel* (Englewood Cliffs: Prentice-Hall, 1973), pp. 1–2.

42. Mervyn C. Alleyne, "Communication Between the Elite and the Masses," in *The Caribbean in Transition: Papers on Social, Political and Economic Development,* edited by F.M. Andic and T.G. Matthews (Rio Piedras, Puerto Rico: University of Puerto Rico, 1965), pp. 12–19.

43. Zora Neale Hurston, *Of Mules and Men* (1935), reprint (New York: Negroes Universities Press, 1969), p. 18.

44. Mervyn C. Alleyne, "Communication Between the Elite and the Masses", p. 1.

45. *Ibid.,* p. 15.

46. Mervyn C. Alleyne, "Language and Society in St. Lucia," *Caribbean Studies,* 1 (April 1961–62), p. 6.

47. *Ibid.,* p. 8.

48. Frantz Fanon, *Black Skin, White Masks,* pp. 109–220.

49. Frantz Fanon, *The Wretched of the Earth* (New York: Grove Press, 1963), p. 190.

50. *Ibid.,* pp. 191–192.

51. *Ibid.,* p. 152.

52. *Ibid.,* pp. 193–194.

53. *Ibid.,* p. 179.

54. *Ibid.*

55. *Ibid.*

56. David Llorens, "The Fellah, The Chosen Ones. The Guardian," in *Black Fire,* edited by LeRoi Jones and Larry Neal (New York: William Morrow and Company, 1968), pp. 169–177.

57. *Ibid.,* p. 171.

58. *Ibid.,* p. 172.

59. *Ibid.,* p. 173.

60. Ossie Davis, "The English Language Is My Enemy," in *Language, Communication, and Rhetoric in Back America,* edited by Arthur L.

Smith (Molefi Asante) (New York: Harper and Row, 1972).

61. Norman E. Whitten, Jr. and John F. Szwed, eds., *Afro-American Anthropology: Contemporary Perspectives* (New York: The Free Press, 1970).

62. *Ibid.,* pp. 63–219.

63. *Ibid.,* p. 19.

64. Karl Reisman, "Cultural and Linguistic Ambiguity in a West Indian Village," in *Afro-American Anthropology: Contemporary Perspectives,* p. 130.

65. *Ibid.,* p. 132.

66. *Ibid.,* p. 136.

67. Roger Abrahams, "Patterns of Performance in the British West Indies," p. 163.

68. *Ibid.,* pp. 166–173.

69. *Ibid.,* p. 163.

70. *Ibid.,* pp. 166–173.

71. *Ibid.,* p. 163.

72. Ethel M. Albert, "Rhetoric, Logic, and Poetics in Burundi: Culture Patterning of Speech Behavior," *American Anthropologist* 64 (October 1964), pp. 35–54.

73. *Ibid.,* p. 36.

74. *Ibid.,* pp. 36–43.

75. *Ibid.,* p. 44.

76. *Ibid.,* p. 46.

77. James Boyd Christensen, "The Role of Proverbs in Fante Culture," in *Peoples and Cultures of Africa,* edited by Elliot P. Skinner (Garden City: Doubleday Natural History Press, 1973), pp. 509–524.

78. *Ibid.,* pp. 511–524.

79. Richard M. Dorson, editor, *African Folklore* (Garden City: Anchor Books, 1972).

80. *Ibid.,* pp. 3–67.

81. Harold, Courlander, *A Treasury of Afro-American Folklore* (New York: Crown Publishers, 1976).

82. Thomas Kochman, editor, *Rappin' and Stylin' Out: Communication in Urban Black America* (Urbana: University of Illinois, 1972), p. xi.

83. Linda E. Wharton, "Black American Children's Singing Games," Ph.D. thesis (Pennsylvania: University of Pittsburgh, 1979).

84. Arthur L. Smith (Molefi Asante), "Markings of an African Concept of Rhetoric," in *Language, Communication, and Rhetoric in Black America* (New York: Harper and Row, 1972).

Arthur L. Smith (Molefi Asante), Socio-Historic Perspectives of Black Oratory," *Quarterly*

Journal of Speech 56 (October 1970), pp. 264–269.

85. Molefi Kete Asante, *Afrocentricity* (Trenton: Africa World Press, 1988).
Molefi Asante, *The Afrocentric Idea* (Philadelphia: Temple University Press, 1987).
Molefi Asante, *Afrocentricity: The Theory of Social Change* (Buffalo: Amulefi, 1980).

86. Arthur L. Smith (Molefi Asante), "Markings of an African Concept of Rhetoric," p. 373.

87. Jack L Daniel, editor, *Black Communication: Dimensions of Research and Instruction* (New York: Speech Communication Association, 1974), p. xiv.

88. *Ibid.*, pp. vii–xiv.

89. Arthur L. Smith (Molefi Asante), "Theoretical and Research Issues in Black Communication," in *Language, Communication, and Rhetoric in Black America* (New York: Harper and Row, 1972), p. 136.

90. Jack L. Daniel, *Black Communication: Dimensions of Research and Instruction,* pp. xi–xii.

91. Jack L. Daniel and Geneva Smitherman, "How I Got Over: Communication Dynamics in the Back Community," p. 33.

92. Paul Carter Harrison, editor, *Kuntu Drama* (New York: Grove Press, 1974).

93. Paul Carter Harrison, *The Drama of Nommo* (New York: Grove Press, 1972).

94. *Ibid.*, p. xi.

95. Oliver Jackson, preface to Paul Carter Harrison, editor, *Kuntu Drama* (New York: Grove Press, 1974), p. xi.

96. *Ibid.*, p. xi.

97. *Ibid.*, p. xi

98. Paul Carter Harrison, *Kuntu Drama,* p. 29.

99. Lorna L. Shaw, "Kumina Dynamics: An Expression of Orature," unpublished dissertation (Howard University, 1991).

100. Eugene D. Genovese, *Roll Jordan Roll: The World the Slaves Made* (New York: Vintage Books, 1974).

101. Leonard Levine, *Black Culture and Black Consciousness* (New York: Oxford University Press, 1977).

102. *Ibid.*, p. ix.

103. *Ibid.*, p. ix.

104. *Ibid.*, p. 291.

105. Solomon Iyasere, "Oral Tradition in the Criticism of African Literature," *Journal of Modern African Studies* 13 (September 1975), p. 108.

106. Solomon O. Iyasere, "The Criticism of African Literature," *Journal of Modern African Studies* 11 (October 1973), p. 448.

107. Iyasere, "Oral Tradition in the Criticism of African Literature," p. 109.

108. *Ibid.*

109. *Ibid.*

110. Leonard Barrett, *Soul Force* (New York: Anchor Books, 1974).

111. Fela Sowande, "Quest of an African World View: The Utilization of African Discourse," in *Black Communication Dimensions of Research and Instruction,* edited by Jack L. Daniel (New York: Speech Communication Association, 1974).
Olive Lewin, "Folk Music Research in Jamaica," in Black Communication: Dimensions of Research and Instruction, edited by Jack L. Daniel (New York: Speech Communication Association, 1974).

112. Some of the notable writers of the diaspora whose works may provide some theoretical base for Afrocentricity are: Molefi Kete Asante, *The Afrocentric Idea* (Philadelphia: Temple University, 1987); Molefi Kete Asante, *Afrocentricity* (Trenton: Africa World Press, 1988); Molefi Kete Asante, *Afrocentricity: The Theory of Social Change* (Buffalo: Amulefi, 1980); Maulana Karenga, *Kemet and the African World View* (Los Angeles: University of Sankore Press, 1986); Cummings, Niles, and Taylor, Handbook on Communication and Development in African and the African Diaspora (Needham Heights: Ginn Press, 1992); James Ward, Afro-American Communication (New York: Kendall-Hunt, 1992); Lorna L. Shaw, Kumina Dynamics: An Expression of Orature (Unpublished Ph.D. dissertation: Howard University, 1991); Leonard Barrett, *Soul Force;* Imgard Bartenieff and Forrestine Paulay, "Dance as Cultural Expression", in *Dance: An Art in Academe,* edited by Martin Haberman and Tobie Miesel (New York: Teachers College Press, 1970); Richard Dorson, *American Negro Folktales* (Greenwich: Fawcett Publishers, 1967); Frantz Fanon, *Black Skin, White Masks;* Susan Feldman, ed., *African Myths and Tales* (New York: Dell Publishing Company, 1963); Melville Herskovits, *The Myth of the Negro Past;* Melville Herskovits, *The New World Negro* (Indiana: Indiana University Press,

1966); Jahnheinz Jahn, *Muntu: The New African Culture* (New York: Grove Press, 1961); John Lovell, Jr., *Black Song: The Forge and the Flame* (New York: Macmillan Company, 1972); Henry Mitchell, *Black Belief* (New York: Harper and Row, 1975); Nicholas Cooper-Lewter and Henry H. Mitchell, *Soul Theology: The Heart of American Black Culture* (San Francisco: Harper and Row, 1968); Geoffrey Parrinder, African Mythology (London: Paul Hamlyn, 1967); Sheila S. Walker, *Ceremonial Spirit Possession in Africa and Afro-America* (Leiden: E.J. Brill, 1972).

The Rhetoric of Western Thought, as we have observed, represents an attempt to focus attention on the creative theoretical insights of European and American rhetoricians over the past three thousand years. But in reading the previous chapters, in addition to the essays on the contributions of women and African American scholars, you may have wondered if there is another point of view different from those we have already examined. The answer to this question is clearly in the affirmative, but it is an answer too detailed and complex to treat effectively here.

It is possible and useful, however, to suggest one point of view different from those we have already examined. To do so, we direct your attention now to a thoughtful essay published by Professor Roichi Okabe of Nanzan University, Nagoya, Japan. Professor Okabe received his undergraduate training in his own country before proceeding to the United States for graduate study; he holds a master's degree from Indiana University and a doctorate from Ohio State. He has authored numerous books, served as a Fulbright scholar, and lectured both in Japan and the United States on cross cultural communication—especially on the theme of Eastern and Western perspectives on discourse theory. Consequently, he is remarkably well qualified to compare two quite different cultural views on communication: the American and the Japanese.

What follows is Dr. Okabe's attempt to assess "how cultural assumptions and values of these two societies characterize the function, scope, and patterns of communication in each." We think you will find his insights both stimulating and suggestive.

Cultural Assumptions of East and West: Japan and the United States*

Roichi Okabe

There has been a growing interest over the past decade in intercultural theory of communication and rhetoric among scholars of the social sciences, philosophy, and the humanities. Many students of communication have become conscious of the critical roles that intercultural perspectives of communication theory assume both theoretically and practically.

Despite this spreading awareness of the importance of the study of communication theory from diverse approaches across national boundaries, the dominant perspective toward communication, and consequently nearly all of the studies in this field, come out of the United States. Very few researchers, for example, have examined the nature, function, and

---

*"Cultural Assumptions of East and West," pp. 21–44 in *Intercultural Communication Theory: Current Perspectives.* Copyright 1983. Reprinted by permission of Sage Publications and the author.

scope of both the theory and the practice of Japanese communication and rhetoric from intercultural perspectives.

The purpose of this chapter is to present one alternative way, namely an Eastern way, of looking at human communication by analyzing and categorizing cultural assumptions, values, and characteristics of communication and rhetoric as they are found in Japanese culture in comparison and contrast with those in the American counterpart.

More specifically, the first part of my chapter will concern itself with a preliminary exploration and analysis of cultural values as found in both societies along the line of Robert L. Scott's nuclear concepts in communication and rhetoric. He lists such concepts as "substance," "form," "strategy," "style," and "tone" as key constituents of communication.[1] This will be followed, in the second section of this study, by an analysis of how cultural assumptions and values of these two societies characterize the function, scope, and patterns of communication in each.

On the basis of the assumption of divergences between the two cultures under discussion, I will set out in this study to describe in dichotomous terms cultural values and assumptions as found in Japan and the United States. All these contrasting assumptions, however, should be viewed as differing in degree or in emphasis rather than as strictly dichotomous in substance. In other words, all these pattern variables should be taken, not as binary distinctions, but as means of pointing out a relative degree of the preponderance of one characteristic over the other. I will, therefore, employ the modifier "predominantly" frequently to indicate relatively high degrees of specific characteristics, as in "predominantly dependent," "predominantly interdependent," and so on.

> The purpose of this chapter is to present one alternative way, namely an Eastern way, of looking at human communication by analyzing and categorizing cultural assumptions, values, and characteristics of communication and rhetoric as they are found in Japanese culture in comparison and contrast with those in the American counterpart.

CULTURAL VALUES IN JAPAN AND THE UNITED STATES

Substance

Robert L. Scott lists rhetorical "substance" as the first nuclear concept in communication, and defines it as "that which enables the speaker to link the stuff of his commitments to those of his listeners."[2] He has in mind value assumptions that speakers and their listeners tend to share.

Values play an important role in rhetorical communication. Speakers or writers will try to link arguments whenever possible to positions generally held by the audience or reader. "An argumentation," the Belgian rhetorician Chaim Perelman asserts, "depends for its premises—as indeed for its entire development—on that which is accepted; that which is acknowledged as true, as normal and probable, as valid."[3] It is fair to assume that in an *intra*cultural setting a communicator and a receiver invariably share some views, desires, and values that can serve as the bases upon which a receiver-conscious communicator builds a receiver-centered case. This assumption, however, does not apply to *inter*cultural communication, where persons of diverse cultural backgrounds interact. This is why an analysis should be made of the cultural values of the Japanese and the Americans that will inevitably characterize the function, scope, and patterns of intercommunication between the two cultures under discussion.

I will here compare and contrast predominant value assumptions held by the Japanese and the Americans concerning their respective society and culture, their attitudes toward nature itself, their human relationships, and their thinking (or thought) patterns.

Values Concerning the Nature of Society and Culture

There are two key concepts for understanding the nature of Japanese society and culture: homogeneity and verticality. Whereas heterogeneity in race, language, habit, and mores is predominant in America, Japan's unusual homogeneity as a people should be emphasized as a key to explaining its culture. One cultural anthropologist, Masao Kunihira, calls Japan an "endogamous society," by which he means that "the members share a great many aspects of their daily life and consciousness."[4] Closely related to this dual concept of homogeneity and heterogeneity is that of verticality and horizontality. "In abstract terms," Chie Nakane observes, "the essential types of human relations can be divided. . . into two categories: *vertical* and *horizontal*."[5] Nakane then attempts to explain through the vertical principle the unique structure of Japanese society, which contrasts with the more horizontal nature of American society.[6]

A horizontal society, typically, is one based on the principle of assumed equality or egalitarianism. "Running through the American's social relationships with others," writes Edward C. Stewart, "is the theme of equality. . . . Interpersonal relations are typically horizontal, conducted between presumed equals."[7] One obvious contrast between Japanese and American societies is the much greater Japanese emphasis on hierarchy.[8] The concept of hierarchy remains fundamental and all-pervasive in Japanese culture, thus coloring its character and determining its shape. Japanese society is divided into numerous groupings, each structured along multiple status layers. This vertical, hierarchical arrangement is quite evident in many organizations, notably government bureaucracies and business firms. Such a speciality of the culture of Japan as the principle of homogeneity and verticality may be attributed to its unique natural conditions, its geographical isolation, and its mild climate. The Japanese have escaped invasions from the outside as well as large-scale famines.

A couple of cultural typologies may serve to explain the above-mentioned characteristics of Japanese versus American cultures. In her remarkable pioneer effort right after World War II to paint a coherent picture of Japanese culture, Ruth Benedict uses a combination of the concepts of "shame" and "guilt." She characterizes Japan as having a shame, rather than a guilt culture such as that of the United States. This means, she explains, that shame before the judgment of the society or the world is a stronger conditioning force than guilt before God. Benedict makes the distinction clear: "True shame cultures rely on external sanctions for good behavior, not, as true guilt cultures do, on an internalized conviction of sin."[9]

Another unique typology should be insightful for a contrastive analysis of Japanese and American cultures. The noted philosopher, Masao Maruyama, describes American culture as being like the *sasara,* a bamboo whisk used in the Japanese tea ceremony and characterized by the outward spreading of many fine wood strands made by carefully slitting one end of a piece of bamboo. He characterizes Japanese culture, on the other hand, as being like the *takotsubo,* or octopus pot, an urn-shaped trap that catches octopi simply by drawing them inside it. American culture, in other words, reaches outward; Japanese culture draws inward. Maruyama cites as one manifestation of the *takotsubo* character the tendency of Japanese scholars to work in a vacuum— that of taking in only what they feel is needed for their own academic pursuits and of never venturing out of their self-sufficient cubicles. While meaningful dialogues in the West are conducted among scholars in diverse branches, the only true communication and information exchange in homogeneous, vertical Japan may be observed within a single cubicle.[10]

To account for the difference between Japanese and American cultures, Maruyama and others offer yet another typology of the "doing" and the "being" orientations.[11] Such American expressions as "getting things done," "How are you doing?" "I'm doing fine—how are you coming along?" all indicate that "doing," as Stewart asserts, "is the dominant activity for Americans."[12] In a feudalistic, vertical society such as that of Japan, an individual's birth, family background, age, and rank tend to be more important than his or her later achievement and development.[13] "What he *is,*" in other words, carries a greater significance than "what he *does.*" For those who have been reared in American culture, peace, for instance, is something that must be built. They face outward to build peace and at the same time work for internal changes that will make peace more effective in the totality of things. In contrast to this American doing/building consciousness, the Japanese see peace as the status quo and something for them to preserve. They think of things happening or being of themselves. Even things that have been de-

> "True shame cultures rely on external sanctions for good behavior, not, as true guilt cultures do, on an internalized conviction of sin."

cided upon are thought of as having happened. Asked what they have been doing, Japanese are likely to answer not "I did such and such," but "Things happen to be so and so."[14]

Still another typology that serves to explain the distinction between the two cultures under consideration is that of "pushing" and "pulling" cultures. The pushing culture, according to Shinya Takatsu, a journalist, has a practical and scientific orientation represented by the development of computers and electronics. The United States represents this sort of culture. Japanese culture, by contrast, is traditionally pulling in nature in that its orientation is humanistic and aesthetic, as seen in the development of its unique, traditional music, art, and literature. Takatsu hastens to add, however, that these two seemingly contrastive modes of cultures should be seen as complementary rather than as symmetrical or diametrically opposed.[15]

Kyoto University Professor Yuji Aida sets forth one last typology to differentiate the American from the Japanese culture: that of the *omote* ("exterior" or "outside") and the *ura* ("interior" or "inside") cultures. In the heterogeneous, egalitarian, *sasara*-type, doing, pushing culture of the United States, there is no distinction between the *omote* and the *ura* aspects of culture. The predominating *omote* aspect is always taken at face value and always carries its own meaning. In the hierarchical, *takotsubo*-type, being, pulling culture of Japan, on the other hand, a clear-cut distinction should always be made between the *omote* and the *ura* dimensions of culture, the former being public, formal, and conventional, and the latter private, informal, and unconventional. The Japanese tend to conceive of the *ura* world as being more real, more meaningful.[16] This tendency of the Japanese to distinguish between the *omote* and *ura* aspects of culture is closely related to their inclination to make the sharp discrimination between belongers to (or "ins" of) a given *takotsubo* group and outsiders (or "outs").[17] At national and international levels, all foreigners are lumped together as *gaijin* (literally "outsiders") and treated as such. This exclusive attitude tends to create, as one journalist puts it, "the Japan-is-different syndrome."[18] This at best frustrates mutual exchange of information and ideas between the insiders and the outsiders in Japan.

Attitudes Toward Nature

The American mode of living is characterized by confrontation with and exploitation of the external world and by humanity's being armed against it. The conquest of natural conditions is the dominant assumption in the United States. Condon calls the American's relationship with nature a "master-slave relationship . . . with man the master of nature."[19] "The American's formidable and sometimes reckless drive to control the physical world,"[20] however, is diametrically opposed to the adaptive attitude of the Japanese toward nature. They tend to look at humanity and nature in total harmony and in eternal inseparability. They have the subtle wisdom to devise comfortable conditions for human living by adapting themselves to their natural surroundings.

Values Concerning Interpersonal Relationships

The value of independence is predominant in the horizontal, doing culture of the United States. The independent "I" and "you" clash in argument and try to persuade each other. They go so far as to enjoy argument and heated discussion as a sort of intellectual game.[21] The principle underlying this high value set on independence is the notion that each individual is solely responsible for his or her fate. What others think and say is of little significance. In contrast, it is the value assumption of interdependence that dominates the stratified, vertical, and being culture of Japan. Here pronouns such as "I" and "you" are truly "relative" in that their correct forms can only be determined in relation to the others in the interaction. Generally, "we" predominates over "I" in Japanese interpersonal relations. What others think and say is of greater importance than what the individual does. This value of interdependence, if taken to the extreme, turns to that of *amae,* namely "dependence, the desire to be passively loved, the unwillingness to be separated from the mother-child circle and cast into a world of objective 'reality.' "[22] The propensity to continue to seek dependent gratification is directly related to Japanese primary association. Commenting on this concept of *amae* as it relates to the social structure, Takeo Doi, originator of the idea, states that "*amae* is a key concept for the understanding not only of the psychological makeup of the individual Japanese but of the structure of Japanese society as a whole. The emphasis on vertical relationships . . . could . . . be seen as an emphasis on *amae.*"[23]

The concept of *amae* also underlies the Japanese emphasis on the group over the individual, the acceptance of constituted authority, and the stress on particularistic rather than universalistic relationships.

There would appear to be two distinct and diametrically opposed cultural concepts affecting both the individual and national cultures of peoples, which James Moloney, borrowing from Hamlet's famous quandry, calls "the 'to be free' concept and the 'not to be free' concept."[24] American political theory, he says, emphasizes individualism, the "to be free" idea. The American value of individualism encourages self-assertion and frank expression of opinions and shows up in the American propensity to argue back when challenged.[25] In the homogenous, vertical society of Japan, on the other hand, the dominant value is conformity to or identity with the group: The Japanese insist upon the insignificance of the individual. The group emphasis has affected the whole gamut of interpersonal relationships in Japan. A group player is more liked than a solo player, for instance. As the old Japanese saying goes, the nail that sticks out gets banged down. The Japanese, therefore, display great cautiousness in expressing personal opinions and in modifying their opinions to be consistent with those of others around them.[26]

In the American model, each individual asserts himself or herself to other individuals who are presumed to be his or her equals. This creates symmetrical relationships, based as they are "on an assumption of likeness, or similarity." The interaction between equals is predominantly the American value assumption. Japanese culture, however, values the contrastive pattern of complementary relationships based "on assumptions of differences, which complement each other to make a whole."[27] John Condon summarizes the key difference between the two cultures under discussion along the dual concept of symmetry and complementality:

> As a culture, Americans place great value on symmetrical relationships, minimizing differences that might suggest inequality. Americans tend not to like titles or honorifics that suggest some superior/subordinate relationship. . . .
>
> Symmetrical relationships maximize similarities of age, sex, role, or status and serve to encourage the apparent differences of each individual as an individual. . . . Complementary relationships [in a culture like that of Japan] maximize differences in age, sex, role, or status

> and serve to encourage the mutuality of the relationship, the interdependence.[28]

Because they are presumed to be equal and symmetrical in their relationships, the Americans tend to maximize their "public self," that is, to expose more of themselves than the Japanese, who are apt to keep their "private self" to a maximum in their interaction with others. As a result, Americans are likely to express their inner feelings and emotions openly, while Japanese tend to conceal them in an effort to maintain harmonious relations with the people around them.[29]

Another aspect of the difference between American and Japanese cultures is found in the diametrical values of informality and formality. Americans tend to treat other people with informality and directness. They shun the use of formal codes of conduct, titles, honorifics, and ritualistic manners in their interaction with others. They instead prefer a first-name basis and direct address. They also strive to equalize the language style between the sexes.[30] In sharp contrast, the Japanese are likely to assume that formality is essential in their human relations. They are apt to feel uncomfortable in some informal situations. The value of formality in the language style and in the protocol allows for a smooth and predictable interaction for the Japanese, "who cannot communicate until they know the status of the other person since the language requires different forms to correspond to the status of the listener."[31]

Contrary to American way of thinking, the Japanese are likely to employ synthetic thinking patterns—synthetic in that they try to "grasp reality in its suchness or isness, or in its totality, seeing things as they are in themselves. . . ."

Values Concerning Thinking (or Thought) Patterns

Cultural differences in patterns of thinking are important issues for both American and Japanese communicators. Analytical thinking, first of all, characterizes the thought pattern of Americans. They tend to analyze and dissect things into elements in order to understand them properly. Their emphasis is upon the parts rather than upon the whole of things. They tend to be quite strong in classification and categorization and to pursue absolute dichotomies such as good and bad, God and the devil, the individual and the whole.

Contrary to this American way of thinking, the Japanese are likely to employ synthetic thinking patterns—synthetic in that they try to "grasp reality in its suchness or isness, or in its totality, seeing things as they are in themselves. . . ."[32] They do not analyze or divide things into categories, so much as they synthesize elements into a unified whole. In this sense, their emphasis is upon the "whole."[33]

Another cultural difference in thinking patterns may be found in the American inclination toward absolutism and in the Japanese tendency toward relativism. In a society that sees itself as made up of independent and equal individuals, as indeed the United States does, any thinking pattern must predominantly be universalistic and absolutistic, applying to all individuals equally. The concepts of right and wrong, for instance, must be clear and invariable, regardless of one's personal status. In a society in which people view themselves primarily as members of groups, however, specific relationships may take precedence over universal principles. Criteria, in other words, may be more situational than absolutistic.[34]

The distinction between another set of thinking patterns, realism and idealism, should also be mentioned here. Realism is factual. It puts its focus on objective facts. This is predominantly the thinking pattern of Americans, who value objectivity, specificity, and precision.[35] In sharp contrast, Japanese thinking is predominantly that of idealism. It puts greater stress on subjective ideas than on objective facts. The Japanese tend to think introspectively and do not show too much interest in the precise details of factual events. The Japanese people, in this sense, are subjective in thinking and orientation.

This discussion of the differences in thinking patterns between the United States and Japan will be concluded with a reference to one last typology— that of "line" versus "point/dot/space." In American culture communication is not established unless the words follow a certain route. The logicality of the English language may be thought of as a line. The listener proceeds toward understanding what the speaker says as he or she follows the coherent, linear route of the speaker. In a heterogeneous and egalitarian society very little is taken for granted in communication. As a result, the logical route should be solidly paved and the listener, too, must take care not to stray from its bounds. The Japanese language, on the other hand, tends to make for a pointlike, dotlike, spacelike thinking. The speaker organizes his or her ideas and thoughts in a stepping-stone mode: The listener is supposed to supply what is left unsaid. In the homogeneous society of Japan much commonality is

taken for granted, so that the Japanese tend to value those loose modes of communication that leave much room for various interpretations.[36]

I have thus far discussed the divergences in rhetorical substance, namely the value assumptions held by American and Japanese communicators. I will now turn to an analysis of how these value assumptions influence the theory and practice of communication and rhetoric as found in American and Japanese cultures.

Form

Robert L. Scott lists rhetorical forms as the second nuclear concept in communication. Form is concerned with the problem of ordering and organizing a discourse.[37] The first difference in discourse organization between the two cultures under discussion is that of the speaker's perspective. If, as in America, the goal of the speaker in relation to his or her audience is confrontation and persuasion, then his or her form should stress those points where he or she differs with his or her opponent. The debater's case is a prime example of a point—a polarized, dichotomous, confrontational mode of organization. If the speaker's goal is harmony and consensus in a homogeneous cultural context, as in Japan, however, the communicative form is likely to be "cautious, tentative, complementary toward the others, incomplete and seeking others to make the position complete."[38] In such an aggregative form, the speaker takes great care in structuring his or her discourse before arriving at his or her point.

Allied closely to this dichotomy between polarization and aggregation in rhetorical form is that of linear and circular forms of argumentation. American logic and rhetoric value step-by-step, chainlike organization, as frequently observed in the problem-solution pattern or in the cause-to-effect or effect-to-cause pattern of organization. In this kind of communicative form, logic is tossed continuously and aggressively between the speaker and the listener, and throughout there is a sense of reinforcing each other's independence. By contrast, Japanese logic and rhetoric emphasize the importance of a dotted, pointlike method of structuring a discourse. No sense of rigidity or logicality is required in the Japanese-speaking society, where there is instead a sense of leisurely throwing a ball back and forth and carefully observing the other's response.

One of the main features of composition in the English language is the construction of a coherent and unified paragraph, a series of sentences that develop one central topic in a clear and forceful manner. Americans are encouraged to start a paragraph with a topic sentence, to develop it with specific details, and to conclude with a return to a general statement in the summary sentence. Rhetorical composition in America values a harmonious proportion between the theme and the details. "As a general rule in English composition and speaking," John Condon aptly points out, "the clearest and most appreciated presentations or explanations are those which contain a balance between the abstract and the specific."[39]

Due to the lack of the paragraph sense on the part of the Japanese, however, I find it difficult, or almost impossible, as an instructor of English and communication, to teach Japanese students of English to write a coherent English paragraph. A paragraph or even a whole composition is usually marked either by a *hosomi* form or by a *zundo* form. *Hosomi,* which literally means "slender," is a way of organizing a discourse with only specific details. *Zundo,* literally "stumpy," is a form of structuring a composition with only general statements. Excessive reliance either on the general or on the specific is a hallmark of form in Japanese rhetoric.

Americans' emphasis on a balance between the general and the specific leads them to place their strongest, most interesting points at the beginning of the series in each major part of a discourse. To put it another way, they tend to follow primacy and anticlimactic principles of organization. By contrast, Japanese communication predominantly favors recency and climactic principles of rhetorical form, saving the most interesting points for the end of the series.[40]

One last distinction in form may be observed in the American emphasis on process versus the Japanese reliance on product. Japanese is often defined as a language of product, a "terminal" language that skips process and goes immediately to a conclusion. The way the Japanese use their language involves what may appear to be leaps in logic. The English language, on the other hand, is described as the embodiment of logic, which is the process itself. Americans value the logical process by which a conclusion is to be drawn. The main difference in rhetorical mode of organization is that Japanese communication is directed toward the object "what" from the beginning, while the English language stresses the steps leading up to the "what," namely the "how" or "why."

Value assumptions influence how each culture views not only form but also strategy in rhetorical communication, which Robert Scott defines as the instruments of rhetoric that the speaker uses for eliciting the intended response from the listeners.[41] Here will be compared and contrasted the way the respective culture looks at three modes of proof in rhetoric, namely ethos, logos, and pathos, and the way each culture under consideration proceeds toward making decisions.

Rhetorical Proof

Since the days of Corax and Tisias, Western rhetorical theorists have been concerned with the role of ethos in communication. During this 2400-year period, Aristotle's view that such dimensions of ethos as intelligence, character, and good will are the most potent means of persuasion has seldom been challenged.[42] Plato, Isocrates, Cicero, and Quintilian all express similar views.[43] It is a surprising fact that almost without exception, modern empirical and experimental studies have demonstrated the theoretical importance of ethos in rhetorical communication.[44]

As a general principle, ethos may be viewed as the dominant factor in rhetorical communication across cultures. However, what constitutes ethos may differ from culture to culture. Here again, the value assumptions of each culture under discussion will give a clue to discovering the ideal constituents of ethos. Americans, for example, still tend to accept such constituents of ethos as intelligence, competence, and character as potent in communication. These qualities are achieved rather than ascribed: the speaker, in other words, has acquired them through his or her own efforts and initiative. The Japanese, on the other hand, have a tendency to subscribe to such ascribed characteristics as seniority, sex, and family background. If the speaker is old, male, and from a reputable family, he may be able to depend on these ascribed qualities in rhetorical communication. Takeshi Naruse observes that in evaluating a person's competence and qualifications, what matters in Japan is not what he or she has learned, but where he or she has learned it—more specifically, what school he or she attended.[45] Thus, as the constituents of the concept of ethos may differ from culture to culture, their influences should be taken seriously in attempting to understand intercultural communication.

The concept of logos provides another example of the difference in rhetorical theory between the two cultures. The American values of specificity, objectivity, and precision tend to lend support to the importance of using as logical proof facts, figures, and quotations from authority. These values also require exactness in citing what others have said.[46] Exact quotation is possible in a society where the unification of spoken and written forms is the rule, and not the exception. This is not the case with Japan, however. Since Japanese culture values the assumptions of subjectivity and ambiguity, the Japanese communicator is inclined to shun relying on specific facts, figures, and quotations from authority. If he or she must resort to quotations, he or she will usually paraphrase rather than quote verbatim what others have said. The main reason for the necessity of paraphrasing is that the separation of spoken and written forms is often the case with the Japanese language.

As has been discussed and analyzed in the section on thinking patterns, Americans value logical consistency, or line logic, in contrast to the extra- and paralogic, or point logic, practiced by the Japanese. Americans, in other words, are more inclined toward hard, mindlike logic than the Japanese, who tend to adopt soft, heartlike logic. As a result, Americans have a tendency to show greater preference for logos, reason, and cognition, whereas the Japanese have a tradition of highly developed words for expressing sympathy, appreciation, and encouragement. The Japanese speaker, therefore, is extremely skillful in expressing complicated emotional nuances, though he or she is weak in employing logic for the precise expression of intents and purposes.[47]

The components of rhetorical proof are thus more complicated than they might first appear to those reared in the tradition of Western rhetoric. They are strongly colored by cultural and national differences. Their nature and function should be analyzed carefully before they can be successfully introduced into intercommunication among cultures and nations.

Decision-Making Strategy

Decisions in American democracy are ideally made by the majority for the greatest good of the greatest number without infringing on the basic rights of the minority or the individual. Open conflict of views and the resolution of differences of opinions through rational discussion and by simple majority voting are both at the heart of the democratic system of the United States. Americans prefer a rational, specific, issue-oriented strategy of decision-making—issue-oriented in that they analyze the problem at hand with little regard to the human relations involved and then select the best possible solution.[48]

The Japanese, on the other hand, assume that differences of opinions can best be resolved and the most suitable decisions made not by argument and voting, but by more subtly seeking a consensus of feeling in a slow, cumbersome, and roundabout manner. Ideally, the Japanese prefer to avoid decisions, if they can, "letting nature take its course as long as the course is acceptable" for the sake of maintaining harmonious relations among members of the group.[49] Making a decision is analogous to resolving a conflict, and the ideas of conflict and confrontation are serious breaches of the Japanese values of harmony and interdependence. This is a diffuse, human-relations-oriented strategy to decision-making.[50] But when they must make a decision to resolve a conflict, the Japanese resort to the unique modes of *nemawashi,* the *ringi* system, and go-betweens.

The Japanese try to involve all relevant parties in the decision-making process. This process is called *nemawashi* or "root binding," which literally means binding the roots of a plant before pulling it out, and refers to the Japanese practice of broad consultation before taking actions for a decision. The functions of *nemawashi* include "to give each group ample time to adjust to the emerging decisions, to explain the goals of the decision and to let them understand the information that leads to this conclusion."[51] Through this method the group is in a position to elicit from its members widespread support for its final solution.

Another popular strategy employed for decision-making is the *ringi* system, which literally means "a system of reverential inquiry about the superior's intentions."[52] This system is the wide circulation of a document to which large numbers of persons affix their seals as a sign that they have seen it and ap-

> The Japanese assume that differences of opinions can best be resolved and the most suitable decisions made not by argument and voting, but by more subtly seeking a consensus of feeling in a slow, cumbersome, and roundabout manner.

proved what it says or proposes. The *ringi* system enables a group to arrive at unanimity and consensus. Referring to the considerable difference between American and Japanese methods of decision-making, Kazuo Nishiyama observes as follows: "The notion of 'decision by a majority' does not exist in the traditional Japanese process of decision-making or *ringi-seido,* because every member concerned must approve the proposal; it must be a unanimous decision. There is no decision, in the American sense, which is obtained through reasoning."[53]

To avoid confrontation and maintain group solidarity, the Japanese also tend to resort to go-betweens. In delicate interactions a neutral person seeks out the views of the two sides concerned and finds ways of resolving differences or else terminates the negotiations without the danger of loss of face on either side.[54]

Style

Rhetorical style is the fourth nuclear concept in communication. Robert Scott defines it as "the way in which language works to embody the communicative intentions of its users."[55] Here, too, the rhetorical canon of style is subject to the influence of cultural values and assumptions.

Reflecting the cultural value of precision, Americans' tendency to use explicit words is the most noteworthy characteristic of their communicative style. They prefer to employ such categorical words as "absolutely," "certainly," and "positively," even to the point of playing the devil's advocate. The English syntax dictates that the absolute "I" be placed at the beginning of a sentence in most cases, and that the subject-predicate relation be constructed in an ordinary sentence.[56] Americans are also inclined to value overstatement, exaggeration, and even oversimplification. They like to use superlative ranking phrases such as "the greatest," "the biggest," "the longest." In their eagerness to oversimplify the reality, they tend to describe it in a dichotomous, either-or pattern. In addition, they lean toward relying on "square words" with "square logic."

By contrast, the cultural assumptions of interdependence and harmony require that Japanese speakers limit themselves to implicit and even ambiguous use of words. In order to avoid leaving an assertive impression, they like to depend more frequently on qualifiers such as "maybe," "perhaps," "probably," and "somewhat."[57] Since Japanese syntax does not require the use of the subject in a sentence, the qualifier-predicate is a predominant form of sentence construction. This omission of the subject often leaves much room for ambiguity. The "I" is not dominant, as in English; its nature is rather determined by its relationship with others. In this sense, it is truly a relative pronoun. Another source of ambiguity in style is found in the preference of Japanese for understatement and hesitation rather than for superlative expressions. Lastly, they are likely to resort to "round words" with associative, "round logic."

Due to the influence of the doing/making orientation in American culture, English sentences are predominantly studded with action verbs. The cultural value of being orientation, on the other hand, requires speakers of Japanese to depend on state verbs that indicate their adherence to the status quo.

A doing-oriented culture is remarkable for its informality, spontaneity, and freedom from adherence to strict stylistic patterns. Americans try very hard to equalize their language and their interpersonal relations, despite differences of age, status, and sex, through an extensive use of informal, colorful, and at times humorous expressions in communication. Humor, in particular, is taken as an effective leveler of differences in interpersonal relations.

It is equally natural for the Japanese to shape their hierarchical relationships through the use of prescribed expressions. Japanese ceremoniousness in style is usually expressed in the varying degrees of honorific language, which differ not only in vocabulary but also in grammar. Failure to choose the correct word may mean offending someone. Consequently, they tend to think it safer to resort to platitudes, cliches, and set phrases than to devise fresh expressions for each interaction. The Japanese, in this sense, are more conscious about the form than about the content of communication.[58]

Another way of looking at the differences in American and Japanese rhetorical styles is to examine the degree of reliance upon what Basil Bernstein calls "elaborated" and restricted speech patterns.[59] In a "low context" culture, namely a "highly individualized, somewhat alienated, fragmented" culture like that of the United States, the lack of shared assumptions requires the American speaker to verbalize his or her message to make his or her discrete intent clear and explicit.[60] Americans are thus more inclined to resort to "the verbal elaboration of meaning."[61] By contrast, Japanese is a typical "high-context" culture, in which "people are deeply involved with each other . . . information is widely shared . . . [and] simple messages with deep meaning flow freely."[62] In such a culture the people have traditionally established and preserved a great number of specific rules of conduct and forms of expression. They do not have to elaborate their speech codes. They can indeed safely depend on restricted codes of speech, which may be taken as "status-oriented speech system . . . [which] reinforces the form of the social difference."[63] With this speech system the Japanese speaker tends to minimize extra- and paraverbal aspects of communication. Bernstein sums up the characteristics of restricted codes as follows:

The "how" of the communication would be important rather than the "what." The discrete intent of the speakers, the "I" of the speakers, would be transmitted not through varying the verbal selections, but through varying the expressive features of the communication, through changes in gestures, physical set, intonation, facial modifications.[64]

My assumption is that differences in style such as these between the two cultures under consideration here must be taken into account for understanding intercultural communication. These are acquired habits indicating widely shared assumptions held by the communicators within a particular culture. Cultural influences on rhetoric and communication are thus more complicated and far-reaching than they might first appear to be.

Tone

I have thus far discussed cultural assumptions of rhetoric as they concern the nuclear concepts of substance, form, strategy, and style. My discussion will now turn to the last nuclear concept, what Robert Scott calls "tone." By tone Scott has in mind "the speaker's attitude toward his listeners."[65]

In American rhetoric the speaker tends to view himself or herself as an agent of change, manipulating and persuading his or her listeners in a confrontational setting. There is a clear differentiation of roles between the speaker and the audience. The speaker is a transmitter of information, ideas, and opinions, while the audience is a receiver of these speech messages. The theory of Western rhetoric has long emphasized the importance of audience adaptation, but this concept, too, carries the implication that audience adaptation is a mere rhetorical tech-

nique always to be viewed from the side of the speaker. The speaker still remains the central, potent agent of attitude change and persuasion. To communicate well means, for the American speaker, to express himself or herself logically and persuasively. Focus on the expressive is a hallmark of American rhetoric.

By contrast, the rhetoric of Japan is remarkable for its emphasis on the importance of the perceiver. The Japanese people, in a sense, are excellent perceivers, capable of accurately tuning in to the faintest of signals. There is not a clear differentiation, but rather an integration of roles between the speaker and the audience. The speaker, therefore, always attempts to adjust himself or herself to his or her listeners. In a culture of *sasshi* or *omoiyari* (both words meaning "considerateness"), to communicate well means, for the Japanese speaker, to understand and perceive the inexplicit, even to the point of deciphering the faintest nuances of nonverbal messages. *Sasshi ga ii,* or "being a good mind reader," and *omoiyari ga aru,* or "being considerate about other's feelings," are both considered virtues in Japanese culture.[66] Impressive or perceptive emphasis remains a potent orientation in the rhetoric of Japan.

The *erabi* ("selective") and *awase* ("adjustive") typology proposed by Kinhide Mushakoji will here serve to illustrate the crucial difference in the concept of tone between speaker-centered and perceiver-centered cultures.[67] The *erabi* or selective view holds that human beings can manipulate their environment for their own purposes, as the speaker consciously constructs his or her message for the purpose of persuading and producing attitude change. *Erabi* means choosing the best from a range of alternatives to effect such change.

The *awase* or adjustive view, on the other hand, assumes that human beings will adapt and aggregate themselves to the environment rather than change and exploit it, as the speaker attempts to adjust himself or herself to the feelings of his or her listeners. *Awase* is the logic not of choosing between but of aggregating several alternatives. Mushakoji succinctly describes communication patterns in *awase* culture as follows:

Awase logic does not depend upon standardized word meanings. Expressions have multifarious nuances and are considered to be only signals which hint at reality rather than describing it precisely. Words are not taken at face value; it is necessary to infer the meaning behind them. In contrast to erabi *culture in which the face value of words is trusted most and one is expected to act on it, in* awase *society it is possible to "hear one and understand ten." It is interesting to note that in Japan it is considered virtuous to "catch on quickly" . . . to adjust to someone's position before it is logically and clearly enunciated.*[68]

The first part of this chapter has thus discussed how cultural values, assumptions, and presuppositions of American and Japanese cultures both reveal and shape the kind of rhetorical theory practiced in each society under the influence of substance composed of value assumptions on the rhetorical concepts of form, strategy, style, and tone.

THE INFLUENCE OF VALUES ON COMMUNICATION

Overall Nature of Rhetoric and Communications

The second part of this chapter will briefly summarize, again in contrastive terms, the overall nature of the theory and practice of rhetoric and communication as understood in the United States and in Japan. It should be stressed once again that these summary views should be taken to indicate differences in degree rather than strict dichotomies in substance.

> The Japanese value harmony and view harmony-establishing and/or harmony-maintaining as a dominant function of communication.

Functions of Rhetoric and Communications

Rhetoric, in the Western sense of the word, is concerned with persuasion pursued at public forums. The prototype of the American speaker consciously uses symbols to create an understanding and to form, strengthen, or change an attitude on the part of his or her listeners. American rhetoric, in this sense, is basically argumentative and logical in nature.[69] It is also confrontational in that the speaker as an independent agent always stands face to face with the listener as another independent agent. Confrontation carries a positive connotation in American rhetoric: It is seen as a dynamic force for the advancement of Western civilization.[70]

The Japanese, on the other hand, value harmony and view harmony-establishing and/or harmony-maintaining as a dominant function of communication. They seek to achieve harmony by a subtle process of mutual understanding, almost by intuition, avoiding any sharp analysts of conflicting views. The result is that Japanese rhetoric functions as a means of disseminating information or of seeking consensus. It is by nature intuitive, emotional, and adaptive.

Dominant Modes of Rhetoric and Communication

There are at least two completely different systems of communication: dialogue and monologue. Dialogue, in the Western sense of the word, aims to clarify the points of disagreement. The dialogical or dialectical mode of communication is a dominant characteristic of American rhetoric and an especially effective means of resolving differences between two parties with diverse interests or backgrounds. Dialogue in this sense of the word, however, will not often appear between Japanese. Even when the mode of communication appears to be dialogical on the surface, its content is no more than alternating monologue; in their eagerness that their views conform, the two sides do not truly engage each other in discussion. Japanese communication tends to be monologic, since Japanese is basically a "chamber" language, not suitable for public discussion or speech at a big hall. In this sense Japanese is quite different from English, which fulfills the requirements of a "public hall" language.[71]

The digital and analogical dimensions of expression proposed by Watzlawick and his colleagues also serve to explain dominant modes of communication.[72] In a digital mode of communication there is no necessary connection between what is expressed and how it is expressed. Since the relationship is arbitrarily assigned, it must be learned. The digital is more characteristic of the American mode of communication. In an analogical mode of expression, however, the relationship between the content and the form is so close that with little training one can guess at the meaning of many analogical forms. The Japanese language is more inclined toward the analogical: its use of ideographic characters, its reliance on onomatopoeia, and its emphasis on the nonverbal aspect.

The excessive dependence of the Japanese on the nonverbal aspect of communication means that Japanese culture tends to view the verbal as only a means of communication, and that the nonverbal and the extraverbal at times assume greater importance than the verbal dimension of communication. This is in sharp contrast to the view of Western rhetoric and communication that the verbal, especially speech, is *the* dominant means of expression.

In a low-context culture, like that of the United States, where very little is taken for granted, greater cultural diversity and heterogeneity are likely to make verbal skills more necessary and, therefore, more highly prized. One of the chief qualifications of a group leader, indeed, is his or her ability of verbal expression. Group leaders should be able to analyze and outline varying positions, clarify their differences, and invite open discussion and confrontation.

In a high context culture such as a Japan's, however, cultural homogeneity encourages suspicion of verbal skills, confidence in the unspoken, and eagerness to avoid confrontation. The Japanese have even developed *haragei,* or the "art of the belly" for the meeting of minds or at least the viscera, without clear verbal interaction. Verbal ability is not necessarily required of Japanese leaders. They are, indeed, expected to perform this *haragei* art.

> The excessive dependence of the Japanese on the nonverbal aspect of communication means that Japanese culture tends to view the verbal as only a means of communication, and that the nonverbal and the extraverbal at times assume greater importance than the verbal dimension of communication.

Other Characteristics of Rhetoric and Communication

The goal of Western societies, including the United States, is a civilization of the dialogue and public speaking. The spirit of Western civilization is the spirit of inquiry. Its dominant theme is the logos. Nothing is to remain undiscussed. Everybody speaks their minds eloquently and persuasively. The exchange of ideas is held to be the path to the realization of the potentialities of each society. America, in this sense, is a communication-active society.

In the tradition of rhetoric and communication, however, Japan stands out in marked contrast to much of the world. The feudalistic, hierarchical society of Japan is most notable for its emphasis on writing and for its total lack of a tradition of public speaking. Modesty, humility, and supression of self are moral ideals in this communication-passive society. These moral qualities lead to a shyness in communication behaviors rare in the age of aggressive self-assertion.

As a corollary to all of this, the Japanese have developed "aesthetics of silence" in place of rhetoric and logic. They tend to view silence as essential to self-realization and sublimation. This is diametrically opposed to the American way of looking at silence as symptomatic of a problem. It is a fairly recent development, and a good sign for students of intercultural communication, though, that in the communication-active American society some attention is being paid to the importance of silence as an emerging area of rhetorical research.[73]

CONCLUSION

The first and second parts of this chapter have stressed the divergence and difference in cultural values, assumptions, and presuppositions as investigated and taught in American and Japanese theories of rhetoric and communication. It has been repeatedly called to mind throughout this chapter that the contrasting views outlined and analyzed here should be taken not as strictly dichotomous in substance but as differing more in degree. Although the main concern of this chapter has been with a comparison and contrast of "A" (for "American")-type theory and "J" (for "Japanese") type theory of rhetoric and communication, this study implies some possibility of A-type theory coming closer to J-type theory and vice versa. This also suggests the possibility of constructing a Z-type theory of communication, an amalgam or an aggregation of both A-type theory and J-type theory, which could bridge the schism in communication among cultures and nations.[74]

My future interest will be in investigating to what extent these seemingly dichotomous assumptions of rhetoric and communication might converge on the continuum and under what conditions this convergence will be made possible. I take it as a good sign for students of intercultural communication that some scholars of an A-type theory have gradually directed their attention to the rhetorical significance of silence, a unique concept in J-type theory. It should be pointed out at the same time that some Japanese reared in J-type theory have found it necessary, or almost inevitable, to approach intercultural communication with something of A-type orientation to communication. They will have to "consciously construct and organize verbal messages" for the purpose of "persuading" their listeners of divergent cultural backgrounds, if they are to be successful in communicating across national and cultural boundaries. They will have to avoid "yes-no" ambiguity and to learn "how to agree to disagree" at international conferences and negotiations.[75]

It is to be hoped that this chapter will respond to the schism that might exist in Western and Eastern communicologists' understanding of intercultural communication and offer one impetus for encouraging joint explorations by communication scholars on both sides of the Pacific as to the possibility of constructing a Z-type theory of cultural rhetoric and communication.

Notes

1. Robert L. Scott, "The Generative Power of Rhetorical Problems," in *The Speaker's Reader: Concepts in Communication* (Glenview, IL: Scott, Foresman, 1969), pp. 2–22.

2. Scott, *The Speaker's Reader,* p. 9.

3. Chaim Perelman, *The Idea of Justice and the Problem of Argument,* trans. John Petrie (New York: Humanities Press, 1969), p. 159. For a discussion of the importance of values in communication, see Wayne C. Minnick, *The Art of Persuasion* (Boston: Houghton Mifflin, 1957), pp. 207–22.

4. Masao Kunihiro, "The Japanese Language and Intercultural Communication," in *The Silent Power: Japan's Identity and World Role,* ed. Japan Center for International Exchange (Tokyo: Simul Press, 1976), pp. 57–58.

5. Chie Nakane, *Japanese Society* (Berkeley: University of California Press, 1970), p. 23.

6. The theme of Nakane's other books is also centered around the vertical principle in Japanese society. See her *Tateshakai no ningenkankei* [Interpersonal Relationships in a Vertical Society] (Tokyo: Kodansha, 1967) and *Tateshakai no rikigaku* [Dynamism in a Vertical Society] (Tokyo: Kodansha, 1978).

7. Edward C. Stewart, *American Cultural Patterns: A Cross-Cultural Perspective* (Pittsburgh, PA: University of Pittsburgh, 1971), p. 46, and Edwin O. Reischauer, *The Japanese* (Tokyo: Charles E. Tuttle, 1977), p. 157.

8. Reischauer, *The Japanese,* pp. 151–157.

9. Benedict, *The Chrysanthemum and the Sword: Patterns of Japanese Culture* (Cleveland, OH: World Publishing Co., 1946), p. 223. See also Bin Kimura, "'Ma' to kojin" ["Space" and the Individual], ed. Takehiko Kenmouchi (Tokyo: Kodansha, 1981), pp. 232–33, and Yujiro Shinoda, *Hokori to nihonjin* [Pride and the Japanese People] (Kyoto: PHP Institute, 1980), pp. 123–52.

10. Masao Matuyama, *Nihon no shiso* [The Intellectual Tradition in Japan] (Tokyo: Iwanami Shoten, 1961), pp. 123–52.

11. Maruyama, *Nihon no shiso,* pp. 153–80: Stewart, American Cultural Patterns, pp. 31–33; John C. Condon and Fathi S. Yousef, *An Introduction to Intercultural Communication* (Indianapolis, IN: Bobbs-Merrill Co., 1975), pp. 71–73, 137; Yuji Aida, *Nihonjin no ishiki kozo* [The Structure of the Japanese Consciousness] (Tokyo: Kodansha, 1972), pp. 36–37; Shichihei Yamamoto, *Nihonjin teki hasso to seiji bunka* [The Japanese Way of Thinking and Political Culture] (Tokyo: Nihon Shoseki, 1979), p. 208. The most recent book on this topic published in Japanese is Yoshihiko Ikegami, *"Suru" to "naru" no gengogaku* [The "Doing" and the "Becoming" Linguistics] (Tokyo: Taishu-kan Shoten, 1981).

12. Stewart, *American Cultural Patterns,* pp. 31–32.

13. Maruyama, *Nihon no shiso,* pp. 158–59.

14. Aida, *Nihon no shiso,* pp. 36–37.

15. *Shinya Takatsu, Hiku bunka osu bunka* ["Pulling" Culture and "Pushing" Culture] (Tokyo: Kodansha, 1977), p. iv.

16. Aida, *Nihonjin no ishiki kozo,* pp. 57–59.

17. Matuyama, *Nihon no shiso,* p. 139.

18. Fumi Saisho, *Nihongo to eigo* [Japanese and English] (Tokyo: Kenkyusha, 1975), p. 11.

19. Condon, *Intercultural Communication,* p. 103.

20. Stewart, *American Cultural Patterns,* p. 59.

21. Reiko Naotsuka, *Obeijin ga chinmoku suru toki: Ibunka kan komyunikeishon* [When Europeans and Americans Keep Silent: Intercultural Communication] (Tokyo: Taishukan Shoten, 1980), pp. 116–17.

22. Takeo Doi, *Anatomy of Dependence,* trans. John Bester (Tokyo: Kodansha International, 1973), p. 7.

23. Doi, *Dependence,* p. 28.

24. James Clark Moloney, *Understanding the Japanese Mind* (Tokyo: Charles E. Tuttle Co., 1954), p. 2.

25. Takao Suzuki, *Kotoba to bunka* [Language and Culture] (Tokyo: lwanami Shoten, 1973), pp. 202–203 and Stewart, *American Cultural Patterns,* pp. 68–71.

26. Shinoda, *Hokori to nihonjin,* pp. 204–5 and Reischauer, *The Japanese,* pp. 127–35.

27. John C. Condon, *Interpersonal Communication* (New York: Macmillan Publishing Co., 1977), p. 52.

28. Condon, *Interpersonal Communication,* pp. 53–54.

29. Dean C. Barnlund, *Nihonjin no hyogen kozo* [The Structure of Japanese Way of Expression], trans. Sen Nishiyama (Tokyo: Simul Press, 1973), pp. 35, 59. See also Barnlund, "The Public Self and the Private Self in Japan and the United States," in *Intercultural Encounters with Japan: Communication—Contact and Conflict,* eds. John C. Condon and Mitsuko Saito (Tokyo: Simul Press, 1974), pp. 27–96.

30. Stewart, *American Cultural Patterns,* pp. 49–50 and Condon, *Intercultural Communication,* pp. 86–87.

31. Stewart, *American Cultural Patterns,* p. 50.

32. Charles A. Moore, *The Japanese Mind: Essentials of Japanese Philosophy and Culture* (Tokyo: Charles E. Tuttle, 1967), p. 290.

33. For a discussion of the relation between the parts and the whole, see Hideo Yamashita, *Nihon no kotoba to kokoro* [The Japanese Language and Mind] (Tokyo: Kodansha, 1979), pp. 33–34.

34. Nobutane Kiuchi, "Fushigi na kuni' nihon o tsukurageta nihonjin" [Japanese Who have Made up a "Wonderland Japan"], in *Nihonjin ni tsuite no jisho* ITen Chapters on Japanese], ed. Yasutaka Teruoka (Tokyo: Chobunsha, 1981), p. 53.

35. John C. Condon, "The Values Approach to Cultural Patterns of Communication," in *Intercultural Encounters with Japan,* p. 150.

36. Shinoda, *Hokori to nihonjin,* pp. 208–15. For a discussion of line like and point like thinking patterns, see Shigehiko Toyama, *Nihongo no ronri* [The Logic of Japanese] Chuo Koronsha, 1975), and *Shoryaku no bungaku* [Omission in Literature] (Tokyo: Chuo Koronsha, 1976).

37. Scott, *The Speaker's Reader,* pp. 6–9.

38. Condon, *Intercultural Communication,* p. 243.

39. John C. Condon, *Words, Words, Words: What We Do with Them and What They Do to Us* (Tokyo: Seibido, 1977), p. 33. For a discussion of the general-specific balance, see also Condon, *Semantics and Communication* (New York: Macmillan, 1966), pp. 39–45.

40. Naotsuka, *Obeijin ga chinmoku suru toki,* pp. 245–45, and Shigehiko Toyarea, *Kotowaza no ronri* [The Logic of Proverbs] (Tokyo Shoseki, 1979), pp. 204–11.

41. Scott, *The Speaker's Reader,* pp. 11–12.

42. Lane Cooper, trans. *The Rhetoric of Aristotle* (New York: Appleton-Century-Crofts, 1932), p. 92.

43. W.M. Sattier, "Conceptions of Ethos in Ancient Rhetoric," *Speech Monographs,* 14 (March 1947): pp. 55–65.

44. For a modern interpretation of the concept of ethos see James C. McCroskey, *An Introduction to Rhetorical Communication,* 3rd ed. (Englewood Cliffs, NJ: Prentice-Hall, 1978), pp. 67–85.

45. Takeshi Naruse, *Kotoba no jika* [The Magnetic Field of Language] (Hiroshima: Bunka Hyoron Shuppan, 1979), p. 60.

46. Shichihei Yamamoto, *Nihonteki hasso to seiji bunka,* pp. 208–11.

47. For a discussion of the relation between reason and emotion see Yuichi Aira, "Shiron 'nihonjin'" [Personal Views on the Japanese], in Teruoka, *Nihonjin ni tsuite no jissho,* p. 177, and Tadanobu Tsunoda, *Nihonjin no no: No No*

hataraki to tozai no bunka [The Japanese Brains: Their Functions in Eastern and Western Culture] (Tokyo: Taishukan Shoten, 1978), p. 85.

48. Kinhide Mushakoji, *Kodo kagaku to kokusai seiji* [Behavioral Sciences and International Politics] (Tokyo: Tokyo University Press, 1972), p. 232.

49. Richard Halloran, *Japan: Images and Realities* (Tokyo: Charles E. Tuttle, 1969), p. 90.

50. Mushakoji, *Kodo kagaku to kokusai seiji,* p. 233.

51. Ezra F. Vogel, *Japan as Number One: Lessons for America* (Cambridge, MA: Harvard University Press, 1979), p. 94.

52. Kiyoaki Tsuji, "Decision-Making in the Japanese Government: A Study of *Ringisei,*" in *Political Development in Modern Japan,* ed. Robert E. Ward (Princeton, NJ: Princeton University Press, 1968), p. 457.

53. Kazuo Nishiyama, "Interpersonal Persuasion in a Vertical Society—The Case of Japan," *Speech Monographs,* 38 (June 1971): p. 149.

54. Condon discusses the role of go-betweens in communication in his *Interpersonal Communication,* pp. 55–58.

55. Scott, *The Speaker's Reader,* p. 13.

56. Hideo Kishimoto, "Some Cultural Traits and Religions," in Moore, ed., *The Japanese Mind,* pp. 110–11.

57. Condon, *Intercultural Communication,* pp. 217–18.

58. Yasushi Haga, *Nihonjin wa ko hanashita* [This Is How the Japanese Spoke] (Tokyo: Jitsugyo no Nihonsha, 1976), pp. 233–34 and Akiko Jugaku, *Nihongo no urakata* [The Background of the Japanese Language] (Tokyo: Kodansha, 1978), p. 29.

59. Basil Bernstein, "Elaborated and Restricted Codes: Their Social Origins and Some Consequences," *American Anthropologist,* 66 (December 1964) (Special Publication): pp. 55–69.

60. Edward T. Hall, *Beyond Culture* (Garden City, NY: Anchor Books, 1976), p. 39.

61. Bernstein, "Elaborated and Restricted Codes," p. 63.

62. Hall, *Beyond Culture,* p. 39.

63. Bernstein, "Elaborated and Restricted Codes," p. 63.

64. Bernstein, "Elaborated and Restricted Codes," p. 61.

65. Scott, The *Speaker's Reader,* p. 14.

66. Takeo Suzuki, *Kotoba to shakai* [Language and Society] (Tokyo: Chuo Koronsha, 1975), pp. 65, 84–85; Takao Suzuki, *Kotoba to bunka,* pp. 201–2; and Aida, *Nihonjin no ishiki kozo,* p. 98.

67. Kinhide Mushakoji, "The Cultural Premises of Japanese Diplomacy," in *The Silent Power,* pp. 35–49.

68. Mushakoji, "The Cultural Premises," p. 43.

69. Condon, *Intercultural Communication,* pp. 190, 213, 232.

70. Hideaki Kase, *Nihonjin no hasso seiyojin no hasso* [The Japanese Way of Thinking and the Western Way of Thinking] (Tokyo: Kodansha, 1977), p. 31.

71. Takehide Kenmochi, "Nihongo to 'ma' no kozo" [The Japanese Language and the Structure of "Space"], in *Nihonjin* to *"ma,"* p. 26, and Shigehiko Toyama, *Hajime ni kotoba ariki* [In the Beginning Was the Word] (Tokyo: Kodansha, 1981), pp. 128–30.

72. Paul Watzlawick, Janet Beavin, and Don Jackson, *Pragmatics of Human Communication* (New York W.W. Norton, 1967).

73. For a discussion of the importance of silence in communication, see Thomas J. Bruneau, "Communicative Silences: Forms and Functions of Silence," ETC, 30 (1973): and Richard L. Johannesen, "The Functions of Silence: A Plea for Communication Research," *Western Speech,* 38 (Winter 1974): pp. 25–35.

74. The terms A-type theory, J-type theory, and Z-type theory are directly taken from a best-selling book by William G. Ouchi, professor of business administration at UCLA, who has most recently proposed the importance of Z-type theory of business management, an amalgam of A-type and J-type theories of organizing and managing businesses. See his *Theory Z: How American Business Can Meet the Japanese Challenge* (Reading, MA: Addison-Wesley, 1981).

75. The *Asahi Shimbun,* an influential daily in Japan, recently commented on the marked change in the communication patterns of the Japanese participants at the Fifth Japan-U.S. Shimoda Conference held in September 1981. The participants from the Japanese side actively expressed their opinions and voiced their disagreements aggressively at times. See *Asahi Shimbun,* Evening ed., September 4, 1981: p. 3.

A Rhetorical and Communication Theory for the 21st Century

Since the 7th edition of The Rhetoric of Western Thought was published at the onset of the 21st Century, we have concluded that the final chapter should look toward the future in an effort to determine the probable direction which rhetorical and communication theory might take in the decades ahead. As an initial step in the construction of this chapter, we invited J. Michael Sproule, a Professor of Communication Studies at San Jose University, to write an essay titled "Toward a Rhetoric for the New Millennium." Dr. Sproule, a distinguished author of books and monographs on rhetorical theory and practice, completed his undergraduate and graduate degrees at Ohio State University, and thus is very familiar with the rhetorical tradition that is featured in The Rhetoric of Western Thought.

As a second step in the formulation of this chapter, we received a copy of Thomas McCain's lecture on "Information and Knowledge On-line: Teaching and Learning in the Communication Age." It was presented at the University of Utah in 1998 as part of the B. Aubrey Fisher Memorial Lecture Series." A copy of the address was sent to us by Robert K. Avery, a Professor of Communication at the University of Utah.

As you read these innovative and provocative papers, several points concerning each study are worthy of special attention. Using American history during the past 200 years as a starting point for his remarks, Michael Sproule surveys such dynamic, developing themes as individual life-style changes, media innovations, varieties of social organization, and communicating in an age of choices. On this latter point, he suggests the need for communicators to find their existential stance and their social or ideological stance. In discussing these ideas, Professor Sproule offers numerous possibilities that will be available to us in a discourse situation in the 21st Century. Finally, he demonstrates how rhetors may locate themselves as millennial communicators.

At the heart of Thomas McCain's lecture on the crucial role that communication may play in knowledge creation and sharing is his belief that "collaboration is a necessary condition for learning with technology." This is necessary, he argues, because we are living in an age of "information abundance." Influenced by his experiences in the laboratory and by his numerous research studies regarding the electronic media, Professor McCain persuasively states that more attention in the learning process should be given to a dialogical view than to the traditional lecture format. A dialogical perspective, he tells us, "starts with the premise that knowledge is something humans acquire through actively creating and organizing their own experiences." This method of collaboration "to solve problems of relevance," he concludes, is what digital technology is all about. The challenge facing us, therefore, "is to act our way into a new way of thinking." With this rationale as a guiding principle, a rhetoric of the future will have a progressively stronger interpersonal communication dimension.

Toward a Rhetoric for the New Millennium

◈

J. Michael Sproule

Millennial idioms such as Y2K and imagery such as Generation X convey the clear sense that ours is a season of accelerating change and renewal. Students of rhetoric easily may find tropes of transformation to designate evolutions in every aspect of the communicative enterprise including speaker (host, website), audience (e-groups, netizens), media (internet world, instant messaging), and public life in general (chatrooms, webcasts). E-terminology is particularly unstable and, therefore, supplies only an uncertain guide to communication in the new century. Taken as a whole, however, innovations in our symbols designating communication suggest the outlines of the rhetorical transactions to be encountered in the next generation. At the very least, the new language seems to promise a world of personal choice that is available at great speed and by means of significant technology.

Choice, speed, and high tech are conditions that seem likely to hold forth well into the millennium, but we realize that they do not describe every aspect of our lives. To fully assess a rhetoric of the new millennium we must consider how choice, speed, and technology relate to the full stream of experiences that are available in our contemporary world. Here it will prove helpful to organize social developments around the three concepts of modernism, *pre*modernism, and *post*modernism. These closely connected terms provide a framework for tracking the evolution of daily life during the last two centuries. The tracks that we find may point to communication pathways of the new century.

PREMODERNISM, MODERNISM, POSTMODERNISM

The choices offered us for the new millennial rhetoric are based on cumulative social changes registered during the last 200 years in the United States. During this time, social arrangements have evolved from a *pre*-modern condition of rural subsistence living to a *modern* national, urban market economy of consumer goods to a *post*-modern arrangement of technological innovation in a diverse society undergoing global migration. These three large-scale social settings—premodernism, modernism, and postmodernism—set the context for what we will experience as communicators in the new century.

*Pre*modern America (here denoting the United States) was largely a rural society based on subsistence farming. With the exception of a small number of large plantations in the South, the landscape of America was that of a spreading quilt of individual farmsteads, usually tended by one family. Owing to poor transportation, farm folk had little incentive to produce more than was needed for subsistence. A small crop surplus might usefully be traded with neighbors for home-produced goods (clothes, tools, or other individual specialties) or to generate a small amount of cash for the payment of taxes. Until the onset of the modern market economy, the basic pattern was that of subsistence and local self-sufficiency.

In the years after the War of 1812, improvements in transportation and the development of factory production using water power extended the cash-and-credit economy to many regions of the U.S. Farmers now produced for the market, growing more than they could consume in the expectation of cash income. Towns matured as farm commodities and factory goods sought buyers.[1] Two generations later, the large metropolitan cities of the early twentieth century represented the epitome of American modernism, a social condition that emphasized organized homogeneity. Notable here were factory assembly lines organized around the One Best Way of doing something and the crush of new immigrants who were expected to "Americanize" (i.e., speak,

Contributed by Mike Sproule.

dress and act similarly to the native-born) as soon as possible.[2]

The transition to *post*modernism accelerated after the 1950s with a rise in ethnic diversity and high technology. In the sphere of immigration, movement into the U.S. increased significantly such that the percentage of foreign-born residents in the U.S. population grew from 4.7 percent in 1970 to 9.3 percent in 1998. Furthermore, beginning in the 1960s, American laws favored non-European populations such that, in 1999, the largest groups of immigrants were Latinos and Asians.[3] During this time various electronic technologies combined to create the wired city. Gradually technology became less an adjunct to urban civilization and more the very environment that shaped experience. In the view of Jacques Ellul, the French theorist, technology rather than people had become the essential atmosphere of society.[4] With each new family of gadgets—television, computer, fax, cell phone, internet—people were more able to create their own personal rhetorical setting. Now there was less need to adapt to immediate neighbors who, because of increased population diversity, were more likely to seem unfamiliar.

Today we inherit a social world that consists of mingled parts of premodernism, modernism, and postmoderism. While no longer dominant, the earliest American hallmarks of family-based subsistence production persist wherever people experience close and strong family life, most notably where there is a family business. More in evidence is the lingering environment of modernism whose presence may be detected whenever we either encounter organizations that march to the beat of fixed operating procedures (e.g., a national food franchise) or find individuals aiming to live similar lives (as in today's gated life-style enclaves). Because we still encounter elements of social premodernism and modernism, today's familiar *post*modern conditions of human diversity mixed with high-tech individuality have not brought about a complete revolution from previous social situations; rather, these postmodern features rep-

> Today we inherit a social world that consists of mingled parts of premodernism, modernism, and postmoderism.

resent the leading edge of social experience. Conditions of premodernism, modernism, and postmodernism coexist today in the United States somewhat as concentric circles. Any given American may simultaneously experience elements of the three social conditions as when a farm kid enrolls in the big-city college, or when an urban factory worker develops an affinity for selling on eBay, or when a youngster who once hung out in an internet chat room now experiences the discipline of the Army.

Choice seems to be the operative word for people such as ourselves whose social world is a pool containing ripples of *pre*modernism, modernism and *post*modernism. We may expect that millennial message makers will roam through a vast variety of available experiences in search of what is personally congenial. Out of a universe of possibilities they will construct an individualized setting of favored ideas and associates. Message makers of the new century may be likened to e-consumers because, like one-click shoppers, they will be searching through a vast range of options, gathering up a shopping basket of choices, and then packaging these personally relevant selections for quick delivery and consumption.

> Message makers of the new century may be likened to e-consumers because, like one-click shoppers, they will be searching through a vast range of options, gathering up a shopping basket of choices, and then packaging these personally relevant selections for quick delivery and consumption.

Having established e-shopping as the millennial metaphor of communication, we are driven to know more about the specific choices available to millennial message makers. These content options will become clearer as we probe key developments in the metamorphosis by which postmodernism grew out of modernism which, in turn, emerged from premodernism. Out of each social transformation came new ways of living, sending symbols, and relating to others. We may turn to three categories of experiences produced by these transitions: (1) life-style changes, (2) media innovations, and (3) varieties of social organization.

INDIVIDUAL LIFE-STYLE CHANGES

The home base of millennial communicators will be the style of life that they fashion for themselves. To assess where we are, and where we are going, it is useful to consider two fundamental ways that our life world differs from that of our predecessors. First, our emphasis is on private life rather than public life and, second, our tendency is to base our self concept on image more than character.

Public versus Private Orientation

The last two hundred years have seen a substantial decline in Americans' interest in community doings with a corresponding rise in a private orientation. These years have seen a growth in individualism, in popular culture, and in the personal consumption of goods.

> In contrast to colonial life's community-centered character, modernism emphasized the individual decision maker as central to society.

From Community to Individual

Colonial times represented the acme of the communal world view. Dwellings consisted of a few large, unspecialized rooms in which people cooked, ate, slept, worked, and visited; people sat on benches instead of individual chairs and ate from common bowls instead of using individual table settings. Outside the individual home, politics, religion, and entertainment all proceeded along communal lines. Voting was a public act in which the gentleman freeholder (viewed as a valid representative of his whole family) announced his choice aloud by voice or publicly added his name to a roster of persons favoring a particular candidate. Religion proceeded on the assumption that Sunday devotions were an exercise of a whole community's responsibility to God. The ungodly actions of one were thought to reflect badly on the whole people, so that individuals would be fined for missing church too frequently. The choicest entertainments frequently were to be found in connection with the community's political and religious gatherings. When crowds came together at town hall, courthouse, or parish church, the occasion often took on the character of a public festival complete with games, contests, and trading.[5]

> The turn from public to private orientation that is reflected in the shift from community performance to solitary consumption has in our era been accompanied by an increasing turn from politics to popular culture.

In contrast to colonial life's community-centered character, modernism emphasized the individual decision maker as central to society. By the early 1800s, family members enjoyed larger houses having more space with rooms frequently designated to specialized functions or to particular persons. Communal benches and bowls were a thing of the past in an age of more available consumer goods.

Throughout the nineteenth century the communal elements of politics, religion, and entertainment also atrophied through ever greater privatization. Ballots became the norm to enable people to register their political choices behind a closed curtain. The triumph of the Revolutionary-era republican political philosophy, under which society was seen as a compact created by individual choice, produced statutes of religious liberty in which godly affairs became strictly a matter of personal selection. The communal character of religion was undermined further by the availability of new church denominations and by the rise of evangelical religion's focus on the individual conversion experience. By 1900, entertainment, too, increasingly had become a matter of single consumers making private selections. Sheet music, and later the spring-wound Victrola, made the musical experience into more of a one-person consumption choice and less a matter of sharing in whatever the neighborhood musicians could cobble together. Public libraries and mass circulation magazines made solitary, silent reading the norm and decreased the practice of reading aloud in groups. By the 1920s, film and radio further acted to make entertainment less a matter of solo or group performance and more an instance of one person selecting an available packaged product.

From Politics to Popular Culture

The turn from public to private orientation that is reflected in the shift from community performance to solitary consumption has in our era been accompanied by an increasing turn from politics to popular culture. The nineteenth century marked the high point of popular interest in politics. Political discussions were an important occasion for exhibiting one's facility for taste and criticism. In our colleges, for example, the most popular groups were the debating and oratorical societies where topics frequently centered on political life. Between the 1890s and the 1920s, however, the performative engagement with political oratory and debate was overtaken in our colleges by the less demanding and more consumer-oriented pleasures of spectator sports and fraternity socializing.[6] The shift from politics to popular culture on our campuses mirrored trends of society at large. Where nineteenth-century Americans closely followed the doings of their favorite political leaders, and felt compelled to keep up with the details of political questions, now this kind of close scrutiny and participation more typically was bestowed upon sports and music. Newspapers reflected the trend. Between the 1890s and the 1920s the percentage of space devoted to serious discussion (editorials and letters) declined around 75 percent and the space devoted to sports increased 47 percent.[7] A broader measure of the decline of political interest has proved to be voter turnout which, in the U.S., has decreased from around 90 percent in the 1880s to about 50 percent in the 1990s.[8]

From Taste to Consumption

The popular consumer culture that began to take shape a century ago has become so familiar that, for many, social status itself now is defined by the proper personal consumption of goods. Most of us declare ourselves to be "middle class," and Americans are most likely to feel suitably middle class if, for example, they live in the right neighborhood, drive the right kind of car, wear stylish clothes, exhibit knowledge about the newest trends in music and dance, and have access to the hottest communication devices. In contrast, until the 1920s, middle-class status was defined less by the individual consumption of goods and more by the public demonstration of proper taste.

In the nineteenth century, showing "taste" meant more than buying the right product; it involved a strong element of personal performance in public. Taste encompassed a range of behaviors including good speech, good manners, and an ability intelligently to discuss important dimensions of social life. Taste was reinforced by polite conversation in which it was assumed that the properly middle-class person

could apply critical standards to the social world. Here it was not enough simply to wear the correct hat or attend the trendiest play because taste represented an inward quality, the ability to receive pleasure from nature or art. The idea here was that one performed outwardly one's internal faculty of taste by being able to discuss why a given product or performance met standards of beauty or good quality. Accordingly, rhetoric textbooks used in the nineteenth century made concepts of taste and criticism central to good communication.[9] Where in the nineteenth century one would discuss proper pronunciation of words and the importance of intelligently discussing literature, art, and music, today we find it risky to label any pronunciation as substandard and we look at communication as an art of getting effects rather than exhibiting a refined character. In our era, taste has become a matter of private choice requiring neither public comment nor validation; the concept has long since disappeared from textbooks of communication.

Since the high point of modernism at the turn of the last century, the shift from community to individual, from politics to popular culture and from taste to consumption together have established individualism as superior to community spirit and action. This proclivity to favor the private over the public has been accompanied by a morality based more on exterior appearance than interior character.

Basing Morality on Character versus Image

The nineteenth-century notion of taste as an inward quality performed outwardly represents a focus on the internal state of the human being just as the consumption of goods emphasizes life as experienced outwardly. Discussions of morality—that is, right versus wrong—also may be based upon inward or outward considerations. Consistent with today's preference for an externalized, consumer-oriented approach to life is the contemporary prevalence of a morality based on received appearances. Another way of putting the point is to say that where morality used to be discussed in terms of interior *character,* now the focus is more on exterior *image.*

Character, as commonly defined, relates to a person's inward orientation to life and includes not only internal virtues (active predispositions to do good) but also qualities of self-discipline and self-control.

In contrast, *image* refers to outside signs or characteristics that are exhibited for measurement by others. Today's preference for image-centered rather than character-based discussions of morality may be examined from a number of vantage points, including the following four. Today's discussions of morality are more likely to focus on (1) material rather than spiritual conditions, (2) ideological rather than religious concepts, (3) role-oriented rather than goal-oriented behaviors, and (4) value-centered rather than virtue-centered notions of life.

From the Spiritual to the Material

A spiritual worldview finds people looking to connect their circumstances to the larger forces "of Nature and of Nature's God" (as Jefferson puts it in the *Declaration*); in contrast, materially oriented people prefer to regard themselves as masters of their own destiny. In early colonial times, people very often searched to find the spiritual meaning of both joyful and painful experiences. A timely rescue could represent God's deliverance; a disaster might signify God's testing of His people. By the early eighteenth century, Americans were less likely to emphasize the spiritual meaning of life's turns and twists and, instead, they were adopting modernism's focus on material causes and criteria.

Illustrative of the spiritual perspective is Mary Rowlandson's narrative account of her capture by Indians in King Philip's war (1675). Despite adversity, Rowlandson felt God's comforting presence. As she reflected on misspent moments of her life, she comprehended a spiritual justice in her dire condition. She found her experiences verified by such scriptural passages as "Thou shalt eat and not be satisfied" (*Micah*, 6.14). She expressed the conviction that her afflictions had positively helped her transcend "the extreme vanity of this World." Reflecting more modern sentiments was Sarah Kemble Knight who kept a diary of her trip on horseback from Boston to New York (1704/1705). Throughout, Knight's narration is more descriptive and factual than Rowlandson's. Although Knight might recur to such expressions as "through God's goodness I met with no harm," more typically she attributed events of her journey to her own decisions about when, how, and with whom to travel. Knight's criteria for the success of her odyssey were not based on any spiritual growth that she experienced but rather her pleasant memories and profitable business arrangements.[10]

> *Character*, as commonly defined, relates to a person's inward orientation to life and includes not only internal virtues (active predispositions to do good) but also qualities of self-discipline and self-control. In contrast, *image* refers to outside signs or characteristics that are exhibited for measurement by others.

> Modernism's tendency to put faith in material more than spiritual causes directly relates to today's preference for ideological (idea-based) rather than religious (God-centered) terms of morality.

From the Religious to the Ideological

Modernism's tendency to put faith in material more than spiritual causes directly relates to today's preference for ideological (idea-based) rather than religious (God-centered) terms of morality. In the biblical version of divinely sanctioned morality, for instance, murder is contrary to one of God's Ten Commandments. Owing to recent social conditions, secular beliefs have added certain ideational refinements to the morality of murder. One recent example has been the concept of "hate crimes." Under the theory of hate crimes, a murder is worse if it was committed by a person who was motivated by hate of the ethnic or life-style group to which the victim belonged. Here society's continuing guilt about racial and sexual discrimination has produced an idea-based morality that departs from the traditional religious view of murder. This reflects today's tendency to make rectitude less a matter of religion and more a matter of public opinion. For this reason, contemporary moral discussions are rife with statistics about behavior and opinion. A key element in the ethics of smoking has become the fact that relatively few people select this behavior, for instance, only 15.8 percent of college students in 1999 reported that they smoked cigarettes frequently. In the "war on drugs," policies seem OK as long as they have majority support; for instance, 78.5 percent of college students believe that employers should be allowed to require drug testing.[11]

The preference for material referents and idea-centered language in our discussions of right and wrong has been accompanied in recent days by a related shift in how we make personal moral choices. On the one hand, we tend to rely more on roles than goals and, on the other hand, to pay more attention to values than virtues.

From Goals to Roles

The environment of subsistence in early America reflected a constant struggle for survival where disaster was ever close at hand due to crop failure or disease. Societies based on survival are easily motivated by such goals as clearing more land or marrying one's children into a better-off family. In today's environment, mere survival is less a problem so that more people make important decisions—such as career and marriage choices—based on what makes them feel good rather than on what keeps disaster at bay. With this greater opportunity for personally empowering choices, however, has come a twofold problem of motivation. First, where people base choices on the pleasure of self-realization (rather than the pain of starvation), they have a weaker stimulus to undertake the difficult effort sometimes required to achieve an objective. Second, the hectic pace and technological character of postmodern life has loosened the strong bonds of family and neighborhood that once helped children form a stable and positive sense of self (even though families now enjoy more material possessions).

Where premodern society demanded that young people contribute to the family, and where modernist schools and factories subjected children to fixed procedures, today we value the child-centered home and the self-concept-enhancing school. Paradoxically, today's ostensibly more nurturing environment often has proved less able to help children systematically identify and pursue goals. The postmodern economy of two-wage-earner families striving for ever more consumer goods has produced a situation where, in the estimation of psychiatrist William Glasser, children increasingly are unable to gain a "satisfactory sense of who they are" from their more fleeting relationships with parents, peers and teachers. Having less home-based support for dedicating themselves to goals, young people increasingly fall into efforts to enact (on their own initiative) various image-enhancing roles seen in popular culture—the sports hero, the cool talker, the hip dancer, the fashion guru, the ultraslim supermodel. Not all are successful in adopting these wholesale identities and so, as Glasser documents, more children than ever have taken on an identity of "failure" and have acted out this frustration in self-destructive or antisocial behavior.[12]

From Virtues to Values

At the same time that personal life choices have become more role-based and less goal-motivated, the framework of value has replaced that of virtue. *Virtue* is a concept that relates to the internal possession of qualities that predispose one to act in a morally straight manner. Classical virtues included proclivities that produced the good society, e.g., friendship and wisdom. Christian virtues represented tendencies to follow God's law as reflected in the four cardinal virtues of justice, prudence, temperance, and courage.[13] In contrast, the concept of *value* originated in the world of economics; it denotes an external measurement of the quality or desirability of an object. Whereas virtue held people to fixed standards based on community or God, values allow a more flexible pursuit of what people, individually or in affinity groups, find desirable. Values relate to a self-chosen good life.[14]

To better understand the implications of a life based on values rather than virtues, we may turn to changes that researchers have found in the diaries of school girls and in the obituaries published by newspapers. A nineteenth-century girl's typical aspirations would be reflected in diary entries to "think before speaking" or to "work seriously." More often found in contemporary diaries are expressions about losing weight or wearing better clothes. Here we find a shift from basing identity on worthy personal qualities (good character) to grounding identity on the projection of outward image (good appearance). The same transition from character to image may be found in how people are described by others in newspaper obituaries. In the nineteenth century, men

> At the same time that personal life choices have become more role-based and less goal-motivated, the framework of value has replaced that of virtue.

were praised on the basis of their virtuous interaction with others in the community, e.g., their patriotism, gallantry, or honesty. Today, the focus is on a person's work career and the attainments of wealth.[15]

One important category of choices for communicators in the new millennium will be the style of life that they desire to pursue. If trends of the past two centuries hold constant, the rhetorical interactions of most Americans will center on individual needs (rather than community concerns), the context will be that of popular culture (instead of politics), and the objective will center upon consuming goods (rather than demonstrating good taste). In this privatized, consumerist environment, moral decisions will focus on material factors (more than spiritual ones), on ideological criteria (more than religious precepts), on role enactment (more than goal attainment), and on self-selected values (more than community- or God-mandated virtues).

Since the millennium promises choices, however, it may be possible for us to construct messages that deviate from the lifestyle tendencies of recent days. Yet going against postmodernism's flow likely will demand a high level of forethought; hereafter will be offered two frameworks of analysis that can help us orient ourselves for communicating in ways that swim against the stream.

> Not only does the millennium offer new lifestyle options, but it beckons with new media of communication. No people are more sensitive to media than are contemporary Americans.

MEDIA INNOVATIONS

Not only does the millennium offer new life-style options, but it beckons with new media of communication. No people are more sensitive to media than are contemporary Americans. Not only do we possess more communication devices than ever before, but we have given media-type labels to experiences that our ancestors considered simply an inevitable part of ordinary life. Thus, "face-to-face" talk now is treated as a particular medium in contrast to "electronic communication"; and "interpersonal communication" similarly is contrasted to the corresponding medium of "mass communication." In the contest for attention at home, the electronic and mass media seem now to be far ahead. In 1899, the at-home media alternatives to face-to-face interaction were individual reading and playing a musical instrument.

In 1999, 36 percent of college-bound teenagers spent six or more hours per day in front of the TV or computer monitor (28 percent reported devoting *no* time to reading).[16] Selection of media becomes ever more possible and necessary even before we leave our homes.

Whereas the premier media of premodern America were oratory and printed pamphlets, postmodernism's dominant devices are electronic. This historical transformation may be seen more clearly by means of four specific evolutions in communication technology: (1) from oral to written—and then to visual, (2) from persuasion to identification, (3) from ritual to reality, and (4) from holism to segmentation.

From Oral to Written to Visual

For upwardly mobile young people in the late 1700s, nothing was more important than becoming an eloquent, powerful, speaker. John Cotton Smith's student diary of 1782 reveals his "thirst for eloquence" based on his having learned of its legendary powers in the hands of Demosthenes of Greece and Cicero of Rome.[17] Oral rhetoric suffused the college curriculum: students translated the works of orators, they declaimed from history's great orations, they participated in forensic disputation (debates), and they prepared and delivered their own orations on themes of their choosing. In addition, students established their own extracurricular oratorical and debating societies and they participated eagerly in student-run plays.

Two generations later, however, writing—both its study and practice—was becoming more central to college life. Students had available a vast new reservoir of print resources, notably novels and newspapers, in a time when the medium of the ear (speech) was losing dominance to that of the eye (the reading of print). The former focus on orators and declamation was slipping away in an atmosphere where increased attention was paid to great literature and to the principles of written composition. Print culture permitted a combination of practical writing and artistic literature that was irresistible for a growing business economy run by upper-middle-class elites.

Textbooks reflected the shift to a print-oriented format in which the model of communication became the expository essay rather than the persuasive speech. The old oral model of organization, found in Cicero, involved a slow general beginning which led into a narration of the situation, a review of arguments, and, finally, an elevated and dramatic peroration. (This format has remained popular with preachers as shown by the "I Have a Dream" oration of the Reverend Dr. Martin Luther King, Jr.). In contrast, when the chief model of communication became the informative essay, the essence of arrangement became the clear statement of the proposition with subordinate arguments concisely presented and directly connected to the theme. Put another way, the narrative and dramatic mode of organization found in orality gave way to writing's abstract and step-by-step arrangement.[18] Organizing became synonymous with outlining. By the 1920s, the format of the essay began to control expectations about oratory when the short, point-by-point business talk became the model of speaking taught in colleges.[19]

The gradual shift from an oral to a print culture which began in the decades before 1800 continued without decisive interruption until the flowering of film in the 1920s and television in the 1950s. Although writing maintained its dominance in the academy—where the book and essay continued as the ultimate media for obtaining or demonstrating expertise—the medium of print began to lose clout in popular pleasures. Popular culture focuses on amusement more than on education, and the visual nature of film and TV may be more easily consumed than print culture's corresponding novels and pulp fiction. Critics now debate about whether the novel has become an obsolete technology in the face of film's power to narrate a story visually.[20] The lure of visual processing has widened its hold with the development of more powerful computers that permit the consumption of pictures as well as print. Although music and voice have become more available in new computers—downloading music onto CD's is a popular pastime—the computer remains a medium of the eye more than of the ear.

> Popular culture focuses on amusement more than on education, and the visual nature of film and TV may be more easily consumed than print culture's corresponding novels and pulp fiction.

From Persuasion to Identification

The twentieth-century turn from writing—a step-by-step process—to pictures that are perceived all at once has a corresponding implication for how people influence one another. Where advocates once amassed arguments in the enumerative style of an essay, literary critic Kenneth Burke observed the more recent practice of influence through identification, where communicators simply associated their cause with the interests of audience members. Instead of listing three reasons why people should donate blood, a speaker might talk about the empathic qualities of blood donors and thereby motivate listeners to take on this role.

Where traditional persuasion required presenting a string of verbal claims, identification sometimes can dispense with words entirely and be achieved by a display of pictures. In this way, a TV commercial might show a SUV climbing a rugged mountain. Even though few consumers ever would take their luxury truck off road, the picture conveys the sense of power and invulnerability that viewers want. In this mode of identification, a communicator displays signs (such as the rugged speed of the vehicle) whereas a traditional persuader would state reasons. William Glasser, psychiatrist, terms our world the "the identity society" because we prefer to identify with role models (people who storm high hills in a shiny SUV) instead of formulating step-by-step goals to attain an objective (finding the most useful transportation available).[21]

> Where traditional persuasion required presenting a string of verbal claims, identification sometimes can dispense with words entirely and be achieved by a display of pictures.

From Ritual to Reality

Ritual plays an important part in the communication patterns of traditional, premodern societies. Ritual observances reinforced customary patterns of behavior as in the rites of courtship whereby—ideally—a man secured the permission of a woman's family before he attempted to win her over. Such a practice corresponded to the historical view that marriage was more a practical connecting of families than a romantic joining of two individuals. Ritual practices of this kind seem irrelevant under the sway of contemporary individualism. Postmodernism tells us that we should aim to take on any role that attracts us—in contrast to rituals of olden days that were thought to bring social harmony by signifying everyone's relatively fixed place in society. As a simple example of ritual-produced harmony, we may think of how in families each member often has his or her customary place at the table or in the car—rather than people always taking whatever seat strikes their fancy.

Oratory in the old sentimental style illustrates how ritual operates in communication. Speeches of a hundred years ago typically included verbal formulas, that is, standard kinds of phraseology that were expected. One such fixed element of style was the tendency of speakers at important public events to invoke high-minded, very general ideals. Audiences accepted idealistic expressions that we, in our cynical era, would tend to dismiss as unrealistic. Consider this excerpt from a Fourth of July oration given in Boston by Edward G. Prescott in 1833.

The enemies of our system, looked back upon former precedents [of ancient Greece and Rome] and predicted our fall. But we have not fallen. Thank God! the stripes yet wave, and the stars are proudly borne on the banner where our fathers placed them.

. . . The beasts of prey have deserted their caves. . . . In their stead are the populous cities, pouring forth their thousands of industrious inhabitants . . . and our Factories gather towns around them. . . .[22]

Not only is Prescott's effusive style—"stripes yet wave"—out of fashion, but the ideas themselves would immediately arouse objections that called attention to discordant actualities. What about the hard conditions faced by workers, deforestation of the environment, and industrial waste? And what about the unmentioned conditions of slavery and women's lack of the vote? Such questions would not reflect the emphasis of 1833 when audiences expected communicators to remind them of things positive and progressive by means of fine sentiments, elegant language, and ideal visions.[23]

Film illustrates another medium in which factuality has triumphed over conventional expression. Here we find today an increasing demand for special effects that have the absolute look of actual life. Early films picked up some of the conventions of stage, where painted sets might suggest a cityscape without presenting it exactly and where violence was stylized and muted. Now movies are set in actual locations and violence is presented in a hyper-detailed manner complete with the simulated tearing of flesh and splattering of blood.

From the Holistic to the Segmented Audience

The transition from community to individual is nowhere better seen than in the ability of communicators to target messages to those segments of the population most likely to respond favorably. The standard communication media of the early nineteenth century—oratory and pamphlets—addressed a presumed whole public. Orators might modify a message depending on where they spoke (e.g., the North versus the South), but they could neither completely control who assembled to hear their remarks nor directly address private appeals to individuals in that audience. The era's pamphlets—which were, in most cases, reprints of speeches—also had to be prepared with a general reading public in mind.

In contrast to the holistic context of earlier communication, today's technology permits messages to be tailored to individuals. Direct mail can target particular households based on family members' known shopping preferences. Even ads in general magazines can be changed to fit the known characteristics of particular communities (as designated by zip codes). Computers allow a combination of selecting the audience and tailoring the appeal. With the advent of e-shopping, ads keyed to one's previous consumption choices pop up as one browses a website.

> The transition from community to individual is nowhere better seen than in the ability of communicators to target messages to those segments of the population most likely to respond favorably.

If trends of the last two centuries hold true, communication in the new millennium is likely to be a situation of the eye holding sway. Focus will be on inducing people to identify with congenial images instead of puzzling through a sequence of persuasive arguments. We may also expect an effort by communicators to be "real" and not to employ ritualistic expressions or rely upon high-minded or romantic notions of life. There will be a decided effort to target receptive audience segments rather than to treat the public as a whole community deliberating over a common message.[24]

Of course, the older media patterns (oral, argumentative, ritualistic, and holistic) remain available for use, today. But making them work in the new millennium will require somewhat greater than average planning (as will hereafter be explained).

VARIETIES OF SOCIAL ORGANIZATION

Choices made by millennial communicators will be influenced not only by people's desired style of life and available media but also by the way that they encounter other people in social life. Here American society's dual emphasis on individualism and materialism presents a paradox. Individualism suggests a focus on the common person, whereas materialism tends to measure people according to a domineering version of the Golden Rule—who has the gold makes the rules. The social context of the new millennial rhetoric can be better understood if we examine both how we value the common person and, further, how the common person marches to materialism. We may turn to three important cultural movements that favor the plain person and three that emphasize how the ordinary individual has been harnessed to a global economy. The three transformations giving greater voice to the everyday American include (1) the shift from aristocracy to democracy, (2) the shift from puritanism to pleasure, and (3) the shift from culture (singular) to cultures (plural).

From Aristocracy to Democracy

Traditional, premodern societies typically are organized on the basis of *aristocracy,* that is, according to

> Choices made by millennial communicators will be influenced not only by people's desired style of life and available media but also by the way that they encounter other people in social life.

the principle that people should behave according to a cultural ideal that is established by society's elite. This social principle may be contrasted to that of *democracy* which emphasizes choice by ordinary individuals and simple majorities.

In premodernism's principle of aristocracy, society's best people (those who represented the cultural ideal) established norms and modeled behaviors to which others felt a need to adhere. The relationship of elites to the mass is well expressed in the dictum of Confucius that the aristocrats should "lead them by virtue, restrain them with ritual." In contrast, democratic leaders emphasize knowing what ordinary people want—and responding to these desires. Leaders pay less attention to courtly ritual and exemplary behavior. In his travels through America in the 1830s, Alexis De Tocqueville, a French aristocrat who was sympathetic to many aspects of popular change, observed how American democracy emphasized the useful and the real, where European aristocracy favored the artistic and the ideal.[25]

De Tocqueville's classic book, *Democracy in America,* presented an extended comparison of societies organized on democratic versus aristocratic precepts. He found each system to bring advantages and disadvantages. In his view, a benefit of aristocracy was that people saw themselves connected to one another by means of a commonly accepted code of practices. Wealthy people, for example, felt an obligation to aid the town's less fortunate. On the other hand, the cost of endowing elites (and masses) with fixed privileges and duties was to keep ordinary people subordinate. De Tocqueville noticed how democracy's people enjoyed greater freedom to change their condition because less weight was given to differences of age, sex and class. For instance, he saw a trend in American families for the father to become less the head (with defined privileges and duties) and more just another member. But democracy's social freedom did not come without its own social cost. Now that people viewed themselves as striving individuals, they saw less reason to personally reach out to other people; folks were more inclined to wait for government to help the needy. In addition to democracy's bringing about a more powerful government apparatus, he also concluded that it promoted a crass materialism. Amassing wealth was democracy's main route to social position whereas, under aristocracy, social recognition also was defined by social rituals. In addition, although a strength of democracy was individual choice, the corresponding danger was that, when choices were tallied, the majority might tyrannize the minority.[26]

From Puritanism to Pleasure

Corresponding to the transition from aristocracy to democracy was a shift from puritanism (an elite-based notion of good) to democratically chosen pleasures. As a philosophy of life, puritanism takes its name from the religious sect that settled the Massachusetts Bay Colony. Puritans saw the nurturing or punishing hand of God in almost every event, from childbirth to attacks by Indians.[27] The Puritans believed that the whole community was in covenant with God, so that everyone had a responsibility to watch for and punish signs of sinfulness in others. Puritans also maintained a clear separation between the elect (those saved by God from eternal damnation) and those sinners who were doomed to hell. Puritans felt a constant need to profess their faith in order to gain assurance that they indeed were a member of the elect.[28]

> Corresponding to the transition from aristocracy to democracy was a shift from puritanism (an elite-based notion of good) to democratically chosen pleasures.

Puritanism clearly represented a species of aristocracy under which God and His elect determined the moral standards. In contrast, democracy brought a tendency to locate morality in the choices, preferences, and decisions of ordinary individuals. The inevitable result has been an increase in personal choices about pleasure. A case in point is the transition from film censorship to film ratings. Complaints about depictions of debauchery in film prompted the movie industry in 1922 set up an organization (Motion Picture Producers and Distributors of America) that promulgated an increasingly specific code of moral standards. Individual state governments and private organizations (e.g., the Legion of Decency of the Catholic Church established in 1934) also weighed in with moral evaluations of cinema. By 1968, the focus had changed from attempting to prohibit particular themes (e.g., drug addiction) and images (usually sexual) to affixing ratings for advisement of the public. The effect was to loosen restraints on the visual gratifications available to audiences.

From Culture to Cultures

The greater freedom of choice available to movie producers since the 1960s has been played out in society's larger transition from an emphasis on culture to a focus on cultures. The older view, that America was a single culture moving from initial diversity to eventual uniformity, is well reflected in Hector De Crevecoeur's *Letters from an American Farmer* (1782). This French immigrant described Americans as a "promiscuous [i.e., mixed] breed" formed by combining a variety of previously unmixed cultures. His focus was on the emergence of a uniquely American outlook and lifestyle that was distinct from any and all of its antecedents. To this view of a singular American culture we may compare the effort of today's multicultural education to present America as a land of separate groups defined along the lines of "race, ethnicity, culture, gender, sexual orientation, religion, and socioeconomic class."[29]

Both views capture obvious realities. On the one hand, Americans do differ along group lines but, on the other hand, Americans find themselves not blending in completely with everybody who shares their group labels. Although the U.S.A. represents neither a unified culture nor a complete nonculture, these two opposing poles of interpretation have had consequences. The older focus on cultural unity in America, when combined with the democracy's tyranny of the majority, led to excessive pressures for people to conform to a somewhat mythical American Way of Life. In this connection, a postmodern notion of multiple cultural experiences not only allows us to recognize America's variety of cultural streams but also permits people to combine the available cultural elements in ways that are personally satisfying. The result is to extend the principle of democracy into the realm of culture. Of course, democracy can devolve into anarchy if individuals or groups focus too inwardly. This was the problem faced by a Los Angeles high school that felt forced to scrap both Black History Month and the Cinco de Mayo celebration. It seems that Latino students angrily perceived that the "other culture" (seen as completely separate) received too lengthy attention.[30]

Although Americans, today, enjoy their democracy of pleasure and culture, they find themselves harnessed to economic trends. Three historical movements in this direction include:

1. a shift from family to popular culture,
2. a shift from an independent middle class to a dependent middle class
3. a shift from citizen of a nation state to cosmopolitan resident of a globalized society.

From Family to Popular Culture

As a way of life (and of looking at life), culture always has been closely connected to the raising of children in the family. The family is the site where people not only first learn how to relate to others, but family life establishes a base line for perceiving the ways of the wider world. Although the family long has functioned as the primary apparatus of cultural reproduction, the modern economy and postmodern panorama have combined to make popular culture an increasingly powerful agent of cultural formation. It has always been the case that, as young people grow up, they begin to test home learning against ideas picked up in the larger environment. But twentieth-century America has seen popular culture—notably the entertainment industry—figuring ever more prominently as a cultural educator.

Sociologists Robert and Helen Lynd compared the home life of Americans in the 1890s and 1920s, finding that young people had become far less home centered. Because of the automobile and movie theater, courtship no longer took place on the front-porch swing. Because of phonograph and radio, young people were less likely to participate in group singing around the family piano. Popular culture divided the family into separate consumption groups such that family reading hours and whole-family parties gave way to separate dances, clubs, and

> Although Americans, today, enjoy their democracy of pleasure and culture, they find themselves harnessed to economic trends.
>
> Three historical movements in this direction include:
> 1. a shift from family to popular culture,
> 2. a shift from an independent middle class to a dependent middle class
> 3. a shift from citizen of a nation state to cosmopolitan resident of a globalized society.

media consumption. As a result of consumer credit and installment buying, mom, pop and the kids all enjoyed a greater range of consumer products—but at the cost of tying the budget more to the fluctuations of the consumer economy.[31]

The penetration of popular culture into families only has increased since the 1920s. Not only has media consumption risen to 50 or more hours per week (TV accounting for most), but children now are raised in homes where fewer people are around. Owing to the decline in the family's control over the cultural learning of children, American parents increasingly must be content with media products that often are attuned to basic instincts—including aggressive speech, confrontational action, and often-stereotypical relationships of people. Film critics, for instance, complain about inarticulate movie heroes who are limited to physical action both in establishing relationships and solving problems.[32]

From an Independent to a Dependent Middle Class

The greater commitment of the family budget to consumer debt can be read as merely sign of a more general shift from an independent middle class to a dependent middle class. Middle-class status used to be defined on the basis of relative economic independence. The old middle class included farmers who, owning their own land, could exercise a degree of personal control over what and how much they produced. Similarly, professionals (lawyers, physicians) and shopkeepers (bakers, blacksmiths) gained some control over their situation because they set fees for specialized services based on recognized competencies. Standing in contrast to the old middle class was the more dependent working class who, in the worst case, bounced from one odd job to another but who, more generally, were entirely dependent for their income on wages set by others.

Under modernism's organizational set up, most professionals now do not set their fees but rather are paid salaries by the employing organization. Middle-class managers can be fired or laid off just as their fellow workers in the factory. For this reason, middle-class status now is defined less by an ability to control one's fees or working conditions and more by attainment of a relatively higher—but quite vulnerable—salary ranking.[33]

From Citizen to Cosmopolitan

Just as postmodern people sometimes find themselves swept along culturally by popular pleasures and economically by dependence on salary or wages, so has the formerly independent citizen of the early republic become a cosmopolitan in postmodernism's global village. A *citizen* enjoys a certain degree of say in a given polity; a *cosmopolitan* is not bound by national borders and, consequently, often has no direct control over the spheres in which he or she operates. The cosmopolitan enjoys the fruits of a diverse world—but at the cost of being, on occasion, an outsider.

The globalization of postmodern economy and culture offers Americans many advantages including wider cultural experiences, international markets for goods, and greater personal mobility. At the same time, the postmodern milieu is one of Americans having less direct control over many cultural and economic decisions that affect them. This postmodern loss of control has been less apparent in the U.S. (as compared to the Third World) because America is at the hub of the new world economy. Brazilian sociologist Alfredo Valladao has coined the expression "World America" to denote today's global condition where lines of culture, finance, and military power converge in the U.S.A.[34]

Today's international flow of capital and goods promises to raise the world's standard of living because of larger, more efficient markets and the ability of national economies to take on specialized roles. For instance, the U.S. will lead the world in high tech but will export low-skill, labor-intensive production to countries where wages are lower. The rub is that American workers are now competing against laborers whose wages and conditions of employment are far below U.S. standards—and

U.S. workers have little direct influence in the matter. At the same time, certain middle-class professionals—such as computer programmers—find that their work can be outsourced to consultants in India or Taiwan. More generally, globalization ties the U.S. economy to those of other regions. For instance, in 1998, the U.S. stock market declined (albeit only temporarily) as a result of a financial turmoil in Asian markets. Similarly, advances in foreign stock markets may lead to higher interest rates in the U.S. as our economy adjusts to world inflation. Global prosperity often comes at the price of wider worries.

Just as the rhetoric of the new millennium will be conditioned by the life style selected by communicators and by the media chosen, Americans of the twenty-first century will relate to each other in an environment in which ordinary people have freedom of action subject to the vicissitudes of national and world conditions.

> Just as the rhetoric of the new millennium will be conditioned by the life style selected by communicators and by the media chosen, Americans of the twenty-first century will relate to each other in an environment in which ordinary people have freedom of action subject to the vicissitudes of national and world conditions.

COMMUNICATING IN AN AGE OF CHOICES

The new millennium beckons with the prospect of limitless options available at our fingertips through new life-style alternatives, through media innovations, and from social trends that promise greater attention to the needs and wants of ordinary people. Now that we have filled out some of the content of the coming age of choice, we return to the question of how millennial message makers will respond to the vast variety of experiences that define their world. Two issues become paramount. First, because today's life-style, media, and social organization are highly individualistic, how can we avoid a confusing chaos of no standards or limits—where nothing can be heard because everyone wants to talk at once? Second, given the many life-style, media, and social-organization transitions of last two centuries, is it possible that these trends are so uni-directional (favoring individualism and materialism) that they nullify our ostensible freedom to select the older, more traditional options?

It appears that *activating choice* will become the essence of communicating in the new millennium. To implement choice, we must overcome its bewildering variety and pressure to go with popular currents. As millions of people e-shop in millions of electronic windows, the result may be feelings of chaos. At the same time, if our preferences deviate too greatly from the general trends of the last generations, we may feel uncertain and out of our time. As a way out of rhetorical chaos and uncertainty, we may turn to two decision-making frameworks that offer some help in negotiating both the breadth and historical depth of our options as communicators in the new millennium. The first of these is a scale of *existential alternatives* that can help us define our internal compass—helping us to find how to communicate in ways that will best allow us to become fully human. The second framework is a *matrix of social philosophies* (or ideologies) that can help us define how best to adapt to the wider society. These two decision-making frameworks—the existential and the social—each provide algorithms (rules of problem solving) for constructing messages in an atmosphere of vast possibility accompanied by relatively few fixed standards. Ultimately, we may measure our success as millennial communicators according to how well we manage decisions existentially and socially.

Finding One's Existential Stance

The condition of our all-too-human existence finds us able to want everything but unable actually to have every good thing at once. As human message makers we find ourselves forced to choose between alternatives that, on the one hand, are both desirable or necessary but, on the other hand, cannot be wholly reconciled. A case in point is the tension between self and others. To the extent that we focus on ourselves, we neglect the needs of others; yet, without good relationships with other people, it is difficult for us to have fully satisfying personal lives.

Self and Other represent two poles of a continuum between which we must position ourselves every time that we make a decision about communication. We may identify any number of similar existential continua; however, for our purposes here it will suffice to focus on six (somewhat overlapping) categories of existential decision. To activate our po-

> As human message makers we find ourselves forced to choose between alternatives that, on the one hand, are both desirable or necessary but, on the other hand, cannot be wholly reconciled.

tential as communicators in the new millennium we will have to make the decisions to locate ourselves between the poles of: (1) acceptance versus change; (2) responsibility versus dependence; (3) opportunity versus oppression; (4) the material versus the spiritual; (5) life as something easy versus life as hard; and (6) openness (sensitivity to others) versus prudence (defensive care of self). By locating ourselves along these continua of possibility, we will define a fixed position from which we may enter rhetorical transitions, making sense of an environment where everything seems otherwise up for grabs.

Acceptance versus Change

Every time that we anticipate communicating with others we straddle the issue of whether to accept things as they are or to change them. How we navigate this dilemma will influence our success in being human. In the movie, *Sunset Boulevard* (1950), a great silent film star, Norma Desmond, faces life as a fifty-year-old whose passion is again to play the young romantic ingenue. She attacks the problem of age by throwing herself at a young lover and undertaking painful cosmetic treatments. Without giving away the plot entirely, let it suffice to say that Norma's subsequent life would have been better if she had avoided the existential trap described by Gabriel Marcel, the French philosopher, who warned against permitting one's function (e.g., the role of film ingenue) to overtake one's larger life.[35] It is hard to build sound relationships when we fail to accept what is inevitable and try to change what cannot be changed.

Responsibility versus Dependence

When life chooses for us, we are dependent; when we must decide for ourselves, we assume responsibility. Both dependence and responsibility can represent desirable choices, but an inability to walk the wire between these two poles often creates problems of when and how to communicate. Two recurring existential questions include (1) where in life *can* we make a difference and (2) where *should* we try to make a difference? For Viktor Frankl these questions literally were a matter of life and death. Trapped in the living hell of the Nazi death camps as Number 119,104, Frankl observed many people surrendering mentally to their seemingly hopeless condition as ill-fed and ill-clad workers who were expected to slowly deteriorate and then be replaced by new victims. Against this background of seemingly no personal control, Frankl developed a powerful philosophy of free will. He observed that few who merely accepted their fate survived for long in the camps. Rejecting the easy and obvious stance of complete victim, Frankl decided that his masters could not, and therefore would not, control his *attitude toward the experience*. By reminding himself that he retained the free will to choose how he would regard his situation, Frankl was able not only to survive the camps but also to write a powerful testament to the possibility of hope against despair.[36] Frankl's discovery is an important one for communicators: where communication with others cannot change the world, our communicating with ourselves can give us a more useful attitude toward the world.

Opportunity versus Oppression

Frankl's powerful message of hope against oppression brings us to the question of how much attention we should give to our opportunities as compared to conditions that oppress us. The liberation movements of the 1960s emphasized the deterministic features of oppression, that is, opportunity denied on the particular bases of race and gender. From a deterministic stance, one either is oppressed or not. On the other hand, viewed from a philosophy of free will—such as that put forth by Frankl—oppression and opportunity are always partly matters of how we choose to view our situation. Frankl's rejection of the (understandable) stance of total victimization may be contrasted to the world as seen in today's "journalism of outrage" in which we are invited each day to search out various external elements that oppress us—persons, institutions, laws.[37]

An important issue facing communicators in the new millennium will be deciding whether opportunity and oppression amount to conditions imposed or attitudes chosen. Where we ignore oppressive conditions, we run the danger of helping preserve them. But on the other hand, too much fine-grained sensitivity to minor irritations can cut us off from useful experiences as in the case, mentioned earlier, of a Los Angeles school scrapping both its Black History Month and Cinco de Mayo celebrations.

The Material versus the Spiritual

As noted earlier, ours often is an age of extreme materialism in which the identities of people, families, organizations, and communities may be determined by marketplace calculations of consumption levels and degrees of prestige recognition. Spiritual considerations atrophy in a time when every human problem seems to call either for a flesh-and-blood expert or a consumable product. Yet present-day hypermaterialism provides an ironic opportunity for those seeking spiritual balance. The desire for some kind of community among people runs strong today. As pointed out by Martin Buber, the existentialist philosopher, our search for community has a spiritual dimension because it represents an urge to stretch beyond our own selves. Once we move from considerations of "I" to those of "You," we enter a realm of vast, unbounded space.[38] The physical needs of others paradoxically provide us with the context in which we can meet our own spiritual needs. Even the most materialistic among us may begin to tap into spirituality when we take cognizance of others in the world who need our help.

Life as Easy or Hard

Should we approach life as something that is supposed to be easy or hard? Premodern cultures experienced more of life's harsh conditions and responded with military-type communication styles in which patriarchs ruled and lower-status men and women deferred. In our own time, when nearly everyone expects to have a say in nearly everything, an assumption has grown up that all aspects of life should accommodate to our personal comfort zone. In such a "culture of entitlement," people expect good things to such an extent that they quickly become angry when confronted with denial or difficulty. For instance, educator Peter Sacks worries that today's students are too ready to treat education as just another consumable product. If education be judged by consumerist standards of price and satisfaction, students may

> To be open to life is to embrace the prospect of hope and to look for a positive value in every moment. Prudence, on the other hand, is based upon our experience that many situations tend to produce pain and, therefore, should be avoided.

cheat themselves by believing that they should not have to put in much effort. It will be a neat trick to balance hard choices with our idealized easy life of consumption.[39]

Openness versus Prudence

To be open to life is to embrace the prospect of hope and to look for a positive value in every moment. Prudence, on the other hand, is based upon our experience that many situations tend to produce pain and, therefore, should be avoided. In our mass-media-saturated era, a defensive or prudent individualism seems as natural as once communitarianism seemed normal. For instance, even by the 1930s, only nine percent of the motives of movie characters were social in nature (e.g., building something in common) as opposed to individualistic (e.g., attaining personal romance or revenge).[40] Contemporary culture bombards us with contradictory ideas about the continuum of sensitivity versus prudence. We are encouraged to avoid the stereotyping of people by being open to each individual regardless of our past experiences with folks who are similar to him or her. At the same time, we are warned of the need to engage in perceptual profiling—to refuse rides from strangers, to walk in pairs at night, to avoid opening e-mail attachments from unknown addresses. As we make choices as communicators in the new millennium, we will confront constantly the existential problem posed by Marcel: How do we remain open to people in the present and hopeful of the future given the accumulated painful experiences of the past?[41] Media may bring us closer to others in the 2000s, but we must on our own find ways to balance a prudent hardness with a openness to the needs and worthiness of others.

As human beings we fashion an internal life of the mind that revolves around many questions of existence: acceptance versus change, responsibility versus dependence, opportunity versus oppression, life's material versus spiritual elements, life's easy versus its hard parts, and the benefits of being open or closing up defensively. Locating ourselves along these existential continua can be a first step as we begin our career as millennial communicators who must deal with the almost limitless stream of life-style, media, and social-practice choices. In other words, a good way to begin building our own rhetoric of the new millennium is to set our internal human compass by deciding where we stand—and what we want to stand for—on the scales of existential experience.

As communicators we must make decisions about what to say, when, where, through what medium, and to whom. It will help if we approach these rhetorical elements by first locating our *existential stance* (a concept derived from that of *rhetorical stance* mentioned elsewhere in *The Rhetoric of Western Thought*). In choosing whether to speak and what to say, it will help to decide whether we should accept things as they are—and how much should we undertake the responsibility for changing them. Whenever we take the risk of communication, we are choosing to embrace opportunity and the good things that life has to offer. Where we keep our ideas close to the vest we hunker down against life's difficult or oppressive conditions. A similar choice is whether to take a material view of things—to use economic criteria to define what is good—or to emphasize our connection with larger forces (world, nature, God, humanity) that operate on us in mysterious ways. These prior existential choices will help decide how much we can risk being open to others and to their ideas without putting ourselves in a defenseless position.

> Just as our communication in the new millennium will be influenced by interior or existential choices, our interactions must take into account the society in which we and others operate.

Finding One's Social (or Ideological) Stance

Just as our communication in the new millennium will be influenced by interior or existential choices, our interactions must take into account the society in which we and others operate. Choices relating to social orientation often are termed *ideologies,* that is, idea frameworks that organize our view of how people and institutions should operate and actually do operate. It is possible to isolate four ideologies—four ways of looking at the world—that have grown up during the time when modernism succeeded premodernism and postmodernism grew from modernism. These are: (1) liberalism, the classic ideology of those oriented to succeeding in the modern free market; (2) socialism, another modern ideology that emphasizes the needs of the less fortunate; (3) conservatism, the lingering ideology of the premodern, premarket society; and (4) liberationism, the postmodern ideology whereby human diversity is treated as vitally important, particularly differences relating to race, ethnicity, sex, disability, and sexual orientation. The social ideology or ideologies that we embrace have a great bearing on what we expect from people and institutions as we engage them through communication..

Although the above four ideology names may not be familiar (and the four treated here can be divided or combined under alternate labels), all of us are immersed daily in the assumptions of these idea systems.[42] In table 1, these systems are organized in a matrix that isolates five aspects of the ideology. In this view, each idea system has a *telos* (or goal), a *hallmark* (a kind of behavior it fosters), an *origination and constituency* (the people who began it or who are favored by it), an *action* (a policy program that it emphasizes), and an *ethos* (an overall feeling that it conveys).

Liberalism

Liberalism emphasizes freedom of individuals to act either in the market economy or in the community at large (note that we talking here about the *classic liberalism* of the late eighteenth century and not the more generalized popular use of the term as something opposite of conservatism). Classic liberalism originated as part of the process by which the free market economy replaced earlier systems of feudal landholding and slave labor. The hallmark of the liberal economy is supposed to be initiative and com-

petition which produces innovation and constantly improving products and services. The constituency of liberalism is the middle class, those people who, by means of property and education, are best ready to compete and to strive for success. The whole system tends toward production—productivity is the action by which the success of a free-market economy is measured. Finally, the ethos or feeling produced by liberalism tends to be that of energy and optimism about the future. This is why the most highly valued contributors to the liberal economy are those people who prepare for the future by educating themselves and saving money for investment.

The common assumption that to succeed you must "sell yourself" relates to communication under the auspices of liberalism. We observe liberalism as the driving rhetorical force whenever we find people trying to promote ideas, products or themselves. When people try to impress others, when they strive to succeed at school or at work, they are operating according to the ideological assumptions of liberalism.

Socialism

Generally the philosophy of socialism is as old as the premodern, feudal practices of communal farming where people jointly worked the fields or ran cattle in the commons. Specifically contemporary socialism grew up as a reaction against liberalism's capitalistic methods of ownership and management. Where liberalism emphasizes the production of goods, socialism focuses on equality (its hallmark) in the distribution of goods (its telos). The constituency of socialism is the working class, people who have less education and property and who, therefore, are less able to function successfully as in-

TABLE 1 MATRIX OF IDEOLOGICAL STANCES

	LIBERALISM	SOCIALISM	LIBERATIONISM	CONSERVATISM
Telos	freedom	distribution	opposing oppression	virtue
Ethos	energy and optimism	care for victims of the economy	care for victims of racism, etc.	solidity and stability
Origins & Constituency	middle class	working class	oppressed groups, enlightened people	elites (various kinds)
Hallmark	initiative and competition	equality	sensitivity	authority and tradition
Action	production	govt. control of economy	official moves against oppression	a decorous style of living

dependent, competitive producers in the economy. Socialism's action agenda has tended to be that of government programs designed to mitigate against the human costs of a focus on production—e.g., medical insurance, unemployment insurance. In societies where socialism has been the dominant ideology, governments have owned and operated the major industries. The overall ethos or feeling of socialism is that of caring for those who may be the victims of productive enterprise.

The ideology of socialism enters the process of communication at several points, notably, wherever the focus is human equality or government action. Also, some media of communication are inherently more oriented to a socialistic world view. Where public speaking and mass communication emphasize an energetic source trying to win over an audience, the media of conversation and group discussion tend to emphasize a more egalitarian give and take.

Liberationism

Although liberationism draws from both liberalism and socialism, this philosophy gained prominence with grass-roots protests of the 1960s—the anti-war (anti-imperialist), civil rights, women's, and gay liberation movements. The objective or telos of the movements was the overthrowing of oppressive systems of thought and action that held back the progress of previously disfavored segments of society. As the movements matured, the hallmark of liberationism became the proper expression of sensitivity toward members of affirmative-action-protected groups. The movements encouraged a vocabulary that emphasized the needs of the oppressed and the proper action of enlightened people (the oppressed and the enlightened amount to the constituency and origins of liberationism). The chief action item of liberationism tends to be administrative or legal proceedings to favor the disadvantaged. Surrounding the entire liberationist project is an ethos or atmosphere of caring and concern for victims.

Because liberationism has played an important part in the transition from modernism to postmodernism, this philosophy has figured many times in the communication practices and patterns of contemporary days. One manifestation of liberationist ideology is the emergence of speech codes on campus to define racist or sexist language—and to prohibit it. The rise of multicultural education and diversity training also represent influences of liberationism. On the other hand, whenever we hear complaints about oppressive "political correctness" (i.e., speech codes and/or diversity issues being used as tools to unfairly stigmatize people or to capture political advantages), we find liber*ation*ism (which emphasizes oppression and concern for victims) undergoing challenge by liber*al*ism (which emphasizes freedom and initiative).

Conservatism

As a system of ideas for living life, conservatism represents a elite-centered philosophy and, therefore, is based on codes of proper, virtuous behavior. Conservative societies are those where a broad consensus exists about what is virtuous and what is not. Because the hallmark of conservatism is authority and tradition, this philosophy requires a system of aristocracy, i.e., a perspective whereby some people are regarded as better reflecting the cultural ideal. Our contemporary society often resists the aristocratic notion that some people are "better" than others; however, the goal of recognizing and rewarding the most accomplished people (those who are the origins and constituency of conservatism) may be found in a number of contemporary social segments—for example, religious organizations, businesses, and some educational settings. Living according to cultural ideals (i.e., decorous living) is the action item most often associated with conservatism. Here conservatism has little trouble labeling certain life styles as "good" or "bad"; in contrast, liberalism would emphasize freedom of choice, socialism the equality of choice, and liberationism the need for sensitivity to many kinds of diversity. The overall feeling or ethos conveyed by conservatism is that of stability (because ideals and virtues do not change) and solidity (because the ideals and virtues enjoy wide support).

Conservatism figures in our communication practices whenever we argue from a position of fixed rights and wrongs. In such a case, we presume the existence of a social tradition or authority upon which we may draw. Concepts of academic excellence, of religious morality, of good business practices all represent the invocation of principles of conservatism. Discussions of proper behavior also presume an accepted cultural standard against which deviations may be measured. Ironically, although postmodern liberationism presents itself as open to diversity, many liberationist proposals have a conservative element. This is because the philosophy of liberationism sets up a hierarchy in which enlightened and sensitive people make up the elite (virtuously celebrating diversity) and unenlightened and insensitive people represent villains.

LOCATING YOURSELF AS A MILLENNIAL COMMUNICATOR

Sampling the life-style, media, and social-organization options accumulated during the previous two centuries will be the joy of millennial communication. Creatively managing this welter of possibility will be the challenge. Already we have looked at how to activate your own choices, first, by locating yourself on the existential continua and, second, by locating yourself in the ideological matrix. It will help, now, to see how finding an existential and an ideological stance applies to an actual rhetorical situation.

The model of millennial communication unfolding here is one of activating choice by means of careful existential and ideological decisions. There are two fundamental ways to see how this model works. One way is to identify a rhetorical moment in your life and reflect on the existential and ideological selections that you made. Another way is to apply the existential and ideological frameworks to the communication of others. For our purposes, here, perhaps the best way to illustrate millennial rhetoric is to undertake the second approach, that is, to examine the stances—existential and ideological—as they pertain to an actual instance of communication. For purposes of illustration, I will focus on communication surrounding the Microsoft rebate offer of January 2000.[43]

The Microsoft corporation of Redmond, Washington devised a consumer rebate program whereby persons who subscribed to its internet service for one, two or three years would receive (at certain electronics stores) an instant rebate of $100, $225, or $400. In the states of California and Oregon, the program permitted people to cancel the internet service at any time without repaying the rebate. In California, people lined up as televisions, VCRs and printers flew off the shelves—and many of these consumers, after exercising their rebate, immediately called Microsoft to cancel internet service.

In the public discussion that followed, two basic lines of thought emerged, each of which reflected different existential and ideological stances. One view of the situation held that it was perfectly OK to take a cash rebate and then negate the principle upon which the rebate was given. This view emphasized

an *existential stance* of determinism (i.e., one just flowed along with Microsoft's momentary lapse of savvy) along with a materialism linked to a sense of oppression (i.e., the rebate just redistributed some of Microsoft's monopolistic profits). Focus also was on taking care of oneself (and not worrying about whether one's actions made society better or worse) combined with a hard prudence (tough luck for Microsoft). Seen along the lines of the *ideological matrix,* those who took the rebate and ran emphasized initiative and competition (getting while the getting was good), distribution (sharing Microsoft's wealth), and overcoming oppression (against a monopoly). The overall tendency was that of the individual responding prudently to a material serendipity. Such an ideological stance was one of liberalism (initiative for self in a competitive environment) combined with a liberationist version of socialism (the little guy striking back against the oppressive corporate world).

According to a second, opposing line of thinking, the take-and-run approach to Microsoft's rebate resulted in a shameful *existential* episode. The buying stampede made Californians look crass (unvirtuously taking advantage of a loophole), selfish (not worrying about taking from others), and dishonest (accepting an offer under false pretenses). Critics also saw a grab-and-get-out strategy as reflecting bad character (people gleefully acting in ways that they would object to loudly under other circumstances) and making the community worse by adding to the world's font of hypocrisy and dishonesty. This existential stance emphasized personal responsibility (instead of one's passively going with the crowd), spirituality (looking for how the self measured up to social or godly standards of good), communitarianism (considering whether one's actions a reflected well or poorly on the community), and sensitivity (viewing Microsoft as an entity deserving of some consideration). Seen from the *ideological matrix,* those who objected to taking the rebate and then canceling internet service emphasized at least two dimensions of liberalism: (1) production (Microsoft should profit from its products) and (2) optimism (resisting a cynical profit taking). This view also extended some of liberationism's sensitivity to a corporation seen as being victimized by a too-trusting policy. More particularly, however, the ideological emphasis was socially conservative with a focus on virtue (e.g., honesty, trustworthiness), on stability (e.g., not acting opportunistically), on decorous living (e.g., self control and courtesy), and on authority and tradition (accepting customary principles of fair play and/or religious prohibitions against stealing).

Just as we may locate the existential and ideological stances involved in the two major sides in the Microsoft rebate dispute, so too can we use these two frameworks either to assess or to plan our own communication with others. In this way, the vast number of life-style, media, and social-organization options can be managed when we set our compass as communicators who activate choice by means of existential and ideological decisions. Neither overwhelmed by options nor carried away by trends, we can prepare messages that represent what we believe is best.

The view of millennial communication given in this essay is one of great possibility combined with great uncertainty. Every epoch in human history has offered new potential—but at the cost of surrender-

> If we locate ourselves existentially, as human beings, and ideologically, as social beings, we will be able to manage what is likely to be a century of choice accompanied by ambiguity.

ing something previously cherished. Modernism brought greater economic wealth and opportunity for self-improvement—but at the cost of communal solidarity. Postmodern has brought a new freedom to shape our individual spaces in personally satisfying ways—but with a loss of comfortable old certainties. Applied to communication, the vast space of postmodern possibility brings feelings of bewilderment and uncertainty mixed with a sense that we ought to be attaining the most prestigious life styles seen in popular culture. Promise tinged with anxiety—this is the sphere of the new millennial rhetoric. Activating preferences in this environment will require finding our rhetorical stance. If we locate ourselves existentially, as human beings, and ideologically, as social beings, we will be able to manage what is likely to be a century of choice accompanied by ambiguity.

Notes

1. David F. Hawke, *Everyday Life in Early America* (New York: Harper and Row, 1989), pp. 31–57 and Charles Sellers, *The Market Revolution: Jacksonian America, 1815–1846* (New York: Oxford University Press, 1991), pp. 3–33.

2. Robert Kanigel, *The One Best Way: Frederick Winslow Taylor and the Enigma of Efficiency* (New York: Viking, 1997); Charles E. Merriam, *The Making of Citizens: A Comparative Study of Methods of Civic Training* (Chicago: University of Chicago Press, 1931).

3. *San Jose Mercury News,* September 17, 1999, p. 18A.

4. Jacques Ellul, *What I Believe,* trans. Geoffrey W. Bromiley (Grand Rapids, MI: William B. Eerdmans, 1989), p. 101.

5. Hawke, passim; Rhys Isaac, *The Transformation of Virginia, 1740–1790* (Chapel Hill, NC: University of North Carolina Press, 1982), pp. 11–42, 58–114; Cortland F. Bishop, *History of Elections in the American Colonies* (New York: Columbia Univeristy, 1893), pp. 140–179.

6. Becky Bradway-Hesse, "Bright Access: Midwestern Literary Societies with a Particular Look at the University for the 'Farmers and the Poor,'" *Rhetoric Review,* 17 (1998), 50–73.

7. Silas Bent, *Ballyhoo: The Voice of the Press* (New York: Boni and Liveright, 1927), p. 42.

8. James S. Fishkin, *Democracy and Deliberation: New Directions for Democratic Reform* (New Haven, CT: Yale University Press, 1991), p. 55.

9. Hugh Blair, *Lectures on Rhetoric and Belles Lettres* (2 vols.: London: W. Strahan, T. Cadell, and W. Creech, 1783), 1:15–40 (there were many American editions of this work) and Edward T. Channing, *Lectures Read to the Seniors in Harvard College,* ed. Dorothy I. Anderson and Waldo W. Braden (Carbondale, IL: Southern Illinois University Press, 1968 [originally published 1856]), 149–184.

10. Cf. "A True History of the Captivity and Restoration of Mrs. Mary Rowlandson" (1677) and "The Journal of Madam Knight" (1704/1705), rpt. in Wendy Martin (ed.), *Colonial American Travel Narratives* (New York: Penguin, 1994), pp. 13, 14, 31, 47, 62.

11. *Chronicle of Higher Education,* January 29, 1999, p. A49.

12. William Glasser, *The Identity Society* (revised ed.; New York: Harper and Row, 1975), pp. 129–138.

13. Alasdair MacIntyre, *After Virtue: A Study in Moral Theory* (2nd ed.; Notre Dame, IN: University of Notre Dame Press, 1984), pp. 151–156, 167, 195; Gertrude Himmelfarb, *The De-Moralization of Society: From Victorian Virtues to Modern Values* (New York: Vintage Books, 1994), pp. 57–58, 241–248.

14. *The Compact Edition of the Oxford English Dictionary* (Oxford, England: Oxford University Press, 1971), 2:3587; Himmelfarb, *De-Moralization,* pp. 9–15.

15. *Chronicle of Higher Education,* November 7, 1997, p. A15; *Antique Week,* July 12, 1999, p. 21B.

16. *Chronicle of Higher Education,* January 29, 1999, p. A49.

17. Cited in Christopher Grasso, *A Speaking Aristocracy: Transforming Public Discourse in Eighteenth-Century Connecticut* (Chapel Hill, NC: University of North Carolina Press, 1999), p. 406.

18. Contrast the treatment of oral organization in the era of Patrick Henry with that of essay writing circa 1900; cf. William Wirt, *Sketches of the Life and Character of Patrick Henry* (9th ed.; Philadelphia: Thomas, Cowperthwait, 1838), pp. 43, 83, 124, 311, 338–339, 381 and Adams S. Hill, *The Principles of Rhetoric* (new ed.; New York: Harper and Brothers, 1895), pp. 177–246.

19. For instance, Wilbur J. Kay, "Course I in Public Speaking at Washington and Jefferson College," *Quarterly Journal of Speech,* 3 (1917), 243.

20. Saul Bellow, *New York Times* (national ed.), October 11, 1999, pp. B1–B2.

21. Kenneth Burke, *A Rhetoric of Motives* (Berkeley, CA: University of California Press, 1950), pp. 24, 55; Glasser, *Identity Society.*

22. Edward G. Prescott, *An Oration Delivered before the Citizens of Boston, on the Fifty Eighth Anniversary of American Independence* (Boston: John H. Eastburn, 1833), pp. 15–16.

23. For more exploration of this point, see Richard Weaver, *The Ethics of Rhetoric* (Chicago: Henry Regnery, 1953), pp. 164–185 and Eric A. Havelock, *The Muse Learns to Write: Reflections on Orality and Literacy from Antiquity to the Present* (New Haven, CT: Yale University Press, 1986), pp. 58–74, especially.

24. See also J. Michael Sproule, "The New Managerial Rhetoric and the Old Criticism," *Quarterly Journal of Speech,* 74 (1988), 468–486.

25. *The Analects of Confucius,* trans. Simon Leys (New York: W. W. Norton, 1997), 2.3; Alexis De Tocqueville, *Democracy in America,* ed. and abridged by Richard D. Heffner (New York: Mentor/Penguin, 1984), pp. 178–179.

26. These points are made, respectively, in De Tocqueville, *Democracy in America,* pp. 232-233, 222, 229–230, 294, 289–314, 210, 112–122.

27. See, for example, "A True History of the Captivity and Restoration of Mrs. Mary Rowlandson" (1677), in Martin, *Colonial American Travel Narratives,* pp. 5–48.

28. Eugene E. White, *Puritan Rhetoric: The Issue of Emotion in Religion* (Carbondale, IL: Southern Illinois University Press, 1972), pp. 3–64, especially.

29. J. Hector St. John De Crevecoeur, *Letters from an American Farmer,* ed. Susan Manning (Oxford, England: Oxford University Press, 1997), Letter III, pp. 40–45, especially; David Schoem, Linda Frankel, Ximena Zuniga, and Edith A. Lewis (eds.), *Multicultural Teaching in the University* (Westport, CT: Praeger, 1995), p. 1.

30. *Palo Alto Daily News,* February 15, 1999, p. 7.

31. Robert S. Lynd and Helen M. Lynd, *Middletown: A Study in Contemporary American Culture* (New York: Harcourt, Brace, 1929), pp. 131–145, 153, 236, 244–245, 254, 257, 265, 280, 287, 487.

32. Tom Shachtman, *The Inarticulate Society: Eloquence and Culture in America* (New York: Free Press, 1995), pp. 100–101, 108–111.

33. A classic treatment may be found in C. Wright Mills, *White Collar: The American Middle Class* (New York: Oxford University Press, 1951), passim.

34. Alfredo G. A. Valladao, *The Twenty-First Century Will Be American,* trans. John Howe (London: Verso, 1996).

35. Gabriel Marcel, *The Philosophy of Existentialism,* trans. Manya Harari (Secaucus, NJ: Philosophical Library, 1956), p. 12.

36. Viktor E. Frankl, *Man's Search for Meaning: An Introduction to Logotherapy* (3rd ed.; New York: Simon and Schuster, 1984).

37. David L. Protess, et al., *The Journalism of Outrage: Investigative Reporting and Agenda Building in America* (New York: Guilford, 1991).

38. Martin Buber, *I and Thou,* trans. Walter Kaufmann (New York: Charles Scribner's Sons, 1970), pp. 55–64, 80, 89, 100, 147, 150.

39. Peter Sacks, *Generation X Goes to College: An Eye-Opening Account of Teaching in Postmodern America* (Chicago: Open Court, 1996).

40. Edgar Dale, *The Content of Motion Pictures* (New York: Macmillan, 1935), p. 185.

41. Marcel, *Existentialism,* pp. 43ff.

42. The number of relevant sources is numberless; however, two references are particularly helpful in making the distinctions noted hereafter: William S. Maddox and Stuart A. Lilie, *Beyond Liberal and Conservative: Reassessing the Political Spectrum* (Washington, D.C.: Cato, 1984) and Paul Berman (ed.), *Debating P.C.* (New York: Dell, 1992), pp. 1–26.

43. *San Jose Mercury News,* January 7, 2000, pp. 1A, 18A and January 8, 2000, pp. 1C, 11C.

Information and Knowledge On-line:
Teaching and Learning in the Communication Age

Thomas A. McCain

Loretta grew up in the hocking hills of Ohio. Her friends and relations were all "hill folk." Loretta's father and most of the adults she knew growing up in the first two decades of this century all worked in the coalmines. She went to school in Murray City, a bend in the road in southeastern Ohio where her other nine brothers and sisters attended school as well. She graduated from high school in 1929 and finally admits to having a bit of trouble with math. But at the time, she mastered what it was that the Murray City public school had to offer—four books worth. During her senior year she had an English book, a business/bookkeeping book, a chemistry book, and a history book; all of which she had to buy, along with paper to write on. She and her classmates spent an entire school year working their way through the information that was in these books; they memorized and recited formulas, poems, and important dates in history. Loretta, who eventually became my mother-in-law, was an educated young woman.

At a recent gathering of our "Monday Night Group" Gabe Singer brought his new bookbag. He's in his first year of high school. The bag holds 35 pounds of books that he is using this term—and that was without his biology book. The old backpack that had served him well last year and still has lots of miles left on it—in the trash heap. It wasn't big enough to hold all of his books for the current grading period for his college prep curriculum.

In a recent visit to the University bookstore I found that one of our undergraduate sophomore courses required nine books for a ten-week quarter.

Quite a contrast in how different times and learning environments treat information and its acquisition. Education in Loretta's day was about mastering known bodies of knowledge—filling-up the student with information—the mind conceived as an empty bucket. For Gabe and his contemporaries it appears that we treat students and their brains as sieves—pouring increasing amounts of information through

Contributed by Thomas McCain.

the holes—knowing that most of the content will pass on through.

- What is happening here?
- What do we know about learning in the information age?
- What role should communication scholars play in the transformation of student learning environments?

WHAT'S HAPPENING?—INFORMATION ABUNDANCE

The information explosion is not a myth. As the literate population has grown, so too has what is available to be read. My lectures about the information age are filled with quotes and aphorisms from the mass media regarding the dizzying rate at which information is generated:

- Humankind's information doubles at least once every five years.
- By the year 2000, 97 percent of what is known will have been discovered or invented since today's college sophomore was born.
- The current half-live of an engineer's knowledge is five years.
- If the trajectory of information generation continues at its present pace, by the year 2020 information available to humankind will double every 73 days.

Granted what counts as "information" includes both Shakespeare's plays and insurance forms. Nonetheless, it is hardly controversial to say that we more often find ourselves overwhelmed with information rather than comforted by it. As Nobel Prize winner Herbert Simon noted, "a wealth of information creates a poverty of attention" (Simon, 1997).

Not only has the amount of information become unwieldy and nearly incomprehensible, so too has the speed with which it is generated. The rate of invention for communication technology has a remarkable history. There is evidence that pre-historic humans were using technology to express themselves at least 45,000 years ago (Marshack, 1999). Some 20,000 years later, the paintings on the walls of the caves in France at Lascaux were left by a society that had stories to tell about their beliefs and their relationships with other animals. Too bad the alphabet hadn't yet been invented so we could understand more clearly what these images mean. It was around 3,500 BCE that evidence indicates that there were humans (the Sumerians) that could write. Just think, it took humans nearly 41,500 years to invent this important communication technology (writing), a length of time nearly unfathomable today. Assuming that the average human life was 30 years, that is about 1,300 lifetimes for humankind to develop from a speaker to a speaker and a writer. The printing press was invented in the middle of the 15th century, some 5,000 years after evidence that we could write—or another 167 lifetimes.

The pattern and speed of invention and change in communication technology in the current century reveals quite a different picture. More innovation to help us extend our world with communication technology has occurred in this last 100 years than through the 450 centuries that separate us from our earliest ancestors. Bill Gates' (1999) new book reflects the new conception of time: *Business @ The Speed of Thought: Using a Digital Nervous System.* The pace of change is accelerating as we live and try to make sense of it. More people are able to communicate in more ways and have access to more information than at any time in human history. But the rate of change for communication technology is not paralleled by a similar rate of change in economic principles, or the rate at which people can read or become wise, nor, for that matter, in how the seven deadly sins are played out. Randal Tobias, former executive with AT&T, put it in perspective when he noted that if the same rate of change that has occurred in networked computing had occurred in the automobile industry, we could buy a Lexis for $2.00 and it could travel at the speed of light for 1,500 miles on a thimble of gas (Tabscott, 1996).

The implication for higher education and communication scholarship is that information overload is the operative mode in which we as students and teachers find ourselves.

Assumption: *Strategies and methods for learning in an era of information abundance require different approaches than can be provided by institutions*

> More people are able to communicate in more ways and have access to more information than at any time in human history.

and processes that were designed for a time of information scarcity.

Here is my simple thesis: digital communication technologies, particularly networked computing, are participating in the alteration of fundamental human communication and learning processes. Communication scholars should provide leadership in helping higher education to understand and transform itself into a learning institution for the 21st Century. There are two aspects of this large problem that require a rationale and action. We should:

■ provide our students with skills in using digital communication tools;

■ transform the context for student learning from a didactic information distribution metaphor to a problem based, chaos generating, and information using metaphor.

Let me first provide a bit of personal history and context for why I have come to believe that skill training and chaos-fostering activity is an appropriate road for dealing with the vicissitudes of learning in the communication age.

THOM'S PERSONAL JOURNEY

When I left the University of Wisconsin in the early 1970s as a freshly minted Ph.D., I set out to become a communication researcher. I remember telling my wife, Jan, during some of our private moments, and in my typically corny way, that I really wanted to "make a significant contribution to the field of communication knowledge." So, I wrote research papers and joined the "Young Turks" of the '70s. My first convention paper was at the Western States Communication Association conference in 1971. The critic on my panel was not overly impressed with my paper, and I was a bit chagrined. According to this critic (who shall remain nameless, though I assure you I remember) the research was not very close to making a significant contribution of any kind. The next panel included someone called B. Aubrey Fisher. His critic thought that his work in small groups was headed in the same direction as mine, toward the "not con-

. . . to understand digital communication technology, is to understand the interdependencies of communication markets, communication technologies and communication policies.

tributing" end of communication scholarship. Aub and I shared a "New York Minute" in the hall commiserating over this before we learned that along with aspiring scholarship in communication we also shared a love for limericks. Before the night was over, "Aye, Aye, Aye, Aye, in China they do it for Chile" was wafting through the hotel halls. We managed to find each other at nearly every convention after that to celebrate our love for both research and a good time. I am honored to be giving the B. Aubrey Fisher Memorial Lecture. His influences have been with lots of us for a long time.

During the 1980s there were three things that happened that led me to the ideas and issues that shape my thinking regarding communication technology and learning: I purchased my first Apple Computer; my family and I lived in Ireland for a year; Jan received her master's degree in Education. The gaining of computer knowledge and skill and the international experience started to shape my thinking regarding an information explosion, and the political, economic aspects of the information rich and the information poor. Jan introduced me to a host of learning theorists and theories, including the work of Howard Gardner and the concept of multiple intelligences and of multiple learning styles. I was on my way to understanding how the networked computer and communication technology could be used in contradictory but mutually helpful ways.

This account of my personal history ends with the current decade of the 1990s, much of which I spent with the Center for Advanced Study in Telecommunications (CAST) at Ohio State. During this period I wrote a briefing paper for the Ohio Board of Regents regarding a state level policy for technology and higher education and became embroiled in the politics of diffusion of digital communication technology. This period crystallized my thinking regarding change, higher education, learning, and interactive technologies. It focused my ideas and actions about communication as an infrastructure of society that led to my litany on the topic: *to understand digital communication technology, is to understand the interdependencies of communication markets, communication technologies and*

communication policies. Diffusion of digital communication technology is about:

- what things cost, who owns what, and what technology most people are using (markets);
- invention of new tools for distribution, storage, and creation of messages (technologies); and
- the politics of communication in the private and public sphere (policy).

Diffusion of digital communication technology is about both continuity and change. As an essentially human process, the adoption of new methods and tools in complex organizations like colleges and universities, will be disruptive and challenging to the status quo. As Steve Gilbert has noted, it will be a "slow revolution" (1996).

Responsible uses of digital communication technology require knowledge and skill that no one person can possibly possess. Collaboration is a necessary condition for learning with technology. I firmly believe that making a difference with digital communication technology for learning requires at least somebody else, usually many more. The 1990s were the time that another "Utah Connection," Steve Acker, and I partnered on numerous projects. Steve (who sees night when I see day) and I have developed several courses and approaches to learning with technology that act as our emergent laboratories for learning about the role of digital technology and student learning. The centerpiece is our course, Communication 140: "Living in the Information Age" http://jac.sbs.ohiostate.edu/co140sp99/archive.htm. We have also embarked on a larger project "MassCommOn-Line", an on-line, continuously updated, multimedia, interactive course and set of resources that introduce students to the markets, technologies, and policies of the mass media and emerging interactive personalized media. We expect it to be available for adoption in 2000.

> Responsible uses of digital communication technology require knowledge and skill that no one person can possibly possess.

WHY SKILLS?

The adoption of digital communication technologies into organizations and existing cultures of practice comes with an inherent tension. On the one hand digital technology is used for efficiency—doing old things more cost effectively, faster, safer, with fewer mistakes, relieving the drudgery that comes from patterned, repetitious, boring human work and activity. At the same time, new intelligent machines, particularly those that are intimately tied to human communication processes, require creativity to help find new ways for thinking about and doing things. Efficiency and Creativity are dialectically opposed in social organizations, colleges included. It is this tension that helps us to understand the process by which organizations transform themselves with the aid of new communication technologies. Shoshana Zuboff (1988) labeled these processes automating and informating when she studied the adoption of intelligent machines in industrial and service organizations. I prefer the terms *efficiency* and *creativity,* for they seem to juxtapose the forces for change in contemporary higher education.

Characteristics of digital interactive technologies do more than improve efficiencies of current processes (transferring messages by the billions); they can change the nature of what is being done, because they provide a new context for accomplishing work. This is particularly true if the work happens to be intellectual work. The necessary condition of this transformation, according to Zuboff (1988) and others (see Nonaka & Takeuchi, 1995) is actual hands-on experience and the development of skill. It is not only the reading of lots of information that makes the Internet and the World Wide Web communicatively important or a powerful facilitator of change in the academy. Rather, it is the multimedia nature of messages and the interactive message production capabilities of the web that are transforming the shape of knowledge. The production of content requires tools and practice. It requires understanding of rules of reading on-line, of storing on-line information, of privileging and qualifying on-line information, of representing facts and opinions in words, pictures, graphs, audio and video. It requires thinking about content in such a way that facts are always current because an author can regularly update them. And it requires thinking about student produced work that is more than the assimilation of knowledge deemed important by others.

The nature of teaching and learning, along with assumptions about the character of knowledge, are part of a lively debate among educators and policy makers. Conventional perspectives support a view of education that resembles the transmissional model of communication in that the teacher, or educational institution, is the creator (or at least controller) of a message, knowledge, and the student is the recipient of that knowledge. Learning occurs when the students acquire the prescribed facts and skills making up a particular content area. The information learned by students is objective, not open to interpretation, so evidence of their learning can be provided through their performance on exams. The teacher serves the role of the gatekeeper controlling the access and distribution of information to the students.

TRANSFORMING THE CONTEXT FOR STUDENT LEARNING

Cognitive research and constructivist theories of learning challenge traditional, transmissional assumptions about education. When information was a scarce resource, the passalong method of knowledge distribution was appropriate. Teachers learned what was important and transmitted it to students who learned it and took tests to prove that they "knew" what they had been taught. The history of the didactic, transmission model of learning is an interesting one (Maxwell and McCain, 1997). It was the product of the industrial age that sought to extend learning to all citizens rather than only the wealthy and privileged. This transmissional view of higher education permeates most every college and university—it is best characterized as an instructional model where the distribution of content is performed by a lecturing professor. Lectures typically happen in a room designed with modern teaching aids (chalkboard and chalk). The professor lectures to rows of chairs, usually bolted to the floor, filled with students who take notes about what the professor says, so that the learners can study the notes to demonstrate mastery of the material on an objective test.

A dialogical view suggests a different understanding of knowledge, that starts with the premise that knowledge is something humans acquire through actively creating and organizing their own experiences. Teaching involves providing content, structuring activities, facilitating group work, and creating a culture of thinking and thoughtfulness (Tishman, Jay, and Perkins, 1993; Brown, 1995). Learning occurs through interaction or dialogue among all participants. Learning depends on teachers situating what is to be taught in terms of the students' experiences, and together they come to mutual understanding, to create new knowledge (Dewey, 1938; Friere, 1993; Jones, Valdez, Nowakowski, & Rasmussen, 1995; Marshall, 1992; Means, 1994; Maxwell & McCain, 1997). This constructivist view of learning reflects the ideas of Delia (1987) and Kelly (1955) in suggesting that cognitive constructs develop through interaction and the way individuals create meaning, construct knowledge, and make sense of their world. Within the constructivist framework, the notion of involvement and personal experience influences one's beliefs and expectations. Assessment within the dialogical approach is based on performance; students are assessed by their ability to demonstrate their knowledge and skills.

The constructivist perspective has tremendous implications for understanding the nature of learning. As such, the dialogical model recognizes knowledge as being socially created through the interaction among teachers and learners and is based upon their previous knowledge, dispositions, and experiences. The students are encouraged to be active explorers, not passive recipients. Instructors coach, facilitate, and model engaged learning. Learning content consists of the building blocks of information and knowledge making up the traditional disciplines, however, these are taken one step further as students are encouraged to apply their knowledge to real-life authentic tasks. A curriculum is project-based with students working collabora-

> A dialogical view suggests a different understanding of knowledge, that starts with the premise that knowledge is something humans acquire through actively creating and organizing their own experiences.

> A curriculum is project-based with students working collaboratively to solve problems of relevance to them and their world.

tively to solve problems of relevance to them and their world. The goal of this model is to help students develop not only basic skills, but also higher order thinking skills, such as critical thinking, problem solving, and communication skills. Evidence of student learning, the basis of assessment, comes in the form of a finished project or presentation, and most often an artifact-representing students' efforts. In much of our work with students on-line, we seek to improve student self-efficacy with digital tools as an indirect indicator of empowerment (McCain, Morris, Green, Al-Najran, 1999).

EXPLICIT AND TACIT KNOWLEDGE ABOUT DIGITAL COMMUNICATION

Is the social activity of teaching and learning in which individuals create and share meaning really different if the information is digital rather than analog? In my view the answer is, yes! Digitized environments not only make teaching and learning activities more efficient, they also can transform the nature of teaching and learning through the creative capabilities of communication technologies. Not only do communication technologies expand the learning content available (thus expediting the distribution of printed information), they introduce an element of currency and accessibility to the content being studied. This feature has the potential to transform teaching and learning—making it more life-like, more interesting, and relevant. Not only do digital technologies expand the circle of learners (thus increasing the efficiency for interactivity), the immediacy of this enhanced exposure, in terms of space and time, can result in broadened horizons, deeper learning experiences, and an appreciation for diversity not realized with traditional text and place-bound interaction.

The informating or creative capabilities of digital communication also can lead to developing tacit knowledge. As opposed to explicit knowledge, tacit, or implicit understanding is not easily articulated and is deeply rooted in action, experience, social values and symbols (Nonaka & Takeuchi, 1995). Tacit knowledge is the stuff for which words won't work. According to Nonaka and Takeucchi, tacit knowledge includes the unspoken rules of culture. It is what you know that can be understood only through hands-on experience. Words seldom capture the smell of sea-air or the sound of wind in a sail. No written description of the WWW communicates the

experience of a MOO or a MUD. Until someone spends time with email, they think it is like sending a letter. "Newbies" to the web are much more likely to print out text copies of mail messages than are those with more time on-line where they have experienced and gained a tacit understanding of email communication. Learning and teaching on-line poses lots of dilemmas. Perhaps the most important thing a teacher and student needs to know about learning on-line is the range of the possible in the on-line contextual environment. Knowing about any context requires experience with it. Knowing how to use new communication technologies creatively to improve and enhance student learning, requires spending time on-line in order to gain an understanding of the tacit ways content, teachers and learners interact with digital content.

DIGITAL DIFFERENCES

Communication technology's creative capabilities extend beyond efficiencies to shifting notions of space and time in ways never before experienced. This challenges the taken-for-granted aspects of when and where things can and should be done. Because of this, they are useful tools for facilitating, encouraging, and even demanding organizational and structural change. This change involves different ways of doing things, of conceiving about things, of imagining and expecting things, and of preserving things as they are. Digital technology takes information and breaks it down into its smallest components. By transforming an analog signal into discrete pieces, digitalization makes it possible to manipulate information, text, graphics, software code, audio, and video in ways never before thought of, thus its informating, transforming, creative capabilities.

The "bit revolution" as Negroponte (1995) refers it to, means that conceptualizing of the possible in communication markets, technology and policy are up for grabs. Copyright, for example, "is a Gutenberg artifact." (p. 58). There are several things which digitalization does to information and messages which fundamentally change its nature from being one of matter (atoms) to being one of bits. First, bits can be mixed together nearly effortlessly; music, text, moving images can be stored, arranged, edited, enhanced, and compressed in an infinite variety of ways with only modest skill. Multimedia is the name for the data which include audio, video and text. In digital form these data and the potential combinations that they afford the user and producer of information, are nearly infinite. The integrative form of multimedia is essentially different from the book, movie, and record form which preceded it. Both teachers and students manipulate information bits, only teachers manipulate information atoms.

The other seemingly innocuous property of digital information is that it creates a new kind of bit—a bit which provides information about itself. There is meta-information about every bit—a header which is transparent to the audience, but which lets the user's computer know about the data. These instructions allow for intelligent use of fragments of messages, starting with something as mundane as what track is playing on a CD player. This new kind of bit, allows for a television program to be not only a program which includes sounds and pictures, but also carries with it a computerized description of itself. For teachers and students, this new ability to create new forms and arrangements of information has never been so profound (Negroponte, 1995).

Use of digital communication technology in teaching and learning activities can provide a mechanism for developing a deeper level of understanding of a process or technique by creating a means for experiencing it first hand. Interactive technologies provide students and teachers the ability to more closely experience real applications, be they viewing a speech in the House of Commons, interacting with scholars studying camera angles, or creating a personal web site on the Internet. When individuals do something rather than discuss or read about it, they learn more. The creative capabilities of digital communication technology create an environment for supporting and encouraging the development of such tacit knowledge in ways that mere efficient distribution of content cannot. Digital communication technologies are not something that can be understood by reading about them, any more than riding a bike can be understood by reading about bikes, or gardening understood through books, or the thrill of a kiss captured through the written word alone. Understanding of digital communication technology requires action-centered experiences that are about both efficiency and creativity.

> The integrative form of multimedia is essentially different from the book, movie, and record form which preceded it.

> Most contemporary academic administrators have little tacit understanding of teaching and learning with technology that they brought with them to the managing process.

TRANSMISSION OR DIALOGUE?

To be sure, digital communication technologies can be used to support either a transmissional or a dialogical view of teaching and learning. Those policy makers, administrators, and teachers comprising the social structure make the choice, but clearly the more exciting possibilities of digital interactive media favor the dialogical model. Access to computers with network connectivity provides students an open window to collect all types of facts, ideas, and tools to apply to their projects that a teacher never may have considered. Through the Internet, individuals can efficiently peruse the world's most acclaimed museums, view texts from libraries all over the world, or join a newsgroup on any imaginable topic. Workstations with desktop publishing software and multimedia capabilities enable students to create and produce professional-looking documents and products. Essentially, digital communication technology does the same thing for students as it does for other users of intellectual works—significantly alters the gatekeeping function. It allows for much more access to ideas and information than was afforded in the traditional classroom and fosters an atmosphere where students are both users and producers of intellectual work.

UNIVERSITY ADMINISTRATION'S DIGITAL CONUNDRUM

Using communication technology in the teaching learning context is indeed resulting in creative new environments for student learning. It is a learning environment that has managers in higher education in a bind, and most administrators don't know it yet. The pressures of budgets and the potential for digital communication technology and distance education to "save money" has most Deans and Deanlets (associate, assistant, vice deans) in a disconnect with contemporary teachers and learners in this regard. Administrators in higher education, appear to be consumed by the need to be efficient and "fill up the pail of knowledge" they are hard pressed to see the creative and "informating" aspects of learning with technology that emerge when intelligent users publish their work. This is so partly because contemporary administrators understand the web as a management tool, rather than a teaching and learning tool. Most contemporary academic administrators have little tacit understanding of teaching and learning with technology that they brought with them to the managing process. Instead, contemporary administrative folks have a tacit understanding of transmissional media and didactic teaching of content, for that is what their experience as student and professor taught them.

In order to maximize the potential for digital communication technologies, one must develop a tacit as well as explicit knowledge of their capabilities. This challenges us to use digital communication technologies to accomplish tasks that are meaningful to learners and that make a difference for a larger audience than a classroom-trapped instructor. The need to work collaboratively with others requires our pluralistic journeys to look for multiple ways through the chaos. Experience is essential to recognizing digital communication technologies' capability to creatively and efficiently transform communication learning processes.

On a personal note, in my thirty some years in academe, nothing has been so provocative, so exciting, so gratifying as the transformation of learning that accompanies students' uses of digital communication technologies. One of the reasons we academics are what we are, is because we were good at being students. Why not find a way to stay in school? As students we all met success in the past. As transformers of the way learning about communication and the world around us can and should occur, we need to be successful in the future. Our discipline and our students need our leadership and example. Loretta needs help in expanding her reading. Gabe needs help in prioritizing and integrating enormous amounts of information. We know that at the very least, we all need practice and timing. It will take skill and understanding. It will include both efficiency and creativity. It requires working with others. It challenges us to celebrate diversity. It requires that we accept chaos. It makes us all wear our learning shirts. Our intellectual legacy is replete with advice that we should think first and act second. In this transformation period of cyberspace, the challenge for us is **to act our way into a new way of thinking.**

Bibliography

Brown, R. G, (1993). *Schools of Thought: How the politics of literacy shape thinking in the classroom.* San Francisco: Jossey-Bass Publishers.

Delia, J. (1987). Interpersonal cognition, message goals, and organization of communication: recent constructivist research. In D. L. Kincaid (Ed.), *Communication theory: Eastern and western perspectives,* (pp. 255–274). San Diego, CA: Academic Press.

Dewey, J. (1938). *Experience and education.* New York: Collier Books.

Friere, P. (1989). *Pedagogy of the oppressed.* New York: Continuum.

Gates, B with Hemingway, C. (1999). *Business @the Speed of Thought: Using a Digital Nervous System,* New York: Warner Books.

Gilbert, S. (1996). Making the most of a slow revolution. *Change,* March/April, 1023.

Jones, B., Valdez, G., Nowakowski, J., & Rasmussen, C. (1995). *Plugging in.* Oakbrook, IL: North Central Regional Educational Laboratory.

Kelly, G. (1955). *The psychology of personal constructs.* New York: North.

Marshack, A. (1999). The art and symbols of ice age man. In David Crowley and Paul Heyer, eds. (1999) *Communication in history: Technology, culture, society.* 3rd ed., New York: Longman.

Marshall, H. (1992). Seeing, redefining, and supporting student learning. In H. Marshall (Ed.). *Redefining student learning,* 1–32. Norwood, NJ: Ablex Publishing Corp.

Maxwell, L., & McCain, T. (1997). Gateway or gatekeeper: Implications of copyright and digitalization on education. *Communication Education, 46,* 141–157.

McCain, T., Morris, S., Green, C., Al-Najran, T. (1999). To do is to empower: relationships between experience with networked computing, efficacy, and attitudes toward life on-line. Paper presented at National Communication Association Convention, Chicago, Illinois.

Means, B. (1994). Using technology to advance educational goals. In B. Means (Ed.). *Technology and education reform,* (pp. 1–22). San Francisco, CA: Jossey-Bass.

Nonaka, I., & Takeuchi, H. (1995). *The knowledge-creating company.* New York: Oxford University Press.

Simon, H. (1997). Designing organizations for an information-rich world, In Donald Lamberton, ed. *The economics of communication and information.* Cheltenham, U. K.: Edward Elgar.

Tabscott, D (1996). *The digital economy: Promise and peril in the age of networked intelligence.* New York: McGraw Hill.

Tishman, S., Jay, E., & Perkins, D. (1993). Teaching thinking dispositions: From transmission to enculturation. *Theory into Practice, 32,* 147–153.

Zuboff, S. (1988). *In the age of the smart machine: The future of work and power.* New York: Basic Books.

Name Index

SUBJECT INDEX